EDUCATIONAL ASSESSMENT OF LEARNING PROBLEMS:
Testing for Teaching

EDUCATIONAL ASSESSMENT OF LEARNING PROBLEMS:
Testing for Teaching

Gerald Wallace
University of Virginia
Stephen C. Larsen
University of Texas

Allyn and Bacon, Inc.

Boston   London   Sydney

The poems for Part 1 and Part 2 are from *The geranium on the window sill just died but teacher you went right on*, by Albert Cullum, copyright 1971, Harlin Quist, Inc., pp. 34, 60. Reproduced with permission of the publisher.

Third printing . . . May, 1979

Library of Congress Cataloging in Publication Data

Wallace, Gerald, 1940–
  Educational assessment of learning problems.

  Includes bibliographies and index.
  1. Educational tests and measurements.
2. Learning ability. I. Larsen, Stephen C.,
1943–   joint author. II. Title.
LB1131.W347   371.2'6   77–27837
ISBN 0–205–06090–0
ISBN 0–205–06089–7 pbk.

For Our Parents

with deep appreciation to

    Rose and John Wallace
    Dorothy Larsen

and with loving memory of

    Earnest Larsen

Contents

Preface

This book provides readers with assessment strategies appropriate for preschool through adolescent students who exhibit various types of learning disorders; each chapter is designed to be useful for preservice teacher trainees as well as those professionals who are currently working in the schools. The diagnostic techniques discussed are not aimed at a particular category of disabled learner, but should be applicable to most pupils who are evidencing school related problems.

Part I of this text provides discussion of the concept of educational assessment as it is now exercised in the schools. Various models of visualizing the assessment process are delineated and discussed. In addition, specific components of formal and informal assessment procedures are presented in some detail to facilitate the reader's understanding of later chapters. Recent legislation that will significantly affect the provisions for services to exceptional children is also considered, as are the implications of this legislation in identification and assessment of, and instructional planning for, handicapped children and youths.

Part II focuses upon the specific assessment techniques used in the areas of reading, written and spoken language, spelling, arithmetic, career education, ecology, and early childhood. In each chapter available standardized tests are specified and their use with students is discussed. These tests were chosen primarily because they are used extensively by professionals throughout the United States and, consequently, teachers need to be aware of their availability and appropriateness for providing educationally relevant data. The main target of the chapters in Part II, however, is to acquaint teachers with the various informal techniques that either are available or can be constructed to determine the instructionally relevant aspects of a student's scholastic problem. In each area—reading, spelling, etc.—descriptions are given of a wide range of evaluative devices, so that teachers working with students with varying degrees of learning disorders and of differing ages may find information that fills their needs. Most of the chapters in Part II conclude with suggestions for increasing one's knowledge and skill in the use of assessment procedures. If any suggestion can be offered the person who is attempting to become skilled in educational assessment, it would be that the techniques must be practiced diligently with as many pupils and in as many situations as possible. Appraisal practices cannot be viewed as a "spectator sport" but, rather, should be seen as the primary vehicle for establishing sound instructional opportunities for students who are not performing at a level that is commensurate with their abilities.

Throughout this book, we have presented information regarding assessment strategies appropriate to preschool through adolescent children. In addition, the chapter on perceptual assessment, although not recommended for use with students who exhibit academic disorders, will provide readers with current theory and research in this highly controversial and possibly instructionally irrelevant area. It is our sincere hope, as teachers read and internalize the material in this text, they will be able to formulate their own philosophies of educational assessment and recognize their unique role in helping children overcome various learning difficulties.

G. W.
S. C. L.

Acknowledgments

We would like to express our appreciation to those who provided us with encouragement and support throughout the completion of this book. We are especially grateful to Mary Poplin, Criss McCuller, Lee Person, Gaye McNutt, John Starkel, and George Maitland, who read parts of the manuscript and recommended many valuable suggestions. Donna Barnsley and Tina Baugher helped with library research and references. Our thanks are also extended to Ann Shaughness, who helped type the manuscript, and Anne LaChance, who was an outstanding graduate assistant and typist throughout the writing of this book. Our children, Chris and T. J. Wallace, and Stephen, Laurel, and Nicholas Larsen, deserve a special note of thanks for understanding our absences while we were writing the book. Finally, we appreciate the constant support and encouragement of our wives, Marti and Patty.

EDUCATIONAL ASSESSMENT OF LEARNING PROBLEMS:
Testing for Teaching

Part 1

DIMENSIONS OF EDUCATIONAL ASSESSMENT

Teacher, come on outside!
I'll race you to the seesaw!
No, you won't fall off!
I'll show you how!
Don't be afraid, teacher.
Grab my hand and follow me.
You can learn all over again!

Albert Cullum

1

Introduction
and Overview

The exaggerated use of assessment measures in schools is a phenomenon of the twentieth century. Historically, the impetus for using various types of tests was provided during World War I (Anastasi, 1976) when there was a pressing need to rapidly classify 1.5 million military recruits with respect to general intellectual levels. Since then, we have witnessed a surge of interest in testing and a corresponding proliferation of educational appraisal techniques. Testing purposes have been modified since World War I. According to Spache (1976), what were once paper-and-pencil techniques measuring certain skills and abilities are now considered to be a series of different educational situations providing the teacher with the opportunity for evaluating various student behaviors in relation to recognized objectives.

The considerable expansion of educational services for handicapped children since World War I made necessary differential assessment of children with learning difficulties. Initially, the diagnostic procedures used with handicapped people were patterned on the traditional medical practice of studying the etiology of a condition and classifying various signs and symptoms according to different disability categories. Consequently, some children with learning handicaps were noted to be *dyslexic,* others were labeled as *brain damaged,* while still others were classified as suffering from *minimal cerebral dysfunction.* Educators and psychologists soon realized that these labels provided very little assistance in remedying the child's learning problem. Kirk (1968), for example, noted that the etiology of a disability was usually not helpful in organizing remedial procedures. At the same time, other writers (Bateman, 1967) recommended that the concept of causation should be deemphasized and that the emphasis should be placed on the specific disabilities being experienced by the individual child.

Over the past few years, the assessment process has become more educationally relevant until today educational evaluations are recognized as a means to gather information about a child in order to set up appropriate teaching strategies. Assessment practices that do not produce guidelines both for instructional objectives and for methods and materials to be used are considered by many to be a waste of valuable time and resources (Wallace & McLoughlin, 1975). In other words, educational assessment results should clearly outline how to teach the child.

The process by which specific skill deficiencies are determined and subsequently remedied has been known, according to Haring and Bateman (1977), as the diagnostic-remedial approach (Bateman, 1967), prescriptive-teaching (Peter, 1965), ability and process training (Ysseldyke & Salvia, 1974), psychometric phrenology (Mann, 1971), and task analysis (Johnson, 1967). To this list can also be added clinical teaching, diagnostic teaching, and psychoeducational assessment. The primary goal in each of these diagnostic-remedial approaches has been to isolate specific skill strengths and weaknesses and recommend various remedial procedures and teaching strategies. Throughout this book we will refer to those procedures as the educational assessment process.

It has been our experience that, just as there are different levels of disability among children, there are different levels of assessment (Otto, McMenemy, & Smith, 1973). In the next section various levels of assessment are described.

LEVELS OF ASSESSMENT

Assessment procedures often are differentially applied according to the severity of each child's specific learning difficulty. All children will *not* require a detailed evaluation involving time-consuming and expensive assessment techniques. In many cases, teachers are able to plan appropriate instructional programs based upon systematic observation and the use of informal teacher-made tests. More intensive assessment procedures are usually reserved for children experiencing severe and prolonged learning difficulties. Most writers in this area (Brueckner & Bond, 1955; Otto, McMenemy, & Smith, 1973; Wilson, 1972) list three specific levels of assessment. However, some amount of overlap must be considered in each of these levels.

The initial level of assessment is often called the *survey* or *general level*. In school this is the *classroom screening level* (Otto, McMenemy, & Smith, 1973). Typically, the child's general classroom performance is measured at this level, and individuals who appear to require more detailed analysis and evaluation are identified.

The intermediate level of assessment usually involves the administration of specific diagnostic tests intended to further identify and examine suspected areas of difficulty. This level focuses on an analysis of particularly troublesome skills and abilities.

The final, most intensive assessment level usually involves a very thorough case study of the child. This level of assessment is usually applicable to children severely handicapped in learning. Very detailed diagnostic techniques are used, including a complete study of the child's home background, school history, health status, and social-emotional history. The primary objective of this level of assessment is to obtain a complete understanding of the child's learning problem by examining and subsequently studying all factors related to the child's specific difficulties.

PURPOSES OF ASSESSMENT

Evaluative techniques generally allow a teacher to make decisions on the basis of information gathered during the assessment process. Decisions may concern individual children, groups of students, or even the relative effectiveness of different methods of instruction (Mehrens & Lehmann, 1969). Among the many reasons for administering tests, Karmel (1970) has listed the following:

- to group children within a particular classroom or to form classroom groups
- to provide special study and remedial instruction
- to evaluate capability and accomplishments
- to foster educational and vocational goals
- to discover educationally and socially maladjusted children
- to measure outcomes of instruction
- to certify pupils' achievements
- to provide material for research

Generally, however, children with specific learning problems are administered various educational assessment techniques for two major purposes: (1) to identify and sometimes label for administrative purposes those children experiencing learning problems who will probably require special educational help, and (2) to gather additional information that might be helpful in establishing instructional objectives and remedial strategies for those children identified as handicapped learners.

Assessment for Identification

During the identification phase of the assessment process, children requiring special help are initially screened and subsequently referred for more intensive appraisal. The typical pattern of identification and referral in most school systems is usually initiated by regular classroom teachers who request help for individual students (Wallace & McLoughlin, 1975). Following the initial referral, children are usually administered a battery of educational and psychological tests to assess academic achievement, intellectual aptitudes, learning abilities, perceptual characteristics, language skills and preferences, motivation, adaptive behavior, and sociocultural variables (Oakland, 1974). Ideally, various emotional and environmental factors are also assessed, and parental and home consultations are arranged.

Following the testing, the results are usually evaluated in terms of the severity of the child's problem. Eligibility for various special education services (e.g., resource room assistance, special class placement, etc.) is also decided at this time. At this point most children are classified according to some special education category (e.g., learning disabilities, educable mentally retarded, etc.).

During the past few years, some aspects of the identification process have been widely criticized. Major objections have been voiced when the evaluation process proceeds no further than identifying the child requiring special assistance. We feel that identification for the purpose of merely classifying the child according to some special education label actually serves no real purpose. Identification under these circumstances actually highlights the inadequacy of the schools and tends to create pressure for inappropriate solutions (Wallace & Kauffman, 1978).

The other frequent objection to the identification process concerns the *sole* use of tests to identify handicapped children. It is now generally recognized that other aspects of a child's behavior are as significant as the child's performance on a standardized test. Consequently, most evaluation procedures also include informal appraisal and observations of the child and consideration of various emotional and environmental variables. Other important variables that should be included involve the relevance of the curricula, teaching methods and materials, peer acceptance, and other extrapersonal factors that influence learning (Oakland, 1974). There is no doubt that assessment practices relying solely on standardized tests will provide an isolated and very limiting view of a child.

Assessment for Teaching

The primary purpose for evaluating children with learning problems should be to gather information that can be used in planning instructional programs for individual children (Myers & Hammill, 1976). The data gathered during the evaluation process should both help the teacher in further understanding a child's specific difficulties and suggest various instructional strategies and procedures. Educational assessment results provide the teacher with an essential *guide* for both planning and implementing instructional programs and techniques.

Many different assessment measures are used in the appraisal process for gathering instructionally relevant information. Collecting systematic observational data and administering a variety of informal teacher-made tests, for example, usually provide more exacting data than do many standardized formal tests. The specific skills and behaviors that are evaluated by informal measures (e.g., visual discrimination of consonants, multiplication of fractions, etc.) generally have been found to be more directly related to ongoing programs of instruction than the skills and abilities measured by most standardized tests (Strang, 1969). Nevertheless, many formal tests are administered to children with learning problems and subsequently analyzed according to the specific skills measured by the tests. As a rule, we have found that the most efficient evaluation process will employ a variety of appraisal techniques, including both formal and informal assessment procedures.

As we have already mentioned, the results from the educational assessment process typically provide the teacher with information for implementing an instructional program. The data will often include levels of instruction, skill strengths and weaknesses, and related behavioral components.

Finally, assessment for teaching implies that evaluative techniques are continually applied in the classroom on an ongoing basis by most teachers. As we will see in Chapter 2, the initial assessment results provide valuable information for programming according to each child's instructional needs, but these recommendations are often modified as the child progresses and his or her specific needs are changed. In this context, assessment becomes an essential part of the entire teaching process in which the teacher continually evaluates the child, not necessarily through formal tests, but by careful observation and various other informal measures. Assessment actually becomes subsumed under the ongoing instructional program, and the process becomes indistinguishable from various other teaching procedures.

ISSUES IN ASSESSMENT

Many different misunderstandings and criticisms concerning assessment principles and objectives have emerged during attempts to implement appraisal techniques in various educational settings. In this regard, Ebel (1975) notes that the reasons tests are criticized are not difficult to find:

> The tests themselves are imperfect. Indeed, some are seriously flawed. They are sometimes used unwisely, misinterpreted, overinterpreted, or handled as weapons rather than as tools. They reflect particular perceptions of the goals of education which not all educators share [p. 83].

We have found that the primary concerns can be categorized into issues involving the personnel completing the assessment, the skills and abilities to be measured, and the specific evaluative techniques that are used in the assessment process. Each of these issues is briefly discussed in the following section.

Who Should Assess?

The issue of *who* should assess the child with learning problems has become a widely debated topic during the past few years. In many school districts, an educational diagnostician or school psychologist is charged with the major responsibility for evaluating all children experiencing serious academic deficiencies within the school system. The results of the evaluative process are incorporated into a diagnostic report, which usually outlines a comprehensive educational plan for remedying the child's learning problems. Depending on the student's educational level, the recommendations are subsequently put into practice by either the regular or special class teacher. However, many educators and psychologists have become disillusioned with this approach to assessment, and in recent years the classroom teacher has taken a more active part in appraising the skills and abilities of the child with learning difficulties.

The passage of the Education for All Handicapped Children Act in 1975 (Public Law 94–142) by the U.S. Congress and the rules and regulations with this law will certainly contribute to continued growth in the quality of assessment services provided for handicapped children. According to MacMillan (1977), the basic rights established by Public Law 94–142 are as follows:

1. *the right to due process,* which protects the individual from erroneous classification, capricious labeling, and denial of equal education
2. *protection against discriminatory testing in diagnosis,* which ensures against possible bias in intelligence tests used with ethnic minority children
3. *placement in an educational setting that is the least restrictive environment,* which protects the individual from possible detrimental effects of segregated education for the handicapped
4. *individualized program plans,* which ensures accountability by those responsible for the education of the handicapped [p. 1].

In addition, Public Law 94–142 rules specifically provide that the team evaluating each handicapped child must include a *regular classroom teacher* or an appropriate equivalent. The new regulations also require observation of the child's academic performance in the classroom. We believe that rules and regulations associated with Public Law 94–142 are noteworthy, due to the increased responsibility of the classroom teacher, and the inclusion of observational data as part of total assessment findings.

According to Burnett (1970), the concept of the teacher as a diagnostician in the classroom is not a new concept. Nonetheless, Myers and Hammill (1976) suggest that the current disenchantment with standardized testing, along with the availability and use of educationally oriented informal tests and an increase in assessment skills, have helped recently to move teachers in the direction of doing a large part of the educational evaluations themselves. Teachers' aides, team teaching, departmentalization, and parent and lay volunteers have also provided teachers with both the time and resources needed to assess the child with individual learning needs (Wallace & Kauffman, 1978).

We feel strongly that regular classroom teachers, resource personnel, and other special classroom teachers should play an important role in the assessment of children with learning difficulties. We agree with Smith and Neisworth (1969) that teachers are in the best position to assess the educational problems of children, because, among other reasons, teachers are in the most desirable situation to observe the *entire* range of student skills and abilities. Teachers usually come to know each child in a classroom quite well and, consequently, are able to distinguish valid samples of characteristic behaviors from isolated incidents, behaviors that occur rarely, or temporary conditions. Behaviors that have been demonstrated to a marked extent over an extended period of time are easily pinpointed by many classroom teachers.

We have found that teachers are quite capable of using both formal and informal assessment procedures. Only limited training is necessary for administering and interpreting many of the formal published tests discussed in subsequent chapters of this book. In addition, many informal teacher-made tests can be similarly constructed and effectively used by teachers in appraising the skills and abilities of children with learning problems. Nevertheless, it has been only recently that colleges and universities have begun to incorporate opportunities for learning various assessment procedures into teacher training programs. Only minimal attention had been given previously to the practical considerations involved in evaluating children *within* the classroom *by* the teacher. However, the increasing number of preservice and inservice training programs dealing with the teacher's role in the assessment process seem to indicate that there is a growing recognition of the needs within this particular training area. Burnett (1970) notes that the diagnostic base for each teacher should probably include the following:

1. skill in selecting the most valuable information available from previous records and files
2. ability to formulate classroom diagnostic procedures capable of increasing the amount of information known about a child's various skills and abilities

3. skill in interpreting the information after the data have been accumulated.
4. ability to make meaningful teaching recommendations for remedying various problems or weaknesses.

In order for assessment to maintain any educational relevance, teachers must take part in the evaluation. On the other hand, teachers should not become involved in the administration and interpretation of noneducational measures such as projective tests (e.g., *Thematic Apperception Test, Rorschach,* etc.) or various individual intelligence tests (e.g., *Wechsler Intelligence Scale for Children, Stanford-Binet Intelligence Scale,* etc.), since these tests require extensive training for proper administration and interpretation. The question of *who* should assess the child with learning problems is best answered by more effectively using the skills of the teacher throughout the educational assessment process.

What Should Be Assessed?

In many schools educational assessment has become an end in itself rather than a means for planning instructional programs (Stephens, 1970; Wallace & Kauffman, 1978). Often improper emphasis has been placed on the grade-equivalent and age-equivalent scores that are obtained from formally published tests. Children are referred to as having an arithmetic age-equivalent score of 7–2, for example, or reading at a 2.4 grade level. We think that the emphasis upon exact scores incorrectly accentuates the least valuable information in terms of planning a remedial program for children with specific learning problems. The detailed information that actually leads to the formulation of the particular score is more important to the teacher. For example, the fact that a teacher knows which letter sounds are known by a child and which sounds are missed on a standardized reading test will probably be more helpful than the teacher's knowledge of the child's grade-level scores. This descriptive skill information provides the teacher with basic data for teaching the child, while grade-level scores are usually too general to use in planning specific teaching sequences.

We believe that the emphasis throughout the evaluation process should be on the specific subskills that comprise each academic skill area. This information can be acquired through either formal or informal tests, but our experience indicates that the administration of informal teacher-made tests is best suited to providing this type of data. Task-oriented informal tests can be constructed easily from any of the various curriculum materials, including workbooks, skill sheets, etc., which are available to most classroom teachers. In addition to being inexpensive, these teacher-made tests are particularly well suited to the needs of children with learning problems because the results from such tests can be directly applied to various programs of instruction.

Specific skill information can also be obtained from some formally published tests when the test administrator carefully examines the student's test performance. In using this procedure, individual test items are analyzed closely for specific errors. Overall findings are then applied to various teaching strategies. Nevertheless, this information might be obtained more easily through the administration of informal teacher-made tests.

The specific skills approach to educational assessment is recommended among professionals because of its applicability to various educational strategies and teaching programs. The information obtained from a specific skills assessment outlines the precise nature of a child's academic difficulties in terms of skill strengths and weaknesses. This information then is used by the teacher to determine the skills in which the child requires direct instruction to overcome particular difficulties. It is important to point out that the specific skills approach seems ideally suited to the needs of children with learning problems because of the very direct relationship between assessment findings and putting into practice various teaching strategies.

Which Assessment Techniques Should Be Used?

The traditional approach in the assessment of children with learning problems has emphasized the use of formal, standardized tests. The wide availability of formal tests, the relative ease of administering them, and the use of normative data are some of the major reasons why these tests have been used extensively within schools. Recently, however, many educators have questioned the sole usage of formal tests to assess children. Questions concerning the overgeneralization of standardized test results and the low reliabilities of many formal tests have been expressed. Nevertheless, the major concern with most standardized tests has been with the very minimal amount of specific teaching information that they provide. Very little data that might be *directly* applied to instructing the child is obtained by the teacher. Instead, the results usually include a general quantitative score (e. g., percentile, grade score, etc.), which is used to compare the student with other groups of children. The exact information concerning specific academic behaviors and skills that encompass day-to-day teaching programs is essentially omitted from most standardized test results.

In attempting to supplement the results of formal tests with more educationally oriented information, many professionals have included different types of informal assessment procedures in the evaluation process. Teacher-made tests and various observational techniques have been particularly useful in this regard. The precision of informal assessment techniques in pinpointing specific skill strengths and weaknesses is viewed as a distinct advantage of this approach. In addition, observations and informal tests can be used as part of a teacher's ongoing teaching program, and the results can be directly applied to various programs and materials used with individual students. In contrast to results from formal testing, the outcome of informal testing is usually directly applicable to teaching the child.

In practice each of the various assessment procedures is usually included in the evaluation. Some of the appraisal techniques are accomplished simultaneously, and one technique may also suggest another (Lerner, 1976). Overlapping among the techniques often makes it difficult to separate them. For example, many teachers include observation as an ongoing technique during all formal and informal testing. It is difficult in these cases to suggest when one assessment technique begins and another ends. Nevertheless, in the vast majority of cases informal assessment approaches probably will provide the most exact data in terms of putting into practice teaching programs and strategies.

The widespread disenchantment with intelligence testing must also be mentioned in our discussion of selecting various assessment techniques. According to Hallahan and Kauffman (1976), all IQ tests are thought to be culturally biased to some degree. The consequent administration of these tests to minority-group children has been questioned in the professional literature. The disproportionate number of minority-group children assigned to lower ability groups and special education classes is often attributed to the discriminatory nature of tests, which reflect only white, middle-class values and abilities. It is also felt that assessment practices are discriminatory when children are not tested in their major language or when examiners are insensitive to relevant characteristics that are evidenced by minority-group children (Oakland, 1974).

These concerns with intelligence testing have caused professionals to consider closely this particular area with regard to assessing all children, especially those with specific learning difficulties. We agree with Hallahan and Kauffman (1976) that IQ tests are neither accurate predictors of educationally relevant behavior nor sensitive guides to the development of educational programs. The focus of attention in selecting various assessment procedures should be on deciding which techniques provide the most educationally relevant information for helping each child overcome his or her specific learning difficulties.

ORGANIZATION OF THE BOOK

Part I of this book has been organized to present more general information and background material for the specific assessment techniques that are discussed in Part II. Chapter 2 presents an overview of various appraisal techniques and assessment models, along with a discussion of some basic technical considerations in testing. The information in Chapter 3 is intended to provide a practical approach to educational assessment. Fundamental testing procedures are discussed, and specific guidelines for using both formal and informal tests are presented with suggestions for interpreting assessment data.

The 10 chapters in Part II describe techniques for assessing children in very specific and essential areas of the school curriculum. Each chapter includes a discussion of the desirable skills that should be included within each area. This is followed by a systematic description and discussion of both formal and informal assessment procedures. Examples of observational scales and teacher-made tests are also included. Most of the chapters conclude with a summary of assessment procedures in each area and a list of suggested teaching activities for applying the information presented.

Though we tend to minimize the use of formally published tests in the assessment process, many of these tests nonetheless are described in this book because they are used extensively within educational settings and can be adapted informally for use in many different situations. It is our belief, however, that the most proficient assessment will include a variety of appraisal techniques.

References

Anastasi, A. *Psychological testing.* (4th ed.) London: Macmillan, 1976.

Bateman, B. Three approaches to diagnosis and educational planning for children with learning disabilities. *Academic Therapy,* 1967, 2, 215–222.

Brueckner, L. J., & Bond, G. L. *The diagnosis and treatment of learning difficulties.* New York: Appleton–Century–Crofts, 1955.

Burnett, R. W. The classroom teacher as a diagnostician. In D. L. DeBoer (Ed.), *Reading diagnosis and evaluation.* Newark, Del.: International Reading Association, 1970.

Ebel, R. L. Educational tests: Valid? Biased? Useful? *Phi Delta Kappan,* 1975, 57, 83–88.

Hallahan, D. P., & Kauffman, J. M. *Introduction to learning disabilities: A psycho-behavioral approach.* Englewood Cliffs, N.J.: Prentice-Hall, 1976.

Haring, N. G., & Bateman, B. *Teaching the learning disabled child.* Englewood Cliffs, N.J.: Prentice-Hall, 1977.

Johnson, D. Educational principles for children with learning disabilities. *Rehabilitation Literature,* 1967, 28, 317–322.

Karmel, L. J. *Measurement and evaluation in the schools.* London: Macmillan, 1970.

Kirk, S. A. Illinois test of psycholinguistic abilities: Its origin and implications. In J. Hellmuth (Ed.), *Learning Disorders.* Vol. III. Seattle: Special Child Publications, 1968.

Lerner, J. *Children with learning disabilities.* (2nd ed.) Boston: Houghton Mifflin, 1976.

MacMillan, D. L. *Mental retardation in school and society.* Boston: Little, Brown, 1977.

Mann, L. Psychometric phrenology and the new faculty psychology: The case against ability assessment and training. *Journal of Special Education,* 1971, *5,* 3–14.

Mehrens, W. A., & Lehmann, I. J. *Standardized tests in education.* New York: Holt, Rinehart and Winston, 1969.

Myers, P. I., & Hammill, D. D. *Methods for learning disorders.* (2nd ed.) New York: John Wiley, 1976.

Oakland, T. Assessment, education, and minority-group children. *Academic Therapy,* 1974, *10,* 133–140.

Otto, W., McMenemy, R. A., & Smith, R. J. *Corrective and remedial teaching.* (2nd ed.) Boston: Houghton Mifflin, 1973.

Peter, L. J. *Prescriptive teaching.* New York: McGraw-Hill, 1965.

Smith, R. M., & Neisworth, J. T. Fundamentals of informal educational assessment. In R. M. Smith (Ed.), *Teacher diagnosis of educational difficulties.* Columbus, Ohio: Charles E. Merrill, 1969.

Spache, G. D. *Investigating the issues of reading disabilities.* Boston: Allyn and Bacon, 1976.

Stephens, T. M. *Directive teaching of children with learning and behavioral disorders.* Columbus, Ohio: Charles E. Merrill, 1970.

Strang, R. *Diagnostic teaching of reading.* (2nd ed.) New York: McGraw-Hill, 1969.

Wallace, G., & Kauffman, J. M. *Teaching children with learning problems.* (2nd ed.) Columbus, Ohio: Charles E. Merrill, 1978.

Wallace, G., & McLoughlin, J. A. *Learning disabilities: Concepts and characteristics.* Columbus, Ohio: Charles E. Merrill, 1975.

Wilson, R. *Diagnostic and remedial reading for classroom and clinic.* (2nd ed.) Columbus, Ohio: Charles E. Merrill, 1972.

Ysseldyke, J. E., & Salvia, J. A critical analysis of the assumptions underlying diagnostic-prescriptive teaching. *Exceptional Children,* 1974, *41,* 181–195.

2

Principles
of Educational
Assessment

The use of a variety of diagnostic techniques to label or categorize children with learning problems has had a long and tumultuous history within the field of special education. Importantly, however, in the past few years we have witnessed an increased effort on the part of many educators to use educational assessment for identifying instructionally useful information. Under these circumstances, assessment data have become a means for planning teaching programs, rather than an end in themselves. The fundamental intent of any educational assessment must be to gather representative data to use later in formulating remedial programs. A number of assessment techniques appropriate for collecting educationally relevant data will be summarized in this chapter.

A DIAGNOSTIC TEACHING PLAN

A complete educational assessment plan should be comprised ideally of four steps: (1) identification procedures, (2) evaluation techniques, (3) development of an education plan, and (4) implementation of teaching strategies. Figure 2-1 schematically describes this assessment process. Each of the steps is discussed in the following section.

Identification

Many different methods are used to identify children with learning handicaps. Some school systems employ district-wide screening programs

FIGURE 2–1   Diagnostic Teaching Flowchart

Level I   Children with suspected education problems, i.e., those that exceed the usual expertise of most regular class teachers, are identified as potential high risk youngsters and referred to some type of diagnostician.

$\downarrow$

Level II   Evaluation of the child's educationally relevant characteristics and the prominent environmental traits that may in some way be associated with obvious or suspected educational problems.

$\downarrow$

Level III   Development of a comprehensive educational plan for the child—one that is based on diagnostic data that have been gathered about him and about his environment.

$\downarrow$

Level IV   Assignment of the child into the most suitable instructional environment as suggested by the educational plan which was generated at Level III.

Source: From *Clinical Teaching: Methods of Instruction for the Retarded* by R. M. Smith. Copyright © 1974 by McGraw-Hill, Inc. Used with permission of McGraw-Hill Book Company.

during which all children within the school system are administered group screening tests. Other schools rely on individual teacher or parental referrals for identifying academically disabled students. In the case of young children, many schools have put into practice preschool and early childhood screening programs (see Chapter 5). Formal and informal assessment devices, along with observational analysis, often have been included during this step of the diagnostic process.

Evaluation

An intensive evaluation of all phases of the child's learning problem usually follows the identification part of the diagnostic process. In some cases, specially trained psychometrists conduct the evaluation. However, most classroom teachers should be allowed to assess the child because of the critical implications usually obtained that could affect teaching the child during this phase of the evaluation. Furthermore, many of the assessment techniques used during evaluations require only minimal training and can be integrated easily into ongoing teaching programs. Gearheart (1976), for example, suggests that no single assessment procedure will fit all cases and circumstances, primarily due to the variety of settings in which diagnostic procedures are put into practice. Many of the techniques used during this stage are reviewed later in this chapter.

Developing a Teaching Plan

Once all of the assessment data are gathered, they are analyzed and developed into a teaching plan for the child. The educational hypotheses formulated during this stage should be based on solid, well-supported data gathered during the evaluation. This step essentially summarizes all that has previously occurred and points the way to remedial or preventive planning (Bateman, 1965). Any data that will be useful in planning an educational strategy are used at this stage, including results from standardized tests and informal teaching programs, observational data, and case-history information.

Implementation

Although the implementation stage of the assessment process includes putting into practice remedial teaching procedures, it might also involve making decisions regarding the educational level of the child. Many children with learning problems will be able to remain in regular classrooms while receiving special instruction from special teachers or from regular classroom teachers. Severely handicapped children, on the other hand, might require temporary special education services, including part-time or full-time classes. Nevertheless, the primary emphasis during this phase should be placed on putting into practice the remedial strategy for helping the children overcome their particular learning handicaps.

COLLECTING ASSESSMENT DATA

The wide variety of methods used to assess children with learning problems are listed in Table 2–1, and the major approaches for obtaining assessment information are discussed in this section. Further reference to each approach by specific content area is provided in subsequent chapters. In many cases, all of these assessment approaches will be used in studying students with learning handicaps. In practice, it will often be difficult to separate one approach from another because of the considerable amount of overlapping among them.

17

TABLE 2–1   Types of Assessment Techniques

A. Objective Tests and Standardized Measures

1. Standardized tests and measures
    a. Achievement tests.
    b. Mental and intelligence tests.
    c. Tests of motor skills and abilities.
    d. Aptitude and readiness tests.
    e. Physiological measures and medical examinations.
    f. Personality and adjustment tests.
    g. Interest inventories and attitude scales.
2. Unstandardized short-answer objective tests.
    a. Simple recall or free response tests.
    b. Completion tests.
    c. Alternate response tests.
    d. Multiple choice tests.
    e. Matching tests.
3. Improved essay types of tests consisting of questions so formulated that they can be scored on a fairly objective basis.
4. Scales for analyzing and rating a performance or a product.
5. Tests involving evaluation of responses using projective methods.

B. Evaluation of Behavior by Less Formal Procedures

1. Problem-situation tests.
    a. Direct experience.
        (1) Experiment to be performed.
        (2) Actual life situation to be met.
    b. Indirect approach.
        (1) Improved essay-type examinations.
        (2) Expressing judgments about described situations.
        (3) "What would you do?"
2. Behavior records concerning in- and out-of-school activities.
    a. Controlled situations.
        (1) Use of checklists, rating scales, score cards, codes for evaluating personality traits, behavior, attitudes, opinions, interests, and so on.
        (2) Self-rating devices, "Guess-Who?"
        (3) Time studies of attention, activities.
        (4) Photographs and motion pictures.
        (5) Stenographic reports.
        (6) Dictaphone and tape recordings.
    b. Uncontrolled situations.
        (1) Log or diary; autobiographical reports.
        (2) Anecdotal records; behavior journals.
        (3) Records of libraries, police, welfare agencies, and so on.
        (4) Still or motion pictures.
        (5) Tape recordings.
3. Inventories and questionnaires of work habits, interests, activities, associates, and the like.
4. Interviews, conferences, personal reports.
    a. With the individual learner himself.
    b. With others, such as parents or associates.

TABLE 2–1   (*Cont.*)

5. Analysis and evaluation of a creative act or product, such as a poem, music, constructions, and so forth.
6. Sociometric procedures for studying group relationships.
7. Evaluation of reactions using projective and expressive techniques.
   a. Psychodrama and play technics.
   b. Free-association tests.
   c. Interpretation of reactions to selected pictures and drawings.
   d. Interpretation of free oral and written expression.
   e. Interpretation of artistic and constructive products.

Source: Leo J. Brueckner, Guy L. Bond, *The Diagnosis and Treatment of Learning Difficulties,* © 1955, pp. 8–10. Reprinted by permission of Prentice-Hall, Inc., Englewood Cliffs, New Jersey.

FORMAL STANDARDIZED TESTS

Standardized tests have been used in educational settings for a long time. Hammill (1971) notes that these tests usually are administered by specially trained persons in settings other than the classroom. In addition, he suggests that

> ... the information acquired is of a decidedly quantitative nature and tends to compare a given child's performance with national or regional normative data. The results, therefore, are often reported in terms of quotients, scaled scores, grade equivalents, or percentiles [p. 343].

General achievement tests and diagnostic tests are among the more commonly used standardized tests. General achievement tests usually are administered to groups of children and therefore provide results of a more general nature. Achievement tests may either sample content in a single subject area (e.g., reading) or consist of a number of subtests in different content areas (e.g., arithmetic, vocabulary, spelling, etc.).

Diagnostic tests, on the other hand, usually are individually administered and are primarily concerned with testing for more specific skills and abilities in various subject-matter areas. For example, a diagnostic reading test probably would include specific subtests in the category of word analysis, such as knowledge of letter sounds, blending ability, syllabication, etc. The results of these tests then would provide the administrator with detailed information concerning a child's strengths and weaknesses in a particular subject-matter area.

A great many tests have been published during the past few decades. Some of the more commonly used tests are listed in Table 2–2. Many of these are discussed in greater detail in later chapters. Other sources of information concerning tests include Buros' *Mental Measurements Yearbook*

TABLE 2–2 Commonly Used Published Tests

Reading	Arithmetic	Spoken Language	Spelling	Written Expression	Early Childhood	Perceptual-motor	Career Education
1. Botel Reading Inventory (Botel, 1962)	1. Diagnostic Tests and Self-helps in Arithmetic (Brueckner, 1955)	1. Houston Test for Language Development (Crabtree, 1963)	1. Gates-Russell Spelling Diagnosis Test (Gates & Russell, 1937)	1. Picture Story Language Test (Myklebust, 1965)	1. Boehm Test of Basic Concepts (Boehm, 1971)	1. Bender Visual-Motor Gestalt Test for Children (Bender, 1962)	1. Career Maturity Inventory (Crites, 1973)
2. Classroom Reading Inventory (Silvaroli, 1973)	2. Key Math Diagnostic Arithmetic Test (Connolly, Nachtman, & Pritchett 1973)	2. The Northwestern Syntax Screening Test (Lee, 1969)	2. Lincoln Diagnostic Spelling Tests (Lincoln, 1955)	2. Sequential Tests of Educational Progress (ETS, 1958)	2. CIRCUS (Anderson, et al., 1974)	2. The Marianne Frostig Developmental Test of Visual Perception (Frostig, Lefever, & Whittlesey, 1964)	2. Differential Aptitude Tests (Bennett, Seashore, & Wesman, 1969)
3. Diagnostic Reading Scales (Spache, 1972)	3. Stanford Diagnostic Arithmetic Test (Beatty, Madden, & Gardner, 1966)	3. Peabody Picture Vocabulary Test (Dunn, 1959)	3. Spellmaster (Cohen & Abrams, 1974)		3. Cooperative Preschool Inventory (Caldwell, 1970)	3. Goodenough Harris Drawing Test (Goodenough & Harris, 1963)	3. General Aptitude Test Battery (U.S. Department of Labor, 1970)
4. Durrell Analysis of Reading Difficulty (Durrell, 1955)		4. The Test of Language Development (Newcomer & Hammill, 1977)	4. Test of Written Spelling (Larsen & Hammill, 1976)		4. Denver Developmental Screening Test (Frankenburg & Dodds, 1970)	4. Bruininks-Oseretsky Test of Motor Proficiency (Bruininks, 1977)	4. Kuder Occupation Interest Inventory (Kuder, 1966)
5. Gates-McKillop Reading Diagnostic Tests (Gates & McKillop, 1962)		5. Utah Test of Language Development (Mecham, Jex, & Jones 1967)			5. Evanston Early Identification Scale (Landsman & Dillard, 1967)		5. Minnesota Vocational Interest Inventory (Clark & Campbell, 1966)
6. Gilmore Oral Reading Test (Gilmore & Gilmore, 1968)							

20

7. Gray Oral Reading Test (Gray & Robinson, 1967)
8. McCullough Word-Analysis Tests (McCullough, 1963)
9. Monroe Reading Aptitude Tests (Monroe, 1935)
10. Roswell-Chall Diagnostic Test of Word-analysis Skills (Roswell & Chall, 1959)
11. Slosson Oral Reading Test (Slosson, 1963)
12. Woodcock Reading Mastery Tests (Woodcock, 1974)

6. First Grade Screening Test (Pate & Webb, 1969)
7. The Meeting Street School Screening Test (Hainsworth & Siqueland, 1969)

5. Motor Free Visual Perception Test (Colarusso & Hammill, 1972)
6. The Purdue Perceptual-Motor Survey (Roach & Kephart, 1966)
7. Auditory Discrimination Test (Wepman, 1958)

6. Nonreading Aptitude Test Battery (U.S. Department of Labor, 1970)
7. Strong-Campbell Interest Inventory (Campbell, 1974)

and *Tests in Print.* The seventh edition of the *Mental Measurements Yearbook,* published in 1972, provides a comprehensive critique of many published standardized tests. *Tests in Print* serves as an excellent bibliography of tests and as an index to the *Mental Measurements Yearbooks.* In addition, *Tests in Print* provides general information concerning grade levels, types of scores provided, publishers, and references to test reviews in *Mental Measurements Yearbooks.*

Limitations of Formal Tests

The increased use of tests within schools actually has been partially responsible for the many poorly constructed tests that have appeared on the commercial market. Regrettably, many of these poorly constructed tests are presently being used in schools. Because of this, each test administrator should make every effort to become aware of both the practical and the technical aspects of individual tests. It is important to know *why* a test is being administered, *what* type of information is expected, and *how* that information is to be used (Mehrens & Lehmann, 1969). In our discussion of specific tests in later chapters, we have attempted to pinpoint the strengths and weaknesses of the tests we have described. Additional sources for this type of information include the *Mental Measurements Yearbook.* Some of the more general limitations and misuses of formal tests are listed also in the following paragraphs.

Overgeneralization of Findings   According to Ekwall (1976), the most flagrant misuse of group standardized tests is using them to make final decisions concerning individual students. It is a common practice in many school districts to label children as *perceptually disordered* or *remedial readers* based upon single test scores. Likewise, many decisions for placing children in special classes or groups are supported only by test scores. In many of these cases, test results obviously have been extended beyond the intended realm of the scores. Test administrators should be aware of this potential misuse of standardized tests, especially as it pertains to interpreting scores from group tests.

Lack of Teaching Information   The vast majority of standardized group tests provide very general information regarding a student's achievement or lack of progress. Most standardized reading tests, for example, indicate that a particular child is reading below grade level. Notwithstanding the importance of this general information, the teacher is provided with basically very little data that can be used in actually *teaching* the child. The more exact information upon which daily instruction is usually formulated is omitted in the results obtained from most formal assessment measures. Grade-level scores (e.g., 3.5) do not describe the specific *behaviors* that encompass that particular score. Instead, the teacher is often forced to gather this information through various informal assessment devices. This lack of teaching information is probably one of the most serious shortcomings of formal tests.

Low Reliability   As discussed in Chapter 1, consistent test results are obtained from tests that are reliable. It is indeed unfortunate that many tests commonly used with children experiencing learning problems are tests with considerably low reliabilities. Many standardized tests do not report any reliability information in test manuals. In our review of specific tests in later chapters, we have attempted to evaluate reliability information for those tests for which it was available.

Child and Administrator Variability   Extreme variation in daily performance is often mentioned as a characteristic of children with learning problems. Attentional difficulties, tendency to be distracted, and hyperactivity are variables that can affect a child's test performance. Consequently, fluctuating test scores often are a result of these reasons, rather than actually being true measurements of academic performance.

Test administrators, too, can cause test variability. Hammill (1971) notes that examiners vary daily in terms of their patience, temperament, and skill. All of these behaviors may affect a child's overall test performance, and it is important that the test administrator is aware of these potential difficulties.

Keeping these misuses and limitations in mind, there are a number of positive aspects of formal standardized tests that should also be mentioned. The ability to compare a child or groups of children with a standardization sample should certainly be considered as an important aspect of standardized tests. Similarly, the relative ease of administration of most formal tests is another advantage. Many standardized tests are very promising when the results of such tests are viewed as just one part of a total evaluation.

INFORMAL TESTS

In contrast to formal standardized tests, most informal tests are administered by the teacher in the classroom. Otto, McMenemy, and Smith (1973) suggest that informal teacher-made tests often are administered when specific data are not available from standardized tests, or to supplement information obtained from standardized tests.

Many types of informal measures may be used for various purposes (Strang, 1969). Some teacher-made tests are specifically designed to assess one particular skill (e.g., shape discrimination, knowledge of place value, etc.), while other informal measures are designed to assess a broad range of skills. Various comprehension abilities, subject-matter knowledge, or even readiness skills are among the wide range of areas that might also be informally measured. Figure 2–2 provides a number of examples of informal tests. Additional teacher-made tests in each area are listed in subsequent chapters. Guidelines for constructing informal tests are discussed in Chapter 3.

Advantages of Informal Tests

There are a number of very important advantages for using teacher-made tests with children experiencing learning problems. Some of these benefits are discussed in the following section.

Similarity to Teaching Programs   Items included in informal tests often approximate the skills and objectives of classroom teaching programs, whereas, as Strang (1969) points out, items on standardized tests too often are remote from the content and skills being taught in a classroom. The data obtained from teacher-made tests usually are quite adaptable to various materials and programs used with individual students. In fact, the instruments that are included as part of this assessment often resemble classroom activities (e.g., classroom assignments, oral exercises, etc.). Furthermore, many informal teacher-made tests actually are constructed from children's books and workbooks and various teachers' manuals. The immediate application of informal test results to classroom teaching is a primary reason for the popularity of these tests among classroom teachers.

Teacher Involvement   The use of assessment procedures by individuals working *directly* with disabled students in an ongoing teaching program also has been recognized as an advantage of informal tests. When compared to visiting diagnosticians and psychometricians, teachers no doubt are in the best position to assess the educational problems of children. In addition to observing the entire range of behavior in many different situations, the teacher is recognized as having stronger rapport with most children than the majority of other adults (Smith, 1969). Furthermore, teachers probably are best prepared to use test results, since one of the primary functions of educational testing is to help plan teaching programs, and this is already part of a teacher's responsibilities. The direct involvement of the teacher in the testing process seems ideally suited to fulfilling this purpose.

Simplicity of Design   Most informal tests are usually very easy to administer, score, and interpret. The amount of time involved in administering them is usually short, and they are relatively inexpensive. Nevertheless, it

FIGURE 2–2   Examples of Informal Tests

Test 1. *Prefixes*

Objective: To assess knowledge of prefixes.

Directions: Direct the child to circle the prefix in each of the following words.

1. uneven	7. indirect
2. reread	8. prepaid
3. unhappy	9. reload
4. misplace	10. inactive
5. inhuman	11. unfair
6. repair	12. disapprove

Test 2. *Regrouping*

Objective: To assess knowledge of regrouping.

Directions: Direct the child to complete each of the following arithmetic examples.

$$
\begin{array}{ccccc}
5\ \ 2 & 6\ \ 7 & 2\ \ 3 & 4\ \ 1 & 6\ \ 5 \\
+\ \ \ 9 & +\ \ 7 & +\ \ 8 & +\ \ 9 & +\ \ 6 \\
\hline
\end{array}
$$

$$
\begin{array}{ccccc}
3\ \ 7 & 5\ \ 3 & 6\ \ 4 & 8\ \ 9 & 7\ \ 5 \\
+2\ \ 4 & +2\ \ 8 & +2\ \ 7 & +6\ \ 2 & +4\ \ 7 \\
\hline
\end{array}
$$

Test 3. *Context Clues*

Objective: To assess knowledge of context clues.

Directions: Direct the child to select the correct word for each sentence.

1. He did not like sour _____.
   (trees, candy, books)
2. Mike saw many _____ at the circus.
   (clowns, trucks, mailboxes)
3. Can you _____ your name?
   (hurry, print, drive)
4. We go _____ in the summer.
   (skating, swimming, sledding)
5. She smiled because she was _____.
   (angry, happy, sad)
6. Mary had a _____ for her birthday party.
   (cake, pencil, car)
7. They live _____ up on a mountain.
   (low, high, middle)
8. "Help him to find his other _____," she said.
   (shoe, nose, hair)

---

is important to point out that many informal tests are difficult to construct. Selecting appropriate test items and sequencing them in order of difficulty are troublesome aspects in constructing teacher-made tests. However, teachers who use these instruments are not burdened by detailed directions, specific time limits, and complicated administrative procedures. Instead, teachers are free to concentrate upon the children's performance. Following the testing, results may be applied to classroom teaching rather than to confusing and often meaningless grade scores, age equivalents, or percentile ranks.

Broader Range of Pupil Progress   The frequent use of informal tests over an extended period of time provides the teacher with an ongoing evaluation of both specific materials and individual achievement (Wallace & Kauffman, 1978). The results provide important input for planning and revising teaching programs during a specific time period. In addition, informal test results serve as a very concise and manageable procedure for reporting pupil progress to parents and other teachers. The range of skills informally evaluated certainly provides a much broader base for communicating student strengths and weaknesses to these individuals.

It is important to note, however, that informal tests actually demand as much precision as standardized instruments during the production of the test and the administration of the test. Furthermore, teachers must carefully interpret informal test results in order to make appropriate educational recommendations. Behaviors noted during informal testing periods should be confirmed by other assessment techniques (e.g., observations, interviews, formal tests, etc.). Effective informal testing necessitates careful planning, administration, and interpretation; otherwise, the results are of little use to teachers.

OBSERVATION

During the past few years, observational techniques have been studied and recommended as an important component of the diagnostic process. Some individuals use observational procedures to confirm the findings of both standardized and teacher-made tests, while others use observational procedures to study certain skills and behaviors untapped by formal tests.

> While observation may take a variety of forms, looking at and recording the behavior of the subject under study are the basic elements in all. Although observation may appear to be a very simple procedure, a great deal of training and experience are required in order for the observer to become skilled at making accurate and meaningful observations. Moreover, observation may range, in terms of sophistication, control, and

precision, from longhand recording of a child's behavior to the use of complicated recording equipment in which the observational data are fed into a computer for qualification and analysis [Medinnus, 1976, p. 3].

Classroom teachers, especially, have many different opportunities throughout a school day to observe children in a variety of settings. Oral reading periods provide an excellent time to note a child's word analysis, word recognition, and various comprehensive skills. The use of the chalkboard allows the teacher an opportunity to survey a number of children simultaneously (Spencer & Smith, 1969). The teacher also may discover many different language skills while observing the child in oral discussion periods, during conversations with other children, and in question-and-answer sessions. Physical education classes and playground activities also provide teachers with excellent opportunities to observe fine and gross motor abilities and a variety of personal and social adjustment skills. Teachers who use any of these situations to note aspects of a child's behavior are usually provided with much information that can be employed readily in planning teaching programs.

Approaches to Observation

Among the number of approaches to observation, three are used extensively with children who experience learning problems. These include *time-sampling techniques, event sampling,* and *rating scales* and *checklists.*

Time-Sampling Techniques   In the time-sampling technique, a teacher records observations only during a specific time interval. This technique usually is recommended when a behavior is difficult to observe, occurs more than 25 times per day, or only occurs in a specific setting, such as during the arithmetic period (Wallace & Kauffman, 1978). Examples of such behaviors might include talking out of turn, hitting other children, reversing letters and words, and jumping out of one's seat. The time-sampling technique provides the teacher with data on the frequency of certain behaviors and the length of time a behavior may persist. An observation form for determining various dependency behaviors is illustrated in Figure 2–3.

Event Sampling   Specific behavioral events (e.g., play episodes, success and failure experiences, etc.) usually are described in detail during an event-sampling procedure. According to Medinnus (1976), event-sampling focuses on a class of behaviors rather than on the occurrence of a specific behavior. Nevertheless, event sampling may be utilized with both frequently and infrequently occurring events. In event sampling the observer describes in as much detail as possible the complete sequence of behavior in the chosen event.

FIGURE 2–3   Time-Sampling Observation Form

Time: 10:00 A.M.
Activity: Outside free play
Age group: Kindergarten

Dependency Behaviors

Time Intervals

	1 minute	2 minutes	3 minutes	4 minutes
Seeking help				
Seeking physical contact				
Seeking proximity				
Seeking attention				

Source: Medinnus, G. R. *Child study and observation guide.* New York: John Wiley and Sons, Inc., 1976, p. 91. Reprinted with permission of the publisher.

Rating Scales and Checklists   The use of either checklists or rating scales during observations usually serves as a means both to organize and to summarize the observations. Cartwright and Cartwright (1974) suggest that checklists and rating scales help the observer to focus attention on specific behaviors and encourage precision in observing. On the other hand, Medinnus (1976) cautions that observers perceive and interpret behaviors differently and rate them in different proportions. Further, numerical ratings provide little information concerning appropriate teaching approaches for working with certain children.

Checklists and rating scales usually are similar in design. Both include a list of behaviors and a place to indicate whether the behavior was observed. Rating scales also provide a means of appraising the behavior being observed. Illustrations of a checklist and a rating scale are provided in Figures 2–4 and 2–5.

Limitations of Observation

It is important to note a number of potential problems with, and limitations of, observation in order that teachers may gain the maximum amount of helpful information from these precedures. Some of the primary problems are listed in the following section.

FIGURE 2–4   Arithmetic Readiness Checklist

Child's Name _____ Date _____

Observer _____

Directions: Place a check mark alongside each behavior observed. Leave the space blank if the behavior was not observed.

_____   1. Discriminates sizes
_____   2. Discriminates shapes
_____   3. Discriminates quantities
_____   4. Understands one-to-one correspondence
_____   5. Counts to 10
_____   6. Counts to 30
_____   7. Understands groups and sets
_____   8. Understands place value
_____   9. Understands arithmetic language
_____   10. Differentiates arithmetic signs
_____   11. Writes numerals to 10
_____   12. Writes numerals to 30

FIGURE 2–5   Language Rating Scale

Child's Name _____ Date _____

Observer _____

Directions: Indicate your rating of the child's language skills according to the
following scale.

5	4	3	2	1	0
Excellent	Good	Average	Fair	Poor	No opportunity to observe

5 4 3 2 1 0   a. *Understands speech sounds*
                      Comments:

5 4 3 2 1 0   b. *Comprehends words*
                      Comments:

5 4 3 2 1 0   c. *Comprehends statements*
                      Comments:

5 4 3 2 1 0   d. *Follows directions*
                      Comments:

5 4 3 2 1 0   e. *Produces speech sounds*
                      Comments:

5 4 3 2 1 0   f. *Formulates words and sentences*
                      Comments:

5 4 3 2 1 0   g. *Grammar and syntax*
                      Comments:

5 4 3 2 1 0   h. *Spoken vocabulary*
                      Comments:

5 4 3 2 1 0   i. *Verbal imagery*
                      Comments:

Teacher Bias   Observations often tell more about the observer than the
individual being observed (Strang, 1969). An observer's beliefs and biases
may only cause the observer to look for what he or she already has in mind
about the student. Observational errors may also be caused by recording
inaccuracies, inappropriate sampling techniques, and preconceived notions
about the student's success or failure. It is important for the observer to be
aware of these potential sources of bias so that observations can be valid
and reliable samples of a student's behavior (Smith & Neisworth, 1969).

Observational Interpretations   Since most observations are only a small
sampling of a student's behavior, it is usually necessary for the observer
to exercise caution when interpreting these observations. Interpretations
should be based upon a number of observations made over an extended

period of time and in conjunction with other assessment data. Careful interpretation of observations will help to guard against overgeneralization of findings and a tendency on the part of some individuals to categorize quickly and label certain behavioral manifestations.

Narrowness of the Data   Observational techniques actually are just one aspect of the total assessment process. The information obtained through observation should be interpreted in conjunction with various informal and standardized test results. Smith and Neisworth (1969) suggest that continual cross-checking of data not only validates certain assessment procedures, but also adds credence to the observations. The use of observational information contributes to a more thorough, accurate, and complete assessment process.

The direct applicability of most observational data to ongoing teaching programs is considered a distinct advantage of this assessment procedure. Observational techniques should be a crucial part of the educational assessment of all children experiencing learning handicaps. The specificity, practicality, and adaptability of these precedures make them indispensable to the process of evaluating children.

TASK ANALYSIS

Task analysis is an additional means for assessing a student's learning needs. According to Wallace and Kauffman (1978),

> ... task analysis may be viewed as a sequence of evaluative activities which pinpoints the child's learning problem and guides the teacher in planning an effective remedial sequence of instructional tasks [p. 105].

During the process of task analysis, a specific task (e.g., jumping rope, printing one's name, telling time, etc.) is broken down into successively smaller component steps until the student's errors in performance are identified precisely and the subskills that must be learned in order to perform the task adequately are known (Hallahan & Kauffman, 1976). A task analysis for dialing the telephone, for example, has been provided by Cartwright and Cartwright (1974), as follows:

> *The task:* The learner will be able to dial a given number on a telephone without making errors and without assistance.

> *Steps in the task:*
> 1. Can recognize numerals 0–9.
> 2. Can recognize alphabet letters A–Z.
> 3. Can differentiate between left and right direction.
> 4. Can pick up receiver and demonstrate how to hold it.
> 5. Can point to the dial and show how to put fingers in holes.
> 6. Can point to the stopper.

7. Can turn the dial with his finger until it is stopped by the stopper.
8. Can put his finger in the hole matching a number he is given and move his finger to the stopper (he has dialed one number).
9. Can dial two numbers in proper order when he is given the two numbers.
10. Can dial more and more numbers in the proper order until he has dialed all seven numbers in a given telephone number.
11. Can repeat step 8 while holding the receiver to his ear.
12. Can repeat steps 9 and 10 while holding the receiver to his ear.
13. Can repeat step 12 going in correct left-to-right order when he is given a written number [pp. 22–23].

Once the component steps of a task have been identified, the child is presented each sequential task and errors are identified until a task is presented that the child can perform without error (Wallace & Kauffman, 1978). Errors are analyzed and, if necessary, further identified. For example, it would probably be necessary to further analyze any errors encountered in step 2 of the example noted earlier in order to identify which alphabet letters the child does not recognize. Further tasks are dependent upon the level of the child's functioning. According to Hallahan and Kauffman (1976), younger or more severely handicapped children require more finely analyzed tasks than older children and those without handicaps.

Following an analysis of a child's errors, the teacher usually designs a remedial program based upon the sequence of skills in the task analysis. Frank (1973), for example, advises that the teacher begin teaching the skills in the task-analysis hierarchy in sequential order following the level at which the child was able to perform all skills correctly. In this way, the task analysis process provides the teacher with each successive teaching step for arriving at a particular objective.

Myers and Hammill (1976) suggest that *sequentiality* and *discreteness* are two of the most important principles of task analysis. Sequentiality refers to the "building-block" theory of skills learning or the principle that the skills of a particular task are learned in sequential order. Each skill is a succession of approximations of the final task. The principle of discreteness relates to the fact that all items must be "discrete enough so that only one element of the task is taught at a time" (Myers & Hammill, 1976, p. 87). For example, in the task analysis for dialing a telephone noted earlier, each of the steps enables the teacher to analyze a specific discrete behavior.

It is interesting to note that the hierarchical nature of task analysis is also a notion that has caused some concern in the professional literature. In the area of reading, Prescott (1971) argues that there is still widespread disagreement among the so-called experts about how children learn to read and the steps involved in the reading process. Others also point out the broad differences among lists of sequential skills. Some, therefore, feel that it is inaccurate to list *the* hierarchy or sequence of skills within a content area. An additional problem often mentioned in relation to task analysis is the considerable amount of time and labor necessary to complete the entire process. This concern becomes particularly appropriate when it is necessary to develop a task analysis for each of the many skills in the educational curriculum.

On the whole, however, task analysis should be considered a very helpful addition to educational assessment procedures. The process basically "allows the teacher to know *what* he wants to teach, *where* he wants to begin, *when* he has succeeded, and *what* the next item should be" (Myers & Hammill, 1976, p. 89).

CRITERION REFERENCED TESTING

The vast majority of published tests in both education and psychology are known as *normative referenced tests;* that is, individual scores are compared to standard or group scores (Hallahan & Kauffman, 1976). Normative referenced tests usually have been administered to groups of individuals of different chronological ages, from different parts of the country, in various grades, and often from both urban and rural areas. *Norms* are then established based upon the various groups included in the sample. Depending upon the type of norms furnished by the test publisher, various comparisons of the performance of individual pupils, classes, grades, schools, and school districts can be made with the academic progress of students throughout the country (Mehrens & Lehmann, 1969).

In *criterion referenced testing,* as opposed to normative referenced testing, an individual's performance is evaluated in terms of an absolute or specific criterion that has been set for the student. Recognition of 90 percent of the prefixes in a list of 50 words, for example, might be the criterion set for one student, whereas the recognition of all sight words in a list of ten words might be the criterion for another student. Other criteria might include spelling 80 percent of a list of words or correctly computing eight out of ten arithmetic examples. According to Hallahan and Kauffman (1976), if a child does not achieve a criterion, then the teacher must consider that either (1) the selected criterion is not appropriate or (2) the student probably needs additional work to complete the required task.

In working with children encountering learning problems, for whom a large part of the instruction is individualized, Proger and Mann (1973) point out that group comparisons are of no real value in terms of teaching a student with uniquely different strengths and weaknesses. Likewise, many norm referenced tests have not included disabled students in standardized samples. Because they are so specific, criterion referenced tests provide the teacher with *exact* information, which is directly applicable to programs of instruction. Prescott (1971) has aptly summarized this type of testing by noting that students' performances are actually evaluated in terms of whether they have achieved or they have failed to achieve specific teaching objectives.

Among the many advantages of criterion referenced testing, Proger and Mann (1973) have included the following: (1) flexibility in using this type of test for various individual requirements; (2) continuous assessment for noting individual student progress; (3) adaptability to any commercially available curriculum; and, most important for the learning handicapped child, (4) judgment of the student relative to his or her own strengths and weaknesses and not to any group performance.

Individuals utilizing criterion referenced tests should nevertheless be aware of a number of potential problems with this type of testing. The setting of inappropriate criteria for individual students has been mentioned as a primary danger in this approach (Hallahan & Kauffman, 1976). In some cases, for example, a student might be unduly struggling with a specific activity because the criterion that was set was too difficult for the student. In such a case, adjusting the criterion to a somewhat more moderate level would certainly facilitate this potential danger. Criteria that are too easy also cause difficulties in many situations. In addition to these problems, another question concerns what to do when the child does not learn the task initially (Gillespie & Johnson, 1974). The usual assumptions of lack of exposure to the task or of inappropriate teaching might be inaccurate with many learning handicapped students.

Finally, it should be noted that an increasing number of curriculum materials with coordinated criterion referenced measures are being used with children experiencing learning problems. The *Wisconsin Design for Reading Skill Development* (see Chapters 8 and 9), for example, has included a criterion referenced test for most of the skills developed in the program. The *Fountain Valley System* and the *Read System* are also based upon specific performance objectives.

CASE HISTORY AND INTERVIEWS

A case history of a student's development and background often will provide tremendous insight into a child's specific learning difficulties. In some cases, home factors may be contributing to the student's disabilities, while in other cases resources in the home may be useful in overcoming the problem (Otto, McMenemy, & Smith, 1973).

Case-history information may be obtained by a variety of methods and techniques. Interviews with the child's parents or adult informants, written completion of case-history forms, or interviews with the child may be necessary depending upon the specific nature of individual cases. Nevertheless, most case-history forms will include information similar to the case-history form illustrated in Figure 2–6.

FIGURE 2–6   Sample Case-History Form

(This information is confidential and for professional use only. Please fill out as completely as possible)

I. IDENTIFYING INFORMATION
    Client's name:

    _____ Age____ Sex____ D.O.B._____
    (first)   (middle)   (last)
    Address:

    _____ Phone_____
    (no. & street)   (city)   (state)   (zip)
    Name of person completing this form:

    _____ Relationship to client_____
    (first)   (middle)   (last)
    Address:

    _____ Phone_____
    (no. & street)   (city)   (state)   (zip)

II. FAMILY HISTORY
    Mother's name:

    _____ Age_____ Occupation_____
    (first)   (middle)   (last)
    Address:

    _____ Phone_____
    (no. & street)   (city)   (state)   (zip)

    Place of employment _____ Bus. Phone _____

    Education _____ Native Language_____
    Father's name:

    _____ Age_____ Occupation_____
    (first)   (middle)   (last)
    Address:

    _____ Phone_____
    (no. & street)   (city)   (state)   (zip)

    Place of employment _____ Bus. Phone _____

    Education _____ Native Language_____
    Preferred person to contact regarding client:

    Name _____ Phone_____

FIGURE 2–6 (*Cont.*)

Names of brothers and sisters	Age	Sex	Grade in school	At home
_____	___	___	_____	_____
_____	___	___	_____	_____
_____	___	___	_____	_____

Language spoken in home_____ Usual language of client_____

Names of relatives or others living in home   Relationship

_____

Relatives who have had speech, language, hearing, or learning problems:

Name	Relationship	Problem
_____	_____	_____
_____	_____	_____

III. MEDICAL HISTORY

Family physician/pediatrician who has primary care of client:

Name _____ Address_____
                                    (no. & street)   (city)   (state)

Phone _____

Does this physician know client is being seen at this Center? _____

General health of client has been _____
                                              (good)   (fair)   (poor)

If fair or poor, explain _____

Date of client's last physical exam _____

Important and/or persistent illnesses, injuries, accidents, and operations. Be sure especially to include convulsive disorders, allergies, ear infections, and contagious childhood diseases:

Condition	Age	Treatment	Length of hospitalization

Has client had high fever? ____ How high____ How long____ Age____

With what illness? _____

Has client had vision checked? _____ By whom_____

Finding _____ Glasses_____

FIGURE 2–6   (*Cont.*)

Any special medical examinations (such as neurological, ENT, Visual)?
Date _____   Place or by whom _____   Specialty _____   Findings _____

Any routine medication? _____ What for?_____

Current medication _____

Current medical problems _____

Note any other medical or physical condition that you think we need to know, such as orthopedic devices (braces, corrective shoes), contact lenses, allergies (e.g., foods that must not be given to client).

IV. BIRTH HISTORY

Mother's health during pregnancy _____
                                       (good)   (fair)   (poor)

Explain _____

List any illnesses, accidents, or surgery mother had during pregnancy

(give month of pregnancy) _____

Any medication mother took during pregnancy (diet pills, tranquilizers, antibiotics, antihistamines, etc.)

Emotional health of the mother during pregnancy _____
                                                    (good) (fair) (poor)

Was Rh incompatibility of parents present? _____

Birthdate _____ Place_____
                     (hospital)   (city)   (state)   (zip)

Pregnancy (mos.)____ Labor (hrs.)____ Induced____ Forceps used____

Medication during delivery _____ Delivery_____
                                        (normal) (breech) (Caesarean)

Birth weight _____ Length of child at birth_____

Condition of child at birth.

Normal ___ Premature___ Cord wrapped around neck___ Jaundiced___

Rh incompatibility _____ Convulsive_____ Blood transfusions_____

Lung problems____ Heart problems____ Hemorrhages____ Other____

Cyanotic (blueish discoloration of skin) _____

Anoxic (lack of oxygen) _____ Incubator_____ How long_____

FIGURE 2–6   (*Cont.*)

Congenital malformations (specify) _____

Injuries at birth (specify) _____

Was oxygen administered to child? _____ For how long? _____

V. INFANT DEVELOPMENT (give age at which child first did following)

Breast fed until _____ Bottle fed until_____ Drank from a cup
(mos.)   (mos.)

at _____ Fed self at_____ Chewed solid foods_____
(mos.)   (mos.)   (mos.)

Compared to others in family, above development was_____
slow   average   fast

Sat with support _____ Sat alone_____ Stood alone_____

Walked _____

Compared to others in the family, motor development was

_____
slow   average   fast

Bowel control _____ Bladder control, day_____ night_____

Responded to sounds ___ Responded to voice___ Made first sound___

Made babbling sounds _____ Said first word_____ Put two or three

words together _____ Answered questions and related facts

verbally _____ Estimate the number of words the child
used at the following ages:

12 months: ___   18 months:___   24 months:___   30 months:___

36 months: ___

Compared to others in the family, speech development was

_____
slow   average   fast

VI. PSYCHOSOCIAL HISTORY

For his or her age, do you consider your child to be socially _____ ,
mature

_____ , _____ ?
average   immature

Check the following that apply to the client:

nail biting _____ thumb sucking_____ bedwetting_____

food faddisms _____ sleeping problems_____ frequent crying_____

FIGURE 2–6   *(Cont.)*

frequent day-dreaming _____ frequent temper tantrums_____

abnormal aggressiveness _____ pronounced disobedience_____

destructiveness _____

Has client been seen by psychologist? ____ At what age?____ Give name

and address _____

Has client been seen by psychiatrist? ____ At what age?____ Give name

and address _____

How is child disciplined? _____

VII. EDUCATIONAL HISTORY

School client presently attends _____
(name of school)

_____   _____
(address)   (grade)

Principal _____ Teacher_____

Client's general school performance _____
(excellent)   (average)   (poor)

Best subjects _____ Most difficult_____

Has client been in a special education classroom? ____ What type?____
   (e.g., MBI, LLD, EMR, TMR, etc.)

Has client ever been retained? _____ What grade?_____ Has client had

special reading instruction? _____ Has client been tested or seen by a

counselor of the school? _____

May this Center contact the school to discuss the client if it is believed

necessary? _____

VIII. SPEECH PROBLEM

What concerns you about the client's speech? (Describe problem):

_____

_____

_____

_____

Who first noticed the problem? _____ When?_____

FIGURE 2–6 (*Cont.*)

Do you think the child has a hearing loss? ____ Has it been tested?____

Where? _____ Results_____

Does child wear a hearing aid? _____ Type_____ Did speech

development ever seem to stop? ____ When?_____ Does the child seem

embarrassed about his or her speech? _____ Has there been a change in

the child's speech within the last 6 months? _____

Describe _____

What efforts have been made to help the child with speech at home?

_____

_____

Has the child had speech or language therapy? _____

Where and when? _____

_____

_____

Results _____

IX. What problems other than speech or hearing does the client have that worry you?

_____

_____

X. COMMENTS

_____

_____

_____

_____

Source: Sample case history form used at the Speech and Hearing Clinic at the University of Texas at Austin. Used with permission.

Written Reports

Written case-history forms most often are used as a preliminary means of gathering information to gain a basic understanding of a child's specific problems. Written reports also may be used when many students are being evaluated or when it is impossible for the parents and teacher to meet in person. An example of a written case history is illustrated in Figure 2–7. It usually is recommended to follow up written reports with either home visits or school interviews.

FIGURE 2–7   Home Information Blank

Date_____

Please supply the information requested below concerning _____

_____. The information will be useful to us in planning the remedial help to be given your child.

1. Has your child any specific difficulties in seeing and hearing? If so, please describe, indicating how recently he has been tested, whether or not he wears glasses, etc.

2. Has your child a general health problem, or a history of health difficulties (other than vision or hearing), which has handicapped him in his work in school? If so, please describe.

3. Did your child have any difficulty in learning to talk? Has he had, or does he now have, any speech problem? If so, please describe.

4. How would you describe your child's general emotional adjustment? For example, is he inclined to be tense and to worry, or is he usually calm and carefree? How does he compare with other children in the family?

5. How would you describe your child's attitude toward reading and toward school? For example, does he like them, dislike them, or doesn't he care? Please describe any changes you have noted in his attitude.

6. Have you attempted to help your child improve his reading either at home or by tutoring? Please describe any specific steps you have taken, materials you have provided, suggestions received from the school, etc.

7. Do you have any suggestions on the probable causes of your child's reading difficulty? If so, please indicate.

8. Has the school ever suggested specific remedial help for your child (such as remedial reading, summer clinic, special tutoring, etc.)?

Source: From *Corrective and Remedial Teaching,* 2nd edition by W. Otto, R. A. McMenemy, and R. J. Smith. Copyright © 1973 by Houghton Mifflin Co. Reprinted by permission of the publisher.

Interviews

Using interviews as a source of information in the diagnostic process can be useful. However, unless there is a specific purpose and plan, interviews can be both unproductive and time consuming. Whether the interview involves a child or the child's parents, a number of guidelines need to be considered. Strang (1969) cautions that an interview should be a conversation with a purpose. Consequently, a broad outline of points to be discussed is usually helpful, according to Ekwall (1976), since more detailed checklists have the disadvantage of structuring the interview to the point where spontaneity is often lost. Ekwall has suggested that the teacher use the following outline for interviewing students:

1. Interests
   1.1 Clubs—church
   1.2 Hobbies
   1.3 Friends
   1.4 How is spare time spent?
2. Student Attitudes
   2.1 Toward his family
   2.2 Toward his school
      2.2.1 Favorite subjects and least liked subjects
   2.3 Teachers
   2.4 Friends
   2.5 His reading problems
      2.5.1 Is he aware of the problem?
      2.5.2 What does he think the problem is?
      2.5.3 How much trouble has he had?
      2.5.4 Why does he have this difficulty?
      2.5.5 What are his suggestions for solutions?
      2.5.6 Does he enjoy reading?
      2.5.7 What does he read?
      2.5.8 Does he go to the library or own books of his own?
   2.6 The student
      2.6.1 How does he feel about himself in relation to other students?

The interpretation of the data and the information gathered during the interview must be completed with extreme caution. Strang (1969) suggests that the interviewer must learn to suspend judgment and to refrain from jumping to premature conclusions. Learning to apply appropriate interviewing techniques takes a considerable amount of time and skill.

CHARACTERISTICS ESSENTIAL FOR ACCURATE ASSESSMENT

There are several concepts that must be discussed in a consideration of either formal or informal assessment. Regardless of the behaviors that are being evaluated, the devices employed to determine their adequacy should possess several characteristics that are essential for efficient use. The most basic of these characteristics may be conveniently grouped under the headings of *reliability* and *validity*. In addition, the interpretation of standardized tests also entails knowledge of *norms* that permits the comparison of one student's score with the scores of a peer group. Each of these components of effective educational measurement will be considered in this section.

Reliability

The term *reliability* is used to refer to the *consistency* of a given testing technique. Acceptable synonyms for reliability would be *dependability, stability, predictability,* and *accuracy* (Kerlinger, 1973). An example of reliability would be persons who are highly consistent in their actions; that is, their behavior could be accurately predicted because of its stability over time. In another vein, if persons are considered inconsistent, then their behavior occurs at random with little observable pattern. They are unpredictable and lack stability. We would say that they are unreliable.

Similarly, assessment techniques also can be reliable or unreliable based upon their variability from one situation to another. In order to determine if a formal or informal test is reliable, the teacher must have some estimate or idea if a score obtained on one person will be consistent across several administrations of the same instrument on different occasions. With formal (i.e., standardized) tests, statistical analyses usually are conducted to specify the level of confidence one may have regarding the reliability of a particular measure. These statistical procedures are derived from *correlating* two sets of test scores from the same instrument. The resultant *correlation coefficient* depicts the degree of *relationship* between the sets of scores (a perfect positive relationship is 1.00 and no relationship is indicated by 0.00). The higher the coefficient is, the more reliable the test is; the lower the coefficient, the more unreliable the test.

When using informal evaluative techniques, teachers are frequently forced to rely upon their own judgment to estimate whether a given device is reliable or not. Through experience teachers should be familiar with the students who they are assessing, as well as with the environment in which the evaluation is being conducted. These features are, of course, very important and lend a great deal of practicality when interpreting the results of the assessment procedures. It is also important to keep in mind, however, that teachers should be certain that the performances of pupils on particular informal tests will be approximately the same on subsequent administrations of those tests. If there is any doubt regarding this point, efforts must be made to continue to retest the students until their "best efforts" are elicited. This can be determined accurately only through a long-term interaction with pupils, which is frequently lacking in typical formal evaluations.

Although the statistical computation of reliability coefficients is not commonly employed in the construction and use of teacher-made techniques, it is an integral part of most standardized tests. In most cases, test manuals devote entire sections to reliability and are used to aid in estimating the reliability of the instrument. The most frequently employed methods of determining a test's reliability are: (1) *test-retest*, (2) *equivalent forms*, (3) *split-half*, and (4) *Kuder-Richardson*. We will now consider each of these methods.

Test-Retest Reliability   One of the most commonly used techniques in determining reliability is the test-retest method. This procedure entails giving the same test to the same group with a specified time interval separating the two administrations. Depending upon the nature of the test, the time interval may extend from several minutes to several years. Regardless of the interval, the two sets of test scores are correlated, and this correlation coefficient permits the estimation of the *stability* of the test over a period of time. If the instrument is stable, students who do well on one administration of the test will also do well on the other administration of the test. To state it another way, the more reliable the device, the more pupils will tend to maintain their same relative positions on the two administrations of the test (Gronlund, 1976). Tests that are stable have large correlation coefficients (e.g., test-retest reliability is estimated to be 0.90 or 0.95). It is not uncommon for standardized achievement tests to report correlation coefficients in the 0.90s.

When attempting to determine a test's test-retest reliability, several important factors should be kept firmly in mind. The length of time interval between administrations will significantly affect the magnitude of the reported correlation coefficient. If the time interval between tests is short, (e.g., a week or less), the coefficients probably will be inflated, because pupils will have recalled some of the answers from one testing to another. It can be expected that as the time interval increases, the correlation coefficient will steadily decrease. The most appropriate time interval between tests will depend upon the type of test and how the results will be used. It is important that teachers seek evidence of reliability that fits the particular interpretation to be made in the school.

Equivalent Forms Reliability   According to Anastasi (1976), one way to avoid the problem of a lengthy time interval in the test-retest method is through the use of alternate forms of the test. In this procedure, reliability is estimated by administering two different but equivalent forms of the test. The two forms are given to the same group of students, and the scores are correlated. This correlation coefficient determines the degree to which the two forms tap the same general information.

The use of equivalent forms is employed primarily to measure an instrument's stability and consistency. The availability of equivalent forms of a test is also helpful for research. For example, equivalent forms may be used as pretests and posttests in follow-up studies to determine the effects of curricular innovation. In addition, alternate forms of a test assist in reducing the effects of possible cheating and coaching, or both.

In attempting to ascertain the reliability of an equivalent form, the teacher should be concerned by the length of time between administering the two forms. In most instances, the time span should be very short; the two tests should be given in *immediate* succession, if possible (Downie, 1958). This is always advisable in order to reduce error variances that are introduced as a result of fluctuations in pupil performance over time. If the interval between administrations is short, reductions in the magnitude of the correlation coefficents due to error variance will be negligible.

Split-half Reliability   One of the most frequently used procedures to determine reliability is the split-half technique. This procedure may be completed by simply administering the instrument one time and then applying a statistical formula. After the test has been given, it is divided into halves by scoring the odd- and even-numbered items separately. This process produces two sets of scores for each student, which when correlated give an estimate of the instrument's "internal consistency." Obviously, the coefficient indicates the extent to which the halves of the test are equivalent.

Gronlund (1976) states that the most usual method of computing split-half reliabilities is through the Spearman-Brown formula:

$$\text{Reliability on full test} = \frac{2 \times \text{Reliability on half test}}{1 + \text{Reliability on half test}}$$

An illustration of how the formula is actually computed can be seen from the following example, where the coefficient between the two halves of the test is 0.70:

$$\text{Reliability on full test} = \frac{2 \times 0.70}{1 + 0.70} = \frac{1.40}{1.70} = 0.82$$

The coefficient of 0.82 indicates the degree to which the full test is reliable where the split-halves correlated 0.70. In general, the higher the correlation coefficient between the two halves of the instrument, the more equivalent are the forms and the more adequate the sampling of the various items.

Kuder-Richardson Reliability Another commonly used method of estimating a test's internal consistency is through the Kuder-Richardson formula. This procedure, similar to the split-half technique, requires only one test administration. Although the test results are divided into halves, a statistical formula is applied based upon the number of correct responses scored by given students. In order to use the Kuder-Richardson procedure accurately, the individual test items should be homogenous (i.e., each item should measure the trait or quality as every other). The test also should be constructed to allow all students the opportunity to respond to every item. If all items are not attempted, the correlation coefficient will be significantly inflated. The Kuder-Richardson method, then, is usually inappropriate for tests in which *speed of response* is an essential factor. Gronlund (1976) feels that the reports in test manuals of Kuder-Richardson analyses should be disregarded routinely *unless* evidence is also provided to show that speed of work is a minimal force in determining a student's test score.

As was stated previously, the test-retest, equivalent forms, split-half, and Kuder-Richardson methods are frequently used to give evidence of a test's reliability. An additional estimate of consistency of performance on a given instrument is *standard error of measurement (SEm)*. The standard error of measurement provides the amount of variation one can expect upon repeated administrations of the same test to a given student. To state it another way, since all persons will vary, at least slightly, on a test from one administration to another, a standard error of measurement gives an estimate of how *variant* the scores will likely be. Such an estimate is useful in determining a pupil's "true" score on a given assessment device.

Most test manuals provide the standard error of measurement. In most cases, it is meant to be used to interpret individual test scores. For example, Jim has just received a score of 70 on a vocabulary test. The standard error of measurement reported in the test manual is 5. What does this mean when the examiner interprets Jim's score? In general, it provides insight into the correct estimate of Jim's "true" (i.e., the score that would be obtained in a perfectly reliable test) vocabulary score. More specifically, we would be confident that 68 percent of all administrations would be +5 or −5 points. That is, if the vocabulary test were administered 100 times, 68 percent of those administrations would result in scores ranging from 65–75 (+10 or −10 points). In addition, in 95 percent of all administrations Jim's score would be between 60–80. At the 99 percent level of confidence, Jim's score would fall somewhere between 55–85 (+15 or −15 points). Using the standard error of measurement, we could be virtually certain that Jim's "true" score would fall between 55–85. It is apparent that teachers and other professionals must be cautious in placing special significance on single test scores without first consulting the standard error of measurement.

Perhaps the most beneficial aspect of the standard error of measurement is that it reinforces the concept that a pupil's test performance should be interpreted as a "band of scores" rather than as a specific score. It prevents professional personnel from becoming too pedantic in using the results of standardized tests. Quite obviously, the larger the standard error of measurement, the less confidence can be placed in the score attained by the student. The smaller the standard error of measurement, the more consistent and reliable is the measurement of the characteristic or trait. In situations in which the educational fate of some children is being decided based on a single test administration, teachers should become acquainted with the standard error of measurement in order to interpret more knowledgeably the true meaning of the test score.

Validity

Whereas reliability refers to the consistency and stability of a test, validity is concerned with what the test measures and how well it does so (Anastasi, 1976). If a test purports to measure the ability to spell a series of words, it should require a pupil to spell words and not to compute mathematical problems. If the test *does,* in fact, appear to measure spelling ability, then it can be thought to possess the rudiments of validity. To what *extent* it is a valid measure of spelling ability may be determined through more detailed study of the test. Depending upon the type of validity, careful inspection of the test, computation of correlation coefficients, and logical reasoning may all give some idea of the *degree* of validity of a particular test. The specific types of validity that are considered in most tests include *content, criterion-related,* and *construct.* The general meaning and procedures for determining these types of validity are presented in Table 2–3. The basic features of content, criterion-related, and construct validity are discussed in the following section.

Content Validity   Content validity refers to the adequacy with which a test covers a representative sample of the behavior or information to be assessed. In essence, in order for an instrument to have content validity, it must contain sufficient items so that it is representative of the topics that it purports to measure. It is self-evident that if a testing device *does not* possess enough items to effectively tap a given area, it could not possibly be valid.

The typical means of determining content validity are through logical analysis and comparison with other tests. Many standardized achievement tests list tables of "specifications" by which examiners estimate how many questions in each content area are needed to adequately measure that area. The items that are finally included in the instrument should roughly correspond to the "specifications" that have been developed for the test. Since

TABLE 2–3   Three Types of Validity

Type	Meaning	Procedure
Content validity	How well the test measures the subject-matter content and behaviors under consideration	Compare test content to the universe of content and behaviors to be measured.
Criterion-related validity	How well test performance predicts future performance or estimates current performance on some valued measure other than the test itself	Compare test scores with another measure of performance obtained at a later date (for prediction) or with another measure of performance obtained concurrently (for estimating present status).
Construct validity	How test performance can be described psychologically	Experimentally determine what factors influence scores on the test.

Source: Gronlund, N. E. *Measurement and Evaluation in Teaching.* New York: Macmillan, 1976. Used with permission of the publisher.

few objective criteria can be applied to judge the apparent relevance or appropriateness of individual items, content validity should never be the sole basis for determining the validity of a measure. Estimates of criterion-related and construct validity must also be attained prior to making this decision.

Criterion-related Validity   Criterion-related validity is used (1) to either compare a test with a valued measure (usually a measurement of the same general characteristics) or (2) to predict the future performance of a student. In both cases, correlation coefficients depicting the degree of relationship between two sets of test scores are employed. As the reader will recall from the earlier discussion of reliability, a coefficient of 1.00 indicates "perfect" relationship and 0.00 denotes no relationship between two variables.

In determining validity by comparing one test with another, an attempt should be made to demonstrate that each device actually assesses the same traits. For example, if a new test of reading is developed, the authors may wish to show that their test is similar to another device that is widely held to be a good measure of reading ability. Consequently, a group of students would be given both tests (within a relatively short time span) and the results would be correlated. If the correlation coefficients were high, it would be possible to say that *if* the accepted and widely used tests were valid, the new instrument must also be, because the students received similar scores on each. If the coefficients were low, the newly developed test would likely be considered not valid, since the students scored differently on it than on the valued device. Of course, this procedure assumes that the criterion (i.e., the widely used and accepted test) is a valid instrument. Hopefully, this will be true; however, many tests have been validated by comparisons with measures that were popular but lacked convincing validity statistics. Teachers attempting to interpret a criterion-related validity reported in test manuals should become familiar with the criterion device in order to make meaningful judgments.

The second form of criterion-related validity is conducted by determining how accurately a test predicts future performance of a student. If a test can predict later performance of a student, it is quite possible that the attributes presumed to be measured do exist and are related to or underlie behavior in certain situations. An illustration of this point would be a school readiness test that is administered routinely to all kindergarten children in a particular school district. The purpose of this test is to estimate which students are high risk for failure in the first grade. At the conclusion of first grade, achievement test scores of all pupils would be correlated with the readiness test scores. A high correlation coefficient would indicate that the readiness test does *predict* well and that its continued use could isolate those students who are most in need of remedial assistance. A small coefficient would indicate that the readiness test is not a good predictor and possibly measures skills that are not essential for successful school performance. In other words, the test is probably not valid.

Criterion-related validity is very helpful in estimating a test's ability to function in certain capacities. Naturally, the criterion must be chosen either for prediction or as a valued measure to ensure that it, in fact, assesses the variables that are of interest. If the criterion selected is invalid or inappropriate, the teacher will obtain little useful data from subsequent analyses.

Construct Validity   When we are concerned with the extent to which an instrument actually measures a psychological quality, we are referring to construct validity. A *construct* is an abstraction or an idea used to explain a facet of behavior. Examples of constructs are intelligence, perception, aptitude, reasoning ability, and cognition. If a test is said to assess intelligence, it is believed that there is such a thing as *intelligence* and that the items incorporated in the test tap behaviors that are indicative of this trait. Proving that a test does measure a given idea is termed *construct validity*.

Gronlund (1976) states that the determination of construct validity involves the following steps:

1. identifying the constructs presumed to account for test performance
2. deriving hypotheses regarding test performance from the theory underlying the construct
3. verifying the hypotheses by logical and empirical means [p. 94].

The methods used in determining construct validity are many and complex. Usually, procedures to accomplish this task revolve around the use of empirical research procedures. A fairly common approach with some tests is to compare results of different groups that are separated on certain characteristics. For example, if a test is used to diagnose the causes of learning disabilities (e.g., to determine if the cause is due to cognitive or perceptual disorders), the test should *discriminate* between learning disabled and normal children. If it does not, one would seriously question the concepts upon which the test is based. In addition, if a remedial program is instituted and the presumed disorder is cured, the test results should be different after the treatment has been completed. If this does not occur, the construct validity of that instrument would certainly be called into question.

Of all estimates of validity, construct validity is, perhaps, the most difficult to ascertain. It is also the one reported least often in most test manuals. However, an estimate of construct validity must be attained (either empirically or logically) prior to confident use of any test. Teachers should refuse to accept as valid the results of any tests that do not clearly state what they are measuring.

Normative Information

The vast majority of standardized tests used in schools provide normative data within their test manuals to aid in the effective interpretation of individual test scores. The inclusion of normative tables permits the comparison of one student's performance with the performance of other pupils who also have taken the test. In this manner, it is possible to pinpoint easily the standing of an individual in comparison to individuals with similar characteristics. It should be noted that in some cases the normative data provided by standardized tests are not suited to the group. In these cases, teachers are encouraged to develop *local norms* to facilitate more accurate interpretation of the results. Interested readers should consult Anastasi (1976) or Gronlund (1976).

The most common means of compiling a table of norms is to convert students' *raw scores* (i.e., total number of correct responses on a subtest or total test) into *derived scores*. Derived scores are numerical reports of test performance on a score scale that has defined characteristics and yields normative meaning (Gronlund, 1976). Teachers are well acquainted with derived scores from the routine administration of standardized achievement tests to students throughout the school year. The most frequently employed derived scores include: age norms, grade norms, percentile norms, and standard score norms. The conversion of raw scores into derived scores is easily done with most standardized tests. The procedure simply entails the use of normative tables in the test manual. The most frequently used types of test norms, their respective derived scores, and their meaning in terms of test performance are given in Table 2-4. Each of these will be discussed in this section.

Grade Norms Grade norms are used in the interpretation of test performance, particularly at the elementary school level. Typically expressed in two numbers, grade norms estimate the average performance on a given test of students at various grade levels. For example, a student may attain 40 correct responses on a mathematics test. By consulting the normative table, the teacher will discover that this raw score is equivalent to a grade norm of 4.3. This figure is interpreted as fourth grade, third month. This means that 50 percent of students in the standardization group that are in the fourth grade received scores above this norm and 50 percent received scores below this norm. If the student who received this score is in the early months of fourth grade, the teacher would estimate that the student's performance is essentially average. If the student is in the eighth grade, the teacher would note that the student's performance on this test is similar to an *average* fourth-grader's score and, consequently, is below what normally would be expected for a typical eighth-grader.

One major drawback of grade norms is that they are not based on equal units of measurement, either on the same scale or on scales of differing instruments. This means that the distance (or rate of growth) from one

TABLE 2–4   Most Common Types of Test Norms

Type of Test Norm	Name of Derived Score	Meaning in Terms of Test Performance
Grade norms	Grade equivalents	Grade group in which pupil's raw score is average.
Age norms	Age equivalents	Age group in which pupil's raw score is average.
Percentile norms	Percentile ranks (or percentile scores)	Percentage of pupils in the reference group who fall below pupil's raw score.
Standard-score norms	Standard scores	Distance of pupil's raw score above or below the mean of the reference group in terms of standard deviation units.

Source: Reprinted with permission of Macmillan Publishing Co., Inc. from *Measurement and Evaluation in Teaching* by N. E. Gronlund, copyright © 1976 Norman E. Gronlund.

grade level to another is not always equivalent. The difference between the grade norms of 6.0–7.0 is probably not the same as between 1.0–2.0. Consequently, grade norms must be interpreted cautiously and used only in a general sense. Perhaps the most beneficial use of these derived scores is to indicate the student's extent of growth in basic curricular areas. In addition, they are also profitable in comparing a student's performance on different educational and psychological tests.

Age Norms   Age norms similar to grade norms are based upon the *average* scores obtained by students of different ages. For example, if a 7-year, 6-month-old student obtains a raw score of 21 on one test, the teacher may interpret this as an age equivalent of 7.6, which means that the *average* score attained by children of 7 years, 6 months is 21. If, however, the student is significantly older and receives the same raw score, the teacher would likely judge the performance to be somewhat below average. If the student is younger, the teacher probably would conclude that the test score indicates above-average performance.

The same limitation of grade norms may also be applied to age norms. The units of measurement are not equal and should be interpreted with great care. This is particularly true with tests designed for secondary schools, as well as with tests designed for adults. The use of these norms at the elementary school level can be helpful, particularly in those areas in which growth patterns seem to be consistent.

Percentile Norms   Percentile norms are used to assist professionals in the interpretation of test scores. The percentile *rank* delineates a student's relative position in a group in terms of the percentage of students who score below him or her. If a student's raw score, for example 75, is converted to a percentile rank of 53, it is possible to conclude that 53 percent of similar students in the normative group fall below this student on the variable being measured. Obviously, it is also possible to conclude that the student's test performance exceeds that of 53 percent of the group.

One major convenience of percentile norms is that it is possible to interpret a student's performance in terms of groups in which the student is a member or desires to be a member. Therefore, it is always necessary to consider carefully the normative group from which the norms were generated. If the normative group does not share similar characteristics to the particular student, it is unwise to attribute any significance to the test score. A related issue is that percentile units are not equal over the total scale. Since most students tend to score near the middle of a distribution, relatively few students will be placed at either extreme. In these instances, a small increase in a test score in the middle ranges may greatly increase a percentile rank, whereas a much larger increase in test performance at the extreme ends of the scale will be needed to affect a similar change in ranking. This is so because of the fewer numbers of scores that occur at the extremes of a scale. Careful interpretation of percentile norms, however, can successfully offset this limitation, since the inequality of units will follow a set pattern and may be managed effectively by a knowledgeable professional.

Standard-score Norms   A very common approach to determining a student's position in a group is through the use of standard-score norms. This procedure indicates how far a given raw score is above or below the mean (i.e., average) of a certain group of scores. Once the average or mean of a group of scores has been established, the *standard deviation* is computed to permit analysis of the actual spread of scores. The student's score, when compared to standard deviation units, is then applied to the normal curve for interpretation (any elementary statistics text contains discussions of the procedure for computing standard deviations and applications to the normal curve). From this analysis, it is possible to estimate the extent to which a student's performance is above or below the average of a normative group.

When utilizing standard score norms, the raw scores are converted into *standard scores*. This process enables the professional to compare efficiently relatively diverse raw scores on a standard scale of measurement. Standard scores usually are expressed as either *z-scores* or *T-scores*. Both types of scores simply permit the interpretation of the number of standard deviation units (+4 or —4 standard deviations is usually maximum) a raw score is below or above the mean of available scores. *Stanines* are also a form of standard scores that are based upon the fact that the distribution of raw scores is divided into nine equal parts. If a student receives a stanine score of 5, this means that the student is located exactly in the center of the distribution. A stanine of 9 means that the student's score is in the upper extreme of the distribution.

Although it is possible to convert easily raw scores into various types of derived scores, the resulting interpretation of a student's performance will be accurate only if the normative group used in the development of the norm is clearly representative of the characteristics that interest the individual student. In order to assure this, the teacher should take the time to inspect carefully the adequacy of the normative group in relation to the purposes for which it is intended. Generally, the test norms should logically be representative of the group being tested. For example, in most instances it is inappropriate to compare the test results of a group of upper-middle-class suburban youngsters with a group of inner-city children regardless of whether they are the same age and are in the same grade. The experiences and opportunities of the two groups will likely be different and, consequently, will affect performance on many types of tests. For this reason, test norms should be described fully in the manual to determine whether accurate interpretations are possible. In addition, the norms established for many well-known devices were generated many years ago and may be out of date. Teachers are always encouraged to check the latest copyright date to ensure that the norms have been updated continually in an effort to keep the test current.

ASSESSMENT MODELS

Many of the previously mentioned techniques have been incorporated into a variety of assessment models. Four somewhat different models are described in the following section. Although each model has distinct features, a number of similarities may also be noted. These components include the use of a variety of assessment techniques, incorporating the classroom teacher into the diagnostic process, and using the assessment data for remedial programs. According to Gearheart (1976), a number of these components usually are necessary for most assessment models to be effective maximally.

Bateman's Diagnostic-Remedial Process

The diagnostic principles outlined by Bateman (1965) are intended primarily to provide information for planning what to do for a given child. Figure 2–8 conceptualizes the five-step process provided by Bateman.

1. *Determining whether a learning problem exists.* The basic intent of the first stage in Bateman's process is to decide whether a significant discrepancy exists between what the student is capable of performing and the student's actual level of achievement. Bateman suggests that it would be somewhat pointless to prescribe remedial procedures for students who are progressing as well as they "should" be.

2. *Describing and measuring the student's problem.* The student's academic difficulties are completely described in the second stage of the process. Various types of assessment procedures, including standardized tests, teacher-made tests, and observational analysis, are used to measure the student's performance. Grade-level scores are not stressed at this stage; instead, determining *how* a student reads or calculates is emphasized.

3. *Analyzing the student's learning problem.* Bateman suggests that experienced clinicians find that this particular stage merges with the behavioral description described in the preceding step. An examination of relevant correlates of the student's learning problem is included in this third stage of the process. One group of correlates, termed *paraconstitutional*

FIGURE 2–8   Stages in the Diagnostic-Remedial Process

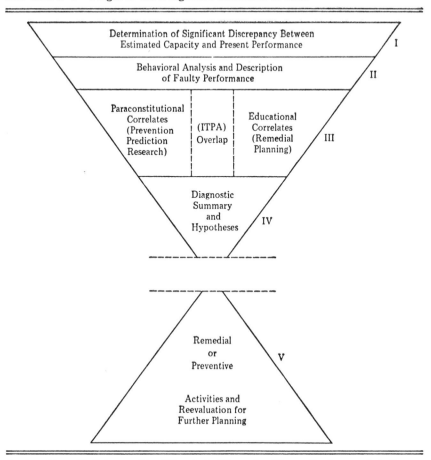

Source: From B. Bateman "An Educator's View of a Diagnostic Approach to Learn-ing Disorders," *Learning Disorders,* V. 1., Special Child Publications, 4535 Union Bay Place N.E., Seattle, WA 98105 © 1965.

factors by Bateman, are considered to be more helpful in preventing or predicting, rather than in remedying learning problems. Grouped within this category would be familial factors, soft neurological signs (motor dif-ficulties, special problems), etc. The other major set of correlates are more directly related to academic performance and include a detailed analysis of a student's strengths and weaknesses (e.g., word-analysis skills, types of written-language errors, etc.). This latter category would be of more help to the teacher in planning remedial programs. Nevertheless, in-formation obtained through study of various paraconstitutional factors certainly would contribute to a more thorough understanding of a student's difficulties.

4. *Formulating educational hypotheses.* The crux of the diagnosis occurs in the fourth step, when all of the assessment procedures have been completed and a hypothesis has been clearly formulated based upon the available information. Bateman believes that the diagnostic hypothesis must avoid technical terms, because they hinder communication. Specific disabilities also should be verified by both objective test data and classroom behavior. Corroborated findings protect the student and the examiner from faulty and inaccurate assumptions. At the same time, it is important that the educational hypothesis lead to specific remedial recommendations.

5. *Remedial programing.* Teaching procedures are planned based upon the previously mentioned diagnostic hypothesis. The teaching plan usually includes specific materials, techniques, and methods, along with suggestions for continual evaluation of the child's progress. In regard to teaching strategies, Bateman believes that the primary focus should be on teaching the student to do what cannot presently be done by using whatever behaviors and techniques will maximize the desired results. Bateman noted a gap between the summary of diagnosis and the remedial planning at the time this particular process was formulated (see Figure 2–3) because of the lack of definitive knowledge and research concerning exactly which techniques most effectively remedy disabilities. It is interesting to note that in recent years very few studies have contributed any additional significant data concerning this particular problem.

The diagnostic-remedial model prepared by Bateman is one that she admits is neither unique nor new. Nevertheless, it has sustained any innovations that have occurred because it represents quite clearly a very sensible and logical process for assessing the needs of handicapped learners.

Diagnostic-Prescriptive Teaching

Diagnostic-prescriptive teaching (DPT) is a method of teaching that emphasizes that good instruction relies upon educationally meaningful diagnosis (Hallahan & Kauffman, 1976). Generally, advocates of this approach attempt to identify a student's specific educational needs through various assessment procedures and then *prescribe* appropriate teaching programs to meet these needs. The nature of the DPT process differs according to individual teachers, but Thomas (1976) suggests that the approach should consist of the following four parts.

1. *Establishing objectives.* Behavioral objectives are considered crucial in the DPT process because they specify the behaviors that will be assessed and later developed. Thomas points out that behavioral objectives also provide evidence that learning has occurred.

2. *Diagnosis.* The diagnostic part of the process attempts to determine

which objectives have been attained and which objectives have not yet been attained by the student. Any of the assessment procedures discussed earlier in this chapter may be used to diagnose educational needs. However, brief, informal probes are usually recommended by most DPT advocates.

3. *Prescribing*. Teaching programs are planned based upon what the student could and could not do in the diagnostic part of the process. Since most prescriptions relate to preestablished behavioral objectives, the vast majority of prescriptions are prepared in advance, and the student is merely directed to the prepared activity (Thomas, 1976). The teacher's major responsibility during this part of the process is to personally instruct students encountering difficulty with various programs.

4. *Criterion measurement*. Once the student has completed the prescribed activities, a measurement is used to determine whether the objective has been attained. Diagnostic tests similar to the evaluation used in the second step of the DPT process might be administered again. However, observations or conferences can also be used to check on the attainment of specific objectives.

DPT may be accurately considered a method of individualizing instruction for children with learning problems. The emphasis throughout most DPT programs involves the achievement of specific task-oriented skills in order to move the student from where he or she is to where the DPT teacher desires the student to be (Ysseldyke & Salvia, 1974). In many ways, the prescriptions may be viewed as a series of assignments for reaching a potential behavior objective (Thomas, 1976).

Finally, it should be noted that organization and record-keeping are important components of most DPT programs. Many different record forms, similar to the form illustrated in Figure 2–9, are used to note student progress. Whether the program is geared to a group or an individual there should be an indication of objectives to be attained, since the behavioral objectives are fundamental to the entire program.

The Assessment Class

In response to the brief and formal evaluation of many students, some school districts recently have implemented a more in-depth and varied evaluation of children through a model known as the *assessment class*. Escovar (1976) describes the assessment class as a self-contained classroom in which children spend the entire school day every day for a 10–20 week period. Class size varies from five to seven students during each 10-week period, and most classes are staffed with specially trained teachers and aides. The class itself is designed, according to Escovar, for any child whose case might have raised questions concerning validity of prior testing, pos-

FIGURE 2–9   Pupil Progress Record Form

Child's name _____

Skill area _____ Dictionary skills _____

Objective	Completion date	Comments
Say alphabet in order		
Alphabetize letters		
Alphabetize words to first letter		
Alphabetize words to second letter		
Alphabetize words to third letter		
Estimate location of a word in the dictionary		
Derive word meaning		
Use guide words		
Interpret syllables		
Interpret accent or stress		
Select word meaning from context		
Interpret pronunciation key		
Use cross reference		
Preferred spellings		
Investigate word origin		

sible emotional involvement, or effectiveness of various teaching strategies.

During the child's placement in the assessment class, various evaluative procedures are employed, and informal assessment and teaching techniques are used continually to verify formal testing results. In addition, different teaching methods and materials are also evaluated in terms of applicability for individual students.

All of the assessment findings and teaching recommendations are shared with pertinent personnel in the student's own school. A detailed teaching plan often accompanies the student's return to school. An important component of the assessment-class model also occurs during periodic follow-up visits by the teacher. During these times, various teaching procedures may be adapted or eliminated according to the student's academic progress.

One of the primary benefits of the assessment-class is that it allows the teacher to study many facets of the child's behavior over an extended period of time. The interaction of the child with many different variables provides a solid base of information from which a number of valuable conclusions can be drawn. Nevertheless, a major weakness of this approach in the past has been the very limited amount of time with which the home teacher was involved with the assessment class. It would seem more logical to involve the teacher more closely during all phases of the evaluation, because this would result in a clearer understanding of the child's problem and would provide important input into the selection of various remedial programs and techniques.

Remedialdiagnosis

In contrast to the more traditional assessment models, *remedialdiagnosis* is described as a procedure to determine the best remedial program on the basis of actual responses to the remedial program (Beery, 1968). The remedial program is grounded in a comparison of various remedial methods in terms of their relative effectiveness for individual students, and not on the basis of test results.

As described by Beery, observation over an extended period of time is emphasized during remedialdiagnosis. Once a relationship has been established between the teacher and the student, a brief evaluation of the student's development is conducted in order to find out what the student needs to learn. However, the major purpose of the assessment is merely to identify which areas are to be studied by means of remedialdiagnosis.

The essence of remedialdiagnosis is that several alternative teaching methods are experimented with as a basis for selecting the best one for each student. The teacher's observations of the student's responses to various teaching methods provide the essential key for selecting particular remedial programs. All efforts are directed through the teacher, who serves as the coordinator for both integrating and applying information from all disciplines. Beery points out that this allows the primary responsibility for the student's education to remain with the classroom teacher.

The concept of remedialdiagnosis is one that may be used by both classroom teachers and remedial specialists. Locating the most appropriate remedial approach for each child is a desired goal and one that probably is a key to remedying various learning problems effectively. In all likelihood, however, the effectiveness of this approach would be enhanced with more specific guidelines regarding judging of the proficiency of remedial methods. Nevertheless, remedialdiagnosis is a very suitable alternative to traditional assessment models that primarily emphasize test results in planning remedial programs.

The assessment of children with learning problems need not be considered the complicated and difficult process it often was considered in the past. Many difficulties with the assessment process have resulted from incorrectly focusing on satisfying the legal definitions of various handicapped children, rather than on gathering relevant information for use in planning teaching strategies for individual children. Any other purpose of educational assessment must be considered secondary to this essential objective.

References

Anastasi, A. *Psychological testing.* New York: Macmillan, 1976.

Anderson, S. B., Bogatz, G. A., Draper, T. W., Jungleblut, A., Sidwell, G., Ward, W. C., & Yates, A. *CIRCUS.* Princeton, N.J.: Educational Testing Service, 1974.

Bateman, B. An educator's view of a diagnostic approach to learning disorders. In J. Hellmuth, *Learning Disorders.* Vol. 1. Seattle, Wash.: Special Child Publications, 1965.

Beatty, L. S., Madden, R., & Gardner, E. F. *Stanford diagnostic arithmetic test* (Level I and Level II). New York: Harcourt Brace Jovanovich, 1966.

Bender, L. *A visual-motor gestalt test and its clinical use.* New York: American Orthopsychiatric Association, 1962.

Bennett, H., Seashore, G., & Wesman, A. G. *Differential aptitude tests.* New York: Psychological Corporation, 1969.

Beery, K.E. *Remedialdiagnosis.* San Rafael, Calif.: Dimensions Publishing, 1968.

Boehm, A. E. *Boehm test of basic concepts.* New York: Psychological Corporation, 1971.

Botel, M. *Botel reading inventory.* Chicago: Follett, 1962.

Brueckner, L. J. *Diagnostic tests and self-helps in arithmetic.* Monterey, Calif.: CTB/McGraw-Hill, 1955.

Bruininks, R. H. *Bruininks-Oseretsky test of motor proficiency.* Circle Pines, Minn.: American Guidance Service, 1977.

Caldwell, B. M. *Cooperative preschool inventory.* Princeton, N.J.: Educational Testing Service, 1970.

Campbell, D. P. *Strong-Campbell interest inventory.* Stanford, Calif.: University of Stanford Press, 1974.

Cartwright, C. A., & Cartwright, G. P. *Developing observation skills.* New York: McGraw-Hill, 1974.

Clark, K. E., & Campbell, D. P. *Minnesota vocational interest inventory.* New York: Psychological Corporation, 1966.

Cohen, C. R., & Abrams, R. M. *Spellmaster.* Exeter, N.H.: Learnco, 1974.

Colarusso, R., & Hammill, D. *Motor free visual perception test.* San Rafael, Calif.: Academic Therapy Publications, 1972.

Connolly, A. J., Nachtman, W., & Pritchett, E. M. *Key math diagnostic arithmetic test.* Circle Pines, Minn.: American Guidance Service, 1973.

Crabtree, M. *Houston test for language development.* Houston: Houston Test, 1963.

Crites, J. W. *Career maturity inventory.* Monterey, Calif.: CTB/McGraw-Hill, 1973.

Downie, N. M. *Fundamentals of measurement.* New York: Oxford University Press, 1958.

Dunn, L. M. *Peabody picture vocabulary test.* Circle Pines, Minn.: American Guidance Service, 1959.

Durrell, D. D. *Durrell analysis of reading difficulty.* New York: Harcourt Brace Jovanovich, 1955.

Ekwall, E. E. *Diagnosis and remediation of the disabled reader.* Boston: Allyn and Bacon, 1976.

Escovar, P. L. Another chance for learning—The assessment class. *Teaching exceptional children,* 1976, 9, 2–3.

Frank, A. R. Breaking down learning tasks: A sequential approach. *Teaching Exceptional Children,* 1973, 6, 16–29.

Frankenburg, W. K., & Dodds, J. B. *Denver developmental screening test.* Denver: LADOCA Project and Publishing Foundation, 1970.

Frostig, M., Lefever, D. W., & Whittlesey, J. R. *The Marianne Frostig developmental test of visual perception.* Palo Alto, Calif.: Consulting Psychologists Press, 1964.

Gates, A. I., & McKillop, A. S. *Gates-McKillop reading diagnostic tests.* New York: Bureau of Publications, Teachers College, Columbia University, 1962.

Gates, A. I., & Russell, D. H. *Diagnostic and remedial spelling manual.* New York: Bureau of Publications, Teachers College, Columbia University, 1962.

Gearheart, B. R. *Teaching the learning disabled: A combined task-process approach.* St. Louis: C. V. Mosby, 1976.

Gillespie, P. H., & Johnson, L. *Teaching reading to the mildly retarded child.* Columbus, Ohio: Charles E. Merrill, 1974.

Gilmore, J. V., & Gilmore, E. C. *Gilmore oral reading test.* New York: Harcourt Brace Jovanovich, 1968.

Goodenough, F., & Harris, D. *Goodenough-Harris drawing test.* New York: Harcourt Brace Jovanovich, 1963.

Gray, W. S., & Robinson, H. M. (Eds.) *Gray oral reading test.* Indianapolis: Bobbs-Merrill, 1967.

Gronlund, N. E. *Measurement and evaluation in teaching.* New York: Macmillan, 1976.

Hainsworth, P. K., & Siqueland, M. L. *Early identification of children with learning disabilities: The meeting street school screening test.* Providence, R. I.: Crippled Children and Adults of Rhode Island, 1969.

Hallahan, D. P., & Kauffman, J. M. *Introduction to learning disabilities: A psycho-behavioral approach.* Englewood Cliffs, N.J.: Prentice-Hall, 1976.

Hammill, D. D. Evaluating children for instructional purposes. *Academic Therapy,* 1971, 6, 341–353.

Kerlinger, F. N. *Foundations of behavioral research.* New York: Holt, Rinehart and Winston, 1973.

Kirk, S. A., McCarthy, J. J., & Kirk, W. D. *Illinois test of psycholinguistic abilities.* (Rev. ed.) Urbana, Ill.: University of Illinois Press, 1968.

Kuder, G. F. *Kuder occupation interest survey.* Chicago: Science Research Associates, 1966.

Landsman, M., & Dillard, H. *Evanston early identification scale.* Chicago: Follett, 1967.

Larsen, S., & Hammill, D. *Test of written spelling.* San Rafael, Calif.: Academic Therapy Publications, 1976.

Lee, L. *The Northwestern syntax screening test.* Evanston, Ill.: Northwestern University Press, 1969.

Lincoln, A. L. *Lincoln diagnostic spelling tests.* Indianapolis: Bobbs-Merill, 1955.

McCullough, C. M. *McCullough word-analysis tests.* Boston: Guinn, 1963.

Mecham, M. J., Jex, J. L., & Jones, J. D. *Utah test of language development.* Salt Lake City, Utah: Communication Research Associates, 1967.

Medinnus, G. R. *Child study and observation guide.* New York: John Wiley, 1976.

Mehrens, W. A., & Lehmann, I. J. *Standardized tests in education.* New York: Holt, Rinehart and Winston, 1969.

Monroe, M. *Monroe reading aptitude tests.* Boston: Houghton Mifflin, 1935.

Myers, P. I., & Hammill, D. D. *Methods for learning disorders.* (2nd ed.) New York: John Wiley, 1976.

Myklebust, H. *Picture story language test: The development and disorders of written language.* Vol. 1. New York: Grune & Stratton, 1965.

Newcomer, P. L., & Hammill, D. D. *The test of language development.* Austin, Tex.: Empiric Press, 1977.

Otto, W., McMenemy, R. A., & Smith, R. J. *Corrective and remedial teaching.* (2nd ed.) Boston: Houghton Mifflin, 1973.

Pate, J. E., & Webb, W. W. *First grade screening test.* Circle Pines, Minn.: American Guidance Service, 1969.

Prescott, G. A. Criterion-referenced test interpretation in reading. *The Reading Teacher,* 1971, 24, 347–354.

Proger, B. B., & Mann, L. Criterion-referenced measurement: The world of gray versus black and white. *Journal of Learning Disabilities,* 1973, 6, 72–84.

Roach, E., & Kephart, N. *The Purdue perceptual-motor survey.* Columbus, Ohio: Charles E. Merrill, 1966.

Roswell, F. G., & Chall, J. S. *Roswell-Chall diagnostic test of word-analysis skills.* New York: Essay Press, 1959.

Sequential tests of educational progress: Writing. Princeton, N.J.: Cooperative Test Division, Educational Testing Service, 1958.

Silvaroli, N. J. *Classroom reading inventory.* (2nd ed.) Dubuque, Iowa: William C. Brown, 1973.

Sloan, W. *Lincoln-Oseretsky motor development scale.* Los Angeles: Western Psychological Services, 1965.

Slosson, R. L. *Slosson oral reading test.* East Aurora, N.Y.: Slosson Educational Publications, 1963.

Smith, R. M. (Ed.) *Teacher diagnosis of educational difficulties.* Columbus, Ohio: Charles E. Merrill, 1969.

Smith, R. M., & Neisworth, J. T. Fundamentals of informal educational assessment. In R. M. Smith (Ed.), *Teacher diagnosis of educational difficulties.* Columbus, Ohio: Charles E. Merrill, 1969.

Spache, G. D. *Diagnostic reading scales.* Monterey, Calif.: California Test Bureau, 1972.

Spencer, E. F., & Smith, R. M. Arithmetic skills. In R. M. Smith (Ed.), *Teacher diagnosis of educational difficulties.* Columbus, Ohio: Charles E. Merrill, 1969.

Strang, R. *Diagnostic teaching of reading.* (2nd ed.) New York: McGraw-Hill, 1969.

Thomas, C. M. *Individualizing instruction.* St. Louis: C. V. Mosby, 1976.

U.S. Department of Labor. Manual for the USES. General Aptitude Test Battery. Washington, D.C.: U.S. Government Printing Office, 1970.

U.S. Department of Labor. Manual for the USES. Nonreading Aptitude Test Battery. Washington, D.C.: U.S. Government Printing Office, 1970.

Wallace, G., & Kauffman, J. M. *Teaching children with learning problems.* (2nd ed.) Columbus, Ohio: Charles E. Merrill, 1978.

Wepman, J. *Auditory discrimination test.* Chicago: Language Research Associates, 1958.

Woodcock, R. W. *Woodcock reading mastery tests.* Circle Pines, Minn.: American Guidance Service, 1974.

Ysseldyke, J. E., & Salvia, J. Diagnostic-prescriptive teaching: Two models. *Exceptional Children,* 1974, *41,* 181–185.

3

A Practical
Approach to Assessment

Assessment results that are useful for teaching are based upon systematic planning and the most efficient testing procedures. Usually, most examiners consider a number of important guidelines throughout the assessment of children with learning problems. The fundamental procedures for using the assessment results are discussed in this chapter. Guidelines for using both formal and informal tests also are presented, along with suggestions for appropriately interpreting assessment data.

ASSESSMENT GUIDELINES

Variety of Appraisal Techniques

In working with children experiencing learning handicaps, teachers frequently tend to use only one specific technique to diagnose the child's difficulties. However, as we have discussed in the preceding chapter, there are many different assessment techniques available to teachers.

As a rule, the information gained through standardized tests (e.g., percentiles, grade scores, etc.) are not precise enough for planning specific teaching programs. The quantitative nature of standardized tests, at best, might indicate general levels of academic functioning and possible areas of difficulty in broad areas such as reading comprehension, arithmetic computation, etc. Nevertheless, many standardized tests are incorporated into the assessment process in order to screen for more detailed diagnostic procedures. In addition, valuable diagnostic information might also be obtained by analyzing a child's responses on specific test items. This point is discussed further in a later section of this chapter.

Observational data and informal teacher-made tests, as compared to standardized measures, usually provide more exact information that may be used in planning remedial strategies. They assess behaviors and skills that are more directly related to a child's actual achievement. In addition, many classroom teachers can participate in the assessment process when informal measures are emphasized.

However, the use of any assessment procedure to the exclusion of all others has many inherent dangers. The individual differences among all children clearly implies that different assessment procedures will be successful with different students. Each diagnostic technique has distinct advantages and disadvantages when used with different types of children in certain situations, and consequently, the best method usually employs a variety of assessment techniques.

Scope-and-Sequence Charts

Specific and concise teaching objectives are essential in planning various assessment procedures and remedial programs. Teaching goals generally are formulated from broad lists of skills and abilities, which are available through curriculum guides, teacher's manuals, and various scope-and-sequence charts. In most instances, these charts and guides provide general information concerning the sequence of skills that children should learn at different levels, grades, or ages. Charts are usually available by subject area in the teacher's manuals accompanying many basic texts. In addition, many local school districts and state departments of education periodically provide curriculum guides for different subject-matter areas. An example of a scope-and-sequence chart in reading is illustrated in Figure 3–1. Many of the following chapters also include examples of scope-and-sequence charts in other areas.

Although the sequence of certain skills and abilities may differ by grade or age level in different charts and guides, the information serves as an excellent guideline for planning a number of assessment procedures. Academic problems initially noted on scope-and-sequence charts may be examined more specifically through the use of either published or teacher-made tests. The sequential listing of skills and abilities on each of the charts and guides serves as an indispensable frame of reference for further questions and concerns about individual learning difficulties. Prospective teaching goals also may be projected by noting the sequence of skills listed on each chart. Essentially, however, the listing of skills becomes a first-level screen for more intensive planning and assessment.

According to Ekwall (1976), a few precautions should be followed in

FIGURE 3–1   Reading Scope-and-Sequence Chart

Skill	Grade Level or Year in School
	1 2 3 4 5 6 7+
Knowledge of Dolch Basic Sight Words (or other similar lists)	
First half	1–3
Second half	2–3
Other Sight Words	1–7+
Other Basic Sight Word Lists	
Configuration Clues	
(Word length, capital letters, double letters, and letter height)	1–4
Context Clues	
(Pictures and words)	1–5
Phonic Analysis	
Single initial consonants (all but soft c and g)	1–4
Soft c	2–4
Soft g	2–4
Initial consonant blends	
bl, br, fl, fr, gr, pl, st, tr,	1–4
cl, cr, dr, gl, pr, sk, sl, sm, sn, tw, sch	1–4
sc, sp, squ, str, thr, shr,	2–4
sw, spl, spr	2–4
dw, wr, scr	3–5
Ending consonant blends	
ld, nd	1–4
nk, ft, st, lt	2–4
ng, nt, mp	2–4
Consonant digraphs	
sh, th (three/this), wh (which/who)	1–4
ch (K/church), ck	2–4
ng	
gh, ph	3–4
Silent consonants	
kn	2–4
gh, mb	2–5
wr	3–5
gn	4–5
Short vowel sounds	
a, e, i, o, u	1–4
Long vowel sounds	
a, e, i, o, u	1–4
Vowel teams and special letter combinations	
oo (look/moon), ea (each/bread),	
ay, eo, ai, ee	2–4
oa (oats, ow(o/cow), ir, ur, or, ar, aw,	
ot (trout), oi, oy, t, er, au, ew	2–5
Rules for y sound	2–4
Vowel rules for open and closed syllables	2–4
Syllable principles (1, 2, and 3)	
1. When two like consonants stand between two vowels the word is usually divided between the consonants.	3–5
2. When two unlike consonants stand between two vowels the word is usually divided between the consonants (unless the consonants are digraphs or blends).	
3. When a word ends in a consonant and "le" the consonant usually begins the last syllable.	
Syllable Principles (4, 5, and 6)	
4. Compound words are usually divided between word parts and between syllables within these parts.	

FIGURE 3–1   *Continued*

Skill	Grade Level or Year in School

Grade Level or Year in School: 1 2 3 4 5 6 7+

- 5. Prefixes and suffixes are usually separate syllables.
- 6. Do not divide between the letters in consonant digraphs and consonant blends.

Structural Analysis
Word endings
ed, ing, 's, d

er, es

est

Word families
all, at, et, em, etc.

Word roots

Contractions
let's, didn't, it's, won't, that's, can't, wasn't, isn't, hadn't

don't, I'll, we'll, I've, he'll, hasn't, haven't, aren't, I'm, he's, we're, you're, what's, there's, she's, wouldn't, she'll, here's

ain't, couldn't, they're, they'd

you'll, she'd, weren't, I'd, you've, you'd, we'd,

anybody'd, there'll, we've, who'll, he'd, who'd, doesn't, where's, they've, they'll

Possessives

Accent Rules[a]

1. In two-syllable words, the first syllable is usually accented.

2. In inflected or derived forms the primary accent usually falls on or within the root word.

3. If two vowels are together in the last syllable of a word, it may be a clue to an accented final syllable

4. If there are two like consonants within a word, the syllable before the double consonants is usually accented.

Suffixes and Prefixes[b]

Dictionary Skills
Say alphabet in order

Alphabetize letters

Alphabetize words to first letter

Alphabetize words to second letter

Alphabetize words to third letter

Estimate location of a word in the dictionary

Derive word meaning

Use guide words

Interpret syllables

Interpret accent or stress

Select word meaning from context

Interpret pronounciation key

Use cross reference

Preferred spellings

Investigate word origin

Parts of speech

▨ Skill Firmly Established   ▨ Skill Extended and Refined (but has been introduced)

[a] *At present no definitive research is available as to which accent generalizations are of high enough utility to make them worthwhile to teach. The four listed here are believed to be quite consistent and also of high utility.*

[b] *The prefixes "a" and "un" should be known by the middle of the third year in school. From that point on, the student should continue to extend and refine his knowledge of prefixes. This extension and refinement would continue throughout his elementary and high school years. The suffixes "er" and "ly" should be known by the middle of the second year of school. From that point on the student should continue to extend and refine his knowledge of suffixes. This extension and refinement would continue throughout his elementary and high school years. (The author suggests that "known" in this case only means that the student recognizes the prefix and/or suffix, but that he not be required to know its meaning.)*

Source: Ekwall, E. E. *Diagnosis and remediation of the disabled reader.* Boston: Allyn and Bacon, 1976, pp. 59–61. Reproduced with the permission of the publisher.

using scope-and-sequence charts. He points out that often there are different levels of development for certain skills. For example, a child who knows various sounds in isolation may not be able to synthesize these sounds into words. The development of many skills and abilities must therefore be considered on a continuum of difficulty and according to different levels of application. Also, no one skill on a scope-and-sequence chart should be considered a prerequisite for a child's learning how to read, write, or calculate. Many children are not able to pronounce isolated sounds but are able to read quite well. Similarly, perfect letter formation is not necessarily a prerequisite for expressing ideas in writing. Nonetheless, scope-and-sequence charts are essential in planning quality programs of assessment and remedy.

Teacher Involvement

It is unfortunate that the concept of educational assessment as practiced in many schools has been misunderstood and inappropriately implemented (Wallace & Kauffman, 1978). Generally, most formal evaluations within a school occur in settings other than regular classrooms (Hammill, 1971). The tests administered during these sessions usually are given by an individual who is not teaching the child (e.g., school psychologist, diagnostician, etc.). The data from the assessment measures are integrated into a report, and the educational implications, if there are any, are shared with the classroom teacher, the special teacher, and the parents (Maitland, 1976).

This type of diagnosis is illogical and unreasonable. Teachers should play an active and central role in assessing *all* children, especially those with difficulties in learning. Our recommendation is based on two reasons: First, teachers are in the best position to assess the *educational* problems of children (Smith & Neisworth, 1969); second, teachers probably are the most active and largest consumers of assessment data.

Since assessment is part of the ongoing teaching process, the teacher is well suited to the role of diagnostician. Daily observational opportunities, informal teaching probes, and various teacher-made tests all provide the teacher with diagnostic information usually unavailable to visiting specialists. Specific behavorial patterns may also be witnessed *over time* and in *actual* teaching situations, rather than during comparatively brief and isolated periods of time. The rapport built up between teacher and student over a period of weeks and months should be considered as another important factor for recommending that the teacher take an active part in the assessment process.

In regard to the teacher as a consumer of diagnostic data, it seems reasonable to recommend that an important role in this process be given to the person working directly with the child. Compared to other professionals, teachers often are better able to use test results and observational information in planning teaching strategies. Putting remedial procedures into practice also has a better chance for success if the recommendations are based on intimate knowledge of classroom organization, available materials, and teaching procedures. In sum, the teacher is an essential key to effective educational assessment.

Continuous Assessment

As an integral part of the remedial process, assessment must be considered as an ongoing procedure for continually gathering relevant information. Meyen (1972), for example, suggests that the initial evaluation must be viewed as a starting point for continuous evaluation. The initial results usually provide information helpful in setting up remedial programs. However, as the child progresses, many of the initial recommendations can be modified or eliminated based upon the child's changing needs. In addition, a number of initial impressions and suggestions that are a result of inaccurate and inappropriate tests might be changed.

Continuous assessment is actually the basis upon which clinical or diagnostic teaching is formulated. Lerner (1976) describes clinical teaching as an alternating teach-test-teach-test process, with the teacher alternating roles between teacher and tester. Units of work and specific skill instruction are taught to the child and evaluated. Continual assessment results provide the teacher with evidence of successful instruction or of faulty learning. As a teaching process, clinical teaching seems uniquely suited to the needs of many children with learning problems. The individualized nature of the teaching procedures provides a personalized teaching program. In addition, the cycle of clinical teaching, as diagrammed in Figure 3-2, requires continual planning and putting into practice teaching tasks based upon an ongoing program of assessment and evaluation.

Continuous evaluation and assessment does not mean that a series of formal tests should be administered to each child. Rather, as we have stated earlier in Chapter 2, many important diagnostic clues may be obtained through informal observations and evaluations of the child. A child's oral reading, for example, might provide an indication of a problem with consonant blends, which is later confirmed by various classroom activities. Specific arithmetic difficulties may be detected while the teacher observes the child working at the chalkboard or while the teacher checks a workbook assignment. Using this type of information in planning teaching programs is a primary goal of clinical teaching. As noted by Heilman (1972), assessment also becomes an essential part of the entire remedial process, not just the prelude to remedial instruction.

FIGURE 3–2   Diagram of the Clinical Teaching Cycle

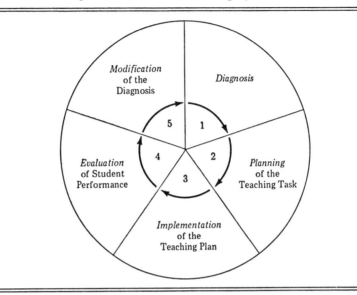

Assess Strengths and Weaknesses

A major part of the emphasis in programs of assessment for children with learning problems often has been placed on the evaluation of a child's deficiencies. Many examiners focused their concern on what the child could not do, rather than on what the child did under particular conditions (Strang, 1969). A summary of the evaluation of a child with learning difficulties, for example, might list all of the specific phonic skills that the child missed on a particular test or all of the words the child misspelled on a spelling test. Many diagnostic tests, in addition, often record students' *areas* of weakness (e.g., auditory difficulties, visual problems, etc.).

A more responsible approach to assessment should include an account of a child's academic strengths. Evaluating and later using these strengths in a remedial program is certainly more reasonable and rational. According to Lerner (1976), achieving goals in learning and acquiring a feeling of success are of prime importance for the child with learning difficulties. Consequently, many remedial specialists recommend that a child's assets serve as the foundation for teaching during the early stages or remedial work while tasks are being planned in the child's areas of disability (Bateman, 1965). This approach allows the child a feeling of immediate success and a mastery of certain tasks.

During both formal and informal periods of assessment, it is especially important for examiners to note the more intact skills and abilities of the child. In addition, examiners should record favorable behavioral strategies and techniques for possible inclusion in eventual remedial programs. Assessment becomes a more positive process when a child's assets, along with deficits, are measured and evaluated by the teacher. Most importantly, the teacher can incorporate many of these assets into planning teaching tasks and programs.

Overtesting

The excessive amount of time teachers spend in assessing children with learning handicaps has become a serious problem in many school districts. Otto, McMenemy, and Smith (1973) believe that overtesting contributes to the gap between diagnostic and remedial efforts because of the subsequent reduction in remedial instruction time. Furthermore, an extensive amount of testing often results in feelings of discouragement and inadequacy on the part of the child, and the consequent loss of rapport between the child and the tester (Ekwall, 1976).

Excessive testing most frequently occurs in cases in which the examiner administers a standard battery of tests to each child evaluated. There are many situations in which, regardless of the child's present problem and referral, each child is administered an intelligence test, a visual-motor perception test, a psycholinguistic measure, and various other achievement tests. Even more astonishing in these cases is the frequent recommendation for further testing once the standard battery has been completed.

All test administrators should refrain from using tests that do not relate directly to planning educational strategies. In this regard, Spache (1976) cautions that the wide use of any test (e.g., the ITPA, Frostig, etc.) does not guarantee validity or value in yielding information that can be directly translated into treatment. Testing results should provide an adequate amount of data for initiating an educational program and for measuring the child's growth over a period of time. Using tests that do not relate to these specific objectives is highly questionable.

Finally, it is important to reiterate that not all the information for understanding a handicapped child will be obtained in the testing at the beginning of a program (Spache, 1976). The continuous nature of the assessment process is intended primarily to assist the teacher in refining and alternating educational strategies based upon the changing and developing needs of the child.

Assessment Findings

Throughout this book, we will emphasize continually the importance of *directly* using assessment results in teaching programs. This is the primary purpose of educational assessment. Regrettably, many test results are improperly applied. As we have mentioned previously, some assessment findings are used as the sole determinant for placing students in special classrooms. The labels that often accompany special class placement are also directly attributable in many cases to test results.

The overgeneralization of standardized test findings has been acknowledged earlier; however, many informal assessment procedures also may be reproached for similar limitations. Observational data, for example, are susceptible to a number of different problems. The inaccurate interpretation of behavior during observations, along with the tendency to formulate generalizations based upon very limited data are both serious issues. Also, important variables are often overlooked during brief and isolated periods of observation.

Another potential problem with informal assessment procedures is the tendency to use teacher-made tests to obtain quantitative scores, such as percentiles or grade scores. Informal tests are not intended to provide specific scores. Information obtained from these measures is more applicable to ongoing teaching procedures. Informal test results, for example, might indicate that the concept of compound words is not understood by some students. The teacher will plan corresponding instructions based upon this knowledge and on the specific test results.

The problem of a *false positive* or a *false negative* diagnosis is also mentioned by Hammill (1971) in a discussion of test results. A false positive diagnosis occurs when the assessment findings inaccurately indicate that the child is encountering a particular problem. In a false negative diagnosis, a child's specific difficulty is not detected during the assessment process. Each of these problems often occurs more frequently than necessary because of the inappropriate selection of many tests, the overgeneralization of assessment findings, the emphasis upon test scores, and the often improper usage of test results for placing students in special classes. It is crucial that all educators become aware of the misuses and abuses of assessment procedures in order to use properly test findings to plan teaching strategies.

Early Assessment

Recently there has been an increased effort among many different disciplines to identify children with learning problems. Educators in particular, have recognized that the earlier a child's learning difficulty is detected the more easily it can be remedied (Wallace & Kauffman, 1978).

Consequently, many school districts have implemented systematic efforts to identify children with learning handicaps. In some cases, screening instruments are administered on a district-wide basis, while in other situations, individual teachers are encouraged to recommend children based upon certain behavioral clusters and other important indicators. It is important, however, that young handicapped learners *can* be identified and subsequently helped to overcome their academic difficulties. Some of the more widely used rating scales, screening tests, observation schedules, and informal tests are discussed in Chapter 5.

Early identification is significant, since most learning problems are often the cumulative results of many deficient components. The interacting effect of various cognitive, language, and socioemotional factors, along with other psychological and environmental variables, frequently can result in a specific learning problem. It is, therefore, vitally important that teachers become aware of behavioral indications of potential difficulties in each of the above mentioned areas. Continued observation and assessment of many maladaptive behaviors often will help to isolate specific skill deficiencies that otherwise might result in more serious academic handicaps.

Assessing All Related Factors

All factors related to children's learning problems must be included in the assessment of children with academic difficulties. Strang (1969) believes that the assessment process should include consideration of ecological factors, as well as various personal factors. Physical, psychological, and socioeducational elements have been mentioned also as other possible components of the assessment process (Ekwall, 1976). In many instances, the evaluation of these related factors will involve a professional other than the teacher or the diagnostician. In the case of the child with visual acuity or hearing impairments, a physician's diagnosis probably will be necessary. Severe personality disturbances, on the other hand, might require the skill of a clinical psychologist.

Nevertheless, the teacher might recognize many interfering factors in the home or neighborhood through periodic home visits or parent interviews or conferences. Teachers seldom will have any direct responsibility or control over home-related problems. However, in some cases, the teacher might refer the family to appropriate community agencies for support and assistance. In other instances, it will be important for the teacher simply to know that the child's academic difficulties are a symptom of a more difficult and involved problem over which the teacher has little control (Ekwall, 1976). Although our primary emphasis in this book is the educational assessment of children with learning problems, we believe that related factors also must be measured adequately.

Multiple Causation

As we have discussed previously, it is usually agreed that the primary purpose of educational assessment is to obtain educationally relevant information for the purpose of planning teaching programs. As such, the study of etiological factors has been a secondary concern during most educational assessments. Nevertheless, it is important to point out that many different factors usually contribute to a child's specific learning problem.

According to Bryant (1972), it is usually advisable to distinguish between the descriptive *manifestations* of the learning problem (e.g., reversal difficulties, poor arithmetic reasoning skills, etc.) and various underlying factors of the learning difficulty (e.g., minimal brain damage, poor nutrition, etc.). Among the more general causative factors, those related to the educational, environmental, psychological, and physiological areas are usually mentioned as the most common (Wallace & McLoughlin, 1975). Consequently, multiple causation is recognized by most professionals in this area; a single causative factor is rarely sufficient in describing the etiology of a learning problem.

The importance of continued study and research within the realm of etiology is well recognized and supported. However, educators, since they are primarily responsible for *teaching* the child, must examine the most relevant factors concerning the student's learning problem. We certainly do not discourage an intensive study of etiology by other professionals in medicine, psychology, and so on; rather, educators must realistically establish priorities in their specific goals in order to teach children effectively. Obviously, this particular objective will be accomplished more efficiently when the assessment process focuses on educationally relevant variables.

USING STANDARDIZED TESTS

Standardized tests are the most widely used assessment techniques for measuring and evaluating a student's academic achievement. Although there are a number of excellent tests from which to choose, the limitations among many of the tests must be seriously considered before selecting a particular test. In addition, many formal tests are misused and severely abused by some examiners. Therefore, a number of important guidelines for using standardized tests are presented in this section.

According to Otto, McMenemy, and Smith (1973), each of the following points should be considered during the process of choosing standardized tests:

1. Define the purpose for testing.
2. Locate suitable tests.
3. Evaluate the test before selecting it.
    Table 3-1 also lists additional items to be considered in analyzing standardized tests.

Testing Objectives

One of the most significant steps in the assessment process is to determine specific testing objectives. *Why* a test is being administered and the information expected to be received from the test are crucial variables that must be clearly outlined prior to selecting any assessment test (Mehrens & Lehmann, 1969). In using standardized tests, assessment choices must be specified further from among the range of formal tests that are commercially available. The use of a group achievement instrument, an individual diagnostic test, or a general survey measure will depend upon the examiner's objectives for a particular student or group of children. For example, a teacher interested in knowing the reading achievement range within a class would probably administer a group reading test. The results of such a test, as noted in Table 3-2, would provide an overall impression of the group's achievement in reading by grade scores. The information also would allow the teacher to group children tentatively for reading instruction. In spite of the importance of this general information, little else concerning an individual child's specific needs can be obtained from this type of test. Essentially, the results from such group tests are limited.

On the other hand, testing objectives that require more specific in-

TABLE 3-1   Items to be Considered in Evaluating a Standardized Test

General facts: Title, author, publisher, designated function.
Reading abilities measured: Are they significant and suitable?
Validity: Does the test measure what it purports to measure?
Reliability: Is the test accurate and consistent?
Diagnostic value: Does it indicate the students' special difficulties and give clues to why they are having these difficulties?
Norms: What types of norms are available? Are they representative of the total population or of certain groups?
Pupil performance: What does the pupil do?
Construction of test: How were the exercises selected?
Manual: Are the directions complete and easily intelligible? Are norms included, uses of the test described, and other data given about test and teaching aids?
Costs:
Mechanical considerations: Is it legible, etc.?

TABLE 3–2   Reading Grade Scores

Grade Scores[a]	Number of Children
7.0–7.9	1
6.0–6.9	2
5.0–5.9	4
4.0–4.9	17
3.0–3.9	3
2.0–2.9	1
	N = 28

[a]A grade score of 4.6 represents the average achievement made by the population used to standardize the test in the sixth month of the fourth grade. Raw scores are converted to grade scores by tables that accompany tests. A raw score of 30 may be equivalent to 4.6, a raw score of 34 to 4.9, and so on.
Source: Karlin, R. *Teaching Elementary Reading: Principles and Strategies.* New York: Harcourt Brace Jovanovich, Inc., 1971, p. 42. Used with permission of the publisher.

formation about a student's reading strengths and weaknesses probably would be best achieved through use of an individual diagnostic reading test. The summary data presented in Table 3–3, for example, illustrates the specific information that might be obtained from such a test. When compared to group measures, individual tests usually provide more practical results in terms of teaching applicability. For example, knowledge of Tom's difficulties with final letter sounds and auditory blending (see Table 3–3) will help the teacher to plan a teaching program for Tom.

In short, a teacher should state clearly testing objectives in order to select the most appropriate assessment technique for each student. Well-defined objectives are important for effective testing procedures and remedial strategies.

Locating Tests

Once specific test objectives have been stated, the teacher should review the available choices of published tests. Among the many sources for locating and sorting out suitable tests, the most useful source, according to Otto, McMenemy, and Smith (1973), is Buros' *Mental Measurements Yearbook.* As mentioned in Chapter 2, the seventh edition of this yearbook was published in 1972. Tests that are available in education and psychology are described fully and evaluated in the yearbook. The critiques are recognized as an excellent source for unbiased and professional information concerning standardized tests.

Tests in Print (Buros, 1974) is an excellent test bibliography and index to the first five yearbooks in the *Mental Measurements Yearbook* series.

TABLE 3–3   Diagnostic Reading Test Scores

Child: Tom	Age: 11 yrs., 3 mos.

Summary of test results

Gates-McKillop Reading Diagnostic Tests

Subtests Administered[a]	Scores/Comments
I. Oral reading	Grade Score = 2.6; halting reading
III. Words: untimed presentation	Very few consistent analytical skills; tends to rely on phonic analysis
V1. Recognizing and blending	Not scorable; many errors in blending the word parts
V2. Giving letter sounds	Missed /t/, /m/, /ĕ,/ /f/
V3. Naming capital letters	Named all correctly
V4. Naming lower-case letters	Named all correctly
VI2. Initial letters	Missed 3 of 19
VI3. Final letters	Missed 12 of 14
VI4. Vowels	Missed 2 of 10
VII. Auditory blending	Errors on 13 of 15; much difficulty
VIII. Auditory discrimination	Difficulty with sounds differing at the end of words

[a]Note: Not all subtests were administered.

The tests listed in *Tests in Print* are described fully, and references to the test reviews in the yearbooks are also provided.

Other sources of test information include publishers' catalogs from which sample specimen sets of tests may be ordered. In addition, many of the following journals often include specific test reviews: *Journal of Educational Measurement, Journal of Educational Research, Journal of Special Education, The Reading Teacher,* and *Perceptual and Motor Skills.*

Test Information

The skills and abilities that various standardized tests measure usually will differ according to specific types of test. Most standardized tests provide little useful information for planning individual teaching strategies. In the majority of cases, the results of these tests will yield data involving general skills and abilities. However, a limited amount of relevant information can be obtained from carefully selected standardized tests. In these situations, the teacher must analyze the test results for the desired data. Wallace and Kauffman (1978) also note that teachers often must translate this test information into teaching procedures, since few standardized tests provide guidelines in this regard.

Individual diagnostic tests usually will provide more exact assessment data than will group achievement tests. Nevertheless, the differences among many diagnostic tests requires careful examination and review in order that the best assessment technique be selected. The various factors measured by specific tests, along with the degree of difficulty of the test, are important considerations in the selection of standardized tests. Many formal tests, for example, are omitted simply because of the difficulty or the range of skills that are included in the test.

An in-depth analysis of a student's test responses often is necessary following the administration of many formal tests. In some cases, a more complete assessment can be attained when test responses are informally studied or when students are asked to explain certain answers. For example, examining particular test items on the *Stanford Diagnostic Arithmetic Test* (Beatty, Madden, & Gardner, 1966) might indicate a specific difficulty in multiplying when a zero appears in the units place of the multiplier, for example

$$\begin{array}{r} 7\ 3 \\ \times\ 2\ 0 \\ \hline \end{array}$$

or a difficulty with number facts involving certain numbers. A detailed analysis of test results obviously has tremendous value in terms of practicality and applicability for teaching procedures. In contrast to grade scores and percentile ranks, almost all of the information gathered in this fashion can be used in *teaching* the child.

Few standardized tests provide relevant information for educating children with learning problems. When these tests are used in the assessment process, teachers often must analyze specific test items in order to understand fully a child's test performance. Consequently, the content of standardized tests must be examined carefully for individual appropriateness prior to the inclusion of these tests in the assessment process.

Time Factors

Many standardized tests are considered inappropriate for children with learning problems because of the long and laborious nature of them. Arrigo (1975) notes that shorter tests probably maintain the children's interest and minimize the opportunity for failure among the low achievers. Many children with learning problems become extremely discouraged during the administration of lengthy tests because of their failure on the more difficult test items. The reliability of a student's performance under these conditions, therefore, must be questioned and certainly considered.

Standardized tests and subtests that are rigidly timed also must be considered as a detriment to children with learning handicaps (Arrigo, 1975). Increased frustration and disappointment often are observed among these children when strict time limitations are imposed for completing various subtests. Reasonable time limits that do not penalize individual children are justified expectations for any standardized test. These factors should be considered when selecting any standardized test.

Reliability and Validity

A standardized test's reliability and validity are among the most important factors to be considered in selecting an assessment battery. As previously discussed, most technical manuals for standardized tests report available reliability and validity information. Serious concern usually is indicated when these data are not available or not provided by the test author(s). Equally important, however, is the assumed ability of test examiners to understand the reported reliability and validity information. This was discussed in the previous chapter.

The concept of *reliability* involves the consistency of scores obtained when the child is examined with the same instrument or with equivalent measures. Although important in test selection, high reliability does not always guarantee that the test is worthwhile (Ekwall, 1976), since a test can be reliable without being valid. Consequently, the concept of *validity* is actually a more central issue.

Validity is probably the most important aspect of the test, since it involves the extent to which the test measures what it was designed to measure. Karlin (1971), for example, asks whether a reading comprehension test could measure comprehension, if questions are limited to just literal meanings. Similarly, word-analysis tests that only measure phonetic analysis are not as valid as tests that measure many types of word-analysis skills.

Considering the importance of validity, it is surprising to note that many tests either report minimal validity data or no validity data at all. This is regrettable, since validity data are some of the most important factors to be considered in selecting a standardized test. In later chapters we will evaluate data for each test reporting this information.

Test Manuals

Most published tests are accompanied by a manual that includes information related to the standardized test. According to Arrigo (1975, pp. 4–5), all of the following are necessary:

1. A description of the subjects and an explanation of what is being measured should be given.
2. Instructions for administering the test must be clear and concise so that the test may be administered to children with varying abilities.

3. Various sample performances should be illustrated and analyzed as an aid in interpretation.
4. Record-keeping should be simple in order to facilitate informal observations of the children's behavior.
5. Scoring should be quick, simple, and precise. All tables should be readily available.
6. Normative data and statistical information on reliability and validity should be available.

In addition, Otto, McMenemy and Smith (1973) suggest that a good manual accompanying the text should include instructions for developing local norms.

Finally, it is important to mention that most publishers offer various types of specimen tests at reasonable cost. These specimen tests are regarded as an excellent way to familiarize oneself with different standardized tests. Ekwall (1976) believes that diagnosticians should make every effort to become familiar with as many tests as possible. He points out that the process of examining new tests and test procedures is an excellent inservice training procedure in itself.

Carefully selected standardized tests can be incorporated into the assessment process when the examiner understands the various limitations of these tests. The results of formal tests must be carefully interpreted, and, also informally analyzed for relevant data to be obtained. In the end, a combination of formal, informal, and observational procedures is probably most useful for assessing children with learning problems.

USING INFORMAL TESTS

Informal teacher-made tests may be used in the classroom for practically any purpose. These tests have a number of distinct advantages for classroom use. According to Heilman (1972), the relatively simple construction of most informal teacher-made tests must be considered a primary advantage. Most of these can be constructed from graded curriculum materials (e.g., workbooks, textbooks, skill sheets, etc.), which are usually readily available to classroom teachers. Also, the informal nature of most teacher-made tests often is considered a distinct advantage for the child with learning problems, because the lack of rigid time limitations and formality help to decrease tension and the lack of motivation among many children. In addition, Ekwall (1976) points out that many standardized tests contain subtests designed to measure skills and abilities that in reality the students do not actually use in the classroom. The informality of most teacher-made tests is also thought to be more closely related to actual classroom instruction.

Another advantage of informal tests is that they are inexpensive and demand no more time for administration and analysis than do most standardized tests (Heilman, 1972). Certainly this is an advantage for many teachers who find that formal tests are either too expensive or time consuming. Finally, informal teacher-made tests offer the very significant benefit of being closely related to ongoing programs of instruction. The results from such tests usually provide exact data, which can be easily and readily applied to various educational procedures and strategies.

Among the many available teacher-made tests, two specific types are used in most classrooms: *informal skill tests* and *informal survey tests*. Each of these is discussed in the following sections.

Informal Skill Tests

Informal teacher-made tests can be prepared for specific skills in each subject-matter area. According to Wallen (1971), these tests usually provide procedures for relating a student's performance in a specific skill to the selection and organization of instruction appropriate for that specific skill. He suggests that specific skill tests are constructed by using various skill objectives. (These skill objectives were noted earlier in this chapter in our discussion of scope-and-sequence charts.) Curriculum guides and manuals also identify skill objectives by grade or age level. Essentially, a specific skill test is constructed by answering the question: *"How does a child, who has attained the specific skill objective, behave?"* (Wallen, 1971).

For example, knowledge of arithmetic signs may be assessed by asking the child to complete an informal test similar to the one shown in Table 3–3. Students who have attained the particular skill probably would be able

FIGURE 3–3   Informal Skill Test for Arithmetic Signs

Directions: Direct the child to write the correct arithmetic sign on each line.

a)	2 _____ 7 = 9		k)	50 _____ 10 = 2 + 3	
b)	4 _____ 3 = 12		l)	15 _____ 6 = 3 × 7	
c)	6 _____ 3 = 5 − 2		m)	18 _____ 8 = 2 × 5	
d)	8 _____ 4 = 2		n)	6 _____ 7 = 45 − 3	
e)	16 _____ 7 = 5 + 4		o)	9 _____ 8 = 6 × 12	
f)	4 _____ 14 = 20 − 2		p)	54 _____ 6 = 3 × 3	
g)	3 _____ 7 = 11 + 10		q)	18 _____ 2 = 2 × 10	
h)	5 _____ 5 = 30 − 5		r)	14 _____ 4 = 2 + 3 + 5	
i)	20 _____ 10 = 2 × 5		s)	49 _____ 7 = 5 + 2	
j)	16 _____ 4 = 2 × 2		t)	6 _____ 6 = 9 × 4	

to complete this teacher-made test successfully. Therefore, it is reasonable to assume that children who correctly finish this test understand the meaning of various arithmetic signs and are able to write them legibly. Teachers are also justified in assuming that children who encounter difficulty with this test probably have not mastered this particular skill. For children with visual-motor difficulties, a multiple-choice format could be used.

Informal skill tests may be constructed in most subject-matter areas by reviewing the skill objectives. To help make most test items valid and reliable, Charles (1972, pp. 333–334) offers the following guidelines for constructing informal tests:

1. Be sure the test directions are very clear.
2. Do not include questions on trivial matters.
3. Use simple wording, language, and sentence structure.
4. Do not include more than one problem in one item.
5. Try to include items that have only one correct answer.
6. Do not use tricky statements or double negatives.
7. Use true-false items that are clearly either true or false, not yes or no, maybe, or sometimes.
8. Do not use words that give hints about correct answers, such as *all, always, none, never, totally, exactly, completely,* and *etc.;* avoid *a, an,* singulars, and plurals before blanks, such as "Toby rode an ————, a large animal of India."
9. Be sure that one item does not give the answer for another item.

An adequate sample must be provided for each skill being measured in order that the test might assess the specific skill accurately. In addition, Karlin (1971) suggests that care should be taken to be sure that the exercises require the children to perform the intended skill. This caution must be especially observed with detailed skill tests, which easily overlap with corresponding abilities.

Informal teacher-made tests also can be sequenced in difficulty from relatively basic tasks to successively more difficult tasks for use with children of varying abilities. In constructing this type of informal test, the teacher merely sequences the test into a series of exercises that are increasingly more difficult. The teacher-made test illustrated in Figure 3–4, for example, progresses from asking the student to note whether the words are alike or different to asking the student to determine the final sound in a word. Teachers are usually able to pinpoint specific skill deficiencies with these informal tests. Spencer and Smith (1969) feel that sequentially based skill tests provide a clue to the exact location in the breakdown of a student's understanding. Each level of the test serves as a subtest of the larger area being assessed. As such, the subtests may be utilized singly or in combination with the other subtests.

FIGURE 3-4   Informal Test for Auditory Discrimination of Final Consonants

1. Direct the child to tell if the following words are alike or different.

   a. did—did   e. hill—him
   b. big—beg   f. car—car
   c. dog—dog   g. map—mat
   d. jam—jar   h. can—cat

2. Direct the child to find the two words with the same sound at the end of the word.

   a. bed, neat, sand   e. car, pan, ten
   b. tall, big, dog   f. frog, hop, lamp
   c. ball, hill, man   g. bus, paint, seat
   d. bank, run, look   h. rib, give, sob

3. Direct the child to pick out the words that end with the same sound as the stimulus word.

   a. *hop*   dog, trip, map, sad, leap
   b. *mat*   but, duck, goat, bump, sit
   c. *dig*   pit, rug, hog, pig, dark
   d. *bed*   lid, tall, mud, red, box
   e. *pain*   den, jam, run, seen, pass
   f. *lick*   fun, duck, bank, but, pet
   g. *tab*   rub, sit, try, but, bib
   h. *ram*   cat, hug, him, fan, dim

4. Direct the child to write the letter that is heard at the end of the stimulus word.

   a. beg   e. rope
   b. skate   f. train
   c. nail   g. book
   d. star   h. mud

Source: We appreciate the assistance of Pauline B. Gotham in constructing this test.

Informal Survey Tests

As compared to informal skill tests, teacher-made survey tests usually are broader in scope. Rather than assessing one specific skill in some depth, survey tests sample a wider range of academic behaviors. Informal reading inventories, commonly referred to as the *IRI*, can be considered a type of reading survey test, which measures word recognition, word analysis, and reading comprehension skills. An example of an IRI is provided in Chapter 8.

Informal survey tests are constructed for broad topics such as arithmetic computation, spelling, and reading comprehension. The content of the test is usually comprised of sample items for each skill included under the broad topic. For example, a survey test of arithmetic computation would include at least several items for various subskills in addition, subtraction, multiplication, and division (see Chapter 12 for an arithmetic survey test). A survey test in reading comprehension similarly would include test items for all types of comprehension, for example, literal, inferential, etc. The informal phonics survey test illustrated in Figure 3–5 incorporates the major components of phonics instruction. This informal test provides the teacher with a good indication of a child's overall phonic knowledge. More detailed information concerning a specific phonic skill (e.g., consonant blends) can be obtained by administering an informal skill test.

INTERPRETING ASSESSMENT DATA

The administration of various assessment instruments in and of themselves provide little useful information unless the data gathered from the assessment techniques are analyzed and incorporated into educational strategies. The crucial and potentially most helpful segment of the assessment process occurs during the analysis of a child's performance.

FIGURE 3–5   Informal Phonics Survey Test

1. Name the following letters:

      t   m   s   f   u   a   p   w   b   y

2. Mark the letter in each row that is the same as the first letter.

      f   c   f   t   p
      m   t   n   p   m
      a   e   u   o   a
      b   d   b   p   r

3. Mark the word in the row that is the same as the first word.

      cat   bat   mat   cat   hat
      may   day   pay   may   way
      fit   hit   sit   kit   fit

4. Mark the word in the row that is different from the other words.

      pan   pan   fan   pan   pan
      hid   hid   lid   hid   hid
      rag   rag   rag   gag   rag

5. Give the sounds of the following letters.

      m   b   s   t   f   r   p

6. Read these words aloud and mark the word that has a different beginning sound.

    boy   book   barn   toy
    pot   put   toe   pig
    man   may   not   mad

7. Read these words aloud and circle the word that has a different ending sound.

    man   fun   ran   hop
    hit   let   bug   hot
    mop   cap   rod   rip

8. Read these words aloud and circle the short vowels that you hear.

    pet   cake   pig   pot   cup
    bag   get   line   hot   pup

9. Read these words aloud and circle the long vowels that you hear.

    lake   wet   pie   hope   cube
    gate   me   nine   told   cut

10. Read these words aloud and circle the word that does not rhyme with the other words.

    rib   sad   fib   bib
    him   dim   Tim   rig
    sit   dip   hit   kit

11. Read these words aloud and circle the silent letters.

    plate   knee   right   crumb   whistle

12. Read these words aloud and circle the word that does not have the same sound as the underlined letter of the first word.

    puff   enough   graph   father   phone   part

13. Read these words aloud and circle the words that have the same sound as the underlined letters of the first word.

    drink   drop   block   drug   dig   draw   drip

14. Read these words aloud and tell the sound of the underlined letters.

    boy   coin   pail   toe   neat   boat

15. Pronounce the following nonsense words:

    lek   gret   tween   blasp
    fring   koop   flable   swite

16. Divide the following words in syllables.

    return   contention   worldly   discontent
    cheerfulness   comfortable   opposite   surgical

Source: We appreciate the assistance of Kathy Marshall in constructing this informal test.

The nature of each child's specific academic difficulties usually influences testing objectives. The objectives, in turn, determine the extent to which various children are evaluated. All children do not require an extensive and prolonged diagnosis by multidisciplinary terms. In most cases, a very straightforward assessment of the child's skill development in the problem area usually is adequate (Otto, McMenemy, & Smith, 1973). For our particular purposes, the two levels of assessment that are generally recognized include the specific skill level of diagnosis and the case-study approach to assessment. The interpretation of assessment information at each of these levels will be discussed in the following sections.

Skill Analysis

The interpretation of assessment data at the skill level of diagnosis is specific and usually relevant to immediate teaching practices. The skills analyzed at this level most often are informally measured by the teacher-made tests described in the previous section of this chapter. Let us look at an example (Figure 3–6). In the case of Paul, an analysis of his errors following an informal subtraction test indicate that his difficulty is in subtracting when a zero is located in a number.

Following the administration of this test, Paul was asked to describe orally his written responses, and the teacher determined that he confused the subtraction of zeros with the multiplication of zeros. Individual practice in subtracting numbers with zeros using sticks was one of the activities the teacher prescribed for Paul.

In Paul's case, the informal skill test provided the teacher with infor-

FIGURE 3–6

Name *Paul*

6 7	4 9	2 8	7 5	8 8
−2 3	−3 0	−1 4	−1 0	−4 5
4 4	1 0	1 4	6 0	4 3
3 4 7	1 9 2	8 8 3	9 7 5	2 7 5
−2 0 1	− 5 0	−5 7 0	−6 2 2	−1 2 0
1 0 6	1 4 0	3 1 0	3 4 3	1 5 0
5 1 3	6 5 4	6 7 6	8 4 5	4 9 7
−2 0 1	−4 2 2	−5 5 0	−2 0 3	− 8 2
3 0 2	2 3 2	1 2 0	6 0 2	4 1 5

FIGURE 3–7

Name: _____

1. tap	may	(tin)	can	soap
2. two	(tax)	book	dog	ever
3. tall	flip	man	(toe)	mop
4. try	swim	here	run	(tip)
5. tab	(toy)	go	bib	son
6. top	cup	(trim)	yes	gone

mation concerning a specific arithmetic difficulty. In many cases, additional data can be gathered with a minimal amount of analysis and interpretation. Mary Ann, for example, was administered the teacher-made test shown in Figure 3–7 to assess visual discrimination of the initial consonant *t*. She was directed to circle the word in each row that begins with the same letter as the stimulus word. Mary Ann's performance on this test indicates that she has attained this specific reading objective. Little else can be interpreted from this test.

In discussing this type of test, Wallin (1971) notes that a child's performance can be interpreted in only two ways: either the student needs or does not need instruction for the skill objective.

We prefer to use these specific skill tests in most educational assessments because of the exact information that is usually obtained. In most instances, the results of the appraised skill require very little analysis, since the child's performance is easily interpreted as having either attained or not attained the particular skill. Specific types of error aid teachers in planning various instructional programs and techniques. In Figure 3–8, for example, a number of different arithmetic errors are provided as illustrations.

Specific skill testing is ideally suited to our concept of continuous evaluation of the child with learning problems. This type of educational assessment embodies many of the principles of clinical teaching, which we discussed earlier. Furthermore, as illustrated in Figure 3–9, the assessed skills are recorded easily for continued examination and review. This particular record form provides the teacher with an excellent tool for evaluating specific consonant sounds.

Specific skill strengths and difficulties also can be gathered and analyzed from a selected number of standardized tests. Many of the formal tests that we describe in subsequent chapters can provide information of an exact nature. In these instances, teachers must go beyond grade scores and percentiles to the child's actual responses for individual test items. An examination of a student's performance on the *Key Math Diagnostic Arithmetic Test* (Connolly, Natchman, & Pritchett, 1973), for example, might yield information as to whether a student's subtraction difficulties involve

FIGURE 3–8   Arithmetic Error Analysis

Child Response	Analysis
1 7 × 2 8 ‾‾‾‾‾ 3 1 5	Possible confusion with regrouping; may not know how to carry.
3 2 2 ᴬ|7 − 2 3 ‾‾‾‾‾ 2 1 1 4	Regroups when it is not necessary.
5 2 × 4 ‾‾‾‾‾ 2 4 7	Probably does not know multiplication combination for 4's.

9 8 r 2
3 ⟍ 2 7 2 6
2 7
   2 6
   2 4
   ‾‾
    2
	Does not record the zero in the answer when unable to divide.

.5 .9 + .6 + .8 ‾‾‾‾ ‾‾‾‾ .11 .17	Probably needs to know that decimals are added differently than whole numbers; needs work with place value and number line.

single-digit numbers, multidigit numbers, regrouping, or decimal numbers. Similarly, a child's specific reading errors on the *Durrell Analysis of Reading Difficulty* (Durrell, 1955) can be ascertained by closely inspecting the performance on each of the various subtests. The diagnostic information obtained through an informal analysis of standardized tests may be applied consequently to educational strategies and ongoing programs of instruction.

Case-Study Analysis

The case-study level of assessment generally is reserved for children with severe learning difficulties. At this level, a detailed study of the individual student's academic performance and behavior is completed for the specific purpose of determining the basic defects that are interfering with effective learning (Otto, McMenemy, & Smith, 1973). Case studies integrate evaluative information from all possible sources. Inferences from test performances are considered in relation to data gained from classroom ob-

FIGURE 3–9   Initial Consonant Sounds Record Form

	b	c	d	f	g	h	j	k	l	m	n	p	r	s	t	v	w	y	z
Joe					✓	✓	✓				✓		✓						
Tim			✓					✓		✓		✓							
Mary Ann	✓					✓					✓	✓	✓	✓	✓				
Don								✓											
Helen		✓	✓			✓	✓				✓	✓	✓	✓					
Peter																			
Carolyn	✓	✓	✓	✓	✓	✓	✓	✓	✓	✓	✓	✓	✓	✓	✓	✓	✓	✓	✓
June																			

servations, daily work assignments, academic potential, previous school experiences, and various home and health records (Beatty, Madden, & Gardner, 1966). Remedial specialists usually are responsible for case studies of individual children, however, many of the basic assessment techniques can also be informally applied by teachers during the course of regular instruction.

All of the information gathered during a case study usually is included in a formal report, which is often included in the child's permanent records. The report usually reflects the efforts of all individuals who have had any responsibilities in the assessment process. Written reports of findings and recommendations will differ according to many factors, including the depth of testing, administrative policies, time considerations, and personal competencies. Nevertheless, Ekwall (1976) has suggested a number of guidelines to be followed in writing case-study reports.

1. Use a type of outline form that will make sections and subsections clearly visible.
2. Include important information but exclude any information that would be of no value in working with the student.
3. Where "impressions" are stated they should be identified as such.
4. List specific test scores and the source of each score.
5. List specific skills needing remediation.
6. Give a brief interpretation of the results of each test that may not be familiar to the person or persons reading the report.
7. Keep sentence structure simple.
8. Use third person when referring to yourself.

9. Make a specific recommendation for the remediation of various difficulties noted.
10. Give exact dates of the administration of each test.
11. Show summary of significant strengths and weaknesses.
12. Include possible causal factors for weaknesses of the student (pp. 377–378).

The analysis and integration of case-study information into educational recommendations and teaching strategies is illustrated in the case of Jimmy. All of the data was gathered and analyzed by a classroom teacher.[1] It should be noted that the educational recommendations from case studies usually are more general than the information gained from specific skill tests.

Jimmy is a 10-year-old boy of normal physical development with no apparent sensory defects. He is the fourth of seven children, all of whom reportedly achieve at average and above-average levels in school. Jimmy's lack of academic progress has concerned his teachers throughout his years in elementary school. In the cumulative record, Jimmy's kindergarten teacher noted his "... immaturity for first-grade work." Nevertheless, he was not retained in kindergarten for another year. Jimmy's present fifth-grade teacher states that he "... is able to complete very few academic tasks without continual help and direction."

In the classroom, Jimmy tends to be extremely inattentive and distracted. He is also inclined to respond quickly during class discussions. His speech patterns are immature in relation to other fifth-graders in the class, and he seldom speaks in whole sentences. Nonetheless, many of Jimmy's verbal comments demonstrate perception and insight. He is very sensitive concerning errors and mistakes that he makes. On a number of occasions, after being called a "retard" by fellow students, he refused to attend school. Jimmy responds well to positive comments, including encouragement and praise. Gross and fine motor skills appear quite normal, and he excels in activities related to sports. Jimmy continues to receive recognition and success in this particular area.

TESTING RESULTS

During periods of formal and informal assessment, Jimmy often seems embarrassed by his academic deficits. He will slump in his chair during particularly troublesome questions. On one occasion, Jimmy tried to conceal his written responses from the teacher. Any timed tests appear to be frustrating to him, and he often becomes restless during extended periods of

[1]We appreciate the skillful assistance of Beverly E. McKee in collecting the data for this report.

assessment. During several periods, Jimmy asked when the testing would be completed. Accordingly, the subtests from most standardized tests were informally administered during periods of instruction, and many timed tests were not timed. Due to Jimmy's frustration, most assessment periods were kept relatively brief.

Reading and Word Analysis

Jimmy's reading can be approximated to be on a first-grade level. He knows most letter names, but very few sounds in isolation. He was unable to decode any new words on three tests—*Gates-McKillop Reading Diagnostic Test, Informal Reading Inventory, Informal Phonics Test*—unless the word was in his sight vocabulary. On the Gates-McKillop flash presentation of words, for example, Jimmy knew *go* and *how,* but he could not decode these same words when they were presented on the untimed subtest immediately following the flash presentation. A number of reversals were also noted on all three reading measures: he called *dook* for *book, on* for *no, tar* for *rat,* and *es* for *see.* He was able to identify initial sounds of some words with fairly good accuracy on the Gates-McKillop; however, medial and final sounds seemed to be completely unknown either in isolation or in analyzing various words. Vowel sounds seemed to confuse him (e.g., *yo* for *you, mate* for *mat,* etc.), and he consistently used long vowel sounds. His sound-blending ability was also poor. Most words that he recognized were known by sight. The results of an informal phonics test indicated a severe problem in this area. Although he was able to discriminate almost all initial consonants, he was only able to discriminate two final sounds, /n/ and /t/.

Arithmetic

Jimmy's arithmetic skills on the *Key Math Diagnostic Arithmetic Test* place him at approximately the third-grade level. During many computations on informal skills, he uses his fingers to count. Jimmy also has some difficulty with various arithmetic symbols and abbreviations. Word problems are very confusing to him because of his severe reading difficulties. On the other hand, Jimmy has an excellent grasp of time and money concepts. His memory for addition and subtraction combinations can be considered quite good. Various multiplication facts are also being learned.

Written Expression and Spelling

Although Jimmy continues to use the manuscript style of writing, his letters are poorly formed and somewhat inconsistent from one writing sample to another. Letter size and spacing also differ within the same word and sentence. Jimmy's sentences are often incomplete, but they do have correct punctuation. His syntax is considerably awkward in many instances. Most importantly, however, Jimmy seems to enjoy the written language experiences that were provided for him.

Few consistent patterns were noted in Jimmy's spelling when he was administered the *Test of Written Spelling*. Both phonetic and nonphonetic words caused him difficulty, and the endings of words seem particularly troublesome. Words that are not memorized appear to be spelled randomly with very little rationale or thought. For example, he spelled *the* and *and* correctly, but spelled *place* as *pukt,* and *baby* as *bket.*

Language Development

The results of the informal language sample and various aspects of diagnostic teaching indicate that Jimmy's receptive and expressive language skills are both poorly developed. He has great difficulty in following directions in the classroom, and he continually asks for instructions to be repeated. He often slurs words together, making many sentences unintelligible. Jimmy usually speaks in short phrases and rarely speaks in whole sentences. Measures of vocabulary understanding were consistently good on the *Test of Language Development.*

ASSESSMENT ANALYSIS

Prior individual intelligence testing indicates that Jimmy has average intellectual capacity, though these scores appear to be depressed because of poor academic performance. His severe language difficulties seem to be a primary source of difficulty for him in the classroom. However, his learning has also been hampered by poor auditory discrimination skills, which seem to have prevented him from functioning adequately in his phonics-based reading program. An adequate sight vocabulary and retention of arithmetic combination facts seem to indicate good memory skills. Successful athletic achievements and an enjoyment of written language activities must also be considered as favorable evaluative findings. Arithmetic functioning, although below grade level, cannot be deemed as serious as Jimmy's language arts difficulties. The arithmetic word-problem deficits, as well as problems with written expression, undoubtedly will improve as Jimmy's language and reading difficulties are remedied. Finally, Jimmy's positive response to praise must be certainly considered an encouraging observation.

EDUCATIONAL RECOMMENDATIONS

Management Techniques

As an overall behavioral strategy, it is important that the teacher be consistently positive with Jimmy. In order to build his confidence and self-reliance, Jimmy needs praise as often as is legitimately possible. Small units of work with which he might be successful should be given to him, and gradually he should be introduced to more difficult assignments. Small steps that require a short amount of attention are probably highly useful with Jimmy. It also is important that Jimmy be helped to understand the various steps and behaviors involved in each task.

Language Arts Instruction

Jimmy's strengths should be capitalized in the area of language arts by use of some of the following techniques:

1. Introduce a language experience approach to reading by having Jimmy dictate stories. Later, encourage Jimmy to write his own short stories. Use all of the stories as a major component of Jimmy's reading instruction.
2. Encourage Jimmy to write or tape stories that capitalize on his athletic ability. He might write or tape stories on ways to improve kicking, catching, or throwing a ball, on rules for different games, and on how to be a good baseball player. Invite other children to read these stories. Later, encourage Jimmy to read stories about great sports individuals.
3. Attempt to increase Jimmy's word-recognition skills by tracing words in various media and by incorporating audio tapes into the reading instruction. Reduce his dependency on phonics by emphasizing the visual components of words (e.g., roots, prefixes, etc.). Work on the linguistic units of words to help reduce the number of meaningless units of information he must process. This approach will also provide Jimmy with a much more solid technique for spelling words.
4. Encourage Jimmy to work with selected children for projects and tutorial assistance in order to increase his ability to communicate.
5. Use selected words from Jimmy's dictated stories as weekly spelling words. Choose linguistically similar words. Integrate Jimmy's word-recognition program in reading with his spelling instruction in order that corresponding skills may be emphasized in both programs.
6. Place frequently reversed words on flash cards for review. Add arrow cues under each word for help (e.g., dog).
7. Do not force Jimmy to use cursive handwriting if he is comfortable in

using manuscript. Tracing various letters and words might help Jimmy in standardizing size and spacing of letters.

Arithmetic

The teacher should use the following techniques to help Jimmy's arithmetic deficiencies.

1. Continue to use manipulative arithmetic materials in working with addition, subtraction, multiplication, and division combinations.
2. Use flash cards and various mnemonic devices to help Jimmy remember arithmetic facts and combinations. Encourage him to use them with other children.
3. Read arithmetic word problems to Jimmy periodically and have him work out the problem orally rather than with paper and pencil.

CONCLUSION

Flexibility is probably the most important feature of the assessment process in terms of practicality and usefulness of results. The employment of a variety of evaluative techniques throughout the appraisal process usually assures the teacher of gathering a maximum amount of relevant information. Otto, McMenemy, and Smith (1973) point out that many standardized and informal assessment measures can be used to complement each other. In many cases, standardized tests provide the needed objectivity, while informal techniques fill in the informational gaps. Consequently, we recommend the use of a variety of assessment techniques in evaluating children with learning problems.

Equally important to the success of the assessment process is the sequence of procedures that are followed throughout the completion of the evaluation. The basic sequence of steps are outlined in Figure 3–10. The inclusion of each step usually results in an organized and effective appraisal of handicapped learners.

Finally, the crucial prerequisite to the implementation of any effective assessment procedure is the knowledge of available sources of information in each academic area. Therefore, each of the succeeding chapters discusses convenient and widely used methods of appraisal in the most important areas of the curriculum. In each chapter, we describe both formal and informal evaluation measures, along with a discussion of instructional goals within each area. The general assessment guidelines outlined in this chapter should serve as a practical foundation for more specific assessment in the academic areas subsequently discussed.

FIGURE 3–10   Sequence of Assessment Steps

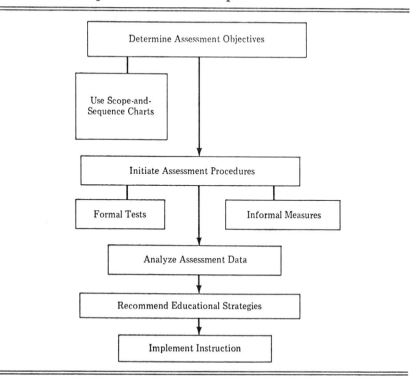

References

Arrigo, H. R. Reading and language arts assessment. *Diagnostique,* 1975, *1,* 3–5.

Bateman, B. An educator's view of a diagnostic approach to learning disorders. In J. Hellmuth (Ed.), *Learning disorders.* Vol. I. Seattle: Special Child Publications, 1965.

Beatty, L. S., Madden, R., & Gardner, E. F. *Stanford diagnostic arithmetic test manual.* New York: Harcourt Brace Jovanovich, 1966.

Brueckner, L. J. *Diagnostic tests and self-helps in arithmetic.* Monterey, Calif.: CTB/McGraw-Hill, 1955.

Bryant, N. D. Subject variables: Definition, incidence, characteristics and correlates. In N. D. Bryant and C. Kass (Eds.), *Final report: LTI in learning disabilities* Vol. 1. U.S.O.E. Grant No. OEG–0–71–4425–604. Project No. 127145. Tucson: University of Arizona, 1972.

Buros, O. K. *Tests in print.* Highland Park, N.J.: Gryphon, 1974.

Charles, C. *Educational psychology: The instructional endeavor.* St. Louis: C. V. Mosby, 1972.

Connolly, A., Natchman, W., & Pritchett, E. *Key math diagnostic arithmetic test.* Circle Pines, Minn.: American Guidance Service, 1973.

Durrell, D. D. *Durrell analysis of reading difficulty.* New York: Harcourt Brace Jovanovich, 1955.

Ekwall, E. E. *Diagnosis and remediation of the disabled reader.* Boston: Allyn and Bacon, 1976.

Hammill, D. D. Evaluating children for instructional purposes. *Academic Therapy,* 1971, *6,* 341–353.

Heilman, A. W. *Principles and practices of teaching reading* (3rd ed.) Columbus, Ohio: Charles E. Merrill, 1972.

Karlin, R. *Teaching elementary reading: Principles and strategies.* New York: Harcourt Brace Jovanovich, 1971.

Lerner, J. *Children with learning disabilities.* (2nd ed.) Boston: Houghton Mifflin, 1976.

Maitland, G. E. Whose child is he—Yours, mine, or ours? *Journal of Childhood Communication Disorders,* 1976, *8,* 15–26.

Mehrens, W. A., & Lehmann, I. J. *Standardized tests in education.* New York: Holt, Rinehart and Winston, 1969.

Meyen, E. L. *Developing units of instruction: For the mentally retarded and other children with learning problems.* Dubuque, Iowa: William C. Brown, 1972.

Otto, W., McMenemy, R. A., & Smith, R. J. *Corrective and remedial teaching.* (2nd ed.) Boston: Houghton Mifflin, 1973.

Smith, R. M., & Neisworth, J. T. Fundamentals of informal educational assessment. In R. M. Smith (Ed.), *Teacher diagnosis of educational difficulties.* Columbus, Ohio: Charles E. Merrill, 1969.

Spache, G. D. *Diagnosing and correcting reading difficulties.* Boston: Allyn and Bacon, 1976.

Spencer, E. F., & Smith, R. M. Arithmetic skills. In R. M. Smith (Ed.), *Teacher diagnosis of educational difficulties.* Columbus, Ohio: Charles E. Merrill, 1969.

Strang, R. *Diagnostic teaching of reading.* (2nd ed.) New York: McGraw-Hill, 1969.

Wallace, G., & Kauffman, J. M. *Teaching children with learning problems.* (2nd ed.) Columbus, Ohio: Charles E. Merrill, 1978.

Wallace, G., & McLoughlin, J. A. *Learning disabilities: Concepts and characteristics.* Columbus, Ohio: Charles E. Merrill, 1975.

Wallen, C. J. Informal testing. In B. Bateman (Ed.), *Learning disorders.* Vol. 4. Seattle: Special Child Publications, 1971.

Part 2

SPECIFIC ASSESSMENT TECHNIQUES

Don't you see my rainbow, teacher?
Don't you see all the colors?
I know that you're mad at me.
I know that you said to color the cherries
  red and the leaves green.
I guess I shouldn't have done it backwards.
But, teacher, don't you see my rainbow?
Don't you see all the colors?
Don't you see me?

Albert Cullum

4

Ecological Assessment

Educational assessment of children experiencing failure in school has shown an increasing ecological trend in recent years, typified by the direct examination of the child *and* the various environments in which the child operates. More specifically, the professional who conducts an ecological assessment attempts to view the child and his or her environment (e.g., the classroom, home, etc.) in its totality rather than as discrete and separately functioning entities. The reason for this is that an individual does not usually act independently of outside forces in any given situation, but is continually responding to a series of situational factors that may or may not be apparent to the casual observer. Such variables as peer pressure, teacher and parent demands, school climate, and the child's own self-concept all have the potential to either "positively" or "negatively" influence a child's academic and social behavior. It is logical that analysis of an underachieving or misbehaving child in *relation* to the environment(s) directly affecting this behavior may yield for the teacher considerable data regarding the nature of an observed problem, as well as suggest remedial strategies that may lead to its eventual amelioration. The purpose of this chapter is to acquaint teachers with the (1) rationale underlying ecological assessment, (2) models useful in conceptualizing a framework in which ecological assessment may be most efficiently conducted, and (3) formal and informal evaluative techniques that are appropriate for studying the child in a variety of environments.

RATIONALE FOR ECOLOGICAL ASSESSMENT

At its most basic level, ecological assessment is geared to an analysis of a student that takes into account the many environments in which the student operates, as well as the student's interactions in those environments. It comes as little surprise to the experienced teacher that the learner affects and is affected by the environment. On any given day a student may appear either quiet or loud; dominant or submissive; cooperative or uncooperative; energetic or passive; and friendly or surly. In many instances, these wide variances in behavior occur with bewildering complexity and speed and, seemingly, without motivation or forethought. It is equally obvious, however, that the behaviors exhibited by a child do not occur in a vacuum. The reactions of teachers, parents, and peers to these relatively normal shifts in behavior will significantly influence whether the behaviors will increase or decrease in frequency. For example, if a student is experiencing difficulty in mastering a particular math lesson and "talks back" to mask discomfort, the immediate response of the teacher frequently will determine if that behavior is exhibited again. If the teacher becomes upset or irritated and responds negatively, the student may feel compelled to continue to "talk back" in order to save face with peers or because this essentially negative interaction is relieving him or her of the necessity of working on the difficult math task. In any event, if this series of interactions among the teacher, student, and peers is not modified or extinguished, it could seriously affect the academic achievement level and emotional status of that student in particular and the entire classroom in general. Obviously, the study of students and their educational setting needs to be considered in cases where moderate to severe learning disorders are evidenced.

Although it is interesting to note the interrelationships between environment and behavior, they are seldom taken into account during consideration of students who are experiencing school failure. In most cases, when a child is observed to be underachieving or acting out in an inappropriate manner, the major area of evaluative focus is only upon the *child*. Frequently, the identified student will be referred to a specialist within the school for intensive diagnostic efforts that are designed to isolate *inherent* disorders or deficits existing within the child that are "responsible" for the learning or behavioral difficulty. Seldom does the educational evaluation attempt to probe those situational factors that may, in fact, have initiated or at least maintained the behavioral patterns that are of concern to the teacher. Newcomer (1977), in discussing the importance of considering the role of the environment in understanding learning failure, states:

> ... the focus on learning problems as strictly child-centered disorders ignores or at least de-emphasizes the fact that learning is an interactive phenomenon and that failure to learn is often intricately associated with breakdowns in a child's relationship with teachers and peers. More succinctly, diagnosing and remediating children's academic difficulties in settings removed from the classroom may not be sufficient if the problems

interfering with learning relate primarily to the types of experiences the child has within the classroom [p. 85].

Possibly many students experience school problems as a result of being unable or unwilling to conform to the demands and expectations of teachers, parents, and peers. If the child is to be assisted in gradually modifying his or her behavior in more acceptable directions (e.g., completing assignments, increasing learning rate, less emotional outbursts, etc.), the behaviors of other individuals in the environment must also be analyzed and altered.

The fact that an educational environment can and does influence the quality and quantity of children's learning has been documented in the literature. In one study, Ruben and Balow (1971) investigated the incidence of children who exhibited academic and behavioral problems in traditional school settings. This study was longitudinal in nature and followed 967 students in kindergarten through third grade. Academic and behavioral disorders were defined as the inability of children to meet adequately the demands of the educational systems in which they were enrolled. The results of this research determined that an incredible 41 percent of the subjects (i.e., 50 percent of the boys and 31 percent of the girls) were classified as being in need of either special class placement, retention, or some special services. Placement in situations other than the regular classroom had been instituted for 24.3 percent of the total study population. It is important to note that pretesting of the 967 subjects demonstrated essentially *normal scores on measures of school readiness, language development, and intelligence.* The authors state

> ... schools and teachers are oriented to a narrow band of expected pupil behaviors which are not consistent with typical behavior patterns of young boys; any pupil ouside of that narrow range is treated as needing special attention. Clearly, the problem is not with the child alone [p. 298].

These data suggest that at least as much diagnostic and remedial intervention needs to be directed toward school environments as toward the individual child.

Much study also has been devoted to exploring the effects of teacher expectations on the academic performance of children. Teacher expectations are inferences or predictions that teachers make about the present and future academic achievement and general classroom behavior of their students. These expectations typically are keyed by certain characteristics of students that may influence the patterns of interactions between teachers and their pupils (Larsen, 1975). Such characteristics as membership in racial and ethnic minority groups, underachievement, sex, and handicapping conditions have all been demonstrated to be strong determinants of teacher behavior (Good & Brophy, 1973). For example, Hoehn (1954), deGroat and Thompson (1949), Morrison and McIntyre (1969), and Good

(1970) have found that low-achieving students received more criticism and less praise than their achieving peers. Not only do teachers address more favorable comments to high-achieving students and more critical comments to low-achieving students, but they also have been found to differ in the number of opportunities for academic responses given to each group. Obviously, these patters of interaction have the potential to significantly affect a child's ultimate scholastic success.

From the foregoing discussion it should be apparent that, if a student is in need of assessment for academic or behavioral reasons, it is essential that various environmental factors be studied to determine their influence in either initiating or maintaining the observed problem. At a minimal level the teacher should be prepared to assess pupil-teacher interaction, pupil-curriculum "match," peer relationships, school and classroom climate, and extraneous variables existing outside the school setting. Unless such evaluations are conducted, it is highly likely that whatever diagnostic and remedial efforts are employed with the child in *isolation* will be largely ineffective. In other words, an ecological assessment should be considered as a vital component of any evaluative effort where the purpose is to delineate those patterns of interaction that may be seriously exacerbating a given school problem.

MODELS OF ECOLOGICAL ASSESSMENT

It is important that teachers, when conducting an ecological assessment, have some conceptual framework to guide them in their data collection. Whatever framework is utilized should permit the systematic collection of descriptive information regarding a child's interactions with the environment. In addition, the ecological assessment should provide some insight into the expectations that students have for themselves and that others have for them. One model appropriate for organizing an ecological assessment has been formulated by Laten and Katz (1975). A description of the five phases recommended in this approach is given below.[1]

1. Initial descriptions of the environment
   A. Engaging the environment for data collection on perceptions of the problem.
   B. Information is gathered from the particular setting(s) in which the problem is most noticeable.

[1]Laten, S., and Katz, G. *A theoretical model for assessment of adolescents: The ecological/behavioral approach.* Madison, Wis.: Madison Public Schools, 1975. Used with permission of authors.

      C. Information is gathered from the settings in which the problem is not noticeable.
2. Expectations
      A. Information is gathered about the expectations of the environments in which the child is experiencing problems.
      B. Information is gathered about the expectations of the environments in which the child is not having problems.
3. Behavioral descriptions
      A. Data is collected on the interactions and skills of the people involved in the problematic situations.
          1. present data
          2. historical data
          3. interactional analysis
          4. functional analysis
      B. Data collected on the interactions and skills of the people involved in successful situations.
          1. present data
          2. historical data
          3. interactional analysis
          4. functional analysis
      C. Assessment of the skills needed by the child to function successfully in different environments.
4. Data is summarized
5. Reasonable expectations are set for the child and for teachers in which the problem is most notable.

    An illustration of an ecological assessment employing this strategy would be the case of Becky, a sixth-grade student who was evidencing certain academic and social problems in school. However, upon closer perusal of her specific behavior patterns, it was evident that the perceived disorder was exhibited only in math and science classes. Her performance in social studies, spelling, and language arts was average, with no reported problems in behavior. Conversations with Becky's math and science teachers indicated that she seemed unwilling to complete assignments, frequently disrupted class discussions, and did not appear to be mastering any of the material that was presented. Both teachers also reported that Becky was an essentially bright child who could "do the work if only she would try." When observing the instructional style of the math and science teachers, it was found that a lecture format was used, and not many small group activities were employed. Mathematical concepts and computations provided the main focus of content for the courses, and students were expected to complete biweekly workbook activities in order to demonstrate knowledge of the material that was discussed during class time.

    Classes in which Becky was *not* experiencing problems were also observed. These classes emphasized a great deal of class discussion and audiovisual aides in the presentation of class content. Students were allowed the freedom to read widely on various topics and to make verbal reports in order to demonstrate their knowledge of concepts presented. Teachers frequently evaluated students in these classes to determine the degree of their mastery of subject content and provided the students with materials that were geared to their particular strengths and weaknesses.

This information, which was obtained during the initial description and expectancy phases of the ecological assessment, assisted in isolating the problem exhibited by Becky and in clarifying the expectations that were held for her in both successful and unsuccessful environments. Further work with Becky indicated that her proficiency in math was at a fourth-grade level and that remedial assistance was required in her math and science classes (Phase 3—Behavioral Description). In addition, it was felt that Becky's disruptive behavior was due to the fact that she was experiencing feelings of failure in those environments. Theoretically, once her math deficiency was overcome, these annoying behaviors would lessen in frequency and intensity. Consequently, Becky's math and science teachers readjusted their expectations and allowed her to work on tasks that were suited to her present skills. Their expectations were gradually modified upward as her abilities increased to the point at which she could perform regular classroom activities (Phases 4 and 5—Summary of Data and Setting of Reasonable Expectations). It was also noted that these teachers were more willing to set alternative expectations for other pupils who were also experiencing academic and social problems in their classrooms.

While this simple, hypothetical example is given only for illustrative purposes, it does demonstrate the framework in which an ecological assessment is usually conducted. First, the problem behavior and the environment in which it is observed is derived from those situations in which the child appears to be functioning appropriately. Second, the expectations of both types of environments are explored and recorded. Behavioral descriptions of the "types" of interactions that occur within the environments of interest are studied, and the skills (academic and behavioral) that are required in each setting are tabulated. Conclusions are drawn from the data collected, and changes in environmental interactions are made to elicit more acceptable behavior from the child. When necessary, the student is helped to acquire those skills that are essential for "normal" learning and social relationships. Ideally, the child is assisted in becoming more efficient in meeting various environmental demands, and the environmental demands, in turn, are modified to insure that they are within the performance capabilities of the child.

Carroll (1974) also has outlined a relatively simple system for conducting an ecological assessment. The major steps recommended in this approach include:

1. *Determining the goal* of assessing the learner and his environment
2. *Develop a conceptual model* for assessing the learner and his environment
3. *Implement the assessment plan* based upon the above concept and model
4. *Evaluate the results* of step 3 and determine the primary learner goals
5. *Develop a set of hypotheses* about the student's learning and emotional characteristics
6. *Develop a learning plan* based upon step 5, the learner characteristics and the learning environment [p. 3–4].[2]

Utilizing the sequences presented in these steps, the teacher attempts to answer a series of questions that relate to the student and the environment(s) in which the student functions. When determining the goals of the assessment process, it is necessary for the teacher to delineate (1) the specific purpose of the evaluation, (2) the specific information that is desired, (3) the method by which it be obtained, and (4) the way in which the information will be used once it is obtained.

The second step, developing a conceptual framework for assessing the learner and the learning environment, is somewhat more difficult and time consuming to carry out. It is the teacher's (i.e., evaluator's) purpose to become aware of the options available within given instructional situations and of the situations that elicit the most appropriate response from the student. The aspects of the environment that are analyzed in depth include such areas as the immediate facility, personnel, curriculum, climate of the classroom, time utilization, and outside resources available to the teacher and the child. Once the professional conducting the evaluation delineates the environmental components to be assessed, each is probed to determine its relevance to the observed problem. Some of the questions that may be useful during this phase of the evaluation are: Are facilities available to provide for large and small group interaction? Are facilities available in the classroom or in the school for crisis intervention? What is the ratio of students to teachers? What materials in the classroom lend themselves to individual study? In there interpersonal "sensitivity" on the part of both the teacher and the children to one another's needs? Is the majority of the classroom work in large group settings, small group settings, or individual settings? The number and type of questions asked will depend upon the particular setting(s) of interest and the specific goals for the assessment that were established during step 1.

According to Carroll, the implementation of the assessment plan may be accomplished by several means. The most common one is systematic observation, and involves either continuous, time-sampling or duration

[2]Carroll, A. W. The classroom as an ecosystem. *Focus on Exceptional Children*, Vol. 6, No. 4, September, 1974.

recording. Examination of various work samples of children may also provide useful information. One method for accumulating data regarding environmental interactions is to spend one full day devoted to following the child or children of interest while completing a diary or anecdotal record of all pertinent activities. When eliciting input to formulate hypotheses about the pupil's learning characteristics, the teacher should feel free to interview the child and any other ancillary personnel who regularly come in contact with the child. Discussions with parents also may provide helpful background information that relates to the child's developmental history. These data can be used to note or to rule out any interfering health factors or pervasive emotional factors that appear to complicate the observed problem. Once the interrelationships between the student and educational setting have been identified, it is possible to make effective judgments regarding the nature of learner-environment "match" and to devise a plan to circumvent or modify those situations that are particularly deleterious to the child.

The two models we have presented are quite useful in conceptualizing a framework in which an ecological assessment may be efficiently conducted. Similar to all models, however, they do not provide the teacher with specific strategies relevant to the successful compilation of interactional data. In order to accomplish this task, it is essential that (1) the particular environmental systems affecting the problem behavior be delineated and that (2) the diagnostic instruments necessary for the collection of relevant data be developed and field tested. Unless these concerns are directly addressed by the teacher, the ecological assessment will not provide the systematic information needed for the development of viable instructional plans. The following sections will discuss these topics with the purpose of relating their use to traditional school settings.

APPROPRIATE DIAGNOSTIC TOOLS FOR USE IN ECOLOGICAL ASSESSMENT

There are many techniques available to the teacher who is interested in conducting an ecological assessment. The selection of which tools to use in a particular situation will vary depending upon the specific data necessary to analyze effectively a child and the learning environment. In general, however, the primary means of gathering ecological data will be through the use of systematic observation, teacher-child interaction systems, checklists and rating scales, and sociometric techniques. Obviously, the *content* of these assessment tools will be modified continually to meet individual needs. We will now present a brief overview of each of these diagnostic tools.

Systematic Observation

The systematic observation of students interacting with their environments can provide the teacher with valid and highly reliable information. The first step in this process is to formulate the specific objective for which the observation is undertaken. Some of these objectives may be to determine how a student behaves in certain situations, the speed with which a child completes a given curricular task, the environmental stimuli that seem to make it difficult for a student to complete an assignment, and so on. Once the behavior(s) to be observed is specified, then a series of guidelines to be followed throughout the entire observational process are needed (Cartwright & Cartwright, 1974). These guidelines include the following:

1. Who will make the observation
2. Who or what will be observed
3. Where the observation will take place (there should be a variety of situations included)
4. When the observation will occur (there should be diversified time periods)
5. How the observation will be recorded [p. 46].

Perhaps the most essential, but somewhat arduous, assignment in the observational process is to *define* succinctly the behavior being observed. It is a common practice in the schools for professionals to describe environmental events in vague and tenuous terms. For example, the description of a student as being "silly" or "mischievous" almost always will cause confusion, because it connotes different images to different people. To one teacher, being "silly" may mean giggling and not completing assignments; to another teacher, being "silly" means fighting and maintaining a generally boisterous activity level. Consequently, using this terms to describe a student's actions will not be very productive in ascertaining whether the "behavior" is interfering with learning. It is apparent that a teacher must delineate the measurable components of the behavior in order to insure that it is accurately observed. Axelrod (1977) demonstrates how to make such a nebulous term as "disturbing others" appropriate for observational purposes:

> In order to make such a term more meaningful, a teacher must break the expression down into smaller, observable units. A teacher might define "disturbing others" as incidents of hitting another student and grabbing another student's possessions. If the teacher wishes to include talking out in class, this is also permissible. The decision as to what the term denotes, however, must be made in advance . . . and the definition must involve behaviors which are observable. One adequate definition of "disturbing others" is . . . grabbing another's objects or work, knocking neighbors' books off desk, destroying another's property, throwing objects at another without hitting, pushing with desk [p. 80].

Once the behavior of interest has been defined in measurable terms, it is possible to determine its occurrence quantitatively. The methods for doing this fall into two general categories: (1) measurement of lasting products and (2) recording of observations. The measurement of lasting products simply entails the tabulation of output of a pupil's work. Such activities as noting the number of words spelled correctly, the correct answers to mathematics questions, and correct punctuation in a written paper are all examples of the measurement of lasting products. Because the product is permanent, teachers may scrutinize it at their leisure. While this technique is certainly not new, it is quite effective in providing one estimate of a student's academic progress.

Recording of observations is utilized to record transitory behaviors, that is, behaviors occurring at one point in time but not at another point in time (Axelrod, 1977). These behaviors do not leave permanent products so they must be measured as they are being exhibited by a student or a teacher. Hand raising, amount of time spent on a task, talking out, and fighting are examples of behaviors that require recording in order to determine the frequency or duration of their occurrence. Chapter 2 discussed two types of recording procedures: time sampling and event recording. Three additional techniques are also commonly employed in the measurement of behavior: (1) *duration recording*, (2) *interval recording*, and (3) *continuous recording*.

Duration Recording   The purpose of duration recording is to provide a measure of time that an individual student engages in a certain behavior. For example, in one case a teacher was interested in determining how long Lee, a preschool student, cried during a morning at school (a 2-hour time period). When the teacher simply recorded the *frequency* or number of "cries," it was found that this behavior occurred only three times. This was not significantly different from other children in the class. However, when the teacher timed the *duration* of each crying period, it was discovered that it lasted on the average of 20 minutes each. Obviously, the accurate interpretation of Lee's crying could only be obtained through duration recording.

The utilization of duration recording must be tempered with caution. With some behaviors it is necessary to use a stopwatch in order to obtain a precise measurement. In addition, the teacher must devote continuous attention to the individual who is being observed. This restriction is not of concern when the person conducting the assessment is not also teaching the class in which the observation is being carried out. When the observer has a variety of other tasks that demand his or her time, the time-sampling procedure may be efficiently employed to obtain results similar to those of duration recording.

Interval Recording   Interval recording is an appropriate technique when it is desirable to determine both the frequency and the duration of a particular behavior. When using this procedure, the observer divides each observation session into equal time periods or intervals. The observer then records the occurrence of the identified behavior during these intervals. In the example given in Figure 4–1, the teacher has recorded whether or not a student was out of his or her seat during 5-second intervals in a 3-minute period.

FIGURE 4–1

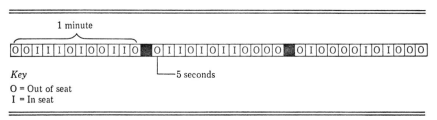

Key
O = Out of seat
I = In seat

In this illustration, the pupil was out of his seat 22 times during the 36 5-second intervals. Similar to duration recording, interval recording has the major disadvantage of requiring the undivided attention of the observer.

Continuous Recording   Continuous recording is sometimes referred to as an *anecdotal record*. The purpose of anecdotal records is to provide brief accounts of events during the day. It is important, however, that the events noted be stated in a factual manner. Wright (1967) has compiled a set of "rules for reporting" on the behavior of children or teachers. The most appropriate of these rules include

1. observing and reporting as fully as possible on the subject's situation
2. never making interpretations that carry the burden of description
3. giving the "how" of everything the subject does
4. giving the "how" of everything done by any person who interacts with the subject
5. whenever possible, stating descriptions of behavior positively.

Although these rules may help to structure the anecdotal record, they must not be permitted to interfere with viewing the behavior of the individual as completely as possible. The primary goal of this approach is to gain a composite picture "of the concrete habitat conditions and the actual behavior of the subject (Wright, 1967, p. 53)."

The systematic observation of environmental events is extremely useful in conducting the ecological assessment. Interested readers should consult any recent texts that provide excellent treatments of different observational procedures that may be employed in the school or the home. We particularly recommend the discussions of Cartwright and Cartwright (1974), Hall (1970), and Axelrod (1977).

Teacher-Child Interaction Systems

For purposes of this chapter, teacher-child interaction systems refer to those formal devices that are designed to codify specific aspects of the communication patterns that exist between the teacher and the child. Virtually all available observation systems are predicated upon several fundamental premises regarding the educational environment, which include:

1. The classroom is an open system, where a myriad of complex interactions are continually taking place.
2. The interaction patterns that do occur are usually overt.
3. The interaction patterns that are observed can be categorized to permit efficient analysis of both their quality and quantity.

While observational systems share essentially the same assumptions regarding purpose and function, they vary greatly in the ease of administration: Some devices require relatively little training on the part of the teacher, whereas other instruments, are quite complicated and entail a training period of 20 hours or more to insure that the technique is adequately mastered. Just as there are differences in the training time of various observational systems, the content of each will vary from focusing upon the transmission of values to measuring the emotional climate within the classroom setting. The type of instrument chosen for use by the teacher will depend upon the particular behavioral patterns of the teacher and child.

An illustration of one classroom observational instrument that has become quite popular is the *Observation Schedule and Record* (OScAR 5) developed by Medley, Schluck, and Ames (1968). The use of the OScAR technique requires the "coder" to observe a classroom environment for 30-minute periods, in sequences of 5-minute intervals. The two major units of verbal behaviors coded are "statements" and "interchanges." Statements are verbal behaviors that do not elicit a response. Teacher statements are classified as affective, procedural, or substantive. Pupil statements are recorded only when one pupil addresses another. Interchanges between the teacher and child are always categorized as initiating with a question and as containing three components: an entry question, a pupil response, and a teacher evaluation of the response. Three types of entry questions are distinguished and are coded as divergent, convergent, or elaboratory. The teacher's response to the student's question (or interchange) is coded into one of six areas: supported, approved, criticized, neutrally rejected, accepted, or not evaluated. In addition to these codes, the OScAR also permits the systematic tabulation of several procedural and managerial teacher behaviors.

Obviously, the OScAR or other observational systems have the capacity to yield a significant amount of classroom interaction data that directly relate to the ways in which a pupil and teacher relate in certain aspects of the instructional process. This device is important because of its sensitivity to the actions of the learner as well as to the teacher. Its use provides specific estimates of the behaviors that actually transpire within the classroom and may point out areas in which the student experiencing failure in school is receiving different responses (potentially negative) from the teacher than his or her achieving peers. It is quite possible that this information will be of help in counseling teachers and arranging optimal learning environments for students.

Because development of the teacher-child interaction system is a relatively new innovation, many teachers may not be familiar with the wide variety of techniques available. A listing of those techniques that are particularly appropriate for classroom use are given later in the chapter. The selection of which device to utilize in a given setting is an additional concern that needs to be addressed by any individual considering the use of observation systems. Herbert and Attridge (1975) have developed a set of criteria that are helpful in determining the adequacy of available instruments. These criteria are organized into three areas: *identifying criteria, validity criteria,* and *practicality criteria.* Identifying criteria helps the teacher solicit information that permits selection of the correct instrument. Validity criteria relates to the empirical evidence available for estimating whether the system represents accurately and consistently the events that it claims to describe. Practicality criteria pertain to the actual administration of the instrument and to the ease with which it is used and the results disseminated. In general, the specific criteria for the identification of observational devices include: (1) the title should be fairly representative of what the instrument does without implying a wider purpose than is warranted; (2) a statement of purpose should be available; (3) the rationale, if any, underlying the device should be made clear; (4) specific applications for which the technique is intended should be clearly stated; and (5) situations in which the instrument should not be used must be specified.

Validity criteria refer to the inference, context, and reliability of the systems. Primarily, teacher-child interaction systems must contain items that are mutually exclusive and should be representative of the dimensions of behavior under study. In addition, the instrument must be highly objective and allow little opportunity for observer inference regarding observed behaviors. The features of the environment in which the observation is taking place should be taken into account and provided for within the existing framework of the instrument. The reliabilities calculated for the system and the conditions under which they were determined must be easily available.

Criteria for practicality involve the ease of implementation of given systems, the complexity of the data-gathering mechanisms required, and the training procedures entailed. Specific criteria include the following factors: (1) codes identifying categories should be simple, easy to remember, and convenient to record; (2) training procedures for observers must accompany the instrument; (3) data-collection and recording procedures must accompany the instrument; (4) procedures for analyzing data should be described and discussed; and (5) costs likely to be incurred in the use of the instrument should be estimated. It is obvious that these points all have implications for validity and should be considered carefully prior to the selection of a device for use in an ecological assessment.

Checklist and Rating Scales

Checklists and rating scales are two commonly employed techniques useful in conducting an ecological assessment. The purpose of these devices is to provide a systematic procedure for obtaining and reporting the judgments of both teachers and pupils. The basic difference between the checklist and the rating scale is the *type* of judgment called for: A rating scale is designed to indicate the *degree* to which a characteristic is present or the *frequency* with which a behavior is observed, whereas the checklist determines the *presence* or *absence* of a particular characteristic or observation of that characteristic. Consequently, the checklist format is not appropriate when delineation of the degree or frequency of occurrence is not an important facet of the ecological assessment.

Of the two types of instruments, the rating scale has the potential to provide the most detailed information regarding the behavior under question. It is important, however, that when devising a rating scale, the teacher should keep several basic principles firmly in mind. These principles directly relate to the selection of the characteristics to be rated, design of the rating form, and conditions under which the ratings are obtained. Gronlund (1976) lists six principles that are of particular import:

1. Characteristics should be educationally significant.
2. Characteristics should be directly observable.
3. Characteristics and points on the scale should be clearly defined.
4. Between three and seven rating positions should be provided and raters should be permitted to mark at intermediate points.

5. Raters should be instructed to omit ratings where they feel unqualified to judge.
6. Ratings from several observers should be combined, wherever possible [p. 444–445].

If these principles are carefully considered by teachers, rating scales can be a valuable tool in structuring and organizing the behavior and social relationships that exist within the school and classroom.

The use of rating scales in the ecological assessment is particularly enhanced by its flexibility of forms. At least three distinct formats are appropriate for use in the educational environment, each of which operates from the same basic scheme. A rating continuum is defined as precisely as possible and a judgment is required to evaluate and rate individuals on certain prescribed traits. All rating forms share the same basic concept of the continuum and differ only in the way in which the traits to be rated are described. The three types of rating scales include (1) the *numerical,* (2) the *descriptive,* and (3) the *graphic.*

Numerical Scales   In numerical scales numbers are assigned to the various levels of each trait and the rater is asked to indicate the degree to which each trait is present. Schertzer and Stone (1971) give an example of one item included on a numerical rating scale:

_____ How would you rate the student's enthusiasm?

1. apathetic
2. rarely enthusiastic
3. sometimes enthusiastic
4. usually enthusiastic
5. intensely enthusiastic.

Once the rater has had the opportunity to consider the trait and choices provided, the most appropriate number is written in the blank provided. Although the numerical rating scale is quite simple, the traits given are generally quite vague, resulting in considerable variation in interpretation by different raters.

Descriptive Scales   Descriptive scales provide lists of illustrative words or phrases from which the rater selects the one most applicable to the individual being evaluated. Typically, the actual questions or traits are preceded by a verbal description that serves to clarify what is being asked. In some instances, it is profitable to elicit comments from the rater so as to further standardize observations. The following is an illustration of a descriptive rating scale provided by Remmers and Gage (1955).

Directions: Place a check mark in the blank before the phrase that represents your evaluation of the pupil.

Is the pupil honest? Can the pupil be trusted to resist temptations to steal, lie, or cheat?

—————— Honest in all situations; never dishonest.

—————— Usually honest; rarely yields to temptation.

—————— Not dependably honest.

—————— Usually dishonest; not to be trusted.

—————— Dishonest in all situations.

Graphic Scales. Graphic scales are distinguished in form by each trait being listed along a horizontal line. In most instances, the characteristic occupies a specific position on the line, but the rater may check between these points if desired. Two types of graphic scales commonly are seen in the schools. The first type simply lists a trait and requires the rater to indicate the extent to which it is observed. No descriptive notations are given. An example of these types is given below.

General Teaching Ability	A	B	C	D	E
	Excellent	Good	Fair	Poor	Lacking

Work Habits	A	B	C	D	E
	Excellent	Good	Fair	Poor	Lacking

The second type utilizes descriptive phrases to identify the points on a scale. This approach permits the teacher great flexibility in alternating the content of a given scale. Schertzer and Stone (1971) provide an example of this type of scale with descriptive phrases.

Leadership					
Actively avoids leadership	Prefers not to lead	Accepts leadership if asked	Occasionaly prefers not to lead	Actively seeks out leadership role

According to Gronlund (1976), the graphic rating scale using descriptive components is most satisfactory for school use. It serves to clarify for both the teacher and the student the types of behavior that represent degrees of progress toward desired learning outcomes. The more specific behavioral descriptions also contribute to increased objectivity and accuracy during the rating process.

As was mentioned previously, checklists (although similar in appearance to rating scales) are concerned with merely determining whether a particular trait is present or absent. Perhaps the most useful purpose of the checklist is in estimating the particular strengths or weaknesses of a child or a teacher. There is no attempt to ascertain the degree to which the characteristics in question are evident. Obviously, the checklist is utilized as an initial means of soliciting assessment data. An example of a checklist that was devised to collect information from parents regarding the problems of their "learning disabled" children is given in Table 4–1. This checklist, although it does not provide detailed information, can be helpful in selecting problem areas that are in need of further study.

Sociometric Techniques

The sociometric technique is used primarily as a means of estimating the degree to which individuals are accepted within a group, of determining the relationships that exist among these individuals, and of discovering the

TABLE 4–1   Parent Problem Behavior Checklist

Directions: Read through the following list carefully and circle the number in front of each statement that describes a problem related to your child.

1. Lacks self confidence
2. Is hypersensitive—feelings easily hurt
3. Is frequently depressed—sad
4. Is easily flustered and confused
5. Is unsure
6. Is very distracted
7. Has short attention span and poor powers of concentration
8. Behavior not predictable—is sometimes good, sometimes bad
9. Exhibits poor muscular coordination—clumsy and awkward
10. Often has physical complaints: headaches, stomachaches, etc.
11. Is nervous and jittery—easily startled
12. Usually feels tired—drowsy
13. Is shy, bashful
14. Is attention-seeking, engages in "show-off" behavior
15. Quarrels and fights with other children
16. Is jealous over attention paid other children
17. Is inattentive to what others say—doesn't accept help and suggestions
18. Is uncooperative in group situations
19. Is distructive in regard to own or others' property
20. Does not respond well to discipline
21. Feels upset about school in general
22. Does not like to be called upon in class
23. Does not seem to be doing the best work possible
24. Requires special attention at school
25. Teacher does not understand his or her problems
26. Teacher does not show interest in his or her disabilities

Source: Larsen S. C. *Parent Problem Behavior Checklist.* Unpublished manuscript, 1972. Used with permission.

structure of the group itself (Northway & Weld, 1967). The majority of sociometric techniques available are quite simple in their construction and administration. In general, these techniques are employed most satisfactorily in groups with defined boundaries, where the individuals know each other at least by name and continue with some cohesion over a reasonable period of time. It is important to note that sociometric techniques also have the potential of measuring the interpersonal attitudes and feelings of specific members of a group.

An example of a sociometric technique that yields information about how individuals within a group feel about each other is the *nomination technique* (Friou, 1972). This strategy is particularly useful in the classroom, because it can assist the teacher in determining "stars" and "isolates" as well as in grouping students for various activities. Each child is required to choose one or more classmate with whom the child would like to play, eat lunch, study, or carry out any other prescribed activity. Respondents may be asked to nominate only one child or as many group members as they wish. When appropriate it is also possible for students to rate their nominations as first, second, or third choice. In addition, the nominating technique also permits the teacher to elicit the names of individuals that are *least* liked or desired by a given child (a procedure helpful in gaining knowledge to help the situation of some children). Some questions that are designed to probe pupils' "rejections" are given below (Blair, 1962):

- With which classmates (2 or 3) do you least like to play?
- Which children get into a lot of trouble?
- Which children do you think are bossy?
- Which children would you not like to eat lunch with?

The nominating technique may also be used to devise a *sociogram*. The sociogram, a device familiar to most educators, consists of a diagram that usually depicts the sociological structure of "likes" and "dislikes" within a classroom (Redl & Wattenberg, 1959). The results of a sociogram can be of help in identifying dominant students in the class structure, the mutually exclusive groups and cliques, the isolates, and the various patterns of social acceptance and rejection. Sociograms can also be profitable in evaluating the effects of a teacher's efforts on changing pupils' social relations. If desired, this technique is adequately flexible for use with an entire grade level (or school population), as well as with a single classroom.

Another category of sociometric techniques entails the *self-report*. This procedure is profitably employed to determine information regarding a student's (1) activities, such as books read, favorite television shows, trips taken, etc., and (2) inner life that concerns feelings, anxieties, interests, etc. Because this information usually is not obtainable by other means, specialized methods, such as a self-report, are sometimes necessary to acquire data regarding this aspect of a child's life.

According to Gronlund (1976), the most ideal method of conducting a self-report is through a personal interview. Although this procedure is malleable depending upon the requirements of the situation, it is extremely time consuming and nonstandardized; that is, the questions and the responses are likely to vary widely from setting to setting. It is recommended that the use of checklists, rating scales, questionnaires, and inventories (a standard set of statements or questions relating to a specific area of behavior) be utilized to structure the interview process.

Projective measures also may be used to estimate students' or teachers' concepts of themselves and their environments. The *Q-Sort*, developed by Stephenson (1953), is one procedure that has been used successfully in school practice (Kroth, 1973). This technique is based upon the theory that individuals have a "real" and "ideal" self and that it is profitable to determine the degree of discrepancy between these two evaluations of self. The individuals being tested are provided with a set of statements that are relevant to the particular situation (e.g., works slowly, asks teacher questions, follows directions, is patient). Once the statements or items have been read, the individuals are asked to place or *to sort* each of them on a formboard that contains nine categories from "most like me" to "most unlike me" in a manner that best represents the individuals' own day-to-day classroom behavior. When this *real sorting* has been completed, the responses are recorded and the individuals are asked to sort the same items as they would *like* to be in daily classroom activities (*ideal sorting*). A comparison of the two sortings is then made to see if there are significant differences between how the individuals actually view themselves and how they would actually like to be perceived. Figure 4–2 presents the formboard commonly employed with the Q-Sort procedure. A sample listing of 25 questions appropriate for Q-Sorting by elementary school children is provided in Table 4–2.

ASSESSING COMPONENTS OF THE LEARNING ENVIRONMENT

The assessment of a student, a teacher, and their ecology can provide valuable insights into understanding instances of learning failure in the classroom. It is indeed surprising that with the accumulation of theories and research that point to the crucial role of the environment in impeding or facilitating children's success in school, a concomitant increase in the number of viable ecological assessment devices has not resulted. With few exceptions, attempts to evaluate the various components of the learning environment that may be influencing a student's academic social development, or both, will need to be teacher constructed and administered. The

FIGURE 4–2   Formboard for the Q-Sort

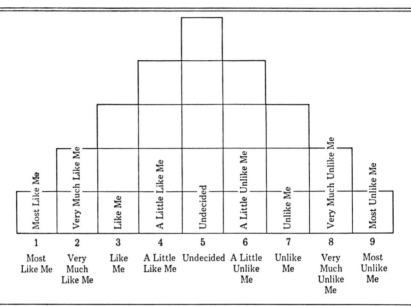

1	2	3	4	5	6	7	8	9
Most Like Me	Very Much Like Me	Like Me	A Little Like Me	Undecided	A Little Unlike Me	Unlike Me	Very Much Unlike Me	Most Unlike Me

Source: Kroth, R. The behavioral Q-sort as a diagnostic tool. *Academic Therapy,* 1973, *VIII,* 317–324. Reprinted by permission or Academic Therapy Publications, San Rafael, California.

use of the assessment tools described in the previous section of this chapter may all be effectively employed to probe those aspects of the environment that may be interfering with a pupil's optimal achievement level and social relationships.

Since ecological assessment is a relatively recent innovation in educational circles, some teachers may be somewhat uncertain as to just how to initiate the total evaluative process. This task may be efficiently accomplished by simply noting those settings in which the pupil operates. Because the vast majority of ecological assessment will be conducted totally within the school, teachers may wish to delineate those situations, for example, social studies, reading, gym classes, in which the student spends a certain portion of time during most school days. Since some of these settings appear to be particularly difficult or troublesome for the pupil and others do not, it is possible to contrast and isolate specific components of the school environment that are in need of more in-depth assessment. This practice of estimating the "fit" of a student into various environmental components has been termed *ecological mapping* (Laten & Katz, 1975).

The mapping of a student's ecology as a first step in a total ecological

TABLE 4–2   Sample Questions to be used in Q-Sorting by Elementary School Children

1. Gets work done on time
2. Pokes or hits classmates
3. Out of seat without permission
4. Scores high in spelling
5. Plays with objects while working
6. Scores high in reading
7. Disturbs neighbors by making noises
8. Is quiet during class time
9. Tips chair often
10. Follows directions
11. Smiles frequently
12. Often taps foot, fingers, or pencil
13. Pays attention to work
14. Works slowly
15. Throws objects in class
16. Reads well orally
17. Talks to classmates often
18. Scores high in English
19. Talks out without permission
20. Rocks in chair
21. Scores high in arithmetic
22. Asks teacher questions
23. Uses free time to read or study
24. Works until the job is finished
25. Walks around room during study time

Source: Kroth, R. The behavioral Q-sort as a diagnostic tool. *Academic Therapy,* 1973, *VIII,* 317–324. Reprinted by permission of Academic Therapy Publications, San Rafael, California.

assessment need not be complicated. An example of this process would be the case of Carol, a 12-year-old girl, who has been reported by one of her teachers as exhibiting "moderate" school problems. Inspection of her records indicates above-average mental ability with average or above-average scores in all academic subject areas. Ms. Lyons, the social studies teacher, has become concerned that Carol recently has lost all interest in the subject, is unwilling to complete any assignments, and does not seem to interact with classmates. Other teachers state that, although Carol's schoolwork has been on a par with her past performance, their major concerns is that they have overheard disparaging comments from other students regarding "the way Carol has been acting." In particular, Mr. Lewis, the gym teacher, has noticed that Carol has gotten into several fights with other girls recently and has had to be referred to the vice-principal for disciplinary purposes. A home visit with Carol's parents reveals no change in the typical routine

FIGURE 4–3

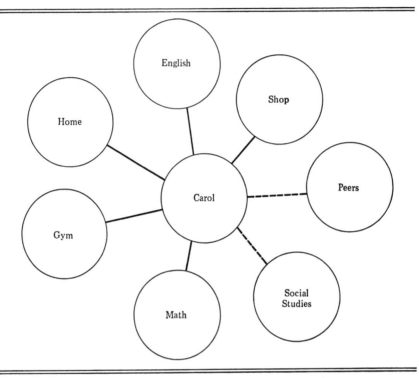

of the home. Neither parent has had any notion that Carol is experiencing trouble at school: her behavior has not changed at home and she has not mentioned any disruptions in her school life.

A preliminary map of the components of Carol's ecology is shown in Figure 4–3. The solid lines connect Carol with classes or settings in which no appreciable difficulty is evidenced; the broken lines illustrate classes or settings in which the reported problem is especially severe. This type of map provides a general overview of Carol's involvements and points out areas in which the ecological assessment can be directed most profitably. Obviously the quantity and quality of Carol's peer relations and teacher interactions need to be carefully probed within the context of her social studies class. The information resulting from this analysis is vital to conceptualize and modify fully those factors that are responsible for Carol's lack of success in school.

Once the ecological map has been completed, it is possible to design techniques that will yield desired data regarding specific environmental settings. Strategies that can be used in specific assessments are presented in the next section. Readers who are interested in a more detailed discussion of ecological mapping are encouraged to consult Laten and Katz (1975).

School and Classroom
Learning Climate

The learning climate of the school and the classroom are two of the most important determinants of how a pupil grows both socially and academically. If the atmosphere of the school and the classroom do not provide encouragement, respect, and emotional support, it is likely that students will lose motivation to perform at a level that is commensurate with their abilities. For this reason, it is sometimes helpful to explore the "learning atmosphere" of the school and the classroom to determine if students are being supplied with an environment that promotes academic achievement and mental health. This information is particularly important for diagnosing and remedying the problems of children who are experiencing school failure.

When assessing the climate of a total school environment, the professional is primarily concerned with determining such variables as communication patterns, role relationships and role perceptions, rewards and sanctions, and general rules and norms that operate within a given facility. According to Fox, Schmuck, van Egmond, Ritvo, and Jung (1975), there are two basic indicators of a "healthy" school climate: effective learning of students and personal satisfaction of the school staff. Those schools with productive climates allow for innovation and, consequently, teachers gain a feeling of confidence and improve their relationships with peers. In those situations in which the climate is unhealthy, there is likely to be evidence of job dissatisfaction, alienation, little or no creativity, frustration, and conformity among staff members. There can be little question that in those schools where the professional climate is not conducive to promoting self-esteem and productivity, pupils' adjustment and achievement will be affected.

There are several major concerns that need to be addressed when the teacher conducts an assessment of the school climate. The manner in which the data are gathered can have significant positive or negative effects on both teachers and administrators. If the desired data are not collected in a straightforward fashion, needed modifications in the school environment will likely be viewed as an intrusion and will be resisted. The following guidelines can provide educators with a viable structure for carrying out the assessment.

1. The people from whom the information is being gathered are aware of why it is being gathered.
2. The persons affected by the school climate believe it is important that this information be gathered.
3. They know about and agree to the way the information is to be used.
4. They have helped to determine the need for gathering the information.
5. They have helped to determine the manner in which the information is being gathered.

6. They are helping to gather the information.
7. They are involved in analyzing and interpreting this information.
8. They are involved in considering actions that seem indicated by the diagnosis.
9. The diagnostic effort is being conducted at a time when it can be viewed constructively by all concerned, rather than as a threatening move by a faction of a potential conflict situation.
10. The diagnostic effort is realistic in scope; it can conceivably contribute to an improvement effort.
11. The diagnostic effort does not compete unrealistically with other time and energy demands.
12. The results of the diagnosis are communicated to various groups in a manner which motivates constructive action, rather than mobilizing resistance to improvement [Fox, et al., 1975, pp 149–150].

The primary ways of collecting data usually entails written responses from various staff members, interviews, and observations. The specific content of the actual diagnostic instruments will depend upon the particular characteristics of the school setting. Such variables as staff responsibilities, behaviors, and resources are potentially important areas of input. The extent to which the community is involved in ongoing school practices is also of concern in some instances. Figure 4-4 presents an example of an instrument that taps one aspect of "typical" staff behavior as it relates to the reactions of the faculty toward one another. In effect, this instrument may provide some estimate of the norms that tend to guide staff behavior in the school building.

Perusal of this scale, when completed by the members of a school faculty, will provide considerable insight into the feelings and expectations of individuals operating within that environment. Similar devices can be easily constructed to probe other aspects of school climate. Teachers in-

FIGURE 4–4   Sample Form for Assessing Aspects of the School Climate

OUR TYPICAL BEHAVIOR

1. Suppose a teacher (let's call him Teacher X) disagrees with something B says at a staff meeting. If teachers you know in your school were in Teacher X's place, what would most of them be likely to do?

Would most of the teachers you know seek out B to discuss the disagreement?

( ) Yes, I think most would do this.
( ) Maybe about half would do this.
( ) No, most would *not.*
( ) I don't know.

Would they keep it to themselves and say nothing about it?

( ) Yes, I think most would do this.
( ) Maybe about half would do this.

FIGURE 4–4   *Continued*

( ) No, most would *not*.
( ) I don't know.

2. Suppose a teacher (let's call him Teacher X) feels hurt and put down by something another teacher has said to him. In Teacher X's place, would most of the teachers you know in your building be likely to . . .

. . . avoid the other teacher?

( ) Yes, I think most would.
( ) Maybe about half would.
( ) No, most would *not*.
( ) I don't know.

. . . tell the other teacher that they felt hurt and put down?

( ) Yes, I think most would.
( ) Maybe about half would.
( ) No, most would *not*.
( ) I don't know.

. . . tell their friends that the other teacher is hard to get along with?

( ) Yes, I think most would.
( ) Maybe about half would.
( ) No, most would *not*.
( ) I don't know.

3. Suppose you are in a committee meeting with Teacher X and the other members begin to describe their personal feelings about what goes on in the school. Teacher X quickly suggests that the committee get back to the topic, and keep the discussion objective and impersonal. How would you feel toward X?

( ) I would approve strongly.
( ) I would approve mildly or some.
( ) I wouldn't care one way or the other.
( ) I would disapprove mildly or some.
( ) I would disapprove strongly.

4. Suppose you are in a committee meeting with Teacher X and the other members begin to describe their personal feelings about what goes on in the school. Teacher X listens to them and tells them his own feelings. How would you feel toward X?

( ) I would approve strongly.
( ) I would approve mildly or some.
( ) I wouldn't care one way or the other.
( ) I would disapprove mildly or some.
( ) I would disapprove strongly.

5. Suppose Teacher X wants to improve his classroom effectiveness. In Teacher X's place, would most of the teachers in your building . . .

FIGURE 4–4 *Continued*

... ask another teacher to observe his teaching and then have a conference afterward?

( ) Yes, I think most would do this.
( ) Maybe about half would do this.
( ) No, most would *not.*
( ) I don't know.

... ask other teachers to let him (Teacher X) observe how the other teachers teach, to get ideas how to improve his own teaching?

( ) Yes, I think most would do this.
( ) Maybe about half would do this.
( ) No, most would *not.*
( ) I don't know.

... have a free and open discussion with his students about his teaching?

( ) Yes, I think most would do this.
( ) Maybe about half would do this.
( ) No, most would *not.*
( ) I don't know.

... ask the principal to observe his teaching and then have a conference afterward?

( ) Yes, I think most would do this.
( ) Maybe about half would do this.
( ) No, most would *not.*
( ) I don't know.

6. Suppose Teacher X disagrees with a procedure that the principal has outlined for all to follow. If Teacher X were to go and talk with the principal about his disagreement, how would you feel about it?

( ) I would approve strongly.
( ) I would approve mildly or some.
( ) I wouldn't care one way or the other.
( ) I would disapprove mildly or some.
( ) I would disapprove strongly.

7. Suppose Teacher X disagrees with a procedure that the principal has outlined for all to follow. If X were to say nothing but ignore the principal's directive, how would you feel about it?

( ) I would approve strongly.
( ) I would approve mildly or some.
( ) I wouldn't care one way or the other.
( ) I would disapprove mildly or some.
( ) I would disapprove strongly.

8. Suppose Teacher X develops a particularly useful and effective method for teaching something. If X were to describe the method briefly at a faculty

FIGURE 4–4   *Continued*

meeting and offer to meet further with any who wanted to know more, how would you feel about it?

(   ) I would approve strongly.
(   ) I would approve mildly or some.
(   ) I wouldn't care one way or the other.
(   ) I would disapprove mildly or some.
(   ) I would disapprove strongly.

Source: Fox, R. S., Schmuck, R., van Egmond, E., Ritvo, M., and Jung, C. *Diagnosing professional climates of schools*. Fairfax, Va.: NTL Learning Resources Corporation, 1975, pp. 71–72. Used with permission of publishers.

terested in acquiring additional references regarding this topic may wish to read Fox, Lippitt, and Schmuck (1964), Corrigan (1969), and Schmuck and Runkel (1970).

Although the assessment of the school environment will provide a general orientation to the organization and administration of the faculty and staff, diagnosing the components of specific *classroom* settings is necessary to secure data regarding the particular problems exhibited by students. It is apparent that pupils tend to respond appropriately to the learning situation when teachers present their methods clearly, take their pupils' point of views into consideration, and frequently check their reactions to classroom activities (Fox, Luszki, & Schmuck, 1966). Students who either misperceive the teachers' intentions or are in situations in which their needs are not being met do not easily become involved in learning activities and fail to utilize their maximum abilities.

Figure 4–5 presents a device that is designed to provide teachers with a general estimate of the classroom climate. The results of this instrument can be tabulated in from 10 to 15 minutes. The content or directions of this form may be altered as needed for different situations. In those cases in which the class (or child) cannot read well enough to complete the device, the teacher may read the items and have the pupils choose the answers that best suit their feelings. At all times it is very important that students be assured of maximum privacy. This, of course, is to elicit answers that are as honest as possible.

When involved with older students who can express themselves in writing, the teacher can simply make up a series of questions that are meant to determine students' reactions to specific types of classroom experiences. For example, a teacher may wish to find out if pupils have suggestions for improving class routine by such questions as:

• "What happens when you have an especially good day at school?"
• "What kind of activities do you enjoy most?"

FIGURE 4–5 Sample Form for Measuring Aspects of the Classroom Environment

Date	_____
Your Number	_____
Class	_____

CLASSROOM LIFE

Here is a list of some statements that describe life in the classroom. Circle the letter in front of the statement that best tells how you feel about the class. *There are no right or wrong answers.*

1. Life in this class with your regular teacher has
   a. all good things
   b. mostly good things
   c. more good things than bad
   d. about as many good things as bad
   e. more bad things than good
   f. mostly bad things

2. How hard are you working these days on learning what is being taught at school?
   a. very hard
   b. quite hard
   c. not very hard
   d. not hard at all

3. When I'm in this class, I
   a. usually feel wide awake and very interested
   b. am pretty interested, kind of bored part of the time
   c. am not very interested, bored quite a lot of the time
   d. don't like it, feel bored and not with it

4. How hard are you working on schoolwork compared with the others in the class?
   a. harder than most
   b. a little harder than most
   c. about the same as most
   d. a little less than most
   e. quite a bit less than most

5. How many of the pupils in this class do what the teacher suggests?
   a. most of them do
   b. more than half do
   c. less than half do
   d. hardly anybody does

FIGURE 4–5   *Continued*

6. If we help each other with our work in this class, the teacher
   a. likes it a lot
   b. likes it some
   c. likes it a little
   d. doesn't like it at all

7. How good is your schoolwork compared with the work of others in the class?
   a. much better than most
   b. a little better than most
   c. about the same as most
   d. not quite as good as most
   e. much worse than most

8. How often do the pupils in this class help one another with their schoolwork?
   a. most of the time
   b. sometimes
   c. hardly ever
   d. never

9. How often do the pupils in this class act friendly toward one another?
   a. always
   b. most of the time
   c. sometimes
   d. hardly ever.

Source: From *Diagnosing classroom learning environments* by Robert Fox, Margaret Barron Luszki, and Richard Schmuck. © 1966, Science Research Associates, Inc. Reprinted by permission of the publisher.

- "Do you feel that you learned a lot today?"
- "Do you feel comfortable when speaking in class?"

These can aid the teacher in forming working hypotheses regarding a classroom in general or a child in particular. Once the questions have been answered, they can be used to stimulate classroom discussion regarding the rationale for establishment of some instructional procedures and possibly regarding how these procedures can be modified to facilitate a more positive learning climate. Teachers will wish continually to reassess the initial responses of students to determine if their first reactions are consistent over time. In addition, students with particularly unusual answers may need individual attention to clarify and possibly to alter their perceptions and expectations. Naturally, the teacher's own astute observational skills used throughout the school day will indicate whether pupils are enjoying the most beneficial learning environment possible.

TABLE 4–3   Sample Listing of Teacher-Child Interaction Systems

1. *Reichenberg-Hackett Teacher Behavior Observation System* (Reichenberg-Hackett, 1962)	Focuses upon nursery school teachers and pupils. Teacher-Behavior is coded according to five major categories.
2. *Teachers Practices Observation Record* (Brown, 1970)	Consists of 62 items grouped into seven categories. Requires little training of observers and possesses high reliability and validity.
3. *Connors-Eisenberg Observation System* (Connors & Eisenberg, 1966)	Is appropriate for use in nursery school and elementary grades. Yields three sets of scores that relate to "episodes," "activities," and "overall judgements."
4. *The Purdue Teacher Evaluation Scale* (Bentley & Starry, 1970)	Is designed to provide junior or senior high school teachers with an evaluation of their performance as seen through the eyes of students.
5. *Classroom Observational Scales* (Emmer, 1971)	Bases observations in 12 variables from "pupil attention" to "enthusiasm." Easily learned and administered.
6. *Flanders' System of Interaction Analysis* (Flanders, 1970)	Is intended to gather data on teacher behaviors that restrict or increase student freedom of action. Focuses upon categories of behavior.
7. *Nonverbal Interaction Analysis*	Provides a method of recording nonverbal behavior in classrooms. Designed to parallel the categories of verbal behavior in *Flanders' System of Interaction Analysis.*
8. *Fuller Affective Interactions Records 33* (Fuller, 1969)	Assesses interpersonal behaviors of preservice teachers and their students. Utilizes five interpersonal dimensions.
9. *Teacher-Child Dyadic Interaction* (Brophy & Good, 1969)	Categorizes each teacher-student verbal interaction. Requires 20 hours of training to be used effectively. An excellent research tool.

Teacher-Student Interaction Patterns

The quality and quantity of interaction between teachers and students frequently is instrumental not only in establishing a particular environmental climate, but also in determining whether effective learning is taking place. The classroom is an extremely busy place where interaction is so complex and subtle that it is sometimes difficult to observe in a consistent fashion. If we consider that as many as 1,000 interpersonal interchanges occur in elementary classrooms each day, it is not surprising that teachers may not be able to monitor them all (Jackson, 1968). In most instances, procedures need to be utilized in order to secure reliable information.

FIGURE 4–6

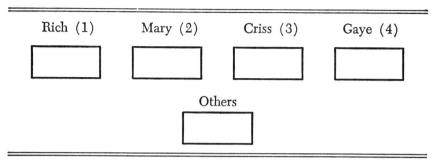

Rich (1)   Mary (2)   Criss (3)   Gaye (4)

Others

Previously one formal observational system (OScAR 5) was presented as an example of a standardized measure appropriate for measuring teacher-student interactions. A number of other instruments also have been produced that may be applied to the classroom setting. Table 4–3 provides a listing of these devices. The rationale for the inclusion of these systems in this table is that they all provide some standardization data and will yield information regarding teacher-child interaction patterns.

In addition to standardized instruments, teachers may utilize informal procedures to collect the same type of information. One informal measure has been devised by Bradfield and Criner (1973). This scale, the *Teacher Attention and Pupil Behavior Scale*, is designed to indicate variations in a teacher's positive and negative attention toward certain students and to record the frequency of those students' *nontask behaviors*. (*Nontask behavior* is defined as any behavior that interferes with completion of a given assignment.) As with most measures that assess teacher-child interaction patterns, it is necessary to generate a code to delineate those behaviors that are of special interest. The code utilized by Bradfield and Criner to indicate the direction of teacher attention and the frequency of the student's nontask behavior is as follows:

P: Teachers attention to *positive* behavior. For example, "That's good" or "Yes, you're right."
N: Teacher's attention to *negative* behavior. For example, "Stop that" or "No, you're wrong."
I: Teacher's instruction (academic or social) to a certain child.
√:   Child's nontask behavior.

The process for administering this scale is quite simple. The first step is to draw five squares, four of which represent the children of interest and one of which indicates all other students in the class (see Figure 4–6). The observation period should last for approximately 10 minutes. During

FIGURE 4–7

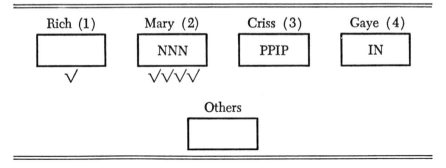

this time, the observer should be in a comfortable position with a clear field of vision of the entire class. As the interactions between the teachers and children are noted, it is possible for the observer to indicate the direction of the teacher's attention and the frequency of the students' nontask behaviors. The observer should place teacher attention codes inside the square of the child receiving attention and the nontask code just below the square of the pupil. An illustration of a completed 10-minute observation period is shown in Figure 4–7.

Child 1 received no direct teacher attention and engaged in nontask behavior on one occasion. Child 2 engaged in nontask behavior four times and was given three negative comments by the teacher during the 10-minute period. Child 3 received the teacher's positive attention three times, direct instruction once, and did not engage in nontask behavior. Child 4 did not engage in nontask behavior and received direct instruction once and negative comment once. By tabulating the total number of times the teacher paid attention to positive and negative behavior and dividing this by 10, it is possible to determine the rate per minute of each type of teacher's attention. It is also possible to ascertain the rate at which nontask behavior is exhibited by counting the total number of times it occurred and dividing by 10. Teachers also may wish to supplement their coding by making written notes regarding the general atmosphere and happenings within the classroom, which frequently are helpful in accurately interpreting and explaining the results of the observational process.

Another method of coding teacher-student interactions has been suggested by Fox, Luszki, and Schmuck (1966). This procedure utilizes a more detailed classification system than the previous technique. Three broad categories of interaction are observed: (1) teacher and the whole class, (2) teacher and individual pupils and (3) pupils and the teacher. Each classification is categorized as to whether it is oriented to work or to social behavior and social control. In addition, the specific nature of each behavior is identified. The following outline classifies the interactions and defines the specifics of each type of behavior.

I. Teacher to the whole class
   A. Work
      1. *Telling and giving information:* transmitting fact, opinion, and the like directly to the whole class about subject matter or related areas of classroom interest
      2. *Giving directions:* telling the class what to do or how to do a particular piece of work
      3. *Asking and indirect probing:* trying to get information from the class or posing questions to the whole class regarding classroom work
   B. Social behavior and social control
      1. *Positive:* indicating to the whole class that its social behavior and control have been good
      2. *Neutral:* giving directions or information with no evaluation implied
      3. *Negative:* indicating to the whole class that its social conduct has not been good
II. Teacher to individual pupils
   A. Work
      1. *Positive:* rewarding comments directed to an individual pupil about an aspect of his work
      2. *Neutral:* comments or questions that are neither rewarding nor punishing directed to an individual pupil about an aspect of his work
      3. *Negative:* punishing comments directed to an individual pupil about an aspect of his work
   B. Social behavior and social control
      1. *Positive:* rewarding comments directed to an individual pupil about his social conduct in the class
      2. *Neutral:* comments or questions that are neither rewarding nor punishing directed to an individual pupil about his conduct in the class
      3. *Negative:* punishing comments directed to an individual pupil about his conduct in the class
III. Pupils to teacher
   A. Work
      1. *Contributions:* pupil remarks, such as elaboration or helpful comments, that add something to class activities or assignments
      2. *Dependent and asking questions:* pupil remarks that either show dependency on the teacher or are questions about work that is to be done
   B. Social behavior and social control
      1. *Complaints:* pupil remarks about conduct of other pupils in the class

FIGURE 4–8   Observation Schedule of a Sixth-Grade Math Class

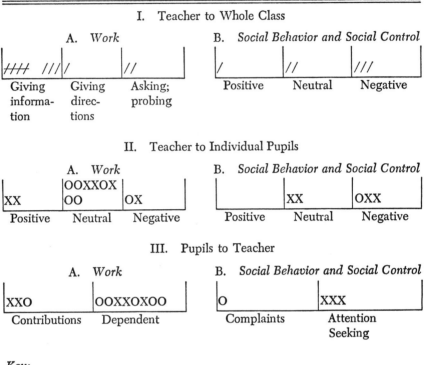

Key:
/ indicates a teacher's statement directed to entire class.
O indicates a teacher's statement directed to or from a girl.
X indicates a teacher's statement directed to or from a boy.

2. *Attention seeking:* pupil remarks aimed at getting attention from the teacher or other pupils, or both [pp. 54–55].[3]

The format presented in Figure 4–8 is suggested for coding the instances of behavior in all categories that occur during a classroom observation period. The entries represent interactions that were collected during one 5-minute period of a sixth-grade math class. The observer marked a category for every observed unit of behavior.

Analysis of the 5-minute observation period indicates that generally the teacher gave information and directions that were delivered in a neutral fashion, received dependency responses, attended more to boys, and elicited statements from boys and girls equally. These findings can be used to

[3]From *Diagnosing classroom learning environments* by Robert Fox, Margaret Barron Luszki, and Richard Schmuck. © 1966, Science Research Associates, Inc. Reprinted by permission of the publisher.

modify a teaching "style," if desired, as well as to provide consistent feedback as to whether behavioral change is progressing in the intended direction.

The utilization of observational systems, both formal and informal, can be quite beneficial in exploring and improving teacher-child interaction patterns. Rating scales and checklists regarding pupils' perceptions of teachers' behavior can also be employed profitably. It is important to keep in mind that, in most instances, it will be necessary for teachers to define carefully those behavioral characteristics (i.e., categories) that are of *interest* in a particular classroom setting. Only rarely will an existing set of categories be appropriate for every situation. Gordon (1966) provides examples of several different classification systems that may be adapted for classroom use.

Peer Relationships

Research in human development and education has indicated that the social position of students within their peer groups influences self-concept, relationships with teachers, and academic performance in specific subject areas (Spaulding, 1964; Friou, 1972). Apparently, students who feel comfortable and at ease with their peers are likely to utilize their various abilities and skills more completely than those who do not. In cases where children are experiencing failure in school, teachers are well advised to evaluate specific aspects of the peer culture to determine its role in facilitating or impeding successful academic and social development, or both.

One means of assessing peer relationship is through the use of behavior rating scales. Table 4–4 provides a listing of selected instruments that tap such variables as group problem-solving skills, seating preferences, and personal-social needs of pupils. These instruments are easily administered and provide the teacher with information regarding certain components of how pupils perceive and react to each other. These rating scales can be adapted for individual classroom use.

In addition to commercially available sociometric instruments, teachers may also construct their own techniques to measure social relations in the classroom. Not only is it possible to determine which pupils are particularly liked or disliked, it is also feasible to determine a child's social power and ability to influence others. It is obvious that virtually all students are adequate judges in measuring competence, helpfulness, and cooperativeness of their peers. Exploring these attitudes may significantly improve a teacher's knowledge of the classroom and the peer interactions that are constantly taking place. One approach to assessing these child perceptions is a modification of the "Guess Who" technique first used by Tyron (1943).

TABLE 4–4   Behavioral Rating Scales for Assessing Peer Relationship

Instrument	Grade Level	Brief Description
1. *Russell Sage Social Relations Test* (Damrin, 1956)	3–6	Provides information regarding the problem-solving skills of various classroom groups.
2. *Syracuse Scales of Social Relations* (Gardner & Thompson, 1959)	5–6; 6–9; 10–12	Pupil rates types of need relationships with classmates and others.
3. *A Class Play* (Bower, 1961)	3–7	Peer rating instrument designed to indicate negative, neutral, and positive influences of others.
4. *The Class Picture* (Bower, 1961)	K–3	Given individually, this scale estimates how students are perceived by their peers.
5. *Ohio Social Acceptance Scale* (Ohio State Department of Education, 1944)	3–6	Consists of six headings: 1. My very, very best friends 2. My other friends 3. Not friends, but okay 4. Don't know them 5. Don't care for them 6. Dislike them Each student is asked to place each of his or her classmates in one of these categories.
6. *Minnesota Sociometric Status Test* (Moore & Updegraff, 1971)	Preschool and early primary grades	Measures social status or acceptance of students by peers. Testing materials on a board with photographs of every child in the peer group. Each student is interviewed and questioned about the photographs.

Fox, Luszki, and Schmuck (1966) have developed an evaluative tool that may be easily employed for this purpose. This device is given in Table 4–5. The authors recommend that instead of asking children to answer these questions by giving the names of their peers, teachers should provide an

TABLE 4–5   Technique for Assessing Certain Attitudes of Students

The People in My Class

It is a job of teachers to find ways to make school life more interesting and worthwhile for all the students in the class. This form is your chance to give the teacher confidential information that will help him to help each pupil. *There are no right or wrong answers.* The way you see things is what counts.

1. Which three persons in this class are most often able to get other pupils to do things? Using your class list, write the numbers of the pupils you select.

   Pupil's number

   The three who are most often able to get others to do things are: _____

   _____

   _____

2. Which three persons in the class do the girls most often do things for?

   Pupil's number

   They are: _____

   _____

   _____

3. Which three persons in the class do the boys most often do things for?

   Pupil's number

   They are: _____

   _____

   _____

4. Which three persons in this class are most cooperative with the teacher and like to do what the teacher wants the class to do?

   Pupil's number

   The three most cooperative pupils are: _____

   _____

   _____

5. Which three persons in this class most often go against the teacher and what he would like the class to do?

   Pupil's number

   The three pupils who most often go against the teacher are: _____

   _____

   _____

6. Which three persons in this class do you think could make the biggest improvement in their schoolwork if they wanted to?

   Pupil's number

   The three who could improve most are: _____

   _____

   _____

7. Which three persons in this class do you think show the most ability to learn new things that are taught in school?

TABLE 4–5 *Continued*

	Pupil's number
The three best learners are:	_____
	_____
	_____

8. Who would you most like to be if you couldn't be yourself but had to be somebody else in this class?

	Pupil's number
Who would you most like to be?	_____
Who else would you like to be?	_____
Who else would you like to be?	_____

Source: Fox, R. S., Luszki, M. B., & Schmuck, R. *Diagnosing classroom learning environments.* Chicago: Science Research Associates, 1966. Used with permission of publisher.

alphabetical listing of class members with a number in front of each name. Each student should receive this list and be encouraged to refer to it when completing the form. Use of this procedure may avoid needless embarrassment for some children.

Depending upon the purpose of the assessment, teachers will find the need to compose different questions for use in the form (for example: "Which children find it hard to sit in class?" "Which children know how to initiate games or other activities so that others join in?" "Which children are always sad, worried, and unhappy and hardly ever laugh or smile?" These are all questions utilized to gain insight into the feelings of students.) This information will prove to be quite valuable when the teacher plans changes in interaction patterns or general classroom routine.

The degree to which students participate in classroom activities may also indicate those who are "leaders," "followers," or "isolates." In particular, observation of small group processes will provide a reliable estimate of which pupils are making the maximum use of participation charts to code the extent of pupils' interaction during group discussions. A participation chart is comprised simply of a list of names of the students and indicates the number of times the students make contributions to an activity. A useful organizational format is to merely list the students' names and mark the number of times a contribution was noted. When desired, the quality of the participations may also be recorded. A completed participation chart for a 15-minute math activity is given in Figure 4–9.

When analyzing this chart, it becomes obvious that children 1 and 4 are providing the majority of positive contributions. Child 5 is essentially "negative" and may be impairing the group's ability to complete its assigned task. Child 3, while not making any contributions, may be unprepared for the activity or may feel uncomfortable in group discussions. In

FIGURE 4–9

Name	Contributions
Activity: Math	
Observer: Mr. Bagley	

Name	Contributions
1. Earnie L.	OOO△O
2. Carol H.	XXO△△△O
3. Katie G.	
4. Bill L.	OOOO△
5. Ann S.	XXXXO
6. Stu E.	△△△

Key
O = relevant contribution made by a student.
X = irrelevant contribution made by a student.
△ = neutral contribution made by a student.

any event, this type of data (when compared to the overall performance of the group) will permit the teacher to either continue the present composition of the group or to modify it in order to ensure reasonable learning and productivity.

Perhaps the most widely known and popular sociometric technique is the sociogram (Gronlund, 1976; Gordon, 1966; and Cartwright & Cartwright, 1974). In effect, the sociogram is a map of the classroom that is used to indicate the children with whom a particular student would prefer to play, study, have lunch, etc. Using this procedure, it is possible for the teacher to generate a graphic picture of the social relations existing in a given group.

The most common approach in administering a sociogram is to devise a series of questions that are of special interest to the teacher. Once the pupils have answered the questions, each child is assigned a number. The numbers representing the children are then arranged in a circular fashion on a sheet of paper. In most cases, the numbers are placed within a small circle. Lines are then drawn between circles to represent choices—positive or negative.

Figure 4–10 presents a sociogram completed on a class of fourth-graders composed of 16 students. This sociogram was derived from the students answering the question, "Who would you most like to work with?" and "Who would you least like to work with?". Numbers 1–10 represent boys, and 11–16 represent girls.

In this class, children 4, 6, and 16 appear to be somewhat popular with their classmates. Child 1 was not selected as either liked or disliked in terms of work relationship and, interestingly, did not make any choices himself.

FIGURE 4–10   Example of a Sociogram

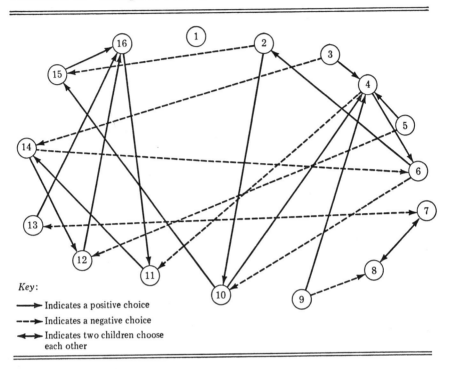

Key:

——▶ Indicates a positive choice

---▶ Indicates a negative choice

◀—▶ Indicates two children choose
each other

Boys apparently prefer to work with boys and girls with girls. In only one instance did a boy (child 10) choose to work with a girl (child 15). All of the girls, with the exception of Child 13 was chosen as a work partner. Of the boys, children 3, 5, and 9 were not selected by any of their classmates. The ranges of "rejections" were fairly evenly distributed with no one singled out as being particularly undesirable.

Information obtained from sociometric devices relating to peer relationships can be helpful for the teacher for a number of reasons. It is possible to determine those students who are in need of improving their interpersonal skills because they are either rejected or ignored by their classmates. Suggestions for grouping pupils according to their abilities and popularity may allow the effective utilization of "high-influence" childen. The knowledge of which students might be most advantageously paired for tutoring is another potentially positive aspect of available sociometric data.

In some classes, the results of a sociometric analysis will point up children who seem to be extremely isolated, unhappy, or socially immature. Obviously, these problems are beyond the scope of professional training of most classroom teachers and should be referred to specialized personnel for in-depth diagnosis and treatment. In cases where the problem seems to be only mild, the teacher can utilize techniques to estimate the students' emotional status at that point in time. The information derived from these procedures can be quite helpful in assisting the students to gain more realistic views of themselves in relation to the interaction of teachers and peers.

One commonly employed strategy for ascertaining a measure of a child's personality or self-concept is the *self-report scale,* which is composed of a series of questions that the children answer about themselves. Self-report scales are totally subjective and apt to be misused if several considerations are not kept firmly in mind: (1) responses can be easily faked; (2) accurate responses require good self-insight; and (3) ambiguity of items may introduce error into the results (Gronlund, 1976). Teachers should not attempt to isolate answers to specific questions for intensive analysis but, rather, should employ the results to gain a general idea of students' personal problems and fears. Although the limitations of the self-report are important, Brandt (1958) has found that students are fairly accurate in assessing themselves, when the task being assessed is something with which they have had experience.

Gordon (1966) has developed a very usable self-report scale, given in Table 4–6. Reportedly, this device assesses attitudes toward school, peers, one's own body and emotions. Children are instructed to mark the scales as they see themselves. For example, the choices for responding to item 1 ("Nothing gets me too mad"/"I get mad easily and explode") are: "If you feel that nothing gets you too mad *most* of the time you would circle the 1. If you feel that most of the time you get mad easily and explode, you would circle the 3, 4, or 5 [p. 73]." Administration of the remaining items is usually self-explanatory. Students should be told truthfully that their responses are confidential and that only honest answers will be of help to the teacher. The items on this scale should be considered as suggestive only, and teachers are encouraged to delete any questions that are inappropriate or add questions that are appropriate to a given situation. Additional readings on self-report techniques may be found in Fox, Luszki, and Schmuck (1966), and Garrett (1965).

USING ECOLOGICAL ASSESSMENT TECHNIQUES

The use of ecological assessment techniques have the potential of providing teachers with educational information that is unattainable through traditional (i.e., child directed) diagnostic procedures. It is crucial, however, that a definite but flexible assessment plan be designed prior to the administration of these procedures. The evaluative plan should consider the

TABLE 4–6 Self-Report Scale to Assess Components of a Student's Self-Concept

How I See Myself

1. Nothing gets me too mad	1	2	3	4	5	I get mad easily and explode
2. I don't stay with things and finish them	1	2	3	4	5	I stay with something till I finish
3. I'm very good at drawing	1	2	3	4	5	I'm not much good in drawing
4. I don't like to work on committees, projects	1	2	3	4	5	I like to work with others
5. I wish I were smaller (taller)	1	2	3	4	5	I'm just the right height
6. I worry a lot	1	2	3	4	5	I don't worry much
7. I wish I could do something with my hair	1	2	3	4	5	My hair is nice-looking
8. Teachers like me	1	2	3	4	5	Teachers don't like me
9. I've lots of energy	1	2	3	4	5	I haven't much energy
10. I don't play games very well	1	2	3	4	5	I play games very well
11. I'm just the right weight	1	2	3	4	5	I wish I were heavier, lighter
12. The girls don't like me, leave me out	1	2	3	4	5	The girls like me a lot, choose me
13. I'm very good at speaking before a group	1	2	3	4	5	I'm not much good at speaking before a group
14. My face is pretty (good looking)	1	2	3	4	5	I wish I were prettier (good looking)
15. I'm very good in music	1	2	3	4	5	I'm not much good in music
16. I get along well with teachers	1	2	3	4	5	I don't get along with teachers
17. I don't like teachers	1	2	3	4	5	I like teachers very much
18. I don't feel at ease, comfortable inside	1	2	3	4	5	I feel very at ease, comfortable inside
19. I don't like to try new things	1	2	3	4	5	I like to try new things
20. I have trouble controlling my feelings	1	2	3	4	5	I can handle my feelings
21. I do well in school work	1	2	3	4	5	I don't do well in school
22. I want the boys to like me	1	2	3	4	5	I don't want the boys to like me
23. I don't like the way I look	1	2	3	4	5	I like the way I look
24. I don't want the girls to like me	1	2	3	4	5	I want the girls to like me
25. I'm very healthy	1	2	3	4	5	I get sick a lot
26. I don't dance well	1	2	3	4	5	I'm a very good dancer
27. I write well	1	2	3	4	5	I don't write well
28. I like to work alone	1	2	3	4	5	I don't like to work alone

TABLE 4-6   *Continued*

29. I use my time well	1	2	3	4	5	I don't know how to plan my time
30. I'm not much good at making things with my hands	1	2	3	4	5	I'm very good at making things with my hands
31. I wish I could do some-thing about my skin	1	2	3	4	5	My skin is nice-looking
32. School isn't interesting to me	1	2	3	4	5	School is very interesting
33. I don't do arithmetic well	1	2	3	4	5	I'm real good in arithmetic
34. I'm not as smart as the others	1	2	3	4	5	I'm smarter than most of the others
35. The boys like me a lot, choose me	1	2	3	4	5	The boys don't like me, leave me out
36. My clothes are not as I'd like	1	2	3	4	5	My clothes are nice
37. I like school	1	2	3	4	5	I don't like school
38. I wish I were built like the others	1	2	3	4	5	I'm happy with the way I am
39. I don't read well	1	2	3	4	5	I read very well
40. I don't learn new things easily	1	2	3	4	5	I learn new things easily

Source: Gordon, I. J. *Studying the child in the school.* New York: John Wiley & Sons, Inc., 1966. Used with permission of publisher. This scale is not to be reproduced without express permission of the author.

characteristics of the students and the specific information desired by the teacher. In some instances, it may be necessary to conduct an ecological assessment because the school problems of some students have become so severe that they are resistant to conventional techniques. On the other hand, it is also possible that similar techniques may provide feedback regarding an innovative teaching method or curriculum plan. In other words, the ecological assessment can be very versatile; it can permit the exploration of positive, as well as negative, elements of the classroom or the school.

In all probability, the effective scheduling of the ecological assessment will encompass the entire school year. Information pertaining to the school climate may be gathered profitably during the first portion of the term, whereas teacher-student interaction patterns and peer relationships may be best employed later in the term when the class has had the opportunity to solidify as a group. In addition, an early evaluation of a student's self-concept may aid the teacher in developing strategies to circumvent possible problems.

One note of caution should be kept in mind regarding the unrestricted use of the ecological assessment. The recent trend in protecting children's civil rights may be a factor in some schools when considering which instruments may be legitimately employed. If there is a question as to whether the data to be collected may, in some way, be detrimental to the children's well-being, the school administration should be consulted. In a similar vein, a teacher must be able, in all cases, to account for why he or she was actually attempting to obtain specific data. As with all educational evaluations, no ecological assessment techniques should be administered unless they are to be used for a well-documented purpose. This caution is made both for the protection of the teacher, as well as, for the student.

Suggested Activities

4–1.   Select and obtain permission to examine a particular student and his or her environment. The student should be experiencing some school-related problems. Under the headings of the five phases of ecological assessment by Laten and Katz (1975), delineate methods, specific procedures, and particular questions to ask or behaviors to note during the assessment. Implement the methods, procedures, and observations, with the student you have chosen, and evaluate your procedures and the obtained results.

4–2.   Select a behavior exhibited by a particular student and record observations for five 1-hour periods. Define the behavior so that it involves concrete, observable actions. Apply two of the three observational recording procedures discussed in this chapter. Graph the results, and discuss the differences in the information gleaned from various recording procedures.

4–3.   For each of the following situations, design a record-keeping form for observational recording of the pertinent behavior. Define the behavior to be recorded.

   a.   Susie is reported to "be constantly talking with her classmates" during class. This is felt to be the reason for Susie's many unfinished assignments as well as for her neighboring classmates' occasional failure to complete assignments.

   b.   On occasion it is noted that John, a second-grade student, resorts to baby talk and thumb-sucking, which is, of course, causing him to have disturbances in his peer relationships.

   c.   Mike rarely participates in class discussions; however, in unstructured activities such as recess and lunch, it is felt that he interacts freely with his peers.

   d.   Sharon's speech therapist wants to obtain some record of the way in which she is pronouncing the *r* sound in class. During therapy the *w* substitution seems to have been ameliorated.

4-4.   Locate and examine some of the behavioral rating scales listed in Table 4–4. Describe these instruments further as numerical, descriptive, graphic, or graphic descriptive in format.

4-5.   Utilize Table 4–1 by having a teacher familiar with the student and the parents complete the form. Discuss any discrepancies between the perceptions of parents and teachers regarding the child's behavior at home and school.

4-6.   Construct and apply one of the sociometric techniques discussed in this chapter, i.e., the nominations procedure, with a sociogram for a group of students or the Q-sort self-report procedure for one individual (see Figure 4–2 and Table 4–2). Summarize results, indicating which students may need intervention or which areas particular students perceive as being difficult.

4-7.   Construct a simple ecological map for three students who reportedly have had some difficulty in school. The map may reflect relationships among individuals or various environments.

4-8.   Construct a checklist that would assist a principal in evaluating the professional climate in the school. Remember to include items that indicate freedom to innovate, peer relationships, general job satisfaction, feelings of confidence, and usefulness. Figure 4–4 may be helpful in initiating ideas for the checklist.

4-9.   Administer Figure 4–5 or a similar instrument to each student within a class or a group. Administer a nominations instrument (a sociometric technique) to the same group or class. Evaluate and summarize the results of each instrument by comparing and contrasting responses made by particular students.

4-10. Select and administer one of the teacher-child interaction systems listed in Table 4–3. Summarize the results and discuss any implications and future recommendations.

4-11. Utilize one of the informal techniques discussed in this chapter for assessing student-teacher interactions. Include the record form, the code utilized, and a discussion of the circumstances under which the data were collected. Follow with a summary of results and any pertinent implications or recommendations.

4-12. Administer one of the behavioral rating scales listed in Table 4–4. Follow with a discussion of any standardized reliability or validity data available.

4-13. Construct an informal instrument for assessing peer relationships. Administer the instrument on two different occasions within 2 weeks to the same group of children. Compare the two administrations and discuss the extent to which the instrument was reliable.

4-14. Develop and administer at least one sociogram to a minimum of five students. Discuss the results and make any recommendations for intervention strategies.

References

Amidon, P. *Nonverbal interaction analysis.* Minneapolis: Paul S. Amidon, 1971.

Axelrod, S. *Behavior modification for the classroom teacher.* New York: McGraw-Hill, 1977.

Bentley, R. R., & Starry, A. R. *The Purdue teacher education scale.* Lafayette, Ind.: Purdue Research Foundation, Purdue University, 1970.

Blair, G. M. *Educational psychology.* New York: Macmillan, 1962.

Bower, E. *The class picture.* Princeton, N.J.: Educational Testing Service, 1961.

Bower, E. *A Class Play.* Princeton, N.J.: Educational Testing Service, 1961.

Bradfield, R. H., & Criner, J. *Classroom interaction analysis.* San Rafael, Calif.: Academic Therapy Publications, 1973.

Brandt, R. The accuracy of self-estimate: A measure of self-concept reality. *Genetic Psychology Monographs,* 1958, *28,* 218–246.

Brophy, J. E., & Good, T. L. *Teacher-child dyatic interaction: A manual for coding classroom behavior.* Austin, Tex.: Research and Development Center for Teacher Education, University of Texas at Austin, 1969.

Brown, B. B. Experimentalism in teaching practice. *Journal of Research and Development in Education,* 1970, *4,* 14–22.

Carroll, A. W. The classroom as an ecosystem. *Focus on Exceptional Children,* 1974, *6,* 1–11.

Cartwright, C. A., & Cartwright, G. P. *Developing observational skills.* New York: McGraw-Hill, 1974.

Connors, K. C., & Eisenberg, L. *The effect of teacher behavior on verbal intelligence in observation Headstart children.* Baltimore: School of Medicine, Johns Hopkins University, 1966.

Corrigan, R. E. *A system approach for education.* Garden Grove, Calif.: R. E. Corrigan Associates, 1969.

Damrin, D. E. *Russell Sage social relations test.* Princeton, N.J.: Educational Testing Service, 1956.

deGroat, A., & Thompson, G. A study of the distribution of teacher approval and disapproval among sixth-grade pupils. *Journal of Experimental Education,* 1949, *18,* 57–75.

Emmer, E. *Classroom observation skills.* Austin, Tex.: Research and Development Center for Teacher Education, University of Texas, 1971.

Flanders, N. A. *Flanders' system of interaction analysis.* Reading, Mass.: Addison-Wesley, 1970.

Fox, R. S., Lippitt, R., & Schmuck, R. *Pupil-teacher adjustment and mutual adaptation in creating classroom learning environments.* U.S. Department of Health, Education and Welfare, Office of Education. Cooperative Research Project No. 1167. Ann Arbor, Mich.: University of Michigan, 1964.

Fox, R. S., Luszki, M. B., & Schmuck, R. *Diagnosing classroom learning environments.* Chicago: Science Research Associates, 1966.

Fox, R. S., Schmuck, R., van Egmond, E., Ritvo, M., & Jung, C. *Diagnosing professional climates of schools.* Fairfax, Va.: NTL Learning Resources Corporation, 1975.

Friou, D. M. The use of peer rating techniques to identify behavioral groups in the classroom. Unpublished manuscript. University of Texas at Austin, 1972.

Fuller, F. *Fuller affective interaction records 33.* Austin, Tex.: Research and Development Center for Teacher Education, University of Texas, 1969.

Gardner, E. E., & Thompson, G. G. *Syracuse scales of social relations.* New York: Harcourt, Brace Jovanovich, 1959.

Garrett, H. E. *Testing for teachers.* New York: American Book, 1965.

Good, T. Which pupils do teachers call on? *Elementary School Journal,* 1970, 70, 190–198.

Good, T., & Brophy, J. *Looking in classrooms.* New York: Harper & Row, 1973.

Gordon, I. J. *Studying the child in school.* New York: John Wiley, 1966.

Gronlund, N. E. *Measurement and evaluation in teaching.* New York: Macmillan, 1976.

Hall, R. V. *Managing behavior.* Lawrence, Kans.: H & H Enterprises, 1970.

Herbert, J., & Attridge, C. A guide for developers and users of observation systems and manuals. *American Educational Research Journal,* 1975, 12, 1–20.

Hoehn, A. A study of social status differentiation in the classroom behavior of 19 third-grade teachers. *Journal of Social Psychology,* 1954, 39, 269–292.

Jackson, P. W. *Life in classrooms.* New York: Holt, Rinehart and Winston, 1968.

Kroth, R. The behavioral Q-sort as a diagnostic tool. *Academic Therapy,* 1973, 8, 317–329.

Larsen S. C. The influence of teacher expectations on the school performance of handicapped children. *Focus on Exceptional Children,* 1975, 6, 1–14.

Laten, S., & Katz, G. A. A theoretical model for assessment of adolescents: The ecological/behavioral approach. Madison, Wis.: Madison Public Schools, 1975.

Medley, D., Schluck, C., & Ames, N. *Assessing the learning environment in the classroom: A manual for users of OScAR 5.* Princeton, N.J.: Educational Testing Service, 1968.

Moore, S., & Updegraff, R. Minnesota sociometric status test. In P. D. Guthrie (Ed.), *Headstart test collection report measures of social skills.* Princeton, N.J.: Educational Testing Service, 1971.

Morrison, A., & McIntyre, D. *Teachers and teaching.* Baltimore: Penguin, 1969.

Newcomer, P. Special education services for the "mildly handicapped." *Journal of Special Education,* 1977, *14,* 85/92.

Northway, M. L., & Weld, L. *Sociometric testing: A guide for teachers.* Canada: University of Toronto Press, 1967.

Ohio State Department of Education. *Ohio Social Acceptance Scale.* Columbus, Ohio: Ohio State Department of Education, 1944.

Redl, F., & Wattenberg, W. W. *Mental hygiene in teaching.* (2nd ed.) New York: Harcourt, Brace Jovanovich, 1959.

Reichenberg-Hackett, W. Practices, attitudes, and values in nursery group education. *Psychological Reports,* 1962, *10,* 151–172.

Remmers, H. H., & Gage, N. L. *Educational measurement and evaluation.* New York: Harper & Row, 1955.

Rubin, R., & Balow, B. Learning and behavioral disorders: A longitudinal study. *Exceptional Children,* 1971, *38,* 293–298.

Schertzer, B., & Stone, S. C. *Fundamentals of guidance.* Boston: Houghton Mifflin, 1971.

Schmuck, R., & Runkel, P. *Organization training for a school faculty.* The Center for Advanced Study of Educational Administration, Eugene, Oreg.: The University of Oregon, 1970.

Spaulding, R. L. Personality and social development: Peer and school influences. *Review of Educational Research,* 1964, *34,* 588–589.

Stephenson, W. *The study of behavior: Q-Technique and its methodology.* Chicago: University of Chicago Press, 1953.

Tyron, C. Evaluations of adolescent personality by adolescents. In R. Baker, J. Kouner, and W. Wright (Eds.), *Child behavior and development.* New York: McGraw-Hill, 1943.

Wright, H. F. *Recording and analyzing child behavior.* New York: Harper & Row, 1967.

5

Early
Childhood Assessment

The identification of learning problems among children during early child-hood has become an increasingly critical issue as evidence continues to accumulate concerning the importance of both early detection and preven-tion of learning difficulties. During the past decade professionals from a wide variety of disciplines have contributed their efforts to the growing number of programs in this area. The increase of both interest and services during the early developmental periods of growth actually can be credited to a variety of sources.

The work of Skeels and Dye (1939) and Skeels (1966) has provided empirical support for the emphasis on early childhood education by demon-strating that environmental modifications during early developmental years certainly can improve a child's later capacity for intellectual and social growth (Payne, Kauffman, Brown, & DeMott, 1974). Additional support has been provided by the scholarly studies of Piaget (1952), Bruner (1961), and Elkind (1969). Their work adds credibility to the belief that early experiences are critical for preparing the child for later learning. El-kind, for example, maintains that early education is important because a child's intellectual growth is cumulative and depends upon early experi-ences. Additional research by Kirk (1958) also has indicated the impor-tance of a child's early environment and the effects that it has on all areas of development.

Some of the most interesting support for early childhood programs has been obtained from laboratory studies with animals. According to Payne, Mercer, and Epstein (1974), the findings of many studies with animals provide a sound rationale for the importance of early experiences. Justifica-tion for early intervention is also noted by Caldwell (1970), who points out that studies with animals suggest that the critical time for manipulation of experiences is during the early infancy of the animals under study.

The important contributions from these and many other sources have certainly helped to focus the attention recently given early childhood education to the point at which the boundaries of this area are constantly being expanded. Kindergarten alone was at one time thought to be the extent of early childhood education. However, increased emphasis upon preschool and nursery school programs, along with the expanded interest in children from birth to 2 years of age, have largely accounted for the current notion that early childhood education includes all programs for children under the age of 9 years (Payne, et al., 1974). Our emphasis in this chapter nevertheless will be concentrated on the preschool and kindergarten child.

Early Childhood Education
Goals

The vast amount of child-development literature suggests that most early childhood programs attempt to emphasize the areas of social, cognitive, motor, language, physical, and perceptual development. Each of these developmental areas also attends to various specifications and growth sequences. The self-help skills of eating, clothing, and personal cleanliness are usually included among the *social development skills,* along with a number of individualization outcomes such as body image, self-image, self-concept, self-esteem, self-determination, and behavioral adjustment to society (Mann, Anfin, & Musey, 1974). Additional specifications for each developmental area are also offered by these same authors in their description of an early childhood, special education teacher preparation program.

Cognitive development usually includes the developmental outcomes of classification, serialization, and making spatial relations. The symbolic functioning of the child, including the ability to solve various problems, is a major goal of development within this area.

The major areas of *motor development* include growth sequences within visual perceptual abilities such as figure-ground perception, discrimination, and constancy. Also included within this area are developmental outcomes in fine and gross motor skills, laterality, directionality, balance, and various movement abilities.

Language development is primarily concerned with the phonological, semantic, and syntactic development of children's language, as well as skills within auditory discrimination and memory, fluency, and other auditory perception areas (Beers, 1974).

A comprehensive listing of additional early childhood education goals is illustrated in Table 5-1. These goals were originally developed based upon a review of the professional literature and interviews with a wide

TABLE 5-1   Taxonomy of Goals of Preschool-Kindergarten Education

The Affective Domain

1. Development of Personality
   A. Shyness-Boldness
   B. Neuroticism-Adjustment
   C. General Activity-Lethargy
   D. Dependence-Independence
   E. Self-esteem
2. Development of Social Skills
   A. Hostility-Friendliness
   B. Socialization-Rebelliousness
   C. Moral Belief and Practice
3. Development of Motivation for Learning
   A. School Orientation
   B. Need Achievement
   C. Interest Areas
4. Development of Aesthetic Appreciation
   A. Appreciation of Art
   B. Music Appreciation

The Intellectual Domain

5. Cognitive Functioning
   A. Spatial Reasoning
   B. Classificatory Reasoning
   C. Rational-Implicational Reasoning
   D. Systematic Reasoning
   E. Attention Span
6. Creativity
   A. Fluency
   B. Flexibility
7. Memory
   A. Span and Serial Memory
   B. Meaningful Memory
   C. Visual Memory
   D. Auditory Memory

The Psychomotor Domain

8. Physical Coordination
   A. Eye-Hand Coordination
   B. Small Muscle Coordination
   C. Large Muscle and Motor Coordination

The Subject Achievement Domain

9. Arts and Crafts
   A. Arts and Crafts Appreciation
   B. Expressive and Representational Skill in Arts and Crafts
10. Foreign Language
    A. Oral Comprehension of a Foreign Language
    B. Speaking Fluency in a Foreign Language
    C. Interest in and Application of a Foreign Language
    D. Cultural Insight through a Foreign Language

TABLE 5-1 *Continued*

11. Function and Structure of the Human Body
    A. Identification of Body Parts and Positions
    B. Growth and Development
    C. Knowledge of Emotional Health
    D. Identification of Self and Surroundings
12. Health
    A. Knowledge of Personal Hygiene and Grooming
    B. Practicing Personal Hygiene and Grooming
    C. Knowledge of Food and Nutrition
    D. Practicing Food and Nutrition
    E. Knowledge of Prevention and Control of Disease
    F. Practicing Prevention and Control of Disease
13. Mathematics
    A. Counting and Operations with Integers
    B. Comprehension of Sets in Mathematics
    C. Comprehension of Numbers in Mathematics
    D. Comprehension of Equality and Inequality in Mathematics
    E. Arithmetic Problem Solving
    F. Measurement Reading and Making
    G. Geometric Vocabulary and Recognition
14. Music
    A. Aural Identification and Music Knowledge
    B. Singing
    C. Instrument Playing
    D. Rhythmic Response (Dance)
15. Oral Language Skills
    A. Oral Semantic Skills
    B. Oral Phonology Skills
    C. Oral Syntactic Skills
    D. Oral Morphology Skills
16. Readiness Skills
    A. General Readiness Skills
    B. Visual Discrimination and Recognition
    C. Auditory Discrimination and Recognition
    D. Kinesthetic and Tactile Perception
17. Reading and Writing
    A. Recognition of Word Meanings
    B. Understanding Ideational Complexes
    C. Oral Reading
    D. Writing
    E. Familiarity with Standard Children's Literature
18. Religion
    A. Religious Belief and Practice
19. Safety
    A. Understanding Safety Principles
    B. Practicing Safety Principles
20. Science
    A. Observation and Exploration
    B. Knowledge of Scientific Facts
    C. Appreciation of the Scientific Approach
    D. Development and Application of Scientific Attitude

TABLE 5–1   *Continued*

21. Social Studies
    A. Community Health and Safety
    B. Cultural-Economic Geography
    C. Democratic Practice
    D. Physical Geography
    E. History

Source: Hoepfner, R., Stern, C., & Nummedal, S. G. *CSE/ECRC preschool/kindergarten test evaluations.* Los Angeles: UCLA Graduate School of Education, 1971.

spectrum of early childhood education practitioners. This table merely provides an outline of these goals, and it is important to note that each goal is operationally defined with some detail in the original source of the taxonomy.

IDENTIFICATION TECHNIQUES

Very few professionals are confident in attempting to identify young learning-handicapped children, even though most agree that early identification is crucial (Keogh, 1970). Consequently, many different techniques have been used for identification purposes, including standardized intelligence tests, developmental scales, medical reports, parental questionnaires, personality measures, informal tests, rating scales, and observational checklists (Barker, 1974). It should be expected then that the current status of early childhood assessment programs continues to be marked by confusing and conflicting reports and recommendations.

According to Keogh and Becker (1973), problems regarding the early identification of children with learning difficulties include, among others, the validity of the predictive measures themselves. They suggest that many dimensions of child development have been considered as possible indicators of later learning problems, mostly with limited success. For example, the broader areas listed in Table 5–1, such as the psychomotor domain, have often been unsuccessfully used as possible predictors of school failure. Jansky and deHirsch (1972) have labeled these approaches as *single variable predictors* and have labeled predictions based upon a combination of variables (e.g., test batteries, readiness tests, etc.) as *multiple variable predictors.*

Single Variable Predictors

Some of the variables that have been used as single measures for predicting learning difficulties include visual perception, visual-motor competence, auditory perception, and skill in oral language, as well as chronological age, sex, intelligence, and emotional status. However, most investigators agree that the utilization of single variables is at best very restrictive.

Visual-motor skills have been widely studied with relation to early identification of learning disabled children. The *Bender Motor Gestalt Test* (Bender, 1938), in particular, has been utilized in many studies, but has not been highly recommended for individual prediction (Keogh, 1965; Keogh & Smith, 1967; Norfleet, 1973). Moreover, in summarizing the usefulness of motor development for predicting learning difficulties, Leydorf (1970) points out that the relationship between motor ability and various academic skills is speculative and that the motor and physical characteristics can rarely serve as adequate predictors of failure in school.

The role of language as a single predictor for identifying children with learning problems also has been widely investigated. Language-related variables were the most significant of the 31 variables measured in the well-known early identification study of Haring and Ridgeway (1967). Nevertheless, the authors infer that each of the tests in the battery, including the language measures, had very limited usefulness when used alone as a predictor of learning problems. Very few common, identifiable learning patterns were revealed by either teacher observation or psychological testing. Jansky and deHirsch (1972) further suggest that additional experimental studies are needed before any definitive decisions can be concluded concerning oral-language deficits and school failure.

A number of writers also have suggested that even intelligence test scores (IQs) be used with caution as predictors of school achievement. The use of these scores with children of lower socioeconomic status, for example, is rarely meaningful because of the very nature of intelligence tests (Jansky & deHirsch, 1972). Further, it is suggested by Keogh and Becker (1973) that there is considerable evidence that can be interpreted as suggesting that intelligence is not necessarily a stable trait in the early years, but may instead be particularly malleable.

In summary, the evidence quite clearly indicates that single variable measures cannot be considered to be consistently reliable predictors of school achievement for young children. Consideration of a combination of variables seems much more realistic and certainly more dependable over a longer period of time. Two single variable measures, the *Boehm Test of Basic Concepts* and the *Evanston Early Identification Scale* are reviewed in the following sections.

Boehm Test of Basic Concepts The *Boehm Test* (Boehm, 1971) is designed to measure a child's mastery of the concepts considered necessary for achievement in the primary grades. Included among the 50 concepts that are assessed are *over, always, between, different,* and *most.* The test is available in two forms, and each form consists of 50 pictorial items arranged in approximate order of increasing difficulty and divided evenly between two booklets. Each test item consists of a set of pictures, about which statements are orally read by the examiner to the children. Each statement briefly describes the pictures and instructs the children to make the picture illustrating the particular concept being evaluated. Concepts are classified according to various categories, including quantity, time, space, and miscellaneous. The cover page from Form A of the test is illustrated in Figure 5–1.

Raw scores on each form may be converted to percentile equivalents for kindergarten, first, and second grade and into various socioeconomic levels. In addition, the author suggests a number of remedial procedures that may be utilized for either individual or group instruction.

The standardization sample consists of over 12,000 students in kindergarten, first, and second grades. Minimal reliability and validity data (norms) are also reported in the manual. However, the author points out that the information is intended as an informal guide rather than as an essential procedure for interpreting test results, since the test was designed as a teaching instrument and not as a predictor of school success or as a means of designating various placements for children within a school.

The Boehm test is a good example of an instrument used with young children that provides very specific information concerning one important aspect of school readiness. When the test is used in this context, the results will be very useful to a teacher for planning an instructional program.

Evanston Early Identification Scale   The Evanston Early Identification Scale (Landsman and Dillard, 1967), which may be administered either individually or in a group, is intended to identify those children who are expected to have difficulty in school. The child is asked to draw the figure of a person. Based on a weighted scale of point values for missing body parts (e.g., mouth, eyes, arms, legs, etc.) the child is classified as *low-risk* (no problems expected in school), *middle-risk* (some difficulty expected in school), and *high-risk* (problems requiring the attention of special personnel can be expected in school). It is recommended that the test be administered to children between the ages of 5–0 and 6–3 years. Although the test is not a diagnostic instrument, the authors provide an excellent discussion of case histories and classroom behavior of high-risk and middle-risk children.

The scale was standardized on 117 children, and the authors note that the test is valid for different socioeconomic groups. Minimal test reliability and validity data are also provided in the manual.

We have found the Evanston scale to be a simple screening device for

FIGURE 5–1   Sample from the Boehm Test of Basic Concepts

NAME_____

Form A

Booklet 2

assessing groups of children. Ferinden and Jacobsen (1970) have found that when this test is used with the reading section of the *Wide Range Achievement Test* (Jastak & Jastak, 1965) the kindergarten teachers obtain almost 90 percent or more accuracy in screening for potential learning disabilities. However, children classified as middle-risk and high-risk will require more extensive evaluation in order for teachers both to fully understand the child's difficulties and to plan appropriate educational programs. Nonetheless, this scale is a very suitable instrument for *screening* larger groups of children for further assessment.

Multiple Variable Predictors

Screening programs based on a combination of variables usually involve one of the following approaches: reading readiness tests, comprehensive test batteries comprised of several subtests, and assessment batteries that are composed of a number of standardized tests.

Among the numerous techniques utilized to screen for reading difficulties, the combination index developed by Monroe (1932) has been widely used and very effective as a diagnostic reading device. The Monroe index involves the use of several standardized tests (e.g., *Gray Oral Reading Test*) and a number of other reading subtests. The Monroe index has been widely recommended as a highly structured screening system (Della-Piana, 1968).

Another type of multiple variable predictor consists of a screening battery that combines various published instruments. In their study, which screened kindergarten children for potential learning disabilities, Ferinden and Jacobsen (1970) found that only the *Wide Range Achievement Test* (Jastak & Jastak, 1965) and the *Evanston Early Identification Scale* (Landsman & Dillard, 1967) were valid instruments for predicting school failure. However, two other instruments could not be reliably used for prediction at this level.

The major work of Jansky and deHirsch (1972) probably is the best known predictive index based upon a combination of variables. The original battery (deHirsch, Jansky, & Langford, 1966) was refined in this later study in order to remedy a number of earlier limitations. The *Screening Index* was developed from a pool of over 19 standardized and informal tests that were used in a 2-year study involving over 400 students. The revised predictive battery identified slightly more than three out of four children who failed in reading at the end of the second grade. The 15–20 minute battery is composed of the five best predicting tests: letter naming, picture naming, word matching (*Gates Reading Readiness* subtest), copying of the *Bender Motor Gestalt* designs, and sentence repetition (*Stanford-Binet Intelligence Scale* subtest). The predictive index can be administered to large populations, which was a major aim of the study.

A type of multiple variable index that has become widely used in the past few years is the screening battery comprised of several subtests. Each of these tests measures a wide variety of the skills considered to be crucial for school success. A number of these tests are described in the following section.

Cooperative Preschool Inventory   *The Cooperative Preschool Inventory* (Caldwell, 1970) is a brief assessment and screening procedure that is designed for individual use with children aged 3–6. It is intended primarily to provide a measure of achievement in areas regarded as necessary for success in school. In addition, the instrument attempts to highlight the degree of disadvantage that a child from a deprived background has at the time of entering school in order to reduce or eliminate any observed deficits.

The inventory consists of 64 items that are scored as *right* or *wrong* by the examiner. Among the test items are those requiring the children to name colors, to copy shapes, to count to 5, to distinguish *more* and *less*, and to identify various body parts. The test may be administered in approximately 15–20 minutes. The items can be grouped according to the following areas: concept activation—numerical; concept activation—sensory; personal-social responsiveness; and associated vocabulary. However, subtest scores are not obtained in the results. The child's number of correct responses are merely converted to a percentile rank for differing chronological ages.

The revised edition of the test was standardized on 1,500 children tested in 150 Headstart classes throughout the United States. Limited reliability and validity data are available in the test manual, including Kuder-Richardson reliability coefficients for age groups ranging from 0.86 to 0.92. The corrected split-half reliability coefficients are reported to range from 0.84 to 0.93.

We recommend this instrument as a good screening tool for measuring certain aspects of school readiness. The test items include particularly relevant behaviors for preschool children. In addition, this relatively brief measure is quite easy to administer and to score. The test manual clearly outlines acceptable responses in a very concise and logical manner.

First-Grade Screening Test   *The First-Grade Screening Test* (Pate & Webb, 1969) is a group test designed to identify children at the end of kindergarten or at the beginning of first grade who will probably experience severe learning problems during their first years in school. The identified children usually will require further individualized evaluation. The test consists of 27 items that sample the child's general knowledge, body image, perception of parental figures, perception of appropriate play, visual-motor coordination, ability to follow directions, memory, and perception of the child's own emotional maturation. Separate booklets for boys and girls are provided.

The test yields a raw score that can be converted to a corresponding percentile for both the end of kindergarten and the beginning of first grade. The authors also recommend the development of local cutting scores for use in referring children for specialized evaluation. It is suggested that these local cutting scores would account for the variability among various school districts in the availability of diagnostic specialists, educational facilities, and goals of first-grade instruction. The authors provide a number of guidelines for developing local cutting scores, along with the general suggestion that a raw score of 15 and below has been found to predict school performance rather efficiently across the country.

The test was standardized on a sample of approximately 3,200 kindergarten students and 5,500 first-grade students. However, Telegdy (1974) provides some evidence to indicate that the children's socioeconomic level affects their performance on this test. In his study of four different school-readiness tests, including the FGST, Telegdy has found that significantly more children in low socioeconomic levels score less well than children in middle socioeconomic levels on all four tests included in the study.

Validity and reliability data are also provided in the manual. Comparisons of FGST scores with various achievement tests are reported in correlations that range from 0.60 to 0.79 for first-grade children. Test-retest reliabilities resulted in 0.82 and 0.84 for various time intervals.

The FGST is a particularly efficient and useful instrument for *screening* groups of children for potential learning handicaps. The 27 test items assess a wide range of both social-emotional and academically related skills that are important for later development. It is important to reiterate, however, that the test will effectively select only those children who will require further evaluation.

CIRCUS CIRCUS (Anderson, Bogatz, Draper, Jungleblut, Sidwell, Ward, & Yates, 1974) is a comprehensive battery of 17 assessment devices for use in nursery school and kindergarten. With the exception of one test, all *CIRCUS* measures may be administered to small groups of children. Fourteen tests are directly administered to children and three measures (questionnaire-type) are completed by the classroom teacher. Most of the *CIRCUS* tests are untimed and may be administered in any order. The complete battery is briefly described in the following paragraphs.

- *What Words Mean*—a 40-item test that measures the child's comprehension of nouns, verbs, and modifiers by having the child mark various pictures.
- *How Much and How Many*—measures the child's understanding of quantitative concepts in areas of counting, rational terms, and numerical concepts.

157

- *Look-alikes*—evaluates visual discrimination by having the child match identical letters, numbers, geometric shapes, and objects.
- *Copy What You See*—measures the child's ability to copy 15 different letters and numbers that are visually presented.
- *Finding Letters and Numbers*—tests the child's ability to recognize and discriminate among capital and lower-case letters and numbers.
- *Noises*—measures the child's ability to associate real-world sounds (e.g., faucet dripping, dog barking, thunder, etc.) with corresponding pictures.
- *How Words Sound*—a 44-item auditory discrimination test that measures a child's knowledge of initial consonants, medial vowels, and final consonants.
- *How Words Work*—tests the child's ability to understand various aspects of functional language including prepositions, conjunctions, and pronouns.
- *Listen to the Story*—is a receptive language measure that tests the child's ability to listen to a narrative and to understand and interpret story events.
- *Say and Tell*—is administered individually; intended to provide a measure of the child's spoken language.
- *Do You Know . . . ?*—is a 32-item measure of the child's general knowledge in six informational areas (e.g., health and safety).
- *See and Remember*—measures visual and associative memory through successively more complex pictures presented at varying time spans.
- *Think It Through*—is a problem-solving test that concentrates on the child's ability to identify problems, to classify and sort objects, to evaluate problem solutions, and to identify the first event in a time sequence.
- *Make a Tree*—measures the child's ability to make appropriately, unusually, or differently a tree from gummed stickers.
- *The Activities Inventory*—is a 60-item measure of the child's approach to classroom activities completed by the teacher. Four major areas are included: physical-motor, academic, role playing and fantasy, and music and art.
- *The CIRCUS Behavior Inventory*—measures the child's reaction to the tests. The teacher completes the 14-item test for each child after the measures have been administered.
- *The Educational Environment Questionnaire*—is also completed by the teacher and provides a description of the class, school or center, and program, as well as self-reports of teacher backgrounds, attitudes, and educational values.

Approximately 3,000 children of nursery school and kindergarten age were included in the standardization sample. Detailed reliability and validity data are also discussed in the manual for each of the CIRCUS tests.

However, no predictive validity information for the tests is included in the manual.

Test scores are converted to sentence reports describing children's competencies. The results help to select children who are experiencing specific difficulties and provide an evaluation of program effectiveness. The authors also suggest that different assessment purposes will entail the use of various subtests or combination of subtests.

There is no doubt that the series of tests that comprise *CIRCUS* can be effectively utilized to measure specific skills deemed important for later school success. The tests are easy to administer and interpret, and contain very concise instructions and guidelines. The fact that the tests may be used singly or in combination is an added advantage for educators particularly interested in evaluating only certain readiness skills. In sum, the *CIRCUS* battery is a good example of an effective multiple variable, early childhood assessment technique.

Meeting Street School Screening Test   The *Meeting Street School Screening Test* (MSSST) (Hainsworth & Siqueland, 1969) is an individually administered screening test for kindergarten and first-grade children. It is specifically designed to identify children who do not possess the necessary language and visual-perceptual-motor skills, or gross motor control for processing the symbolic information in the traditional school curriculum.

The MSSST is based on Osgood's (1957) model of information processing. The test is comprised of three subtests: the Motor Patterning test measures movement patterns and awareness of the body in space; the Visual-Perceptual-Motor test surveys visual discrimination, visual memory, reproduction of geometric and letter forms, and understanding of spatial and directional concepts; and the Language subtest measures how a child listens, remembers, sequences, and formulates language.

Raw scores are converted to scaled scores for each subtest and to a total test score according to the children's chronological ages. Normative tables are provided for the age range 5–0 to 7–5 years. A profile of scores also is available for comparing an individual child's performance with expectations for his or her age. In addition, the test authors provide a number of suggestions for using appropriate cut-off scores to predict those children who are in high-risk categories for learning disabilities.

Minimal information concerning the standardization sample is provided in the test manual, along with a number of studies describing various reliability and validity data. The predictive validity data as reported by the authors are basically sound and quite encouraging.

As one of the earliest standardized tests for identifying young children with learning disabilities, the MSSST is recognized as a very fine approach for assessing high-risk children. The detailed discussion of early identification programs, as well as the information provided for interpreting scores, must certainly be considered as additional advantages for using the test.

Rating Scales

The use of multiple variable predictors generally have been viewed as more dependable and successful than the use of single variable predictors. Nevertheless, the multiple variable predictors have been recommended cautiously because of their relatively low predictive validity and their lack of relevance to educational programs and materials (Keogh & Becker, 1973). Somewhat in reaction to these findings, recently teachers have begun using rating scales to a greater extent for predictive purposes. Bryan and McGrady (1972) have noted the advantages of rating scales, some of which are economy of time and money, teacher involvement, intensive evaluation of a few children, evaluation of areas not usually testable, and the opportunity to identify specific areas of disability despite a child's overall adequate performance. The promising results from a variety of studies have also lent some support to this approach.

The study by Haring and Ridgeway (1967), which was mentioned earlier in this chapter, for example, concludes that kindergarten teacher ratings were effective predictors of children with learning problems. Similarly, in an informal study, Rochford (1970) notes that 95 percent of the children who later developed learning difficulties were identified as early as in kindergarten by their teachers. Keogh and Smith (1970) found teacher ratings to be consistently significant when correlated with achievement scores in second through sixth grades. In their longitudinal study of teacher rating effectiveness for identifying high-risk children, Ilg and Ames (1964) also report a high correlation between kindergarten teacher ratings and sixth-grade achievement.

The use of kindergarten teachers' anecdotal records as predictors for learning difficulties was investigated by Cogwill, Friedland, and Shapiro (1973). Based upon the teachers' descriptions of various children's traits and quantitative differences in behavior, the results indicate that anecdotal comments do distinguish many learning disabled children.

In addition to teacher rating scales, parents are sometimes asked to complete questionnaires regarding their children. The results are subsequently utilized as general guidelines for program planning and further evaluation. Three parent-administered screening instruments are described in Table 5–2.

In sum, the use of rating scales to identify children with learning problems has been more closely studied in recent years. Most scales have been found to be fairly accurate for predicting school success or failure. More

TABLE 5–2   Parent-administered Screening Instruments

Name	Age Range	Description
Parent Readiness Evaluation of Preschoolers (Ahr, 1968)	3–9 to 5–8 years	Parent administers to child verbal and performance sections and many subtests, including general information, memory for words, reproducing numbers, knowledge of syntax and grammar, etc.
Preschool Attainment Record (Doll, 1967)	6 months to 7 years	Parent is interviewed concerning eight categories of child's developmental behavior: ambulation, manipulation, rapport, communication, responsibility, information, ideation, and creativity.
School Readiness Survey (Jordan & Massey, 1969)	4–6 years	Parent administers to child a survey in seven sections, including number concepts, discrimination of form, color naming, symbol matching, speaking vocabulary, listening vocabulary and general information.

objective teacher perceptions have been generally noted when structured guidelines or forms have been provided. Two specific methods for systematic observations are described in the following sections.

Rhode Island Pupil Identification Scale   The *Rhode Island Pupil Identification Scale* (Novack, Bonaventura, & Merenda, 1972) is primarily designed to help the classroom teacher identify children with learning problems. The scale is comprised of 40 items that reflect the behaviors often found in the presence of school failure. The scale is divided into two parts: Part I is composed of 21 items that deal with behaviors readily observable in the classroom; Part II is composed of 19 items that involve behaviors evaluated through examination of a child's written work. Each item is rated on a 5-point Likert scale by the classroom teacher. The complete scale is illustrated in Figure 5–2.

Over 800 subjects in kindergarten through the second grade comprised the standardization sample. The sample was chosen to be representative of children in these grades in terms of age, sex, state geographic location, race distribution, and ethnic origin. Test-retest reliability coefficients range from 0.755 to 0.988, and very encouraging concurrent and predictive validity data are reported by the authors (Novack, Bonaventura, & Merenda, 1973).

Although this scale does not yield information concerning specific cutoff scores, it does provide the classroom teacher with an assessment

FIGURE 5–2   Rhode Island Pupil Identification Scale

Observation period: from_____ to _____

Observer _____

Name _____ Age_____ _____
                                                         years   months

Sex _____ Grade _____

School _____

City _____ State_____

Instructions: For each item on this form, rate the pupil being evaluated according to the following scale:

1 = never   2 = rarely   3 = occasionally   4 = frequently   5 = always

If during any observation period no opportunity has arisen for the task to be performed, leave the item blank.

Part I refers to behavior which can normally be observed in the classroom. Part II deals with behavior which is most readily observable through written work.

Part I
____ a. Has difficulty cutting.
____ b. Has difficulty pasting.
____ c. Bumps into objects.
____ d. Trips over self.
____ e. Has difficulty catching a ball.
____ f. Has difficulty jumping rope.
____ g. Has difficulty tying shoes.
____ h. Has difficulty buttoning buttons.
____ i. Breaks point of pencil.
____ j. Has difficulty sitting still.
____ k. Has difficulty standing still.
____ l. Has short attention span.
____ m. Gives the appearance of being tense.
____ n. Has difficulty remembering what is seen.
____ o. Has difficulty remembering what is shown.
____ p. Cries.
____ q. Fails to take reprimands well.
____ r. Has difficulty understanding directions.
____ s. Tends to be discouraged.
____ t. Tends to give up.
____ u. Tends to avoid group activity.
____ v. Has difficulty completing assignment in allotted time.

____ PART I SCORE

Part II
For items with an asterisk (*) indicate item and describe the error on the back of the page. Record any additional errors not indicated on check sheet.
____ a. Has difficulty staying within lines when coloring.
____ b. Produces work which varies in quality.
____ c. Demonstrates poor handwriting on papers.

____ d. Erases on papers.
____ e. Turns in papers which are dirty.
____ f. Has difficulty writing within lines.
____ g. Starts writing in the middle of the paper rather than from the left margin.
____ h. Mirrors and/or reverses letters, numbers, words, or other forms in copying.*
____ i. Mirrors and/or reverses letters, numbers, words, or other forms when visual stimulation is not provided.*
____ j. Runs words or parts of words together in copying.*
____ k. Runs words or parts of words together when visual stimulation is not provided.*
____ l. Omits or substitutes letters, words, and/or numbers in copying.*
____ m. Has difficulty with the names of letters and/or numbers.*
____ n. Omits or substitutes letters, words, and/or numbers when no visual stimulation is provided.*
____ o. Has difficulty completing written work in the time allotted.
____ p. Has difficulty grasping number concepts.
____ q. Has difficulty arranging numbers vertically.
____ r. Has difficulty with addition and subtraction.
____ s. Makes omissions, substitutions, or reversals of letters, numbers, and/or words in reading.*

____ PART II SCORE

____ TOTAL SCORE FOR PARTS I & II

Editor's Note: Persons wishing to use this scale should contact the senior author, Harry S. Novack.

Source: Novack, H. S., Bonaventura, E., & Merenda, P. F. *Rhode Island pupil identification scale.* Providence, R.I.: Authors, 1972. Used with permission.

device that helps to systematize classroom observations. Since the observed behaviors reflect actual classroom practices, the resulting data can be readily utilized in working with various children. Furthermore, the conciseness, brevity, and relatively simple administration and interpretation of the scale must also be considered as additional advantages for using this instrument.

The Pupil Rating Scale: Screening for Learning Disabilities   The purpose of the *Pupil Rating Scale* (Myklebust, 1971) is to identify children with learning disabilities. Classroom teachers rate children in five areas:

- *Auditory Comprehension:* comprehending word meanings, following instructions, comprehending class discussions, retaining information
- *Spoken Language:* vocabulary, grammar, word recall, storytelling—relating experiences, formulating ideas
- *Orientation:* judging time, spatial orientation, judging relationships, knowing directions
- *Motor Coordination:* general coordination, balance, manual dexterity
- *Personal-Social Behavior:* cooperation, attention, organization, reaction to new situations, social acceptance, responsibility, completion of assignments, tactfulness

Each rating is based on a 5-point scale of behavioral description. A score of 3 is an average rating, whereas scores of 1 and 2 are below average. Above-average ratings are scores of 4 or 5. Each behavioral item is clearly defined and clarified. Scores are derived by simply adding the numbers that have been circled by the teacher.

The research sample for the scale consisted of over 2,000 third- and fourth-grade students. The author suggests that these results may be considered normative for these grades and age groups. However, the scale may also be utilized effectively with children at younger ages and grade levels, since the item descriptions are widely applicable to various age groups.

Scores may be analyzed according to specific items or areas of behavior. In addition, the *auditory comprehension* and *spoken language* scores may be added to obtain a single score for verbal facility. Similarly, the areas of *orientation, motor coordination,* and *personal-social behavior* may be added together for a nonverbal learning score. A total scale score may also be obtained by adding the scores in all areas.

The rating scale was actually one of the most reliable screening procedures that resulted from the Myklebust and Boshe (1969) screening project in learning disabilities. It is a highly efficient procedure for screening children who have learning difficulties, but each identified child likely requires further individualized evaluation. The scale is often used as the initial step in attempting to identify learning disabled children.

Developmental Screening Tests

Some early childhood tests that are used to screen high-risk children are based on various developmental sequences. These tests usually can be given to very young children because of the range of skills and behaviors that are measured. Two developmental screening tests, the *Denver Developmental Screening Test* and the *Valett Developmental Survey of Basic Learning Abilities,* are reviewed in the following section.

Denver Developmental Screening Test The *Denver Developmental Screening Test* (Frankenburg & Dodds, 1970) is widely used on individual children and is primarily intended to aid in the early detection of delayed development in children aged 2 weeks through 6 years and 4 months. The test consists of 105 items arranged in the following four sections:

- *Personal-Social:* tasks indicating the child's ability to get along with people and take care of himself or herself
- *Fine Motor-Adaptive:* items indicating the child's ability to see and use his or her hands to pick up objects and draw
- *Language:* tasks indicating the child's ability to hear, carry out commands, and speak
- *Gross Motor:* items indicating the child's ability to sit, walk, and jump.

In the *Denver Developmental Screening Test* age scales in months from 1 to 24, and in years from 2½ to 6 are found across the top and bottom of the test form. Each of the test items is represented on the test form by a horizontal bar placed along the age continuum to indicate the ages at which 25 percent, 50 percent, 75 percent, and 90 percent of the children in the standardization sample passed an item. The number of items that are administered vary according to the age of the child. Generally, however, each section of the test is continued until the child has three failures in each of the four test sections. In scoring the test, a *delay* in development is considered to happen when the child fails any item that 90 percent of the children normally can pass at a younger age. According to the number of delays in each section, the results can be interpreted as *abnormal, questionable,* and *normal.* It is advised that individuals be rechecked whose results are either abnormal or questionable after approximately 2–3 weeks. Further professional help is recommended for children who continually score in these two categories.

The test was standardized on over 1,000 children between the ages of 2 weeks and 6.4 years with separate norms for boys and girls, and on children whose fathers were in white-collar or blue-collar jobs. Reliability and validity data that have been reported in the literature reveal generally favorable results, notwithstanding the fact that the test was standardized on a limited, regional sample with very few minority-group children.

The Denver test is an excellent screening device that is relatively simple to administer and interpret. The test may be administered without special training in psychological testing, and the accompanying manual provides very concise directions for scoring and interpreting responses. We believe the test is a very useful tool for the early detection of children with developmental problems.

Valett Developmental Survey of Basic Learning Abilities   The *Valett Developmental Survey* actually consists of 273 items that have been arranged on an ascending scale of difficulty in seven different areas. Selected tasks are grouped according to motor integration and physical development, tactile discrimination, auditory discrimination, visual-motor coordination, visual discrimination, language development and verbal fluency, and conceptual development. Developmental norms from various sources are also listed for children aged 2 through 7 for each task on the survey.

The survey is intended to provide the teacher with a classification of selected developmental tasks in the previously mentioned areas of development. The survey is administered by scoring + when the skill item has been attained, − when the skill item has not been attained, and ± when the skill item has been partially attained. An overall score is obtained by noting the number of correct items. It is also suggested that a developmental level may be estimated for each area through use of the developmental norms provided for each skill item.

Specific scoring criteria are not provided in the manual, nor is any information available concerning reliability and validity. Nevertheless, the survey can serve as a clue for educational programming and as a guide for teaching specific skills. On the other hand, Mann (1971) particularly questions the seven skill areas and the placement of specific items within each category.

The lack of normative data and definitive guidelines for administering, scoring, and interpreting the results can be considered serious limitations of this instrument. The survey should be considered as a general guideline for reviewing a limited number of developmental tasks.

Informal Published Batteries

A type of multiple variable index that has become increasingly popular in screening for high-risk children is the informal assessment battery. These nonstandardized instruments usually include several subtests that measure skills considered to be important for early school success. Three examples of informal published batteries are discussed in the following section.

Pre-reading Screening Procedures   One of a series of screening tests by Slingerland (1969), the *Pre-reading Screening Procedures* is intended for children who have not yet been introduced to reading. All of the screening tests are group measures designed to identify children experiencing specific language-learning disabilities. The specific purpose of the prereading screening measure is to find children of average to superior intelligence who may have difficulty in reading, writing, and spelling unless preventive measures are employed.

The prereading screening measure is comprised of seven subtests for group administration and two supplementary tests requiring individual testing. The subtests are briefly described below:

- Test 1 *Visual—Discrimination of Letter Forms*
  In a series of exercises the child is asked to find the letter(s) matching a stimulus letter(s).
- Test 2 *Visual—Discrimination of Word Forms*
  The child is asked to find a match for a stimulus word.
- Test 3 *Visual—Visual Perception Memory*
  After viewing a card with a symbol or word on it for 6–10 seconds, the child is asked to mark a symbol from among four choices.
- Test 4 *Visual-Motor—Copying*
  The child is asked to copy six different combinations of symbols, letters, or numerals.
- Test 5 *Visual-Motor—Visual Perception Memory*
  After viewing a symbol for 6–10 seconds, the child is asked to draw it from memory. Ten different symbols are used.
- Test 6 *Auditory—Discrimination*
  The child is asked to note by making different marks (e.g., // or XX) whether the words pronounced by the examiner are the same or different.
- Test 7 *Letter Knowledge*
  The child is requested to mark, among four choices, the letter named by the teacher.

The two supplementary tests are recommended specifically for children evidencing speech and language deficits. The Echolalia Test requires the child to repeat a series of words pronounced by the examiner, while the Reproducing a Story subtest requires the child to retell a story already told by the examiner.

Although the test is not standardized, a 5-point rating scale was developed on the basis of administering the test to approximately 400 children in different parts of the country. Each of the subtests is individually rated according to *high, M+, M, M—,* and *low.* In addition, a number of guidelines are provided for evaluating specific types of errors, such as reversals, inversions, rotations, and distortions. It is also suggested that the quality of a child's errors is as important as the number of errors that are made.

The Slingerland screening tests have become widely used in certain areas of the country. The specific nature of the subtests provide classroom teachers with educational information that is often immediately useful in planning instructional programs. Furthermore, the remedial techniques developed by Orton-Gillingham (cf. Myers & Hammill, 1976) are recommended by the test author as probably the best program of instruction for children performing poorly on these screening tests. Nevertheless, these tests should be very carefully used, since information concerning both reliability and validity is not available. In many cases, the screening procedures probably will need to be supplemented by additional evaluative data gathered by the classroom teacher or other school personnel.

Psychoeducational Evaluation of the Preschool Child   The *Psychoeducational Evaluation of the Preschool Child* (Jedrysek, Klapper, Pope, & Wortis, 1972) is a structured testing and educational procedure that was designed to assess a child's level of achievement in five areas of functioning. The evaluation can be used with any child functioning at a preschool level, and for whom an educational plan is being formulated. The authors clearly state that this instrument is intended to supplement the information obtained by means of standardized tests. The focus of the evaluation is on careful observation and response, along with functional analysis and achievement capacity (the level at which a child can achieve). Examiners are encouraged to observe simultaneously and systematically the child's total behavior while responding. The emphasis is on exploring *how* the child arrives at a solution and on determining impaired areas of functioning.

The evaluation consists of 41 items in the five areas of (1) physical functioning and sensory status, (2) perceptual functioning, (3) competence in learning for short-term retention, (4) language competence, and (5) cognitive functioning. The main items within each area or section are sequentially arranged in order of difficulty, culminating in the level appropriate for first-grade entrance. They are presented in sequential order unless the task becomes too difficult for the child. If the task is too difficult, *probes* are presented that permit both lateral and downward modification of the main item requirements. For example, if a child is unable to fit together two halves of a circle, the procedure may be demonstrated by the examiner. If the child still cannot do this, the child may be presented with a more practical and concrete representation of the tasks (e.g., picture of a cat cut in half) and then asked to put the pieces together.

The educational evaluation provides no normative data, since this is not considered to be consistent with the purpose of the evaluation. It is recommended that the results be used to formulate teaching goals and to develop teaching programs. The teaching probes seem particularly well suited to this purpose, since the probes foster teaching styles and approaches that are effective for individual children.

The manual is actually an extension and elaboration of Haeussermann's (1958) text. The evaluation guidelines are clearly outlined in the manual, and an explanation of test procedures and materials is provided. The educational evaluations of three different children are also presented, which provides the examiner with a solid foundation for administering and using the results in planning teaching programs.

A Program for the Early Identification of Learning Disabilities *A Program for the Early Identification of Learning Disabilities* developed by Petersen (1970) is an informal assessment battery comprised of 24 items and specifically designed for kindergarten and first-grade children experiencing academic difficulties. The child's skills are measured in each of the following areas: general information, language development, auditory discrimination and perception, ability to listen and follow directions, visual perception, eye-hand coordination, fine motor functioning, tactile perception and kinesthetic performance, laterality and directionality, spatial and temporal relationships, memory, ability to change set, organizational ability, task orientation, manner of relating to others, stamina, gross motor functioning, body concept, recognition and comprehension of the printed word, and number concepts and functioning.

The assessment instrument is an outgrowth of the author's wide experience with learning disabled children, and is intended as an aid to classroom teachers in planning educational experiences for these children. Consequently, no attempt has been made to establish norms. The author does provide a number of excellent guidelines and suggestions for programming educational materials and techniques in each of the various areas investigated on the test.

A structured observational guide is also provided with the evaluation. The examiner notes the child's behavior in 14 different areas, each of which is discussed in the manual.

The results of this informal evaluation provide the teacher with an overall knowledge of a child's abilities in most of the important skill areas in kindergarten and first grade. More importantly, the results can be used in working with learning disabled children in schools.

Teacher-made Tests

Despite the evidence supporting the use of classroom teachers as a first-level screening for early identification of high-risk children (Keogh, Tchir, & Winderguth-Behn, 1974), teacher-made tests have been limited to either rating scales or checklists. Most checklists tend to reflect the developmental-skills point of view, and few have varied in content since relatively little is known about the kinds of behaviors that can predict school success or failure (Karlin, 1971; Keogh, et al., 1974). Figure 5-3 is an illustration of a typical readiness checklist used by many teachers to assess behaviors of young children.

The results of a completed child-growth checklist are used either to screen for further assessment or to guide the teacher in educational planning. The checklist illustrated in Figure 5-3, for example, provides a list of behaviors that can be included easily in most early childhood programs for children experiencing various difficulties. On the other hand, many checklists also serve to alert teachers about children with more severe difficulties. In these cases, the advice and counsel of specialists within a school district invariably will be required.

In addition to checklists and rating scales, classroom teachers can evaluate specific readiness skills by constructing informal tests. These objective tests measure skills closely related to learning tasks. Consequently, the results from these teacher-made tests often are directly applicable to teaching programs. Informal tests can be constructed for almost any readiness skill. (The list of goals in Table 5-1 can be used as a general reference for test topics.) Three examples of informal tests are illustrated in Figure 5-4, each of which measures skills directly related to teaching programs. The results provide the teacher with useful information both for personalizing teaching and for incorporating data into actual teaching procedures. This type of teacher-made test continues to hold tremendous promise for assessing young children.

USING EARLY CHILDHOOD
ASSESSMENT TECHNIQUES

The early identification of children with learning problems is a complex issue. The difficulties associated with the selection of appropriate screening instruments certainly can be considered a crucial component of the identification process. However, in addition to various psychometric procedures, Keogh (1972) has suggested that nonpsychometric variables specific to various situations should also be considered. Among the suitable alterna-

FIGURE 5–3   Child-growth Checklist

Name of Child _____

School _____   Date _____

I. *Motor Growth*

	Satisfactory	Unsatisfactory	Further Assessment Required	Comments
1. Prints name				
2. Cuts with scissors				
3. Throws and catches balls				
4. Walks on balance beam				
5. Knows left-right				
6. Skips, hops, jumps				
7. Knows body parts, positions				
8. Ties shoes				

II. *Language Growth*

1. Follows directions				
2. Is attentive				
3. Converses with peers				
4. Fluent in vocabulary				
5. Aware of sequential order				
6. Able to formulate ideas				
7. Uses complete sentences				
8. Able to retell stories				

III. *Social-Emotional Growth*
1. Shares
2. Cooperates
3. Shows self-control
4. Works independently
5. Responsible, dependable
6. Participates in group activity

IV. *Cognitive Growth*
1. Matches pictures
2. Classifies objects
3. Counts
4. Recognizes shapes, sizes, and colors
5. Identifies similarities and differences
6. Retains information
7. Recognizes rhyming words
8. Comprehends logically

V. *Physical Growth*
1. Good health
2. Vision
3. Hearing

FIGURE 5–4   Examples of Informal Readiness Tests

Shape Discrimination
Direct the child to mark the shape that is not the same as the other shapes in each row.

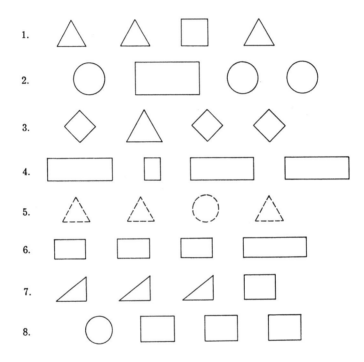

tives, Keogh views favorably the use of teacher-rating scales and any of the informal task-related tests that we have described. Similarly, another model proposed by Feshback, Adelman, & Fuller (1974) places considerable emphasis not only on the teacher's evaluation but also on the discrepancy between a child's competencies and those required for success in first-grade classrooms to which a child is assigned.

Early childhood assessment programs should not operate within a vacuum, but instead should be viewed as a means of furthering individual growth and development (Keogh, 1970). A major problem with many screening programs is that the identification merely serves as a label for the child. Identification programs not tied to teaching programs and procedures must be considered both unrealistic and unwarranted. A close relationship should exist between diagnostic procedures and educational programs. We do a considerable disservice to children if screening programs are not followed by well-conceptualized intervention programs (Frankenburg, 1973).

FIGURE 5–4   *Continued*

Verbal Fluency

Give the child an object to feel that cannot be seen (e.g., placed in a paper bag), and then ask the child to describe the object.

Examples of Objects:

ball, spoon, pencil, sandpaper, salt, rock

Examples of Examiner Questions:

How does it feel?
How small is it?
Name some things you can do with it.
What is it made of?
Describe how it tastes or smells.
Why is it necessary to have it?

Quantity Discrimination

Direct the child to mark the box with the greatest number of objects.

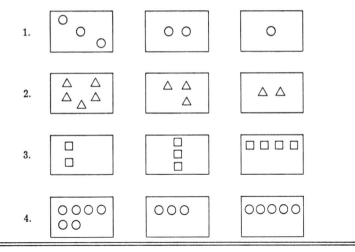

The measurement of a range of behaviors is both necessary and recommended. A knowledge of the educational tasks the child is required to perform in school, along with a task analysis of learning problems and the situational variables in different schools, must be considered an important part of the evaluation process (Wallace & McLoughlin, 1975).

A considerable amount of available evidence suggests that *careful* early childhood assessment is effective in identifying many children who are high risk. The number of alternatives for measuring readiness behaviors that we have presented in this chapter should be closely examined in order to match each child to the most appropriate technique. Once the teacher accomplishes this, it is likely that the teacher will be able to form effective intervention strategies.

Suggested Activities

5–1.   Mary Beth is an active, healthy 5-year-old girl. She presently is attending a private, all-day kindergarten, in which she is experiencing some difficulty in readiness activities. Her poor, fine-motor co-ordination prevents her from adequately completing many cutting, coloring, and pasting tasks. In addition, she cannot distinguish various geometric shapes, nor can she count accurately above 5. During observation periods in the classroom, Mary Beth appears to be outgoing and eager to participate even when she experiences difficulty with a task. She seems to play well with other children, though her verbal interactions with them are minimal. Mary Beth's speech and language are immature in both quality and quantity, and she often speaks in sentences of two or three words.

Outline an assessment plan for Mary Beth. Include both formal and informal measures in your evaluative procedures, and discuss the type of data you expect to gather from them.

5–2.   Mrs. Taylor, the resource teacher at the El Rancho Elementary School, has been asked to design a screening tool for identifying young children with high-risk behaviors. The faculty at El Rancho specifically has requested a checklist questionnaire that could be completed by parents when they register their children for kindergarten.

Organize the checklist, and discuss the criteria you will use to select children requiring further evaluation.

5–3.   Choose one skill from the taxonomy of goals for preschool and kindergarten children listed in Table 5–1 (e.g., auditory memory) and design an informal test to measure that particular skill in young children. Evaluate the effectiveness of the test after administering it to a child.

5–4.   Construct a teacher-rating scale that can be used by first-grade teachers as a first-level screening for identification of children with learning problems. Be sure that the rating scale is concise and that you can administer it easily. Also, include the range of behaviors that usually are noted in observing children with potential learning difficulties.

5–5.   Examine specimen copies of several formal early childhood measures discussed in this chapter. Review the readiness skills measured by each test and indicate the type of child for whom the test is best suited. Consult Buros' *Mental Measurement Yearbook* and the test manual in regard to research studies that have used the test and for each test's predictive validity. Discuss the strengths and weaknesses of each test.

5-6.   Administer one of the tests in Figure 5-4 to a child who may have learning problems. Examine the results in terms of implications for further formal or informal assessment. List the specific remedial teaching tasks that you can use to help the child.

5-7.   During informal observations of 5-year-old Brad, Mrs. Wilson has noticed that Brad encounters difficulty in rhyming words and in discriminating differences among various initial consonant sounds. Brad also has problems in following directions and with any activity that involves auditory sequencing.

Outline a thorough assessment program for Brad and discuss the information you desire to gather from this evaluation plan.

5-8.   Many professionals have recognized the importance of assessing various social-emotional variables in the early identification of children with learning problems. However, in practice, very few social-emotional factors actually are incorporated into available early childhood screening instruments. Construct an observational checklist that can be used by an elementary school teacher to appraise these skills and discuss various remedial techniques for children exhibiting social-emotional problems.

5-9.   Edward's first-grade teacher, Mrs. Logan, has observed that Edward usually experiences severe problems in most writing and drawing activities. He often tightly clutches the pencil, resulting in letters that are either too small or too large. He encounters many difficulties while attempting to print on a line, and his letters are often incorrectly slanted. Edward cannot color within the lines of a drawing, nor can he duplicate a peg design. Mrs. Logan recently has noticed that Edward's writing improves when he is given the opportunity to trace the letters and words before writing them.

Outline additional appraisal techniques that might be necessary and list the remedial teaching procedures that will enable Edward to overcome his particular difficulty.

5-10. Five-year-old Victor was referred for evaluation because of his almost total lack of verbal communication in the kindergarten classroom. Formal and informal testing and classroom observations indicate that Victor has normal hearing and that he understands information verbally presented in class. Although he does not experience difficulties with articulating, Victor encounters problems in expressing various concepts verbally. His communication in the classroom usually involves one- or two-word replies, or responses of printing and gesturing.

Outline a teaching program for Victor, along with additional evaluative information that you might be able to gather during diagnostic teaching periods. List both long- and short-term teaching goals.

References

Ahr, A. E. *Parent readiness evaluation of preschoolers.* Skokie, Ill.: Priority Innovations, 1968.

Anderson, S. B., Bogatz, G. A., Draper, T. W., Jungleblut, A., Sidwell, G., Ward, W. C., & Yates, A. *CIRCUS.* Princeton, N.J: Educational Testing Service, 1974.

Barker, E. Early identification and intervention of learning disabilities. Unpublished manuscript, University of Virginia, 1974.

Beers, C. Early identification of learning disabled children. Unpublished manuscript, University of Virginia, 1974.

Bender, L. *A visual-motor gestalt test and its clinical use.* New York: American Orthopsychiatric Association, 1938.

Boehm, A. E. *Boehm test of basic concepts.* New York: Psychological Corporation, 1971.

Bruner, J. The act of discovery. *Harvard Educational Review,* 1961, *31,* 31–32.

Bryan, T., & McGrady, H. Use of a teacher rating scale. *Journal of Learning Disabilities,* 1972, *5,* 199–206.

Caldwell, B. M. *Cooperative preschool inventory.* Princeton, N.J: Educational Testing Service, 1970.

Caldwell, B. M. The rationale for early intervention. *Exceptional Children,* 1970, *36,* 717–727.

Cogwill, M., Friedland, S., & Shapiro, R. Predicting learning disabilities from kindergarten reports. *Journal of Learning Disabilities,* 1973, *6,* 577–582.

deHirsch, K., Jansky, J. J., & Langford, W. S. *Predicting reading failure.* New York: Harper & Row, 1966.

Della-Piana, G. M. *Reading diagnosis and prescription: An introduction.* New York: Holt, Rinehart and Winston, 1968.

Doll, E. A. *Preschool attainment record.* Circle Pines, Minn.: American Guidance Service, 1967.

Elkind, D. Preschool education: Enrichment or instruction? *Childhood Education,* 1969, *46,* 321–328.

Ferinden, W. E., & Jacobsen, S. Early identification of learning disabilities. *Journal of Learning Disabilities,* 1970, *3,* 589–593.

Feshbach, S., Adelman, H., & Fuller, W. W. Early identification of children with high risk of reading failure. *Journal of Learning Disabilities,* 1974, *7,* 639–644.

Frankenburg, W. Increasing the lead time for the preschool age handicapped child. In M. Karnes (Ed.), *Not all little wagons are red.* Arlington, Va.: Council for Exceptional Children, 1973.

Frankenburg, W. K., & Dodds, J. B. *Denver developmental screening test.* Denver, Colo.: LADOCA Project and Publishing Foundation, 1970.

Frankenburg, W. K., & Dodds, J. B. The Denver developmental screening test. *Journal of Pediatrics,* 1967, *71,* 181–191.

Haeussermann, E. *Developmental potential of preschool children.* New York: Grune & Stratton, 1958.

Hainsworth, P. K., & Siqueland, M. L. *Early identification of children with learning disabilities: The Meeting Street School screening test.* Providence, R.I.: Crippled Children and Adults of Rhode Island, 1969.

Haring, N., & Ridgeway, R. Early identification of children with learning disabilities. *Exceptional Children,* 1967, *33,* 387–395.

Ilg, F. L., & Ames, L. B. *School readiness: Behavior tests used at the Gesell Institute.* New York: Harper & Row, 1964.

Jansky, J., & deHirsch, K. *Preventing reading failure.* New York: Harper & Row, 1972.

Jastak, J. F., & Jastak, S. R. *The wide range achievement test.* Wilmington, Del.: Guidance Associates, 1965.

Jedrysek, E., Klapper, Z., Pope, L., & Wortis, J. *Psychoeducational evaluation of the preschool child.* New York: Grune & Stratton, 1972.

Jordan, F. L., & Massey, J. *School readiness survey.* (2nd ed.) Palo Alto, Calif.: Consulting Psychologists Press, 1969.

Karlin, R. *Teaching elementary reading: Principles and strategies.* New York: Harcourt, Brace Jovanovich, 1971.

Keogh, B. K. The Bender Gestalt as a predictive and diagnostic test of reading performance. *Journal of Consulting Psychology,* 1965, *29,* 83–84.

Keogh, B. K. Introduction and overview. *Journal of Special Education,* 1970, *4,* 309–311.

Keogh, B. K. Psychological evaluation of exceptional children: Old hangups and new directions. *Journal of School Psychology,* 1972, *10,* 141–146.

Keogh, B. K., & Becker, L. D. Early detection of learning problems: Questions, cautions, and guidelines. *Exceptional Children,* 1973, *40,* 5–11.

Keogh, B. K., & Smith, C. Visuo-motor ability for school prediction: A seven year study. *Perceptual and Motor Skills,* 1967, *25,* 101–110.

Keogh, B. K., & Smith, C. Early identification of educationally high potential and high-risk children. *Journal of School Psychology,* 1970, *8,* 285–290.

Keogh, B. K., Tchir, C., & Winderguth-Behn, A. Teachers' perceptions of educationally high-risk children. *Journal of Learning Disabilities,* 1974, *7,* 367–374.

Kirk, S. A. *Early education of the mentally retarded.* Urbana, Ill.: University of Illinois Press, 1958.

Landsman, M., & Dillard, H. *Evanston early identification scale.* Chicago: Follett, 1967.

Leydorf, M. Physical-motor factors. In B. K. Keogh (Ed.), *Early identifica-*

tion of children with potential learning problems. *Journal of Special Education*, 1970, *4*, 313–320.

Mann, L. Review of the Valett developmental survey of basic learning abilities. In O. K. Buros (Ed.), *The seventh mental measurement yearbook*. Highland Park, N.J.: Gryphon, 1971.

Mann, M., Anfin, C., & Musey, H. *Child development center curriculum: Child program for the early childhood special education teacher preparation program*. Charlottesville, Va.: School of Education, University of Virginia, 1974.

Monroe, M. *Children who cannot read*. Chicago: University of Chicago Press, 1932.

Myers, P. I., & Hammill, D. D. *Methods for learning disorders*. (2nd ed.) New York: John Wiley, 1976.

Myklebust, H. R. *The pupil rating scale: Screening for learning disabilities*. New York: Grune & Stratton, 1971.

Myklebust, H., & Boshe, B. *Final report: Minimal brain damage in children*. U.S. Public Health Service Contract 108–65–142. Evanston, Ill.: Northwestern University Publications, 1969.

Norfleet, M. The Bender Gestalt as a group screening instrument for first grade reading potential. *Journal of Learning Disabilities*, 1973, *6*, 383–388.

Novack, H. S., Bonaventura, E., & Merenda, P. F. *Manual to accompany Rhode Island pupil identification scale*. Providence, R.I.: Authors, 1972.

Novack, H. S., Bonaventura, E., & Merenda, P. F. A scale for early detection of children with learning problems. *Exceptional Children*, 1973, *40*, 98–105.

Osgood, C. E. *Contemporary approaches to cognition*. Cambridge, Mass.: Harvard University Press, 1957.

Pate, J. E., & Webb, W. W. *First grade screening test*. Circle Pines, Minn.: American Guidance Service, 1969.

Payne, J. S., Kauffman, J. M., Brown, G. B., & DeMott, R. M. *Exceptional children in focus: Incidents, concepts, and issues in special education*. Columbus, Ohio: Charles E. Merrill, 1974.

Payne, J. S., Mercer, C. D., & Epstein, M. H. *Education and rehabilitation techniques*. New York: Behavioral Publications, 1974.

Petersen, W. *A program for the early identification of learning disabilities*. Seattle: Special Child Publications, 1970.

Piaget, J. *The origins of intelligence in children*. New York: International Universities Press, 1952.

Rochford, T. Identification of preschool children with potential learning problems. In R. Reger (Ed.), *Preschool programming of children with disabilities*. Springfield, Ill.: Charles C. Thomas, 1970.

Skeels, H. M. Adult status of children with contrasting early life experience.

Monographs of the Society for Research in Child Development, 1966, 31 (3), 1-65.

Skeels, H. M., & Dye, H. B. A study of the effects of differential stimulation on mentally retarded children. Convention Proceedings, American Association on Mental Deficiency, 1939, 44, 114-136.

Slingerland, B. H. Pre-reading screening procedures. Cambridge, Mass.: Educators Publishing Service, 1969.

Telegdy, G. A. The relationship between socioeconomic status and school readiness. Psychology in the Schools, 1974, 11, 351-356.

Valett, R. E. Valett developmental survey of basic learning abilities. Palo Alto, Calif.: Consulting Psychologists Press, 1966.

Wallace, G., & McLoughlin, J. A. Learning disabilities: Concepts and characteristics. Columbus, Ohio: Charles E. Merrill, 1975.

6

Perceptual Assessment

Many professionals consider the development of perceptual abilities in children an essential prerequisite to academic achievement. This belief has become so widespread in schools that batteries of "perceptual" tests are administered routinely to students evidencing scholastic failure. If it is determined that the children suffer from a form of perceptual dysfunction, they may be placed in programs designed to remedy the disorder. Members of the perceptual school believe that, once the perceptual problem has been corrected or circumvented, it is then possible for the student to learn in an efficient manner. Inversely, they believe that, if the hypothesized disorder is not remedied, the diagnosed academic failure will continue.

Although perceptual theories have received much attention in schools, it is important to note that serious questions have arisen regarding their use. In general, criticisms have centered around the inability of their proponents actually to delineate what constitutes "perception" or a "perceptual disorder." In addition, perceptually oriented tests and training programs have not facilitated academic achievement. At best, perceptual assessment should be considered experimental, with little empirical support of its usefulness in schools. Consequently, we do not recommend the use of these techniques except for research. The reason for devoting a chapter to perceptual methodology is that it is used widely in schools. Teachers must be aware of the basic premises of this approach so that they can formulate their own positions regarding the efficacy of perceptual practices and can evaluate its effectiveness when applied to children in their own classrooms.

The purpose of this chapter is to acquaint teachers with (1) the concepts of perceptual assessment, (2) standardized and informal perceptual assessment procedures commonly employed with underachieving children, and (3) a summary of research regarding the relationship of perception to academic achievement.

PERCEPTUAL DISORDERS
IN CHILDREN

One of the most popular beliefs regarding children who experience difficulty in school is that their academic failure is due to underlying perceptual disorders. The effect of these perceptual disorders is that various sensory information gleaned from the environment is not conveyed to the brain in a consistent and integrated manner. Children who are thought to suffer from deficiencies in perceptual development frequently are described as "not seeing" or "not hearing" the same as other children or as lacking in such skills as "laterality," "directionality," "visual closure," "ocular pursuit," and "temporal-spatial relations." So widespread is the belief that perceptual efficiency underlies successful learning that many school systems routinely assess all incoming 5- and 6-year-old children for deficiencies in perceptual development. As an outgrowth of these screening activities, schools have established classes for students of all ages who have been judged "perceptually handicapped."

Although many educators and psychologists espouse a perceptual basis for school failure, other professionals have seriously questioned the relevancy of this position. The primary reason for dissatisfaction with the use of perceptual diagnosis and training activities is that there is little research evidence to support the contention that a relationship exists between perceptual functioning and academic achievement. In addition, most of the activities designed to remedy perceptual disorders do not appear to address themselves to the particular curricular skill deficiency of the student (i.e., reading, spelling, arithmetic, etc.) and may, in fact, detract from teaching efforts to attack *directly* the observed deficiency. To illustrate the point that remedial efforts that are undertaken should focus upon school-related tasks rather than upon perceptual skills presumed to be *prerequisites* to academic proficiency, Karlin (1971) states,

> It seems that the ability to discriminate among letter and word forms has a greater influence upon the ability to recognize words than the ability to see differences and similarities among nonverbal forms. If children are weak in recognizing letters, it would seem appropriate to provide training in letter forms; if they are weak in discriminating between words, then training with words ought to be provided. Experiences directly related to tasks children are expected to perform should be more productive than experiences which might have some tangential relation to the task [p. 81].

181

It is axiomatic that much controversy exists as to whether perceptual diagnosis and remedies should be incorporated as an integral part of the school curriculum. Before teachers make a decision regarding the usefulness of these techniques, they need to acquire insight into what actually is thought to constitute the *perceptual process,* as well as into what the characteristics are of children who come to be labeled "perceptually handicapped." This information is an essential first step in determining the ultimate usefulness of current perceptual theory and practices.

The Perceptual Process

The process of *perception* relates to a person's ability to extract relevant sensory data from the environment and relay it in a consistent and integrated fashion to the higher levels of the central nervous system (i.e., brain). In order to accomplish this task, the person must possess (1) sensory organs that are receptive to stimulation, (2) peripheral nerve tracts that are capable of accurately transmitting the sensory information received by the eyes, ears, taste buds, etc., to higher neurological levels, and (3) a brain that permits the integration of these sensory data. If the perceptual processes are functioning appropriately, the person is able to "make sense" out of the environment and, by relying upon past experience, continually to increase learning efficiency. For example, a 2-week-old infant probably is unable to distinguish between the auditory stimuli of a dog barking, a hand clapping, and a mouth whistling if all are produced at the same level of intensity. However, as the infant matures and gains in experience, the infant eventually will be able to make fine discriminations, such as between the sounds /b/ and /p/, fine gradations in color, and minute variations in cutaneous stimulation. Consequently, it is possible to assume that with adequate perceptual functioning a person is able to imbue stimuli with such properties as form, size, texture, color, intensity, pitch, timbre, etc. According to advocates of perceptual theory, the ability to "perceive" these attributes is essential in varying degrees to cognitive development as well as to all later academic achievement.

Although the preceding discussion may be helpful in gaining knowledge of the physical operation of perceptual processes, it does little to provide a clear and concise definition of what actually constitutes perception. It is indeed surprising that after years of concentrated research in this area, there is still no general agreement on a definition of *perception.* Differing theorists have conceptualized perception as being comprised of psychological characteristics ranging from mere sensation to the highest level of cognitive functioning. Obviously, this lack of agreement on terminology and definition hampers the uninitiated reader from forming a clear perspective of what actually constitutes perception. Hammill (1975) makes an astute

182

observation in a discussion of the different theories regarding perception. He states,

> To some theorists, the entire receptive process is called "perception." To others, a distinction is made between sensation," i.e., the passive reaction of the receptor cell (a reaction not involving memory), and "perception," i.e., the remainder of the process. Others write only of "sensation" and "cognition" and perception is subsumed under "cognition." Still other theorists distinguish between "sensation," "perception," and "cognition." The processes that involve thinking, meaningful language, or problem solving are assigned to "cognition," while those dealing with the nonsymbolic, nonabstract properties of the stimuli, e.g., size, color, shape, texture, or sequence, are relegated to "perception" [p. 204].

In light of the ambiguity that exists regarding the characteristics of perception, we have accepted the position of Strauss and Lehtenen (1947), who were early pioneers in the development of perceptual theory as currently employed in schools. To these investigators perception is a discrete mental function that lies between sensation (i.e., nervous activity of the sense organs) and thought (i.e., the highest form of symbolic activity). The primary function of the perceptual process is to give "meaning and significance to a given sensation and therefore acts as a *preliminary* to thinking (Strauss & Lehtinen, 1947, p. 28)." According to this theory of perception, the person organizes, mediates, integrates, and interprets the sensory stimuli that constantly impinge upon him or her. However, it is important to note that this information, in and of itself, is not essentially meaningful; it merely provides the "raw material" necessary for higher-level cognitive functioning. Wepman (1967) also espouses this view and comments that the perceptual levels of learning ". . . underlie the conceptual level and provide the basic precepts upon which concepts are built, and they must be understood and clarified before the conceptual level is focused upon (p. 353)."

This view of the role of perception in learning is, by far, the one most frequently used in psychometric tests measuring perceptual adequacy in children. These tests are comprised of items that are geared to tap a child's responses to nonmeaningful stimuli (e.g., matching geometric forms, recalling strings of digits, differentiating between nonsense shapes and sounds). Advocates of this approach reason that, if academic failure is exhibited, measurement of these "lower level" (i.e., perceptual) skills will frequently provide insight into *how the child learns.* This information is considered basic to understanding, evaluating, and remedying the core of the school-related problem. Evidence from research regarding the efficacy of this theory when applied to academic failure will be discussed later in this chapter.

Perceptual Disorders

Perceptual disorders are considered by many to be one of the primary problems confronting underachieving children. Deficiencies in perceptual functioning may be derived from any source that interferes with the effective use of sensory stimulation. The cause most commonly mentioned is the dysfunction of the central nervous system (Wepman, 1967; Zigmond & Cicci, 1968; Kephart, 1960; and Frostig, 1975). To these writers all learning is, basically, a neuropsychological manifestation, and the mechanism of learning is accomplished through activity of sophisticated neurological functioning. If the central nervous system is faulty, the child's perceptual ability will be impaired. Eisenson (1966), in discussing perceptual deficiencies in children as a result of dysfunction of the central nervous system, states that four essential perceptual processes frequently are impaired. These include:

> ... (1) the capacity to receive stimuli that are produced in sequential order; (2) the capacity to hold the stimuli in mind, to hold the sequential impression so that its components may be integrated into some pattern; (3) the capacity to scan the pattern from within so that it may be compared with other impressions or other remembered patterns; and (4) the capacity to respond differentially, meaningfully to the perceptual impression [p. 25].

Although not all children who evidence perceptual disabilities are brain damaged, the disabilities when present will greatly increase the probability of such dysfunctions (Wepman, 1975).

Other conditions that have been mentioned as causing perceptual disorders include mental retardation, defects in sensory acuity, gross motor problems, emotional disturbance, and lack of eye and hand dominance (Lerner, 1976; Wold, Kane, & Koetting, 1969). In addition, Kephart (1960) has posited that many children exhibit perceptual disorders because they are not offered enough opportunities to experiment with objects at a concrete level. The reason for this dilemma is that our increased technology has become too complex for some children to understand and manipulate concrete objects at early stages of learning. If increased cognitive demands are placed on children with no accompanying increase in the practice of elementary auditory, visual, and motor skills, perceptual disorders may be evidenced by many children entering school. These children, according to some perceptual theorists, are likely to become slow learners.

The psychological characteristics of students who are suffering from perceptual disorders are reported in the literature. As with the definition(s) of perception, these characteristics tend to be vague and do little in the way of providing teachers with relevant information regarding the child's demonstrated school failure, that is, underachievement. Cruickshank (1975) has commented that most descriptions of perceptual disorders focus on *what it is not.* It is his contention that, in order to fully appreciate the complexity of perceptual disorders, professionals must become more concerned with *what it is.* Cruickshank has listed the findings of a committee that studied perceptual "mal-development." The major characteristics of perceptual disorders include an inadequate ability to

> ... (1) recognize fine differences between auditory and visual discriminating features underlying the sounds used in speech and the orthographic forms used in reading; (2) retain and recall those discriminated sounds and forms in both long and short term memory; (3) order them sequentially both in sensory and motor acts; (4) distinguish figure-ground relationships; (5) recognize spatial and temporal orientations; (6) obtain closure; (7) integrate sensory information; (8) relate what is perceived to specific motor functions [p. 73].

Other professionals also have delineated the symptoms indicative of perceptual disorders. Bush and Waugh (1976) state that it is necessary that the teacher be aware of motor-movement patterns as precursors to normal perceptual disorders. Bush and Waugh (1976) state that it is necessary that development include

1. poor visual-motor coordination
2. poor body balance while walking forward, backward, or sideways
3. lack of skill in jumping and skipping
4. difficulty in perceiving self in time and space
   a. will not be able to tell time at the appropriate growth period
   b. will not know readily the parts of the body
   c. will be clumsy in relation to other children
   d. will not readily respond to directions of right and left—a laterality problem.
5. difficulty in making normal rhythmical movements in writing and may tend to increase or decrease the size, shape, color, or brightness
6. uneven or jerky ocular movement
7. trouble with object constancy—with size, shape, color, or brightness
   a. letters may become reversed—*d* becomes *b*, for example
   b. difficulty in establishing consistent responses; that is, may know how to spell or read a word one day but not on the next [Bush & Waugh, 1976, p. 312].

In describing the characteristics of children exhibiting perceptual disorders, theorists espousing a perceptual orientation rely heavily upon the use of psychological constructs to interpret the cause of disorders. For example, if a student has difficulty in mastering basic sound-symbol relationships during the beginning stages of reading, a professional with a perceptual orientation may diagnose the problem by stating that the disorder stems from an inability to integrate auditory and visual stimuli, primarily as they relate to the ability to discriminate. To these professionals, the constructs of integration and auditory and visual discrimination are psychological functions representative of physiological brain activity. These and other perceptual constructs are (1) *inferred* from the student's activity (i.e., test score), (2) not directly observable, (3) open to wide interpretation, and (4) have a questionable empirical relationship to actual academic performance. For this reason, teachers should be extremely cautious when presented with psychological theories used by professionals in the school to explain *why* their students are failing to achieve academically. Teachers should endeavor to derive (1) explicit definitions for each theory used, (2) the method used in determining that the student is experiencing trouble in this area, and (3) the educational or instructional usefulness of the diagnosis. In other words, teachers have an obligation to insure that the diagnostic and remedial procedures employed with their students will relate to the area in which the child is experiencing failure. If teachers are in doubt about the meaning or relevance of the perceptual characteristics applied to children in their classrooms, they are advised to conduct their own assessment of the deficiency or to attempt to increase their own knowledge and understanding of perceptual theory. Hallahan and Cruickshank (1973) present a thorough discussion regarding the historical perspectives of the perceptual-motor theory and the efficacy of commonly used perceptual-motor assessment devices and training programs.

PERCEPTUAL MODALITIES

One of the cornerstones of perceptual theory revolves around the concept that certain modalities (i.e., pathways of learning) must be functioning before successful learning can occur. According to this theory, a modality refers to a discrete neural pathway through which perceptual information information is transmitted to the cerebral cortex, it is used as the basis for information is transmitted to the cerebral cortex, it is used as the basis for complex symbolic behavior. Although many receptive systems operate within human beings, the modalities of primary importance for educational purposes include auditory, visual, and motor (tactile-kinesthetic) (Reger, Schroeder, & Uschold, 1968). Perceptual theorists believe that children develop *different* abilities to learn by eye, ear, or motor movement (i.e., a preferential modality). Consequently, educators must determine the child's *type of learning*, or the modality, for learning prior to selecting teaching strategies for various curricular areas (Wepman, 1967). For this reason, most of the assessment devices available to measure perceptual skills are geared to determining the adequacy of the auditory, visual, and tactile-kinesthetic modalities. The remainder of this section will provide an introduction to each of these perceptual modalities.

Auditory Modality

The effective functioning of the *auditory modality* (pathway) for learning depends upon many factors. The first of these factors involves a peripheral system capable of transmitting auditory stimuli to the brain. The mechanisms that are responsible for this task include the external, middle, and inner ear (which receives sound waves and processes them for transmission to the brain), as well as the VIII cranial nerve (Zigmond & Cicci, 1968). Once the auditory stimuli pass through the three parts of the ear, the VIII cranial nerve (or *auditory nerve*) transforms the stimuli into electrochemical impulses that are sent, by an indirect route, to the cerebral cortex for interpretation. If any of these operations do not perform adequately, the child is unable to make maximum use of auditory data. In these situations the child may be diagnosed as "perceptually deficient," or "perceptually handicapped" (Wepman, 1975).

The psychological interpretations of specific auditory perceptual skills vary widely among authors (Wallace & McLoughlin, 1975). Myklebust (1954) defines auditory perception as the ability to select pertinent sounds from the environment. This definition, although vague, is typical of most definitions offered by perceptual theorists. The means by which an individual uses selected sounds from the environment is through the operation of many discrete psychological skills that mediate a given auditory signal. Flower (1968), Chalfant and Scheffelin (1969), and Messing (1968) discuss lists of these skills. A composite list of important auditory perceptual skills includes:

1. *auditory awareness*—determination if sounds are or are not present
2. *auditory discrimination*—ability to distinguish between and among such variables as intensity, pitch, phonemes, and words
3. *auditory memory*—recall of strings of digits, words and/or sentences
4. *auditory figure-ground*—selection of and attention to relevant auditory stimuli from diverse background noise
5. *auditory blending*—synthesis of component sounds into syllables or words

The development of these and other auditory perceptual skills depends, to a great extent, on the child's early exposure and teaching. Barsch (1967) feels that listening proficiency is mainly a function of the demands placed upon the auditory mechanism. The more verbal stimulants (and, consequently, auditory stimulants) there are in a child's environment, the more highly developed the auditory perceptual skills will be. According to Chaney and Kephart (1968), the degree to which these skills are present influences academic achievement, particularly in the area of the language arts.

187

Visual Modality

Historically, the visual pathway for learning has received considerably more professional attention than has the auditory pathway. Whereas the auditory signal is usually transitory and difficult to control experimentally, the *visual modality* tends to be permanent and more amenable to later analyses (Kidd & Kidd, 1966). In general, *visual modality* refers to the ability of the eye to form an image of an object and transmit that image to the visual centers of the brain. This process entails the passage of light rays from the object through the cornea, pupil, and lens on their way to the retina (the rear portion of the eyeball). When light hits the light-sensitive cells of the retina, it stimulates the optic nerve, which is responsible for carrying the resultant electrical impulses to the visual cortex for use in complex learning and behavior.

In discussing visual perception, theorists differentiate between *acuity* and *perception*. Getman and Hendrickson (1966) define *acuity* as the "result of all sensori-motor actions that take place in the end organ (the eye) that will provide for the clarity of the light pattern that strikes the retina (p. 156)." Visual perception, according to Goins (1958), is the phenomenon by which visual stimuli are "apprehended" by the mind through the medium of the eye. Apparently, the processing of visual stimuli involves a series of actions or steps that lead to successful learning. Chalfant and Scheffelin (1969) state that the individual first receives visual stimuli and then orients the eyes to the light source, scans the object, identifies and integrates the dominant cues, and formulates hypotheses regarding the object as it is perceived. The components of visual perception that permit these operations include

1. *visual discrimination*—ability to note differences and similarities among forms, letters, and words
2. *spatial relationships*—determination of the positions of objects in space
3. *visual-motor integration*—integration of perceived visual stimuli with movements of the body parts
4. *visual figure-ground*—ability to focus upon selected figures and to screen out irrelevant stimuli in the background
5. *visual memory*—recall of a sequence of several visually presented items or recollection of the primary features of one stimulus
6. *visual closure*—identification of a figure when only a few fragments are presented

The development of visual perceptual skills has been a source of interest to professionals in many fields of study. Gesell, Ilg, and Bullis (1949) stress the effects of movement in learning effective visual skills. One of the fundamental skills the child needs to develop is use of the body parts in relation to concrete objects. More specifically, the child's ability to experience the environment depends upon learning efficient motor movements by using the visual mechanism as a "steering" device. At its more sophisticated level, some professionals believe that visual perception affects the manner in which a child performs in the classroom, in particular, reading achievement (deHirsch, 1957).

Tactile-Kinesthetic Modality

The *tactile-kinesthetic, haptic,* or *motor-perception* modality refers to information acquired through the sense of touch and movement. This modality, in and of itself, is not considered to be of primary importance in learning (Wepman, 1967; Getman & Hendrickson, 1966). It is mentioned frequently, however, as an essential factor in the development of other, presumably more important, perceptual systems. Kephart (1960) and Barsch (1966) both indicate that basic motor patterns must be established *prior* to the effective use of perceptual information. According to them, the child must develop a variety of skills that include posture, maintenance of balance, eye-hand coordination, laterality, body awareness, locomotion, and ocular control as a means of exploring and understanding the environment. Because the tactile-kinesthetic modality (i.e., skills that comprise effective motor movement) is considered an essential ingredient of most perceptual activities, the literature is replete with such terms as "perceptual-motor," "visual-motor," etc. The use of these terms indicates that the teacher should consider the crucial element of motor functioning when conceptualizing any part of the perceptual process.

Chalfant and Scheffelin (1969) list two major types of information derived from the tactile-kinesthetic modality. The first involves the sense of *touch* (i.e., tactile). The information obtained via this system includes

1. geometric information concerning surface area of size, shape, and angles
2. surface texture
3. qualities of consistency such as hard, soft, resilient, or viscous
4. pain
5. temperature
6. pressure [p. 41]

The second relates to data accrued through body *movement* (i.e., kinesthetic), such as

1. dynamic movement patterns of the trunk, arms, legs, mandible, and tongue
2. static limb positions or postures
3. sensitivity to the direction of linear and rotary movement of the skull, limbs, and entire body [p. 41]

Whereas very few tests have been designed to measure exclusively tactile-kinesthetic proficiency, many tests of visual perception include items that purport to tap various *haptic skills* (i.e., the sense of touch without utilization of vision). These evaluative techniques will be discussed in the next section of this chapter.

ASSESSMENT OF PERCEPTUAL-MOTOR DISORDERS

The evaluation of perceptual-motor disorders in children usually is attempted to discern the underlying cause of an academic problem *or* to determine if a student is sufficiently ready to profit from formal teaching efforts. In addition, the measurement of perceptual abilities and their relation to learning has been the subject of recent attention by researchers. Regardless of the purposes for assessing perceptual functioning, it is evident that this type of psychological testing is a common practice in many schools. As with all aspects of diagnostic intervention, the teacher needs to direct attention toward the formulation of objectives regarding the specific information desired. Hammill (1975) feels that, when perception is studied in the schools, professionals must concern themselves with certain questions that, when answered, will yield information regarding a particular perceptual problem. These questions include the following:

1. Do I wish to assess perception, perceptual-motor integration or both?
2. Am I interested in a particular perceptual skill; e.g., discrimination, figure-ground, or closure, or in overall perceptual ability?
3. Is the measure appropriate for the prospective sample; i.e., are the children physically able to respond, and is the test too easy or too difficult?
4. Is the measure reliable enough to be used for educational purposes; i.e., as the basis for diagnosing the problem of an individual child, or for research purposes?
5. Is the information to be derived worth the time to administer the device? [pp. 206–207].

The answers to these questions may be supplied through the use of standardized or informal assessment tests. Standardized tests include those that provide normative data and that contain specific directions for administering them. Teachers construct informal tests for use in classroom situations. The purpose of this section is to discuss techniques that are commonly used and strategies appropriate for both standardized and informal assessment.

STANDARDIZED TESTS

A large number of standardized instruments have been produced that measure various perceptual abilities. In general, these tests focus upon the assessment of specific modalities, including the (1) visual, (2) auditory, and (3) motor. It is important to note that, although the theory of perception usually is thought of as being a receptive process, auditory and visual-perception tests frequently require relatively complex motor or vocal *responses* by the subject who is being evaluated. Such auditory and visual tasks as reproducing geometric shapes, tracing complicated figures, putting pieces of a puzzle together, and giving verbal descriptions of stimuli that are seen or heard can influence a test score significantly and give a distorted picture of perceptual skills. For this reason, the teacher should carefully scrutinize each perceptual assessment test to be used in order to ensure that the responses required are within the performance capabilities of the child. A list of commonly employed perceptual tests that assess the visual, auditory, and motor modalities is given in the next section.

Visual-Perception Tests

The measurement of visual perception abilities in children and in adults has received attention from educators and psychologists. Visual-perception development has been thought to be directly related to brain functioning. In some cases, "depressed" performance in this specific skill has been used in the diagnosis of cerebral dysfunction, epilepsy, and some forms of psychosis (Graham & Kendall 1960). In addition, visual perception frequently is thought to be a prime factor in the failure of children in school. As a result, measures of visual-perception ability are employed in standard test batteries that evaluate learning and behavior problems. Colarusso and Gill (1975–1976) have listed the criteria for consideration in selection of visual-perception assessment tests. These considerations include such variables as the degree of reliability and validity, response requirements, administration time, nature of scoring procedures, and appropriateness of normative data. Tables 6–1, 6–2, and 6–3 summarize visual-perception tests that are used frequently in the schools. Table 6–1 lists the mechanical elements of the measures, including age-ranges, number of subjects upon which norms are based, whether the test is administered to groups or individuals, and whether the test employs consumable materials. Table 6–2 provides the reliability of the tests with interpretations concerning the statistical acceptability of the reliabilities. Table 6–3 offers a description of the components of each test and the specific skill areas evaluated. Teachers may find the tables particularly helpful when they attempt to determine the adequacy

191

TABLE 6-1 Summary of Data on Selected Tests or Visual Perception

Title	Author	Number of Items	Administration Time in Minutes	Age Range	Norms	Group (G) or Individual (I)	Consumable Materials
Bender Visual-Motor Gestalt Test	Bender, L.	9	7–15	4–11	1104	I	No
Chicago Test of Visual Discrimination	Weiner, P. Wepman, J. Morency, A.	9	10–15	6–8	90	G, I	No
Developmental Test of Visual-Motor Integration	Beery, K. Buktenica, N.	24	10–15	2–15	1039	G, I	Yes
Developmental Test of Visual Perception	Frostig, M.	72	30–60	4–8	2116	G, I	Yes
Eye-Motor Coordination	Maslow, P.	16	15–20	4–8	2116	G, I	Yes
Figure-Ground	Lefever, D.	8	15–20	4–8	2116	G, I	Yes
Form Constancy	Whittlesey, J.	32	10	4–8	2116	G, I	Yes
Position in Space		8	5	4–8	2116	G, I	Yes
Spatial Relationships		8	5–10	4–8	2116	G, I	Yes
Illinois Test of Psycholinguistic Abilities	Kirk, S. McCarthy, J. Kirk, W.	40	8	2–10	1000	I	Yes
Visual Closure		25	15–20	2–10	1000	I	No
Visual Sequential Memory							
Memory-for-Designs Test	Graham, F. Kendall, B.	15	5–10	6–80	341	I	No
Metropolitan Readiness Tests	Hildreth, G. Griffiths, N. McGauvran, M.						
Matching		14	5–6	5–6	12231	G	Yes
Copying		14	7	5–6	12231	G	Yes

Test	Author						
Motor-Free Visual Perception Test	Colarusso, R. Hammill, D.	36	8–10	4–8	883	—	No
Perceptual Achievement Forms	Lowder, R.	7	10	6–8	1510	—	No
Primary Visual-Motor Test	Haworth, M.	16	10–15	4–8	500	—	No
Purdue Perceptual-Motor Survey	Roach, E. Kephart, N.	22	60	6–18	200	—	No
Revised Visual Retention Test	Benton, A.	10	5	8–44	600	—	No
Slosson Drawing Coordination Test	Slosson, R.	12	10–15	5–adult	200	G, I	Yes
Wechsler Intelligence Scale for Children	Wechsler, D.						
Total Performance		177	50–60	5–15	2200	—	Yes
Picture Completion		20	10	5–15	2200	—	No
Block Design		7	15	5–15	2200	—	No
Object Assembly		7	12	5–15	2200	—	No
Coding		45 (A) 93 (B)	3 (under 8) 2 (over 8)	5–15	2200	—	Yes
Mazes		8	10	5–15	2200	—	Yes

Source: Colarusso, R. P., & Gill, S. Selecting a test of visual perception. *Academic Therapy*, 1975–1976 XI, 157–167. Reprinted by permission of Academic Therapy Publications, San Rafael, California.

193

TABLE 6–2   Reliabilities of Selected Tests of Visual Perception

Title	Test-Retest	Split-half	Kuder Richardson	Hoyt's	Inter-scorer
Bender Visual-Motor Gestalt Test	.60–.66	—	—	—	.88–.96
Chicago Test of Visual Discrimination	.35–.68	.69–.72	.78–.93	—	—
Developmental Test of Visual-Motor Integration	.80–.87*	—	—	—	.96
Developmental Test of Visual Perception	.69	.78–.89	—	—	—
Eye-Motor Coordination	.29–.39	.59–.60	—	—	—
Figure-Ground	.33–.39	.91–.96	—	—	—
Form Constancy	.67–.74	.67–.77	—	—	—
Position in Space	.60–.63	.35–.70	—	—	—**
Spatial Relationships	.52–.67	.65–.85	—	—	—**
Illinois Test of Psycholinguistic Abilities					
Visual Closure	.57–.82	—	—	.49–.71	—**
Visual Sequential Memory	.12–.71	—	—	.51–.96	—**
Memory-for-Designs Test	.72–.90	.92	—	—	.93
Metropolitan Readiness Tests					
Matching	—	.82–.86	—	—	—**
Copying	—	.79–.85	—	—	—
Motor-Free Visual Perception Test	.77–.82*	.81–.84	.71–.82	—	—**
Perceptual Achievement Forms	—	—	—	.64–.73	.58–.99
Primary Visual-Motor Test	.82	—	—	—	.82–.98
Purdue Perceptual-Motor Survey	.95	—	—	—	—
Revised Visual Retention Test	.85	—	—	—	.95
Slosson Drawing Coordination Test	.96	—	—	—	—
Wechsler Intelligence Scale for Children					
Total Performance	—	.86–.90	—	—	—**
Picture Completion	—	.59–.68	—	—	—**
Block Design	—	.84–.88	—	—	—**
Object Assembly	—	.63–.71	—	—	—**
Coding	—	.60	—	—	—**
Mazes	—	.75–.81	—	—	—**

*Acceptable test-retest reliability by age level.
**Test uses objective scoring procedure.
Source: Colarusso, R. P., & Gill, S. Selecting a test of visual perception. *Academic Therapy*, 1975–1976 XI, 157–167. Reprinted by permission of Academic Therapy Publications, San Rafael, California.

TABLE 6-3   Description of Components of Selected Tests of Visual Perception

Title	Motor Free	Response Required	Skill Area Tested
Bender Visual-Motor Gestalt Test	No	Copy geometric forms and patterns	Visual-motor integration
Chicago Test of Visual Discrimination	Yes	Match geometric forms	Visual memory; visual discrimination
Developmental Test of Visual-Motor Integration	No	Copy lines and forms	Visual-motor integration
Developmental Test of Visual Perception	No		Visual-motor integration; visual perception
Eye-Motor Coordination	No	Draw lines	Visual-motor integration
Figure-Ground	No	Outline figures	Figure-ground; visual-motor integration
Form Constancy	Yes	Outline figures	Form constancy
Position in Space	Yes	Mark matching item	Spatial relationships
Spatial Relationships	No	Draw line to sample	Spatial relationships; visual-motor integration
Illinois Test of Psycholinguistic Abilities			
Visual Closure	Yes	Mark partially hidden common objects	Visual closure
Visual Sequential Memory	Yes	Pattern reconstruction	Visual sequential memory
Memory-for-Designs Test	No	Copy geometric forms	Visual memory; visual-motor integration
Metropolitan Readiness Tests Matching	Yes	Mark matching geometric and letter-like items	Visual discrimination
Copying	No	Copy geometric and letter-like figures	Visual-motor integration
Motor-Free Visual Perception Test	Yes	Identify geometric and letter-like forms	Visual perception
Perceptual Achievement Forms	No	Copy geometric designs	Visual-motor integration; visual discrimination
Primary Visual-Motor Test	No	Copy designs	Visual-motor integration
Purdue Perceptual-Motor Survey	No	Copy forms and patterns; perform gross-motor tasks	Visual-motor integration
Revised Visual Retention Test	No	Copy geometric forms	Visual-motor integration
Slosson Drawing Coordination test	No	Copy geometric forms	Visual-motor integration
Wechsler Intelligence Scale for Children			
Picture Completion	Yes	Identify picture with missing parts	Visual closure
Block Design	No	Make block pattern	Visual discrimination
Object Assembly	No	Make whole from parts	Visual closure
Coding	No	Mark different shapes	Visual discrimination; visual-motor integration
Mazes	No	Trace a maze	Visual-motor integration

Source: Colarusso, R. P., & Gill, S. Selecting a test of visual perception. *Academic Therapy,* 1975–1976 XI, 157–167. Reprinted by permission of Academic Therapy Publications, San Rafael, California.

of various tests that may be applied routinely to students. Descriptions of representative visual-perception tests are given to acquaint teachers more fully with assessment tests in this area. Figure 6–1 presents examples of items that are found in various standardized visual-perception tests.

Memory-for-Designs Test

The Memory-for-Designs Test (Graham & Kendall, 1960) measures visual-perception ability, primarily as it relates to memory. The test is composed of 15 nonsense designs, which are shown to the subject in a graded sequence (5-second presentations). The test requires that the subject reproduce the design from memory. The examiner judges the responses subjectively on a scale from 0–3 by comparing them with sample drawings provided in the test manual. A raw score is obtained by adding the points obtained for all 15 drawings and then correcting it for age and intelligence and comparing it to the norm tables.

The norms for this test were derived from the scores of 825 carefully selected individuals including normal, brain-injured, psychotic, and idiopathic epileptic persons ranging in age from 8.5 to 60 years. Based upon the subjects used in this procedure of deriving norms, it is possible to interpret a subject's score as falling into *normal, borderline,* or *critical,* with respect to probable brain disorders. Apparently, no validity figures have been compiled for this device. Graham and Kendall recommend that a clinical or school psychologist, neurologist, pediatrician, or other person with comparable training in the area of brain disorders administer this test.

Bender Visual-Motor Gestalt Test

The *Bender Visual-Motor Gestalt Test* (BVMGT) (Bender, 1938) is similar in format to the *Memory-for-Designs Test.* The BVMGT is composed of nine geometric figures that the subject is required to draw from memory or reproduce while the stimulus is present. A number of forms have been developed for children from ages 4 through 11. Although this instrument is used primarily to measure visual-perception abilities, it also has been employed to evaluate social and emotional adjustment, intelligence, and brain damage. Administration of this test is relatively simple, but a trained clinical psychologist should both administer and interpret it. The reliabilities of this test (see Table 6–2) are quite low and should be carefully considered prior to use in educational settings. Readers interested in alternative scoring procedures for the BVMGT are encouraged to consult Koppitz (1964, 1968).

FIGURE 6–1 Examples of Visual-Perception Tasks

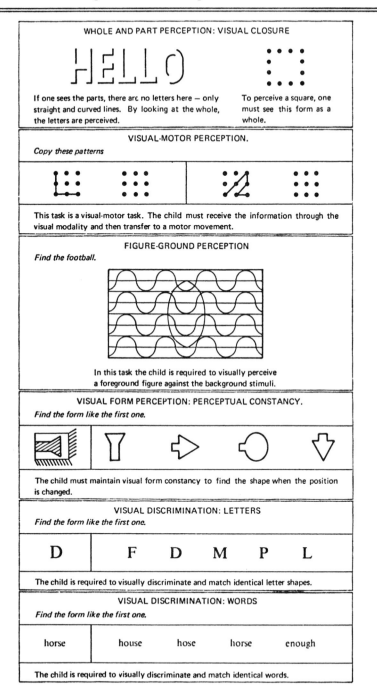

Developmental Test
of Visual-Motor Integration

The *Developmental Test of Visual-Motor Integration* (VMI) is a very popular technique for assessing visual-motor functioning in children and adolescents. Beery and Buktenica (1967) have developed a series of 24 geometric forms that the child should reproduce while the forms are still present. The forms presumably are sequenced in such a fashion as to detect transition of visual-perception skills from one stage of development to the next. Reportedly, the VMI is appropriate for children from 2 to 15 years of age; however, it is also used with children in preschool and in early primary grades. When used for screening purposes, the VMI may be administered in group settings. The manual accompanying the test provides detailed scoring criteria for judging the adequacy of a student's response. The VMI is different from most tests of visual perception because it appears to possess reliability coefficients of sufficient magnitude that it can be used with confidence.

Motor-Free Test of Visual Perception

The *Motor-Free Test of Visual Perception* (MVPT) (Colarusso & Hammill, 1972) is an example of a test that does not require complicated motor responses by the child. The 36 items included in the MVPT require matching a given stimulus with one of four alternatives and selecting the one of four alternatives that is different from the others. In all items the child indicates a response by pointing to the alternative chosen. The visual-perception constructs measured by this test include spatial relationships, visual discrimination, figure-ground, visual closure, and visual memory. This test was standardized on a sample of 881 children 4 through 8 years of age. Adequate reliability and validity statistics have been compiled that indicate the MVPT is essentially a well-constructed assessment test. The manual supplies specific directions for the teacher to administer and interpret the test. Interestingly, Colarusso and Hammill do not recommend that their device be used to understand the causes of academic underachievement. Rather, they state that

> ... this test is offered to those who wish to estimate visual perceptual ability in children. ... No claims are made regarding the relationship of the ability tapped to reading or any other school skills; actually our validity findings suggest that little commonality exists between the MVPT and measures of school achievement and intelligence [p. 21].

Obviously, this finding is important to educators and would undoubtedly be applicable to other tests of visual perception.

The Marianne Frostig
Developmental Test
of Visual Perception

The *Marianne Frostig Developmental Test of Visual Perception* (DTVP), developed by Frostig, Lefever, and Whittlesey (1964), measures five distinct perceptual skills: (1) eye-motor coordination; (2) figure-ground; (3) form constancy; (4) position in space; and (5) spatial relations. Each of these skills is represented in a separate subtest within this test. An examiner can administer this test to individuals and groups, but must have proper training before using it. Normative data are available for normal children between the ages of 4 and 8. The DTVP is best used as a screening device for nursery-school, kindergarten, and first-grade children and as a clinical device for older children who evidence signs of learning disabilities. The teacher also can use the results of this test as the basis for designing perceptual training programs to assist students in overcoming aspects of failure in school.

The DTVP is the most popular visual-perception test available and, consequently, is the most thoroughly researched. The two most important negative findings regarding this test are that (1) the individual subtests seem to lack sufficient reliability to be useful in school practice and (2) the DTVP measures, at most, only two distinct perceptual factors (Hammill, Goodman, & Wiederholt, 1971; Corah & Powell, 1963; Olson, 1968; Sprague, 1965; and Boyd & Randle, 1970). Even though available research strongly questions the usefulness of the DTVP to identify high-risk children, it is still routinely administered in many schools. Teachers should be aware of the shortcomings of this test (and all standardized tests) prior to using their findings in planning teaching programs. Readers wishing to find a detailed summary of research on the DTVP should refer to Hammill and Wiederholt (1972) and Mann (1972).

A number of additional tests designed to assess visual-perception abilities also have been produced. Although these tests are not used as widely as the ones mentioned above, teachers should be aware of their existence for future reference. These tests include the *Slosson Drawing Coordination Test* (Slosson, 1967); *The Primary Visual Motor Test* (Haworth, 1970); *Chicago Test of Visual Discrimination* (Weiner, Wepman, & Morency, 1965); and *Southern California Figure-Ground Visual Perception Test* (Ayers, 1966). Subtests also have been used to tap visual-perception ability. Some of these subtests include Matching and Copying from *The Metropolitan Readiness Tests* (Hildreth, Griffiths, & McGauvran, 1969); Visual Attention Span for Objects and Visual Attention Span for Letters from the *Detroit Tests of Learning Aptitude* (Baker & Leland, 1935); Visual Closure and Visual Sequential Memory from the *Illinois Test of Psycholinguistic Abilities* (Kirk, McCarthy, & Kirk, 1968); and Picture Arrangement, Block Design, Object Assembly, and Coding from the *Wechsler Intelligence Scale for Children* (Wechsler, 1974).

Auditory-Perception Tests

When reviewing tests of auditory perception, it becomes apparent immediately that little attention has been devoted to this skill when compared with visual perception. It seems logical to conclude that the reason for this lack of auditory-perception assessment tests stems from mechanical difficulties in designing reliable and valid test items. According to Hammill (1975), the auditory abilities most commonly assessed in schools are auditory discrimination and auditory-sequential memory. Auditory discrimination is evaluated by requiring a child to differentiate between pairs of words or nonsense syllables that have minimal differences (e.g., rat-pat or ōmā-ōtā). Auditory-sequential memory is assessed by asking the child to repeat strings of digits, nonsense syllables, or words. In addition to these tests, several recent tests that propose to assess auditory perception in a wider fashion have been developed. This section will provide descriptions of tests of auditory-perception abilities most frequently employed to assess disorders in this area.

The Goldman-Fristoe-Woodcock Test of Auditory Discrimination　The *Goldman-Fristoe-Woodcock Test* (Goldman, Fristoe, & Woodcock, 1970) is intended to assess speech-sound discrimination under conditions of quiet and noisy backgrounds. The two subtests are administered individually via tape recordings. The child's task is to view four separate pictures and to select the one that represents the word spoken. The words for each of the four pictures differ only slightly (e.g., goat, coat, boat, and throat). Obviously, a child's lack of familiarity with the objects in the pictures will affect significantly the overall test score. The test manual provides suggestions for determining a child's knowledge of the concepts involved in the examination procedure.

The *Goldman-Fristoe-Woodcock Test* was standardized on 745 subjects ranging from 3 to 84 years of age. Percentile norms are provided for 32 separate age levels extending from 3 years, 8 months to over 70 years. Although the reliabilities of the two subtests are acceptable (i.e., 0.81–0.87), validity is questionable. The reason for the questionable validity is that the authors make no attempt to correlate scores with other auditory-discrimination devices because, in their opinion, the other tests appear inadvertently to measure factors other than auditory discrimination. One suggested use of this test is screening of students who are suspected of suffering from serious auditory-perception disorders; however, the authors make no claim for the predictive usefulness of the test results.

Auditory Discrimination Test   The *Auditory Discrimination Test* (ADT) developed by Wepman (1958), is intended to identify students in the primary grades who are experiencing difficulties in auditory discrimination. The procedure for administering this test is quite simple. The student listens to the examiner say pairs of words and indicates whether the words are the same or different (e.g., dump-dumb; car-car). Performance on this task indicates a child's ability to use the auditory modality and provides a method of comparing progress over time. Regrettably, confident interpretation of ADT is difficult, because no description of the normative population is given in the manual. In addition, Blank (1968) has found that failure on this instrument occurs because frequently the child does not comprehend the concepts of *same* or *different*, not because the child has an auditory discrimination disorder. For these reasons, the results of ADT should be viewed with some caution and used only as an informal measure of auditory skills.

Screening Test for Auditory Perception   The *Screening Test for Auditory Perception* (STAP) is a group-administered test designed to "detect weaknesses rather than strengths in aural perception (Kimmell & Wahl, 1969, p. 3)." STAP contains five subtests, which measure the ability to perceive the difference between (1) long and short vowel sounds; (2) initial single-consonant sounds and blends; (3) rhyming and nonrhyming words; (4) retaining and identifying rhythmic sequences; and (5) words with only subtle phonemic differences. As with the *Auditory Discrimination Test,* the sample used to establish the norms is described inadequately, and no reliability or validity figures are provided in the test manual. Hammill (1975) states that, in view of these shortcomings, teachers' professional judgments probably are as accurate as this test.

Goldman-Fristoe-Woodcock Auditory Skills Test Battery   The *Goldman-Fristoe-Woodcock Auditory Skills Test Battery* (Goldman, Fristoe, & Woodcock 1976) provides a comprehensive, diagnostic, auditory-perception test battery for individuals from 3 years of age to adulthood. Four primary auditory skills are measured through 12 separate subtests. These skills include: (1) auditory selective attention—ability to listen in the presence of noise that is varied in type and intensity; (2) auditory discrimination—ability to discriminate between speech sounds; (3) auditory memory—ability to recall sequences of auditory stimuli and content from an orally presented story; and (4) sound-symbol—ability to mimic, recognize, analyze, blend, and associate (i.e., read and spell) various auditory and visual stimuli. This test relies heavily upon visual stimuli in its administration, which has the potential for seriously affecting any conclusions regarding a person's auditory-perception ability. More than 7,000 subjects were employed in the normative process. The normative group ranges from 9 to 18 years of age and were somewhat unreliable in their responses; however, the majority of reported reliability coefficients for other ages was generally acceptable (reaching a magnitude of at least 0.80). Estimates of content and construct validity are provided in the test manual.

A number of other standardized tests contain subtests that tap various auditory-perception abilities. Teachers should be familiar with these instruments since they are frequently included in test batteries that evaluate learning handicaps of underachieving children. *Auditory-sequential memory* (i.e., recalling in sequence what is heard) is a commonly assessed perceptual skill that is presumed to be directly related to school performance. The typical method of measuring this skill is to require the subject to repeat the order of items presented in a sequential order. Examples of auditory-sequential memory tasks include repeating the days of the week, a series of digits, and words in a sentence. Subtests that assess this skill include Auditory Sequential Memory from the *Illinois Test of Psycholinguistic Abilities* (Kirk, McCarthy, & Kirk, 1968); Oral Directions, Oral Commissions, and Auditory Attention Span from the *Detroit Tests of Learning Aptitude* (Baker & Leland, 1935); and Digit Span from the *Wechsler Intelligence Scale for Children* (Wechsler, 1974).

An additional auditory-perception skill of interest to school personnel is *auditory blending*. This ability historically has been linked to reading performance in children. The usual means of assessment is to ask the child to listen to components or parts of words (e.g., c-a-t) and then to say the complete word. While a significant relationship between auditory blending and academic achievement never has been demonstrated conclusively, many reading tests routinely include subtests to measure this ability (see Chapter 8). Other instruments that evaluate this skill include the *Roswell-Chall Auditory Blending Test* (Roswell & Chall, 1963) and the Sound Blending subtest of the *Illinois Test of Psycholinguistic Abilities* (Kirk, McCarthy, & Kirk, 1968).

Motor Tests

Relatively few tests of motor ability are available for use in the schools. When these skills are evaluated, they are assessed through the use of informal techniques. Rosner (1975) states that "testing general motor skills is simple . . . standardized tests are available but, in my opinion, these are not necessary (p. 92)." In some instances, however, it is necessary to measure formally a child's motor proficiency in order to obtain a score that is used primarily to justify placement of a child in special classes (Cratty, Ikeda, Martin, Jennett, & Morris, 1970). The standardized tests most commonly used for this purpose are discussed in the next sections.

The Oseretzky Tests   The Oseretzky tests employed in schools are derived from a device developed in Moscow's Psychoneurological Institute during the 1920's. Although the original purpose of these tests was to determine "motor idiocy" in Russian children and adults, subsequent revisions used in Europe and the United States are designed to provide a general estimate of gross and fine motor abilities. Readers interested in an historical perspective of the Oseretzky tests, as well as critical reviews of current forms of the instrument, are referred to Morris and Whiting (1971).

Although many forms of this test have been used with children, the most popular revision, *The Lincoln-Oseretzky Motor Development Scale* (Sloan, 1954), which consists of over 40 individual items, is appropriate for students between 6 and 14 years of age. Examples of the skills tapped include motor speed, balance, dynamic coordination, general coordination, synkinesia (i.e., overproduction of "associated movements"), and jumping. As would be expected, many of the skills assessed in this revision are similar and probably do not merit being listed as discrete subtests. Factor analytic studies conducted by Vandenberg (1964) have, in fact, demonstrated that there is great overlapping of the skills assessed in the Lincoln-Oseretzky Scale. In addition, very little information is provided regarding reliability or validity.

A more recent modification of the Oseretzky tests is the *Bruininks-Oseretzky Test of Motor Proficiency* (Bruininks, 1977). This test is an improvement over earlier versions, since more complete standardization data have been accumulated and the age ranges have been extended to include children from 4 to 18 years of age. The instrument must be individually administered and includes items that assess both fine and gross motor control. The specific subtests include (1) running speed and agility, (2) balance, (3) bilateral coordination, (4) strength, (5) upper-limb coordination, (6) response speed, (7) visual-motor control, and (8) upper-limb speed and dexterity. Test results are reported as age equivalents and percentile ranks, and are used to estimate a child's general motor ability and provide a basis for comparisons with the normative population on the individual subtests. A total of 892 subjects between 3 and 18 years of age were used in the standardization sample. Test-retest reliability for the subtests is generally below 0.80. Those teachers who use this test should take this into account, since this level of reliability is questionable (Gronlund, 1976). Validity figures indicate that the test does provide a fairly accurate estimate of developmental changes in motor development. This test also can differentiate successfully between achieving and underachieving students. Few data are offered to support this claim, however.

Cratty Perceptual-Motor Battery   The *Cratty Perceptual-Motor Battery* (Cratty, 1970), although it is not as well known as the Oseretzky tests, is frequently used to assess motor development in children. The subtests incorporated into this battery include (1) body perception, (2) gross agility (movement in a vertical plane), (3) balance (static posturing), (4) locomotor agility (movement in a horizontal plane), (5) tracking (catching), and (6) throwing (Cratty, 1975). *Averages,* instead of norms, have been computed for this measure. Scores are reported for children 4 to 10 years of age. Stanines also have been developed to aid interpretation of a child's performance. The individual subtests appear to be reliable; only one was found to be less than 0.80 (using the test-retest procedure). Cratty states that research findings, as yet unpublished, indicate that the test battery significantly discriminates between a group of normal children and a group of children clinically designated as neurologically impaired. It is interesting to note, however, that the two subtests within the gross agility category do not correlate highly and that there is some question regarding the levels of difficulty between the teaching and the catching measures (Cratty, 1975). Cratty feels that further refinements of the instrument are necessary before all subtests can be used with confidence.

Other tests are available to assess motor ability in children and adolescents. The *Frostig Movement Skills Test Battery* (Opert, 1967) is available commercially, but is significantly hampered by normative, reliability, and validity problems. The *Fleishman Motor Ability and Fitness Scales* (Fleishman, 1964) contains norms drawn from adolescents 12 to 18 years of age. These scales tap grip strength, throwing, running, pull-ups, broad-jumps, sit-ups, and general agility. Both the *Preschool Attainment Record* (Doll, 1966) and *The Denver Developmental Screening Test* (Frankenburg & Dodds, 1967) include subtests that assess gross-motor development in children under 6 years of age.

INFORMAL ASSESSMENT TECHNIQUES

The methods employed in the assessment of perceptual disorders can take many forms. When the teacher evaluates a child to place the child in a remedial class, a battery of standardized tests usually is administered to "justify" the placement. However, when a teacher has responsibility for planning a perceptual-based remedial program, it is almost certain that the teacher will need to conduct an informal evaluation in order to derive the specific information necessary to plan the program effectively. The informal assessment consists of devices constructed and administered by the teacher, which pinpoint particular deficiencies in the child's visual, auditory, or motor "pathways" of learning. The content of the informal assessment will vary from teacher to teacher, largely as a result of divergent opinions and theories regarding the particular skills that make up the perceptual modalities. For this reason it is essential that teachers, prior to initiating the informal evaluation, carefully consider their own philosophy regarding perceptual assessment and training. In addition, teachers should clearly delineate the *specific information desired* regarding the child's perceptual disorder before beginning the assessment process. If teachers do not attend to these points, the information collected will be of little use in planning the remedial program. The remainder of this section will discuss some informal assessment techniques that are employed for estimating gross proficiency in the visual, auditory, and motor "perception" modalities.

Informal Assessment of the Visual Modality

The single most important facet of the informal evaluation is the teacher's observations of a student while the student engages in various classroom activities. This is particularly true in cases in which teachers have not yet determined whether the exhibited problem is, in fact, "perceptual" in nature. Teachers will find that this phase of the evaluation is simplified when a checklist of behaviors is used to structure observations. The format and content of checklists undoubtedly will vary depending upon the perceived problem of the student and the needs of the teacher. It should be noted, however, that the time and effort required to devise specific checklists will be well spent if only information that is considered necessary in the planning of the remedial program is collected.

Figure 6–2 presents a sample checklist that is geared toward evaluating

FIGURE 6–2   Sample Checklist for Visual-Perception Skills

	Yes	No
1. Notices likenesses and differences	____	____
2. Discriminates between colors and knows names	____	____
3. Matches shapes and forms	____	____
4. Solves simple puzzles	____	____
5. Copies name, shapes, etc.	____	____
6. Reproduces a simple bead pattern from memory	____	____
7. Uses obvious visual cues in the environment	____	____
8. Mimics at least three visually presented acts in sequence	____	____
9. Drawing and coloring are equal to peers	____	____
10. Completes work when presented on a "crowded" paper	____	____
11. Works close to paper or desk	____	____

the adequacy of visual-perception modality. It is apparent that failure in any of these tasks does not necessarily mean that a child is suffering from a visual-perception disorder. Factors such as poor visual acuity, problems with motor control, unfamiliarity with school-related tasks, or simple disinterest can all cause a student to *appear* to have some type of visual-perception disorder. Obviously, a teacher must observe a child in numerous situations and conditions in order to verify that a perceptual problem does, in fact, exist. If a problem does exist, careful analysis of accumulated data will direct the teacher to *components* of the visual-perception process that need to be remedied. Some commonly assessed visual-perception skills are listed in the next few sections.

Ocular Motility To many educators advocating a perceptual orientation toward understanding of school problems, the visual skill of *ocular motility* is essential to efficient learning. *Ocular motility* refers to the control of and coordinated movement of the eyes. Students with problems in this area have difficulty following a moving object with equal binocular movements of the eyes. Spache and Spache (1969) state that when ocular-motility disorders are evidenced,

> ... the child does not receive exactly the same images from both eyes since they may not bear upon the same objects. These conflicting images are reflected in inaccurate perception and discrimination and if persistent or severe, lead to a tendency to suppress or ignore one of the images. ... Practically every thorough study of child vision indicates that these various difficulties in binocular coordination are highly significant in reading failure at almost all ages of children [pp. 250–206].

The informal assessment of ocular motility is quite simple if the teacher keeps in mind that the objective of the evaluation is to determine if the eyes move in a coordinated and "nonjerky" fashion. Mann and Suiter (1974) feel that additional indices of ocular-motility disorders are: (1) crossing of the eyes, (2) excessive squinting, redness, or watering of the eyes, and (3) straining of the eyes to see clearly. Techniques that are easily employed to measure this ability include suspending a ball (or similar object) in front of the child at eye level. The object suspended is slowly swung to and fro, in circles, and side to side approximately 15 inches from the child's face while the child follows it with the eyes. During this process, the teacher carefully notes the student's ocular motility to ascertain whether the eyes are working in a fluid and easy manner.

Another simple technique is to ask the child to focus the eyes on various points at differing distances (test for convergence). To accomplish this the teacher holds a pencil approximately 12 inches from the child's face and asks the child to look from the pencil to an object on the wall or blackboard. It is important that the child focus clearly with each eye movement. If difficulties are observed, there is a strong possibility that ocular motility disorders exist. When a teacher notes the presence of such disorders, the teacher should refer the student to the school nurse or other medical personnel for an in-depth diagnosis.

Form Perception   *Form Perception* is considered to be essential for school readiness. In essence, this skill relates to the child's ability to perceive objects as whole, or in their entirety. This skill is so important that many reading workbooks designed for primary grades include activities to "teach" this skill. It is interesting to note, however, that research has not yet shown conclusively that form perception is related to reading performance (Larsen & Hammill, 1975). Nevertheless, assessment of this skill is frequently attempted in schools.

Perhaps the most straightforward method of evaluating form perception is for the teacher to ask the student to recognize or trace simple configurations, cut out geometric forms, and color within the lines (Spache & Spache, 1969). The ability to complete puzzles successfully is a good indication of skill in form perception, as is drawing pictures of objects, events, animals, etc., accurately. Matching or sorting objects by shape (e.g., shapes may be made of cardboard, masonite, or paper) is another assessment strategy. The same task also can be conducted using letters or words when reading instruction is begun.

Visual Memory   *Visual Memory* refers to a child's ability to store and recall information presented visually. To measure this skill a teacher may test recall of stimuli visually presented out of sequence or may focus upon a child's ability to remember a specific sequence of objects or figures (i.e., visual sequential memory). A simple method of evaluating nonsequential visual memory is to place 6–10 common items (e.g., ball, pencil, eraser, etc.) in front of a child for approximately 20 seconds. After covering or removing the objects, the teacher asks the child to say or write down what was seen. If written responses are used, the teacher should not be concerned with such factors as penmanship or spelling. Many variations of this procedure can be used creatively. For example, if a more difficult task is required, the teacher can present an increased number of items, or the teacher can remove one or two of the items and ask the child to identify what is missing.

Another technique to tap visual memory is to show the child a geometric figure for 3–5 seconds, remove it, and have the child duplicate it from memory. Although the complexity of the figures will depend upon the age and ability of the student, Lott, Hudak, and Scheetz (1975) have found that the following shapes are reproduced correctly by most children at the following ages:

3 years	circle
4 years	cross
5 years	square
6–7 years	triangle
7 years	diamond

When administering this test, the teacher should take care to ensure that the child's motor ability is adequate before making a judgment regarding perceptual proficiency.

The measurement of visual sequential memory can be accomplished by techniques similar to those just described. The major differences are (1) the stimuli to be used are shown in a specified order and (2) the child must recall the stimuli in the exact sequence in which they were presented. If the teacher asks the child to imitate a series of actions he or she has just performed, this will provide an estimate of the skill. Bailey (1975) suggests that the teacher give the children a number of cards with sequences of directions written on each card. The child is required to recall the directions in proper order. The use of regular playing cards also may be a useful diagnostic tool. After placing four or five cards in front of a child, the teacher asks the child to study them for 5 seconds. Once the cards are turned over the child must recall them in sequential order. Cards with pictures, numerals, syllables, or words on them also may be used for variation. Increasing the number of cards per presentation is necessary with older children. Usually, students are able to remember 7–8 cards by 12 years of age.

As was mentioned earlier in this chapter, the specific visual-perception abilities measured will depend solely upon the orientation and needs of the teacher. Some professionals have been concerned with such variables as the perception of length, size, color, and shape. Smith (1969) has devised evaluation strategies for each of the skills adapted from the work of Montesori (1965). These techniques, presented in Table 6–4, are conducted easily in most classroom situations. Teachers desiring additional suggestions regarding informal testing of visual-perception skills may consult Bailey (1975), Valett (1969), Jedrysek, Klapper, Pope, and Wortis (1972), and Mann and Suiter (1974).

Informal Assessment of the Auditory Modality

As with visual perception, the informal assessment of the auditory modality usually is initiated through careful classroom observation. Observation should take place during those times in which the child is engaged in regu-

TABLE 6–4   Assessment of Various Visual-Perception Skills

Dimension Assessed	Suggested Evaluative Activity
1. Perception of Length	Provide the child with several rods or sticks (Cuisennaire Rods, for example) of varying lengths. Ask the child to tell which of two rods is longer, and which is shorter. Gradually increase the complexity of the task by requiring finer visual discriminations and by using objects other than rods. Have the child group rods according to similar lengths.
2. Perception of Size	Using objects of the same color and shape but varying in size, such as large blocks, ask the child to point to the smallest, the next largest, and so on, until the appropriate ordinal relationship has been shown among a set of objects. In this activity the child does not need to respond verbally or to move, just to point; thus minimizing the influence of the association and expressive components of the perceptual-motor process. As the child gains skill in this task, it can be complicated by adding other objects, or by varying shape and color as well as size.
3. Perception of Color	Display a series of plates in different colors. Ask the child to point to the appropriate color as you name it. Use widely different colors initially, gradually increasing the difficulty of the task by using more similar plates. Eventually the teacher might ask a child to point to all of the red objects in a picture. This task is more difficult than the former activity.
4. Perception of Shape	Using various geometric forms, have the youngster identify the one which is most round, square, or pointed. Later, have him pile the shapes so that those that are round are in one pile, square in another pile, and so on. This activity, as well as use of the simpler geometric forms which can be inserted into appropriate slots, will be helpful in analyzing a child's perception of differences in shape.

Source: Smith, R. M. Perceptual-motor skills. In R. M. Smith (Ed.), *Teacher diagnosis of educational difficulties.* Columbus, Ohio: Charles E. Merrill, 1969. Used with permission of the publisher.

lar curricular activities. Characteristics of auditory-perception disorders frequently are thought to include such behaviors as (1) inability to attend to normal environmental sounds, (2) inability to discriminate among differing sounds, and (3) inability to locate the source of sounds (Vance & Han-

FIGURE 6–3   Sample Checklist for Auditory-Perception Skills

	Yes	No
1. Does the child turn or cup one ear to the speaker? (hearing)		
2. Does the child fail to answer to his name from behind? (hearing)		
3. Voice (hearing)		
excessively loud _____		
excessively soft _____		
monotone _____		
4. Does the child consistently ask to have words repeated? (hearing)		
5. Does the child have difficulty repeating a clapped sequence? clap-clap clap-clap (memory-sequence)		
6. Does he fail to follow more than one direction? (memory-sequence)		
7. Does he fail to remember the sounds of things: animal, home, or nature (memory)		
8. Does he fail to follow the rhythm in band playing activities (memory-sequence)		
9. Is he unable to pay attention when there is noise in the room? (figure-ground)		
10. Does the child fail to tell the difference between human vs. non-human sounds? (discrimination)		
11. Does the child fail to tell when sounds are the same or different? (discrimination)		
12. Is he unable to locate the source or direction of sound? (localization)		
13. Does he fail to understand that the sound "m" in the word "man" is the same as the sound of "m" in the word "mop"? (auditory—auditory association)		
14. Is he unable to identify most of the letter sounds? (auditory—visual associative memory)		
15. Is he unable to identify most of the letter names? (auditory—visual associative memory)		

Source: Mann P. H., & Suiter, P. *Handbook on diagnostic teaching.* Boston: Allyn and Bacon, 1974. Used with permission of the publisher.

kins, 1975). Performance on these and other auditory skills affects many children's school performance. The use of checklists to delineate specific auditory-perception skills is useful in structuring observations and in pinpointing areas in need for further study. Figure 6–3 is an example of an auditory-perception checklist that can be modified easily to meet the particular needs of individual children.

Once a teacher observes a child exhibiting behaviors that may indicate auditory-perception difficulties, the teacher can then undertake a more complete analysis. This may be accomplished by isolating and assessing the proficiency of particular auditory skills. Sabatino (1967; 1973) has reported upon an experimental version of an evaluative technique that can help teachers to conceptualize the auditory perceptual process and to devise strategies for measuring specific behaviors. The *Test of Auditory Perception* contains six subtests that are designed to provide a composite view of auditory-perception functioning. The subtests include: (1) recognition of sounds, (2) recognition of words, (3) immediate memory of digits, (4) immediate memory of speech, (5) rhythmic structures, and (6) auditory comprehension of speech. This test is nonstandardized; however, Sabatino (1967) presents research results, which suggest that the instrument can be useful in clinical situations. Teachers can modify this device easily for possible application within the classroom.

Rosner (1975) also has described a technique to assess auditory-perception skill. The skill that the *Test of Auditory Analysis Skills* (TAAS) evaluates is the ability to break words into syllables. This skill is important to the child in learning to read. When giving the TAAS, the teacher begins by giving a demonstration item to introduce the testing procedure. The demonstration item is presented as follows: the teacher says, "Say *cowboy*." A short pause is given to permit the child to respond. The teacher then says, "Now say it again but don't say *boy*." The correct answer is *cow*. If the student has no difficulty with this item, the teacher moves on to another demonstration and the remainder of the 13-item test. The TAAS test items are given in Table 6–5. Rosner suggests that the test be terminated after the child makes two successive errors in order to avoid frustrating the child. The TAAS score is the total number of *correct* responses attained by the child. Rosner also provides a table that helps the teacher interpret an individual child's score (see Table 6–6). Use of this table is quite simple; when a child receives a TAAS score of 10, his or her auditory-perception skills are considered satisfactory if the child is in the second grade or below. If the child is in a higher grade, this score would be considered substandard.

Whereas the results of this test may be indicative of auditory-perception ability, the test score itself probably will be of little educational usefulness. In most instances, the teacher must conduct additional evaluations in order to isolate specific disorders more fully. Examples of such evaluations are presented below.

TABLE 6–5   Test Items for the TAAS

A	Say **cowboy**	Now say it again, but don't say **boy**	**cow**
B	Say **steamboat**	Now say it again, but don't say **steam**	**boat**
1	Say **sunshine**	Now say it again, but don't say **shine**	**sun**
2	Say **picnic**	Now say it again, but don't say **pic**	**nic**
3	Say **cucumber**	Now say it again, but don't say **cu (q)**	**cumber**
4	Say **coat**	Now say it again, but don't say /k/ (the **k** sound)	**oat**
5	Say **meat**	Now say it again, but don't say /m/ (the **m** sound)	**eat**
6	Say **take**	Now say it again, but don't say /t/ (the **t** sound)	**ache**
7	Say **game**	Now say it again, but don't say /m/	**gay**
8	Say **wrote**	Now say it again, but don't say /t/	**row**
9	Say **please**	Now say it again, but don't say /z/	**plea**
10	Say **clap**	Now say it again, but don't say /k/	**lap**
11	Say **play**	Now say it again, but don't say /p/	**lay**
12	Say **stale**	Now say it again, but don't say /t/	**sale**
13	Say **smack**	Now say it again, but don't say /m/	**sack**

Source: From the book, *Helping children overcome learning difficulties* by Jerome Rosner. Copyright © 1975 by Jerome Rosner. Used with permission of the publisher, Walker and Company.

TABLE 6–6   Guidelines for Interpreting the Results of the TAAS

TAAS Score	Expected for Children in
1	Kindergarten
2	Kindergarten
3	Kindergarten
4	Grade 1
5	Grade 1
6	Grade 1
7	Grade 1
8	Grade 1
9	Grade 1
10	Grade 2
11	Grade 2
12	Grade 3
13	Grade 3

Source: From the book, *Helping children overcome learning difficulties* by Jerome Rosner. Copyright © 1975 by Jerome Rosner. Used with permission of the publisher, Walker and Company.

Auditory Recognition   Recognition of sounds (auditory recognition) is the most basic of all auditory abilities (Kaluger & Kolson, 1969). The objective in evaluating this skill is to determine if a child is capable of identifying auditory stimuli that commonly occur in the school or the home. To conduct evaluations in this area, a teacher may tape-record the sounds of a vacuum cleaner vacuuming, a dog barking, a person typing, a piece of paper tearing, and scissors cutting and then ask the child to name them. In addition, the noises produced by various animals may be used as stimuli if the child is familiar with them. For example, the *meow* of a cat, *oink* of a pig, or *moo* of a cow frequently are used to measure this ability.

A more subtle task is to tape-record classroom sounds that are not identified as easily and to require the child to name the object making the noise. The dropping of a pencil, stapling of papers, writing on a chalkboard, turning on of lights, and dripping of a water faucet are all appropriate for measuring auditory recognition. Vance and Hankins (1975) suggest using items placed in small containers, which then are shaken either by the teacher or the child. The child is asked to identify the contents of the jar by listening to the sounds the containers make. Items that can be used include stones, chalk, sand, or a breakfast cereal. The teacher also may ask the child to sit facing away from him or her and then initiate a series of sounds (e.g., hand claps, pencil taps, etc.). The teacher then asks the child to tell how many sounds were heard or to repeat the particular pattern of sounds that were made. These and other activities can provide an estimate of a child's auditory recognition.

Auditory Memory   *Auditory memory* is the ability to retain stimuli presented auditorially. Tasks required of the child may entail remembering nonordered events or recalling stimuli in a specific sequence. An illustration of simple memory assessment is to ask a child to follow a single command, such as "Come here," "Go to the door," or "Sharpen your pencil." Asking the child to read a short paragraph or a complete story and then to answer questions, such as "Who is the story about?" "What happened?" or to retell the story also will assess auditory memory.

The measurement of sequential memory is similar to auditory memory in that the child must recall material presented auditorially in the particular order in which it was heard. The most widely used technique to evaluate this skill is dictation of a series of digits to the child, who then must recall and repeat the exact sequence orally. The number of digits included in each presentation varies depending upon the age of the child. Lott, Hudak, and Scheetz (1975) state that two tries should be allowed the child on each item before the teacher concludes that the child cannot complete the task. According to them a child's performance may be judged on the basis of the following guidelines:

2 years	2 digits
3 years	3 digits
4–5 years	4 digits
6–9 years	5 digits
10+ years	6 digits

Variations of this assessment strategy are devised easily to test auditory-sequential memory. For example, the teacher may say a series of letters or words and ask the child to repeat them orally or write them on a sheet of paper. If the child is older, the repetition of complete sentences also can be used to measure this ability. Following a series of verbal directions is also an acceptable indication of sequential memory. Asking the child to write or say an address, to follow directions for baking a cake, or to recite the days of the week all can be used by the teacher during the course of daily classroom activities. Bailey (1975) recommends the use of this old childhood game:

First person: I'm going to the store, and I'm going to take a coat.
Second person: I'm going to the store, and I'm going to take a coat and hat.
Third person: I'm going to the store, and I'm going to take a coat, hat, and . . . , etc.

Each child recalls in sequence the objects taken by the previous children, in addition to his or her own. The activity continues until the children experience difficulty. Creative teachers will have no problem in devising other techniques appropriate for measuring skill in auditory-sequential memory.

Auditory Discrimination *Auditory discrimination* refers to the ability to perceive differences, if any, between at least two auditory stimuli. This ability is believed to be related to the development of proficiency in speaking, as well as to the mastery of basic skills during beginning language arts instruction. Consequently, the measurement of auditory discrimination frequently is attempted with children who experience problems in academic achievement. In addition, many "readiness" tests routinely given to 5- and 6-year-old children include items designed to evaluate this skill in order to estimate the children's potential for success in school.

The informal assessment of auditory discrimination may be undertaken easily by the teacher. One of the most basic evaluative methods is to determine if a child can differentiate between sounds that are "soft" and sounds that are "loud." However, the teacher must make certain that the child understands the concepts of "different" and "same." These concepts are essential for the child to attain before the teacher can initiate more sophisticated strategies. Once it is clear that the child understands what these terms mean, the teacher can have the child practice using a pitch pipe or other instrument that easily produces sounds of different pitch or intensity levels.

The most commonly used testing method for measuring auditory discrimination is to tell the child to shut the eyes and to listen to the pairs of words that will be spoken. Once the child hears the words, he or she must indicate whether they are the "same" or "different." Initially, some pairs may be markedly different (e.g., cow-horseshoe) and later can gradually become similar until they are only differentiated by a single sound (e.g., car-tar). The teacher can use words that are within the child's vocabulary or words that are unknown to the child. Some professionals suggest that pairs of nonsense syllables should also be used to vary the testing procedure.

Another method is to give verbally a list of words to the child, most of which will begin with the same letter (e.g., toy, top, etc.). The child is then asked to indicate each time a word does not begin with *t*. With younger children, use of such actions as the clapping of hands or the raising of arms is helpful because they are simple actions and can hold the children's attention.

An additional method consists of the teacher pronouncing a word while emphasizing the beginning, middle, or ending sound. After it is certain that the child has perceived the emphasized sound correctly, the teacher asks the child to give other words that include the same sound in the position in which the sound was heard. Obviously, this technique will be effective only with children who have the capability to perform the task. If a child is deficient in such areas as articulation and vocabulary, other procedures should probably be used.

Although the preceding activities can be used successfully in the assessment of auditory-perception abilities, teachers may wish for various reasons to measure such constructs as auditory closure, figure-ground, or blending. A number of publications contain suggestions for training these skills, which may be adapted easily for evaluation. Interested readers should consult Lerner (1976), Flower (1968), and Bush and Giles (1969) for additional information on this topic.

Informal Assessment
of the Motor Modality

The measurement of motor ability in children frequently is the initial step in diagnosing children who are experiencing difficulty in school. In the past motor ability alone was thought to be directly related to academic achievement. For example, students who were judged to be clumsy or uncoordinated in kindergarten and first grade were believed to be predisposed to scholastic failure. Recent research, however, negates the assumption that general motor skills are *directly* linked to school achievement (Hallahan & Cruickshank, 1973; Cratty, 1970). Rosner (1975), in a discussion of the relationship of motor abilities to learning problems, has made this astute observation:

> General motor skills have been associated with learning problems for some time. In fact, when professionals first became aware of the child with

learning disability, the major treatment methods emphasized general-motor training activities that helped the child become better coordinated. As time passed, it became clear that good motor skills, in themselves, were not the answer. We all know too many beautifully coordinated illiterates and too many clumsy geniuses to support that position [p. 80].

If the assessment and subsequent remedy of motor skills do not result in increased academic performance, why then are they of concern to educators? The answer to this question lies in the fact that to perceptual theorists adequate motor ability is necessary for developing higher levels of perceptual and cognitive skills. Theoretically, as a child grows from infancy to early childhood, motor exploration and experimentation become the *foundation* upon which all later learning is based (Kephart, 1960). Gradually, as the child gains a working knowledge of the environment, auditory and visual-perception skills become increasingly important in transmitting and organizing relevant sensory stimulation. In effect, the auditory and visual modalities assume the role of motor movement as the primary mode(s) of learning. For example, very young children may be able to sort cardboard squares, circles, and triangles only when permitted to touch them and feel their various shapes. Later, after the *concept* of what constitutes a square, a circle, and a triangle has been learned through motor exploration, a child will be able to differentiate these geometric shapes by simply looking at them (i.e., by using the visual modality). According to perceptual theory, if appropriate motor concepts are not learned, the child will use other (i.e., later developing) perceptual channels only with extreme difficulty. Consequently, if a child is experiencing difficulty in forming various concepts (e.g., recognizing letter forms), the perceptually oriented teacher may be concerned with whether the child has acquired the necessary motor skills upon which the concepts are based. If the child is deficient in these skills, the teacher may conclude that auditory and visual perception might also be affected. Until these deficiencies are evaluated and remedied, efficient learning is virtually impossible.

The assessment of motor ability in children often is conducted through informal, nonstandardized tests. Generally, the behaviors of interest to the teacher are concerned with differentiating body parts, dynamic balance, laterality (internalized awareness of sidedness), directionality, awareness of space and time, and body image. One informal survey evaluating motor performance and its relation to perceptual awareness is *The Purdue Perceptual-Motor Survey* (PPMS) (Roach & Kephart, 1966). This survey provides activities that elicit behaviors indicative of skills in the areas of (1) balance and posture, (2) body image and differentiation of body parts, (3) perceptual-motor matching, (4) ocular control, and (5) form perception. In total, 22 scorable items divided into 11 subtests are presented. For the most part, few specialized materials are required in the administration of the survey.

For teachers who may not be familiar with the assessment of motor skills, Chaney and Kephart (1968) have developed checklists that enhance the ability to observe specific motor skills. A portion of one of these checklists appropriate for monitoring most basic motor movements is given in Table 6–7. The specific activities needed to administer the skills optimally are provided in this table. The reader should note that this list closely approximates the general categories of behavior listed in the *Purdue Perceptual-Motor Survey* and can be used as a separate assessment device in and of itself or in conjunction with the PPMS to validate observations.

Teachers can also develop techniques designed to estimate motor ability to supplement commercial tests. Traditional physical education activities can be adapted easily for evaluation. Determining a child's skill in tumbling, jumping rope, handling objects, running obstacle courses, and playing ball will yield information concerning general movement patterns. In most instances, the teachers' strategies are as accurate and reliable as any standardized tests currently available.

One of the basic means of assessing motor ability is to ask the child to move the parts of the body upon command. Usually, the teacher states the body part to be moved, and then gives the command to move. The child holds this position until the teacher gives the command to go back to the original position. Simple commands should be given to permit the child to learn the procedure. Over time, increasingly complex commands can be given in order to identify the motor sequences that are particularly easy or difficult for a given child. Simple commands may include the directions "left leg forward—move," (pause) "back"; "right arm forward—move," (pause) "back." More complicated motor commands may include unilateral, bilateral, or cross-lateral limb movements. Examples of these activities are: left arm, left leg forward (unilateral); both arms forward (bilateral); and right arm, left leg forward (cross-lateral).

A similar evaluative technique consists of asking the child to imitate the movements of the teacher. The student should be standing with feet approximately 8–12 inches apart for balance, with arms hanging loosely at the sides. The teacher makes clear and explicit movements with the arms and legs in various positions. Gradually, arm and leg movements in various combinations are imitated by the children. The children are told to imitate the movements on the opposite side the teacher is making them (e.g., right side for the teacher, left side for the children). For some children it may help if the teacher introduces the activity as a game in which they will win points for making correct responses or lose points for making incorrect responses. At no time, however, should the game become so competitive that the children feel that they are losing. The object of this procedure, of course, is to elicit the children's best efforts.

Identification of body parts is an ability that can be measured in children. To accomplish this task, the teacher asks the children to touch various

TABLE 6–7   Observations of Basic Motor Movements

Movements and Points to Observe	Comments

I. DIFFERENTIATION

  A. *Head Control* (child on his back on the floor)

    1. Observe head position as child pulls up to sitting position. Hold a pole (broomstick) for the child to pull on. Head should lift easily and first, shoulders should follow. Note if:

      a. Shoulders tense and lift first with head lagging behind. ☐

      b. Head is "tied into" the shoulders and all lift as a unit. ☐

    2. Observe child's ability to lift only the head while lying on back and on stomach. Can he easily lift his head and look about? Note if:

      a. It is necessary to tense the whole body first. ☐

      b. There is tension in other limbs. ☐

      c. Child is unable to lift or move head. ☐

  B. *Trunk Differentiation* (child on his stomach or back as required)

    1. Can the child differentiate at the waistline? Can he lift knees and move them from side to side touching floor while keeping shoulders on the mat? Can he pivot the upper trunk without moving hips and legs? (The pivoting can be done by swaying back and forth or on the stomach; the elbows or hands can be used to propel the upper trunk back and forth in a semicircle.) Note if:

      a. Child cannot move upper trunk without involving or moving lower trunk. ☐

      b. Child cannot move lower

TABLE 6–7   *Continued*

Movements and Points to Observe	Comments

trunk without involving or moving upper trunk. ☐

2. Can the child differentiate the four quadrants of the trunk? Can he enervate and move a shoulder or hip without involv-ing other parts of the body? (Have the child try a variety of hip and shoulder movements.) Note if:
   a. To move one leg at the hip the other leg becomes in-volved and moves also. ☐
   b. To move one arm at the shoulder the other shoul-der, the head, or a leg becomes involved in the movement. ☐
   c. A quadrant can be moved alone but the remainder of the body tenses. ☐

3. Since true differentiation pre-supposes that differentiated parts can also be used in com-bination, it is well to check and see if the child can move parts of the body simultaneously. Note if:
   a. The thrust or movement is not truly bilateral— that is, if one side has more thrust or seems to lead the other.
      Bilateral hip thrust. ☐
      Bilateral shoulder thrust. ☐
   b. Upper trunk cannot move without involving the lower trunk, and reverse. ☐

4. Simultaneous unilateral move-ment of shoulders and hips can also be explored and observa-tions made as in B.3. above.
   a. Right shoulder and hip. ☐
   b. Left shoulder and hip. ☐

C. *Limb Differentiation* (child on stom-ach or back as required)

TABLE 6–7   *Continued*

Movements and Points to Observe	Comments
1. Requires a variety of arm and leg movements in all directions close to the body and in full extension. (Give the child a goal to reach toward or follow with hand or foot.) Note if:	

a. The child can move his hands into tasks only if the upper arms are kept close to the body and all movement comes from the elbows. ☐

b. He uses a fully extended arm with little or no elbow movements. ☐

c. Movements back and forth between the two extremes are rigid, jerky and uncontrolled. ☐

d. There are areas in which the limb cannot move with ease. ☐

e. The child cannot cross the "midline" of his body without moving the head or trunk. ☐

f. The child changes hand or foot at the midline or acts as if he would like to do so. ☐

If the child's problem is basically one of inadequate differentiation it will be quite evident at this point. If, however, he has passed the above tests but has failed such items as angels and jumping on the PMS, it would suggest that differentiation is hampered by a lack of adequate balance or that the child has not learned to use the differentiated parts in combination.

Source: Chaney, C. M., & Kephart, N. C. *Motoric aids to perceptual training.* Columbus, Ohio: Charles E. Merrill, 1968. Used with permission of the publisher.
Authors' Note: Although in this table the pronoun "he" is used exclusively, it should *not* be interpreted to mean that girls are excluded from this evaluative technique.

parts of the body with both hands without looking at their bodies or other children. Children should stand facing the teacher, who makes such commands as (1) "touch your head," (2) "touch your ears," (3) "touch your toes," (4) "touch your shoulders." Once the children understand the commands, they can verbalize the movement as it is being done. For example, if the children say, "I am touching my *(correct body part)*" at the appropriate time, this helps the teacher find out if the children can identify parts of their bodies.

Many materials can be adapted by teachers for use in evaluating the motor ability of children. Crawling and creeping, floor-ladder activities, stepping stones, and obstacle courses can all be used as assessment strategies. Readers may wish to consider the procedure listed by Cratty (1975), Humphrey (1965), Wickstrom (1970), and Mosston (1965) when they formulate evaluative techniques in this area.

PERCEPTION AND ACADEMIC ACHIEVEMENT

To some educators and psychologists the adequacy of perceptual development in children is directly related to academic achievement. This hypothesis is based almost exclusively upon clinical experiences of professionals who put their theories into practice by generating standardized tests and teaching programs appropriate for perceptual diagnosis and remedies. That this approach has become popular is attested to by the fact that between 1936 and 1970 perceptual programming has become unquestionably the most widely used method of evaluating low-achieving children (Hallahan & Cruickshank, 1973).

Regrettably, the rise of perceptual tests and materials has not been accompanied by pertinent research to validate its usefulness in schools. In fact, extensive reviews of the literature and research studies have raised serious doubt regarding whether this method of assessment and teaching should even continue to be used with students exhibiting academic failure. For example, commonly used perceptual tests have been shown (1) to lack the necessary power to differentiate between low- and normal-achieving children and (2) to be unreliable predictors of which children are likely to exhibit difficulties in school (Cohen, 1969; Hartman & Hartman, 1973; Black, 1974; Bryan, 1974; Vellutino, Steger, DeSetto, & Phillips, 1975; Newcomer & Hammill, 1975; and Sowell, 1975). In addition, programs designed to remedy perceptual disorders have been demonstrated to be nonproductive (Robinson, 1971; Hammill, 1971; Hammill & Wiederholt, 1972; Hammill, Goodman, & Wiederholt, 1974; Hammill & Larsen, 1974; and Larsen,

Parker, & Sowell, 1976). Unquestionably, teachers should be aware of relevant research findings prior to making decisions as to whether perceptual activities should be used with their students.

One of the primary tenets of perceptual theory is that impairment of the skills underlying the auditory and visual modalities will interfere significantly with the learning. In order to arrive at this assumption, it is necessary to believe that a high positive relationship exists between perceptual skills and academic achievement levels. If such a relationship does not exist, it is obvious that perceptual disorders, as measured, cannot be considered seriously as a factor in cases of learning failure. Two recent studies explore the relationship between measured auditory and visual-perception skills and school achievement, particularly reading (Hammill & Larsen, 1974; Larsen & Hammill, 1975). The results of these studies may be helpful for teachers in developing their own positions regarding perceptual diagnosis and remedies.

The first study focused upon those studies that use correlational statistical procedures and that deal with the relationship between measures of reading and measures of auditory discrimination, memory blending, and auditory-visual integration (Hammill & Larsen, 1974). In total, 33 suitable studies that reported in excess of 300 individual correlation coefficients have been located. The studies are evenly distributed among all elementary grade levels. The results of this review have failed to validate the assumption that certain auditory-perception skills, as measured, are necessary for the reading process and that children actually fail to read well because of defects in this area. In other words, a certain percentage of students who score adequately on tests of auditory perception experience difficulty in learning to read, and an equally sizable percentage who do poorly on these same tests have no problems in reading.

The second study also deals with research that employs correlational procedures but considers only those that probe the relationship of academic achievement and visual-perception development (Larsen & Hammill, 1975). The specific perceptual skills of interest include visual discrimination, spatial relations, memory, and auditory-visual integration. Sixty appropriate studies have been found that generate over 600 coefficients suitable for analysis. As with auditory perception, the visual skills are found to have only a minimal relationship to learning. The conclusion of this review is that the time and expense currently devoted to visual-perception testing and training should be reevaluated seriously if the purpose of their use is to improve academic achievement. Apparently, the assumption held by many theorists that adequate perceptual functioning (i.e., as measured in schools) is a prerequisite to academic achievement is not supported by available research. This observation is further supported by the fact that Larsen, Rogers, and Sowell (1976) were unable to differentiate statistically between normal-achieving students and those that had been labeled as "learning disabled" on commonly used tests of auditory- and visual-perception abilities. It is interesting to note that the learning disabled children as a group received somewhat *higher* scores than their matched peers on the majority of tests administered.

Considering the fact that little empirical data exists to support the supposition that perceptual ability is related to academic achievement, it is not surprising that various perceptual *training* programs also have been shown to be less than successful in improving learning. Hallahan and Cruickshank (1973), in a review of 42 studies that attempt to train perceptual abilities, state that, because of serious methodological errors, no definite conclusions can be drawn regarding the efficacy of perceptual training. Careful perusal of their review, however, indicates that the "better designed" research studies are *far more likely* to produce negative results than are the poorly conducted studies. Myers and Hammill (1976), after extensively reviewing 105 research studies that were concerned with the effects of perceptual training, demonstrate that little support now exists for the continued use of these programs to facilitate achievement levels of students. Recent efforts in this area of research tend to support the findings of Myers and Hammill. For example, Wilson, Harris, and Harris (1976), in a well-controlled study that focuses on the effects of an auditory-perception remedial program on school performance, have found that increasing competency in auditory perception *does not* improve a student's proficiency in either reading or spelling any more than does instruction in traditional types of reading activities.

At the present time it appears that the tendency of some professionals to emphasize a perceptual orientation to understanding learning problems is unsupported by available research. For this reason, we do not advocate or recommend the use of either perceptual tests or training techniques in work with students exhibiting academic failure. If the purpose of remedial diagnosis and programming is to improve the curricular areas of reading, spelling, arithmetic, written or spoken language, time devoted to determining perceptual proficiency wastes time and energy on the part of both the teacher and the child. Until such time as supporters of these techniques offer more substantive research, we must consider perceptual assessment and remedies as unproven, experimental, and unrelated to any aspect of learning. It is our sincere hope that teachers will become familiar with research in this area (1) to make their own decisions regarding the status of perceptual theory and educational strategies and (2) to acquaint professional colleagues with the apparent viability of such approaches. It is only through this process that teachers will be relatively certain that the diagnostic and teaching efforts initiated will relate directly to increasing the academic achievement of children.

References

Ayers, J. *Southern California figure-ground visual perception test*. Los Angeles: Western Psychological Services, 1966.

Bailey, E. J. *Academic activities for adolescents with learning disabilities*. Evergreen, Colo.: Learning Pathways, 1975.

Baker, H. J., & Leland, B. *Detroit tests of learning aptitude*. Indianapolis: Bobbs-Merrill, 1935.

Barsch, R. H. Teacher needs—motor training. In W. M. Cruickshank (Ed.), *The teacher of brain-injured children*. Syracuse: Syracuse University Press, 1966.

Barsch, R. H. *Achieving perceptual-motor efficiency*. Seattle: Special Child Publications, 1967.

Bender, L. *The Bender visual motor Gestalt test for children*. New York: American Orthopsychiatric Association, 1938.

Beery, K., & Buktenica, N. A. *Developmental test of visual-motor integration*. Chicago: Follett, 1967.

Black, F. W. Achievement test performance of high and low achieving learning disabled children. *Journal of Learning Disabilities*, 1974, *7*, 179–182.

Blank, M. Cognitive processes in auditory discrimination in normal and retarded readers. *Child Development*, 1968, *39*, 1091–1101.

Boyd, L., & Randle, K. Factor analysis of the Frostig developmental test of visual perception. *Journal of Learning Disabilities*, 1970, *3*, 253–255.

Bruininks, R. H. *Bruininks-Oseretzky test of motor proficiency*. Circle Pines, Minn.: American Guidance Service, 1977.

Bryan, T. Learning disabilities: A new stereotype. *Journal of Learning Disabilities*, 1974, *7*, 304–309.

Bush, W. J., & Giles, M. *Aids to psycholinguistic teaching*. Columbus, Ohio: Charles E. Merrill, 1969.

Bush, W. J., & Waugh, K. W. *Diagnosing learning disabilities*. Columbus, Ohio: Charles E. Merrill, 1976.

Chalfant, J. C., & Scheffelin, M. A. *Central processing dysfunctions in children: A review of research*. NINDS Monograph, No. 9. Bethesda, Md.: U. S. Department of Health, Education and Welfare, 1969.

Chaney, C. M., & Kephart, N. C. *Motoric aids to perceptual training*. Columbus, Ohio: Charles E. Merrill, 1968.

Cohen, S. A. Studies in visual perception and reading in disadvantaged children. *Journal of Learning Disabilities*, 1969, *2*, 498–507.

Colarusso, R., & Hammill, D.D. *The motor free test of visual perception*. San Rafael, Calif.: Academic Therapy Publications, 1972.

Colarusso, R., & Hammill, D. D. *The motorfree test of visual perception*. San Rafael, Calif.: Academic Therapy Publications, 1972.

Corah, N. L., & Powell, B. J. A factor analytic study of the Frostig developmental test of visual perception. *Perceptual and Motor Skills*, 1963, *16*, 59–63.

Cratty, B. J. *Perceptual and motor development in infants and children.* New York: Macmillan, 1970.

Cratty, B. J. *Remedial motor activity for children.* Philadelphia: Lea & Febiger, 1975.

Cratty, B. J., Ikeda, N., Martin, M., Jennett, C., & Morris, M. *Movement activities, motor ability and the education of children.* Springfield, Ill.: Charles C. Thomas, 1970.

Cruickshank, W. M. The psychoeducational match. In W. M. Cruickshank and D. P. Hallahan (Eds.), *Perceptual and learning disabilities in children.* Vol. I. Syracuse: Syracuse University Press, 1975.

deHirsch, K. Tests designed to discover potential reading difficulties at the six year old level. *American Journal of Orthopsychiatry*, 1957, *27*, 566–576.

Doll, E. A. *Preschool attainment record.* Circle Pines, Minn.: American Guidance Service, 1966.

Eisenson, J. Perceptual disturbances in children with central nervous system dysfunctions and implications for language development. *British Journal of Disorders of Communication*, 1966, *23*, 23–30.

Fleishman, E. A. *The structure and measurement of physical fitness.* Englewood Cliffs, N.J.: Prentice-Hall, 1964.

Flower, R. M. The evaluation of auditory abilities in the appraisal of children with reading problems. In H. K. Smith (Ed.), *Perception and reading.* Newark, Del.: International Reading Association, 1968.

Frankenberg, W. K., & Dodds, J. B. *The Denver developmental screening test. Journal of Pediatrics*, 1967, *71*, 181–191.

Frostig, M. The role of perception in the integration of psychological functions. In W. M. Cruickshank and D. P. Hallahan (Eds.), *Perceptual and learning disabilities in children.* Vol. I. Syracuse: Syracuse University Press, 1975, pp. 115–148.

Frostig, M., Lefever, D., & Whittlesey, J. *The Marianne Frostig developmental test of visual perception.* Palo Alto, Calif.: Consulting Psychologists, 1964.

Gesell, A., Ilg, F., & Bullis, G. E. *Vision, its development in infant and child.* New York: Paul B. Hoeber, 1949.

Getman, G. N., & Hendrickson, H. H. The needs of teachers for specialized information on the development of visumotor skills in relation to academic performance. In W. M. Cruickshank (Ed.), *The teacher of brain-injured children.* Syracuse: Syracuse University Press, 1966.

Goins, J. T. Visual perceptual abilities and early reading progress. *Supplementary educational monographs.* Chicago: The University of Chicago Press, 1958.

Goldman, R., Fristoe, M., & Woodcock, R. *The Goldman-Fristoe-Woodcock test of auditory discrimination.* Circle Pines, Minn.: American Guidance Service, 1970.

Graham, F. K., & Kendall, B. S. Memory-for-designs test. *Perceptual and Motor Skills,* 1960, *11,* 147–190.

Gronlund, N. E. *Measurement and evaluation in teaching.* New York: Macmillan, 1976.

Hallahan, D. P., & Cruickshank, W. M. *Psychoeducational foundations of learning disabilities.* New York: Prentice-Hall, 1973.

Hammill, D. D. Evaluating children for instructional purposes. *Academic Therapy,* 1971, *6,* 53–58.

Hammill, D. D. Assessing and teaching perceptual-motor processes. In D. D. Hammill and N. Bartel (Eds.), *Teaching children with learning and behavior problems.* Boston: Allyn and Bacon, 1975.

Hammill, D. D., Goodman, L., & Wiederholt, J. L. Appropriateness of the developmental test of visual perception when used with economically disadvantaged children. *Journal of School Psychology,* 1971, *9,* 430–435.

Hammill, D. D., Goodman, L. & Wiederholt, J. L. Use of the Frostig DTVP with economically disadvantaged children. *Journal of School Psychology,* 1974, *9,* 430–435.

Hammill, D. D., & Larsen, S. C. The effectiveness of psycholinguistic training. *Exceptional Children,* 1974, *41,* 5–15.

Hammill, D. D., & Larsen, S. C. The relationship of selected auditory perceptual skills and reading ability. *Journal of Learning Disabilities,* 1974, *7,* 429–436.

Hammill, D. D., & Wiederholt, J. L. Review of the Frostig visual perception test and the related training program. In L. Mann and D. Sabatino (Eds.), *The first review of special education.* Vol. 1. Philadelphia: JSE Press, Grune & Stratton, 1972.

Hartman, N. C., & Hartman, R. Perceptual handicap or reading disability? *The Reading Teacher,* 1973, 684–695.

Haworth, M. R. *The primary visual motor test.* New York: Grune & Stratton, 1970.

Hildreth, G. H., Griffiths, M., & McGauvran, M. E. *The metropolitan readiness tests.* New York: Harcourt, Brace Jovanovich, 1969.

Humphrey, J. H. *Child learning through elementary school physical education.* Dubuque, Iowa: William C. Brown, 1965.

Jedrysek, E., Klapper, A., Pope, L., & Wortis, J. *Psychoeducational evaluation of the preschool child.* New York: Grune & Stratton, 1972.

Kaluger, G., & Kolson, C. *Reading and learning disabilities.* Columbus, Ohio: Charles E. Merrill, 1969.

Karlin, R. *Teaching elementary reading.* New York: Harcourt, Brace Jovanovich, 1971.

Kephart, N. C. *The slow learner in the classroom.* Columbus, Ohio: Charles E. Merrill, 1960.

Kidd, A. H., & Kidd, R. M. The development of auditory perception in children. In A. H. Kidd and J. L. Riviore (Eds.), *Perceptual development in children.* New York: International Universities Press, 1966.

Kimmell, G. M., & Wahl, J. *The screening test for auditory perception.* San Rafael, Calif.: Academic Therapy Publications, 1969.

Kirk, S., McCarthy, J., & Kirk, W. *Illinois test of psycholinguistic abilities.* Urbana, Ill.: University of Illinois Press, 1968.

Koppitz, E. M. *The Bender-Gestalt test for young children.* New York: Grune & Stratton, 1964.

Koppitz, E. M. *Psychological evaluation of children's human figure drawings.* New York: Grune & Stratton, 1968.

Larsen, S. C., & Hammill, D. D. The relationship of selected visual skills to school learning. *Journal of Special Education,* 1975, *9,* 281–291.

Larsen, S. C., Parker, R., & Sowell, V. *The effectiveness of the MWM program in developing language abilities.* Unpublished manuscript, The University of Texas at Austin, 1976.

Larsen, S. C., Rogers, D., & Sowell, V. The usefulness of selected perceptual tests in differentiating between normal and learning disabled children. *Journal of Learning Disabilities,* 1976, *9,* 85–91.

Lerner, J. *Children with learning disabilities.* Boston: Houghton Mifflin, 1976.

Lott, L., Hudak, B., & Scheetz, J. *Strategies and techniques for mainstreaming: A resource room handbook.* Monroe, Mich.: Monroe County School District, 1975.

Mann, L. Marianne Frostig developmental test of visual perception. In O. K. Buros (Ed.), *The seventh mental measurement yearbook.* Highland Park, N.J.: Gryphon, 1972.

Mann, P. H., & Suiter, P. *Handbook on diagnostic teaching.* Boston: Allyn and Bacon, 1974.

Messing, E. S. Auditory perception: What is it? In J. Arena (Ed.), *Successful programming: Many points of view,* Fifth Annual Conference Proceedings, Association of Children with Learning Disabilities. San Rafael, Calif.: Academic Therapy Publications, 1968, 439–452.

Morris, P. R., & Whiting, H. T. A. *Motor impairment and compensatory education.* Philadelphia: Lea & Febiger, 1971.

Mosston, M. *Developmental movement.* Columbus, Ohio: Charles E. Merrill, 1965.

Myers, P. I., & Hammill, D. D. *Methods for learning disorders.* New York: John Wiley, 1976.

Myklebust, H. R. *Auditory disorders in children: A manual for differential diagnosis.* New York: Grune & Stratton, 1954.

227

Newcomer, P., & Hammill, D. D. *Psycholinguistics in the schools.* Columbus, Ohio: Charles E. Merrill, 1975.

Olson, A. V. Factor analytic studies of the Frostig developmental test of visual perception. *Journal of Special Education,* 1968, 2, 429–433.

Opert, R. E. *Frostig movement skills test battery.* Palo Alto, Calif.: Consulting Psychologists Press, 1967.

Reger, R., Schroeder, W., & Uschold, K. *Special education: Children with learning problems.* New York: Oxford University Press, 1968.

Roach, E., & Kephart, N. C. *The Purdue perceptual-motor survey.* Columbus, Ohio: Charles E. Merrill, 1966.

Robinson, H. *Perceptual training—Does it result in reading improvement?* Paper presented at the annual convention of the International Reading Association, Atlantic City, April 1971.

Rosner, J. *Helping children overcome learning difficulties.* New York: Walker, 1975.

Roswell, F., & Chall, J. *Roswell-Chall auditory blending test.* New York: Essay Press, 1963.

Sabatino, D. A. The construction and assessment of an experimental test of auditory perception. *Exceptional Children,* 1967, *35,* 729–737.

Sabatino, D. A. Auditory perception: Development, assessment, and intervention. In L. Mann and D. A. Sabatino (Eds.), *The first review of special education.* Philadelphia: JSE Press, 1973.

Slosson, R. I. *Slosson drawing coordination test.* East Aurora, N.Y.: Slosson Educational Publications, 1967.

Smith, R. M. Perceptual-motor skills. In R. M. Smith (Ed.), *Teacher diagnosis of educational difficulties.* Columbus, Ohio: Charles E. Merrill, 1969.

Sowell, V. *Efficacy of psycholinguistic testing and training.* Unpublished manuscript, The University of Texas at Austin, 1975.

Spache, G. D., & Spache, E. B. *Reading in the elementary school.* Boston: Allyn and Bacon, 1969.

Sprague, R. Learning difficulties of first grade children diagnosed by the Frostig visual perception tests: A factor analytic study. *Dissertation Abstracts,* 1965, *25,* 4006–A.

Strauss, A., & Lehtinen, L. *Psychopathology and education of the brain-injured child.* New York: Grune & Stratton, 1947.

Valett, R. E. *Programming learning disabilities.* Palo Alto, Calif.: Fearon, 1969.

Vance, H. B., & Hankins, N. E. Teaching interventions for defective auditory reception. *Academic Therapy,* 1975, *11,* 69–78.

Vandenberg, S. G. Factor analytic study of the Lincoln/Oseretzky. *Perceptual and Motor Skills,* 1964, *19,* 23–41.

Vellutino, F., Steger, J., DeSetto, L., & Phillips, F. Immediate and delayed recognition of visual stimuli in poor and normal readers. *Journal of Experimental Child Psychology,* 1975, *19,* 223–232.

Wechsler, D. *Wechsler intelligence scale for children.* New York: Psychological Corporation, 1949. Revised WISC-R, 1974.

Weiner, P. S., Wepman, J. M., & Morency, A. S. A test of visual discrimination. *Elementary School Journal,* 1965, *65,* 330–337.

Wepman, J. M. *Auditory discrimination test.* Chicago: Language Research Associates, 1958.

Wepman, J. M. The perceptual basis for learning. In E. C. Frierson and W. B. Barbe (Eds.), *Educating children with learning disabilities: Selected readings.* New York: Appleton-Century-Crofts, 1967.

Wepman, J. M. Auditory perception and imperception. In W. M. Cruickshank and D. P. Hallahan (Eds.), *Perceptual and learning disabilities in children.* Vol. II. Syracuse: Syracuse University Press, 1975.

Wickstrom, R. L. *Fundamental movement patterns.* Philadelphia: Lea & Febiger, 1970.

Wilson, S. P., Harris, C. W., & Harris, M. L. Effects of an auditory perceptual remediation program on reading performance. *Journal of Learning Disabilities,* 1976, *9,* 670–678.

Wold, R. M., Kane, M., & Koetting, J. F. Dominance—fact or fantasy: Its significance in learning disabilities. In R. M. Wold (Ed.), *Visual and perceptual aspects for the achieving and underachieving child.* Seattle: Special Child Publications, 1969.

Zigmond, N., & Cicci, R. *Auditory learning.* San Rafael, Calif.: Dimensions Publishing, 1968.

7

Spoken-Language Assessment

The acquisition of language, which is so frequently taken for granted in the developing child is, perhaps, the most remarkable intellectual accomplishment of a human being. Not only does use of language represent one of the uniquely human characteristics, it also serves as an essential prerequisite to all phases of academic achievement. In order for children to develop a linguistic system that is adequately functioning, they must master the rules of phonology, morphology, syntax, and semantics, all of which are components of spoken language. If for any reason a child is experiencing problems in receiving or expressing verbal stimuli, the teacher must probe the areas of the deficiency in order to plan appropriate remedial strategies. To accomplish this, it is necessary that the teacher be familiar with a variety of formal and informal devices available for assessing spoken-language disorders. This chapter will acquaint teachers with (1) the dimensions of language development, (2) the factors influencing linguistic proficiency, (3) the stages or milestones in normal language acquisition, and (4) the techniques appropriate for assessing problems with the spoken language.

DIMENSIONS OF LANGUAGE

At its most basic level *language* is defined as a system of verbal symbols (words) that people use to communicate with one another (Carroll, 1964). The ability to create and use language is one of the most distinctive features of human beings. Without language the transmission of shared meanings, values, and traditions would be virtually impossible. The pervasiveness

230

of language in all areas of human behavior has been discussed by Lang-acker (1968). He states:

> Language is everywhere. It permeates our thoughts, mediates our relation-ships with others, and even creeps into our dreams. The overwhelming bulk of human knowledge is stored and transmitted in language. Language is so ubiquitous that we take it for granted, but without it, society as we know it would be impossible. [p. 1].

Because language is an essential component of human behavior, it is apparent that the teacher must consider carefully a child's language pro-ficiency when assessing the various aspects of the child's failure in school. In order to accomplish this task, teachers must be aware of the general sequence of language development, as well as the discrete linguistic skills that are necessary for adequate linguistic performance. In the next sections we will discuss language development and the aspects of phonology, mor-phology, syntax, and semantics.

Language Development

According to Bartel (1975), one of the major obstacles to understanding the nature of language arises from individuals failing to make a distinction between speech and language. The term *speech* is meant to describe the *oral* or *spoken* utterances of human beings to convey meaning. The term *language* is used to describe the general knowledge a person possesses of the linguistic concepts upon which all speech is based. If an internal lan-guage system has not been developed, meaningful speech is impossible.

Many authors have noted that the distinctions between speech and language are related to the psychological terms *competence* and *perfor-mance* (terms first used by Chomsky, 1957). Competence is the speaker-hearer's inherent knowledge of language, and performance is the observable use of language in concrete situations (Chomsky, 1965). It is important to note that linguistic competence itself never can be observed or mea-sured directly. It is possible only to infer that it is or is not present in a child "on the basis of the child's understanding and production of sentences" (Bartel, 1975, p. 156). Consequently, the use of language (i.e., exhibited performance in speech, oral reading, and writing) is the primary means by which professional people can assess a child's mastery of various language concepts. Efficient measurement of *spoken* language ability relies upon a teacher's understanding of the levels of linguistic usage shown by children. Table 7–1 outlines the ages at which gross linguistic performances occur in most children. It is obvious that as the child grows older the com-plexity of observed utterances increases markedly.

In order to develop language proficiency, a child must (1) be physio-

TABLE 7-1   Ages at Which Gross Linguistic Performances Occur

Age	Vocalizations
Birth	Cry and other physiological sounds
1–2 months	Cooing sounds as well as cry
3–6 months	Babbling as well as cooing
9–14 months	First words as well as babbling
18–24 months	First sentences as well as words
3–4 years	Use of all basic syntactical structures
4–8 years	Correct articulation of all speech sounds in context

Source: From *The development of speech* by Paula Menyuk, copyright © 1972. The Bobbs-Merrill Company, Inc.

logically mature, and (2) receive appropriate stimulation and reinforcement from the immediate environment. The most important physiological mechanisms necessary for language development include functioning central and peripheral nervous systems (Wood, 1969). These neurological systems are responsible primarily for transmitting sensory stimuli to the brain (e.g., auditory and visual images) in a consistent and efficient manner and for making possible the specific motor movements necessary for discrete articulation and sound production. In addition, the sensory information that is relayed to the central nervous system (i.e., brain) must be organized, integrated, and stored in such a manner that the child gradually will develop a core of experiences that will facilitate understanding and use of the spoken language. Once a child has received, organized, and *internalized* common events in the environment, behavior becomes more purposeful. For example, it is not unusual for an infant, during the first 12 months of life, gradually to be able to play meaningfully with a toy car, truck, doll or to follow simple commands and become aware of the rules in the home. It can be said that when the child progresses through these early stages of learning (before the advent of spoken language) he or she is developing an internal language, which frequently is referred to as *inner language* (Goldstein, 1948; Vygotsky, 1962). Inner language serves as a bridge between thought and spoken language, orients the child to the environment, and provides verbal imagery for words and concepts. It is through the attainment of inner language that a child establishes the necessary linguistic competence to master spoken language, reading, writing, spelling, and other language arts. If, for any reason, linguistic competence is not attained, progress in academically related tasks most certainly will be negatively affected.

Although it generally is held that inner language is essential to all later stages of language development, it should be noted that inner language it-

FIGURE 7-1   The developmental hierarchy of a person's language system.

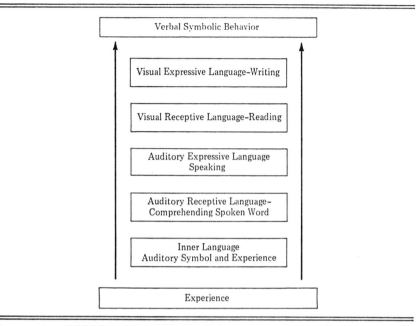

Source: From Myklebust, H. R. *The psychology of deafness.* (2nd ed.) New York: Grune & Stratton, 1964. Reprinted by permission of the author and the publisher.

self never can be observed directly (Dale, 1976). It is possible to infer only that a child possesses inner language on the basis of how the language symbols actually are received or expressed. For this reason it is important that teachers be aware of the stages of normal language development in order to determine if the child has attained adequate inner language. Myklebust (1960) has stated that children master five developmental levels that lead to language proficiency. A graphic illustration of Myklebust's developmental hierarchy is presented in Figure 7-1. The first level in this model involves the acquisition of an internal language system or inner language. The second level entails making associations between auditory symbols and experience, which results in comprehension of spoken words (auditory receptive language). At the third level auditory expressive language is demonstrated through the use of speech. In the final stages the development of reading (visual receptive language) is followed by expressing printed words through writing (visual expressive language).

Throughout the entire process of language development, children must first receive and then integrate a myriad of sensory data in order to develop the necessary competence to express themselves through speech or writing. The fundamental rule in conceptualizing the acquisition of language is that meaningful input (reception) always precedes output (expression)

(Berry, 1969). The distinction between *receptive* and *expressive language* is of great importance when we attempt to assess a child's abilities in spoken language.

Components of Language

In order to develop the competence to understand and use spoken language, the child must first master several basic elements that are prerequisite to this ability. The major *components* or *elements* of language usage include (1) *phonology*, (2) *morphology*, (3) *syntax*, and (4) *semantics* (Berry, 1969). It is the combination of these four elements that adds a distinctive structure and meaning to language. Myers and Hammill (1976) state, "the languages of communities, such as English, Japanese, Russian, etc., become distinctive when the sound systems, syntactic rules, and semantic structures of those languages are generated and reinforced within the community (p. 162)." Teachers must be aware of the different components of language to assess their role in cases of spoken-language disorders.

Phonology   Phonology is the study of the sound system that constitutes spoken language; *phonemes* refer to the *specific sounds* that make up a language. In and of themselves, phonemes have no meaning, but must be produced in such a fashion that they conform to standards of accepted usage within a language. For example, the phonemes /t/ and /d/ are meaningless by themselves, but if they are interchanged in a word they will significantly alter its meaning (e.g., toe—doe). Consequently, children must learn to comprehend adequately and to produce individual phonemes as a prelude to normal language development. Obviously, if a child does not perceive differences in the various phonemes and produces them in a distorted fashion, language usage will be impaired substantially.

Even though most adults when speaking produce phonemes with ease and consistency, it should not be thought that the phonological system is simple and easily attained. In most instances the English phonemes are similar and are differentiated only by slight differences (Jakobsen & Halle, 1956). The "minimal pairs" of /b/—/p/, /t/—/d/, /k/—/g/, /f/—/v/, etc., are produced in exactly the same place in the mouth and are only distinct in that one sound in each pair is voiced (by vibrating the vocal folds), whereas the other sound is unvoiced (no vibration of the vocal folds). It is truly amazing that most children at a very early age are capable of meaningful discriminations between these and other phonemes, with regard to comprehension and production of them. For this reason it is possible that no language uses all of the possible phonemic variations available. Brown (1965) points out:

Phonemes are for the most part vowels and consonants, and they correspond roughly to the letters of an alphabet writing system. Phonemes are not in themselves meaningful; they are semantically empty. No language uses very many. The range in languages of the world is from about fifteen to about eighty-five, with English using forty-five. Probably the number is small because it is advantageous to use only sounds that can be easily produced or identified [p. 247].

Morphology *Morphology* is the study of the smallest *meaningful* units of language *(morphemes)*, which cannot be divided into smaller units without destroying their meaning. For example, the word *book* contains only one morpheme. It would be impossible to divide this word into smaller components and still maintain its basic integrity as a word. However, when the plural marker *s* is added to the word *book* (i.e., *books*), a change in meaning occurs. Consequently, the word *books* is composed of two distinct morphemes, each of which is essential to an understanding of the concept of "two or more books."

The analysis of morphemic elements includes the study of grammatical markers used in language to specify concepts, such as plurality (marked by *s* for regular nouns), verb tense (marked by *ed, ing,* etc.), and shifts from adjective to adverb (marked by *ly*) (Myers & Hammill, 1976). In some instances, morphemes are highly irregular: *woman* plus the plural morpheme becomes *women; rise* with the past-tense marker becomes *rose; mouse* plus the plural morpheme becomes *mice.* The reader can easily generate many other examples to illustrate this point.

Syntax *Syntax* relates to the arrangement of words into meaningful phrases and sentences. In this instance, the ordering of words can have great impact upon the meaning of a given sentence or a phrase. For example, the sentence, "Are you going?" implies a specific question. However, a simple reordering of the words to "You are going." markedly alters the meaning of the original sentence. It is apparent that children must learn the importance of proper ordering of words within a sentence to facilitate adequate receptive and expressive language.

According to Bartel (1975), knowledge (i.e., competency) of syntax permits a person (1) to distinguish grammatical from ungrammatical sentences, (2) to go beyond the superficial nature of sentences and perceive the meaning that lies beneath the surface, (3) to generate an infinite number of sentences using a set number of rules, (4) to understand sentences that never have been heard before, and (5) to recognize ambiguities in sentences. Syntax undoubtedly plays a vital role in the production and understanding of language. If a child has difficulty in the acquisition or use of syntactical rules, oral language development likely will be disorganized and difficult to understand.

Semantics Semantics refers to the *meaning* of words and sentences. Whereas other components of language have been studied extensively, semantics has received considerably less attention. However, it is possible to state that initially a child develops associations between words and common objects in the environment. Most young children quickly demonstrate knowledge of semantics by learning the appropriate verbal symbols for such common objects as dog, ball, dish, and book. They use these words appropriately in the process of communication and in the same situations in which adults use them. However, as demands for increased sophistication in language usage are made upon the child, it is necessary for the child to rely increasingly upon the situational and linguistic context in which the word is used. Clark (1974) among others has demonstrated that the way in which young children comprehend terms describing relationships, such as prepositions, is partially a function of the total context in which they hear the prepositions. Consequently, not only must children master simple word meanings, but also they must have competency in using each component of language in order to derive the most meaning from a given phrase or sentence.

FACTORS AFFECTING LANGUAGE DEVELOPMENT

The normal development of language is dependent upon a combination of factors. Initially, in order for a child to acquire a language system, the child must possess an intact nervous and muscular system that permits understanding and use of the phonological, morphological, syntactical, and semantic components of language. Many internal and environmental factors are associated with the level of proficiency with which some children use verbal symbols in communication. The purpose of this section is to discuss the most important factors that directly influence the development of language.

Intelligence

Intelligence is perhaps the most important determinant in the development of language, since it affects both the ability to mimic verbal symbols, as well as to understand the meaning of them (Ausubel & Sullivan, 1970). McCarthy (1960) has found that accelerated language development is one of the most striking characteristics of intellectually gifted children. As early as in the first 2 years, a small but positive relationship seems to exist between the observed level of infant language and later measures of intelligence (Winitz, 1964).

Just as above-average intelligence facilitates language development, so a lack of mental ability negatively affects overall linguistic competence. Undoubtedly, individuals who are mentally retarded are slower in exhibiting language skills because they do not possess the necessary intelligence to develop linguistic competence or an inner language, or both. Consequently, a mentally retarded child usually will demonstrate language behavior typical of younger children (McWilliams, 1966). However, delayed language development is not always a sign of below-average intelligence. Many normal and intellectually gifted children use language late for reasons unrelated to mental ability (Newland, 1960). It is imperative that teachers be aware of the effects of intelligence on language so that they can consider the potential of these effects when they assess spoken-language disorders.

Environmental Stimulation

The quality and quantity of contact that children have with adults is a significant variable in their language development (Cazden, 1966). The language delays of children who come from lower socioeconomic levels concern many educators and psychologists. Bereiter and Engelman (1966) have determined that preschool disadvantaged children use less verbal communication than their advantaged peers. McConnell and Robertson (1970) have interpreted this finding to mean that communication in these homes tends to be restricted and characterized by parental language intended mainly to control the children's behavior and to express emotions. In addition, language in these environments is seldom used to explain or inform.

Bernstein (1961) also has noted major differences in the language systems used by children in upper and lower socioeconomic levels. In most instances, the speech and language of individuals from lower socioeconomic levels consist of a "linguistic code" that is geared to sharing experiences and attitudes in their social relationships, but that lacks the conceptual levels necessary for reasoning, analyzing, and forming complex explanations. It is not surprising, then, that language development of children from lower socioeconomic levels tends to be more basic and less elaborate than that of children from environments where language is used in a supportive way (John, 1963).

Children who have hearing deficiencies also are deprived of their environmental stimulation that supports the development of adequate language skills. It is obvious that if a child has a hearing loss, which impairs the reception of linguistic symbols, the child will be slower in developing language than children who do not have a hearing loss. According to Eisenson and Ogilvie (1971), children with mild to moderate hearing impairments, especially if the impairments are recognized early, may speak quite competently if they are given appropriate attention and training. The significance of this problem is increased greatly when we consider that 5 percent of school-aged children have hearing levels outside the range of normal (Davis & Silverman, 1960). Every teacher must be observant continually for signs of hearing loss among students and always consider this variable when they assess spoken-language disorders.

Central Nervous System Functioning

As was mentioned previously in this chapter, an intact central nervous system (CNS) is an essential prerequisite to normal language development. The adequately functioning CNS permits the reception, modification, interpretation, and storing of sensory information from the immediate environment. The knowledge regarding the environment that is derived from these experiences provides the basis for inner language, which provides the basis for all later forms of spoken and written communication. In those instances in which children have sustained significant neurological impairments, deficiencies in most forms of language behaviors frequently are noted.

The term often used to identify children with neurological disorders and linguistic disturbances is childhood *aphasia.* In the literal sense, aphasia means *without language* or *without speech.* In most situations, the label aphasia is used to designate relatively severe disorders in the comprehension and production of spoken and written language. The characteristic features of abnormal language development of the aphasic child have been described by Eisenson and Ogilvie (1971):

> A characteristic feature of the language development of aphasic children, aside from the initial retardation, is unevenness of ability. Even after this child begins to use language, he does not show the expected increments or the "ordered" pattern by which most children increase their linguistic abilities for day-to-day communication .... They may show parallel disparities in learning to read and write. The result may be that even after the children are in the mid-primary grades, their educational achievements are so uneven as to cause considerable concern to their teachers, their parents, and to themselves [p. 404].

The major difference between the language development of aphasic children and of children who are mentally retarded or come from nonstimulating homes is the *disordered* nature in which language is acquired and used. Whereas the mentally retarded and nonstimulated children demonstrate relatively even (although *delayed*) patterns of development, aphasic children will demonstrate erratic patterns of development (McConnell & Robertson, 1970). For example, comprehension skills, both auditory and visual, may be completely normal; however, the ability to express oneself using appropriate sentence structure (i.e., syntax) may be impaired significantly. Although many authorities now feel that *classifying* children as *brain-damaged* or *aphasic* is useless from an educational standpoint, they encourage teachers to become familiar with the potential effects and terminology associated with deviant neurological functioning to increase their ability to communicate with other (noneducational) personnel in the schools.

Emotional Development

In order to develop an adequate language system, a child must possess the necessary emotional integrity to respond appropriately to the immediate environment (Berry, 1969). At a basic level an infant must recognize and respond to the human voice as a prerequisite to normal language development. Once an infant becomes comfortable with the voices of parents, internalization and assimilation of verbal utterances takes place and provides a bridge between the environment and the child. It is through the processes of internalization, integration, and assimilation that the ability to abstract and to conceptualize becomes possible (Myklebust, 1954).

It is axiomatic that if a child is emotionally impaired and cannot or does not relate to individuals in the environment, serious language disturbances may result. In some situations in which emotional disturbances are obvious and severe, children may be diagnosed as *autistic, childhood schizophrenic,* etc. These affective disturbances usually are classified as "psychotic disorders of childhood" (Vetter, 1969). The language behavior of such children tends to be syntactically disordered, repetitious, egocentric, and obsessive (Wolff & Chess, 1965).

In less serious cases of emotional maladjustment, language development may be near normal; however, the child may feel secure enough to communicate with only one or two individuals in the environment. In addition, Oswald (1963) has noted that many disturbed children also exhibit deviant vocal qualities (e.g., in pitch, timbre, quality, etc.) that may interfere with effective communication. Lorenz and Cobb (1954) report that neurotic children demonstrate a lower than normal use of connectives, prepositions, interjections, and adjectives. There can be little doubt that socioemotional integrity is an essential ingredient for normal language development. Teachers are well advised to consider this variable when they assess any aspect of spoken language disorders.

DEVELOPMENTAL STAGES IN THE
ACQUISITION OF LANGUAGE

Prior to understanding and assessing deficiencies in spoken language, teachers must become aware of the behaviors that are indicative of normal language development. As with all other areas of human development, behaviors associated with language acquisition progress through various stages—usually from the gross to the complex. As the child becomes increasingly more sophisticated in his or her use of language, comprehension and production of language gradually resembles that of the adult. The speed and efficiency with which the child passes through the various stages of language development are used by professionals to assess the adequacy of the receptive and expressive aspects of language usage.

The major developmental stages through which a child progresses in acquiring linguistic competency have been the topic of intensive study for 50 years (Dale, 1976). In most situations the first 12 months of a child's life are spent in a sequence of *prelinguistic* (i.e., utterances made *prior* to the use of true words) *vocalizations* that seem to provide the basis for all later language development (Eisenson, 1963). The first two stages of prelinguistic vocalization are (1) *undifferentiated crying* and (2) *differentiated crying*. The undifferentiated cry is the initial reaction to the environment, including the first cry at birth, and is reflexive and generalized in its manifestation. By the fifth week, however, the infant's cries become more differentiated in tonal quality and loudness. Eisenson states,

> . . . the sensation of hunger—caused, among other things, by a contraction of the muscles of the stomach—results in changes of *all the muscles* of the body, including those involved in the production of speech sounds. These changes, when accompanied by vocalization, give rise to the type of cry which we come to recognize as a hunger cry, characterized and distinguished from others by its rhythms [p. 191].

Apparently, a "tuned-in" mother is able to distinguish the two distinct cries of her 6- to 10-month-old infant as either stimulated by pain or by fatigue.

By the second or third month, most normal infants enter into the third level of prelinguistic utterance, *babbling*. This stage of linguistic development is characterized by vocal play during which sounds are produced at random. During this period of babbling infants primarily are stimulating themselves rather than responding to environmental sounds. The sounds that are produced in this stage include the vowel /ae/ as in *cat* and the consonants /k/, /g/, /h/, /p/, /m/, and /b/.

The fourth and fifth levels of prelinguistic vocalization include *lallation* and *echolalia*. Lallation is defined as the infant's tendency to repeat or imitate intentionally his or her own random sounds. Echolalia usually begins in the eighth or ninth month when the infant purposefully imitates sounds made in the environment (e.g., the sounds of the vacuum cleaner, car, or of adults talking) but *without* apparent meaning. According to Eisenson (1963), the levels of lallation and echolalia are of crucial importance to language usage because "during these stages the child acquires a repertoire of sound complexes which ultimately he will be able to produce at will, and which he must have before he can learn to speak or acquire language in the adult sense (p. 195)."

Shortly after reaching 1 year of age, most children begin to use single words with meaning. At this point the words tend to be nouns; verbs are used a bit later. Reinforcement by adults or older siblings in the environment is very important in maintaining a supportive environment for the child's language development. At 18 months of age the vast majority of normal children begin to use simple two- and three-word sentences (McNeill, 1966). When children have demonstrated this initial step in the acquisition of basic syntax, it can be assumed that the vocalizations are orderly, rule governed, and are *not* imitations of adult utterances (Braine, 1963; Brown & Bellugi, 1964; and Miller & Ervin, 1964). By 30 months of age, according to McNeill (1966), most children have achieved a high level of linguistic competency in relation to syntactical usage.

During the ages of 5 and 6 the child continually refines and adapts all the components of language usage. Over 2,500 words have been incorporated into the child's vocabulary by this time, and the average length of spoken sentences consists of approximately 4.5 words. The child's use of language tends to be quite egocentric in that first-person pronouns are very frequently used to indicate his or her own interests, feelings, and motivations (Piaget, 1971). Articulation of sound also continually increases in efficiency. Consonant sounds that require more complex muscular functioning (e.g., /s/, /r/, /th/) are gradually articulated with ease and consistency.

When the child enters school linguistic functioning becomes more complex and adult-like. Spoken-language proficiency becomes highly correlated with the other language arts. Loban (1963), in a longitudinal study, has demonstrated that children who speak in an efficient and effective manner also rank well in written language and in reading. Children who score below average on any one of the measures also tend to score below average on the other two. As the children progress to higher grades the relationship among the language arts *increases.* Apparently, growth in one area of language ability reinforces growth in other areas.

The reader should be aware that this discussion of the various stages of language acquisition is not intended to be complete. McNeill (1966) provides a complete discussion of this topic, which should be of value to any interested professional. The following table compiled by Bartel (1975) presents a summary of the primary milestones noted in the acquisition of linguistic comprehension and production. It is hoped that readers will refer to this table when they conceptualize the process of language development.

TABLE 7-2 Developmental Stages of Language Acquisition

Age	General Characteristics	Purpose of Vocalization	Vocabulary	Sentence Length	Phonology	Syntax	Comprehension
1–4 weeks	Undifferentiated crying						
4–6 weeks	Differentiated crying	Shows pleasure, distress					Responds to human voice by attending
6 wks.–6 mos.	Babbling—vocal play, calling, gurgling	Shows pleasure, distress			Mostly front vowels /g/, /k/, /l/		
6–9 mos.	Lalling—intonation present, syllables are present	Getting attention, socialization			Mostly front vowels, some syllables /m/, /n/, /p/, /b/		Responds to human speech by smiling and vocalizing, may understand some words or intonations, verbal syncretism
9–12 mos.	Echolalia—repetition of sounds made by self and others	Responds to adult stimulaton—self-satisfaction	Sometimes first word appears		Consonants begin to exceed vowels		Inner language (Myklebust), some receptive ability—will do patta-cake or wave "bye-bye"
12–18 mos.	Intentional use of speech, beginning of true speech	Generalized use of vocabulary, e.g., "dada" might mean "daddy is coming," "where's daddy," "I want my daddy"	1–20 words, nouns, verbs, adjectives, adverbs	1 word	Monosyllabic or disyllabic		Responds to simple commands, understands words, phrases, e.g., "no," "Come"

18–24 mos.	Intentional, meaningful speech	Satisfaction of needs, exploration of environment, egocentric speech	Up to 300 words	2-word sentences appear, beginnings of form-class differentiation, begins use of nouns	Consonants: mostly initial and medial; final pronunciation rarely inconsistent	Uses simple rule, sentence (pivot or modifier) + open or lexical item	Uses input from adults for inducing his own grammatical rules. Comprehends more than he produces. — Understands tense, basic numerical concepts, e.g., "many," "few," but doesn't produce these. Can understand rudimentary causality
2–3 years	Speech becoming more intelligible and differentiated, sometimes beginning of stuttering	Satisfaction of needs, exploration of environment, egocentric speech. Words still general in content	Up to 900 words	3–4 words	Masters two thirds adult speech sounds	Simple and compound sentences, differentiation of pivot class to demonstratives, adjectives, determiners, expanded noun phrase, conjunctions such as "and" appear; begins to use auxiliary verb "is," subject-predicate appears, plural suffix /s/ appears	
3–4 years	Language becoming more developed and refined by adult standards	Language used for narration, explaining, requesting. Beginning of speech to describe imaginary events	Up to 1,500 words, relatively fewer nouns, more adjectives, adverbs, pronouns, conjunctions, prepositions	4–8 words	Most double consonant blends (e.g., gr, mp, bl, rt) appearing, some triple consonant blends (mpt, mps) present, most single phonemes except /j/, /s/, /v/, and final l and t	Past tense appears, overgeneralization of inflectional markers, e.g., "ed," "s"; negative transition appears: questions such as "What that thing go there?" produce complete simple-active-declarative kernel sentences	Understands more numerical concepts, e.g., "two" or "three," comprehends most adult structure except complex embedding and ambiguous sentences

TABLE 7-2 *Continued*

Age	General Characteristics	Purpose of Vocalization	Vocabulary	Sentence Length	Phonology	Syntax	Comprehension
4–5 years	Language becoming complete in structure and form, more abstract	Decline of egocentric speech, growth of true communication, information seeking	Up to 2,500 words	Up to 7 + words	Final /s/, /sh/, /ch/, additional double and triple consonant blends appear, occasional reversal of sounds	Most basic rules mastered, produces grammatical sentences including most transformations, uses comparatives, uses all parts of speech correctly	Knows most common opposites, definitions of common words, verbal syncretism decreasing, uses many "how," and "why" questions in response to statements by others
5–6 years	Continued development and refinement	Information-seeking, name-calling, contradicting, arguing	2,500 + words	Average 4.5 words	/th/ (unvoiced) sound, additional double and triple consonant blends	Syntactical development essentially complete, except for complex embedding and ambiguities	Understands 6,000 words (estimate), shows inner logic, some abstracting and categorizing
6–7 years	Language becoming increasingly symbolic	Begins to read and write	Likes to use big words, increasing in size and complexity	Average 6.5 words	/th/ (voiced) sound, additional double and triple blends; all phonology mastered by most girls and some boys	Speech made up of: nouns 17%, verbs 25%, adjectives, 7.6%, adverbs 10%, pronouns 19%, conjunctions 2.6%, prepositions 7.6%, interjections 1%, articles 8.3%	Can use picture dictionary, can define and explain words, anticipates closure in speech of others, understands time and seasons, left-right

244

| 7 + years | Fluent usage | Likes to use big words, increasing in size and complexity | Master of last sounds /-kt/, /-tr/, /-sp/ | Most errors now are common to child's cultural environment, e.g., use of double negative | Understands cause and effect relationship |

Source: Bartel, N. Assessing and remediating problems in language development. In D. D. Hammill & N. Bartel (Eds.), *Teaching children with language and behavior problems.* Boston: Allyn and Bacon, 1975. Adapted by the authors from Berry (1969), Lewis (1936), McCarthy (1954), McNeil (1970), Metraux (1950), Templin (1957) and from other sources.

ASSESSMENT OF SPOKEN-LANGUAGE DISORDERS

For most children development of spoken-language abilities occurs with remarkable speed and ease. As normal children grow older they demonstrate increasingly complex behaviors that indicate the acquisition of both receptive and expressive language usage. The degree of competency that a child develops in spoken language skills will influence later academic achievement. Consequently, if a child is exhibiting school-related problems, the teacher must be prepared to assess components of spoken language to determine if deficiencies in this area are contributing to academic failure.

A multitude of techniques to assess aspects of spoken language are available. The major categories into which these techniques are divided include (1) standardized tests and (2) informal teacher-made tests. These tests and techniques will be outlined in the next section.

STANDARDIZED TESTS

The standardized measures available to assess spoken language share several common characteristics. These characteristics include specific directions for administering and scoring the tests, a set of fixed items designed to measure an aspect of spoken-language behavior, and norms that have been established to permit comparison of an individual's score with the scores of groups who have taken the test. The principal types of standardized tests available to assess spoken-language proficiency are those that (1) provide a *comprehensive* view of all language functioning and (2) measure *specific* components of linguistic performance (e.g., phonology, linguistic structure, or semantics). In addition to these, some standardized tests have been produced that assess language behavior, but they should not be considered as true measures of language development; rather, these tests assess what has become known as "correlates" of language functioning (Dickson, 1974). The factors that are assessed in these tests include perception, cognition, and motor ability. Teachers should be aware of the strengths and weaknesses of all three types of tests when they attempt to determine if a student is deficient in spoken language.

Comprehensive Tests of Language Ability

Comprehensive tests of language ability are very useful in assessing general linguistic skill. The measures that are currently available to accomplish this task have been constructed within a developmental framework. Normative data are available for each test, which permits a comparison of a child's score with that of a group that also has taken the test. As with most tests that attempt to measure a wide range of skills, comprehensive tests of language ability do not provide an in-depth diagnosis of language problems. These measures perhaps are best used to provide a general estimate of language behavior and to point out specific areas that are in need of more thorough assessment. The reader is encouraged to carefully review each test that we will now discuss in order to determine the particular linguistic constructs upon which each is based.

The Houston Test for Language Development   The Houston Test for Language Development (Crabtree, 1963) is divided into two parts to allow the linguistic assessment of children from 6 months to 6 years of age. Part I consists of a checklist to be completed by an observer who has ready access to the child. This part is designed for very young children from 6 months to 3 years of age. The categories of language assessed include accent, melody of speech, gesture, vocabulary, sound articulation, dynamic content, and grammatical usage. The accompanying manual provides specific directions for administering items, including the particular behaviors that are to be observed. The score sheet for Part I is shown in Figure 7–2.

Part II consists of a kit of materials (e.g., dolls), which assist the teacher in eliciting free running speech, to be used with children from 3 to 6 years of age. Some of the 18 areas tapped in this part include vocabulary, auditory judgments, temporal content, syntax, self-identity, etc. The normative data provided for *The Houston Test for Language Development* are based upon the scores of 215 children from 6 months to 6 years of age. While the standardization data are minimal, a teacher can learn to administer and interpret this instrument easily. The results of this test are probably best used to gain an informal estimate of a child's language development, which then can be used to plan teaching programs.

The Utah Test of Language Development   The Utah Test of Language Development (Mecham, Jex, & Jones, 1967) is designed to assess expressive and receptive verbal language skills in children from 1 to 15 years of age. Although this test originally was constructed for use with brain-damaged children, it can be used also with children who do not have observable organic impairment but who do give evidence of language disorder. The 51 items in this test have been selected from other standardized tests. The general categories of language measured include repetition of digits, naming of colors, naming of pictures, copying designs, length of sentences, vocabulary, responding to simple commands, and reading. The standardization sample for *The Utah Test of Language Development* consisted of 273 normal subjects ranging from 1 to 14 years of age. Since this sample is comprised of less than 20 children from each age level, the results of this

FIGURE 7–2   Score Sheet for Part I

Scoring Sheet: The Houston Test for Language Development

Name _____ Birthdate _____ Sex _____

Parents _____ Address _____

Date of Test _____ Examiner _____

Referred By _____ Reason for Referral _____

Items	Age in Months					
	6	12	18	24	30	36
Smiles	X					
Vocalizes back vowels	X					
"Talks" to inanimate objects	X					
Attends to voice	X					
Blows bubbles	X					
Laughs out loud	X					
Controls volume	X					
Squeals	X					
Uses vocal grunt	X					
Holds out arms to be taken		X				
Vocalizes syllables		X				
Repeats syllables		X				
Imitates sounds		X				
Uses reflexive jargon		X				
Responds to "bye, bye"		X				
Uses 2–3 words		X				
Will pat-a-cake		X				
Understands inhibitions		X				
Converses in jargon			X			
Points to indicate wants			X			
Uses 10 or more words			X			

FIGURE 7–2   *Continued*

Items	Age in Months					
	6	12	18	24	30	36
Identifies parts of doll			3	5		
Obeys prepositions				1	2	3
Names pictures			1	8	11	16
Points to pictures			5	10	15	19
Articulates labials				X		
Articulates dentals					X	
Articulates velars						X
Uses three-word sentence				X		
Verbalizes action					X	
Uses pronoun I					X	
Gives four lines from memory						X
Tells what happened						X
Names his sex						X
Gives full name						X
Announces his action						X
Protests inaccuracies						X

Scoring Summary

Age in Months	Item Value	No. Items Passed	Score
6	.666		=
12	.666		=
18	1		=
24	1		=
30	1		=
36	.6		=

TOTAL SCORE =

Basal Age (Age at which all items were passed) =

Upper Age (Highest age at which any item is passed) =

Language Age (Total Score from Score Summary) =

test must be viewed with some caution. The scores obtained from this instrument are intended to be translated into a language-age equivalent. No attempt is made to provide information in the form of a profile or to classify the types of errors made by the child. In most situations, this test can be administered in 45 minutes.

The Test of Language Development   Of all the tests providing a comprehensive measure of language ability, *The Test of Language Development* (TOLD) (Newcomer & Hammill, 1977) is, perhaps, the most highly standardized. This test is composed of five principal and two supplemental semi-independent subtests, each of which taps a different component of spoken language. The TOLD is used with children ranging in age from 4.0 to 8.11 and can be administered by any professional who has adequate contact with the child. The five principal subtests measure aspects of semantics and syntax, and include: (1) *picture vocabulary*—assesses the extent to which a child understands the meanings associated with words (receptive semantics); (2) *oral vocabulary*—measures the ability of the child to give oral definitions to common words (expressive semantics); (3) *grammatic understanding*—assesses the ability of the child to comprehend syntactical form and grammatical markers (receptive syntax); (4) *sentence imitation*—taps the ability of the child to reproduce correct sentences (receptive syntax); (5) *grammatical completion*—measures the ability of the child to comprehend and use certain common morphological forms and inflections (receptive and expressive syntax). The two supplemental subtests focus upon the phonological skills of word discrimination and word articulation.

The research support for the TOLD is extensive, and three types of reliability were employed in constructing the test; i.e., internal consistency, stability, and standard error of measurement. Newcomer and Hammill indicate that the coefficients associated with the individual subtests were greater than 0.80 at most age levels. Content, item, concurrent, and construct validity statistics are reported in a separate volume. None of the reported coefficients are below 0.69. The TOLD's norms are based upon the performance of 1,014 children. Approximately 40 minutes are required for administration.

The Michigan Picture Language Inventory   *The Michigan Picture Language Inventory* (MPLI) (Wolski, 1958) is individually administered to children from 4 to 6 years of age. The test first assesses comprehension and then expression. In addition to deriving total scores for reception and expression, the test also taps various word classes, which include: (1) singular and plural nouns, (2) personal pronouns, (3) possessives, (4) adjectives, (5) demonstratives, (6) articles, (7) adverbs, (8) prepositions, and (9) verbs and auxiliaries. The procedure to administer this portion of the MPLI is complex and, although untimed, requires a substantial amount of time to administer.

Tests of Language Correlates

As can be noted from the preceding discussion, there are many tests available that measure different facets of language ability. It should be noted that these tests have as their primary focus the assessment of a child's skills as they relate to the comprehension and use of phonology, morphology, syntax, and semantics. Proficiency in these areas is fundamental to normal language usage and must be the primary consideration in an assessment of deficiencies in linguistic performance (Lenneberg, 1967; Menyuk, 1971; Whitaker, 1971). Teachers must be judicious when they select tests of spoken language and must be sure that whatever test they choose adequately taps these linguistic constructs.

This concern for the selection of true language measures becomes complicated when we consider that some popular tests attempt to assess linguistic competence but, in fact, center upon factors that are more appropriately labeled as language correlates. Although measurement of these abilities may be of some value in understanding the child as a total person, they should not be viewed as viable linguistic tests. It is important that educators be aware of the content and theoretical constructs of these tests so that they do not waste time in assessing variables that will not yield usable data relevant to a child's true *language* abilities. Two tests that fall into the category of measuring language correlates are *The Illinois Test of Psycholinguistic Abilities* and the *Slingerland Screening Tests for Identifying Children with Specific Language Disabilities*.

Illinois Test of Psycholinguistic Abilities   The *Illinois Test of Psycholinguistic Abilities* (ITPA) (Kirk, McCarthy, & Kirk, 1968), as the name implies, is a test designed to measure the psycholinguistic skills of children from 2 years, 4 months to 10 years, 3 months of age. *Psycholinguistics* is defined as the study of language systems used in human communication and thinking—in particular, the manner in which individuals acquire and use such systems (Deese, 1970). The ITPA attempts to measure psycholinguistic skill through three basic dimensions: (1) channels of communication—the auditory-vocal and visual-motor modalities through which the content of communication is presumed to flow; (2) psycholinguistic processes—reception, organization, and expression; and (3) levels of organization—representational (a more complex mediating process) and automatic (less voluntary but well organized and integrated). The 10 subtests and 2 supplemental subtests constituting the ITPA are listed below.

1. Auditory Reception
2. Visual Reception
3. Auditory Association
4. Visual Association
5. Verbal Expression
6. Manual Expression
7. Grammatical Closure
8. Visual Closure
9. Auditory Sequential Memory
10. Visual Sequential Memory
11. Auditory Closure
12. Sound Blending.

While the construction of the ITPA seems to be thorough, there is serious question as to whether it actually measures true psycholinguistic ability. Carroll (1972) states that

> It requires some stretching of meaning to call the ITPA a measure of psycholinguistic abilities. . . . The title of the ITPA is a misnomer, and users should be cautioned to look carefully at the true nature of the test, which might less misleadingly have been named something like the Illinois Test of Cognitive Functioning [p. 442].

The only subtest that can be said to assess linguistic functioning is Grammatical Closure (Newcomer & Hammill, 1976). The ITPA provides a notion of a child's general perceptual and mental abilities, but it should not be used if the assessment goal is obtaining data relevant to specific language proficiency or academic achievement. Readers interested in more thorough critiques of the ITPA are referred to Wiederholt (in press), Rosenberg (1971), Weener, Barrett, and Semmel (1967), and Newcomer and Hammill (1976).

Slingerland Screening Tests for Identifying Children with Specific Language Disabilities The purpose of the *Slingerland Screening Tests* (Slingerland, 1970) is to screen young children for potential language impairments that relate to reading, writing, spelling, and speaking. Nine subtests are used to measure such variables as visual copying, visual memory, visual discrimination, auditory memory, auditory perception, and auditory-visual association. Additional tests can be administered if desired. These measures include oral sentence completion, retelling a brief story, and word repetition. The accompanying manual provides directions for scoring the tests as well as suggests interpretations for different patterns of errors.

As with the ITPA, the Slingerland should not be considered a true measure of linguistic ability. The constructs of auditory and visual perception and cognition, which underlie the vast majority of items on both tests, have a questionable relationship to either language development or later academic achievement (Hammill & Larsen, 1974; Larsen & Hammill, 1975; Newcomer & Hammill, 1976; Larsen, Rogers, & Sowell, 1976; Sowell, 1976). Consequently, these tests have little demonstrated theoretical or empirical validity as they pertain to school performance. When attempting to assess phonological, morphological, syntactical, or semantic functioning, teachers are well advised to select other, more appropriate tests.

Tests for Measuring Components of Language

The teacher wishing to evaluate a child's spoken-language usage has many standardized instruments from which to choose. Comprehensive tests of language ability can provide a broad picture of linguistic performance; however, frequently it is necessary to conduct an in-depth analysis of specific aspects of language. This will be the case in situations in which a child has exhibited particular problems in comprehension or use of phonology, linguistic structure (i.e., morphology and syntax), and semantics. A number of tests are available that assess each of these specific areas.

Tests of Phonology

As will be recalled from an earlier section in this chapter, phonology refers to the nonmeaningful sound system that constitutes spoken language. The tests that are available to measure a child's competence in phonology usually focus upon sound articulation (expressive language) and auditory discrimination (receptive language). Since tests of auditory discrimination are described in Chapter 6, only measures of *articulation* will be dealt with at this point. Two commonly used tests include the Templin-Darley Tests and the Goldman-Fristoe Test.

The Templin-Darley Tests of Articulation   The Templin-Darley Tests of Articulation (Templin & Darley, 1960) is one of the most popular set of tests available to assess ability of articulation. These tests are diagnostic in nature; however, a designated 50 items may also be used for screening purposes. The specific test items tap the child's ability to produce vowels, diphthongs, single consonants (in initial, medial, and final positions of words), and consonant blends in varying combinations. During the test the child is required to say a series of single words that contain a test sound or a combination of sounds in a specific position. When these are not articulated properly, the child is given a correct pronunciation of the word and asked to repeat it. By using this measure the teacher also can evaluate the degree of intelligibility of a child's conversation. Age norms have been established for this set of tests, which permit the determination of whether a child's ability to articulate is above or below average in comparison to peers.

Goldman-Fristoe Test of Articulation The purpose of *The Goldman-Fristoe Test of Articulation* (GFTA) (Goldman & Fristoe, 1969) is to evaluate a child's production of consonant sounds. In total the GFTA makes use of three assessment subtests. The first subtest, *sounds-in-words,* consists of 35 familiar pictures; children are required to name the pictures and respond to questions about some of them. All single consonant sounds in the English language are tested, with the exception of /zh/. The second subtest, *sounds-in-sentences,* provides a systematic means of assessing sound production in a context similar to that found in conversation. Two narrative stories are read aloud by the examiner and illustrated by sets of five and four pictures, respectively. The child is asked to recount each story in his or her own words, using the pictures as memory aids. The *stimulability* subtest, the third subtest, determines if phonemes that were articulated incorrectly are now articulated correctly when the child is given maximum stimulation. Norms are provided for children from 3 to 8 years of age. Indepth instructions are provided for scoring and interpreting the test results.

Tests of Linguistic Structure

A second component of language performance is the comprehension and use of various *linguistic structures.* Linguistic structure refers to the manner in which children use various aspects of morphology and syntax. Some commonly used standardized tests designed to assess *linguistic structure* include the *Carrow Elicited Language Inventory, Developmental Sentence Analysis, Northwestern Syntax Screening Test,* and *Test for Auditory Comprehension of Language.*

Carrow Elicited Language Inventory The purpose of the *Carrow Elicited Language Inventory* (CELI) (Carrow, 1974) is to provide a means for evaluating a child's control of grammar. The CELI consists of 52 stimuli, which include 51 sentences and 1 phrase. The teacher reads a series of sentences to the child and asks the child to *imitate* exactly what he or she hears. (These responses must be taped by the examiner). The sentences and phrases range in length from 2 to 10 words, with an average of 6 words. Of the 51 sentences, 47 are in the active voice and 4 are in the passive voice; 37 are affirmative and 14 are negative; 37 are declarative and 12 are interrogative; and 2 are imperative. A summary of grammatical forms included in the CELI are presented in Table 7–3. In addition to a total-error score, subscores are obtained for each grammatical category. Adequate reliability and validity statistics are reported in the accompanying manual. The average time for administration, transcription, and scoring is 45 minutes.

Developmental Sentence Analysis   Of all tests available to assess syntactical structure, *Developmental Sentence Analysis* (DSA) (Lee, 1974) is, perhaps, the most comprehensive and thorough. DSA is a method for devising a detailed and readily quantified and scored evaluation of a child's use of standard English grammatical rules. The procedure for administration of the DSA is to elicit spontaneous speech from the child while the child is in conversation with an adult. *Developmental Sentence Analysis* consists of two separate procedures, Developmental Sentence Types (DST) and Developmental Sentence Scoring (DSS). The DST is used to classify presentence phrases (when either a subject or predicate is missing) and to indicate if grammatical structure is developing in an orderly manner before basic sentences emerge. A group of 100 phrases is collected with the DST procedure. The classification chart for judging the presentence phrases is given in Table 7–4. The horizontal and vertical classification of this chart permits the examiner to assess the *diversity* of phrases spoken as well as the specific *linguistic composition* of the phrases.

The DSS is designed to analyze the grammatical structures found in complete sentences. A group of 50 complete sentences is needed for analysis with the DSS technique. A sentence is complete if it has a noun and a verb in a subject-predicate relationship. The speech sample must be a group of consecutive phrases, and no repeated sentences are permitted in the final scoring. Specific directions are given for scoring syntactical development in both the DST and DSS procedures. The statistical data provided includes (1) a cross-sectional study of DSS language samples from 200 children between the ages of 2.0 to 6.11, which was used to establish a normative base for the instrument; (2) estimates of internal consistency; and (3) item analyses of the DSS procedure. Information is also provided regarding the differences in development of syntax between male and female children.

Northwestern Syntax Screening Test   The *Northwestern Syntax Screening Test* (NSST) (Lee, 1969) is designed to provide a quick estimate of a child's level of syntactical comprehension and use. The age norms provided for the NSST are from 3 years, 11 months to 7 years, 11 months. In total, 40 items are used to test syntactical ability: 20 items assess the child's receptive ability by requiring the child to look at four pictures and indicate

TABLE 7–3   Summary of *CELI* Grammatical Forms

Form	Number
Pronouns	41
Indefinite (it, no one, everyone, both, what, whatever)	9
Personal	
1st & 2nd person (I, me, my, mine, you)	12
3rd person (he, she, her, hers)	10
Plural (we, they, their)	7
Demonstrative (those, that)	2
Reflexive (himself)	1
Prepositions (to, by, in, between, under, on, with)	14
Contexts: modifying copula *is*	4
modifying auxiliary *is* + *ing*	2
modifying auxiliary *is* + *ed*	2
modifying main verbs	6
Conjunctions (and, because, if, or, before, than, that)	7
Articles (the, a)	41
Contexts: occurring initially	16
occurring medially	25
Adverbs (fast, where, outside, how, down, up, now)	9
Wh-Questions (where, why, whose)	5
Negative (not, n't)	13
Contexts: with copula	2
with auxiliary	8
with modal	3
Nouns	
Singular	50
Plural	9
Adjectives and Predicate Adjectives	7
Verbs	103
Main Verbs (uninflected, *s*, *ed*)	46
Contexts: singly	14
with auxiliary + (neg)	17
with modal + (neg)	5
with infinitive	5
with auxiliary + neg + infinitive	2
with modal + auxiliary + neg	1
with modal +auxiliary + infinitive	1
with gerund	1
Copula ('s, is, are, been)	14
Contexts: singly	11
with neg	2
with modal + auxiliary	1
Auxiliary (am, is, are, has, have, has been, have been, do, does, did)	26
Contexts: with verb (ing, ed) + (neg)	20
with neg + verb + infinitive	2
with modal + neg + verb	2
with modal + verb + infinitive	1
with modal + copula	1

TABLE 7–3   *Continued*

Form	Number
Modal (can, could, will, would, may)	8
Contexts: with verb + (neg)	5
with auxiliary + copula	1
with neg + auxiliary + verb	1
with auxiliary + verb + infinitive	1
Infinitives	8
Gerunds	1

Source: From *Carrow Elicited Language Inventory* by E. Carrow, 1974, Copyright 1974 by Learning Concepts. Reprinted by permission.

the one that is most appropriate after a sentence is spoken by the examiner; and 20 items assess the child's expressive ability by having the child repeat sentences originally spoken by the examiner as the examiner points to various pictures. The norms are based on 344 children from middle-class families in which standard English is spoken. Suggestions are provided in the accompanying manual to aid the examiner in interpretation of scores, and procedures are provided to aid in scoring the child's responses.

Test for Auditory Comprehension of Language   The *Test for Auditory Comprehension of Language* (TACL) (Carrow, 1973) takes approximately 20 minutes to administer and is used with children from ages 3 years, 11 months to 6 years, 11 months. The TACL assesses oral-language comprehension without requiring language expression from the child. The test consists of 101 reproductions of line drawings, which represent categories and contrasts that can be designated by form classes and function words, morphological constructions, grammatical categories, and syntactical structures. The form classes and function words assessed are nouns, verbs, adjectives, adverbs, and prepositions. Morphological constructions are formed by adding *er* and *ist* to free morphs such as nouns, verbs, and adjectives. Grammatical categories that are tested include contrasts of case, number, gender, tense, status, voice, and mood. Syntactical structures of predication, modification, and complementation also are evaluated. Percentile ranks are provided for interpretation of individual test scores. A particularly notable feature of the TACL is that it also can be administered in Spanish, although norms are only available for the English version. The language categories measured by the TACL are presented in Table 7–5. A 25-item screening test also is available but, unfortunately, it must be bought separately.

TABLE 7–4   The Developmental Sentence Types (DST) Classification of Presentences

	Noun	Designator

Single Words	car Daddy kitty-cat
	truck Mommy Santa Claus
	cookie girl hot-dog
	Basic sentence elaborations:
	  Plural: *books, cars, men*
	Basic sentence modifications:
	  Pronoun: *me, something, nobody*
	  Question: *book? car? truck (right?)*
		here, there
		this, that
		it
		Basic sentece elaborations:
		  Plural: *those, these*
		Basic sentence modifications:
		  Question: *this? that? here? there?*

	Noun Elaboration	Designative Elaboration

2-word Combinations	Noun phrase
	  Article: *a car, the truck*
	  Possessive: *Daddy car, Billy truck*
	  Quantifier: *more car, other truck, two boy*
	  Adjective: *big car, dirty truck, red shoe*
	  Attributive: *baby bear, police car*
	Basic sentence elaborations:
	  Plural: *the cars, more trucks*
	  Additive: *car truck, Mommy Daddy*
	  Adverb: *now car, truck too, car again*
	  Subject-object: *doggie bone, Daddy ball*
	  Subject-locative: *car garage, Mommy window*
	Basic sentence modifications:
	  Pronoun: *this one, my truck, her cookie*
	  Negative: *not car, not truck, not this*
	  Question: *a car? another truck (OK?)*
	  Wh-question: *what car? which one?*
	  Conjunction: *and car, and truck, and this*
		Designator + noun
		  here car, there truck, this car, that truck, it car, it truck
		Basic sentence elaborations:
		  Plural: *these cars, there trucks*
		  Adverb: (*that again* = noun + adverb)
		  (*there now, here again* = fragments)
		Basic sentence modifications:
		  Pronoun: *here something, there one*
		  Negative: (*not this* = noun + negative)
		  (*not here, not there* = fragments)
		  Question: *that truck? this car (right?)*
		  Wh-question: *what this? who that?*
		  Conjunction: (*and this* = noun + conj.)
		  (*and here, and there* = fragments)

Constructions	Noun phrase
	  my big car, some more trucks, a red box
	Noun phrase + prepositional phrase
	  the car in front, the spot on the floor
	Quantifier + prepositional phrase
	  all of them, some of the other cars
	Basic sentence elaborations:
	  Plural: *some other cars*
	  Adverb: *now the car, the other truck too*
	  Additive: *the car the truck*
	  Subject-object: *the doggie another bone*
	  Subject-locative: *the car the garage*
	Basic sentence modifications:
	  Pronoun: *his other truck, all of mine*
	  Negative: *not the car, not that one*
	  Question: *the other car? the boy too (huh?)*
	  Wh-question: *what big car? which other one? how much milk? how many cookies? how about that one? what about me?*
	  Conjunction: *and the car, car and truck*
		Designator + noun phrase
		  here another car, there a truck
		  this a red car, that my truck
		  it a big car, it my truck
		Basic sentence elaborations:
		  Plural: *here some cars, these big cars*
		  Adverb: *there car too, here car now*
		  Additive: *there Mommy Daddy*
		Basic sentence modifications:
		  Pronoun: *that somebody car, here his car*
		  Negative: *that not car, this not a truck*
		  Question: *that a car? this a car (right?)*
		  Wh-question: *who that boy? what that one?*
		  Conjunction: *here a car and truck*

Source: Lee, L. *Developmental sentence analysis.* Evanston, Ill.: Northwestern University Press, 1974. Used with permission of the publisher.

TABLE 7-4 *Continued*

Descriptive Item	Verb	Vocabulary Item
big, pretty, broken, fixed *one, two, more* *on, off, up* Basic sentence elaborations: None Basic sentence modifications: Pronoun: *my, his* Question: *red? big (huh?)*	*sleep, eat, walk, fall* (*look, lookit, wait, stop* = imperative sentence) Basic sentence elaborations: Verb elaboration: *going, fell* Basic sentence modifications: Negative: *can't, won't* (*don't* = imperative sentence Question: *see? eat (OK?)*	*yes, no, OK, sh, hey, hi* *bye-bye, night-night, oh-oh* Basic sentence elaborations: Adverb: *again, now, too* Basic sentence modifications: Question: *huh? right? OK?* Wh-question: *what? who? where? when? how? why?* Conjunction: *because*

Predicative Elaboration	Verbal Elaboration	Fragments
Noun + descriptive item *car broken, truck dirty* *light off, TV on* *car there, truck here* Basic sentence elaborations: Plural: *cars here, lights on* Basic sentence modifications: Pronoun: *that pretty, it* *big something here,* *another on* Question: *car broken?* *it gone (right?)* Wh-question: *where car?* *what here? who there?*	Verb + object: *hit ball* Verb + locative: *sit chair* Verb + particle: *fall down* (Noun + verb = sentence: *baby sleep, that go, it fall*) Basic sentence elaborations: Verb elaboration: *saw car* Plural: *eat cookies, see cars* Adverb: *eat now, fall too* Basic sentence modifications: Pronoun: *see it, find one* Negative: *not fall, can't go* Question: *see it? go home?* Wh-question: *where go?* *what take? what find?* (*who go? what come?* = sentence) Conjunction: *and sleeping* Infinitive: *wanna go, gonna go*	Basic sentence elaborations: Prepositional phrase: *for Daddy, in car* Plural: *on chairs, in car* Adverb: *too big, all gone, up now, here again, right here, over there* Basic sentence modifications: Pronoun: *to you, in it* Negative: *not big, not here* Question: *in here? all gone (huh?)* Conjunction: *and big, but dirty, and here*

| Noun phrase + descriptive item: *the car broken, a truck dirty, this light off, the TV on, other car there, a truck here, car in garage, hat on head, Spot a good dog, Tom bad boy* Basic sentence elaborations: Plural: *all cars broken* Adverb: *light off now car here too, truck too dirty* Double locator: *car over there* Basic sentence modifications: Pronoun: *he bad boy, it off now* Negative: *this not broken* Question: *it off now? car over there (huh?)* Wh-question: *where that one? who in car? what color car? what in here?* Conjunction: *car and truck here* | Verb + object: *eat the cookie* Verb + locative: *put the table* Verb + particle + noun: *take off hat, turn on light* (Noun phrase + verb = sentence *the car go, a boy eat*) Basic sentence elaborations: Verb elaboration: *goes in barn* Adverb: *see car now, go in too* Basic sentence modifications: Pronoun: *want it now* Negative: *not fall down* Question: *see that one? eat more cookies (OK?)* Wh-question: *where put car? what take out? what find here? what doing to car?* Conjunction: *and find car* Infinitive: *wanna see it, gonna go home, gotta find it* | Words in series: *1, 2, 3, 4, etc.* *dog, cow, pig, etc.* Basic sentence elaborations: Prepositional phrase: *in the car, for the boy* Plural: *on the chairs* Adverb: *in car too, back over there* Basic sentence modifications: Pronoun: *on my head* Negative: *not in it* Question: *in here too? in the car (right?)* Conjunction: *and for me* |

TABLE 7–5   The Test for Auditory Comprehension of Language

Form Classes and Function Words	Items
Nouns	1–10, 29, 30
Adjectives	11–28
Verbs	31–38
Adverbs	39–41
Demonstratives	42–43
Prepositions	44–49
Interrogatives	82–84
Morphological Constructions	
Noun/Noun + Derivational Suffix "er"	50, 51
Verb/Verb + Derivational Suffix "er"	52
Noun/Noun + Derivational Suffix "er" + Masculine Suffix	53
Adjective/Adjective + Derivational Suffix "er," "est"	54–56
Noun/Noun + Derivational Suffix "ist"	57, 58
Grammatical Categories	
Gender and Number, Pronoun	59–63, 65
Number, Noun	66–69
Number, Verb	70, 71
Tense, Verb	64, 72–77
Voice, Verb	78–81
Status, Verb	85–88, 98
Syntactical Structure	
Imperative Mood	89, 90
Predication, Noun-Verb Agreement	91, 92
Complementation	95
Modification	93, 94, 96
	97, 99, 100
Coordination	101

Source: From *Test for Auditory Comprehension of Language* by E. Carrow, 1973, Copyright 1973 by Learning Concepts. Reprinted by permission.

Tests of Semantics

A third component of linguistic ability relates to the child's mastery of *semantic structures.* Although the definition of *semantics* refers to the meaning of words *and* sentences, tests designed to tap semantics mainly focus upon the comprehension and use of words. In fact, these measures may be more accurately labeled *tests of vocabulary.* Frequently used measures of semantics include the *Peabody Picture Vocabulary Test* and *Ammons Full-Range Picture Vocabulary Test.*

Peabody Picture Vocabulary Test   The *Peabody Picture Vocabulary Test* (PPVT) (Dunn, 1965) is widely used to evaluate the child's comprehension of words. The stimulus items are a series of four pictures. Each picture is presented in order, and the child is required to indicate the picture that best represents a stimulus word spoken by the examiner (e.g., cow, block, key, skirt, catching, tying, pouring, sewing). The norms for the PPVT are based on ages ranging from 2 years to adulthood. Although it is possible to generate an IQ scale from this test, users are cautioned to employ this test only for purposes of assessing vocabulary. The PPVT can be administered easily by the teacher and requires approximately 20 minutes to administer.

Ammons Full-Range Picture Vocabulary Test   The *Ammons Full-Range Picture Vocabulary Test* (APVT) (Ammons & Ammons, 1958) is similar in format to the PPVT. This instrument measures general intelligence as well as vocabulary comprehension. The APVT contains four pictures, which are shown to the child. As the examiner says a word, the child indicates which of the pictures best represents the given word. The APVT is not as well standardized as the PPVT, nor are the cartoon-like drawings in this test particularly clear. Norms for this test begin at 2 years of age.

INFORMAL ASSESSMENT TECHNIQUES

As we have noted, there are many standardized tests available for measuring various aspects of spoken language. There is little doubt that these tests provide helpful information in pinpointing general areas of deficiency. It is our belief, however, that in order to gain useful data relevant to a child's spoken-language problem a teacher must rely primarily upon interviewing, observational, and teaching skills. Depending upon the severity of the language disorder, a teacher should be prepared to design a series of structured situations that will permit analysis of the child while the child engages in a variety of language activities (i.e., *diagnostic teaching*). Regardless of whether the child is in preschool or elementary grades, a period of diagnostic teaching frequently is necessary to isolate those factors that are interfering with efficient language usage. Language scales and diagnostic training batteries also may assist teachers in structuring their observations and in gleaning useful information. The purpose of this next section is to discuss useful, informal assessment procedures that are appropriate for the evaluation of receptive and expressive language.

Diagnostic Teaching

Diagnostic teaching is the process that permits a teacher to analyze a child's behavior while the teacher engages in teaching. In cases of suspected language deficiency the teacher is interested particularly in finding those areas that impede *as well as* facilitate linguistic usage. In general, this process may extend in time from as short as 4 weeks to as long as 1 full school year or longer. The amount of time devoted to the diagnostic teaching depends completely upon the specific goals the teacher establishes and the severity of the disorder. Obviously, diagnostic teaching should not be concluded once the teacher has derived some initial findings regarding a child's particular problem; rather, it will be beneficial only if it is extended over the entire time that the child receives special assistance. It is necessary to continue the diagnostic teaching in order to ensure that whatever teaching activities have been instituted as a result of initial observations are still appropriate and that the documentation of the child's progress still provides input for further decision making regarding assessment and remedial programs.

The diagnostic teaching should vary in content, depending upon the language characteristics of individual children. Regardless of what direction is taken, it is necessary for teachers (1) to keep accurate records and (2) to be thoroughly familiar with developmental milestones associated with normal language functioning. Several examples of scales and checklists are provided later in this chapter to assist teachers in recording relevant behaviors associated with language. The need for professionals to be aware of schedules of language development is self-evident, because without such knowledge it is extremely difficult to judge accurately whether observed behaviors deserve special attention with regard to a child's environment or chronological and mental age. Teachers are encouraged to review the stages of language acquisition carefully before they initiate any diagnostic teaching. Those who wish to find additional sources of developmental schedules relating to language should consult McNeill (1966; 1970), Carroll (1961), Templin (1957), and McCarthy (1960).

Once the teacher has developed an efficient record-keeping system and has become familiar with the stages of language acquisition, controlled interactions with the child can begin. Berry (1969) suggests that, in most instances in which there is a language problem, teachers should secure a case history of the child, because very likely it will yield data pertinent to the problem. This case history can be obtained from the children's parents or, in some instances, from the children themselves. After the teacher obtains the case history, then the teacher can set up interactions with the child that will elicit particular language samples for later analysis. Throughout the entire phase of diagnostic teaching, continual monitoring of gains in spoken language documents progress and guides future interactions with the child.

Case History   The primary purpose of a case history is to obtain insights into the history of a child's language development. In most situations, particularly where the problem is relatively severe, the case history is invaluable in obtaining (1) a perspective of the early stages of the disorder, (2) the physical or emotional conditions that may have caused the problem (e.g., learning problem), (3) the manifestation of the language disorder in environments other than the school or clinic, and (4) clues about how to stimulate the child in the most productive manner in order to assess and remedy the situation. When the teacher attempts to conduct an interview with a parent (or an older child) to secure a case history, care must be taken to first prepare a set of specific questions that clearly relate to the problem at hand. In cases in which a teacher conducts a number of interviews, it is necessary to develop a standard form that can be adapted to meet the needs of a given situation. Frequently, after the initial interview and first few diagnostic teaching sessions, teachers will want to secure additional information periodically from the parents in order to validate their own observations.

The physical environment in which the case history is taken should be free from distraction and conducive to putting parents at ease. Questions should be asked in a straightforward manner and with a purpose. It is important that parents should not feel as if they are on trial and or that questions are designed to find fault with them. Rather, the questions always should be directed at securing information that relates to the observed language disorder. For example, some important questions would be:

- When did the child speak his or her first words?
- Does the child have a history of upper respiratory infections that caused hearing problems?
- Were there severe emotional upsets in the home during the first few years of the child's life?
- Do siblings also evidence language problems?
- Has the child's language problem been evaluated previously?
- When did the parents first notice, if at all, that something was wrong?
- Were there long periods in the child's life during which no language was used?
- At what level is the child's social relationship with peers, siblings, and parents?

Answers to these and other questions frequently will provide teachers with data that (1) gives a feeling about the child and the language problem; (2) isolates particular linguistic areas in need of assessment and remedying; (3) gives an indication if additional personnel should be consulted (e.g., psychologist, speech therapist, physician, etc.); and (4) suggests techniques that might be used in developing rapport with the child. If the case-history interview is planned and conducted with empathy and care, it may well be one of the most important and informative facets of the total language evaluation.

Eliciting Language Samples Once the teacher has obtained the case history, a series of diagnostic teaching situations need to be instituted to pinpoint specific linguistic deficiencies. In most instances, children will, after a period of casual interactions, readily exhibit a wide range of verbalizations. On the other hand, some children will evidence hesitation in speaking, and these children present the teacher with a significant problem, especially if the children's lack of language usage is long-term. In these cases, the teacher will have to be creative in structuring situations that are conducive to speaking.

In situations in which a child hesitates in speaking, perhaps the best rule to remember is never to attempt to *force* the child to speak. The teacher should always try to elicit normal and representative speech from the child. In order to accomplish this with children who are capable of speaking but reluctant to use speech, it may be necessary to devote three or four sessions to setting the stage for language usage. Teachers need not be discouraged if a long period of time is required to establish effective relationships with children; rather, teachers should view this time as helpful for systematically observing other relevant nonverbal behaviors (e.g., motor development, social relationships, complexity of free play, etc.).

Many authors have suggested techniques for eliciting language from children. In general, these procedures entail the creative use of such common objectives as toys, picture books, fruit, musical instruments, and in some cases, even small animals. Frequently, the teacher may find that bringing other, more verbal children into the diagnostic teaching session will reduce the tension of the situation and will provide a more supportive environment. Leaving a group of children alone (while tape-recording the session) with a group of toys or a pet will often provide the teacher with new insights into a child's true language ability. Readers who are interested in further reading regarding methods for eliciting language are encouraged to consult Lee (1974), McCarthy (1930), Menyuk (1969), and Johnson, Darley and Spriesterbach (1963).

Once the teacher has established a satisfactory relationship with the child so that the child feels free to communicate verbally, it is helpful (although not essential) to tape-record the sessions. The tape-recordings can be invaluable when the teacher attempts (1) to select the language areas to analyze in depth; (2) to validate the initial diagnostic conclusion(s); and (3) to evaluate the success of subsequent remedial programs. As in all phases of the diagnostic teacher program, the teacher should endeavor from the very beginning to record observed impressions of the problem in order to facilitate discovery of those areas that need attention most. A form such as the one presented in Figure 7–3 can be used to categorize and summarize the teacher's first impressions of the linguistic areas in which the child seems to be particularly strong or weak. Note, however, in this form that the area of *phonology* refers to the child's ability to comprehend or

FIGURE 7-3

Child's Name _____

Phonology		Linguistic Structure					Semantics					Sentence Length			
Vowels	Conson-ants	Grammati-cal Cate-gories	Sentence Complexity	Verb Tense	Sentence Forms	Inflec-tional Markers	1–50 Words	50–300 Words	300–1,500 Words	1,500–2,000 + Words	2-Word Sentences	3–4 Word Sentences	4–7 Word Sentences	7 + Sentences	

produce the vowels and consonants necessary for the efficient use of words. *Linguistic structure*, the components of morphology and syntax, relates to the child's use of grammatical categories (nouns, verbs, pronouns, articles, etc.), verb tense, complexity of sentences (simple, complex, or compound), sentence form (interrogative, declarative, imperative, etc.) and inflectional markers such as *ed*, and *s*. *Semantics* is meant to categorize the number of words comprehended or used by the child. *Sentence length* refers to the average number of words used by the child in producing sentences. Teachers are encouraged to adapt this form to their specific needs. The relative normality of a given child's performance in each of these areas can be determined by reviewing the developmental stages presented in Table 7–2. Once the teacher has considered each of the categories on this or a similar form, a complete analysis of the results helps determine which of the components of phonology, linguistic structure, or semantics are most in need of immediate and careful analysis. The following sections outline procedures for eliciting specific language samples appropriate for the assessment of these three linguistic components.

Phonology If articulating individual phonemes is a problem for a child, it is necessary that the teacher determine the specific sounds that are particularly troublesome. When available, standardized tests such as those described earlier in this chapter may be used. When necessary, however, teachers can construct their own tests to examine these troublesome areas. Johnson, Brown, Curtis, Edney, and Keaster (1967) recommend the following procedures for assessing a child's problems with articulating phonemes:

1. eliciting and observing a carefully controlled sample of the person's spontaneous speech
2. noting carefully any articulation errors that occur and record a description of them
3. checking the results of this procedure by observing less formal, conventional speech
4. determining whether or not the person can imitate, as isolated sounds, those sounds on which he habitually makes errors in test words or running speech.[1]

The materials for testing may include a series of pictures with which the child is familiar. The pictures (i.e., words) chosen should include all of the sounds used in the English language. The child is asked to say the word in isolation, and the particular sound(s) tested in that word are scored as either correctly or incorrectly produced. Teachers may wish to consult

[1]From p. 136, *Speech handicapped school children*, 3rd Edition by Wendell Johnson et al. Copyright © 1967 by Harper & Row, Publishers, Inc. By permission of the publisher.

Eisenson and Ogilvie (1971) for a complete example of specific words and scoring procedures appropriate for testing proficiency in articulation.

To interpret the results of any articulation test, the teacher should be aware of the ages at which children master individual sounds. Templin (1957) has indicated that all sounds of the English language are produced with ease and efficiency by most normal children at 8 years of age. Individual consonant sounds should be correctly produced at the following ages:

3 years	/m/, /n/, /ng/, /p/, /f/, /h/, /w/, /y/	6 years	/t/, /th/, /v/, /l/
		7 years	/th/ (unvoiced), /z/,
4 years	/k/, /b/, /d/, /g/, /r/		/zh/, /j/
5 years	/n/, /s/, /sh/, /ch/		

Teachers will find that when they assess articulation, a careful notation system is helpful to describe impressions of the child's speech. Johnson, et al. (1967) suggests that the following criteria be used to categorize observations of efficiency of articulation.

A. Overall frequency of misarticulations
   1. Few errors
   2. Errors rather numerous
   3. Many errors
B. General consistency of misarticulations
   1. All error sounds misarticulated consistently
   2. Occasional correct articulation of error sounds
   3. Frequent correct articulations of error sounds
   4. No consistent errors—general inaccuracy of articulation
C. Degree of interference with communication
   1. No interference
   2. Slight interference—some listeners may react negatively
   3. Moderate interference—most listeners would react negatively
   4. Extreme interference—speech very hard to understand or is quite unintelligible.[2]

A number of diagnostic articulation tests have been constructed to provide a comprehensive view of articulatory ability. *A Deep Test of Articulation* (McDonald, 1964) is designed to test consonant sounds with stimuli that approximate conversational speech. The test is available in picture and sentence forms so that they may be used with children of all ages. Avant and Hutton (1962) have devised a measuring tool that allows assessment of articulation in connected speech and also provides an estimate of general vocal quality. The child is required to read a short passage

[2]From p. 139, *Speech handicapped school children*, 3rd Edition by Wendell Johnson et al. Copyright © 1967 by Harper & Row, Publishers, Inc. By permission of the publisher.

that emphasizes those sounds occurring most frequently in the English language and those that are most often found to be used incorrectly. Specific instructions are also provided for scoring errors produced by the child. Either of these techniques may be easily incorporated into the diagnostic teaching format.

Linguistic Structure   One area of language functioning that frequently requires attention during diagnostic teaching is *linguistic structure*. As we have discussed previously, linguistic structure refers to the comprehension and use of morphology and syntax. If a child experiences problems in linguistic structure, he or she will have difficulty also in following even simple conversations and will misuse grammatical units of speech, use sentence forms that a younger child would use, and, in severe cases, be almost lacking in all meaningful communicative skills. Although the informal diagnosis of morphology, syntax, and semantics can be carried out simultaneously, it is imperative that teachers be selective in the techniques that they use to elicit language samples so that they will obtain successfully whatever data they desire.

Perhaps the most comprehensive assessment device of language structure yet developed is the *Developmental Sentence Analysis* (Lee, 1974). This procedure was described earlier because it possesses the qualities of a standardized test, but it is also a powerful diagnostic tool. Lee has provided detailed directions for using the results of this test to formulate objectives appropriate for remedial purposes. Two major factors to be considered with regard to this test, however, are that it requires an understanding of basic psycholinguistic theory and terminology and it is time consuming to carry out. Regardless of these two factors, the *Developmental Sentence Analysis* still remains one of the most viable assessment devices available to professionals concerned with linguistic deficiencies in children. Lee points out the need for careful analysis of a child's problem as a prelude to successful intervention. She states:

> Developmental Sentence Analysis is a time consuming procedure, but it yields information that is essential to the planning of effective clinical teaching. The day has passed when clinicians can rely on informal judgments on parents' reports as valid indicators of a child's language development. The days are also passed when clinicians can merely hope for syntactic development to occur through the simple exposure of a child to a verbal input. Language stimulation is not enough. It is necessary to have a plan. Developmental Sentence Analysis provides a clinical procedure for assessing a child's developmental level, for selecting appropriate goals in lesson planning, and for measuring progress throughout the period of interventional teaching when the main emphasis is on the learning of grammatical structure [p. 201].

Teachers who consistently are confronted with children who demonstrate significant language disorders are advised to become familiar with this approach and to employ it judiciously during periods of diagnostic teaching.

Another procedure that has been developed to assess a specific aspect of linguistic structure is the Berko experimental test of morphology (Berko, 1961). According to Wiig and Semel (1976), knowledge of morphology directly influences word formation and the ability to interpret changes in word meanings when morphemes (smallest meaningful units of language) are combined. The Berko procedure, in an attempt to measure knowledge of morphological forms, uses 33 test items (composed of nonsense words): 10 measure the rules for formulating noun plurals; 8 measure past tense; 3 measure singular possessives, plural possessives, and derivation; 2 measure third-person singular of verbs and adjectival inflection; and one measures progressive tense and compound words. The actual items on this instrument consist of a series of line drawings depicting a series of both real and nonsense figures. For example, in the testing procedure used to measure past tense the teacher would present a picture of a man doing calisthenics. The teacher then would say, "This is a man who knows how to do 'mot.' He is 'motting.' He did the same thing yesterday. What did he do yesterday? Yesterday he _____." The child is asked to supply the missing word that incorporates the correct morphological form for each item. In experimental studies Berko found that first-grade children were capable of making consistent and orderly responses to the items, even to the point of pronouncing inflectional endings with elaborate care. Apparently this procedure has diagnostic validity, because it has been shown to differentiate between mentally retarded and normal children (Newfield & Schlanger, 1968) as well as between learning disabled and normal children (Wiig, Semel, & Crouse, 1973). Teachers will find that this informal test provides usable teaching information when used with children who exhibit difficulties in following morphological rules.

An additional aspect of linguistic structure that frequently requires the teacher's attention is the comprehension and production of syntactical forms. It has been our experience that one of the most productive ways to test a child's skill in these two areas is through the use of a stimulating object (e.g., toy) that interests the child. Many individuals have recommended that a doll house or a ranch set be used in diagnostic teaching situations because these toys are usually interesting to children and provide maximum opportunities for verbal interactions between the child and the teacher. The procedure for using these objects is quite straightforward: the teacher asks the child, through simple commands, to arrange furniture and people or animals in the doll house or ranch set. As the teacher develops rapport with the child, the commands to place the furniture, people, animals, etc., in their proper places gradually increase in complexity. For example, the initial request might be to "put the table in the kitchen," or to "put the horse in the corral." After a period of time, the commands can be as complex as "take the largest table and put it in the children's bedroom." By paying careful attention to the wording of the commands (i.e., syntax), a teacher can gain valuable estimates of a child's syntactical *comprehension.*

Berry (1969) suggests a picture-story technique to evaluate the *production* of syntax and semantics in children from 5 to 8 years of age. The materials used in this procedure include a series of 11 pictures that depict a sequence of actions about which a portion of a story is told. The teacher sets the pictures in front of the child and proceeds to tell a story; the child is encouraged to follow by viewing the sequential drawings. When the child is apparently comfortable with the activity, the teacher stops and says, "You finish making up the story. Here are the pictures to help you." The teacher tape-records the child's subsequent verbalizations. If the child is reluctant to begin or stops after a few sentences, the teacher can gently question the child to spur him or her on. The dimensions of the child's language that are assessed include (1) the level of ideas, (2) lexical elements (words), (3) functional elements, (4) linguistic form, (5) melody pattern, and (6) articulatory proficiency. Table 7–6 includes an outline of each of these dimensions, which if carefully applied should assist the teacher in formulating an in-depth evaluation of the child's phrases. This outline also can be used to evaluate the content of *any* story that has been told by a child. Hopefully, upon completion of this and similar tasks teachers would be able to derive a complete profile of the child's language ability in order to formulate teaching goals.

TABLE 7–6

===

I. Substance of Language: Ideational Levels
   A. Enumeration
      1. Names of people, objects, physical surround
      2. Simply reproduces visual situations
   B. Literal description
      1. Presents formless, disorganized bits of information
      2. Describes only what he sees without attempting to establish relations or continuity
      3. Groups information according to some plan
   C. Imaginative description
      1. Introduces unseen figures and objects which are incorporated in the story
      2. Employs deliberate invention of details: romancing
      3. Reflects syncretistic understanding (whole is understood before parts are understood)

TABLE 7–6   *Continued*

    D. Interpretation: Level I
      1. Interprets concrete details and relates them to the plot of the story
      2. Reflects little egocentric thought
      3. Attempts to explain events and motives of action
    E. Interpretation: Level II
      1. Introduces forms of analysis; synthesis of ideas and events in perception
      2. Introduces imaginative and abstract materials suggested by the picture sequence
      3. Abstracts qualities or meanings from stimuli; forms constructs transferable from situation to situation, using materials that are tangible, abstract, or numerical

  II. Language Behavior
    A. Enjoys verbalizing about exploits and behavior of the child adventurer
    B. Develops precepts logically from sense impressions
    C. Identifies with the child in the story in some respects
    D. Uses speech to elaborate new connections
    E. Uses gestures, mimicry, movement, demonstration to accompany language
    F. Uses communicable logic (guided by memories of earlier reasoning and by expressed deduction)
    G. Uses loose referential lexical meanings (*He needs to*_____ instead of *He wants to*_____)
    H. Uses rigid language structure
    I. Uses egocentric logic (no real connections)
    J. Shows anxiety, inability to tolerate visual or auditory stimuli (defense against anxiety)
    K. Uses autistic language: highly organistic; grotesquely imaginary

 III. Use of Lexical Elements of Language. Content words: Nouns, Verbs, Adjectives
    A. Word use
      1. Total number of words used in each class
      2. Limits choice of words to semantic class
      3. Uses quantitative words correctly (some, any, several)
      4. Uses noun substitutes
    B. Word Substance: Qualitative assessment of perceptual value

 IV. Use of Functional Elements of Language: Structure Words
    A. Uses prepositions and conjunctions
    B. Uses interrogatives
    C. Uses noun determiners
    D. Uses auxiliaries
  V. Use of Linguistic Form
    A. Sentence type, complexity, and elaboration
      1. Total number of complete sentences
      2. Total number of complex sentences employing:
        a. modifying phrases
        b. subordinate clauses

TABLE 7–6 *Continued*

    3. Total number of compound sentences
    4. Preponderant sentence types: Interjectional? imperative? interrogative? declarative?
  B. Grammar and syntax
    1. Uses atypical word order:
      a. inverts subject-verb-object order
      b. makes remote inversions
      c. makes attempt to fit words into syntactic frame
    2. Uses incomplete sentences:
      a. interrogative fragments
      b. interjectional phrase fragments
    3. Uses verbs not in agreement with subject
    4. Omits auxiliary
    5. Makes errors in formation of tense
    6. Uses double negative
    7. Misuses nouns and pronouns
    8. Makes errors in formation of plural forms of nouns
    9. Makes errors in gender

VI. Prosody: Melody of Speech
  A. Uses a rhythm that is:
    1. conversational
    2. measured
    3. staccato
    4. tachyphemic
  B. Employs intonation patterns that:
    1. are appropriate to meaning
    2. are stereotyped, meaningless, atypical
    3. follow morphemic sequences
  C. Stress is:
    1. placed on proper morphemic units
    2. expressed by changes in:
      a. pitch-stress
      b. duration
      c. intensity

VII. Articulation and Resistance to Articulatory Disintegration
  A. Distorts, omits, or substitutes consonantal phonemes
  B. Distorts, omits, or substitutes vowel phonemes
  C. Confuses phoneme order
  D. Maintains articulatory proficiency throughout story
  E. Articulatory disintegration is notable:
    1. in long sentences
    2. at end of story
    3. with increase of excitement or anxiety

Source: From Mildred Freburg Berry, *Language disorders of children: The bases and diagnoses,* © 1969, pp. 235, 245, 248–250. Reprinted by permission of Prentice-Hall, Inc., Englewood Cliffs, New Jersey.

Semantics Semantics refers to the meaning that is conveyed by a combination of words or sentences. Obviously, an estimate of a child's meaningful use of sentences can be derived from using many of the activities described in the section dealing with the linguistic structure. Teachers also can use the Peabody Picture Vocabulary Test informally to evaluate receptive vocabulary. In addition to these techniques, a number of word games can be used to study a child's comprehension and production of vocabulary.

An example of a game appropriate for assessing semantic development is one in which the teacher presents an object and then asks the child to give names of other objects that are similar to it. Berry (1969) gives a list of some words that could be used in this game, and some equivalent ones:

1. bed—sofa, couch, cradle
2. pencil—pen, chalk, crayon
3. bicycle—cycle, motorcycle, trike, scooter
4. lady's dress—robe, gown, suit, frock
5. letter—postcard, newspaper, package

Regardless of the stimulus words chosen, the teacher should accept any likenesses that are reasonable, given the child's age and background.

A similar activity to the one just described consists of the teacher stating a sentence and asking the child to say something that means the same thing. For example, the teacher may say, "The girl jumped"; the child's response might be, "The girl hopped." By carefully selecting items, the teacher should be able to obtain information regarding the child's knowledge of words. It is important to keep in mind that it may take several sessions and careful demonstrations to prepare the child adequately for this task.

A slightly different technique has been described by Rosenberg and Cohen (1967). With this technique the teacher seats two children in positions in which they cannot see each other, but are close enough physically so that they can hear each other speak. One child is given an object (e.g., a toy horse, or a shoe) and asked to describe it to the other child. The teacher observes the verbal interactions between the two children for signs of good or poor vocabulary usage. Of course, the teacher can carry out this technique with only one child in order to control the content of the vocalization or interject words that are of special interest. Teachers will find that this game is appropriate for children of school age.

Although the techniques discussed in this section may be helpful in assessing components of language development, they are certainly not intended to be a complete list. Teachers are limited only by their own creativity in devising strategies for the diagnosis of language problems. Teachers may wish to consult Bangs (1968), Valett (1969), and Gray and Ryan (1973) for discussions of language activities that may be easily adapted for evaluative purposes.

Record Keeping   One of the most important aspects of diagnostic teaching is continuous record-keeping of initial diagnostic conclusions and any subsequent changes in the child's linguistic abilities. The case-history interview is one method of collecting relevant data regarding the child's problem. However, once the diagnostic teaching has begun, it is necessary for the teacher to record consistently the teaching methods employed and the child's responses in order to be certain that progress is being maintained at an optimal level. In addition, the continual input from each session provides valuable insights into selecting the most advantageous methods of evaluating and teaching individual children.

Perhaps the most basic way to record observations is to keep a log or a journal of events that have occurred during each session. This type of record keeping is not standardized in format, but it will frequently yield extremely useful data appropriate for formulating long-term teaching objectives.

In addition to the journal, teachers also may find it necessary to keep more detailed records of a child's performance on specific linguistic variables. It is impossible to plan the exact content of each session prior to it, but teachers need to develop appropriate forms based upon the objectives that have been established for each child. Table 7–2 contained a sample form that can be used during initial interaction(s) with the child to outline the primary and secondary language problems. Additional forms are presented in Figures 7–4 and 7–5. The information provided in Figure 7–4 concerns the *comprehension* of verbal information by children from 3 to 8 years of age. Although this form is not meant to be applicable for all children, it can be adapted easily for use with a wide variety of problems. Figure 7–5 deals with the components of phonology, syntax, and semantics as they relate to *spoken* language. A teacher can select one of the items listed in this figure for more intense observation and continuously record diagnostic impressions during a period from a few days to several weeks.

It will come as little surprise to the reader that diagnostic teaching is used primarily with children who exhibit moderate to severe disorders of language ability. Certain aspects of diagnostic teaching, however, can be applied to situations in which the problem is mild and requires only a limited period to isolate the problem areas. The checklist presented in Figure 7–6 is intended to be completed by the classroom teacher to determine individual language readiness of kindergarten and first-grade children. By comparing a high-risk child with a normal child, the teacher should be able to make valid judgments regarding the adequacy of the child's general language proficiency.

FIGURE 7–4   Form to Measure Comprehension of Spoken Language

Name _____

Age (C A) _____

Original enrollment date _____

Recorder _____

Key

A   Yes, or very good
B   Better than average
C   Average
D   Below average
E   No, or poor
√   Inconsistent
O   No opportunity to observe

Date of Record

Responds only to gestures (A or E)						
Makes appropriate gestural response in speech reading to: That's all I have; No more, etc. (A or E)						
Responds better to speech with gestures than to speech alone (A or E)						
Responds to words and phrases (A or E)						
Responds to speech continuum (A or E)						
Responds to speech when he is not looking at speaker (A or E)						
Responds to speech in background of noise (A or E)						
Comprehends morphemic sequences only at slow rate (A or E)						
Comprehends morphemic sequences at normal rate (A or E)						
Responds better to speech with gestures than to speech alone (A or E)						
Mimics facial and articulatory movements of speaker when attending (A or E)						
Taps rhythm of jingle or nursery rhyme						

FIGURE 7–4   *Continued*

Anticipates meaning of phrase or sentence						
Attends quickly, purposively to verbal stimuli (A or E)						
Attends only to fringe areas of speech, not to central cues (A or E)						
Exhibits tension or anxiety when attending to speech (A or E)						
Comprehends single linguistic structure (word order); syntax						
Comprehends vocabulary appropriate to age						
Reflects insight into problems (inner logic) (What must you do when: hungry, sleepy, cold, etc.)						
Tells what happens (comprehension of current events)						
Announces future action (comprehension of future events)						

Source: From Mildred Freburg Berry, *Language disorders of children: The bases and diagnoses,* © 1969, pp. 235, 245, 248–250. Reprinted by permission of Prentice-Hall, Inc., Englewood Cliffs, New Jersey.

FIGURE 7–5   Form to Measure Phonology, Semantics, and Syntax of Spoken Language

Name _____

Age (C A) _____

Original enrollment date _____

Recorder _____

Key

A Yes, or very good
B Better than average
C Average
D Below average
E No, or poor
√ Inconsistent
O No opportunity to observe

FIGURE 7–5   *Continued*

	Date of Record							
Has two-word sentences (A or E)								
Has more than two-word sentences (A or E)								
Imitates phrase sequences without distortion (A or E)								
Repeats sentences of 12–13 syllables (A or E)								
Uses only simple sentence structure (A or E)								
Uses complex sentence structure (A or E)								
Responds without lag to questions (A or E)								
Voluntarily asks for objects by name								
Uses plurals correctly								
Uses pronouns but in incorrect case (A or E)								
Uses pronouns correctly								
Uses past tense in proper form								
Uses subject-verb in agreement								
Articulates phonemic sequences but omits or distorts some phonemes (A or E)								
Articulates phonemic sequences accurately (e.g.: Rain goes pitter patter; My puppy plays with kitty.)								
Confuses phoneme or word order (A or E)								
Omits little words in sentence (A or E)								

FIGURE 7–5   *Continued*

Often has unintelligible speech (A or E)							
Uses single words and phrases (A or E)							
Has meager vocabulary (A or E)							
Has vocabulary appropriate to C.A.							
Demonstrates prosody in contextual expression							
Often has cluttered speech (A or E)							
Gives full name (A or E)							
Names his sex (A or E)							
Misnames objects, people (A or E)							
Names objects, people correctly (A or E)							
Voice abnormally loud (A or E)							
Voice abnormally soft (A or E)							
Pitch changes follow shifts in meaning							
Loudness changes follow shifts in meaning							
Voice is monotonous (A or E)							
Voice is harsh (A or E)							
Voice is nasal (A or E)							
Voice is breathy (A or E)							
Speech rhythm is measured (A or E)							
Speech rhythm is irregular (explosive)							

FIGURE 7–5   *Continued*

Imitates speech rhythm of others							
Enjoys act of speaking							
Responds easily to salutation, etc.							
Verbalizes purposively							
Verbalizes rarely (A or E)							
Uses variety of sentence forms (declarative, interrogative, etc.)							
Uses grammar appropriate to C.A.							
Tells story demonstrating semantic relations							
Imitates melodic expression of others (pitch-stress, duration, etc.)							
Articulatory stability maintained throughout story							
Articulation patterns disintegrate before end of story (A or E)							
Reflects intent to remember and replicate story exactly as it is printed							
Tells essential features of story							
Puts together string of nonessential features (A or E)							
Recalls more nonessential than essential cues of story (A or E)							
Recalls essential cues of story							
Demonstrates immediate recall							

Source: From Mildred Freburg Berry, *Language disorders of children: The bases and diagnoses,* © 1969, pp. 235, 245, 248–250. Reprinted by permission of Prentice-Hall, Inc., Englewood Cliffs, New Jersey.

FIGURE 7–6   Inventory of Language Skills

	Yes	No
Hearing		
Does he respond to his name?		
Does he respond to simple questions?		
Does he ask to have questions repeated?		
Speech		
Does he speak clearly and distinctly enough to be heard?		
Does he repeat spoken words correctly?		
General Skills		
Does he listen attentively?		
Does he follow simple oral directions?		
Does he listen to stories with understanding?		
Does he listen when other children are talking?		
Does he express himself in telling about his art pictures?		
Does he express simple ideas in complete sentences?		
Does he tell a story in sequence?		
Does he predict outcomes of a story?		
Does he ask the meanings of words and signs?		
Does he show an interest in books?		

Source: Burns, P. C., Broman, B. L., & Wantling, A. L. *The language arts and childhood education.* (2nd ed.) Chicago: Rand McNally, 1971. Used with permission of the publisher.

The process of record keeping, in certain instances, need not be the sole responsibility of the teacher. If older children with mild to moderate handicaps are involved, the children can check their own problem areas. Figure 7–7, in a questionnaire format, summarizes the major skills involved in listening for meaning. If some children have difficulties in paying attention during class time, a teacher can ask them to complete this form and indicate those areas in which they feel weak. The teacher can fill out an identical form for each child and then compare the results. The teacher can have a subsequent conference with the student and point out the areas in which inprovement is needed. This may do a great deal to alleviate the observed problem. Any teacher will recognize that the possibility for generating many such simple, student-oriented questionnaires involving language ability is virtually endless.

Language Scales

In some cases teachers will find that a child's language problem is not severe enough to warrant an intensive evaluation procedure such as diag-

FIGURE 7–7   Checklist for Listening

	Yes	No
1. Did I remember to get ready for listening?		
a. Was I seated comfortably where I could see and hear?		
b. Were my eyes focused on the speaker?		
2. Was my mind ready to concentrate on what the speaker had to say?		
a. Was I able to push other thoughts out of my mind for the time being?		
b. Was I ready to think about the topic and call to mind the things I already knew about it?		
3. Was I ready for "take-off"?		
a. Did I discover in the first few minutes where the speaker was taking me?		
b. Did I discover his central idea so that I could follow it through the speech?		
4. Was I able to pick out the ideas which supported the main idea?		
a. Did I take advantage of the speaker's clues (such as first, next, etc.) to help organize the ideas in my mind?		
b. Did I use my extra "think" time to summarize and take notes—either mentally or on paper?		
5. After the speaker finished and the facts were all in, did I evaluate what had been said?		
a. Did this new knowledge seem to fit with the knowledge I already had?		
b. Did I weigh each idea to see if I agreed with the speaker?		

If you marked questions *No,* decide why you could not honestly answer them *Yes.*

Source: Kopp, O. W. The evaluation of oral language activities: Teaching and learning. *Elementary English,* 1967, *44,* 117. Copyright © 1967 by the National Council of Teachers of English. Reprinted with permission.

nostic teaching. The use of language scales that are either commercially produced or teacher made can be a convenient tool for classifying and recording the linguistic skills of a child. The ultimate effectiveness of these language scales depends upon the care with which they are prepared and used. As with other evaluative instruments, teachers should view critically any scale with regard to the appropriateness of the behaviors observed in relation to the specific information needed for preparing teaching programs.

If properly used, language scales can serve several important functions: (1) they can direct observations toward specific aspects of linguistic ability; (2) they can permit a common frame of reference for comparing a group of children on the same language characteristics; and (3) they can provide a systematic method for recording observations.

Several language scales that can be obtained commercially or found in journals are summarized in Table 7–7. In general, these scales tend to be

TABLE 7–7 Language Scales

Scales	Components Assessed	Ages
Communication Evaluation Chart (Anderson, Miles, & Matheny, 1963)	Receptive and expressive language	3 months to 5 years
Infant speech and language development (Boone, 1965)	Receptive and expressive language	1 to 24 months
Developmental Potential of Preschool Children (Haeussermann, 1958)	Receptive and expressive language; designed for use with cerebral-palsied children	2 to 4½ years
Vineland Social Maturity Scale (Doll, 1953)	Social competence; some language items included	Birth to 25 years
The Verbal Language Development Scale (Mecham, 1959)	Questionnaire format for receptive and expressive language	Birth to 25 years
Rating Scale for Evaluation of Expressive, Receptive and Phonetic Language Development in the Young Child (D'Asaro & John, 1961)	Receptive, expressive, and phonological language development	4 weeks to 6 years
Preschool Language Scale (Zimmerman, Steiner, & Evatt, 1969)	Auditory comprehension; general verbal ability	1½ to 7 years
Assessing Language Skills in Infancy (Bzoch & League, 1971)	Receptive and expressive language	Birth to 3 years
The Callier-Azusa Scale (Stillman, 1976)	Measures wide range of behaviors, including receptive and expressive language; developed for multihandicapped children	Birth +
The Basic School Skills Inventory (Goodman & Hammill, 1975)	One subtest taps general language	4 to 7 years
Language Motivating Experiences for Young Children (Engel, 1969)	Receptive and expressive language of multihandicapped children	Birth +

developmental in nature; that is, the linguistic behaviors observed extend from infancy to adulthood. Teachers are encouraged to review as many scales as possible to gain a perspective of the range of items that are often included to evaluate language usage. Frequently, teachers may wish to combine various aspects of different scales to adapt them to their own assessment objectives and to provide data that are more relevant for identification of problems and establishing remedial programs.

If we look carefully at Table 7-7, it becomes apparent that many scales are available that assess linguistic competency. It is possible, however, that, when desired scales are inaccessible or not appropriate for existing needs, teachers will construct their own devices to use in the school or the clinic. Teachers are advised to review the stages of language development again, which are presented in Table 7-2. In addition to the sources mentioned earlier in the chapter, interested readers may also wish to consult Lenneberg (1967), Gesell and Amatruda (1947), and Berry (1969) for in-depth discussions of the stages of language acquisition.

Once the teacher has become familiar with the stages of normal language development, he or she will need to determine the specific purposes for using the language scale. For example, one teacher may need only a general scale to find those children who need more intensive evaluations (e.g., diagnostic teaching); on the other hand, another teacher may need a scale that yields detailed information regarding one aspect of a child's use of linguistic structure (i.e., morphology and syntax). Table 7-8 is a sample language scale designed to be used with kindergarten and first-grade children. The scale was developed to isolate those children who will profit from language experiences supplementing those offered in the regular classroom. It is Gately's opinion that proficient receptive and expressive language usage is a prerequisite to later academic achievement. When administering this scale, the teacher simply observes each child for a short period of time and notes those skills that the child has or has not yet mastered. In addition to supplying cues for planning appropriate intervention strategies and suggesting possibilities for teaching groups of children, the completed scales also provide a basis on which to evaluate the child's progress over time.

Language scales also can be used to assess a specific area of language usage systematically. An example of this is given in Figure 7-8. In this case the teacher was interested in assessing a child's usage of verb structure in spoken language. As with the previous scale, the teacher administers the instrument by observing the child's expressive language and recording whether the child has command of the behavior under question. Once a teacher has compiled the information requested on this scale, it is possible to make a reliable and accurate judgment regarding a child's knowledge and use of verbs. With proper observation, it is possible to construct useful language scales for every aspect of language ability.

TABLE 7–8   A Sample Language Scale for Assessing General Linguistic
Abilities in Kindergarten and First-Grade Children

I. Reception
A.[1] When music is played (or sung by the assessor), child is able to "freeze" like a statue when the music stops

A.[2] When shown a picture, child can name and give the beginning sound orally of four out of seven objects in the picture

A.[3] Given a box of eight crayons, child is able to select the crayons that have the "l" sound in their names (purple, yellow, black)

B. Given verbal directions, child is able to follow them ("Go touch the window."; "Touch your head."; "Touch your toes.")

C. Given an assortment of blocks of different colors, child is able to choose the block in the color given orally by the assessor

Notes:

II. Noting Relationships or Association
A. Given pairs of pictures showing things that are usually associated (shoes and socks, brush and comb, bread and butter), which are mixed up, child is able to match the pictures in pairs

B. When asked how two or more things are alike (e.g., "In what way are a horse and a cow alike?"—concrete likenesses; legs, eyes—abstract similarities; both live on a farm, work for a man, and are animals), child is able to tell about concrete and abstract likenesses.

C. Given three riddles presented orally by the assessor, child is able to complete them successfully ("He delivers letters to our homes; he is a _____."; "She helps sick people; she is a _____.")

D. Presented pictures in two classification areas, child is able to select and place them in proper category (household items, farm animals, things we wear, etc.)

Notes:

III. Expression
A. Presented with action pictures, child is able to make up a story telling what might be happening

B. When asked to act out a role, child is able to perform the activity (show what a farmer does when he is cutting wood; show what a carpenter does when she is sawing a board.)

Notes:

IV. Integration Tasks
A. When shown a picture, and when oral sentences are given with one word in the sentence in sound blending, child is able to pick out object in the given picture, in sounds only ("There is a b-a-l-l in the picture.")

B. When shown a card with dots that form a figure, child is able to identify the form before finishing the figure by connecting the dots with lines

Notes:

V. Memory
A. When shown a picture and told a story about it, child is able to tell the story back to the assessor

TABLE 7–8   *Continued*

B. When given a series of directions to follow, child is able to perform them ("Stand up, clap your hands, stomp your feet, and sit down.")
C. When a box is drawn on the board with two or three objects inside, child is able to reproduce it immediately after it is erased by the assessor
D. When given directions orally, child is able to follow them ("Walk to the door, turn around three times, and skip back.")
E. When shown a picture from a picture dictionary or a catalogue, child is able to recall at least three objects after picture has been removed from view

Notes:

Source: We acknowledge Margaret Gately for permitting us to use this informal scale.

Diagnostic Training Batteries

A third method of informally assessing language disorders is through the use of *diagnostic training batteries.* Diagnostic training batteries usually contain a series of materials and activities that (1) permit an evaluation of receptive and expressive language and (2) provide teaching strategies designed to remedy the deficient areas. Although many of these batteries have been produced for use in reading and mathematics, only recently attention has been devoted to language problems in children. One of the most complete diagnostic training batteries yet devised is the *Environmental Language Intervention* (MacDonald, 1976). The model upon which this system is based is "directed toward children who have yet to use sentences in conversation and play and is directed downward behaviorally to children yet to display essential components of language and communication (MacDonald, 1976, p. 16)." There are three major assessment strategies used in the Environmental Language Intervention program, each of which will be discussed in this section.

FIGURE 7–8   A Sample Language Scale for the Assessment of Verb Usage in Spoken Language

1. Commands   _____
   Verb: Noun
   Open the door.

2. Action statements present progressive   _____
   Noun: *be* Verb + *ing*
   The boy is running.

FIGURE 7–8 *Continued*

3. Answer and ask question: What is Noun doing? _____
   What: *be:* Noun: doing?
4. Answer and ask question: Who is running? _____
   Who: *be:* Verb + *ing*
5. Plurals _____
   Noun: *be:* Verb + *ing*
   They are running.
6. Verbs of the senses _____
   Noun: Verb + Adverb
   The sun feels hot.
7. Past tense regular verbs _____
   Noun: Verb
   The boy played.
8. Past tense irregular verbs _____
   Noun: Verb
9. Past tense question forms _____
   What did _____ do?
   What did _____ see?
   Who saw _____?
10. Negative *not* with past tense _____
    Noun₁: *do: not:* Verb Noun₂
    The boy did not kick the ball.
11. Verb *give* + *to* imperative and past tenses _____
    and question form
    $N_1 + V + N_2$ to N_3
    Mary, give the book to John.
    What did N_1 do?
12. Question form with *be* and pronoun *it* _____
    (use with all previous forms)
    John, put the book on the table.
    Is the book on the floor? No, it is on the table.
    Is the book on the table? Yes, it is.
    Is the car red? No, it is blue.
                    Yes, it is.
13. Question form with *do* _____
    Did John put the book on the table?   *Yes, he did.*
                                            No, he put it on the floor.
    Did John give the book to Mary?   *Yes, he did.*
                                            No, he gave it to Jimmy.
14. Transformations _____
    John bought a balloon.
    The balloon is red.   *John bought a red balloon.*
    That is a flower.
    The flower is blue.
    The flower is little.   *That is a little blue flower.*

FIGURE 7–8   *Continued*

We went to the zoo.
We went yesterday.   We went to the zoo yesterday.
15. Adverbs of manner   _____
    Noun + Verb + Preposition + Noun + Preposition + Noun
    We rode to the farm on a bus.
16. Future tense: *will* + Verb   _____
    N_1 + *will* + Verb + Article + N_2
    We will make jello.
17. Verb *have*   _____
    N_1 + *have* + Noun
    I have a ball.
    Mary has a ball.
18. Question form + *have*   _____
    What do you have?   A book.
    What does Mary have?   Mary has a book.
    Who has the thimble?   John.
19. Verb *have* + Adjective + Noun   _____
    N_1 + Verb + Adjective + $Noun_2$
    The cat has soft fur.
    What has soft fur?   The cat.
    What does the cat have?   Soft fur.
    Does the cat have soft fur? Yes, it does.
    Does a cat have a short tail? No, a cat has a long tail.
20. *Going to* + Verb   _____
    be + *going to* + Verb
    I am going to get a crayon.
21. *Like to* + Verb   _____
    I like to swim.
22. *Can* + Verb   _____
    I can write.
23. *Could* + Verb   _____
    I could run to the store.
24. *Be* + Verb + *ing*   _____
    I am going downtown.
25. *Made* + Pronoun + Verb   _____
    He made me mad.
26. *Think that* + Noun + Verb   _____
    I think that Mary left.
27. Indirect Object taught as transformation   _____
    Mary gave the book to John.
    Mary gave John the book.
28. *Why* question with Infinitive *to* + Verb in answer _____
    Why did the boy go to the library?   To get a book.
    Why did the boy go to the store?   To buy some groceries.

Source: We appreciate the assistance of Libby Dogett in constructing this scale.

Parent-Child Communication Inventory   *The Parent-Child Communication Inventory* (PCCI) was developed by MacDonald (1973) with the intention of permitting home-based language assessment prior to intervention by professionals. This system relies heavily upon parents' observations of their child's language usage in the home. Two tasks are asked of the parents: (1) to report from memory any behavior that is pertinent to language development (i.e., eye contact, meaningful play, social relationships, motor development, language production, etc.) and (2) to conduct and report upon an assigned activity that is meant to assess a particular skill. MacDonald (1976) illustrates the procedure:

> For example, for "verbal imitation" PCCI asks parents to report prior observations of this child imitating sounds of language. Then the parents are instructed to carry out an activity designed to elicit verbal imitations from the child. In this way, by providing the professional with information about the child and the child's interactions with parents at home, PCCI helps the professional design an environmentally relevant, formal evaluation at the same time that it establishes the family as the initial and integral part of the assessment and training process [p. 21].

After the PCCI has been completed by the child's parents, the professional assessment begins. The professional assessment procedures include the *Environmental Prelanguage Battery* and the *Environmental Language Inventory.*

Environmental Prelanguage Battery   The *Environmental Prelanguage Battery* (EPB) (Horstmeier & MacDonald, 1975) is composed of a sequenced set of procedures that assess the prelinguistic behaviors that are necessary for language development. At the initial stage of assessment the EPB is devoted to determining a child's general readiness skills (e.g., attending to task, response rate, stimulability). After these readiness skills have been established, the EPB is directed at determining the level of symbolic play activities as a prerequisite to language usage. A series of structured interactions with the child assesses receptive language. In addition, this battery provides discrete evaluative activities for imitating sounds and words.

Environmental Language Inventory   The *Environmental Language Inventory* (ELI) (MacDonald & Nickols, 1974) focuses upon the evaluation of expressive language delays through rules, context, and generalization. Syntactical *rules* of interest are those that have been shown to govern the early two-word phrases of normally developing children. The assessment of the *context* of children's verbalizations takes into account linguistic (semantic and grammatical structures) and nonlinguistic (gestures) cues that enrich verbal expression. *Generalization* of phrases in a wide range of settings is an important variable in language usage. The ELI samples the child's language in imitation, play, and conversation. A child's performance can alert the teacher to the most appropriate modes for generalizing emerging language.

INTERDISCIPLINARY RELATIONSHIPS AND SPOKEN-LANGUAGE ASSESSMENT

Throughout this chapter, we have focused on the role of the teacher in assessing spoken-language disorders. We have not intended, however, to imply that teachers should overlook other professionals in the schools who may possess knowledge and expertise in diagnosing and remedying language disorders. In many cases, a speech pathologist, psychologist, physician, or reading specialist can offer valuable assistance, particularly in the areas of administering standardized tests and structuring observations of a child's language usage. It is also helpful for teachers to find out if there are specialized personnel available in their schools prior to initiating the language evaluation. When possible, a team of professionals should be assembled to help plan and carry out the most appropriate methods for analyzing a child's language disorder.

Although a team approach is certainly desirable, teachers must be prepared to rely primarily on their own skills, because specialized personnel may not be available immediately, may not have the time to participate, or may not be competent enough to be of help in the evaluation. If a teacher is confronted with the task of organizing and conducting the entire evaluation alone, the teacher should try not to become discouraged or feel helpless. Regardless of whether other professionals are involved or not, the teacher is the one most intimately involved with the child and, consequently, is most closely attuned to the information required for efficient program planning. It is imperative that the teacher recognize his or her own unique insights into the character of the child's problem, because without these insights *any* attempts at meaningful and relevant assessment will be futile. Furthermore, if the teacher does not assume a major responsibility for coordinating and managing the language assessment, the child's special learning needs will not be met.

The initial phases of the teacher's evaluation usually can be carried out within the confines of the regular classroom. By observing the child's interactions with peers and adults and by using a form similar to the one in Table 7–2, the teacher will obtain data not available from standardized tests. The activities that we discussed earlier under the heading diagnostic teaching can be applied during many of the small group sessions that are part of every classroom. A language evaluation need not entail teachers spending an excessive amount of time with the children. More often, when teachers become familiar and comfortable with the basic principles of language development, they will discover a number of other children who can profit from systematic assessment and instruction in spoken-language usage. Without doubt, teachers can and should endeavor to identify, assess, and remedy the majority of language problems evidenced in the classroom. As many teachers will realize, if this does not occur, some children will be deprived of the opportunity to achieve at a level that is commensurate with their abilities.

Suggested Activities

7-1.   In September Ms. McCuller, a first-grade teacher, was assigned two 6-year-old students. These students, Jim and Rich, appear to have oral language problems. Neither student has ever been noted speaking in complete sentences. Ms. McCuller feels that she will need to conduct an educational assessment in order to learn more about the source of these language problems before she selects appropriate remedial procedures. Because both Jim and Rich are also new to the school district, there is no background information available; therefore, Ms. McCuller has decided to conduct a parent interview. Hopefully, this procedure will allow her an opportunity to visit their homes and possibly obtain other useful information.

Construct a parent interview form that would be helpful to Ms. McCuller in obtaining the necessary information and in determining whether the deficits are due to generally low-mental ability, lack of environmental stimulation, or other factor(s) unrelated to these two.

7-2.   In some instances useful information regarding a child's language development can be obtained directly from parents. Using Table 7-1, construct a short (one page or less) information form that parents of kindergarten children can fill out when they register their children for school. This form will assist teachers in early detection of language problems.

7-3.   Ms. Person is the principal of the only elementary school in a small rural school district. She and several members of her teaching staff have become concerned with the poor oral-language skills evidenced by some students entering first grade. These teachers have decided to provide special assistance for these pupils in kindergarten and first grade that would be devoted to increasing oral-language skills. In order to select the children who need the assistance, Ms. Person has decided to outline in checklist format the possible factors leading to poor language development and to use this checklist as an initial screening device.

Construct a short checklist that the teaching staff can complete on each student. The device will, hopefully, identify all high-risk students, as well as students who may need attention from professionals outside the teaching staff (e.g., medical doctors, speech therapists, etc.).

7-4.   In September, Mr. Gray, a first-year preschool teacher, was asked to identify those students in his class who may need speech therapy. Because Mr. Gray has only had limited exposure to preschool children, he sometimes has difficulty understanding the speech of some of his students. He feels sure that the majority of his students do not need speech correction and that in a short time he will be able to distinguish between normal and abnormal speech in 4-year-olds.

Using the phonology column of Table 7–2, construct a list of words, phrases, and sentences that a preschool teacher like Mr. Gray could have a student imitate in order to obtain information regarding the adequacy of a student's pronunciation skills.

7-5.   You have just been selected by Oscar Buros, Editor of the Mental Measurement Yearbooks, to write a review of the *Test of Language Development*. Obtain a copy of the TOLD for examination. Review the format of other Buros' reviews of similar measures and the discussion of acceptable standardization, reliability, and validity criteria (located in Chapter 2) and then write a thorough review of this test.

7-6.   Obtain and administer one of the tests of linguistic structure discussed in this chapter to two children. Begin the analysis of the data by listing each error the student makes and the type of error it represents (e.g., verb tense, etc.). Summarize major areas of difficulty based upon your error analysis. Provide a short discussion of the appropriateness of these results in light of the reliability, validity, and standardization data given in the accompanying manuals.

7-7.   Select one test that measures vocabulary skills and review the standardization, reliability, and validity data presented in the accompanying manual. Discuss the strengths and weaknesses of the test and any recommended uses and cautions one might have when interpreting the results.

7-8.   Criss is completing her master's work in language therapy at a university. She has recently become interested in the *Developmental Sentence Analysis* and feels she may want to use it when she starts her job in the schools. Because she feels that obtaining a good language sample is critical to proper use of this analysis, she has decided to work with three 8-year-old children in order to obtain experience in eliciting language samples from elementary school pupils.

Outline three discrete methods Criss might employ to accomplish this task. Be specific in discussing the procedures of each method.

7–9. Develop and execute several procedures for eliciting a language sample from six students, and then describe the methods used in each. After you describe the methods, discuss the most and least successful methods. What were the factors and variables that may have affected the success or failure of each?

7–10. Elicit and record a language sample that consists of a minimum of 100 phrases from a student. Use Figure 7–3 to analyze the sample within the basic areas of phonology, linguistic structure, semantics, and sentence length. Once you have analyzed the sample thoroughly, list any areas you found to be deficient.

7–11. Select either the Berko, Lee, or Berry approach to assessing a child's linguistic structure. Apply the selected procedure to the assessment of one child. Outline the specific procedure and the materials you have used. Then prepare a detailed sketch of the skills the student has and skills the student either does not have or did not demonstrate during the assessment.

7–12. Obtain and administer one of the language scales listed in Table 7–7. Using the accompanying manual and other information gained regarding spoken language, formulate instructional objectives that need to be met by the student. The usefulness of the test results, of course, will vary depending on the specific purposes of the scale.

References

Ammons, R., & Ammons, H. *Full-range picture vocabulary test.* Missoula, Mont.: Psychological Test Specialists, 1958.

Anderson, R., Miles, M., & Matheny, P. *Communication evaluation chart.* Cambridge, Mass.: Educators Publishing Service, 1963.

Ausubel, D. P., & Sullivan, E. V. *Theory and problems of child development.* New York: Grune & Stratton, 1970.

Avant, V., & Hutton, C. Passage for speech screening in upper elementary grades. *Journal of Speech and Hearing Disorders,* 1962, 27, 40–46.

Bangs, T. E. *Language and learning disorders of the pre-academic child.* New York: Appleton-Century-Crofts, 1968.

Bartel, N. Assessing and remediating problems in language development. In D. D. Hammill and N. Bartel (Eds.), *Teaching children with language and behavior problems.* Boston: Allyn and Bacon, 1975.

Bereiter, C., & Engelman, S. E. *Teaching disadvantaged children.* Englewood Cliffs, N.J.: Prentice-Hall, 1966.

Berko, J. The child's learning of English morphology. In S. Saporta (Ed.), *Psycholinguistics.* New York: Holt, Rinehart and Winston, 1961.

Bernstein, B. Social class and linguistic development: A theory of social learning. In F. Halsy (Ed.), *Education, economy, and society.* New York: Free Press, 1961.

Berry, M. *Language disorders of children.* New York: Appleton-Century-Crofts, 1969.

Boone, D. Infant speech and language development. *Volta Review,* 1965, 67, 414–419.

Braine, M. D. The ontogeny of English phrase structure: The first phase. *Language,* 1963, 39, 1–13.

Brown, R. W. *Social psychology.* New York: Free Press, 1965.

Brown, R. W., & Bellugi, U. Three processes in the child's acquisition of syntax. *Harvard Educational Review,* 1964, 34, 133–151.

Burns, P. C., Broman, B. L., & Wantling, A. L. *The language arts and childhood education.* (2nd ed.) Chicago: Rand McNally, 1971.

Bzoch, K. R., & League, R. *Assessing language skills in infancy.* Gainsville, Fla.: Tree of Life Press, 1971.

Carroll, J. B. Language development in children. In S. Saporta (Ed.), *Psycholinguistics.* New York: Holt, Rinehart and Winston, 1961.

Carroll, J. B. *Language and thought.* Englewood Cliffs, N.J.: Prentice-Hall, 1964.

Carroll, J. B. A review of the Illinois test of psycholinguistic abilities. In O. K. Buros (Ed.), *Seventh Mental Measurement Yearbook.* Highland Park, N.J.: Gryphon, 1972.

Carrow, E. *Test for auditory comprehension of language.* Austin, Tex.: Learning Concepts, 1973.

Carrow, E. *Carrow elicited language inventory.* Austin, Tex.: Learning Concepts, 1974.

Cazden, C. B. Subcultural differences in child languages: An interdisciplinary review. *Merrill-Palmer Quarterly,* 1966, 12, 185–219.

Chomsky, N. *Syntactic structures.* The Hague: Mouton Press, 1957.

Chomsky, N. *Aspects of the theory of syntax.* Cambridge, Mass.: MIT Press, 1965.

Clark, E. V. Some aspects of the conceptual basis for first language acquisition. In R. L. Schiefelbusch and L. L. Lloyds (Eds.), *Language perspectives—acquisition, retardation and intervention.* Baltimore: University Park Press, 1974.

Crabtree, M. *The Houston test for language development.* Houston: The Houston Test Company, 1963.

Dale, P. S. *Language development.* New York: Holt, Rinehart and Winston, 1976.

D'Asaro, M., & John V. Rating scale for evaluation of expressive, receptive and phonetic language development in the young child. *Cerebral Palsy Review,* 1961, 22, 3–4.

Davis, H., & Silverman, S. R. *Hearing and deafness.* New York: Holt, Rinehart and Winston, 1960.

Deese, J. *Psycholinguistics.* Boston: Allyn and Bacon, 1970.

Dickson, S. *Communication disorders: Remedial principles and practices.* Glenview, Ill.: Scott, Foresman, 1974.

Doll, E. *Vineland social maturity scale.* Minneapolis: Educational Test Bureau, 1953.

Dunn, L. *Peabody picture vocabulary test.* Circle Pines, Minn.: American Guidance Service, 1965.

Eisenson, J. *The psychology of communication.* New York: Appleton-Century-Crofts, 1963.

Eisenson, J., & Ogilvie, M. *Speech correction in the schools.* New York: Macmillan, 1971.

Engel, R. *Language motivating experiences for young children.* Van Nuys, Calif.: DFA Publishers, 1969.

Gesell, A., & Amatruda, C. *Developmental diagnosis.* (2nd ed.) New York: Paul B. Hoeber, 1947.

Goldman, R., & Fristoe, M. *Goldman-Fristoe test of articulation.* Circle Pines, Minn.: American Guidance Service, 1969.

Goldstein, K. *Language and language disturbances.* New York: Grune & Stratton, 1948.

Goodman, L., & Hammill, D. D. *The basic school skills inventory.* New York: Follett, 1975.

Gray, B., & Ryan, B. *A language program for the nonlanguage child.* Champaign, Ill.: Research Press, 1973.

Haeussermann, E. *Developmental potential of preschool children.* New York: Grune & Stratton, 1958.

Hammill, D. D., & Larsen, S. C. The relationship of selected auditory perceptual skills to reading ability. *Journal of Learning Disabilities,* 1974, 7, 429–436.

Horstmeier, D. S., & MacDonald, J. D. *Environmental prelanguage battery.* Nisonger Center Technical Report, Columbus, Ohio, 1975.

Jakobsen, R., & Halle, M. *Fundamentals of language.* The Hague: Mouton Press, 1956.

John, V. The intellectual development of slum children: Some preliminary findings. *American Journal of Orthopsychiatry,* 1963, 33, 813–822.

Johnson, W., Brown, S. F., Curtis, J. F., Edney, C. W., & Keaster, J. *Speech handicapped school children.* New York: Harper & Row, 1967.

Johnson, W., Darley, F. L., & Spriesterbach, D. C. *Diagnostic methods in speech pathology.* New York: Harper & Row, 1963.

Kirk, S., McCarthy, J., & Kirk, W. *The Illinois test of psycholinguistic abilities.* (Rev. ed.) Urbana, Ill.: University of Illinois Press, 1968.

Kopp, O. W. The evaluation of oral language activities: Teaching and learning. *Elementary English,* 1967, 44, 117. Used with permission.

Langacker, R. W. *Language and its structure.* New York: Harcourt Brace Jovanovich, 1968.

Larsen, S. C., & Hammill, D. D. The relationship of selected visual perceptual skills to school learning. *Journal of Special Education,* 1975, 9, 281–291.

Larsen, S. C., Rogers, D., & Sowell, V. The usefulness of selected perceptual tests in differentiating between normal and learning disabled children. *Journal of Learning Disabilities,* 1976, 9, 85–91.

Lee, L. *Northwestern syntax screening test.* Evanston, Ill.: Northwestern University Press, 1969.

Lee, L. *Developmental sentence analysis.* Evanston, Ill.: Northwestern University Press, 1974.

Lenneberg, E. *Biological foundations of language.* New York: John Wiley, 1967.

Loban, W. D. *The language of elementary school children.* Champaign, Ill.: National Council for Teachers of English, 1963.

Lorenz, M., & Cobb, S. Language patterns in psychotic and psychoneurotic subjects. *A.M.A. Archives of Neurology and Psychiatry,* 1954, 72, 665–673.

MacDonald, J. D. *Parent-child communication inventory.* The Nisonger Center, Columbus, Ohio, 1973.

MacDonald, J. D. Environmental language intervention. In F. Withrow and C. Nygren (Eds.), *Language, materials and curriculum management for the handicapped learner.* Columbus, Ohio: Charles E. Merrill, 1976.

MacDonald, J. D., & Nickols, M. *Environmental language inventory manual.* Columbus, Ohio: Ohio State University, 1974.

McCarthy, D. The language development of the preschool child. *Child Welfare Monographs,* No. 4. Minneapolis: University of Minnesota Press, 1930.

McCarthy, D. Language development. *Monograph of Social Research and Child Development,* 1960, 25, No. 77, 5–14.

McConnell, F., & Robertson, J. B. Auditory perceptual skills of culturally disadvantaged children. In M. Romportl (Ed.), *Proceedings of the Sixth International Congress of Phonetic Research.* Prague: Academia, 1970.

McDonald, E. T. *A deep test of articulation.* Pittsburgh: Stanwix House, 1964.

McNeill, D. Developmental psycholinguistics. In F. Smith and G. A. Miller (Eds.), *The genesis of language.* Cambridge, Mass.: MIT Press, 1966.

McNeill, D. *The acquisition of language.* New York: Harper & Row, 1970.

McWilliams, B. J. The language handicapped child and education. *Exceptional Children.* 1966, 32, 221–228.

Mecham, M. *The Verbal language development scale.* Circle Pines, Minn.: American Guidance Service, 1959.

Mecham, M., Jex, J. L., & Jones, J. D. *Utah test of language development.* Salt Lake City: Communication Research Associates, 1967.

Menyuk, P. *Sentences children use.* Cambridge, Mass.: MIT Press, 1969.

Menyuk, P. *The acquisition and development of language.* Englewood Cliffs, N.J.: Prentice-Hall, 1971.

Menyuk, P. *The development of speech.* Indianapolis: Bobbs-Merrill, 1972.

Miller, W. R., & Ervin, S. M. The development of grammar in child language. In U. Bellugi and R. W. Brown (Eds.), *The acquisition of language. Monograph of Social Research and Child Development,* 1964, *29,* 9–35.

Myers, P., & Hammill, D. D. *Methods for learning disorders.* (2nd ed.) New York: John Wiley, 1976.

Myklebust, H. *Auditory disorders in children.* New York: Grune & Stratton, 1954.

Myklebust, H. R., & Boshes, B. Psychoneurological learning disorders in children. *Archives of Pediatrics,* 1960, *77,* 247–256.

Newcomer, P. L., & Hammill, D. D. *Psycholinguistics in the schools.* Columbus, Ohio: Charles E. Merrill, 1976.

Newcomer, P. L., & Hammill, D. D. *The test of language development.* Austin, Tex.: Empiric Press, 1977.

Newfield, M. U., & Schlanger, B. The acquisition of morphology by normal and educable mentally retarded children. *Journal of Speech and Hearing Research,* 1968, *4,* 693–706.

Newland, T. E. Language development of the mentally retarded child. *Monograph of Social Research and Child Development,* 1960, *25,* No. 77, 71–87.

Oswald, P. F. *Soundmaking.* Springfield, Ill.: Charles C. Thomas, 1963.

Piaget, J. *The language and thought of the child.* New York: World Publishing, 1971.

Rosenberg, S. Problems of language development in the retarded. In H. C. Haywood (Ed.), *Social-cultural aspects of mental retardation.* New York: Appleton-Century-Crofts, 1970.

Rosenberg, S., & Cohen, B. D. Toward a psychological analysis of verbal communication skills. In R. L. Schiefelbusch, R. Copeland, and J. D. Smith (Eds.), *Language and mental retardation.* New York: Holt, Rinehart and Winston, 1967.

Slingerland, B. H. *Slingerland screening tests for identifying children with specific language disabilities.* (2nd ed.) Cambridge, Mass.: Educators Publishing Service, 1970.

Sowell, V. *The efficacy of psycholinguistic training through the MWM program.* Unpublished manuscript, University of Texas at Austin, 1976.

Stillman, R. *The Callier-Azusa scale.* Dallas: The University of Texas at Dallas, 1976.

Templin, M. *Certain language skills in children.* Minneapolis: University of Minnesota Press, 1957.

Templin, M. C., & Darley, F. L. *The Templin-Darley tests of articulation.* Iowa City: Bureau of Educational Research and Service, University of Iowa, 1960.

Valett, R. E. *Programming learning disabilities.* Palo Alto, Calif.: Fearon, 1969.

Vetter, H. J. *Language behavior and psychopathology.* Chicago: Rand McNally, 1969.

Vygotsky, L. *Thought and language.* Boston: MIT Press, 1962.

Weener, P., Barrett, L. S., & Semmell, M. I. A critical evaluation of the ITPA. *Exceptional Children, 1967, 33,* 373-380.

Whitaker, H. A. *On the representation of language in the human brain.* Edmonton, Alberta, Canada: Linguistic Research, 1971.

Wiederholt, J. L. A review of the Illinois test of psycholinguistic abilities. In O. K. Buros (Ed.), *Eighth mental measurement yearbook.* Highland Park, N.J.: Gryphon, in press.

Wiig, E. H., & Semel, E. M. *Language disabilities in children and adolescents.* Columbus, Ohio: Charles E. Merrill, 1976.

Wiig, E. H., Semel, E. M., & Crouse, M. A. The use of morphology by high-risk and learning disabled children. *Journal of Learning Disabilities, 1973, 6,* 457-465.

Winitz, H. Research in articulation and intelligence. *Child Development, 1964, 35,* 287-297.

Wolff, S., & Chess, S. An analysis of the language of fourteen schizophrenic children. *Journal of Child Psychology and Psychiatry, 1965, 6,* 29-41.

Wolski, W. *The Michigan picture language inventory.* Ann Arbor, Mich.: The University of Michigan Press, 1958.

Wood, N. E. *Verbal learning.* San Rafael, Calif.: Dimensions Publishing, 1969.

Zimmerman, I., Steiner, V., & Evatt, R. *Preschool language scale.* Columbus, Ohio: Charles E. Merrill, 1969.

Word-Analysis
Assessment

Millions of children in the United States experience difficulties in reading despite the inordinate number of special teaching programs and innovative teaching materials and techniques available, and the specialists who are prepared to work with these children. In fact, some writers have suggested that reading difficulties continue to be the most prevalent cause of failure in school (Strang, 1969).

The reasons children fail in reading have been studied and discussed professionally since the nineteenth century (Morgan, 1896). Medical personnel, for example, often have suggested that some type of brain dysfunction is responsible for the reading difficulty termed *dyslexia* (Orton, 1937), whereas school factors, such as inappropriate materials, often have been mentioned by educators. The classic and highly respected study by Robinson (1946), however, concludes that multiple factors probably are responsible for reading failure, some of which are difficulties related to education, environment, psychology, society, and physiology. Bond and Tinker (1967) believe that these factors interact as part of a pattern, and that in all but the mildest cases contribute to the difficulties evidenced by these children.

DEFINITIONS OF READING

There are many different definitions of *reading*, along with many misconceptions of which skills are involved in the reading process. Some writers have suggested that reading actually is synonymous with *word-calling*.

These writers believe that reading occurs if a person pronounces words correctly, even if the person does not understand what has been read. Recently, however, the *nature of language* also has begun to play an important role in various definitions of reading. Goodman and Niles (1970), for example, view reading as a psycholinguistic process in which there is a great deal of interaction between thought and language.

Most definitions of reading reflect the theoretical positions and philosophical beliefs of the authors. Consequently, Spache and Spache (1969) believe that no one definition of reading will be accepted unanimously. They see reading as a multifaceted process which can be described at various times and developmental stages as a visual act, a perceptual process, a communication component, a reflection of cultural background, and a thinking process. At one stage, for example, the child might be concerned primarily with differentiating one symbol (letter) from another; later, the child might be concerned with advanced comprehension skills, such as critical reading and evaluation of the reading material. Nevertheless, the child is involved in reading even though he or she is using skills from different developmental stages.

STAGES OF READING

Generally, children progress in reading as they progress in developmental stages. The components of the stages of reading have been outlined by many writers, for example, Kaluger and Kolson (1969) and Harris (1970). We have found that most of the outlines of reading stages present similar patterns of reading development from preschool through adulthood, with the exception of some minor differences. Bush and Huebner (1970) provide the following stages of reading.

1. *The Prereading Stage.* This stage is a period of preparation for reading and usually occurs from birth to age 6. The language activities in the child's immediate environment play an important role during this stage. The amount and type of language that a child hears and then uses during this period of growth certainly contributes to later reading achievement. Some children actually learn to read by themselves or with minimal assistance toward the end of this stage.

2. *The Beginning Reading Stage.* This formal stage of reading instruction, which has been called by some the *real reading stage,* usually occurs in kindergarten through second grade depending upon a child's ability and the educational philosophy of the individual school district. This period is characterized by instruction in forming sound-symbol relationships and decoding words. There is considerable variation in approaches during this

stage; basal readers, programmed reading, language-experience approaches, and word analysis are among the many techniques used. Lerner (1976) points out that the greatest number of innovations and changes have taken place and the most research has been done at this stage.

3. *The Beginning Independent Reading Stage.* This stage is a period of limited independence in reading. It occurs when a child begins to analyze a number of unknown words. Seated activities increase, and the child begins reading library books, which provide a measure of growth during this reading stage.

4. *The Transition Stage.* This stage can occur in grades 2 through 4, as reading in both the content areas and supplementary reading increases. However, teacher guidance is still necessary, since the child is only beginning to be faced with complex ideas in higher-level reading material.

5. *The Intermediate or Low Maturity Stage.* This stage, which occurs during the intermediate grades, is marked by increasingly more advanced comprehension skills and use of a wider range of reading materials. All phases of reading grow during this period.

6. *The Advanced Reading Stage.* The characteristics of mature reading often emerge during junior and senior high school. At this stage, the student has mastered most word-identification techniques and advanced comprehension and study skills and has become more proficient in reading for different purposes at varying rates.

READING SKILLS

The skills that are necessary for a child to read well are learned gradually as the child progresses through the reading stages. Among the multitude of reading skills that are necessary, most may be classified as *word-analysis skills* or *comprehension skills*. In this chapter, we will be concerned primarily with word analysis, whereas Chapter 9 will concentrate on comprehension skills. It should be noted that the purpose of reading is to understand what an author has written, but this cannot be attained unless the person can recognize and analyze the words that comprise reading passages. We have, therefore, organized our discussion according to these two broad areas of reading.

Word-analysis skills are used to find meanings for unknown words. According to Heilman (1968), word-analysis skills may be grouped into the following five categories:

1. *Word Form.* This category includes all the configurations that make a word unique in appearance, including its length and any special features, such as double letters or tall letters (e.g., ball, tent, etc.). These character-

istics usually become less important as children expand their reading vocabulary.

2. *Structural Analysis.* The structure of a word, including the root, prefix, or suffix, is sometimes very helpful in analyzing a new word (e.g., rereading, unsure, singer, etc.). The group of skills within this category are often taught in conjunction with phonic-analysis skills.

3. *Contextual Clues.* Children use skills of contextual analysis when they attempt to analyze unknown words through the context in which they are used (e.g., the baby had a bottle). Contextual clues are applied more easily when children read for meaning.

4. *Pictorial Clues.* Pictures are often used by both children and adults to help analyze unknown words. Heilman indicates that pictures actually help children focus attention on meaning and supplement a story in which children know only a limited number of words.

5. *Phonic Analysis.* The ability to associate sounds with particular symbols (phonic analysis) has been the center of controversy in reading for many decades. Fry (1972) points out that probably no other concept or word associated with reading causes more emotional response than does *phonics.* Many reading experts believe that phonic-analysis skills are the most important ones for reading well, whereas others suggest that the approach is no more significant to later success in reading than any of the other word-analysis skills. We believe that Heilman's (1968) volume provides an excellent discussion for placing phonics in a proper perspective.

The skills that make up word analysis are many and varied. Together, these skills comprise a major component in the process of learning to read. It is important that teachers become familiar with these skills, since they are precisely the ones children must learn in order to read (Karlin, 1971). Similarly, an organization of these skills into a scope-and-sequence chart will provide the teacher with a means for both locating and assessing specific reading deficiencies. The word-analysis skills listed in the scope-and-sequence chart that we presented in Chapter 3 (see Figure 3–1) are based upon an analysis of five basal readers. The continuity of development across grade levels for some skills is necessary since the authors of various basal readers do not introduce all skills in the same sequence or at the same grade level (Ekwall, 1976).

The word-analysis skills shown in Figure 3–1 provide the teacher with a complete guide for both assessing and teaching these reading skills. Interaction among skills is provided for in the sequence by noting those skills that are extended and refined over a number of grade levels. The teacher can use the listed skills in selecting standardized tests, as a guide for observing children, and as a checklist for constructing informal assessment tests. Further suggestions for using this scope-and-sequence chart will be discussed later in this chapter.

ASSESSING WORD-ANALYSIS SKILLS

There are a variety of techniques available to teachers for assessing and analyzing problems with word analysis, and these are described in this section. In most cases, the method or technique used for collecting data will depend upon the specific information that is required by the teacher. Information concerning the level of reading of an entire class, for example, would be best obtained from a group reading achievement test. The need for detailed information concerning a particular student's skills, on the other hand, might be better obtained from an individual diagnostic reading test or an informal teacher-made test.

The use of different assessment techniques also depends upon the specific difficulties the child encounters, the availability of specialized services, and the educator's ability to use diagnostic tools (Wilson, 1972). Therefore, in Table 8–1 we present the most widely used sources for diagnostic information in reading. The type of information that the teacher can obtain from each source is also described.

FORMAL ASSESSMENT TECHNIQUES

General Reading Tests

Standardized reading tests are among the most widely used instruments for assessing children's reading achievement. These tests are standardized because they have been administered to large numbers of representative students, which formed the basis for developing norms for comparative purposes. Because the tests are standardized and the data obtained from the test results are objective, they have wide appeal among educators. General achievement batteries with reading subtests and group reading survey tests are the most popular standardized tests used in reading.

A general achievement battery provides an overall estimate of a child's achievement in various school subjects. The reading sections of these batteries are limited to testing vocabulary and comprehension skills. Intensive assessment of reading skills is not the purpose of these tests. They should be administered when only an overall measure of reading achievement is necessary. Table 8–2 lists several general achievement batteries with reading sections. A number of these tests require individual administration.

In comparison to the achievement tests listed in Table 8–2, there are group survey tests that measure reading skills exclusively. These tests usually provide the teacher with a *general range* of reading abilities. Ac-

TABLE 8–1   Sources of Information on Reading Assessment

Sources, Methods, and Instruments	Kinds of Information Obtained	What Was Learned about an Individual Student, Dick
1. School records	Scores on previous intelligence and achievement tests; school marks in all subjects; family size, economic and social background, language spoken, visual, auditory, and general health information; attendance; change of schools.	Dick is the oldest of seven children. His family is of low-middle socioeconomic status; white, Irish and German extraction. Poor English, but no foreign language is spoken. Kuhlmann-Anderson IQ 110; no recorded health problems; good attendance at the same school. Dick has done consistently poor work through the first year of high school.
2. Classroom observation of students engaged in oral reading, in group discussion, and other classroom activities	Success in completing a given assignment; oral and silent reading performance; indications of attitudes toward reading, school, and himself; interests; relations with other students; speaking vocabulary and sentence structure; uses made of reading; changes in attitudes, points of view, and behavior.	Dick seems to make no real effort to learn new and difficult words. He glides over them and does not stop to analyze or remember them. Even after the teacher has pointed out obvious errors in spelling, Dick makes the same errors again. On the same page he will spell a word both correctly and incorrectly. Other pupils choose him in games. Woodworking is his favorite subject.
3. Interest inventories and questionnaires	Reading interests and other interests.	Dick's main interest is sports. He checked several reading interests, but may just have thought this was the thing to do.
4. Reading autobiography and other introspective reports	Family reading habits, his own past and present reading interests, his analysis of his reading difficulties.	The family does little reading; Dick has read little in the past. At present he says he enjoys reading books on aviation.
5. Daily schedule	How he spends his time: in outdoor activities, TV, movies, chores, part-time work; alone, with friends, with family; kinds and amount of reading.	Most of Dick's free time was spent playing outdoors. After supper he usually watched TV. During the days recorded he did no voluntary reading.
6. *Dolch Basic Sight Word Test*	Sight recognition of basic words, words that he needs to study.	Dick failed to recognize at sight about one-fourth of the Dolch basic vocabulary.

TABLE 8–1 *Continued*

Sources, Methods, and Instruments	Kinds of Information Obtained	What Was learned about an Individual Student, Dick
7. Informal tests and group reading inventory	The free or creative-type response yields information about the pupil's approach to reading and inferences as to how his mind works when he reads. The short answer or multiple-choice questions give understanding of other aspects of comprehension.	Dick could not read independently books above the sixth-grade level. He picked out a few scattered ideas but saw no relation or sequence among them. He was able to identify most of the main ideas and supporting details in the multiple-choice questions. He made no application of the ideas to his own life.
8. Standardized reading tests	Different tests yield different kinds of information: speed of reading easy material, speed-comprehension ratio, special vocabulary in each subject, sentence and paragraph comprehension, ability to use index and reference material.	On the subtests as reported on the *Iowa Silent Reading Test,* Dick's vocabulary, sentence meaning, and directed reading seem to be very poor. He used the index well but slowly, had surprisingly high ability to get the main idea of a paragraph. His total reading score was at the 33rd percentile.
9. Listening comprehension tests	Relation between listening comprehension and silent reading comprehension on comparable material.	Dick comprehended much better when he listened than when he read.
10. Diagnostic spelling test	Grade level of spelling ability, kinds of errors made.	Dick's spelling is about sixth-grade level; he is not word-conscious.
11. Classroom projective techniques, e.g., incomplete sentences, pictures	Attitudes toward self, family, and clues as to emotional conflicts, worries, etc.	Dick gave repeated indications of fear of failure and dislike of school.

Source: From *Diagnostic teaching of reading* (2nd ed.) by R. Strang. 1969. McGraw-Hill Book Company.

cording to Karlin (1971), the teacher can use the information obtained from these tests to compare a class's reading achievement with that of the general population, to group children for instruction, and to indicate the rough growth of groups and individuals. Very often group results also are used as an indicator of need for further testing. For example, the child whose scores are particularly low or uneven may require additional assessment so that the teacher can fully understand the child's instructional needs.

TABLE 8–2   Achievement Tests with Reading Sections

Test	Grade Level	Reading Skills
California Achievement Test (Tiegs & Clark, 1963)	K–14	Vocabulary, comprehension
Comprehensive Tests of Basic Skills (CTB/McGraw-Hill, 1968)	K–12	Vocabulary, comprehension
Metropolitan Achievement Tests (Durost, Bixler, Wrightstone, Prescott, & Balow, 1971)	2.5–9.5	Word knowledge, reading
Peabody Individual Achievement Test (Dunn & Markwardt, 1970)	K–12	Reading recognition, comprehension
SRA Achievement Series (Thorpe, Lefever, & Naslund, 1968)	1–9	Vocabulary, comprehension
Wide Range Achievement Test (Jastak & Jastak, 1965)	Preschool and up	Letter and word recognition

Similarly, test results that do not reflect a child's performance in reading may require further analysis.

There are some things about these group tests that teachers should keep in mind. These instruments basically are screening measures that indicate a child's general range of reading abilities. The results are more reliable when they are applied to a group rather than an individual child (Kaluger & Kolson, 1969). In addition, these tests tend to overestimate a child's reading levels, especially the child who is in an upper elementary grade (Duffy & Sherman, 1973). Some common group tests are listed in Table 8–3.

Diagnostic Reading Batteries

Most diagnostic reading tests are highly specialized and must be administered individually. They usually provide detailed information concerning a child's strengths and weaknesses in various subskills of reading. Obviously, not all children require an intensive appraisal of reading skills. Administration of these tests, therefore, is reserved for those children who are experiencing severe reading difficulties. In some cases classroom teachers who have become familiar with the procedures for administering, scoring, and interpreting the tests can administer these tests (Smith, 1974).

TABLE 8–3   Group Reading Tests

Test	Grade Level	Skills Measured
California Reading Tests (Tiegs & Clark, 1970)	1–14	Vocabulary, reading comprehension
Gates-MacGinitie Reading Tests (Gates & MacGinitie, 1965)	1–9	Vocabulary, comprehension, speed, and accuracy
Iowa Silent Reading Tests (Greene, Jorgansen, & Kelley, 1956)	4–14	Rate, comprehension, directed reading, word meaning, sentence meaning, paragraph comprehension and location of information
Silent Reading Diagnostic Tests (Bond, Clymer, & Hoyt, 1955)	3–6	Word recognition, syllabication, root words, word elements, beginning sounds, letter sounds, and rhyming
Stanford Diagnostic Reading Tests (Karlsen, Madden, & Gardner, 1966)	2.5–8.5	Comprehension, vocabulary, auditory discrimination, syllabication, beginning and ending sounds, blending, and sound discrimination

In other cases, however, specialists who are trained and experienced in intensive diagnosis should administer these tests.

Generally, the diagnostic reading batteries include multiple subtests measuring word recognition, word analysis, and related reading skills (e.g., auditory synthesis, auditory discrimination, etc.). We will review three major diagnostic reading batteries in this section.

Gates-McKillop Reading Diagnostic Tests   The *Gates-McKillop Reading Diagnostic Tests* (Gates & McKillop, 1962) is a battery of reading skills available in two forms, each of comparable difficulty. We suggest that teachers administer the subtests in no particular order and only to those children who need a thorough diagnosis.

Each of the two forms of the *Gates-McKillop* consists of eight subtests, some of which contain several parts. The cover page of the pupil record booklet (see Figure 8–1) lists the complete series of subtests. We list each subtest in the following section.

1. Oral Reading
2. Words: Flash Presentation
3. Words: Untimed Presentation
4. Phrases: Flash Presentation

FIGURE 8–1   Cover Page from Gates-McKillop Reading Diagnostic Tests

PUPIL RECORD BOOKLET	FORM **1**	**G A T E S - M c K I L L O P** **READING DIAGNOSTIC TESTS** ARTHUR I. GATES ANNE S. McKILLOP Professor Emeritus of Education Professor of Education Teachers College, Columbia University Teachers College, Columbia University

Pupil's Name _____ School _____ Date _____

Pupil's Age _____ Birthday _____ Grade _____ Examiner _____ Teacher _____

AGE, GRADE, INTELLIGENCE	1 Raw Score	2 Grade or Other Score	3 Rating	READING AND OTHER TESTS Date Given	1 Raw Score	2 Grade or Other Score	3 Rating ( ) ( )
1 Chronological Age				1 _____			
2 Grade Status (A.G.)				2 _____			
3 Binet ___I.Q. _____ MA			(Date Given)	3 _____			
4 _____ I.Q. _____ MA				Average Silent Reading Gr. (ASRG)			

READING DIAGNOSTIC TESTS

I. Oral Reading (OR)			( ) ( )	V. Knowledge of Word Parts			(OR)
Total Score				1. Recognizing and Blending Common Word Parts			
Analysis of Total Errors							
a. Omissions, Words		%		2. Giving Letter Sounds			
b. Additions, Words		%		3. Naming Capital Letters			
c. Repetitions		%		4. Naming Lower-Case Letters			
d. Mispronunciations (g through k)		%					
Analysis of Mispronunciations				VI. Recognizing the Visual Form of Sounds			
e. Full Reversals							
f. Reversal of Parts				1. Nonsense Words			
g. Total Wrong Order (e+f)				2. Initial Letters			
h. Wrong Beginnings				3. Final Letters			
i. Wrong Middles				4. Vowels			
j. Wrong Endings							
k. Wrong Several Parts				VII. Auditory Blending			
II. Words: Flash Presentation			( ) ( )	VIII. Supplementary Tests			( )
III. Words: Untimed Presentation				1. Spelling 2. Oral Vocabulary 3. Syllabication			
IV. Phrases: Flash Presentation				4. Auditory Discrimination 5. _____			

5. Knowledge of Word Parts
    a. Recognizing and Blending Common Word Parts
    b. Giving Letter Sounds
    c. Naming Capital Letters
    d. Naming Lower-Case Letters

6. Recognizing the Visual Form of Sounds
    a. Nonsense Words
    b. Initial Letters
    c. Final Letters
    d. Vowels
7. Auditory Blending
8. Supplementary Tests
    a. Spelling
    b. Oral Vocabulary
    c. Syllabication
    d. Auditory Discrimination

The *Gates-McKillop* is recognized as a very complete diagnostic test of word-analysis skills. The major advantages to this battery are the variety of reading tasks included in the test and the specific aids that are offered for analyzing a child's strengths and weaknesses (Della-Piana, 1968). However, the length and laborious nature of the test have been cited as major disadvantages. Other limitations include the omission of a reading comprehension subtest and the lack of instructions for eliminating certain tests (Spache, 1976).

We have found that the *Gates-McKillop* is an excellent diagnostic reading test because of its range of word-analysis skills included in the subtests. Gates and McKillop do not offer any reliability or validity data for the test; consequently, the test is best used informally with children experiencing severe deficiencies in word analysis.

Notwithstanding the limitations mentioned, we believe that the *Gates-McKillop* is probably the most complete diagnostic reading test commercially available.

Durrell Analysis of Reading Difficulty The *Durrell Analysis of Reading Difficulty* (Durrell, 1955) is for children at the nonreading through sixth-grade reading levels. It consists of a series of tests in oral and silent reading, listening comprehension, word recognition, and word analysis, plus supplementary tests in visual memory and auditory analysis of word elements, spelling, and handwriting. The test provides grade-level scores that the teacher enters on a profile chart. In addition, the teacher can note the nature of particular reading deficiencies on the *Check List of Instructional Needs* (see Figure 8–2). Durrell feels that the information included on the checklist has more teaching value than do the norms of the test.

The *Durrell Analysis* includes the following 10 subtests:

1. Oral Reading
2. Silent Reading
3. Listening Comprehension
4. Word Recognition and Word Analysis
5. Naming Letters—Identifying Letters Named—Matching Letters

FIGURE 8–2   Checklist of Instructional Needs

NON-READER OR PREPRIMER LEVEL	PRIMARY GRADE READING LEVEL	INTERMEDIATE GRADE READING LEVEL
Needs help in:	*Needs help in:*	*Needs help in:*
1. Listening comprehension and speech	1. Listening comprehension and speech	1. Listening comprehension and speech
__ Understanding of material heard	__ Understanding of material heard	__ Understanding of material heard
__ Speech and spoken vocabulary	__ Speech and spoken vocabulary	__ Speech and oral expression
2. Visual perception of word elements	2. Word analysis abilities	2. Word analysis abilities and spelling
__ Visual memory of words	__ Visual memory of words	__ Visual analysis of words
__ Giving names of letters	__ Auditory analysis of words	__ Auditory analysis of words
__ Identifying letters named	__ Solving words by sounding	__ Solving words by sounding syllables
__ Matching letters	__ Sounds of blends, phonograms	__ Sounding syllables, word parts
__ Copying letters	__ Use of context clues	__ Meaning from context
3. Auditory perception of word elements	__ Remembering new words taught	__ Attack on unfamiliar words
__ Initial or final blends		__ Spelling ability
__ Initial or final single sounds	3. Oral reading abilities	__ Accuracy of copy Speed of writing
__ Learning sounds taught	__ Oral reading practice	__ Dictionary skills: Location, pronunciation,
4. Phonic abilities	__ Comprehension in oral reading	meaning
__ Solving words	__ Phrasing (Eye-voice span)	_____
__ Sounding words	__ Errors on easy words	_____
__ Sounds of blends — phonograms	__ Addition or omission of words	
__ Sounds of individual letters	__ Repetition of words or phrases	3. Oral reading abilities
5. Learning rate	__ Ignoring punctuation	__ Oral reading practice
__ Remembering words taught	__ Ignoring word errors	__ Comprehension in oral reading
__ Use of context clues	__ Attack on unfamiliar words	__ Phrasing (Eye-voice span)
6. Reading interest and effort	__ Expression in reading	__ Expression in reading Speech skills
__ Attention and persistence	__ Speech, voice, enunciation	__ Speed of oral reading
__ Self-directed work	__ Security in oral reading	__ Security in oral reading
7. Other	_____	__ Word and phrase meaning
_____	_____	_____
_____	_____	_____
_____	4. Silent reading and recall	4. Silent reading and recall
_____	__ Level of silent reading	__ Level of silent reading
	__ Comprehension in silent reading	__ Comprehension in silent reading
	__ Attention and persistence	__ Unaided oral recall
	__ Unaided oral recall	__ Unaided written recall
	__ Recall on questions	__ Recall on questions
	__ Speed of silent reading	__ Attention and persistence
	__ Phrasing (Eye movements)	__ Word and phrase meaning difficulties
	__ Lip movements and whispering	__ Sentence complexity difficulties
	__ Head movements Frowning	__ Imagery in silent reading
	__ Imagery in silent reading	
	__ Position of book Posture	5. Speeded reading abilities
	_____	__ Speed of reading (Eye movements)
	_____	__ Speed of work in content subjects
	5. Reading interest and effort	__ Skimming and locating information
	__ Attention and persistence	6. Study abilities
	__ Voluntary reading	__ Reading details, directions, arithmetic
	__ Self-directed work Workbooks	__ Organization and subordination of ideas
		__ Elaborative thinking in reading
		__ Critical reading
		__ Use of table of contents References
		7. Reading interest and effort
		__ Voluntary reading
		__ Variety of reading
		__ Self-directed work

Source: Reproduced from the *Durrell Analysis of Reading Difficulties,* Copyright © 1937, 1955 by Harcourt Brace Jovanovich, Inc. Reproduced by special permission from the publisher.

6. Visual Memory of Words—Primary/Intermediate
7. Sounds
    a. Hearing Sounds in Words/Primary
    b. Learning to Hear Sounds in Words
    c. Sounds of Letters

8. Learning Rate
9. Spelling
   a. Phonic Spelling of Words
   b. Spelling Test
10. Handwriting

The accompanying manual does not provide any information on reliability, validity, or standardization procedures. Nevertheless, users of the complete battery feel that the test is adequate for assessing all but the most severe reading difficulties (Otto, McMenemy, & Smith, 1973). The test itself is easily administered and scored, and clear and concise directions are included in the manual.

We have found that the *Durrell* test is comparable to the *Gates-McKillop* in terms of offering complete word-analysis and word-recognition tests. The major difference between the two is the addition of a silent reading subtest in the *Durrell*. We also have found the Durrell manual to be useful in organizing remedial teaching and planning teaching programs.

Diagnostic Reading Scales The *Diagnostic Reading Scales* (Spache, 1972) are a series of integrated tests developed to provide a standardized, individualized evaluation of skills in oral reading, silent reading, and auditory comprehension. The scales consist of three-word recognition lists, 22 reading passages of graduated difficulty, and eight supplementary phonic tests. The tests are intended to be used with children in elementary grades and older children with reading difficulties.

The word lists that make up the first unit of the test assess a child's skills in word recognition and word analysis, and determine the level at which reading passages should be initiated. The three-word lists, graduated in difficulty, consist of 50 words in the first list and 40 words each in the other two lists.

The 22 reading passages are used to determine a child's reading level. Oral reading errors (e.g., omissions, substitutions, additions, etc.) are recorded by the examiner, and comprehension is checked by asking seven to eight questions following each passage. These results are used to determine the reading levels (from three) for each student: (1) *instructional level*—implies the level at which the child should be exposed to both classroom practice and reading materials; (2) *independent level*—indicates the level at which the child can read supplementary and recreational reading materials independently; and (3) *potential level*—indicates the level at which a child can progress under favorable conditions once various mechanical difficulties are remedied.

Eight supplementary phonic tests are intended to provide detailed information concerning the child's phonic knowledge and word-analysis skills. The tests assess each of the following phonic skills: (1) consonant sounds, (2) vowel sounds, (3) consonant blends and digraphs, (4) common syllables or phonograms, (5) blending, (6) letter sounds, (7) initial consonant substitution, and (8) auditory discrimination. The phonic tests actually are intended to be an inventory of phonic skills and to provide specific teaching clues.

Detailed reliability and validity data are provided in the accompanying manual; however, normative data are not described. The *Diagnostic Reading Scales* are very similar to the *Gates-McKillop* and the *Durrell* tests, in that each of these is a completely organized program for diagnosing individual reading skills. Nevertheless, it is important to note that the concept of reading levels provided by Spache may be confusing, since the levels are somewhat different than those used by most writers in this field.

In sum, each of the three tests described in this section is a good example of a complete diagnostic battery. The *Gates-McKillop* is the best overall measure of specific word-analysis skills. All three tests are highly recommended for appraising specific reading skills. We agree with Otto, McMenemy, and Smith (1973) that selected subtests from any or all of the batteries would be used more frequently than an entire battery.

Specialized Word-Analysis Tests

Several reading tests are intended primarily to measure specific word-analysis skills. A profile of a child's ability to use phonetic and structural analysis skills can be obtained from these tests. Among those available in this area are three that are highly representative of specialized word-analysis tests: the *Botel Reading Inventory*, the *McCullough Word Analysis Tests,* and the *Wisconsin Tests of Reading Skill Development: Word Attack*. Other word-analysis tests are listed in Table 8–4.

Botel Reading Inventory   The three tests which comprise the *Botel Reading Inventory* (Botel, 1962) include Word Recognition, Word Opposites, and the Phonics Mastery Tests. The tests were developed as informal measures to provide an estimate of a child's reading level during periods of teaching, free reading, and frustration and to estimate a child's phonics proficiency.

The Word Recognition Test is the only test that must be individually administered. It consists of 20 words for each of eight reading levels from prekindergarten to fourth grade. Figure 8–3 illustrates the words from the first three levels. The child continues reading from each level until he or she falls below 70 percent on two successive levels.

The Word Opposites Test is a group test that gives an estimate of a child's reading comprehension. In each of the 10 levels of the test, the child must find the opposite of the first word in a line of other words.

TABLE 8–4   Additional Individualized Word-Analysis Tests

Test	Grade Level	Skills Measured
California Phonics Survey (Brown & Cottrell, 1963)	7–13	Long vowels, short vowels, and other vowels; consonant blends and digraphs; consonant-vowel reversals; configuration; word endings; negations; opposites; sight words and rigidity.
Phonics Knowledge Survey (Durkin & Meshover, 1964)	All	Letter names; consonant sounds; long and short vowels; vowel generalizations; consonant blends; digraphs; vowel combinations; syllabication; beginning consonant combinations; and special sounds.
Roswell-Chall Diagnostic Test of Word-Analysis Skills (Roswell & Chall, 1959)	2–6	Consonants and consonant digraphs; short vowel sounds; vowel combinations; final e rule and syllabication rules.
Sipay Word-Analysis Tests (Sipay, 1974)	All	Letter names; symbol-sound association; consonant, vowel, consonant trigrams; initial and final consonant blends and digraphs; vowel combinations; open syllables; final e rule; silent consonants; visual blending; contractions; and others.

For example,

> front   under   back   up   little

The test can be administered as a reading or a listening test. If it is used as a listening test, the Word Opposites will indicate a discrepancy between the child's reading performance and reading potential.

The Phonics Mastery Test enables the teacher to identify sounds that a child knows and those with which the child is having difficulty. The test is presented in four levels; the first three levels are intended for grades 1–3. The goal for each level is 100 percent mastery. Level A tests mastery of initial consonant sounds, consonant blends, consonant digraphs, and rhyming words; level B tests mastery of vowel sounds; level C tests mastery of syllabication level; and level D tests recognition of phonetic elements in nonsense words. This last level can also serve as a quick screening test for phonic skills. If the child successfully passed level D, there would be no need to administer the preceding levels of the test.

FIGURE 8–3   Word Recognition Test

PRE-PRIMER	PRIMER	FIRST
a	all	about
ball	at	as
blue	boat	be
come	but	by
father	do	could
get	duck	fast
have	find	friend
house	girl	guess
in	he	hen
it	kitten	how
little	like	long
make	now	mitten
mother	out	never
not	put	old
play	saw	party
ride	stop	sat
see	thank	some
to	there	tell
want	three	tree
will	train	walk

Source: Excerpted from the Word Recognition Test of the *Botel Reading Inventory* by Dr. Morton Botel. Copyright © 1970 by Follett Publishing Company. Used by permission of Follett Publishing Company.

Botel does not offer any normative data or information concerning reliability and validity. We recommend that teachers use the test informally as a survey of individual pupils. Furthermore, the fact that the test can be administered to a group is an added advantage, even though a more thorough diagnosis would be necessary for a severely disabled reader. The *Botel Reading Inventory* can be used as a preliminary screen for the more detailed diagnostic tests (*Gates-McKillop, Durrell,* etc.) discussed in the previous section.

McCullough Word-Analysis Tests The McCullough Word-Analysis Tests (McCullough, 1963) are designed for either individual children or groups of children at all levels. The tests originally were published as measures related to classroom teaching, and consequently were standardized on only a small population of children.

Each of the seven tests contains 30 test items. The tests include the following:

1. *Initial Blends and Digraphs*—tests the child's ability to hear a consonant blend or digraph, and to identify the letters that make the sound.
2. *Phonetic Discrimination*—evaluates the child's ability to hear sounds.
3. *Matching Letters to Vowel Sounds*—assesses the child's ability to hear vowel sounds and to identify the letters that make these sounds.
4. *Sounding Whole Words*—tests the child's ability to identify consonant and vowel sounds and to blend these sounds into words.
5. *Interpreting Phonetic Symbols*—tests the child's ability to use a pronunciation key.
6. *Dividing Words into Syllables*—evaluates the child's ability to apply eight syllabication rules in the division of words.
7. *Root Words in Affixed Forms*—tests the child's ability to divide a word structurally into prefix, roots, and suffix.

Raw scores can be converted to percentile ranks for each of these tests, for some tests combined, and for a total score on all seven tests. Minimal normative data, along with reliability coefficients (0.94 to 0.96 for the total test), are briefly discussed in the accompanying manual. McCullough also suggests various remedial aids for which each of the test results can be used. Teachers will find these tests useful in determining a child's structural and phonic skills for word analysis.

Wisconsin Tests of Reading Skill Development The Wisconsin Tests of Reading Skill Development: Word Attack (Kamm, Miles, Van Blaricom, Harris, & Stewart, 1972) consists of 38 brief tests, each of which is keyed to a specific *word-attack skill.* The tests are available at four different levels of difficulty, all of which are appropriate for individual or group administration. The word-attack skills correspond to those skills taught in kindergarten through third grade: sight vocabulary, rhyming, consonants, vowels, base words, plurals, and syllabication.

Each of the tests has a criterion reference, and individual performance is evaluated in terms of criterion behaviors rather than comparisons to group performances. Consequently, the tests help teachers to identify those word-attack skills that a child has not yet mastered. In this regard, the tests are good indicators of those specific skills that need to be taught. The teacher also can use them to monitor a student's progress. The reliability coefficients for each of the tests is reported to be 0.80 or better, which we feel is quite acceptable for brief tests of this type.

Word-Recognition Tests

The administration of graded word lists to estimate a child's word-recognition ability and general reading level recently has become very popular. Reading scores are based on the child's ability to pronounce words at different levels of reading difficulty. The graded word lists usually consist of 15–20 words for each of the 10–12 reading levels from primer to high school.

The tests are usually administered by finding the word list for which the child can pronounce all words correctly (labeled the *basal list*) and by continuing until the *ceiling list* or the list in which the child mispronounces or is unable to read all the words is found. Raw scores on each test are subsequently converted to reading levels.

Although graded word lists are helpful in locating a child's *general* reading level, nonetheless they sample only a few words at each level, and all commercially available word lists include different words. They serve very little purpose for the severely disabled reader who would probably need a more thorough analysis of his or her reading skills.

Among the available graded word lists, each of the following is widely used and similar in design: *San Diego Quick Assessment Tests* (LaPray & Ross, 1969), the *Botel Reading Inventory* (Botel, 1962), the *Diagnostic Reading Scales* (Spache, 1972), and the *Slosson Oral Reading Test* (Slosson, 1963).

Additional Published Tests

Several published reading tests that are widely used in assessing children with learning problems cannot be placed in any of the categories previously discussed in this chapter. Two of these tests include the *Woodcock Reading Mastery Test* and the *Gray Oral Reading Test*.

Woodcock Reading Mastery Tests The *Woodcock Reading Mastery Tests* (Woodcock, 1974) consist of five reading tests individually administered to children in kindergarten through the twelfth grade. The five tests include Letter Identification, Word Identification, Word Attack, Word Comprehension, and Passage Comprehension. Two alternate forms of the battery are available. A description of each of these tests follows:

1. *Letter Identification.* The test contains 45 items that measure a child's ability to name the letters in the alphabet. Letters are arranged in order of difficulty according to eight different classes.

2. *Word Identification.* The test consists of 150 words sequenced in difficulty from words found in beginning reading programs (e.g., *is, come, the,* etc.) to those found in twelfth-grade classes (e.g., *grandiose, picayune, beatitude,* etc.). The child is asked to name the word.

3. *Word Attack.* This test contains 50 nonsense words, arranged in order of difficulty, that the child must identify. Most consonant and vowel sounds, common prefixes and suffixes, and frequent misspellings of vowels and consonants are represented.

4. *Word Comprehension.* Seventy items are included on this test. An analogy format is used, and each analogy consists of a double pair of words, which measures the child's knowledge of word meanings. The child is asked to read the first pair of words in the analogy, then the first word of the second pair, and finally tell the examiner a word that would complete the analogy correctly. For example,

listen—hear   observe— ——————

During the test, the child reads the words silently.

5. *Passage Comprehension.* In this test, the child silently reads a passage in which a word is missing and then gives the examiner an appropriate word for the blank space. The 85 items range in difficulty from phrases and short sentences to detailed two-sentence paragraphs. The child must draw upon different word-analysis and comprehension skills to supply the missing word in the passage.

Results from these five tests can be combined to provide a composite index of a child's overall reading skill. In addition, each of the tests establishes a basal level (five consecutive correct responses) and a ceiling level five consecutive errors). Raw scores can be converted to traditional normative scores, such as grade scores, age scores, percentile ranks, etc. However, Woodcock places more emphasis on the specially designed *Mastery Scale,* which predicts the child's relative success with reading tasks at different levels of difficulty.

Detailed standardization information is provided in the accompanying manual. Separate norms are available for boys and girls, as well as for groups. Procedures also are available for adjusting norms to the socioeconomic level of any community. Validity and reliability data are described;

split-half reliabilities, calculated at several grade levels, fall in the 0.90 to 0.99 range.

The Woodcock tests are relatively easy to administer, score, and interpret. The results provide the examiner with an overall indication of a child's ability in each of the areas tested. However, a more detailed analysis of a child's skill areas often is necessary if the child is experiencing severe reading difficulties.

Gray Oral Reading Test   The *Gray Oral Reading Test* (Gray & Robinson, 1967) consists of 13 reading passages. The group of tests is available in four forms, all of which are similar in organization, length, and difficulty. The first three reading passages are appropriate for children in first grade, the next five, for children in second to sixth grades, and the last five passages each increase in difficulty by two grade levels. Difficulty is increased by the range and diversity of vocabulary, length and complexity of sentences, and maturity of concepts. With the exception of children in the beginning levels, most children can read at least five or more passages.

Oral-reading errors are recorded by the examiner as teacher aided, gross mispronunciations, partial mispronunciations, omissions, insertions, substitutions, repetitions, and inversions. The total number of errors the child makes and the time in seconds the child uses to read each passage determine the grade equivalent in oral reading. Four literal comprehension questions are also included for each passage, but these scores are not used in determining the grade-equivalent score.

Limited standardized information is included in the accompanying manual, even though the standardization is considered tentative. Separate norms are provided for boys and girls, along with minimal validity information and reliability coefficients ranging from 0.969 to 0.983 among the four forms of the test. The manual also provides a number of excellent suggestions for detecting various patterns of errors throughout the test. Spache (1976) questions the use of an oral-reading test with children at grade levels in which oral reading plays a very small part in both teaching and placing the child in reading groups. His concern actually involves the desirability of employing an oral-reading test with children who silently read almost exclusively. Unfortunately, this is a question to which very few professionals have addressed themselves. We believe, nevertheless, that educators need to be aware of this.

INFORMAL ASSESSMENT TECHNIQUES

Much of the information necessary for properly instructing children with reading difficulties is available to the teacher through the use of informal measures. In this section, we will discuss the range of informal techniques that teachers will find useful.

Observations

The use of observational procedures as a basic technique in assessing reading problems has been suggested by noted authorities in this field for some time (Strang, 1969; Tinker & McCullough, 1975). Ongoing, day-to-day observations of children provide teachers with information that often cannot be measured by standardized reading tests. Oral-reading periods, written-seatwork assignments, group-instruction periods, and oral-discussion periods seem to offer the best opportunities for collecting observational data, and observations during these periods often provide the teacher with varied information concerning the child's reading interests and attitudes, along with information involving specific word-analysis errors and reading comprehension skills. Observational data also can be used to confirm the results of other tests that the teacher may have administered to a child.

The information obtained during these observations must be recorded systematically in order for it to be beneficial to the teacher. According to Strang (1969), record-keeping can take either of two forms: dated observations that are recorded and periodically summarized or a checklist. The checklist probably is the one most widely used, since it surveys the entire range of reading skills. (Figure 8–4 provides an example of a checklist used to record reading information.) After the checklist has been completed, the teacher is able to isolate a child's particular strengths and weaknesses exhibited in various areas.

Another example of a reading-skills checklist is given in Figure 8–5. When a child has attained each of the specific skills in this checklist the teacher notes this by inserting the date in the space next to the skill. These observations then provide the teacher with a record of a child's progress in the mastery of these skills and the sequence in which they were learned. More important, the observations are an additional source of assessment data that may be used in conjunction with other information to provide the best possible program of instruction for the child.

In addition, Barbe (1961) has designed a series of checklists that are useful in observing various reading skills. The checklists are available through the sixth-grade reading level for sight-word recognition, word analysis, comprehension, oral reading, silent reading, and rate of reading.

It should be noted that observations must be interpreted with particular care. Interpretations should be based upon current, multiple observations that have occurred over an extended period of time. In addition, it is suggested that observations should be supplemented by data from either formal or other informal tests. For a complete discussion of observational skills refer to Cartwright and Cartwright (1974).

FIGURE 8–4   Reading Diagnosis Checklist

	3rd Check	2nd Check	1st Check		
1				Word-by-word reading	
2				Incorrect phrasing	
3				Poor pronunciation	
4				Omissions	
5				Repetitions	
6				Inversions or reversals	
7				Insertions	ORAL READING
8				Substitutions	
9				Basic sight words not known	
10				Sight vocabulary not up to grade level	
11				Guesses at words	
12				Consonant sounds not known	
13				Vowel sounds not known	
14				Blends, digraphs or diphthongs not known	
15				Lacks desirable structural analysis	
16				Unable to use context clues	
17				Fails to comprehend	ORAL SILENT DIFFICULTIES
18				Unaided recall scanty	
19				Response poorly organized	
20				Low rate of speed	
21				High rate at expense of accuracy	SILENT READING
22				Voicing-lip movement	
23				Inability to skim	
24				Inability to adjust reading rate to difficulty of material	
25				Written recall limited by spelling ability	OTHER RELATED ABILITIES
26				Undeveloped dictionary skill	
27				Inability to locate information	

TEACHER _____
SCHOOL _____
NAME _____
GRADE _____

D Difficulty recognized
P Pupil progressing
N No longer has difficulty

The items listed above represent the most common difficulties encountered by pupils in the reading program. Following each numbered item are spaces for notation of that specific difficulty. This may be done at intervals of several months. One might use a check to indicate difficulty recognized or the following letters to represent an even more accurate appraisal:

Source: Ekwall, E. E. *Locating and correcting reading difficulties.* Columbus, Ohio: Charles E. Merrill Publishing Co., 1970. Reproduced with permission of the publisher.

FIGURE 8–5   Primary Reading Checklist

Name: _____

Observer: _____

Directions: Indicate when the behavior was observed to occur by placing the date in the blank next to the item. If the behavior is not observed, do not make any mark.

_____ 1. Listens to short stories (about five minutes duration) without interrupting

_____ 2. Uses simple sentences in his conversation

_____ 3. Tells about a sequence of three actions he has performed in correct order

_____ 4. Looks at picture books from front to back consistently

_____ 5. Looks at a row of written information from left to right

_____ 6. Follows a series of three directions given to him orally

_____ 7. Says letter names when shown cards with letters printed on them

_____ 8. Tells what will happen next in an unfinished story

_____ 9. Tells the main idea of a story after he has read it silently

_____ 10. Repeats short rhymes he has heard a number of times

_____ 11. Dictates his own three- or four-sentence story to the teacher

_____ 12. Illustrates his own stories appropriately

Source: Cartwright, C. A., & Cartwright, G. P. *Developing observation skills.* New York: McGraw-Hill, 1974, p. 110. Reprinted with permission of the publisher.

Interviews

A teacher's interview with a child is an additional informal assessment technique that can be used beneficially. During this interview it is possible for the teacher to gather information concerning reading attitudes, interests, and specific data about word-analysis skills.

According to Ekwall (1976), each of the following guidelines will help to make an interview successful:

1. make the interviewee comfortable
2. use open-ended questions
3. give the interviewee time to think
4. refrain from expressing negative judgment or attitudes
5. avoid the use of technical terms
6. promise only what you know you can accomplish
7. do not undersell your own knowledge and abilities
8. avoid the use of words that might offend older students

9. avoid the use of overly personal questions
10. refer to yourself in the first person
11. ask only one question at a time
12. remember that children usually have an inaccurate perception of time and numbers

Most interviews must be planned carefully so that the results can be both interpreted and used. Bush and Huebner (1970), for example, suggest that a checklist for each area to be measured (e.g., word analysis, comprehension, appreciation, etc.) should be used. Some amount of structure during the interview also provides a more systematic assessment. Wallace and McLoughlin (1975) suggest that an interviewer ask the following questions before informally measuring word-analysis skills:

1. What word analysis skills does the child use?
2. How extensive is the child's sight vocabulary?
3. What *consistent* word-analysis errors does the child make?
4. Does the child depend upon one word-analysis skill (e.g., sounding words out)?
5. Does the child consistently distort or omit particular words or parts of words?
6. Does the child read too quickly, too slowly, or word by word?

Informal Reading Inventories

One of the most widely used informal assessment procedures is the Informal Reading Inventory (IRI). As originally described by Betts (1946), the IRI consists of a carefully graded series of 100–150 word reading passages, usually ranging from preprimer through eighth-grade levels. The selections usually are selected from reading books with which the child has had little or no contact. As the child reads aloud, the teacher records mistakes in word recognition and word analysis that are subsequently analyzed to see if there is a pattern to the errors. After the child reads each passage, the child answers a series of questions that test comprehension of the content of the reading passage.

According to Johnson and Kress (1965), administration of an IRI can determine the reading level at which a child can function independently, the point at which the child can profit from instruction, the level at which the child becomes completely frustrated, and the level at which the child comprehends what is heard. The IRI also can determine the child's specific reading strengths and weaknesses and serves as an evaluation of progress when inventories are administered periodically.

The specific criteria that are applied to each of the reading levels are shown in Table 8–5 and also discussed in the following paragraphs.

TABLE 8–5   Standards for Informal Reading Inventory

Reading Level	Word Recognition	Comprehension
Independent	99%	90% and above
Instructional	95%	75% and above
Frustration	90% and below	50% and below
Hearing comprehension		75% material read to student

Independent Level   The level at which the child reads orally in a natural conversational tone is the *independent level*. The child's reading at this level also is free from any symptoms of difficulty, such as finger-pointing or lip-moving. Reading is rhythmical and well phrased. Extensive supplementary reading for enjoyment and information is possible at this level. As noted in Table 8–5, material at this level is read with 99 percent accuracy in word recognition (1 error per 100 words) and with a comprehension score of at least 90 percent.

Instructional Level   The *instructional level* is the level at which the child probably can profit from teacher guidance through classroom teaching. Little tension is noted in a child's oral reading at this level, and the child can use most word-recognition techniques easily. The child usually reads with 95 percent accuracy in word recognition (1 error per 20 words) and a comprehension score of at least 75 percent.

Frustration Level   The *frustration level* is the level marked by many errors and refusals. The child is usually quite tense at this level, since the material is too difficult to read, and comprehension is often less than 50 percent. It is recommended that the test be terminated at this level.

Hearing Comprehension Level   In the *hearing comprehension level* the child comprehends 75 percent of the material read aloud by the examiner. This level is a good indication of the vocabulary and language structure that the child understands.

Informal reading inventories have the advantage of being relatively easy to administer and interpret. Powell (1971), for example, notes that the "strength of the IRI is not as a test instrument but as a strategy for studying the behavior of the learner in a reading situation and as a basis for instant diagnosis in the teaching environment (p. 121)." In addition, the procedure is both inexpensive and easily used as a supplement to various standardized tests. The adaptability of the IRI for different assessment purposes must also be mentioned as an advantage. Table 8–6 summarizes the advantages and disadvantages of using the IRI.

TABLE 8–6   Pros and Cons of the IRI

Pro	Con
Easy to construct by selecting samples from a basal series.	Only true if we assume that almost any basal at any level is similar to most others.
Selections from basal are the most realistic testing material.	Not true for reading programs of a nonbasal nature, that is, individualized, language experience, and so on.
Selections from basal reflect exact grade levels.	Basal readers vary widely in reflecting the usual materials of a grade level.
If child makes more than five word recognition errors per 100 words, the selection is too difficult for instructional purposes.	Apparently an arbitrary standard, particularly if applied regardless of pupil's comprehension.
Child should show at least 75 percent comprehension at instructional level.	True; in basal-type materials pupils are apt to show at least this degree of comprehension.
Independent reading level is that at which child reads with 99 percent oral accuracy and 90 percent comprehension.	If we follow these standards, pupils cannot use materials in his areas of interest, or resource books, as dictionaries, encyclopedias, and the like.
Frustration level is that at which child reads with 90 percent oral accuracy and less than 75 percent comprehension.	Is relatively meaningless. Once the instructional level is established, any level above this is frustrating (according to current practice!)
Almost any teacher can frame appropriate comprehension questions.	Typical teachers' questions demand only recall of detail. Besides, without item analysis, how do we know that questions discriminate between good and poor comprehenders?
The IRI provides a body of diagnostic information to the teacher.	Unless she collects and analyzes 75–100 errors, no accurate diagnosis of skills is possible.
The average teacher can administer and interpret the IRI.	Very doubtful. Studies of teacher skill in recording an oral reading test indicate that she does not even hear a sizeable proportion of errors. Also assumes teacher has broad knowledge of reading skills and the reading process.

Source: Spache, G. D. *Investigating the issues of reading disabilities.* Boston: Allyn and Bacon, 1976, p. 305.

An IRI for the first through sixth grades, which is based on selections from *My Weekly Reader,* is illustrated in Table 8–9. Comprehension questions of both a factual and inferential nature are included, along with vocabulary questions.

TABLE 8–7   Individual Reading Inventory (Teacher's Record Form)

Some seeds travel
in the water.
Some seeds travel
in the air.
Some seeds travel
on animals.
Some seeds travel
on people's clothes.[a]

First Grade: "How Seeds Travel"
Questions:
   1. What are these sentences about? (2 points)
   2. How do some seeds travel? (2 points)
   3. Why is it good for seeds to travel? (2 points)
   4. What does *travel* mean? (1 point)
   5. Give a sentence using the word *travel*. (1 point)

Total no. words: 23   Accuracy:
   No. words correct: 90% (21)[b]
   No. errors: 95% (22)
Reading time (wpm):   Comprehension score:

Autumn is a busy time
in the north.
Autumn is harvest time.
Potatoes are dug in autumn.
Corn is picked in autumn
Many crops are being harvested.[c]

Second Grade: "Autumn's Harvest Time"
Questions:
   1. What are these sentences about? (2 points)
   2. What kind of a time is autumn in the north? (1 point)
   3. What is dug in autumn? (1 point)
   4. What is picked in autumn? (1 point)
   5. Why is autumn a busy time? (2 points)
   6. What does *harvest* mean? (1 point)
   7. Use *harvest* or *harvested* in a sentence. (2 points)

Total no. words: 27   Accuracy:
   No. words correct: 90% (24)
   No. errors: 95% (27)
Reading time (wpm):   Comprehension score:

 The U.S. Army has been buying dogs. The dogs are German shepherds. The Army needs 200 dogs. The dogs will help guard top-secret Army camps.
 The Army tests the dogs before buying them. Army dogs cannot be afraid of noise. They must be smart and able to obey orders.[d]

[a]*My Weekly Reader,* vol. 39, ed. 1, p. 3, Oct. 2–6, 1961.
[b]The figures in parentheses are the number of words correct to make 90 and 95 percent accuracy.
[c]*My Weekly Reader,* vol. 31, ed. 2, p. 1, Sept. 18–22, 1961.
[d]*My Weekly Reader,* vol. 31, ed. 3, p. 13, Sept. 25–29, 1961.

TABLE 8–7   *Continued*

Third Grade: "Dogs Guard Army Camps"
Questions:
1. What are these paragraphs about? (2 points)
2. How many dogs does the Army need? (1 point)
3. What kind of dogs does the Army buy? (1 point)
4. What must the dogs be able to do? (2 points)
5. Why does the Army need dogs? (1 point)
6. What does *guard* mean? Give a sentence using the word *guard*. (1 point)
7. What does *top-secret* mean? (1 point)
8. Use *top-secret* in a sentence. (1 point)

Total no. words: 51   Accuracy:
  No. of words correct: 90% (46)
  No. errors: 95% (48)
Reading time (wpm):   Comprehension score:

     A giant, four-engine airplane swoops low over a burning forest in California. A "water bomb" drops from the plane. Soon, the roaring blaze is out.
     A helicopter flies slowly over a newly cut forest in Minnesota. As the helicopter moves, it leaves behind a trail of small seeds.[e]

Fourth Grade: "How Airplanes Help"
Questions:
1. What are these paragraphs about? (2 points)
2. What does the airplane drop on the burning forest? (1 point)
3. How do helicopters plant new forests? (2 points)
4. What does the "water bomb" do? (2 points)
5. What does *swoop* mean? (1 point)
6. Use *swoop* in a sentence. (2 points)

Total no. words: 49   Accuracy:
  No. of words correct: 90% (44)
  No. errors: 95% (47)
Reading time (wpm):   Comprehension score:

     The big jet screeches as its engines turn. It takes off with a roar and climbs swiftly into the sky.
     Inside the plane, the passengers hear only a muffled sound of the jet's powerful engines. The takeoff is so gentle that travelers may not even know when the plane lifts off the ground. The jets fly at from 450 to 600 miles an hour. Travelers can go from New York to Chicago in two hours. They can travel from coast to coast in five to six hours.[f]

Fifth Grade: "Facts about Jet Planes"
Questions:
1. What are these paragraphs about? (2 points)
2. What sound does the big jet make when its engines begin to turn? (1 point)
3. How fast do jets fly? (1 point)

[e]*My Weekly Reader,* vol. 43, ed. 4, p. 1, Sept. 25–29, 1961.
[f]*My Weekly Reader,* vol. 44, ed. 5, p. 1, Nov. 27–Dec. 1, 1961.

TABLE 8–7 *Continued*

4. How long do jets take to go from New York to Chicago? (1 point)
5. How long do jets take to go from coast to coast? (1 point)
6. Why is it so quiet inside the jet? (2 points)
7. Give an example of a *screech* and a *muffled sound.* (2 points)

Total no. words: 87   Accuracy:
  No. words correct: 90% (78)
  No. errors: 95% (82)
Reading time (wpm):   Comprehension score:

      Kruger Park is a wild animal preserve. The fence around the park will keep the animals in and unlicensed hunters out. The fence is one of the steps being taken to protect wild life in African countries.
      Africa's wild life has been disappearing at an alarming rate. One wild-life expert says it is possible that all large animals will be gone from the continent within the next ten to twenty years.[g]

Sixth Grade: "Protection of Wild Life in Africa"
Questions:
1. What are these paragraphs about? (2 points)
2. Where is Kruger Park? (1 point)
3. Why is there a fence around the park? (2 points)
4. Why are steps being taken to protect wild life in Africa? (2 points)
5. In how many years may all large wild animals be gone from Africa? (1 point)
6. What is a wild animal preserve? (1 point)
7. What is a continent? (1 point)

Total no. words: 69   Accuracy:
  No. words correct: 90% (62)
  No. errors: 95% (66)
Reading time (wpm):   Comprehension score:

[g]*My Weekly Reader,* vol. 16, ed. 6, p. 1, Oct. 2–6, 1961.
Source: From *Diagnostic teaching of reading* by Ruth Strang, 1969. McGraw-Hill Book Company. Reproduced with permission of the publisher.

    Several published IRIs, such as the *Classroom Reading Inventory* and the *Standard Reading Inventory,* are also available.

Classroom Reading Inventory   The *Classroom Reading Inventory* (Silva-roli, 1973) is composed of graded word lists, graded oral paragraphs, and a graded spelling survey. The inventory is recommended for children in second through eighth grades, and it provides the teacher with information concerning a child's *independent, instructional, frustration,* and *hearing capacity* reading levels. The teacher is also able to informally assess a child's word-recognition, word-analysis, and comprehension skills.

The graded word lists consist of 20 words for each of eight reading levels from preprimer to sixth grade. The child reads each list until he or she mispronounces or indicates 5 of the 20 words (75 percent) are unknown in a particular grade level.

The highest level at which a child successfully pronounces all 20 words in a list provides the starting level for the graded oral paragraphs. This section of the test consists of eight reading passages sequenced in difficulty from preprimer to sixth grade. As the child reads each selection, the examiner analyzes and records the child's word recognition errors according to repetitions, insertions, substitutions, omissions, and need for assistance in pronouncing words. Following the oral reading of the passages, the child answers five comprehensive questions dealing with facts, inferences, and vocabulary contained in each selection.

The spelling survey section of the inventory consists of 15 words for each of seven levels from first to seventh grades. This test is discontinued at the level at which the child misses 5 of the 15 words.

Since this is not a standardized test and normative data are not provided, the inventory results are informally used in organizing reading programs. Silvaroli suggests that elementary school teachers without prior individualized diagnostic experience in reading use this inventory. It is furthermore suggested that the information provided by the inventory is intended primarily for *instructional,* not classification, purposes.

Analysis of Oral Reading Errors   As noted earlier, the IRI can also be used to assess word-analysis and word-recognition skills. Errors are recorded according to a systematic procedure similar to the system outlined in Table 8–8. Later examination of these errors often will reveal various patterns of strengths and weaknesses that might provide a basis for remedial instruction. The coded passage in Table 8–8, for example, indicates that the child might be encountering difficulties in looking at the entire word (e.g., *present* for *preserve, fender* for *fence*) and might be omitting some words. Karlin (1971) believes that these recorded inventories are the most accurate method of estimating a child's instructional level.

An alternate method for analyzing oral-reading errors is based upon the work of Goodman (1965) and his professional associates. In their analysis of oral-reading errors (which they call *miscues*), the emphasis is placed on the nature of the miscue itself instead of on the number of errors made by the child. Goodman and his colleagues believe that miscues are grammatical substitutions based on the syntactical and semantic information from the context and the redundancy of the language (Goodman, 1970). The *Reading Miscue Inventory* (Goodman & Burke, 1972) differs from other diagnostic instruments in that the analysis is qualitative as well as quantitative. Miscues are considered to be serious only when they alter the meaning of what is written. The miscue inventory also provides the teacher

TABLE 8–8   A Marking System for Oral-Reading Errors

Type of Error	Rule for Marking	Examples
1. Omissions	Encircle the omissions.	She did (not) like the cake(s).
2. Substitutions and mispronunciations	Write in the substituted or mispronounced word.	go Everyone ~~went~~ to the movies on ~~Sunday~~ night. Saturday
3. Insertions	Write in the insertions.	go with Please ^help me ^carry the table.
4. Repetitions	Draw a wavy line beneath the repeated word(s).	He came to the <u>back</u> <u>door</u>.
5. Words aided or unknown	Underline the word(s).	The <u>new</u> car was brown and <u>white</u>.
6. Inverted word order	Draw an elongated line between the inverted words.	Sam was/not very nice.
7. Words self-corrected	Make a check above the word.	✓ The forest (was) close to the ~~house~~.

Example of a Coded Passage

present   fender
Kruger Park is a (wild) animal ~~preserve~~. The fence (around) the park
bad   fender
will (keep) the animals in and (un)licensed ^hunters out. The fence is one
wet   ✓
of the (steps) being taken to protect ~~wild~~ life in (African) countries.

with considerable information concerning the child's strengths, from which programs of instruction can be planned.

Teacher-made Tests

Additional information concerning a child's reading abilities and deficiencies can be obtained from informal teacher-made tests. According to Otto, McMenemy, and Smith (1973), the data obtained from these tests often are more useful to the teacher than the data obtained from standardized tests, since informal tests focus on the reading behavior that may be relevant at any given time. Teacher-made tests most often are used when a quick, informal estimate concerning a specific skill is required, or when published tests are unavailable or lack essential data for assessing particular problems.

Many teacher-made tests are constructed by using standardized tests as guides. Durkin (1976) recommends that teachers study the content of diagnostic tests since they offer information concerning different reading skills. Reading scope-and-sequence charts (see Figure 8–1) also will help teachers in constructing informal tests, since these charts include the skills that comprise a large part of the day-to-day instruction in reading.

The examples of teacher-made tests found in Table 8–9 illustrate several methods for measuring specific reading skills either individually or in small groups. The sequence of steps provided by Brueckner and Bond succinctly describe the process of informal test construction:

1. Specify clearly what outcome is to be evaluated.
2. Define the outcome in terms of observable behavior or characteristics of the learner.
3. Prepare test items or test situations by which the behavior or characteristics can most readily be evaluated.
4. Secure some kind of record of the behavior exhibited in the test or test situation.
5. Analyze the information secured and judge the significance of the findings [1955, p 14].

Teacher-made tests are excellent measures for determining whether children have obtained behavioral reading objectives. Wallen (1972) suggests that informal tests be viewed as a working definition of the objective. In other words, the child who attains the objective should behave in the manner described in the informal test.

USING WORD-ANALYSIS
ASSESSMENT TECHNIQUES

Many of the diagnostic procedures discussed in this chapter and listed in Table 8–1 will be useful to teachers working with children who are experiencing learning problems. It will not be necessary to assess or to administer a standardized test to every child. Each of the assessment procedures outlined in this chapter has certain limitations and strengths when used in various situations with specific children.

Before selecting the appropriate assessment technique, the examiner must define the specific purpose for using the assessment technique. Some techniques are better suited to certain objectives; the teacher interested in knowing the general reading level of a class, for example, probably will want to use a reading survey test. On the other hand, the teacher who requires more extensive data concerning a child's reading will use detailed diagnostic tests. Once the purpose has been established, the teacher's primary concern will be to select the most appropriate assessment technique for meeting that purpose.

TABLE 8-9   Examples of Teacher-made Tests

Auditory Discrimination of Final Consonants

1. Tell me if these words are the same or different.

   a. bad—bag   f. tall—tap
   b. kite—kick   g. jam—jar
   c. can—cat   h. hill—him
   d. jump—jump   i. mat—mat
   e. dad—dog   j. lab—lap

2. Tell me the two words that have the same sound at the end.

   a. bed, neat, sand   f. frog, hop, lamp
   b. tall, big, dog   g. bus, paint, seat
   c. ball, hill, man   h. rib, give, sob
   d. bank, run, look   i. and, mend, well
   e. car, pan, ten   j. gab, dad, cub

3. Raise your hand when I say a word that *ends* with the same sound as the first word.

   a. *hop*   dog, trip, mop, sad, leap
   b. *mat*   but, duck, goat, bump, sit
   c. *dig*   pet, rug, hog, pig, dark
   d. *bed*   lid, tall, mud, rod, box
   e. *pain*   den, jam, run, seen, pass
   f. *lick*   fun, duck, bank, but, pet

Visual Discrimination of Initial Consonants

1. Circle the words in each row that begin with the same letter as the first word.

   b. *fat*   baby   top   fork   me   foot
   a. *trip*   goat   tag   like   hat   took
   c. *ball*   boy   dog   girl   bike   duck
   d. *drum*   pig   book   dark   baby   kick
   e. *map*   nat   milk   cart   ever   may
   f. *nut*   hat   meet   nose   beat   none
   g. *good*   gum   pear   quit   give   rest
   h. *see*   zoo   son   root   some   ton

2. Underline each word that begins with the same letter as *dog*.

   big   deal   book
   bark   pump   dumb
   dump   deep   tack
   dig   bite   dairy

3. Draw a line from each letter to a word that begins with the same letter.

   f   mop
   w   rug
   e   stop
   m   wall
   r   fake
   s   eat

Knowledge of Synonyms

1. Circle a word in each row that means the same as the first word.

   a. *hot*   dry   rainy   warm   stop
   b. *rip*   drive   tear   airplane desk

TABLE 8-9   *Continued*

c. *start*	begin	dull	kitten	book
d. *small*	tree	desk	big	little
e. *cash*	money	sweater	key	paper
f. *man*	trunk	male	safe	car

2. Give a synonym for each of the following words.

a. skinny	f. answer
b. happy	g. sweet
c. journey	h. jump
d. new	i. quiet
e. angry	j. error

Knowledge of Compound Words

1. Draw a line to separate the two words that make up each of the following compound words.

a. airplane	f. hilltop
b. teapot	g. sharpshooter
c. cowboy	h. meanwhile
d. windmill	i. northwest
e. breakfast	j. backstop

2. Draw a line from the word in the first column to the word in the second column that completes the compound word.

a. day	fly
b. snow	time
c. birth	meal
d. snap	corn
e. house	ball
f. rain	day
g. oat	made
h. home	shot
i. pop	coat

In selecting an assessment procedure, the teacher should also consider the validity and reliability of each instrument, along with the applicability of the normative data and the skills measured. The assessment technique that will involve the most economical use of time and that will also test a child's specific reading difficulties is recommended by most reading authorities (Bond & Tinker, 1967). Teachers often will find that a combination of approaches meets the needs of most children. Observations are supplemented by either informal or standardized tests, and many diagnostic instruments must be accompanied by teacher-made tests in order to provide a complete assessment. Strang's (1969) beliefs in this regard seem particularly appropriate:

> The cautious, flexible, purposeful, appropriate use of informal and standardized tests, insightfully interpreted, will yield much valuable diagnostic information [p. 143].

Suggested Activities

8–1. Peter is an 8-year-old boy who recently moved to the Jones School District from another state. Although his previous school records have not yet arrived, his parents have told his teacher that Peter experienced some reading difficulties in his former third-grade classroom. In order to provide the teacher with some general information concerning Peter's word-analysis skills, construct an informal observational checklist that can be used for noting these skills during an oral-reading period.

8–2. Recently, Ann's first-grade teacher noticed that Ann sometimes reverses certain letters and words while reading orally. No other reading difficulties have been observed, and Ann is presently reading at grade level. Construct an informal skills test to help Ann's teacher specifically analyze which letters and words are reversed.

8–3. Obtain specimen copies of two published word-analysis tests discussed in this chapter. Carefully review each test and compare them to see which reading skills each one measures. Indicate the type of child for whom each test would be most applicable. Compare the tests according to available normative data and reliability and validity information. List the advantages and disadvantages of each test.

8–4. Donald is a fifth-grade boy of normal intellectual ability who was referred for evaluation because of his severe reading difficulties. The classroom teacher is particularly interested in educational suggestions and recommendations for remedial programming. Donald is reported to have experienced reading problems since his first year in school. His first-grade teacher reported that Donald did not know the names of the letters of the alphabet by the end of the school year, and each succeeding teacher has noted corresponding reading difficulties.

   Donald's present teacher reports that he is functioning at first-grade reading level with some knowledge of letter sounds and that he has a sight vocabulary of approximately 100 words. Based upon this information, outline an assessment program for Donald. List the techniques that might be used, along with reasons for using these specific instruments. Be sure to discuss assessment objectives and the type of information that the teacher would obtain from your recommendations.

8–5. Select a formal word-analysis test discussed in this chapter, and consult the latest edition of Buros' *Mental Measurements Yearbook* for further description and evaluation. Critique the test based upon the information provided in this chapter and in the Buros volume.

8–6. Patti is a sixth-grade student who was administered the following informal word list. Summarize her untimed word-analysis skills, and suggest an appropriate teaching strategy.

Word	Response
afraid	after
always	away
everyone	everyone
morning	morning
whispered	whisper
mosquito	mosquito
behavior	behave
standard	standout
sponge	sprong
through	tough
medical	medicine
straight	strange

8–7. As a high school teacher working with reading disabled students, Mr. Sheperd is continually frustrated by the inappropriateness of most formal word-analysis tests for older students functioning at a primary reading level. Design an informal word-analysis test that can be used with these students and that will provide Mr. Sheperd with an accurate assessment of each student's skills.

8–8. Obtain a specimen copy of a word-analysis test discussed in this chapter. Examine each subtest and carefully read the accompanying test manual. Observe the test being administered, and, when possible, practice administering procedures with other adults or children. Note particularly troublesome subtests, and pay specific attention to various behaviors exhibited by the child. Suggest how certain subtests can be informally evaluated and analyzed for additional information.

8–9. The following graded paragraphs were administered to Sam, a second-grade student, during an Informal Reading Inventory. Examine Sam's performance, and discuss possible areas of strength and weakness.

Some seeds travel in (the) water.
                              ate
Some seeds travel in the air.
                    no
Some seeds travel on animals.
              no   cloth
Some seeds travel on people(s) clothes.

+	1. What are these sentences about?
+	2. How do some seeds travel?
+	3. Why is it good for seeds to travel?
+	4. What does travel mean?
+	5. Give a sentence using the word travel.

does   not

Autumn is a busy time in the north.

trim

Autumn is (harvest) time.

Potatoes are dug in autumn.

The

ᴧCorn is picked in autumn.

corn   bring   having

Many crops are being harvested.

+	1. What are these sentences about?
corn picking	2. What kind of time is autumn in the north?
+	3. What is dug in autumn?
+	4. What is picked in autumn?
+	5. Why is autumn a busy time?
didn't know	6. What does harvest mean?
no response	7. Use harvest or harvested in a sentence.

us

The U.S. Army has been buying dogs. The dogs

giving   sheps   wants

are German shepherds. The Army needs 200 dogs.

pot

The dogs will help to guard top-secret Army

colonels   trys

camps. The Army tests the dogs before buying

after

them. Army dogs cannot be afraid of (noise).

sure   always

They must be smart and able to ᴧobey orders.

+	1. What are these paragraphs about?
lots	2. How many dogs does the Army need?
sheps	3. What kind of dogs does the Army buy?
didn't know	4. What must the dogs be able to do?
didn't know	5. Why does the Army need dogs?
+	6. What does guard mean? Give a sentence using the word guard.
+	7. What does top-secret mean?
+	8. Use top-secret in a sentence.

8–10.   Administer one of the teacher-made tests illustrated in Table 8–9 to a child who is experiencing specific reading difficulties. Examine the results in terms of further assessment that might be required, and implications for remedial teaching.

8–11. On the basis of various formal assessment procedures and informal observations, it was determined that 9-year-old Barbara was experiencing difficulty in remembering almost all sight words. Her third-grade teacher reports that Barbara can apply various phonetic and structural-analysis skills appropriately while reading orally but that the continual application of these skills has slowed down her reading considerably. Describe a number of teaching tasks that might help Barbara, and briefly outline an overall teaching plan for increasing sight-word recognition.

8–12. After being administered a number of informal tests and subtests of published instruments, 9-year-old Greg evidenced difficulty in various aspects of sound blending. He was able to identify individual sounds in the initial, medial, and final positions but was unable to blend these sounds into words. While analyzing a specific word Greg would generally identify the initial sound and guess at the remainder of the word, even though usually he was familiar with other parts of the word when they were presented separately. It was also noted that Greg lacked versatility in using other word-analysis skills. He depended upon sounding-out and guessing at various word parts. Based upon this data, outline an initial teaching strategy for Greg. List any information that might be gathered during diagnostic teaching periods, along with a number of short- and long-term goals for Greg.

References

Barbe, W. B. *Educator's guide to personalized reading instruction.* Englewood Cliffs, N.J.: Prentice-Hall, 1961.

Betts, E. A. *Foundations of reading instruction.* New York: American Book, 1946.

Bond, G. L., Clymer, T., & Hoyt, C. J. *Silent reading diagnostic tests.* Chicago: Lyons & Carnahan, 1955.

Bond, G. L., & Tinker, M. A. *Reading difficulties: Their diagnosis and correction.* (2nd ed.) New York: Appleton-Century-Crofts, 1967.

Botel, M. *Botel reading inventory.* Chicago: Follett, 1962.

Brown, G. M., & Cottrell, A. B. *California phonics survey.* Monterey, Calif.: California Test Bureau, 1963.

Brueckner, L. J., & Bond, G. L. *The diagnosis and treatment of learning difficulties.* New York: Appleton-Century-Crofts, 1955.

Bush, C. L., & Huebner, M. H. *Strategies for reading in the elementary school.* New York: Macmillan, 1970.

Cartwright, C. A., & Cartwright, G. P. *Developing observation skills.* New York: McGraw-Hill, 1974.

Comprehensive tests of basic skills. Monterey, Calif.: CTB/McGraw-Hill, 1968.

Della-Piana, G. M. *Reading diagnosis and prescription: An introduction.* New York: Holt, Rinehart and Winston, 1968.

Duffy, G. G., & Sherman, G. B. *How to teach reading systematically.* New York: Harper & Row, 1973.

Dunn, L. M., & Markwardt, F. C. *Peabody individual achievement test.* Circle Pines, Minn.: American Guidance Service, 1970.

Durkin, D. *Teaching young children to read.* (2nd ed.) Boston: Allyn and Bacon, 1976.

Durkin, D., & Meshover, L. *Phonics knowledge survey.* New York: Teachers College Press, Columbia University, 1964.

Durost, W., Bixler, H., Wrightstone, W., Prescott, B., & Balow, I. *Metropolitan achievement tests.* New York: Harcourt Brace Jovanovich, 1971.

Durrell, D. D. *Durrell analysis of reading difficulty.* New York: Harcourt Brace Jovanovich, 1955.

Ekwall, E. E. *Locating and correcting reading difficulties.* Columbus, Ohio: Charles E. Merrill, 1970.

Ekwall, E. E. *Diagnosis and remediation of the disabled reader.* Boston: Allyn and Bacon, 1976.

Fry, E. B. *Reading instruction for classroom and clinic.* New York: McGraw-Hill, 1972.

Gates, A. I., & MacGinitie, W. *Gates-MacGinitie reading tests.* New York: Teachers College Press, Columbia University, 1965.

Gates, A. I., & McKillop, A. S. *Gates-McKillop reading diagnostic tests.* New York: Bureau of Publications, Teachers College Press, Columbia University, 1962.

Goodman, K. A linguistic study of cues and miscues in reading. *Elementary English Review,* 1965, *42,* 639–643.

Goodman, K. S. Analysis of oral reading miscues: Applied psycholinguistics. *Reading Research Quarterly,* 1969, *5,* 9–30.

Goodman, K. S. Reading: A psycholinguistic guessing game. In H. Singer and R. Ruddell (Eds.), *Theoretical models and processes of reading.* Newark, Del.: International Reading Association, 1970.

Goodman, K. S., & Niles, O. S. *Reading process and program.* Champaign, Ill.: National Council of Teachers of English, 1970.

Goodman, Y. M., & Burke, C. I. *Reading miscue inventory: Manual procedure for diagnosis and remediation.* New York: Macmillan, 1972.

Gray, W. S., & Robinson, H. M. (Eds.). *Gray oral reading test.* Indianapolis: Bobbs-Merrill, 1967.

Greene, H. A., Jorgansen, A. N., & Kelley, V. H. *Iowa silent reading tests.* New York: Harcourt Brace Jovanovich, 1956.

Harris, A. *How to increase your reading ability.* (5th ed.) New York: McKay, 1970.

Heilman, A. W. *Phonics in proper perspective.* (2nd ed.) Columbus, Ohio: Charles E. Merrill, 1968.

Jastak, J. F., & Jastak, S. R. *Wide range achievement test.* Wilmington, Del.: Guidance Associates, 1965.

Johnson, M. S., & Kress, R. A. *Informal reading inventories.* Newark, Del.: International Reading Association, 1965.

Kaluger, G., & Kolson, C. J. *Reading and learning disabilities.* Columbus, Ohio: Charles E. Merrill, 1969.

Kamm, K., Miles, P. J., Van Blaricom, V. L., Harris, M. L., & Stewart, D. M. *Wisconsin tests of reading skill development: Word attack.* Minneapolis: National Computer Systems, 1972.

Karlin, R. *Teaching elementary reading: Principles and strategies.* New York: Harcourt Brace Jovanovich, 1971.

Karlsen, B., Madden, R., & Gardner, E. F. *Stanford diagnostic reading tests.* New York: Harcourt Brace Jovanovich, 1966.

LaPray, M., & Ross, R. The graded word list: Quick gauge of reading ability. *Journal of Reading,* 1969, *12,* 305–307.

Lerner, J. *Children with learning disabilities.* (2nd ed.) Boston: Houghton Mifflin, 1976.

McCracken, R. A. *Standard reading inventory.* Klamath, Ore.: Klamath Printing, 1966.

McCullough, C. M. *McCullough word-analysis tests.* Boston: Ginn, 1963.

Morgan, W. P. A case of congenital word-blindness. *British Medical Journal,* 1896, *2,* 1,387.

Orton, S. *Reading, writing, and speech problems in children.* New York: Norton, 1937.

Otto, W., McMenemy, R. A., & Smith, R. J. *Corrective and remedial teaching.* (2nd ed.) Boston: Houghton Mifflin, 1973.

Powell, W. R. The validity of the instructional reading level. In R. E. Leibert (Ed.), *Diagnostic viewpoints in reading.* Newark, Del.: International Reading Association, 1971.

Robinson, H. *Why children fail in reading.* Chicago: University of Chicago Press, 1946.

Roswell, F. G., & Chall, J. S. *Roswell-Chall diagnostic test of word-analysis skills.* New York: Essay Press, 1959.

Silvaroli, N. J. *Classroom reading inventory.* (2nd ed.) Dubuque, Iowa: William C. Brown, 1973.

Sipay, E. R. *Sipay word-analysis tests.* Cambridge, Mass.: Educators Publishing Service, 1974.

Slosson, R. L. *Slosson oral reading test.* East Aurora, N.Y.: Slosson Educational Publications, 1963.

Smith, R. M. Clinical teaching: *Methods of instruction for the retarded.*

(2nd ed.) New York: McGraw-Hill, 1974.

Spache, G. D. *Diagnostic reading scales.* Monterey, Calif.: California Test Bureau, 1972.

Spache, G. D. *Diagnosing and correcting reading difficulties.* Boston: Allyn and Bacon, 1976.

Spache, G. D., & Spache, E. B. *Reading in the elementary school.* (2nd ed.) Boston: Allyn and Bacon, 1969.

Strang, R. *Diagnostic teaching of reading.* (2nd ed.). New York: McGraw-Hill, 1969.

Thorpe, L. P., Lefever, D. W., & Naslund, R. A. *SRA achievement series.* Chicago: Science Research Associates, 1968.

Tiegs, E. W., & Clark, W. W. *California achievement test.* Monterey, Calif.: CTB/McGraw-Hill, 1963.

Tiegs, E. W., & Clark, W. W. *California reading test.* Los Angeles: California Test Bureau, 1970.

Tinker, M. A., & McCullough, C. M. *Teaching elementary reading.* (4th ed.) Englewood Cliffs, N.J.: Prentice-Hall, 1975.

Wallace, G., & McLoughlin, J. A. *Learning disabilities: Concepts and characteristics.* Columbus, Ohio: Charles E. Merrill, 1975.

Wallen, C. J. *Competency in teaching reading.* Chicago: Science Research Associates, 1972.

Wilson, R. M. *Diagnostic and remedial reading for classroom and clinic.* (2nd ed.) Columbus, Ohio: Charles E. Merrill, 1972.

Woodcock, R. W. *Woodcock reading mastery tests.* Circle Pines, Minn.: American Guidance Service, 1974.

Reading Comprehension Assessment

The area of reading comprehension is a controversial field of study. Most authorities agree that comprehension is a vital component of the reading process; however, there is little consensus among these experts in regard to definitions, theories, or components of reading comprehension. Consequently, the literature is often confusing and contradictory and contains very few universal understandings and agreements (Durkin, 1976). Nevertheless, some authorities have developed comprehension models and taxonomies that have influenced the formulation of definitions. Some of these are discussed in the following section.

COMPREHENSION MODELS AND SKILLS

One of the most widely discussed comprehension models was developed by Spache (1963) based upon Guilford's model of the structure of the intellect. The intellectual abilities that Guilford has classified as *operations* (cognition, memory, convergent thinking, divergent thinking, and evaluation) and *products* (units, classes, relations, systems, tranformations, and implications) have been translated into specific reading behaviors by Spache.

On the other hand, the Barrett taxonomy of cognition and effective dimensions of reading comprehension is quoted by Clymer (1968) as divided into five major skill categories or levels, including literal comprehension, reorganization of ideas or information explicitly stated, inferential comprehension, evaluation or judgment, and appreciation. Each of these

TABLE 9–1 The Barrett Taxonomy: Cognitive and Affective Dimensions of Reading Comprehension

1.0 Literal Comprehension
  1.1 Recognition
    1.11 Recognition of Details
    1.12 Recognition of Main Ideas
    1.13 Recognition of a Sequence
    1.14 Recognition of Comparison
    1.15 Recognition of Cause-and-Effect Relationships
    1.16 Recognition of Character Traits
  1.2 Recall
    1.21 Recall of Details
    1.22 Recall of Main Ideas
    1.23 Recall of a Sequence
    1.24 Recall of Comparisons
    1.25 Recall of Cause-and-Effect Relationships
    1.26 Recall of Character Traits
2.0 Reorganization
  2.1 Classifying
  2.2 Outlining
  2.3 Summarizing
  2.4 Synthesizing
3.0 Inferential Comprehension
  3.1 Inferring Supporting Details
  3.2 Inferring Main Ideas
  3.3 Inferring Sequence
  3.4 Inferring Comparisons
  3.5 Inferring Cause-and-Effect Relationships
  3.6 Inferring Character Traits
  3.7 Predicting Outcomes
  3.8 Interpreting Figurative Language
4.0 Evaluation
  4.1 Judgments of Reality or Fantasy
  4.2 Judgments of Fact or Opinion
  4.3 Judgments of Adequacy or Validity
  4.4 Judgments of Appropriateness
  4.5 Judgments of Worth, Desirability, and Acceptability
5.0 Appreciation
  5.1 Emotional Response to the Content
  5.2 Identification with Characters or Incidents
  5.3 Reactions to the Author's Use of Language
  5.4 Imagery

Source: Barrett, T. C. Taxonomy of cognitive and affective dimensions of reading comprehension. Unpublished paper, Madison, Wis. Used with permission.

major areas is further extended into specific types of tasks for reading that the teacher can subsequently use. An outline of this taxonomy is provided in Table 9–1.

A detailed model of reading comprehension by Gray has been modified by Robinson (1966). This model consists of five major aspects: word perception, comprehension, reaction, assimilation, and speed of reading. The skills required for the various aspects of reading were Robinson's primary concern, not the process of reading or the techniques of reading instruction.

The influence of psycholinguistics also has been noted recently because there have been many suggestions involving reading comprehension from experts within that realm (Smith, 1973). Psycholinguists believe that only a small part of the information that is necessary for reading comprehension comes from the printed page. The reader's knowledge about language, reading, and words, and what the reader brings to the printed page, also will have a tremendous impact on comprehension. Similarly, it is important to psycholinguists that reading be understood as an extension of natural language development.

Finally, many models are based upon the belief that a hierarchical sequence of skills must be employed in reading comprehension. However, different writers often give different outlines of what is involved in comprehension (Tinker & McCullough, 1975). For example, Duffy and Sherman (1973) identify five categories of skills, including word meaning, organization and structure, fact-inference, and evaluation or judgment. Another widely accepted classification of comprehension is offered by both Smith (1963) and Karlin (1971). They suggest that the three levels of comprehension are *literal, interpretive,* and *critical.*

According to Huus (1971), the reader grasps the material as a whole at the *literal* level of comprehension: the reader can usually outline, paraphrase, or summarize the ideas expressed by the author. Huus believes that the parrot-like repetitions at this level are similar to what goes on in schools.

The skills involved at the *interpretive* level of comprehension usually include finding cause-and-effect relationships, detecting the main idea, and drawing conclusions. Karlin (1971) describes this level as reading "between and beyond the lines" for the implied meanings. Huus (1971) concludes that many facets of meaning, including content, theme, character development, style, and relationships of various types, can be obtained through interpretation.

The *critical* level of comprehension, as an extension of interpretive reading, includes judging accuracy, distinguishing between fact and opinion, and using analysis skills more thoroughly. This is usually considered the highest level of comprehension, at which the reader compares the material with his or her total conceptual background (Kaluger & Kolson, 1969).

Among the many available lists of reading comprehension skills, the sequence provided by the Baltimore City Public Schools (1972) is typical.

1. noting main ideas and details
2. identifying story elements

3. analyzing characters
4. recognizing language usages
5. determining sequence
6. forming sensory images
7. seeing relationships
8. comparing and contrasting
9. identifying tone and mood
10. anticipating outcomes
11. recognizing the author's purpose
12. evaluating and making judgments

Each of these skills can be applied across grade levels for children at certain ages, thus providing a scope-and-sequence chart for reading comprehension skills.

A potential difficulty in using these lists, however, has been pointed out by Spache and Spache (1969). They provide evidence to indicate that comprehension is a more general process and not one necessarily composed of 50 or more discrete skills that automatically make up the total act of comprehension. Additional arguments are provided by Niles (1968), who believes that the number of skills to be taught probably could be reduced if teachers, among others, understood the essentials of the comprehension process.

FACTORS AFFECTING COMPREHENSION

Before attempting to outline some of the important considerations in appraising comprehension skills, it would be helpful if we discuss briefly a number of factors influencing the degree of comprehension, most of which will be relevant to both the type and thoroughness of the assessment used.

The *nature of the reader* is a strong factor in affecting the reader's comprehension level. The reader's background and experience, interest, motivation, physical condition, and reading ability all should be considered. The child who finds the reading material uninteresting probably will not pay as close attention to it as the child who finds the reading material both fascinating and absorbing. Similarly, the reader who has a varied and extensive reading background probably will find more success than the reader who has a more limited background of experiences and exposure to reading.

The *reader's purpose* also must be viewed as an important factor influencing comprehension. Some readers experience problems with comprehension because they are unable to adjust their comprehension according to the various types of material they are reading. The degree of comprehension when reading for pleasure, for example, certainly is quite different from the intense comprehension necessary when studying for a final examination.

The *type of material* that is read may also affect comprehension. Reading passages that are too difficult for a student will influence the level of comprehension negatively. Students may attend to the technical aspects of reading, such as word analysis, when the reading material becomes too involved and puzzling. A lack of emphasis often is noted when students struggle with the recognition of new words. Complicated language patterns and styles also will contribute to comprehension problems of many students because the emphasis must be placed on reading aspects other than comprehension.

The extent to which a student comprehends various reading material will be affected by all of these factors. Consequently, each factor must be considered individually in an attempt to determine the reasons for reading comprehension problems.

ASSESSING READING COMPREHENSION DIFFICULTIES

The confusion and disagreement that were mentioned with respect to a definition of the components of reading comprehension undoubtedly have been partially responsible for the dearth of information regarding the assessment of various comprehension skills (Otto, McMenemy, & Smith, 1973). Obviously, any consensus regarding the measurement of reading comprehension skills must await some general agreement concerning a definition of comprehension and the components involved in the process.

Most attempts at evaluating reading comprehension traditionally have used a combination of approaches, since few single forms of evaluation provide completely reliable and valid assessments. According to Gilliland (1974), information on a student's comprehension skills usually has been obtained from standardized reading tests (both group and individual), informal observations, and teacher-made tests. Each of these techniques will be discussed in the following sections.

Group Standardized Tests

Fry (1972) points out that there is no consistent agreement among users of standardized tests on which skills comprise reading comprehension; each test seems to measure different abilities. Vocabulary knowledge and general comprehension usually are the skills most often appraised. However, other tests may assess rate of comprehension, understanding of sentences or paragraphs, and rate of reading. Most group standardized tests do not classify various subskills of reading comprehension beyond vocabulary and general comprehension (Ekwall, 1976). Therefore, very few tests measure higher-order comprehension skills, such as critical reading. The majority of comprehension tests require literal comprehension: the student responds with factual information about a reading passage.

Group standardized tests are usually valuable to teachers when they want to determine an overall comprehension level of a class. The results of these tests provide the teacher with *general* information concerning comprehension strengths and weaknesses for groups of children and serve as an index for measuring reading improvement over a specific period of time. Table 9–2 lists some group reading tests with comprehension sections. The *Stanford Diagnostic Reading Test—Level II* is described in some detail in the following paragraphs because it emphasizes reading comprehension components.

TABLE 9–2   Group Tests with Comprehension Sections

Test	Comprehension Section	Grade Level
Developmental Reading Tests (Bond, Balow, Clymer & Hoyt, 1965)	*Primary:* Vocabulary, general comprehension, specific comprehension	1–3
	Intermediate: Basic vocabulary, reading to retain information, reading to organize, reading to evaluate-interpret, reading to appreciate, average comprehension	4–6
Gates-MacGinitie Reading Tests (Gates & MacGinitie, 1965)	Vocabulary, comprehension, and speed and accuracy	1–9
Iowa Test of Basic Skills (Lindquist & Hieronymus, 1956)	Vocabulary, comprehension, work-study skills	3–9
Nelson Reading Test (Nelson, 1962)	Vocabulary, comprehension	3–9
Stanford Diagnostic Reading Test—Level II (Karlsen, Madden, & Gardner, 1966)	Literal and inferential comprehension	4.5–8.5
Traxler Silent Reading Test (Traxler, 1942)	Story comprehension, word meaning, paragraph meaning, total comprehension	7–10

Stanford Diagnostic Reading Test—Level II   The *Stanford Diagnostic Reading Test—Level II* consists of six reading subtests and provides normative data for students in the middle of the fourth grade (4.5) to the middle of the eighth grade (8.5), although the test may be used also with students performing poorly at other grade levels. Figure 9–1 provides a schematic description of how the six subtests relate to each other.

The authors of this test believe that vocabulary, rate of reading, and word recognition are skills subordinate to the ultimate goal of reading instruction—reading comprehension. The vocabulary subtest assesses the understanding of the meaning of words, whereas the three word-recognition subtests assess the ability to determine what words are being read. The last subtest, rate of reading, evaluates the speed at which meaning is comprehended.

In the reading comprehension subtest the authors have attempted to assess both literal and inferential comprehension. Both of these parts are scored separately. The series of reading passages and questions require understanding of content, perception of important details, and ability to draw reasonable inferences. The general reading level is obtained from the total score of these two parts. In addition, this subtest provides a base line from which one can judge any of the other subtests.

Raw scores on the subtests can be converted into stanines, and the reading comprehension total score may be interpreted in terms of a grade score, since this subtest best represents a student's overall reading performance. In addition, the authors provide an extensive and particularly valuable section in the accompanying manual that discusses how to interpret the test results for different types of students. The clinical applica-

FIGURE 9–1   Schematic Diagram of the Stanford Diagnostic Reading Test

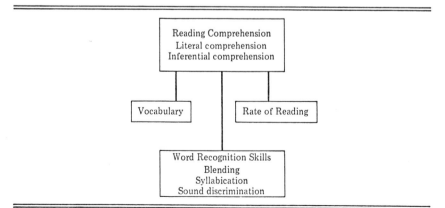

Source: Karlsen, B., Madden, R., and Gardner, E. F. *Stanford Reading Diagnostic Test Manual for Administering and Interpreting.* New York: Harcourt Brace Jovanovich, 1966, p. 4.

tions and the suggestions for remedial instruction are also very helpful. Furthermore, a computer program is available for analyzing each student's profile of subtest scores in order to place the student into a group with common strengths and weaknesses.

Over 12,000 individuals have been included in the standardization program. Split-half reliability coefficients reported in the test manual range from 0.72 to 0.97 for Level II subtests for various grade levels.

We believe that the Stanford test provides a good estimate of paragraph comprehension. The inclusion of both literal and inferential comprehension and the variety of subject-matter content are recognized as important advantages of this test.

Individual Diagnostic Tests

Diagnostic tests that are individually administered have the distinct advantage of providing the examiner with detailed information concerning a student's specific reading strengths and weaknesses. As mentioned in Chapter 8, the administration of diagnostic reading tests should be reserved for children experiencing severe reading difficulties, since these tests usually provide exact data and are very time consuming to administer.

Only a limited number of the diagnostic reading batteries discussed in Chapter 8 include sections that measure reading comprehension. Diagnostic tests that have comprehension sections are listed in Table 9–3. However, it is important to note that, although these tests assess reading

TABLE 9–3   Diagnostic Tests with Comprehension Sections

Tests	Comprehension Sections	Grade Level	Group or Individual
Botel Reading Inventory (Botel, 1962)	Word opposites	1–12	G/I
Diagnostic Reading Scales (Spache, 1972)	Comprehension questions following oral reading	1–8	I
Durrell Analysis of Reading Difficulty (Durrell, 1955)	Silent reading, listening comprehension	1–6	I
Gilmore Oral Reading Test (Gilmore & Gilmore, 1968)	General comprehension	1–8	I
Woodcock Reading Mastery Tests (Woodcock, 1974)	Word comprehension, passage comprehension	K–12	I

comprehension, not all include normative data for these subtests. The *Botel Reading Inventory,* for example, is an informal measure, and the Word Opposites subtest in the *Inventory* is actually used as an estimate of comprehension.

In addition to these diagnostic reading batteries, a number of diagnostic tests are available *primarily* for assessing reading comprehension skills. The three discussed in the following section are unique in this regard, because each is essentially a measure of reading comprehension providing a detailed analysis of skills within this area.

Reading Diagnostic Record for High School and College Students   The *Reading Diagnostic Record for High School and College Students* is an informal test of reading comprehension consisting of four paragraphs read orally by the student. The examiner records any oral reading errors, such as additions or mispronunciations and observes the student's phrasing, intonation, and use of stress. Strang (1969) points out that these skills indicate the student's understanding of the language structure of the selection. After the student reads the passage, comprehension is assessed by having the student answer an unstructured question, such as *"What did the author say?"* Additional comprehension questions evaluate the student's ability to grasp the main idea and important details, to interpret, to draw inferences and conclusions, and to explain the passage. However, it is suggested that these questions be varied for individual situations. A suggested scale for rating the reading passages is also provided in another publication (Strang, 1969).

Strang believes that the free, unstructured response, unlike those received from the usual standardized test questions, offers the examiner an opportunity to evaluate each student's unique approach to reading. Stilted views of the reading passage, rather than creative responses based upon personal experience, can be compared and analyzed for planning various teaching programs. Strang asserts that many students have not learned to read with the intent to understand, remember, and communicate, but rather have learned just to recall words.

In addition to providing information about the child's reading comprehension, the diagnostic record is also organized to summarize other reading data. The record provides space for outlining information relevant to the problem that is available through other sources (e.g., educational history, medical reports, etc.). Another section of the record suggests further information that might be gained through interviews and observations. Figure 9–2 illustrates the outline provided in the record for studying the students' developmental and educational history.

The diagnostic record is an excellent source for gathering and organizing all of the data pertinent to a student's reading problem. Although the reading passages are intended for older students, the other parts of the

FIGURE 9–2

V. DEVELOPMENTAL AND EDUCATIONAL HISTORY
(Aspects that might have bearing on the individual's
reading ability)

A. Autobiographical Sketch of Reading History
(Written or dictated by the student; the written autobiog-
raphy may be supplemented in an interview.)
Attach autobiography here.

B. History of Interest in Reading
(Obtained in interview with student and parent if possible.)

At what age did individual begin to read?

What method or methods were used in teaching the
child to read?

Schools attended during first six grades?

When were difficulties in reading first noted?

What types of difficulties were first noted?

Describe any remedial work that has been done.

How much of the student's time has been spent in reading?

B. History of Interest in Reading (Continued)
What has been his attitude toward reading?

What is his attitude now?

Account for changes in attitude.

What kinds of books did he read at different periods
of his life?

Describe the environment in which he usually reads at
home. Does he have privacy? Good light?

What has been the attitude of his parents and other
members of his family toward his reading?

Does reading play an important part in their lives?

How much use is made of the public library?

What kinds of books are there in the home library?

Other significant information:

From Ruth Strang, *Reading Diagnostic Record for High School and College Students*. (New York: Teachers College Press, 1952), pp. 6–7.
Reprinted with permission of the publisher.

record may be used with a child of any age. The reading passages and accompanying questions can also be extended or adapted for students of different ages and grades. The nature of the record is informal and flexible and it is absent of any quantitative data such as grade-level scores or percentile rankings.

Gilmore Oral Reading Test   Gilmore Oral Reading Test (Gilmore & Gilmore, 1968) consists of 10 reading passages that measure accuracy, comprehension, and rate of oral reading for children in first through eighth grades. Five comprehension questions to test recall are asked after each reading passage.

The examiner asks the child to read a passage two grade levels below his or her present grade level. If less than two errors are made, the examiner asks the child to read each successive passage until 10 or more errors are made on one paragraph. In addition to asking comprehension questions, the teacher also records any oral-reading errors, including omissions, mispronunciations, additions, and hesitations. Specific directions for recording each of these errors are suggested in the accompanying manual. Unlike oral-reading errors, the child's responses to the questions are not considered as a measure for terminating the test.

Grade-level scores and stanines are provided for accuracy, comprehension, and rate of oral reading. A general rating, ranging from poor to superior, is also available for each child's actual grade level. Standardization information, including reliability coefficients and validity data, is also described in the test manual. The reliability coefficients for comprehension range from 0.53 to 0.60 and are considered unacceptable by some reading experts (Spache, 1976).

The Gilmore test is an example of a standardized oral-reading test that can be used effectively to measure at least one component of reading comprehension. Additional comprehension skills can be assessed through teacher-made questions. Otto, McMemeny, and Smith (1973) also have mentioned that the *Gilmore Oral Reading Test* can be very useful as a model for teachers devising their own informal oral-reading tests.

Wisconsin Tests of Reading Skill Development: Comprehension   The *Wisconsin Tests of Reading Skill Development: Comprehension* (Kamm, Miles, Van Blaricom, Harris, & Stewart, 1972) is an individualized program providing a framework for reading instruction; it is not intended to be used as an entire reading program. The comprehension tests are similar in design to the word-attack tests described in Chapter 8. They are available at five different levels of difficulty and may be administered either individually or in groups.

These tests deal only with those skills requiring convergent thinking: establishing cause-and-effect relationships, using context clues to derive word meanings, drawing conclusions, and judging relevance. Each of the tests is an independent unit that focuses upon the student's time limitations and other structured procedures that tend to inhibit a student's performance. The comprehension tests generally correspond to those skills used in kindergarten through sixth grade.

As mentioned during our discussion of word-attack skills, the tests do not provide any group referenced norms. Individual performances are evaluated in terms of certain behavioral objectives (criterion-referenced), with the student usually expected to respond correctly to at least 80 percent of the items in any given test.

The comprehension tests, with reliability coefficients of 0.80 or better, are ideally suited to the needs of teachers who find it necessary to determine which specific comprehension skills have and have not been mastered by the children. Appropriate instruction is planned more easily once these questions have been answered. The Wisconsin tests focus on pertinent component skills that together provide a realistic and effective assessment of comprehension beneficial in planning teaching programs.

Informal Tests

The ongoing evaluation of comprehension skills upon which daily teaching is often based is measured mainly by the use of informal tests (Tinker & McCullough, 1975). These tests usually provide the teacher with the exact information necessary to evaluate specific difficulties encountered by students. Informal tests are used more extensively in reading comprehension than in other areas because there are only a few available standardized tests that assess reading comprehension in any depth. Among the types of informal tests available for providing informal data on reading comprehension, we have found that the *checklist,* the *informal reading inventory,* and the *cloze procedure* are widely used.

Checklists Some writers have noted that checklists can be used advantageously for recording the presence or absence of specific behaviors in particular curriculum areas (Cartwright & Cartwright, 1974). We have also suggested previously that checklists may survey a general range or a specific list of skills. Most checklists are comprised of a list of behavioral statements with a space for recording whether the behavior was attained.

In reading comprehension, checklists may be used to indicate either individual or group progress for any range of skills. Figure 9–3, for example, provides an illustration of a checklist for recording the attainment of various critical reading skills. This checklist can be used to record the continuous progress of children within a class. Tinker and McCullough (1975) point out that the number and variety of items rated depend upon the

FIGURE 9–3   Critical Reading Skills Checklist

Chris	Tim	Steve	Laurel	
✓	✓		✓	Establishes cause and effect
✓		✓	✓	Anticipates outcomes
✓		✓	✓	Draws conclusions
✓		✓	✓	Distinguishes fact from opinion
✓	✓		✓	Makes inferences
✓			✓	Establishes sequence
✓			✓	Forms opinions
✓		✓	✓	Compares and contrasts
✓		✓	✓	Evaluates and solves problems
			✓	Reacts to mood and time
			✓	Supports opinions with relevant data
		✓		Judges statements
✓		✓	✓	Analyzes character
✓		✓	✓	Judges Accuracy
✓		✓	✓	Recognizes persuasive statements

	Comments		
	Having difficulty mastering these skills	No problems	

teacher and the particular reading objectives that are emphasized in the teaching.

Informal Reading Inventories   Although we have discussed specific guidelines for informal reading inventories (IRI) in Chapter 8, it should be reiterated that IRIs can be used for appraising various aspects of reading comprehension. Each reading selection in an IRI usually is followed by a series of questions on comprehension. These questions often measure understanding of vocabulary, ability to grasp the main idea, noting of stated facts, and sometimes the ability to make inferences. The responses are then used to establish the child's independent, instructional, and frustration levels (see Table 8–5).

A well-recognized advantage of the IRI is its adaptability for different purposes. Depending upon specific needs and interests, the teacher may ask only questions on vocabulary or only inferential comprehension questions. Nevertheless, it has been our experience that teachers tend to prepare questions that require primarily literal comprehension. In this regard, Valmont (1972) has suggested a number of guidelines for preparing IRI questions. Among the many recommendations, Valmont suggests that the examiner ask the most important questions first, and state the questions so that they start with *who, what, when, where, how,* and *why.* The questions also should approximate the order in which the appropriate information is presented in the passage. Good examples of the range of comprehension questions are provided in a number of published IRIs (McCracken, 1966; Silvaroli, 1973).

The *Reading Miscue Inventory* (RMI) (Goodman & Burke, 1972) is somewhat of a reaction to the informal reading inventory and also provides a procedure for evaluating reading comprehension. However, in the RMI the children are asked to retell in their own words a story that they read orally. This retelling is then scored according to character analysis, events, plot, theme, specifics, generalizations, and major concepts. The reader is referred to Goodman and Burke (1972) for a more thorough discussion of the RMI.

Cloze Procedure The *cloze procedure* is another informal technique that can be used to measure both reading levels and comprehension. In this technique, the child is presented a reading passage of 100–250 words with every fifth word omitted (starting with the second sentence) and is asked to fill in the missing words or synonyms. The missing words usually are replaced with lines of uniform length, and all punctuation is left intact. The cloze procedure can be administered either individually or in groups. In a group administration, the children are instructed to fill in the missing words. Figure 9–4 illustrates the cloze procedure. The excerpt is taken from the twelfth book of the *Chandler Reading Program.*

The child's reading levels are obtained by converting correct responses to percentages. However, currently there is some controversy about scoring synonyms as correct responses. Furthermore, unlike the scoring procedures for informal reading inventories, little agreement has been reached about scoring cloze passages. Ekwall (1976) suggests the following:

• Independent Reading Level—57 percent and above
• Instructional Reading Level—44–56 percent
• Frustration Reading Level—43 percent and below

According to Gilliland (1974), the cloze procedure is an excellent means of evaluating a student's comprehension. He points out that, in addition to being able to determine reading levels, the examiner also can determine whether a student understands material of a certain type or on a particular subject. Hafner (1965) also suggests that cloze errors may be examined according to linguistic components, cognitive types, and reasoning skills. Additional evidence by Bormuth (1969) indicates that cloze test scores do correlate with standardized tests of reading comprehension. However, Duffy and Sherman (1973) believe that the technique should be used judiciously, since results are sometimes misleading depending upon various features of the selected reading passage. Furthermore, a child needs

FIGURE 9-4   Cloze Procedure

The New Flashlight

Jerry walked to school by himself because he liked to think about things on the way to school. Sometimes the things he __1__ about were not important. __2__ today he was thinking __3__ something very important, and __4__ was talking to himself __5__ it.

"I've got a __6__ !" Jerry said to himself. " __7__ last I've got a __8__ of my very own! __9__ what a flashlight!"

For __10__ long time, everyone in __11__ family but Jerry had __12__ flashlight. Jerry thought about __13__ great big flashlight that __14__ father had in the __15__ of the car.

Jerry __16__ it was a funny __17__ flashlight. It looked something __18__ a lunch box with __19__ big white light on __20__ end and a little __21__ light on the other __22__ .

You didn't hold it __23__ your hand. If you __24__ a flat tire at __25__ , you put the big __26__ down on the street. __27__ big white light let __28__ see to work on __29__ tire, and the little __30__ light flashed on and __31__ to show people in __32__ cars that you were __33__ .

Correct Answers:
1. thought   2. But   3. about   4. he   5. about   6. flashlight   7. At   8. flashlight 9. And   10. a   11. Jerry's   12. a   13. the   14. his   15. back   16. thought 17. looking   18. like   19. a   20. one   21. red   22. end   23. in   24. had   25. night   26. flashlight   27. the   28. you   29. the   30. red   31. off   32. other 33. there

---

Source: Take another look, Chandler Reading Program. New York: Noble and Noble, Publishers, Inc., 1969. Reproduced with permission.

more than just reading skills to write in a correct answer (Gillespie & Johnson, 1974).

Teacher-made Tests

In addition to providing a measure of student progress over a specific period of time, informal, teacher-made tests can be very beneficial for assessing various comprehension skills. Wilson (1972) has suggested that, among the variety of uses, teacher-made tests can be designed to measure the comprehension skills needed for certain school subjects (e.g., science and social studies), as well as for general reading. In addition, informal tests can be constructed to determine a child's ability with specific skills. However, teachers must be reminded to include enough items to adequately sample the particular skill and to be sure that the items actually measure the skill that is being evaluated. Wallen (1972), for example, believes that teacher-made tests in comprehension are more difficult to construct than those in other areas because comprehension skills are not as clearly observable as word-analysis skills. Therefore, teachers must carefully consider the selection of reading passages and the development of test questions when they construct informal reading comprehension tests.

The teacher-made tests illustrated in Figure 9–5 are good examples of why they are helpful to teachers, since the results are very applicable to ongoing teaching programs. These tests often deal with reading skills that the child must use daily, whereas Strang (1969) points out that standardized test items often are remote from the content and skills taught in many classrooms.

Finally, it should be noted that published workbook comprehension exercises can be used as a guide for constructing informal tests. The variety of exercises found in these workbooks, including true-false, completion, multiple-choice, and matching tests, provide a solid basis for formulating teacher-made tests. In many instances, the workbook exercises can serve easily as informal tests themselves by using them as a measure of comprehension ability over a period of time. We believe that all of these informal measures are valuable for teachers in planning teaching programs for children experiencing problems in reading comprehension.

USING READING COMPREHENSION ASSESSMENT TECHNIQUES

Any thorough evaluation of student achievement in reading comprehension must include both formal and informal measures of this skill. Unlike other areas of the curriculum, published tests alone will not measure the important components of reading comprehension sufficiently. The relatively few published tests in this area make it almost imperative that informal measures become an important part of diagnostic batteries in reading comprehension.

Most evaluations of a child's comprehension can be initiated through an analysis of performance on group reading achievement tests. The results of such tests usually will indicate to the teacher which children may require further evaluation. Using these data as guidelines, the teacher will then collect additional information by informally observing the child during teaching periods, discussion periods, and independent work activities. An analysis of work samples and administration of an informal reading inventory probably will provide additional detailed information that will contribute to further understanding of the child's particular problem. In many cases, further appraisal through individualized reading comprehension tests or teacher-made tests may be necessary in order to pinpoint specifically the

FIGURE 9–5   Teacher-made Tests in Reading Comprehension

Cause and Effect Relationships

Directions: Read each sentence below and decide the season that best fits the description in the sentence. Write the season on the line following the sentence.

summer   fall   winter   spring

1. Susan put on a warm coat and mittens. _____
2. John got the rake out of the shed. _____
3. Mary and Ann decided to go for a swim to cool off. _____
4. Rufus slipped on the icy steps. _____
5. The beavers were cutting down trees to build up a good supply of food. _____
6. The groundhog stuck its head out of the hole and decided it was warm enough to stay. _____
7. Jake was glad to be back in school again. _____
8. The creeks were full from the melting snow. _____
9. Susan and Sandy lay on the sand to get a tan. _____
10. The pumpkins were ripe and needed to be picked. _____

Main Idea

Tom likes to read, but Joe would rather play ball. They both liked to watch TV.

What is the main idea of this story?

    a. Tom's books
    b. things that Tom & Joe like to do
    c. how to keep busy

Grandmother and grandfather are coming to our house for a visit. Mother is baking a cake for them. Dad is fixing the front porch.

What is the main idea of the story?

    a. getting ready for grandmother and grandfather
    b. baking a cake
    c. fixing the porch

Yesterday we went to the circus with our scout troop. We left our seats to go get some popcorn and when we got back we couldn't find our group. There were so many people and so many other scout groups that we became confused. A clown walked by us and saw that we were worried. He helped us find our seats by looking at our ticket stubs.

Tell me the main idea of this story in your own words.

Noting Details

Sue was only in the sixth grade, but she was sure that she wanted to be a doctor when she grew up. She talked with her teacher and her school counselor. They told her where she could get more information about medical

FIGURE 9–5 *Continued*

---

careers and how she could prepare for the future. Sue began to take notes on information she received. The counselor also suggested that she talk with the librarian about ordering films and books from the media center. Sue soon realized from her reading that she must work especially hard in math and science, and she began to work harder in her school subjects.

1. What grade was Sue in?
   a. high school
   b. fifth grade
   c. sixth grade

2. Who did Sue talk to about being a doctor?
   a. her doctor
   b. her teacher and counselor
   c. her parents

3. What subjects are important for becoming a doctor?
   a. spelling and writing
   b. science and math
   c. music and art

Source: We acknowledge the skillful assistance of Gregory Muzik and Erma Young Smith in constructing these informal tests.

nature of the child's difficulties. In all cases, however, each additional assessment technique used should help the teacher to understand more clearly the comprehension problem; otherwise, the assessment procedures are of no practical value to either the child or the teacher.

The wide usage of informal assessment techniques in reading comprehension seems due in part to the obvious difficulties of actually testing what Wallen (1972) views as the "child's translation of language to thought (p. 234)." The flexible use of informal techniques, such as teacher observations and teacher-made tests in natural settings, provides more realistic information for planning sound remedial programs. Nevertheless, it is important that teachers do not completely disregard the few published instruments that are available in this area. Some standardized measures can be used to give balance to the assessment battery, because in some instances the published tests provide a better measure for a particular purpose. In the end, the objectives of a reading program, the needs of the individual students, and the skills of the teacher will determine the type of assessment technique that will be used with individual students.

Suggested Activities

9-1. Mr. Parks is an eighth-grade English teacher who recently has noticed that a group of 10–12 students of average ability in his class are experiencing some difficulty in distinguishing fact from opinion.

   Design a group test that Mr. Parks can administer to these students in order to further analyze this particular skill.

9-2. Mrs. Long is a high school resource-room teacher working primarily with students of average to above-average intellectual ability who are reading on the first- to second-grade reading level. Mrs. Long has experienced some difficulty in locating a general reading comprehension test on the primary level that holds the interest of her pupils.

   Construct an informal reading comprehension test to assist Mrs. Long. She is primarily interested in measuring each child's literal and inferential comprehension abilities.

9-3. Mrs. Cohen, a third-grade teacher, informally has observed that a group of children within her class experience difficulty in using context clues even though each child's overall comprehension level is considered at grade level.

   Design an informal test that can be used to appraise a student's ability to apply context clues, and discuss possible intervention strategies for children experiencing difficulty in this area.

9-4. Design an informal vocabulary test by selecting a minimum of 20 words from a graded text in a particular content area (e.g., science, social studies, etc.). Ask the child the meaning of the words through either open-ended or multiple-choice questions. Sample lists from a number of sequentially graded texts will enable the teacher to measure a child's vocabulary understanding over various levels of difficulty.

9-5. When the passages in the reading text were no longer accompanied by illustrations or picture clues, Mr. Hansen observed that a small group of his second-graders began to experience various reading comprehension difficulties.

   List the evaluative procedures that Mr. Hansen might use to further pinpoint specific comprehension difficulties, and describe any teaching procedures designed to help a child with this problem.

9-6. The ability to summarize and synthesize has been listed by Barrett (see Table 9-1) as an important reading comprehension ability. Discuss the various informal assessment techniques that can be used to measure this particular skill. Be sure to note the different assessment techniques that can be applied by classroom teachers in ongoing teaching programs.

9-7. Frank, a seventh-grader, silently has read the following graded paragraphs and has responded orally to each of the comprehension questions.

Examine Frank's answers and suggest possible teaching strategies for increasing his reading comprehension skills.

> A giant four-engine airplane swoops low
> over a burning forest in California. A
> "water bomb" drops from the plane. Soon,
> the roaring blaze is out.
> A helicopter flies slowly over a newly
> cut forest in Minnesota. As the helicopter
> moves, it leaves behind a trail of small
> seeds.

1. What are these paragraphs about?
   Seeds
2. What does the airplane drop on the burning forest?
   bombs
3. How do helicopters plant new forests?
   by flying over forests
4. What does the "water bomb" do?
   don't know
5. What does swoop mean?
   go down low
6. Use swoop in a sentence.
   Some birds swoop down to get food.

> The big jet screeches as its engines turn.
> It takes off with a roar and climbs swiftly into
> the sky.
> Inside the plane, the passengers hear only a
> muffled sound of the jet's powerful engines. The
> take-off is so gentle that travelers may not even
> know when the plane lifts off the ground. The jets
> fly at from 450 to 600 miles an hour. Travelers
> can go from New York to Chicago in 2 hours. They
> can travel from coast to coast in 5 to 6 hours.

1. What are these paragraphs about?
   jets
2. What sound does the big jet make when its engines begin to turn?
   don't know
3. How fast do jets fly?
   very fast, faster than regular airplanes.

4. How long does it take to go from New York to Chicago?
   5 hours
5. How long does it take to go from coast to coast?
   don't know
6. Why is it quiet inside the jet?
   the thickness of the plane
7. Give an example of a *screech* and a *muffled* sound.
   a. A car sometimes screeches.
   b. A muffled sound is like when you have ear muffs on your ears.

9–8.   During oral discussion periods, Mrs. Shaw has observed that 9-year-old David continually encounters difficulty in predicting the outcome of stories read by his fourth-grade reading group. The results of an informal test in this area have verified that David does anticipate inappropriate outcomes even though he is able usually to note specific details and recognize the main idea of a story.

List a number of remedial tasks to help David, and outline an overall teaching strategy.

9–9.   The cloze procedure was used in the following paragraph to informally measure the reading comprehension ability of the children in Mr. Kingsbury's third-grade classroom. Examine the represented performance of one child in this class and evaluate his reading comprehension (see also Figure 9–4 for the correct answers).

The New Flashlight

Jerry walked to school by himself because he liked to think about things on the way to school. Sometimes the things he 1. did about were not important. 2. Not today he was thinking 3. again something very important, and 4. he was talking to himself 5. about it.

"I've got a 6. idea!" Jerry said to himself. "7. How last I've got a 8. idea of my own!" 9. He what a flashlight!"

For 10. a long time, everyone in 11. the family but Jerry had 12. Jerry flashlight. Jerry thought about 13. it great big flashlight that 14. his father had in the 15. bus of the car.

Jerry 16. was it was funny 17. laughing flashlight. It looked something 18. not a lunch box with 19. a big white light on 20. back end and a little 21. small light on the other 22. piece.

Source: Take another look, Chandler Reading Program. New York: Noble and Noble, Publishers, Inc., 1969.

9–10.   Following the administration of an informal reading comprehension test, Bruce's fifth-grade teacher concluded that Bruce was encountering difficulty in both recognizing and in recalling the main idea of paragraphs. In responding to questions of this type, Bruce usually uses the concluding sentence of the paragraph as the major reference for his response.

Based upon this information, outline a teaching strategy for Bruce. List any additional evaluative information that might be necessary.

References

Baltimore City Public Schools. *Sequential listing of reading skills.* Baltimore: Baltimore City Public Schools, 1972.

Bond, G. L., Balow, B., Clymer, T., & Hoyt, C. J. *Developmental reading tests.* Chicago: Lyon & Carnahan, 1965.

Bormuth, J. R. Factor validity of cloze tests as measures of reading comprehension ability. *Reading Research Quarterly,* 1969, *43,* 358-365.

Botel, M. *Botel reading inventory.* Chicago: Follett, 1962.

Cartwright, C. A., & Cartwright, G. P. *Developing observation skills.* New York: McGraw-Hill, 1974.

Clymer, T. What is reading?: Some current concepts. In H. Robinson (Ed.), *Innovation and change in reading instruction: Sixty-seventh yearbook of the National Society for the Study of Education.* Chicago: University of Chicago Press, 1968.

Duffy, G. G., & Sherman, G. B. *How to teach reading systematically.* New York: Harper & Row, 1973.

Durkin, D. *Teaching young children to read.* (2nd ed.) Boston: Allyn and Bacon, 1976.

Durrell, D. *Durrell analysis of reading difficulty.* New York: Harcourt Brace Jovanovich, 1955.

Ekwall, E. E. *Diagnosis and remediation of the disabled reader.* Boston: Allyn and Bacon, 1976.

Fry, E. *Reading instruction for classroom and clinic.* New York: McGraw-Hill, 1972.

Gates, A. L., & MacGinitie, W. H. *Gates-MacGinitie reading tests.* New York: Teachers College Press, Columbia University, 1965.

Gillespie, P. H., & Johnson, L. E. *Teaching reading to the mildly retarded child.* Columbus, Ohio: Charles E. Merrill, 1974.

Gilliland, H. *A practical guide to remedial reading.* Columbus, Ohio: Charles E. Merrill, 1974.

Gilmore, J. V., & Gilmore, E. C. *Gilmore oral reading test.* New York: Harcourt Brace Jovanovich, 1968.

Goodman, Y. M., & Burke, C. I. *Reading miscue inventory: Manual procedure for diagnosis and remediation.* New York: Macmillan, 1972.

Hafner, L. Importance of cloze. In E. T. Thurstone and L. E. Hafner (Eds.), *The philosophical and social basis for reading 14th yearbook.* Milwaukee, Wis.: National Reading Conference, 1965.

Huus, H. Critical aspects of comprehension. *Elementary English,* 1971, *48,* 489–494.

Kaluger, G., & Kolson, C. J. *Reading and learning disabilities.* Columbus, Ohio: Charles E. Merrill, 1969.

Kamm, K., Miles, P. J., Van Blaricom, V. L., Harris, M. L., & Stewart, D. M. *Wisconsin tests of reading skill development: Comprehension.* Minneapolis: National Computer Systems, 1972.

Karlin, R. *Teaching elementary reading: Principles and strategies.* New York: Harcourt Brace Jovanovich, 1971.

Karlsen, B., Madden, R., & Gardner, E. F. *Stanford diagnostic reading test—Level II.* New York: Harcourt Brace Jovanovich, 1966.

Lindquist, E. F., & Hieronymus, A. N. *Iowa test of basic skills.* Boston: Houghton Mifflin, 1956.

McCracken, R. A. *Standard reading inventory.* Klamath, Oreg.: Klamath Printing Co., 1966.

Nelson, M. J. *Nelson reading test.* Boston: Houghton Mifflin, 1962.

Niles, O. J. Comprehension skills. In M. A. Dawson, *Developing comprehension including critical reading.* Newark, Del.: International Reading Association, 1968.

Otto, W., McMenemy, R. A., & Smith, R. J. *Corrective and remedial teaching.* (2nd ed.) Boston: Houghton Mifflin, 1973.

Robinson, H. M. The major aspects of reading. In H. A. Robinson (Ed.), *Reading: Seventy-five years of progress.* Supplementary Educational Monographs No. 96. Chicago: University of Chicago Press, 1966, 22–32.

Silvaroli, N. J. *Classroom reading inventory.* (2nd ed.) Dubuque, Iowa: William C. Brown, 1973.

Smith, F. *Psycholinguistics and reading.* New York: Holt, Rinehart and Winston, 1973.

Smith, N. B. *Reading instruction for today's children.* Englewood Cliffs, N.J.: Prentice-Hall, 1963.

Spache, G. D. *Toward better reading.* Champaign, Ill.: Garrard, 1963.

Spache, G. D. *Diagnostic reading scales.* Monterey, Calif.: California Test Bureau, 1972.

Spache, G. D. *Diagnosing and correcting reading disabilities.* Boston: Allyn and Bacon, 1976.

Spache, G. D., & Spache, E. B. *Reading in the elementary school.* (2nd ed.) Boston: Allyn and Bacon, 1969.

Strang, R. *Reading diagnostic record for high school and college students.* New York: Teachers College Press, Columbia University, 1952.

Strang, R. *Diagnostic teaching of reading.* (2nd ed.) New York: McGraw-Hill, 1969.

Tinker, M., & McCullough, C. M. *Teaching elementary reading.* (4th ed.) Englewood Cliffs, N.J.: Prentice-Hall, 1975.

Traxler, A. E. *Traxler silent reading test.* Indianapolis: Bobbs-Merrill, 1942.

Valmont, W. J. Creating questions for informal reading inventories. *The Reading Teacher,* 1972, 25, 509–512.

Wallen, C. J. *Competency in teaching reading.* Chicago: Science Research Associates, 1972.

Wilson, R. M. *Diagnostic and remedial reading for classroom and clinic.* (2nd ed.) Columbus, Ohio: Charles E. Merrill, 1972.

Woodcock, R. W. *Woodcock reading mastery tests.* Circle Pines, Minn.: American Guidance Service, 1974.

10

Spelling Assessment

The ability to spell is one of the most basic and essential skills within the language arts curriculum. It is interesting to note, however, that in comparison with reading, spelling has received little attention by educators. The trend to reduce spelling to a minor subject in the curriculum is regrettable, because poor spelling certainly distracts from the effectiveness of any form of written communication. For this reason, students who experience difficulties in learning to spell should be carefully identified and steps should be taken to assist them in overcoming their difficulties. The process by which a teacher assesses and ultimately remedies a student's spelling difficulties depends upon the severity of the problem, the student's concept skills necessary for proficient spelling, the student's attitude toward spelling, and the instruments available that measure spelling ability.

This chapter will acquaint teachers with (1) a basic overview of the nature of spelling, (2) factors related to successful spelling, (3) processes by which children learn to spell, and (4) various devices and strategies appropriate for assessing spelling difficulties. It is our feeling that, in order to assess spelling disorders adequately, the teacher must understand the idiosyncratic nature of English orthography and the skills that must be attained in order to master it. Knowledge of available spelling tests is also essential for the teacher who is planning appropriate intervention strategies. Informal teacher-made assessment tests are treated in detail to ensure that the data teachers derive from them are related directly to school practice.

THE NATURE OF ORTHOGRAPHY

At its most basic level, *spelling* may be defined as the ability to arrange properly letters into words that are necessary for effective written communication. Implicit in this definition is that an adequate speller must possess knowledge regarding the manner in which *phonemes* (speech sounds of oral language) are represented by *graphemes* (letter symbols of the written code, or *orthography*). Regardless of whether the person attempts to spell a word in oral or written form, first the functional correspondence of sounds to letters must be understood before effective spelling is attained (Westerman, 1971; Boyd & Talbert, 1971).

In order that educators fully understand the nature of spelling, they must become familiar with the *alphabetic* principle that underlies spelling. In essence, this principle states that each phoneme in a language has its own unique graphic counterpart. In languages in which there is a nearly one-to-one correspondence between a sound and its letter symbol, the task of learning to spell is simple and straightforward. According to Hanna, Hodges, and Hanna (1971), a student attempting to spell in an alphabetically consistent language needs only (1) to determine which sounds are contained in a word and the order in which they occur, (2) to know what grapheme represents each sound, and (3) to write the graphemes in the same order in which the sounds occur in the word. A good example of a language that is highly consistent alphabetically is Hawaiian. This language is composed of 13 phonemes and 12 graphemes. Obviously, the Hawaiian-speaking child only needs to hear or say the various sounds of a word and to correctly transcribe them into the alphabetically regular graphemes in order to spell Hawaiian words correctly.

Unfortunately, the phoneme-grapheme relationships in English are somewhat less consistent than other languages, and they are especially apparent when one considers that there is a minimum of 251 ways of graphemically representing the 40+ English phonemes (Feigenbaum, 1958). If our language were alphabetically consistent, the sound /k/ would be represented by only one letter or grapheme. In actual practice, however, there are 11 different ways of spelling the /k/ sound (e.g., cash, bask, character, keep, biscuit, etc.). Another example is the long /ē/ sound, which is spelled at least 12 ways in common words and *only* about 1/5 of the time is the letter *e* alone (e.g., leave, see, ski, believe, key, etc.). The reasons for the obvious inconsistencies of English spelling are many and vague. Glim and Manchester (1975) state that, perhaps, the most likely reasons for these inconsistencies are:

1. English words come from many diverse sources. In doing so, they preserve the graphic conventions found in different spelling systems. For example, the French "eau" is preserved in plateau, bureau, and tableau.
2. The spelling of English words tends to ignore changes in sound, especially when word changes result from a shift in stress. Consequently, related words may look more alike than they sound, such as: finite, infinite; Christ, Christmas; crime, criminal.

3. The pronunciation of English words has changed without corresponding graphic changes, so that words originally distinct in pronunciation are now homophonous, such as knight, night; wright, rite, write, right; and bough, bow.
4. The current pronunciations of words are not at all clearly represented in writing as, for example, "sure" /shur/, and even more so, "machine" /ma shēn/ [pp. 1–2].

Consequently, educators traditionally have tended to view English spelling as haphazard, with no useful structure for guiding students to become efficient spellers. In the past learning to spell by rote was used: each word in a spelling lesson was memorized and repeated upon command during a weekly spelling test (Westerman, 1971). It is important to note, however, that recent research has demonstrated that, although English orthography certainly is not consistent, it does possess sufficiently consistent phoneme-grapheme correspondences (rules) so that they can be used in spelling diagnosis and instruction. Otto, McMenemy, and Smith (1973) state:

> In light of recent findings of linguistic research, it appears valid to conclude that the English spelling system is considerably more regular than it formerly was assumed to be. These latest findings argue strongly for the teaching of generalizations as the logical emphasis in a spelling program. Linguistics presents an illuminating picture of the alphabetic nature of the English language . . . and the systematic way in which these letters pattern in the English orthography [p. 253].

The primary studies that have influenced current thought regarding the nature of English orthography were conducted at Stanford University (Hanna, Hanna, Hodges, & Rudorf, 1966). Essentially, the purpose of this research was to analyze basic phoneme-grapheme (sound-letter) relationships of 17,000 commonly used words, as well as to study the structure of the English language in general. If it could be demonstrated that our language is, in fact, based upon regular relationships between phonemes and graphemes, a major reconceptualization of traditional spelling diagnosis and curriculum would be warranted.

The study by Hanna, et al. was divided into two phases. In Phase I computer technology was used to analyze the sound-letter relationships in 17,000 commonly used words with the intention of clarifying the alphabetic nature of English spelling. The results of this phase of the research demonstrated that, contrary to traditional viewpoints, English orthography is far from chaotic. According to Hanna, et al., English orthography " . . . is based upon relationships between phonemes and graphemes—relationships which are sometimes complex in nature which, when clarified, demonstrate that English orthography, like that of other languages, is largely systematic (p. 76)." It was found, for example, that the vast majority of consonants have single spellings that are used 80 percent or more of the time in the 17,000 words investigated. Although vowels are not as consistent, it was determined that their spelling could be predicted with reasonable accuracy when one considers such factors as position and stress within words.

Although the insights gained from Phase I were important, it was still not clear whether the observed phoneme-grapheme rules could be useful in the actual spelling of words. Consequently, the authors undertook Phase II, in which a computer was programmed to predict the spelling of the 17,000 words by using the orthographic insights gained from Phase I. The rules that were used to program the computer were based upon four basic factors: (1) simple correspondences between phonemes and graphemes; (2) the effects of *where* (i.e., position) a phoneme occurs in a syllable; (3) the effects of *stress* upon the choice of a letter to represent a sound; and (4) immediate environment of the sound within a word. An example of how environment can affect spelling is: when the /f/ sound follows the /s/ sound it is always spelled with a *ph* rather than the letter /f/ (e.g., sphere, sphinx).

The major findings of Phase II demonstrated that of the total number of words, a surprising 49.8 percent (8,346 words) were spelled without error. Additional analysis showed that 6,332 words (37.2 percent) were spelled with only one error, 1,941 (11.4 percent) with two errors, and 390 (2.3 percent) with three or more errors. Further study of the errors made by the computer indicate that a child with a simple mastery of certain rules of *morphology* (i.e., word formation including prefixes and suffixes) would have had little difficulty in correctly spelling many of the words missed. According to Hodges and Rudorf (1966), teaching a child the principles of affixation and compounding would eliminate many of the errors that the computer had made.

It was apparent from the results of this study that one of the primary factors underlying spelling ability is the understanding of the linguistic nature of orthography. Although many educators correctly believed that many words in the traditional spelling curriculum could be aptly described as "spelling demons" (words that do not conform to any phonological or morphological rules, or that conform to rules of little practical utility), it can no longer be denied that there does exist a considerable body of words that are governed by rules to the extent that the knowledge of these rules would be useful. This fact seems particularly significant in light of research that has demonstrated that over one-half of children's writing consists of the repetition of 100 words and that 4,500 words make up nearly 99 percent of the words used by all writers (Otto, McMenemy, & Smith, 1973). Examples of productive phoneme-grapheme relationships that were documented in the Hanna, et al. study are given in Table 10–1. Each of these correspondences, when occurring in a specific part of a word, were spelled consistently over *90 percent* of the time by the computer. It is assumed that an adequate speller would have an intuitive grasp of these and other productive rules in order to spell proficiently.

In the research now available regarding spelling, it is clear that in

TABLE 10–1   Productive Phoneme-Grapheme Relationships

Phoneme	Grapheme		Example
Vowels			
/ĭ/	i	in all positions	hit
/ĕ/	e	in medial positions	bet
/ă/	a	in all positions	sat
/ŏ/	o	in all positions	lot
/ə/	u	in all positions	luck
/ī/	i-e	in medial positions when next phoneme is word-final	lime
/ē/	e	in syllable final position	legal
/oi/	oy	in word final position	boy
/ou/	ow	in all positions	sow
/ȯ/	o	in all positions	loss
/u̇/	u	in all positions	full
Consonants			
/b/	b	in all positions	bat
/p/	p	in all positions	put
/t/	t	in initial positions if unaccented syllable and followed by /ə/	tie
/d/	d	in all positions	doe
/g/	g	in all positions	gone
/th/	th	in all positions	the
/v/	v	in all positions	leave, vote
/ks/	x	in all positions	box
/l/	l	in all positions	lump
/le/	le	in all positions	fable
/m/	m	in all positions	map
/n/	n	in all positions	now
/ng/	ng	in word final position	king
/r/	r	in all positions	ran
/hw/	wh	in all positions	where
/h/	h	in all positions	how
/ch/	ch	in all positions	church, nature
/w/	w	in all positions	wax
/zh/	si	in all positions when followed by /ə/	vision

diagnosing spelling errors the teacher must take into account both the regularity and irregularity of the phoneme-grapheme relationships of the English language. The traditional concept that the majority of English words must be learned by rote is undoubtedly true in many cases; however, it is equally true that a large number of words do conform to generalized rules. In any event, if diagnosis of spelling is to be effective it should assess a student's ability (1) to use those phoneme-grapheme rules that are easily applied to a large number of words, (2) to spell those words that are homonyms, in which correct spelling depends upon the meaning of the word, and (3) to spell those words that are so irregular that they must be learned primarily by memorization (e.g., forecastle, colonel, iron).

FACTORS INFLUENCING
SPELLING ABILITY

As we have seen, the ability to spell is very complex and multifaceted. For all practical purposes, it is impossible to isolate the various factors that operate during the act of correctly spelling a word. However, there are prerequisite behaviors that must be manifested by a child prior to the initiation of formal spelling instruction. These prerequisite behaviors include: (1) adequate vision and hearing acuity; (2) fine motor skills that permit successful manipulation of a pencil when copying a word or a sentence; (3) acceptable pronunciation for establishing reliable sound sequences within a word; (4) recognition of and ability to name the letters of the alphabet; (5) knowledge of the meaning of a word before the spelling of it is attempted; and (6) desire to successfully communicate in written form. It should be clearly noted that although all prerequisites need not be present for minimal proficiency in spelling simple words, they all will need to be attained if a child is ever to communicate in written form with ease and confidence.

Considerable evidence is available regarding the fundamental skills necessary for effective spelling. Predominantly, this evidence supports the belief that an understanding of the various phoneme-grapheme relationships is essential in learning to spell. Aaron (1959), when studying spelling in the fourth and eighth grades, concluded that

> The fact that spelling of phonetic syllables was the largest contributor to the estimate of the spelling of non-phonetic words as well as those which were phonetic indicates that phonetic skills may be important in the spelling of all words. . . . Another important predictor of spelling success was that of visual analysis of words. This latter test may be referred to as one of structural analysis [p. 141].

It is apparent that skills in phonetics and structural analysis are crucial to spelling success. Hildreth (1955), following the same logic, states that the ability to reason from analogy and the ability to generalize frequently are observed as characteristics of good spellers.

A more detailed analysis of the elements of spelling ability was conducted by Hunt, Hadsell, Hannum, and Johnson (1963), who discovered that

Previous workers in the field of spelling seem to have identified four factors, besides general intelligence, that affect the ability to spell English words. These factors are: (1) the ability to spell words that are phonetic; (2) the ability to spell words that involve roots, prefixes, suffixes, and the rules for combining; (3) the ability to look at a word and reproduce it later; and (4) the ability to spell the demons.[1]

These researchers accorded phonological and morphological factors primary importance in efficient spelling, and they also recognized that attention needs to be directed toward those words (i.e., *demons*) that must be mastered primarily through memorization.

Implications regarding necessary skills of good spellers are available from the studies conducted by Hanna, et al., which were discussed at some length previously in this chapter. Rudorf (1966) isolates the major variables that must be considered when one evaluates a student's proficiency in spelling. These variables include:

1. discriminate between the phonemes of the language;
2. identify graphemic options of each of the sounds;
3. identify syllables in oral speech and reproduce them in writing;
4. recognize stress when present;
5. relate phonemes to their immediate environment;
6. recognize morphemes such as roots, affixes and inflections;
7. utilize certain principles of morphophonemics (how word parts are joined and how morphemes change in combination to form words);
8. to relate meaning (as determined by syntax) to spelling [p. 54].

The major conclusion drawn from this study is that successful spellers must use a *variety* of skills when they attempt to spell words; the more skills they have mastered, the more efficient they will become in dealing with English orthography. Inversely, if students do not spell well, efforts at diagnosis must explore systematically those specific factors that have been proven necessary for spelling proficiency. Obviously, educators must become knowledgeable of these factors in order to plan effective diagnostic and remedial programs.

SPELLING MODELS AND SEQUENCE OF SKILLS

The successful diagnosis of spelling errors requires a great deal of expertise on the part of the teacher. Although knowledge of English orthography and of those skills necessary for spelling ability are useful, it does not explain

---

[1]From Hunt, B., Hadsell, A., Hannum, J., & Johnson, H. W. The elements of spelling ability. *Elementary School Journal*, 1963, 63, 342–349. Reprinted by permission of The University of Chicago Press.

what children actually *do* when they are engaged in spelling a word. It is essential that teachers have access to and use a theoretical model of spelling behavior in order to understand and to manage effectively problems that frequently occur in school. Hammill and Noone (1975) state that an overall grasp of a model is necessary if ". . . the teacher is to know how and where breakdowns in spelling occur and what might be done to correct or bypass problem areas (p. 90)."

One of the most complete models yet devised has been postulated by Personke and Yee (1966). In essence, this model uses an information-processing system that consists of five logical phases: (1) *initial input processing*—determining the problem to be solved; (2) *information processing* prior to deciding what courses of action to consider and take; (3) *decision making*—analyzing what information is available and acting through chosen channels; (4) *executing selected behavior*—spelling a word; and (5) *feedback of information* through internal or external sources.

The basic assumption of this model is that all spelling behavior is initiated by the need to spell a word, which may derive from a spelling lesson, a wish to write a personal note, or a need to complete a written language arts assignment. Once the student *needs* to spell a word, regardless of whether the word is familiar or not, two input mechanisms are available to perform the task correctly. The first mechanism is *internal input,* which entails learned responses, the ability to generalize phonological rules, word-attack skills, attitudes, and habits of proofreading. If the use of internal skills is not adequate, then *external input* may be employed, which includes asking the advice of others and the use of dictionaries, books, and charts. Although the operation of the internal and external input, as used in this model, is apparent to any teacher, the *processing channels* that are necessary for effectively using all input (i.e., correctly spelling a word) are less obvious.

The processes that are viewed as being of prime importance are as follows:

- *Memory channel*—The student uses only internal input to spell a word and to determine if it is correct.
- *Memory-kinesthetic detour*—The student spells words with no conscious thought of overlearning (i.e., in, the, or, etc.).
- *Checking channel*—The student makes use of outside sources (external input) prior to writing the word.
- *Proofreading channel*—The student, after writing the word, checks spelling through external input.
- *Proofreading rewrite bypass*—The student, if discovering a word is spelled incorrectly, rewrites the word after consulting external sources.

Shores and Yee (1966) contend that the processes are not exclusive and that all must be employed in a complimentary fashion if a student is to be able to spell a wide variety of words. If a spelling program or curriculum

TABLE 10–2   Processes Necessary for Aspects of Spelling

Channel	Strengths	Weaknesses
Memory kinesthetic detour channel	Quickest, most efficient; allows one to write without thinking, an eventual goal in spelling	Useful only for stored words; words are reinforced whether right or wrong, leading to problems of "negative practice"
Memory channel	Responses likely correct due to more careful information processing	Requires unconscious thought, provides "conceptual break" in writing process
Checking channel	Speller always has correct response due to checking before writing; only correct response is fed back to memory drum	Conceptual break greatest due to time loss in finding information
Proofreading channel and Proofreading rewrite detour	Less conceptual break; more chance of active problem solving by using own sources first	Disadvantage of possibly reinforcing an incorrect written response that eventual correct response may not eliminate; can alleviate this problem by not assuming first response correct

Source: Westerman, G. S. *Spelling and writing.* Sioux Falls, S.D.: Adapt Press, Inc. 1971. Used with permission of the publisher.

emphasizes only a few of these processes, the student would not be able to manage all of the spelling situations encountered. The major strengths and weaknesses of the various processes, as summarized by Westerman (1971) are given in Table 10–2.

Additional, less complex models of spelling behavior are available to educators (Peters, 1970; Poplin, 1976; Westerman, 1971). These models tend to be behavioral because they stress such factors as correct verbalization, motor skill handwriting speed, letter sequence, and attention to word form. One assumption running through all of the models is that there are numerous abilities and skills that must be integrated before efficient spelling ability can be obtained. Regardless of which theoretical model a teacher adopts, the teacher should make every effort to explore the diverse skills necessary for proficient spelling.

Although the specific skills and the sequence in which they are presented vary from one model to another, there are certain broad guidelines that a teacher can follow when constructing diagnostic devices or planning

TABLE 10–3 Sequence of Skills Used in One Basal Spelling Series

I. Auditory recognition of phonemes
  A. Consonant sounds
    1. The eighteen primary consonant sounds: *b, d, f, g, h, j, k, l, m, n, p, r, s, t, v, w, y, z*
    2. The *sh, ch, wh, th,* and *ng* sounds
II. Graphemic representation of phonemes
  A. Consonant sounds
    1. The regular consonant sounds
    2. *sh, ch, ng, wh,* and *th* sounds
    3. *nk* spellings of the *ngk* sounds
    4. *c, k, ch,* and *ck* spellings of the *k* sound
    5. *s* spelling of the *s* and *z* sounds
    6. *gh* and *ph* spellings of the *f* sounds
    7. *wh* spelling of the *hw* sound
    8. *x* spelling of the *ks* sounds
    9. *g* spelling of the *g* and *j* sounds
    10. Consonant sounds spelled with double letters
    11. Silent consonants
  B. Vowel sounds
    1. Short vowel sound regularly spelled in initial or medial position
    2. Long vowel spelled by
      a. Single vowel at the end of a short word in open syllables
      b. Two vowels together
      c. Vowel-consonant-silent *e*
      d. *ow* spelling of long *o* sound
      e. *ay* spelling of long *a* sound
      f. Final *y* spelling of long *e* sound
      g. Final *y* spelling of long *i* sound
    3. Additional vowel sounds and spellings
      a. *oo* spelling of *ie* and *ii* sounds
      b. *ow* and *ou* spellings of the *ou* sound
      c. *oy* spelling of the *oi* sound
      d. Vowel sounds before *r*
    4. Unexpected spellings
      a. Single vowel spellings (e.g., kind, cost)
      b. Vowel-consonant-silent *e* (e.g., give, done)
      c. Two vowels together (e.g., been, said)
      d. Miscellaneous (e.g., they, eye, could, aunt, etc.)
    5. The *le* spelling of the *əl* sound
III. Using morphemes to make structural changes
  A. *s* or *es* plural
  B. Changing *y* to *i* before *es*
  C. *ing* ending
    1. With double consonants
    2. With dropped silent *e*
  D. Adding *er* and *est* endings
  E. *er* noun agent ending
  F. Adding *d* or *ed* ending
  G. Using final *s* to show possession
  H. *s* or *es* for third person singular
  I. Irregular plural noun changes

TABLE 10–3   *Continued*

J. Using the number suffixes
K. Using suffixes to change the parts of speech
L. Using prefixes to change meanings
IV. Devices to aid spelling recall
   A. Syllabication
   B. Recognizing compounds
   C. Recognizing rhyming words, homonyms, and antonyms
   D. Alphabetizing
V. Miscellaneous
   A. Vowel-consonant/consonant-vowel syllabication
   B. Vowel/consonant-vowel syllabication
   C. Remembering irregular spellings
   D. Spelling compounds by parts
   E. Spelling contractions and possessives
   F. Spelling abbreviations
   G. Capitalization of proper nouns
   H. Spelling by analogy

Source: Excerpted from *Basic goals in spelling,* Fourth Edition, by W. Kottmeyer and A. Claus, copyright 1972, with permission of Webster/McGraw-Hill.

remedial programs. The first assumption is that virtually all curriculum plans for teaching spelling now include a heavy emphasis upon the mastery of certain linguistic skills (phoneme-grapheme relationships, morphological variations, etc.). A typical sequence of skills designed by Dr. William Kottmeyer to promote proficiency in spelling is given in Table 10–3.

The various linguistic skills play a major role in learning to spell, but other factors must also be considered to assure that what is learned will be useful as well as generalizable. For example, it is important that a student be proficient in the spelling of days of the week, holidays, months of the year, proper nouns, and commonly used homonyms. The ability to proofread effectively (sometimes referred to as *proofspelling*) and to use a dictionary also are viewed as spelling skills and must be considered when assessing general spelling proficiency. Discussion of how these or other lists of skills can be used in a comprehensive diagnostic effort is provided in the following sections.

ASSESSMENT OF SPELLING DIFFICULTIES

When a student is first observed to be exhibiting spelling difficulties, the teacher will use a variety of assessment techniques to determine the severity of the problem and to pinpoint specific patterns of error. As a first step in the assessment of spelling difficulties, the teacher must become thoroughly familiar with the diversity of instruments available. The actual instruments chosen will depend upon whether the teacher is determining only a general or an in-depth estimate of spelling ability. In either case, it is essential that the teacher clearly define the objectives of the assessment in order to select an appropriate instrument. Hammill and Noone (1975) state that selection should be based upon the following three considerations:

1. Know what the test measures and what its limitations are before giving it to a child. For example, what type of children were used for the standardization and what is the reported reliability and validity of the test.
2. Be prepared to supplement the test where possible with other measures.
3. Use informal evaluation techniques whenever specific information about the child's spelling abilities are required as a guide to planning a remedial program [p. 96].

In general, spelling tests may be grouped into three broad categories: (1) standardized achievement tests that provide grade equivalent, percentile, or other normative data but do not attempt to yield diagnostic information; (2) nonstandardized achievement and diagnostic tests that are made up of a wide variety of divergent spelling lists; and (3) informal teacher-made instruments that are diagnostic in nature and relate to the specific needs of the individual teacher, student, and learning environment. Each of these categories will be discussed in this section.

Standardized Achievement Tests

The majority of standardized achievement tests available are designed to provide only a general estimate of spelling ability. No attempt is made in these instruments to provide the teacher with detailed information regarding the specific patterns of errors exhibited by individual students; rather, achievement tests usually yield a single score that is then compared to a set of standardized norms. As a result of this process, teachers are able to determine if a student is spelling above or below the average of local or national standardization sample used in establishing norms. The relative performance of a student is interpreted in the form of grade equivalents, percentiles, spelling ages, and stanines.

The manner in which spelling is measured will vary among instruments. Two main techniques often are used: *dictated-word* and *proofreading*. In the dictated-word test, the student is instructed to write words that are presented orally by the examiner, then used in a sentence, and orally presented again. The major characteristic of this technique is that the student must write the dictated word without the benefit of reference material or scratch paper.

The proofreading approach entails presenting the student with a series of words that may or may not be misspelled. The student is required to determine which of the words are spelled incorrectly or indicate that all are spelled correctly. In some instances the stimulus words are various spellings of the same word (as in the Peabody Individual Achievement Tests) or are composed of differently spelled words (as in the Comprehension Test of Basic Skills).

A list of the most commonly used standardized achievement tests with spelling sections is listed in Table 10–4. The type of spelling assessment procedure (dictated-word or proofreading) used and the appropriate grade levels are also provided.

When a teacher selects a standardized spelling test, he or she must pay careful attention to the reported reliability and validity sections of the in-

TABLE 10–4   Achievement Tests with Spelling Sections

Test	Procedure for Assessing Spelling	Grade Levels
Test of Written Spelling (Larsen & Hammill, 1976)	Dictated-word	1–8
Comprehensive Tests of Basic Skills (CTB/McGraw-Hill, 1968)	Proofreading	2–12
California Achievement Tests (Tiegs & Clark, 1970)	Proofreading	1–12
Stanford Achievement Tests (Madden & Gardner, 1972)	Proofreading	1–9
Peabody Individual Achievement Test (Dunn & Markwardt, 1970)	Proofreading	K–12
Iowa Test of Basic Skills (Hieronymus & Lindquist, 1971)	Proofreading	1–9
Metropolitan Achievement Tests (Durost, et al., 1970)	Dictated-word Proofreading	2–4 4–9
SRA Achievement Series (Thorpe, Lefever, & Nasland, 1974)	Proofreading	1–12
The Gray-Votaw-Rogers General Achievement Tests (Gray, Votaw, & Rogers, 1963)	Dictated-word Proofreading	1–3 4–9
Wide Range Achievement Test (Jastak & Jastak, 1965)	Dictated-word	3–12
The Iowa Test of Educational Development (Lindquist & Feldt, 1959)	Proofreading	9–12
McGraw-Hill Basic Study Skills: Spelling (Raygoz, 1970)	Proofreading	9–12

strument. Shores and Yee (1973) have stated that, of the frequently used achievement tests, relatively few report adequate statistics demonstrating that the measures will provide highly consistent and valid results. In addition, the teacher should consider the manner in which spelling is assessed in light of the particular information desired. Otto, McMenemy, and Smith (1973) feel that the dictated-word test is more difficult and, perhaps, more valid than the proofreading test.

Test of Written Spelling One instrument that we feel has particular strength is the *Test of Written Spelling* (TWS), (Larsen & Hammill, 1976). Contrary to other achievement tests, this dictated-word test is based upon educational theories that research has confirmed to be valid, specifically, those findings of Hanna, et al., cited previously in this chapter. Each word included in this instrument was selected because it is used in 10 commonly employed basal spelling series and it tests the ability of students to spell words that are linguistically consistent *as well as* those that are not (i.e., demons). Categorizing words as predictable and unpredictable represents a major departure from current tests that have no discernible construct validity. The selection of words from commonly used basal programs ensures that the items used in the TWS are actually taught in the schools.

The TWS was standardized on 4,500 children who resided in 22 states. The three types of normative data available, based upon the performance of these children, are spelling ages, grade equivalents, and spelling quotient. The spelling ages and grade equivalents permit the interpretation of students' scores with regard to how well they have performed in comparison to children of the same age and grade. The spelling quotient provides the teacher with an additional estimate of how well students are achieving. The reliability and validity of the TWS are amply demonstrated. This feature of the instrument is quite impressive when compared to the reported reliability and validity of other achievement tests (see Shores and Yee, 1973, for a thorough discussion of this topic).

Although the TWS is designed to provide only a general estimate of spelling ability, a discussion of the way in which results can be interpreted also is provided in the accompanying manual. Samples of spelling profiles of individual learners are discussed in detail. Sources of additional information regarding informal diagnostic techniques are given, which teachers should find useful in attempting to locate or initiate more in-depth diagnostic strategies.

Nonstandardized Achievement and Diagnostic Tests

The second category of assessment techniques is described as nonstandardized achievement or diagnostic tests. The basic criteria for inclusion in this category are that these tests (1) have been published; (2) provide inadequate or no statistical data to permit the comparison of a student's score with the performance of children of the same age or grade level; (3) have selected the spelling items from a wide range of word lists and basal spelling programs (frequently unspecified); and (4) supply the teacher with some indication of general spelling level or diagnostic information. For the most part, the tests included in this section are general in nature and, consequently, should be considered carefully prior to being used in the classroom.

Three instruments that provide both achievement and diagnostic information have been developed by Kottmeyer (1959), Betts (1956), and Mann and Suiter (1974). The common component of these tests is that they are made up of lists of words that have been grouped by grade levels. The words incorporated in each list were selected from various basal spelling programs and are, presumably, representative of spelling vocabularies taught in schools. Determining a grade-level score is accomplished *not* by comparing a student's performance with a normative group, as with standardized achievement tests, but rather, by administering the graded-word lists until a student has reached the level at which further testing is unnecessary (i.e., no more words are likely to be spelled correctly). The level at which the student spells approximately 90-100 percent of the words correctly is considered to be an accurate reflection of the *achievement level* for that student. In addition to the achievement score obtained from these tests, minimal suggestions for analyzing errors can be obtained.

The shortcomings of these spelling measures are readily apparent and should be outlined for teachers who are contemplating using them in their classrooms. The first of these shortcomings centers on the lack of standardization data, a result of which is that one is forced to assume that the graded-word lists do, in fact, adequately sample the words taught at those grade levels. It should be kept in mind that the devices by Kottmeyer (1959) and Betts (1956) were constructed in the 1950's, and it is questionable that their word lists are still applicable today. The Mann and Suiter instrument does not specify the various series that were used in selecting their word samples. Consequently, it is impossible to make an efficient judgment as to whether their word lists would be applicable for use in classrooms.

The diagnostic suggestions supplied in these assessment devices tend to be vague and too general in scope. It is questionable that if the diagnostic suggestions for analyzing errors are followed, sufficient data will be obtained to adequately plan remedial programming. If teachers desire to gain a general estimate of a student's achievement, a standardized test should be employed, because it will at least give teachers information about specific procedures that were followed in generating the derived scores (e.g., selection of sample subjects, types of scores provided, etc.). If a teacher does not wish to use a standardized test, but still desires an achievement score, we recommend the use of an informal spelling inventory. (It will be discussed in the following section of this chapter.)

Gates-Russell Spelling Diagnosis Test   Another test that frequently has been mentioned as providing a variety of diagnostic information is the *Gates-Russell Spelling Diagnostic Test* (Gates & Russell, 1940). This instrument measures nine areas that Gates and Russell claim are related to spelling ability: spelling words orally; word pronunciation; giving letters for letter sounds; spelling one syllable; spelling two syllables; reversals; word attack; auditory discrimination; and the effectiveness of visual, auditory, kinesthetic, or combined methods of study. Whereas a few of the subtests probably yield diagnostic information, Spache (1953) states that available research on this test does not ". . . justify the use of some of the individual tests of the battery. The tests were chosen by a priori reasoning and retained in the published form without any critical examination of their validity or reliability [p. 200]." Apparently, the Gates-Russell test can be used as an initial step in observing spelling difficulties, but should not be considered as a complete diagnostic battery in and of itself.

Lincoln Diagnostic Spelling Test   The *Lincoln Diagnostic Spelling Test* (Lincoln, 1955) was designed to measure three facets of spelling: Pronunciation, enunciation, and use of rules. Norms are provided in the form of percentile ranks, but the number of subjects used to standardize the measure is exceedingly low across all grade levels. The diagnostic data provided are equally suspect, and it is doubtful that they would be of any substantial help to a teacher. Specific rules included in the test are vague and superficial in nature. Plessas (1965), in reviewing this test, concludes that ". . . the *Lincoln Diagnostic Spelling Test* is best used as a general measure of spelling performance with some analytical features to assess deficiencies in the use of certain spelling rules among students [p. 326]."

Spellmaster   A published comprehensive, diagnostic spelling test that does promise to be useful for teaching is *Spellmaster* (Cohen & Abrams, 1974). This test has been field tested with over 2,500 students ranging in age from kindergarten through adulthood. Three categories of words are included in *Spellmaster:* regular words, irregular words, and homonyms. The regular words are those that contain dependable phoneme-grapheme correspondences. Irregular words (commonly referred to as *demons*) are those that must be memorized whole or in part, since their spelling violates basic phonological and morphological rules. Homonyms are separated because their spelling, which may be either regular or irregular, must be learned in conjunction with their meaning.

The authors of this program also have provided a very helpful scope-and-sequence chart that contains all the regular phonic and structural

TABLE 10–5   Scope-and-Sequence Chart for Diagnostic Tests

	AUDITORY		AUDITORY PLUS VISUAL			CONCEPTUAL		
Test Level	1	2	3	4	5	6	7	8
Avg. Grade Level	K-3	1-4	2-5	3-6	4-7	5-8	6-9	7-10
Consonants	b d f g h l m n p r t v y	s z w	c j k x qu			c: city g: germ		
Beginning Blends	dr- gr- tr- pl- fl-	sw- sp- sl- st- str- spr- spl-						
Ending Blends	-mp -nd -ft -lt -nt		-st -nt -lf -nd -mp	-nk				
Digraphs		ch sh th ng	wh					ph: phrase ch: ache
Vowels	short a e i o u	short a e i o u	ai, ay, a-e ee, ea, e-e igh, y, i-e, ind oa, ow, o-e, old	u-e: cube	u-e: rule -y: envy	ie: field ei: receive schwa (ə):*	y: system	i: stadium i: companion
Vowel Digraphs				oo: pool	oo: hood ea: ready			
Diphthongs				oi: join ou: cloud ow: down aw: claw	oy: joy ew: chew	au: sauce		
"r" & "l" control				ar, er, ir, ur er, ear are, ire, ore all				
Prefixes				un- re-	pre- en- mis- ex- a- in-	con- per- com-		Derivational Doubling; immature
Suffixes		-s: chops	-s: wheels -ing -ed -es	-er -est -ly -ful -y	-tion -ive	-ent -en -ant	-ment -ous -ness -sion	-ance -ence -ible -able -fully -ally -ssion
Endings					-et: target -ic: public -al: signal -le: poodle	-ey: kidney	-us: cactus	
Syllables:** open and closed							open: ti-ny closed: gos-sip	
Generalizations						ck-k ch-tch ge-dge		
Advanced Phonics								ti: cautious ci: social tu: future
Contractions							mustn't they've	
Rules							1 Dropping e: hope-hoping 2a. Doubling final consonants (monosyllabic): hop-hopping 3. Changing y to i: funny-funnier	2b. Doubling final consts (polysyllabic): open-opening begin-beginner
Sample Words	lap rug flop yet mint	sang chops brush spent bathtub	mean loaded junk painting waxes	refuse smartest fired join loudly	loyal ahead expensive strangle prescribe	loosen freckle computer belief launched	skinny scaring cloudiness sympathy enormous	fortunately immortal forbidden phrase architect
Total Test Words	20	20	40	40	40	40	40	40

* The "schwa" is a neutral vowel sound in an unaccented syllable.
** Open syllable ends in a vowel making the vowel long: mo/ment, pu/pil. Closed syllable ends in a consonant making the vowel short: sad/dle, pup/py.

Source: Cohen, C. R., & Abrams, R. M. *Spellmaster, spelling: testing and evaluating book one.* Exeter, N.H.: Learnco Inc., 1976.

elements tested. (See Table 10–5.) In using this chart, a teacher selects the initial level for diagnostic testing. Even if a teacher chooses not to use the *Spellmaster* program in its entirety, this chart will help provide a framework by which informal tests can be made to meet the specific needs of individual classrooms and children.

Other parts of the *Spellmaster* program include student-response sheets, class-data charts for profiling the performance of an entire class, and individual progress records for specific pupils. An additional part is a *correlation chart*, which outlines the phonic and structural elements tested and demonstrates where they are taught in seven commonly used basal spelling programs. This feature of the *Spellmaster* allows it to be used effectively for programming appropriately graded remedial instruction in most classroom situations.

In summary, the majority of available nonstandardized achievement or diagnostic tests provide the teacher with minimal information appropriate for planning teaching programs. The primary weaknesses of these techniques are (1) that the grade-equivalent scores are based upon inadequate or nonexistent statistical data and, consequently, must be viewed with suspicion and (2) that the diagnostic information is frequently vague and unsubstantiated by any empirical data. The *Spellmaster* program overcomes these handicaps because it does not specify grade-level spelling ability and provides in-depth error analysis of a student's specific spelling difficulties. If teachers do not have access to the *Spellmaster* but wish to assess students' spelling needs, it is likely that they will develop their own diagnostic techniques. Methods for accomplishing this task will be discussed in the following section.

Informal Spelling Assessment

The third category of spelling assessment involves the use of teacher-made tests. Undoubtedly, these tests will provide more usable information regarding a student's level and specific needs than either the commercially available achievement or diagnostic tests. At its most efficient level, the informal assessment should clearly outline the relevant skills a student has or has not mastered, pinpoint patterns of errors, provide direction for systematic remedial instruction, and permit a nonsubjective measure to gain as the pupil moves from task to task.

The procedure by which a teacher conducts an informal assessment will vary depending upon the diagnostic information desired. Typical informal strategies, however, usually incorporate (1) a period of structured observation that includes the use of checklists and specific skill sequences, (2) informal spelling inventories that determine grade-level placement in particular basal series and specific skill deficiencies, and (3) specialized diagnostic techniques if they are deemed necessary.

Observation One of the most readily available strategies for assessing spelling errors is structured observation when students are engaged in behaviors related to spelling. The behaviors to be observed, of course, will need to be specified in order for this technique to be optimally successful. Brueckner and Bond (1966) have produced a good set of guidelines for systematically observing a student:

1. Analysis of written work, including test papers
   a. Legibility of handwriting
   b. Defects in letter forms, spacing, alignment, size
   c. Classification of errors in written work, letters or tests
   d. Range of vocabulary used
   e. Evidence of lack of knowledge of conventions or rules
2. Analysis of Oral Responses
   a. Comparison of errors in oral and written spelling
   b. Pronunciation of words spelled incorrectly
   c. Articulation and enunciation
   d. Slovenliness of speech
   e. Dialect and colloquial forms of speech
   f. Way of spelling words orally:
      1) Spells words as units
      2) Spells letter by letter
      3) Spells by diagraphs
      4) Spells by syllables
   g. Rhythmic patterns in oral spelling
   h. Blending ability
   i. Giving letters for sounds or sounds for letters
   j. Technique of word analysis used
   k. Quality and error made in oral reading
   l. Oral responses on tests or word analysis
   m. Analysis of pupil's comments as he states orally his thought process while studying new words
3. Interview with Pupil and Others
   a. Questioning pupil about methods of study
   b. Questioning pupil about spelling rules
   c. Questioning pupil about errors in convention
   d. Securing evidence as to attitude towards spelling
4. Questionnaire
   a. Applying checklist of methods of study
   b. Having pupil rank spelling according to interest
   c. Surveying use of written language
5. Free Observation in Course of Daily Work
   a. Securing evidence as to attitudes towards spelling
   b. Evidence of improvement in the study of new words
   c. Observing extent of use of dictionary
   d. Extent of error in regular written work
   e. Study habits and methods of work
   f. Social acceptability of the learner
   g. Evidences of emotional and social maladjustment
   h. Evidences of possible physical handicaps
6. Controlled Observation of Work on Set Tasks

a. Looking up the meanings of given words in dictionary
b. Giving pronunciation of words in dictionary
c. Writing plural forms of derivations of given words
d. Observing responses on informal tests
e. Observing methods of studying selected words.[2]

Systematic observation can supply very valuable information to the teacher about a student's particular spelling problems. The application of the guidelines just listed, either in their entirety or in modified form, should result in a list of discrete student behaviors that interfere with proficient spelling. At this point, a checklist may be of assistance in further isolating specific patterns of errors.

One example of a spelling checklist has been provided by Partoll (1976). The purpose of it is to identify skills that are indicative of students in need of remedial assistance, as well as the skills in which students are deficient. The Partoll checklist is provided in Figure 10–1.

Although numerous spelling checklists have been published for classroom use, the teacher often will find the need to construct a checklist to meet his or her own particular needs. To perform this task, we recommend the use of the series of skills that are employed in the basal series used in that particular school. Earlier in this chapter we listed the series of skills used in *Basic Goals in Spelling*. By taking these or similar sequences of skills reported in other basal programs, teachers can construct their own criterion-referenced checklists that would extend from a first- through sixth-grade level. It would then be possible (1) to determine the skills not yet mastered by a student, (2) to determine the most appropriate level at which remedial instruction should begin; (3) to profile an entire class in order to group pupils effectively, and (4) to evaluate the progress of individual students continually in relation to their acquisition of the skills necessary for effective spelling. Regardless of how a particular spelling series (i.e., sequence of skills) is used by a teacher, it is essential that the teacher possess a thorough understanding of the rationale emphasized in the program. If this understanding is not attained, effective informal assessment will be very difficult, if not impossible.

Informal Spelling Inventory   The purpose of the Informal Spelling Inventory (ISI) is to determine a student's general achievement level and to isolate specific patterns of errors that are exhibited when the student spells particular words. The differences between the informal inventory and standardized and nonstandardized achievement tests are that the inventory is teacher-made and does not attempt to compare a student's score with a normative group; rather, emphasis is focused upon placing the stu-

[2]Leo J. Brueckner and Guy L. Bond, *The diagnosis and treatment of learning difficulties* © 1955, 369–370. Reprinted by permission of Prentice-Hall, Inc., Englewood Cliffs, New Jersey.

FIGURE 10–1   Checklist for Specifying Spelling Errors

_____	1. Consonant sounds used incorrectly (specify letters missed)
_____	2. Vowel sounds not known
_____	3. Sounds omitted at beginning of words
_____	4. Sounds added at the beginning of words (e.g., a blend given when a single consonant required)
_____	5. Omission of middle sounds
_____	6. Omission of middle syllables
_____	7. Extraneous letters added
_____	8. Extraneous syllables added
_____	9. Missequencing of sounds or syllables (transposals like "from" to "form"
_____	10. Reversals of whole words
_____	11. Endings omitted
_____	12. Incorrect endings substituted ("ing", for "en" or for "ed")
_____	13. Auditory confusion of *m/n, th/f, s/z,* or *b/d* or other similar sounds
_____	14. Phonetic spelling with poor visual recall of word appearance
_____	15. Spelling laborious, letter by letter
_____	16. Poor knowledge of "demons" (*e.g.,* one, iron, forecastle)
_____	17. Spells, erases, tries again, etc., to no avail
_____	18. Reversals of letter shapes *b/d, p/q, u/n,* or *m/w*
_____	19. Spelling so bizarre that it bears no resemblance to original; even pupil cannot read his own written words
_____	20. Mixing of upper and lower case letters
_____	21. Inability to recall how to form either case for some letters
_____	22. Spatial placement on line erratic
_____	23. Spacing between letters and words erratic
_____	24. Poor writing and letter formations, immature eye-hand coordination
_____	25. Temporal disorientation: slowness in learning time, general scheduling, grasping the sequence of events in the day and those
_____	26. Difficulty in concept formation; not able to generalize and transfer readily to abstract "the rules and the tools"

Source: Partoll, S. F. Spelling demonology revisited. *Academic Therapy,* 1976, XI, 339–348. Used with permission of the author and the publisher.

dent at the appropriate level in a basal program (i.e., specific skill sequence). If the words included on the ISI are chosen with care, an error analysis can be conducted that will specify the particular deficiencies of an individual student.

Mann and Suiter (1974) provide a set of simple and straightforward directions for constructing an ISI, which include selecting a sample of words from each basal spelling book of a given spelling series. The teacher should choose 15 words from the grade 1 book and approximately 20 words from the grades 2 through 8 books. Mann and Suiter suggest that to select the words, the teacher should determine the number of words taught at a particular level and divide this figure by 20. For example, if there are 500 words in a book, we would divide by 20, which would yield 25. Therefore, the list would consist of every twenty-fifth word in the book.

An example of an ISI derived from the spelling vocabulary taught in a basal series is given in Table 10–6. The words were selected from *Spell Correctly* (Benthul, Anderson, Uteck, Biggy, & Bailey, 1974).

When administering the informal spelling inventory, the teacher should begin at the first level for all children from grades 4 and below. Any students who are in grades 5 and above should begin with the third-level words. The teacher should use the dictated-word format when administering the test: (1) say the word in isolation, (2) use the word in a sentence, and (3) repeat the word again. The testing should be continued until the student misses six words in a row.

In order to determine achievement and teaching levels, a suggested set of criteria are helpful. The achievement level can be located by finding the highest level at which a score of 90–100 percent is obtained. The teaching level is that highest level at which a score of 75–89 percent is obtained. For example, if Donny spelled 93 percent of the Level IV words correctly and 81 percent of the Level V words correctly, his achievement level would be the fourth level and instruction should be initiated at level five.

At the conclusion of the informal spelling inventory, a careful analysis of the various errors yields profitable information. The manner in which the error analysis is conducted will vary depending upon the teacher's needs. A sample of some patterns of error has been suggested by Edgington (1968).[3] They may aid the teacher in structuring the error analysis, and include:

1. Addition of unneeded letters (e.g. *dresses*)
2. Omissions of needed letters (e.g. *hom* for *home*)
3. Reflections of a child's mispronunciation (e.g. *pin* for *pen*)
4. Reflections of a child's dialectical speech pattern (e.g. *Cuber* for *Cuba*)
5. Reversals of whole words (e.g. *eno* for *one*)
6. Reversal of vowels (e.g. *braed* for *bread*)
7. Reversal of consonant order (e.g. *lback* for *black*)
8. Reversals of consonant or vowel directionality (e.g. *brithday* for *birthday*)
9. Reversals of syllables (e.g. *telho* for *hotel*)
10. Phonetic spellings of nonphonetic words or parts thereof (e.g. *cawt* for *caught*)
11. Wrong associations of a sound with a given set of letters, such as *u* has been learned as *ou* in you
12. "Neographisms" such as letters put in which bear no discernible relationship to the word dictated
13. Varying degrees and combinations of these or other patterns

[3]Edgington, R. But he spelled them right this morning. *Academic Therapy*, 1968, *3*, 58–59. Used with permission of the author and the publisher.

TABLE 10–6   ISI Developed upon the Basal Program *Spell Correctly*

Level II	Level III	Level IV
1. am	1. able	1. across
2. bake	2. belong	2. anyhow
3. boy	3. came	3. bench
4. chin	4. duck	4. brush
5. down	5. fork	5. church
6. fast	6. hay	6. curve
7. go	7. jar	7. drink
8. he	8. kitten	8. everyone
9. hot	9. mile	9. flow
10. jet	10. nice	10. gold
11. lot	11. pony	11. held
12. man	12. seed	12. kitchen
13. on	13. sky	13. mix
14. ran	14. study	14. number
15. sand	15. tar	15. pail
16. stop	16. tie	16. ranch
17. trip	17. trap	17. sharp
18. us	18. van	18. tooth
19. when	19. wagon	19. windy
20. yes	20. wrote	20. young

Level V	Level VI	Level VII	Level VIII
1. accident	1. abroad	1. abnormal	1. abdicate
2. autumn	2. adventure	2. amusement	2. applause
3. belt	3. attractive	3. burden	3. butcher
4. build	4. chapter	4. captain	4. chaotic
5. cellar	5. cycle	5. clumsy	5. curiosity
6. crumb	6. desire	6. democracy	6. delicate
7. duty	7. employ	7. enemies	7. evict
8. feather	8. favorite	8. fifteen	8. galaxies
9. ghost	9. gain	9. generalize	9. hydrogen
10. height	10. however	10. hundred	10. legalize
11. lake	11. jury	11. intelligent	11. motivate
12. meal	12. lunar	12. knowledge	12. pecans
13. own	13. nervous	13. metric	13. prologue
14. pledge	14. owner	14. nourish	14. revision
15. rent	15. perfect	15. pioneer	15. squire
16. search	16. prove	16. quirk	16. tactics
17. streaming	17. shake	17. reject	17. umbrella
18. thirstiest	18. tank	18. scarce	18. vivid
19. wasn't	19. usually	19. telephone	19. vision
20. yearn	20. yourself	20. wrecked	20. woven

Teachers who are interested in determining a student's spelling errors may also wish to review the abilities that are related to success in spelling, because knowledge of these abilities (discussed earlier in this chapter) will assist the teacher during observations as well as with error analysis.

Specialized Diagnostic Techniques At the conclusion of the achievement and diagnostic portion of the spelling assessment, the teacher may still find the need to use additional techniques to further analyze a particularly difficult spelling problem. Two highly usable strategies include the *cloze procedure* and what frequently has been referred to as diagnostic teaching.

The *cloze procedure*, which has been discussed in Chapter 7, is a very versatile diagnostic tool. In this technique a student is required to fill in a missing word from a sentence or the missing letter(s) in a word. Examples of this procedure would be:

The boy bounced the (ball).
h_sp_tal (hospital).

According to Cartwright (1969), the cloze procedure would be used in assessing specific spelling difficulties as well as in evaluating a student's knowledge of spelling rules (phoneme-grapheme correspondences). To illustrate this, a teacher may wish to measure a student's understanding of the silent *e* rule (making the media vowel *long*). Performance on the following items would give the teacher some idea as to whether the student has mastered this skill.

1. The m_l_ (male) lion has a m_n_ (mane).
2. The store has a s_l_ (sale) on bicycles.
3. The boy played a musical instrument called a fl_t_ (flute).
4. What is the correct t_m_ (time)?
5. How do you _s_ (use) this tool?

If a student exhibits difficulty in completing these items, a multiple-choice format can be used. For example:

1. The b____ ran across the street.
   a. oi
   b. oy
   c. ou
   d. y

2. Come to my h____se.
   a. ow
   b. o
   c. ou
   d. au

3. Use the ____ to open the door.
   a. kee
   b. key
   c. kie
   d. kea

4. Be at home at ____.
   a. nun
   b. non
   c. none
   d. noon

The cloze procedure, although it is a useful technique in assessing spelling, also has several limitations that should be kept firmly in mind. Students will not fill in blanks if they do not know the word. It would be safe to assume that if the word is not part of a student's oral language, it should not be used as a stimulus item. In addition, the reading level employed in the items should be kept to a minimum to avoid penalizing the child who has problems with word-attack or comprehension skills. If these restrictions are kept in mind, the cloze procedure can be a viable assessment strategy.

Another useful technique is diagnostic teaching. Generally, this approach involves the careful observation of a student's efforts to perform academic tasks; particular strengths and weaknesses are noted; alternative ways of completing the task are shown; and demonstrated progress is evaluated. Anderson and Groff (1968) outline several specific tasks that will aid the teacher in gaining a clear perspective of a student's ability to deal with different spelling activities, which may be viewed as variations of the more traditional forms of spelling tests. Anderson and Groff's suggestions include asking the student to:

1. circle or underline vowels in certain words
2. mark long or short vowels in certain words
3. select the words of more than one syllable
4. mark word accent and divide into syllables
5. write abbreviations of words
6. alphabetize words
7. change all single words to plurals
8. show contraction or possession
9. demonstrate ability to generalize from practiced to new words.

After the teacher has gained some insight from these structured tasks, a period of direct teaching is initiated to determine the most efficient manner by which the student masters necessary skills. Otto, McMenemy, and Smith (1973, pp. 266–267) give a detailed outline of a diagnostic teaching procedure for spelling. The teacher must

1. develop a step-by-step teaching plan that will lead logically to mastery of a desired spelling objective
2. discuss the plan with the student to ensure understanding and co-operation
3. select the most appropriate materials to conduct the individual lessons
4. evaluate the student's demonstrated skill acquisition (if any)
5. modify the program as needed.

Obviously, this diagnostic teaching plan will yield useful information regarding a student's particular spelling disorder. As with all assessment activities, the ultimate objective is to provide appropriate data that are directly applicable to teaching. There is little doubt that specialized assessment strategies are of significant assistance to the teacher who chooses to use them.

USING SPELLING ASSESSMENT
TECHNIQUES

Because educational assessment must relate directly to remedial programming, all attempts to assess spelling difficulties must be based upon *specific goals* that have been established for individual students. Without these goals it is highly probable that the assessment process will not meet the need for which originally it was designed (Horn, 1954).

If the goal of the teacher is to determine the achievement level of a particular student or group of students, a number of commonly available standardized achievement tests would be adequate. However, in making a final selection, the reliability, validity, and normative aspects of these tests should be perused carefully in order to locate the tests that will best meet the needs of the school environment. The teacher using standardized tests should realize that administering these tests will not yield diagnostic information that outlines specific skill deficiencies.

In most instances, the teacher will need to conduct a more in-depth evaluation of a student's spelling problems. Regardless of whether it is necessary to determine a student's ability to use the dictionary, knowledge of rules, association of letters with sounds, or proofreading of written material, the teacher should construct his or her own assessment technique. An obvious first step in constructing such a test would be to observe and analyze a student's written work. These relatively simple and straightforward strategies can (and usually do) provide invaluable data regarding probable skill deficiencies, as well as the areas for teaching. The use of the Informal Spelling Inventory and error analysis will further expand the teacher's insight into those factors that are either impeding or facilitating a student's achievement in spelling. Obviously, the teacher needs to be creative in all phases of the spelling assessment. Making maximum use of the student's total efforts in written communication activities is essential to ensure that whatever information is gleaned during the assessment will be a reliable estimate of typical spelling behavior.

Suggested Activities

10–1. The teaching staff of Washington Elementary School recently has become concerned with the poor performance of their students on the spelling subtest of achievement tests administered during the past 2 years. They have decided to inspect their spelling text to detect differences from other textbooks.

Select any two spelling series (grades 1–3 or grades 4–7), and briefly outline the sequence in which spelling skills are presented (such as the one presented in Table 10–3). Conclude with a summary of the similarities and differences in which the skills are presented by grade level.

10–2. Using Table 10–3 construct an informal spelling test that would indicate the spelling ability of a given student. The test should be one that could be used as a placement for the child in the appropriate level of *Basic Goals in Spelling* (Kottmeyer & Claus, 1974).

10–3. Three fifth-grade teachers of Poe Middle School are initiating a new creative writing program. They have decided to group the students by ability into three classes. One of the criteria to be used is spelling ability. They have decided to use a standardized achievement test in spelling to begin their assessment.

Use Table 10–4 to locate and examine several standardized instruments. On the basis of your examination, write a recommendation to the staff for the selection of a specific test.

10–4. Using the scope-and-sequence chart presented in Table 10–5, construct an informal testing device that is appropriate for six consecutive grade levels. Administer the instrument to four children, and determine the specific skills that the children have not mastered.

10–5. Obtain samples (two from each student) of original compositions composed by a class of third-graders. Apply Figure 10–1 to analyze spelling errors within the compositions.

10–6. Select two consecutive levels of any basal spelling series. Using the sequence of skills presented in the two levels construct a checklist similar to the one found in Figure 10–1. Analyze the original compositions of three different students for spelling errors.

10–7. Don, a first-grade student, was given Level II and III of the ISI developed from the *Spell Correctly* series (see Table 10–6).

Use his responses listed below to conduct an error analysis, and suggest skills that need immediate attention. Then place him at an appropriate point within this series.

1.	am	1.	abel
2.	bake	2.	belon
3.	boy	3.	came
4.	chin	4.	duck
5.	down	5.	forke
6.	fas	6.	hay
7.	go	7.	jor
8.	he	8.	kittin
9.	hot	9.	mik
10.	jet	10.	nise
11.	lot	11.	ponee

12.	man	12.	sede
13.	on	13.	ski
14.	ran	14.	stude
15.	san	15.	tor
16.	stop	16.	ti
17.	trip	17.	trap
18.	us	18.	van
19.	wen	19.	wagun
20.	yes	20.	rote

10–8. Select 10 spelling words, and design two informal devices, using the cloze procedures illustrated in this chapter. Administer both devices to the same group or class of students. Summarize by comparing the results of the two assessments. Later, dictate these same words and note any differences in results.

10–9. Locate one student having problems in spelling. During the course of 2 months, plan to work with the student at least twice a week. Carefully plan your assessment procedure so that it is similar to the suggested techniques for diagnostic teaching presented in this chapter. Write an in-depth report, analyzing those skills needing remedying and those remedial strategies you found most successful with this particular student.

References

Aaron, I. E. The relationship of selected measures to spelling achievement at the fourth and eighth grade level. *Journal of Educational Research,* 1959, *53,* 138–143.

Anderson, P. S., & Groff, P. J. *Resource materials for teachers of spelling.* (2nd ed.) Minneapolis: Burgess, 1968.

Benthul, H. F., Anderson, E. A., Uteck, A. N., Biggy, M. V., & Bailey, B. L. *Spell correctly.* Morristown, N.J.: Silver Burdett, 1974.

Betts, A. E. What about spelling? *Education,* 1956, *76,* 3–6.

Boyd, G. A., & Talbert, E. G. *Spelling in the elementary school.* Columbus, Ohio: Charles E. Merrill, 1971.

Brueckner, L. J., & Bond, G. L. *The diagnosis and treatment of learning difficulties.* New York: Appleton-Century-Crofts, 1966.

Cartwright, G. P. Written expression and spelling. In R. M. Smith (Ed.), *Teacher diagnosis of educational difficulties.* Columbus, Ohio: Charles E. Merrill, 1969.

Cohen, C., & Abrams, R. *Spellmaster,* Exeter, N.H.: Learnco, 1974.

CTB/McGraw-Hill. *Comprehensive tests of basic skills.* New York: CTB/McGraw-Hill, 1968.

Dunn, L. M., & Markwardt, F. C. *Peabody individual achievement test.* Circle Pines, Minn.: American Guidance Service, 1970.

Durost, W., Bixler, H., Wrightstone, J., Prescott, G., & Balow, I. *Metropolitan achievement tests.* New York: Harcourt Brace Jovanovich, 1970.

Edgington, R. "But he spelled them right this morning!" *Academic Therapy,* 1968, *3,* 58–59.

Feigenbaum, L. H. For a bigger better alphabet. *High Points,* 1958, *40,* 34–36.

Gates, A., & Russell, D. *Gates-Russell spelling diagnostic test.* New York: Columbia University Press, 1940.

Glim, T. E., & Manchester, F. S. *Basic spelling: A rationale.* New York: J. B. Lippincott, 1975.

Gray, H., Votaw, D. F., & Rogers, J. L. *The Gray-Votaw-Rogers general achievement tests.* Austin, Tex.: Steck-Vaughn, 1963.

Hammill, D. D., & Noone, J. Improving spelling skills. In *Teaching children with learning and behavior problems.* Boston: Allyn and Bacon, 1975.

Hanna, P. R., Hanna, J. S., Hodges, R. E., & Rudorf, E. H. *Phoneme-grapheme correspondences as cues to spelling improvement.* U.S. Department of Health, Education and Welfare. Washington, D.C.: U.S. Government Printing Office, 1966.

Hanna, P. R., Hodges, R., & Hanna, J. S. *Spelling: Structure and strategies.* Boston: Houghton Mifflin, 1971.

Hieronymus, C., & Lindquist, A. P. *Iowa test of basic skills.* Boston: Houghton Mifflin, 1971.

Hildreth, G. *Teaching spelling.* New York: Holt, Rinehart and Winston, 1955.

Hodges, R. E., & Rudorf, E. H. Searching linguistics for cues for the teaching of spelling. In T. D. Horn (Ed.), *Research on handwriting and spelling.* Champaign, Ill.: National Council of Teachers of English, 1966.

Horn, E. *Teaching spelling.* Department of Classroom Teachers, National Education Association of the United States, 1954.

Hunt, B., Hadsell, A., Hannum, J., & Johnson, H. W. The elements of spelling ability. *Elementary School Journal,* 1963, *63,* 342–349.

Jastak, J. F., & Jastak, S. R. *Wide range achievement test.* Wilmington, Del.: Guidance Associates, 1965.

Kottmeyer, W. *Teachers guide for remedial reading.* St. Louis: Webster, 1959.

Kottmeyer, W., & Claus, A. *Basic goals in spelling.* New York: McGraw-Hill, 1974.

Larsen, S. C., & Hammill, D. D. *Test of written spelling.* Austin, Tex.: Empiric Press, 1976.

Lindquist, E. F., & Feldt, L. S. *The Iowa test of educational development.* New York: Science Research Associates, 1959.

Madden, R., & Gardner, E. F. *Stanford achievement tests.* New York: Harcourt Brace Jovanovich, 1972.

Mann, P. H., & Suiter, P. *Handbook in diagnostic teaching.* Boston: Allyn and Bacon, 1974.

Otto, W., McMenemy, R. A., & Smith, R. J. *Corrective and remedial teaching.* Boston: Houghton Mifflin, 1973.

Partoll, S. F. Spelling demonology revisited. *Academic Therapy,* 1976, *11,* 339–348.

Personke, C., & Yee, A. A model for the analysis of spelling behavior. *Elementary English,* 1966, *43,* 278–284.

Peters, M. L. *Success in spelling.* Cambridge: W. Heffer and Sons, 1970.

Plessas, G. P. Review of the Lincoln Diagnostic Spelling Test. In O. K. Buros, *The Sixth Mental Measurement Yearbook.* Highland Park, N.J.: Gryphon, 1965.

Poplin, M. A model of spelling behavior. Unpublished manuscript, University of Texas at Austin, 1976.

Raygoz, B. F. *McGraw-Hill basic study skills: Spelling.* New York: McGraw-Hill, 1970.

Rudorf, E. H. Measurement of spelling ability. In T. D. Horn (Ed.), *Research on handwriting and spelling.* Champaign, Ill.: National Council of Teachers of English, 1966.

Sequential test of basic skills, Palo Alto, Calif.: Educational Testing Service, 1958.

Shores, J. H., & Yee, A. Spelling achievement tests: What is available and needed? *Journal of Special Education,* 1973, *7,* 301–310.

Spache, G. Review of the Gates-Russell Spelling Diagnosis Test. In O. K. Buros, *The Fourth Mental Measurement Yearbook.* Highland Park, N.J.: Gryphon, 1953.

Thorpe, L. P., Lefever, D. W., & Nasland, R. A. *SRA achievement series.* New York: Science Research Associates, 1974.

Tiegs, E. W., & Clark, W. W. *California achievement tests.* New York: CTB/McGraw-Hill, 1970.

Westerman, Gayle S. *Spelling and writing.* Sioux Falls, S.D.: Adapt Press, 1971.

11

Written-Expression Assessment

Written expression is one of the highest forms of communication. In order to become proficient in written expression, a person must develop skills and abilities in all of the other areas that comprise the language arts: competency in speaking, reading, spelling, handwriting, capitalization, punctuation, word usage, and grammar. Consequently, when we consider the complexities of written expression, it comes as little surprise that many students experience significant difficulties in mastering the complexities of this area. When a teacher observes that a student is exhibiting problems in written communication, it is necessary to plan and conduct an assessment that will outline the pattern of strengths and weaknesses, which will then become the basis for teaching intervention. It is important that the teacher have expertise in various assessment techniques, both formal and informal.

This chapter will familiarize teachers with (1) the factors that affect written expression; (2) skill sequences that are used when written expression is taught in school; and (3) various devices and strategies useful in assessing written-expression disorders. Knowledge in each of these areas is essential to effectively analyze and remedy writing difficulties.

FACTORS AFFECTING WRITTEN EXPRESSION

As with all other subject areas within the language arts curriculum, written expression is a highly complex and multidimensional skill. This complexity is apparent when we consider that the ability to convey thoughts in writing adequately depends upon the successful acquisition of *all* previous stages of language development (Wallace & McLoughlin, 1975; Black, 1968; and Johnson & Myklebust, 1967). Prior to mastering the intricacies of written expression, a student must have some knowledge and expertise in listening, speaking, spelling, handwriting, punctuation, and capitalization. Difficulties in any of these areas will likely interfere with the normal acquisition and uses of written expression. This section will acquaint teachers with the factors that directly affect the manner in which children learn to express themselves through written symbols.

Spoken Language

The adequate development of basic language concepts in human beings is indispensable to all phases of academic growth, and this development usually follows a relatively set pattern. Initially, the child learns to listen and to understand language before it is possible to express ideas through speech. In addition, the child must acquire an ability to speak prior to acquiring the ability to write competently. Although children will exhibit these language behaviors at different ages, they are attained in the same general sequence (Ferris, 1971). The teacher must take into account these prerequisite speech patterns before assessing a student's readiness for written-language instruction.

The ability to convey ideas via speech develops relatively early in children. Although spoken language seems to be acquired with precision and ease by most children, its normal development should not be taken for granted by parents or teachers. The processes by which children are able to express themselves verbally are so complex that no one has yet unraveled these mental processes involved in normal speech development. Black (1968) states,

> Learning to speak, which we commonly take so much for granted, is probably the most remarkable intellectual feat the ordinary man accomplishes. Sophisticated research on phonetics and acoustics, the physiology and neurology of speech, only heightens the marvel. The delicacy and subtlety of control involved in as commonplace an utterance as "Pass the salt, please" present analysis and explanation problems that still baffle experts.[1]

In assessing a student's ability to write, it is essential that the teacher consider the relationship between spoken and written language. Specifically, speech precedes writing and, consequently, a student who can speak a clear, concise sentence exhibits a skill that is basic in learning how to

[1]From *The Labyrinth of Language* by Max Black. © 1968 by Encyclopedia Britannica, Inc. Reprinted by permission of Praeger Publishers, Inc., New York.

write. Conversely, if a student's speech patterns are choppy, unclear, or garbled, it is likely that the student's writing will be the same. For example, if a child says, "I ain't got none," he or she will probably write this sentence in the same way. Attempts to induce children to write at a level that is more sophisticated than their habitual speech patterns are largely unrealistic (Ferris, 1971). The point is that although it is inappropriate to delay writing instruction until a student has established excellent speech habits (if this ever occurs), the adequacy of a student's speech must be considered if the teacher attempts to assess or remedy disorders of written expression.

Mechanical Aspects of Written Expression

Once a student begins a structured sequence of written expression, the student will soon discover that it is necessary to conform to certain conventions of English that have been established by generations of writers: *handwriting, capitalization, punctuation,* and *format.* These conventions must become automatic for even the very young student. Students must become conscious of the fact that proper use of these tools aids in the clear expression of thought, and at the same time enables them to interpret a writer's message.

Handwriting   Handwriting (frequently referred to as *penmanship*) is indispensable to written expression. Regardless of how well organized the written passage may be, it will not convey a thought adequately unless it is presented in a legible fashion. Variables such as letter formation, spacing, alignment, slant, and quality of line all directly affect legibility (Freeman, 1915). Obviously, the development of gross- and fine-motor control and hand-eye coordination are necessary for legible handwriting. However, although legible handwriting is indispensable to written expression, teachers should keep in mind that good penmanship is only a *tool* for achieving effective communication. What is *primary* are the ideas expressed; the style and language of the written passage are of foremost importance only when they are so deficient that they interfere significantly with coherent written expression.

Punctuation and Capitalization   Like handwriting, the skills of *punctuation* and *capitalization* must be mastered to facilitate development of proficient written language. Even young students are able to recognize that capital letters stress words of special significance and punctuation marks help to avoid misreading the sentence. According to Donoghue (1971), "It is through the use of punctuation that the writer tries to convey meaning to the reader without benefit of the help which a speaker has—gestures, pitch, stress, juncture, and facial expression (p. 233)." Commas, exclamation points, periods, hyphens, question marks, apostrophes, and colons are used (1) to show relationships between sentences and words, (2) to shorten words, (3) to add emphasis, or (4) to indicate omissions. It is apparent that inappropriate use of punctuation and capitalization will result in, at most, distortion of the message (i.e., idea) that is meant to be conveyed, and least, loss of readability.

Format   The *format* of written language refers to the manner in which a person has *organized* his or her thoughts. Organization entails the appropriate use and combinations of sentences, paragraphs, and specific conventionalized forms of written communication (e.g., headings of a standard business letter). Donoghue (1971) lists these major conventions, which must be mastered:

1. Place the date and name on all papers.
2. Maintain straight margins of a specific width.
3. Leave space at the top and bottom of the page, between the heading and body, between words and between sentences.
4. Indent the first word of each paragraph.
5. Observe the six-part form for business letters: heading, inside address, greeting, body, closing, and signature.
6. Observe the five-part form for friendly letters: heading, greeting, body, closing, and signature.
7. Observe the forms for both topic and sentence outlines, indenting main parts with Roman numerals.
8. Prepare a simple bibliography in the intermediate grades, listing articles from magazines and encyclopedias as well as books [p. 236].

Knowledge of these conventions will undoubtedly enhance the overall effectiveness of any written communication.

Sentence and Paragraph Sense

Although handwriting, punctuation, capitalization, and format are important to written language, they definitely play a secondary role in relation to the quality of *ideas* that are expressed. According to Myklebust (1965), Hammill (1975), and West (1966), factors such as productivity, syntax, content, and organization of thoughts must be considered when a teacher assesses and tries to remedy disorders in written language. At its most basic level, meaningful writing is a *thinking process*, usually developed from a firm base in spoken language. It is essential that both teachers and students see written expression in this manner, for an idea poorly clarified in the mind and speech of a writer also will tend to be disorganized on paper.

Two important facets of meaningful writing include writing sentences and paragraphs. In writing sentences a student must become aware of the diverse syntactical patterns available for expressing ideas. Lefevre (1970) also emphasizes the importance of syntactical knowledge in the language arts when he states, "sentence comprehension—sentence sense—is the beginning of reading comprehension as well as of the ability to write compositions (p. 83)." Students must be exposed to a lot of appropriate reading material in order to acquire acceptable syntactical models.

In addition to writing coherent sentences, students must also combine, categorize, and classify ideas in paragraph form. Many pupils experience a great deal of difficulty in connecting ideas within and among paragraphs (Otto, McMenemy, & Smith, 1973). This problem is likely due to a faulty conception about the function of a paragraph. A paragraph should be a cogent *unit of thought* containing complete sentences that qualify and support the main assertion. Obviously, students attempting to write paragraphs must have acquired an ability to organize ideas and clarity of thought in order to convey meaning adequately. Students who exhibit problems in putting sentences in a logical order undoubtedly will find it very difficult to write meaningful paragraphs.

SKILLS NECESSARY FOR WRITTEN EXPRESSION

As has been noted previously, before a student demonstrates competency in written expression, the student must be proficient in listening, speaking, spelling, reading, handwriting, punctuation, capitalization, format, and logical thinking. There can be little question that assessing and remedying disorders in written expression are difficult because they require a great deal of expertise on the part of the teacher. To acquire the necessary expertise to assess and remedy these disorders a teacher must become thoroughly familiar with the skills that lead to the ability to express oneself adequately via the written word. These skills will be discussed in the next section.

Of all the language activities taught in elementary and secondary schools, written expression is by far the most difficult for pupils to master successfully. Written expression, unlike speech, entails communicating ideas without the aid of facial expressions, tone, or gestures. In fact, every writer is aware that the more one wishes to convey an idea (e.g., because its significance and importance are critical), the more arduous writing becomes.

TABLE 11–1   Minimal Skills Necessary for Successful Written Expression

Logical Sequence and Demonstration of Relationships

	Grade Levels					
	1	2	3	4	5	6
1. Establish a controlled purpose for composition to determine the relevancy of ideas under consideration	X	X	X	X	X	X
2. Arrange ideas according to						
a. Order of importance	X	X	X	X	X	X
b. Spatial order	X	X	X	X	X	X
c. Time sequence	X	X	X	X	X	X
d. Cause and effect	X	X	X	X	X	X
3. Draw a simple comparison or contrast between two objects	X	X	X	X	X	X
4. Draw a simple comparison or contrast between two ideas		X	X	X	X	X
5. Understand and demonstrate relationships between valid evidence and generalization				X	X	X
6. Write in informal or formal style according to need		X	X	X	X	X
7. Be aware of steps of the composition process as a means of ordering thoughts		X	X	X	X	X
8. Recognize and produce						
a. Narrative prose		X	X	X	X	X
b. Descriptive prose		X	X	X	X	X
c. Expository prose			X	X	X	X
d. Argumentative prose					X	X
e. Poetry		X	X	X	X	X
Conventions of Written Expression						
1. Produce legible markings in						
a. Manuscript writing	X	X	X			
b. Cursive writing				X	X	X
2. Recognize and produce						
a. Correct punctuation	X	X	X	X	X	X
b. Correct capitalization	X	X	X	X	X	X
3. Be aware of appropriate format for different types of written composition (business letter, friendly note, report, etc.)	X	X	X	X	X	X
4. Draw conclusions regarding the adequacy of written composition by proofreading	X	X	X	X	X	X

Source: Adapted from the *Elementary composition curriculum guide,* 1967. Clover Park School District No. 400, 5214 Steilacoom Blvd., Lakewood Center, Wash. 98499.

In order to assist students in acquiring effective written communication, it is necessary to present them with the skills shown in Table 11–1.

This list of skills should provide the teacher with a broad overview regarding the various components of written communication. The teacher should keep in mind, however, that the specific scope-and-sequence chart will vary depending on the particular program or method of instruction used in a school. According to the Florida State Department of Education, the major *factors* that are stressed in teaching the logical sequence and demonstration of relationships in most English programs include:

1. *narrowing* compositions by determining what to put in and what to leave out of their writing
2. *ordering* of ideas through such techniques as contrast, chronology, comparison, cause-effect, question-answer, or example-generalization
3. *focusing* of a written product so that it conveys information or induces a mood
4. *personalization* of written material by the use of appropriate vocabulary and alternative form
5. *thinking responsibly* to make compositions as reliable and accurate as possible.

The specific skills emphasized in presentation of the conventions of written expression are more consistent across basal programs. The reason for this consistency is that handwriting, punctuation, capitalization, and format are relatively mechanical and do not require the abstraction necessary in establishing a logical sequence and demonstrating relationships within a written composition. For example, although handwriting is vital to normal written communication, it is secondary to the actual organization and expression of ideas. The goals and objectives of handwriting shown in Table 11–2 were derived from several common curriculum guides and will give teachers some insight into the various factors involved in teaching this particular skill.

The sequence in which capitalization and punctuation are taught varies slightly in different schools; however, the basic information presented will be consistent across basal programs. The particular skills in capitalization that students should attain prior to leaving elementary school have been outlined by Greene and Petty (1967), and are meant to indicate only those that are required for *minimal* competency in this area.

Grade One
    a. The first word of a sentence
    b. The child's first and last name
    c. The name of the teacher, school, town, street
    d. the word "I"

TABLE 11–2   Goals of Handwriting Instruction in Grades 1–6

Kindergarten and First Grade

1. Children exhibit familiarity (both through discussion and frequency of use) with writing as a form of communcation. This suggests that the teacher will use labels, charts, and stories dictated by children to accompany pictures.
2. Children learn to write their names and usually master the basic shapes used in writing. Many will be able to write short notes, stories, invitations, holiday greetings, etc., and most will be able at least to copy these from the chalkboard.
3. At the conclusion of the first grade most children master the alphabet, (upper and lower case letters).
4. Most children correctly write numbers to 10.

Second and Third Grades

1. A majority of children achieve mastery of the alphabet to the extent that they can write original stories, reports, etc. By the end of second grade handwriting is truly functional for most students.
2. Children are more skillful in spacing words and letters. Writing tends to be neater, more legible, and attractive.
3. Transition to cursive writing is made in second or third grade. Certain elements of joining letters, introduction of slant, etc., are taught to an entire class while individualized approaches are used for individual children when needed.
4. Although children make the transition from manuscript to cursive writing, basic skills in manuscript writing are maintained. Many children continue to use the manuscript form for independent writing activities because of its speed and ease.
5. Children learn the rudiments of punctuation, paragraph sense, format, etc.
6. In the third grade, pens are introduced as writing instruments.

Fourth, Fifth, and Sixth Grades

1. Children continually achieve mastery of cursive writing and establishing individual writing styles.
2. Manuscript writing is maintained for labeling, map work, and charts. All children are encouraged to retain this skill throughout elementary school.
3. Children acquire the objectivity necessary for evaluation of their own handwriting. Increased emphasis is placed upon self-help and individual responsibility for handwriting improvement in the intermediate and upper grades. Proofreading receives continuing emphasis through the sixth grade.
4. Functional competency is achieved in fields related to handwriting such as punctuation, paragraphing, identification and placement of topic sentences, etc.
5. Pens (ballpoints) are used with as much ease and fluency as pencils. Fountain pens also may be used if desirable.

Source: Adapted from Lamb, P. *Guiding children's language learning* © 1971, pp. 212–214. Reprinted by permission of William C. Brown Company, Publishers, Dubuque, Iowa.

Grade Two
  a. Items listed for Grade one
  b. The date
  c. First and important words of titles of books the children read
  d. Proper names used in children's writings
  e. Titles of compositions
  f. Names of titles: "Mr.," "Mrs.," "Ms.," "Miss"

Grade Three
  a. Items listed for Grades one and two
  b. Proper names: month, day, common holiday
  c. First and important words in titles of books, stories, poems
  d. First word of salutation of informal note, as "Dear"
  e. First word of closing of informal note, as "Yours"

Grade Four
  a. All that is listed in preceding grades
  b. Names of cities and states in general
  c. Names of organizations to which children belong, as Boy Scouts, Grade Four, etc.
  d. Mother, Father, when used in place of the name
  e. Local geographical names

Grade Five
  a. All that is outlined for previous grades
  b. Names of streets
  c. Names of all places and persons, countries, oceans, etc.
  d. Capitalization used in outlining
  e. Titles when used with names, such as President Lincoln
  f. Commercial trade names

Grade Six
  a. All that is outlined for preceding grades
  b. Names of the Deity and the Bible
  c. First word of a quoted sentence
  d. Proper adjectives, showing race, nationality, etc.
  e. Abbreviations of proper names and titles

Compared with capitalization skills, those related to punctuation are more numerous and used with discretion. Punctuation marks are used to assure that what is intended to be communicated to the reader is, in fact, communicated. Incorrect use of the punctuation marks will interfere significantly with or distort the meaning of almost any written passage. This is even more obvious when the written message becomes more complex. The uses of punctuation marks, as shown in Table 11–3, are usually acquired by most elementary-school children.

TABLE 11–3   Listing of Major Punctuation Rules

The Period

1. At the end of a declarative and an imperative sentence (although the terms "declarative" and "imperative" may not necessarily be taught)
2. After abbreviations and initials
3. With numbers or letters preceding a list in outline
4. With numbers or letters to help indicate items in a list of words or sentences or longer thought units even if the items are not included in an outline

The Comma

1. After the greeting in a personal letter and after the closing in a personal or business letter
2. Between the date of a month and the year
3. After the name of a city where it is written directly to the left of the name of the state
4. With words or groups of words in a series
5. After "yes" or "no" when used as a part of an answer
6. In a sentence containing a direct quotation (to separate the quotation from the rest of the sentence unless a question mark or an exclamation point sets the quotation off from the rest of the sentence)
7. After a word or group of words, other than a sentence, which shows some, but not as much, surprise or expresses moderately strong feeling
8. After the name of a person addressed
9. With appositives
10. After the last name of a person if it is written before the first name, as in an alphabetical list

The Question Mark

1. After an interrogative sentence
2. After a direct quotation in question form given as part of a sentence

Quotation Marks

1. In a direct quotation to set off the exact words of the speaker
2. Around the title of a story (but not of a book) or of an article

The Exclamation Point

1. At the end of an exclamatory sentence
2. After a single word that shows surprise or expresses strong feeling
3. After a word or group of words expressing strong feeling given as a direct quotation

The Apostrophe

1. In a contraction
2. In a possessive noun

The Hyphen

1. Between syllables if a word is divided at the end of a line so that one or more syllables occur at the end of one line and the remaining syllable(s) at the beginning of the next line
2. In a compound word, including compound nouns, adjectives, and numbers

TABLE 11–3   *Continued*

The Colon

1. After the salutation in a business letter
2. Between the hour and minutes when expressing the time of day, as in 9:30 a.m.

Underlines

With a title of a book or magazine when used as part of a sentence, in hand-written or typewritten form

Source: Dallman, M. *Teaching the language arts in the elementary school.* (3rd ed.) Dubuque, Iowa: 1976, pp. 111–112. Reprinted by permission of the publisher.

When we review the uses of punctuation marks, it is clear that they are important enough to be taught. The grade levels at which they are introduced are listed below:[2]

Grade One
    a. Period at the end of a sentence which tells something
    b. Period after numbers in any kind of list

Grade Two
    a. Items listed for Grade one
    b. Question mark at the close of a question
    c. Comma after salutation of a friendly note or letter
    d. Comma after closing of a friendly note or letter
    e. Comma between the day of the month and the year
    f. Comma between name of city and state

Grade Three
    a. Items listed for Grades one and two
    b. Periods after abbreviations
    c. Period after an initial
    d. Use of an apostrophe in common contraction, such as isn't, aren't, don't
    e. Commas in a list

Grade Four
    a. All items listed for previous grades
    b. Apostrophe to show possession
    c. Hyphen separating parts of a word divided at end of a line
    d. Period following a command
    e. Exclamation point at the end of a word or group of words that makes an exclamation
    f. Comma setting off an appositive

[2]From Greene, H. A. and Petty, W. T. *Developing language skills in the elementary school,* Fifth Edition. Boston: Allyn and Bacon, Inc. 1975.

g. Colon after the salutation of a business letter
h. Quotation marks before and after a direct quotation
i. Comma between explanatory words and a quotation
j. Period after outline Roman numeral

Grade Five
a. All items listed for previous grades
b. Colon in writing time
c. Comma to indicate changed word order
d. Quotation marks around the title of a pamphlet, chapter of a book, and the title of a poem or story
e. Underlining the title of a book

Grade Six
a. All items listed for previous grades
b. Comma to set off nouns in direct address
c. Hyphen in compound numbers
d. Colon to set off a list
e. Comma in sentences to aid in making meaning clear

Once a student demonstrates mastery over the organization and sequencing of ideas within a written composition and is able to write them in correct form, then the student will acquire competency in written expression. At this point, the student also must have developed the habit of effective self-editing and proofreading (Wallace & McLoughlin, 1975). Beginning in first grade, pupils should be taught to depend upon themselves, so that they will find errors of expression and correct them. Greene and Petty (1967) state that a student must be encouraged to "... carefully examine what he has written in terms of selection of the ideas or information, effectiveness of organization, clarity of expression, and courtesy to the readers, including legibility of writing, correct punctuation, and acceptable usage (p. 221)."

ASSESSMENT OF DISORDERS
IN WRITTEN EXPRESSION

At a relatively early age most students are able to express thoughts in writing. The ability to accomplish this task, even at a seemingly simple level, requires that a student possess minimal competency in the following: (1) adequate spoken language; (2) organization of thought processes; (3) knowledge of the grammatical and syntactical aspects of written language; (4) proficient spelling (see Chapter 10); (5) motor control for good handwriting (i.e., penmanship); and (6) familiarity with the conventions of sentence and paragraph sense, capitalization, and punctuation. Deficiencies in these areas may interfere significantly with successful written expression. Teachers must be prepared to assess any or all of these components when they first observe students experiencing difficulties in written expression. The method by which teachers conduct an assessment depends upon the specific needs of teachers and students.

Assessment techniques that measure aspects of written expression may be divided into two broad categories: (1) standardized tests that yield either achievement or diagnostic data and (2) informal teacher-made tests that are designed to relate specifically to educational planning and intervention. Each of these categories will be discussed in this section.

STANDARDIZED TESTS

The vast majority of standardized tests available to teachers are geared to provide only a general estimate of ability in written expression. The most common of these standardized tests yield general achievement information. Other tests, although fewer in number, do provide some diagnostic data applicable for planning remedial programs.

Achievement Tests

The primary purpose of standardized achievement tests is to compare a student's performance with statistically derived standardization norms. After the comparison is made, a teacher is able to determine if a pupil's written expression is "on par" with the standardization sample used in establishing norms for the test. Usually, a student's score is reported in the form of grade equivalents, percentiles, etc. It should be noted that there is no attempt to supply the teacher with specific error patterns that could be used in formulating teaching plans.

There are several points a teacher should keep in mind when interpreting a score received from a standardized achievement test. In most instances, the assessment of written expression in these tests is limited to requiring a student to read a series of phrases to determine if there are mistakes in capitalization, punctuation, or word usage. No attempt is made to analyze a passage actually written by a given student. An example of how one component of written expression (i.e., word usage) is usually assessed on achievement tests is given in Figure 11-1. The student is asked to read the first three sentences and determine if any mistakes are evident. If one is present, the student is instructed to mark the appropriate blank on the record sheet. If no mistakes are present, the student marks the

FIGURE 11–1   Sample Item for Word usage Included on Many Standardized
Achievement Tests

Sample Question	*Answer*
1. Will you come with me?	① ② ● ④
2. We went to the store.	
3. She bring me the toy.	
4. No mistakes.	

"no mistakes" column. A similar format is used to assess other aspects of written expression.

The most commonly employed standardized achievement tests with written expression sections are listed in Table 11–4. The grade levels and various aspects of written expression that are measured in each instrument are also provided.

When selecting a standardized achievement test, the teacher should carefully preview a variety of tests and choose the one that will best meet his or her needs. Aspects of reliability and validity should also be considered to ensure that the chosen test will yield data that are consistent across time and that actually measure true components of written expression. In addition, teachers should remember that, in order to perform adequately on

TABLE 11–4   Achievement Tests with Written Expression Sections

Tests	Components Assessed	Grade Levels
Comprehensive Tests of Basic Skills (CTB/McGraw-Hill, 1968)	Word usage, mechanics,[a] and grammatical structure	1–12
California Achievement Tests (Tiegs & Clark, 1970)	Word usage, mechanics, and grammatical structure	3–12
Stanford Achievement Tests (Madden & Gardner, 1972)	Mechanics and grammatical structure	3–9
Iowa Test of Basic Skills (Hieronymus & Lindquist, 1971)	Word usage and mechanics	1–9
SRA Achievement Series (Thorpe, Lefever, & Nasland, 1974)	Mechanics and grammatical structure	2–9
Metropolitan Achievement Tests (Durost, et al., 1970)	Word usage, mechanics, and grammatical structure	3–9

[a]Mechanics includes punctuation and capitalization.

a standardized achievement test, a student *must* be able to read at or near grade level. The scores of any student who has obvious reading problems should be disregarded or interpreted with great caution. A student with reading disorders requires a carefully constructed informal evaluation in order that a valid estimate of his or her skills in written expression will be ascertained.

Diagnostic Tests

Although written expression is a skill valued in today's society, little effort has been devoted to constructing diagnostic tests. At present, only two tests have been located that supply usable information for planning instruction. These tests include the *Picture Story Language Test* and the *Sequential Test of Education Progress*.

Picture Story Language Test   The *Picture Story Language Test* (PSLT) (Myklebust, 1965) was developed for the purpose of studying written expression (both developmentally and diagnostically). In this test a student is presented a picture and asked to write a story. The resulting composition is then evaluated according to *productivity, correctness,* and *meaning. Productivity* is defined as the amount of language expressed (i.e., length); in particular, the number of words, sentences, and the number of words per sentence are computed. *Correctness* (i.e., syntax) furnishes an indication of the student's word usage, word endings, and punctuation. *Meaning* refers to the actual content that is conveyed within sentences. The total scores are derived from (1) counting the number of words, number of sentences, and words per sentence; (2) determining the accuracy of word usage, of word endings, and punctuation (a rating procedure); and (3) counting errors of additions, omissions, substitutions, and word order. Once scores for each of these areas have been calculated, they are converted into age equivalents, percentiles, and stanines.

It is our opinion that the PSLT can be used in gaining a clearer understanding of how students express themselves in writing. However, teachers should use the information obtained from this instrument in a strictly informal fashion. Hammill (1975) and Anastasiow (1972) have raised serious questions regarding the adequacy of the reliability and validity information of the PSLT. Consequently, the scores derived from this test should be interpreted with great caution. It is recommended that teachers use the PSLT only as an informal, observational technique.

Sequential Test of Educational Progress   Another standardized diagnostic test is the *Sequential Test of Educational Progress* (STEP) (Educational Testing Service, 1958). The STEP includes items that fall into the following five categories:

1. *organization*—ordering of ideas, events, facts, etc.
2. *conventions*—syntax, word choice, punctuation, and spelling
3. *critical thinking*—detection of unstated assumptions, cause-and-effect relationships, and anticipation of the needs of readers
4. *effectiveness*—adequacy of emphasis and development, exactness of expression, economy, simplicity, and variety
5. *appropriateness*—choice of a level of usage suitable to purpose and reader (i.e., using the right tone and appropriate vocabulary).

In most instances, the items included in the STEP require the student to select appropriate changes to correct a given passage. The student must identify errors in the items presented and select a revision that most satisfactorily solves the observed problems. The written passages upon which the items are based were drawn from materials actually written by students in schools (most were graded as poor or failing). The subject matter is presented in the form of reports, letters, essays, minutes of meetings, or directions.

Although the STEP does not include analysis of a student's own writing (a criticism of standardized achievement tests), the inclusion of the additional task of selecting appropriate revisions to correct errors is helpful in gaining a more in-depth view of disorders in written expression. Special normative tables permit comparison of average grade performances in a specific school with average grade performances in other schools. Analysis of specific error patterns assists teachers in planning teaching intervention. If teachers find it necessary to use a standardized diagnostic test, we recommend that they use it primarily to structure observations that can be verified by the passages actually written by students. Specific suggestions for constructing informal tests to assess written expression disorders will be presented in the following section.

INFORMAL ASSESSMENT
TECHNIQUES

The ultimate goal of any writing instruction is to prepare students to convey their thoughts adequately. The steps through which students pass in order to accomplish this goal are fairly standard in most schools. Initially, students are encouraged, both individually and in groups, to dictate stories to the teacher. In the primary grades, spelling and handwriting skills have not developed to the point that permits independent writing, but over time, students begin to copy the compositions that have been dictated to them and are capable of rudimentary additions peculiar to their own individual interests. At a somewhat later level students engage in independent writing activities that take many forms, for example, stories, reports, and poetry. Throughout this process, knowledge of punctuation and capitalization also is mastered and eventually used correctly with little thought or effort. By the fourth grade most students are capable of writing well-structured paragraphs.

In some instances, students do not pass through these stages successfully. When students exhibit disorders in written expression, the teacher should initiate informal assessment to outline the specific problems. The first step in conducting an informal assessment entails obtaining a representative sample of the student's written work. Once this has been secured, an analysis of the following areas can be undertaken:

1. general composition, including evidence of purpose, content, and organization as well as sentence and paragraph development
2. appropriate diction (word choice) that permits a clear discussion of the topic selected
3. mastery of the rules that underlie the use of capitalization and punctuation
4. quality of handwriting.

Table 11–5 provides a sample profile of components of written expression that can be used with an individual or an entire class. These profiles enable a teacher to isolate the particular problem(s) that a student is experiencing and provides a record by which improvement can be documented over time. The value of structuring the analyses of written work is that although a subjective interpretation is always required, a method of standardizing observations (the main purpose of the profile), helps to promote reliable and valid informal assessment. The major components outlined in Table 11–5 can be evaluated as follows:

1. *purpose*—main ideas unclear or missing, too broad, lacking in significance, or poorly stated
2. *content*—ideas unsupported, lack specifics, unrelated to the subject, or taken from another source
3. *organization*—introduction and conclusions poorly stated, ideas randomly presented, transitions inappropriately used
4. *paragraphs*—paragraphs inadequately developed
5. *sentences*—sentences are fragmented, consist of dangling modifiers, lack variety, show problems with tense, subject-verb agreement, and pronoun-antecedent agreement
6. *word choice and usage*—vocabulary inappropriate, clichés, tone ineffective

TABLE 11-5   Sample Profile of Written-Expression Components

| Pupils' Names | Composing | | | | | | Mechanics | | |
	Purpose	Content	Organization	Sentences	Paragraphs	Word Choice and Usage	Capitalization	Punctuation	Handwriting

7. *capitalization*—incorrectly used in titles, proper nouns, words for deity, etc.
8. *punctuation*—italics, period, comma, exclamation point, quotes incorrectly used
9. *handwriting*—does not permit quick and easy reading in either manuscript or cursive style.

It should be clearly noted that the profile given in Table 11–5 (and descriptions of the major components) are merely suggested and should be modified to meet the specific needs of individual classrooms.

Although general profiles are useful in gaining a broad understanding of a pupil's mastery of written expression, it may be necessary to perform an in-depth assessment of particularly troublesome areas. The more abstract components of written expression (i.e., purpose, content, and organization) must be judged in relation to the student's intelligence, experiences, and motivation to communicate. Essentially the teacher must formulate minimal competencies or objectives and determine the extent to which students are or are not meeting them. Readers are referred to the guidelines established by West (1966) and Cartwright (1969) when they outline these minimal competencies.

Other elements of written expression are more mechanical in nature and lend themselves more readily to objective assessment. It must be kept in mind that usefulness of the techniques discussed depends upon obtaining representative samples of a student's written work and carefully analyzing them for error patterns. It is essential that teachers be familiar with the rules upon which the conventions of written expression are based.

Word Usage

Word usage (i.e., grammar) is important in effective written expression. The manner in which the teacher views grammar will determine the types of errors that the teacher will assess. Burns (1974) has proposed a minimal list of errors that may be included in an analysis of word usage, which are presented in Table 11–6.

When using an analysis chart the teacher has the option to record the particular error made or the number of times an error is made. In addition, a teacher may wish to devise examples for the items listed on the chart. For example, a student is likely to be judged to be deficient in word usage if the patterns (see Table 11–7) are noted in the written composition (Burns, 1974). Teachers are encouraged to modify this chart to reflect their own specific needs. However, it is essential that teachers assess word usage so that they will fully understand a student's competency in this area.

TABLE 11–6   Analysis of Written Usage

Pupils' Names	Verbs				Pronouns			Adjectives/ Adverbs			Words				
	Tense form	Tense shift	Agreement	Auxiliary missing	Subject or object position	Pronoun/adjective	Antecedents	Form	Confusion	Article	Comparison	Addition	Omission	Substitution	Plural	Substandard

Source: From Paul C. Burns, *Diagnostic teaching of the language arts* © 1974, p. 101. Reproduced by permission of the publisher, F. E. Peacock Publishers, Inc., Itasca, Illinois.

Punctuation

For some students, learning the punctuation marks is very difficult (Greene & Petty, 1967). The reason for this difficulty may be that the teacher does not point out the similarities between punctuation in written expression and the intonations, pauses, and other conventions used in oral communication. In any event, when a teacher notices inaccurate punctuation, a specific analysis of error patterns must be initiated.

A teacher may be aided by knowledge of the most frequent punctuation errors that students make in written compositions. Furness (1960) has listed the seven most common errors, and these are outlined in Table 11–8. This list should assist the teacher in making a quick and accurate assessment of a student's punctuation skills.

An additional procedure for evaluating punctuation skills is offered

TABLE 11–7   Sample of an Analysis Chart

Items	Example of Errors
Verbs	
1. Tense form	He seen it.
	I have come home.
	Bill come home.
2. Tense	Inappropriate shift between sentences.
3. Agreement	They was here.
4. Auxiliary missing	He standing there.
Pronouns	
1. Subject or preposition object	Him did it.
	With Sam and I he went.
2. Demonstrative adjective	Them books are mine.
3. Unclear antecedents	Mary and Jane were there and she saw him do it.
4. Form	Our'n, her'n
Adjectives / Adverbs	
1. Confusion (*good for well*)	Everything went good.
2. Article (*a for an*)	She and I go to an store.
3. Double comparison	He is more bigger than I am.
Words	
1. Additions	This here dog is pretty.
2. Omissions	She went the movie.
3. Substitutions	Sally sat on the there.
4. Plurals	The two boy played.
5. Nonstandard	I ain't going there.

by Burns (1974). In this procedure the teacher prepares a series of short sentences and paragraphs, in which punctuation rules (e.g., commas, semicolons) are used. The teacher dictates the passages, the pupils write them, and then the teacher analyzes the written passages for weak spots. In most instances, the student's performances closely approximate their spontaneous writing. This method of assessment is far more accurate than having students analyze a series of prepared passages and merely indicate errors in punctuation that are evident.

As with other areas of written expression, we recommend that teachers use a record-keeping system for noting punctuation errors. Table 11–9 can be used in this regard. It is recommended that the numerals associated with Dallman's listing of punctuation items listed in Table 11–3 be used to indicate specific errors under each heading. This method will permit teachers to record quickly and succinctly the specific mistakes in students' punctuation.

TABLE 11–8   Common Errors in Punctuation

Errors		Possible Causes
1. Omission of period at end of sentence	a. b. c. d.	Carelessness Indifference Poor observation Haste
2. Omission of period	a. b. c.	Carelessness Insufficient practice Lack of "abbreviation conscious-ness"
3. Failure to use a colon	a. b.	Intellectual immaturity Lack of sensitivity to emotional overtones of written materials
4. Omission of question mark after question	a. b.	Carelessness Indifference
5. Failure to set off nonrestrictive clause by a comma	a. b.	Lack of appreciation of a suspension of thought Lack of observation
6. Failure to set off a series by commas	a. b. c. d.	Carelessness Lack of writing experience Lack of attention to details Misunderstanding of the concept of "series"
7. Lack of commas setting off an appositive	a.	Failure to understand the relation of the insertion to the sentence proper

Source: Furness, E. L. Pupils, pedagogues, and punctuation. *Elementary English,* 1960, 187–189. Copyright © 1960 by the National Council of Teachers of English. Reprinted by permission of the publisher and the author.

Capitalization

Compared to punctuation skills, those skills related to use of capital letters are neither as complex nor as numerous. The most frequent capitalization error made by students is using capital letters when they are not appropriate. Learning about capitalization consists of when *not* to use them as well as when to use them (Ferris, 1971). It is obvious, however, that unless students master the rules of capitalization, the general appearance and clarity of their writing certainly will be diminished.

To review the rules of capitalization, teachers are referred to the previous section on capitalization in this chapter; they must become familiar with these rules in order to assess a student's usage of capital letters ade-

TABLE 11–9   Analysis of Punctuation Errors

Pupils' Names	Period	Comma	Semicolon	Colon	Quotation mark	Apostrophe	Question mark	Hyphen	Underlining

Source: Paul C. Burns, *Diagnostic teaching of the language arts* © 1974, p. 90. Reproduced by permission of the publisher, F. E. Peacock Publishers, Inc., Itasca, Illinois.

quately. A convenient method of isolating errors is to construct a chart that permits efficient analysis of a student's written work. A sample chart is presented in Table 11–10. Teachers are encouraged to adapt the items in this chart to their own classroom needs. It is important that when analyzing a student's knowledge of capitalization rules, efforts must be made to ensure that the written samples used are truly representative of the student's everyday work. However, the most important aspect of assessment is to keep detailed records of a student's errors that allows efficient remedial teaching.

Sentence and Paragraph Sense

The most elemental aspect of written expression is the development of sentence and paragraph sense. In other words, students must be able to recognize the various syntactical patterns available for expressing thoughts in sentences and the manner in which sentences are combined to form a well-

TABLE 11–10   Analysis of Capitalization

Pupils' Names	First word of sentence	The word "I"	Proper names	Titles	Proper adjectives	First word of quotation	Words for the deity	Appropriate abbreviations	Salutation and closing of letter	Words such as mother, father when used as a name	Trade names

articulated thought. If these two elements are not learned, any efforts at written expression will be fruitless.

The development of sentence sense is exceedingly difficult for some pupils. Lefevre (1970) feels that the most efficient method of developing this ability is to deemphasize the traditional ways in which grammar has been taught in the schools. He states,

> It is not helpful to insist, as some teachers still do, that every sentence must have a subject and predicate, and must also "express a complete thought." Rather than attempt to lay down an abstract verbal prescription that means little or nothing to the learner, it is preferable to allow him over a generous period of time, to develop his own inductive definition of "sentence" by associating the term with varied examples of sentences with common components [p. 168].

Apparently, a pupil must establish an internal concept of sentence structure, which, when used, will result in an acceptable sequence of words conveying a unit of thought. In time, students learn that a sentence *must* have a subject and a verb that agree in number and tense. More complex sentence structures are learned as a student's knowledge and experience increase.

The primary function of a well-written paragraph is to categorize and classify ideas. The ideas expressed in sentences also must be sequenced in a logical fashion. The ability to write unified, cogent paragraphs is a very difficult task for most students, and teachers must be vigilant continually for any observed unusual difficulties.

The major goals of writing effective paragraphs have been specified by Dallman (1976):

1. Knowledge of what a paragraph is.
2. Knowledge of the characteristics of a good paragraph.
3. Knowledge of the importance of the use of good paragraphs.
4. Skill in the use of topic sentences.
5. Skill in making all sentences in a paragraph contribute to its central thought.
6. Skill in relating points in the correct order.
7. Skill in using good beginning sentences.
8. Skill in using good ending sentences.
9. Skill in making transitions from one paragraph to another.[3]

Although a broad listing of goals is useful in understanding what constitutes a good paragraph, it does little to help the teacher analyze a student's work for apparent weaknesses. At least six elements should be considered when a pupil's performance in writing good paragraphs is charted. The teacher should ask the following questions in order to outline patterns of difficulty:

1. Does the paragraph deal with only one topic?
2. Are the major points of the paragraph presented in a correct sequence?
3. Does the paragraph have a beginning sentence that adequately introduces the idea to be discussed?
4. Does the paragraph have an end sentence that concludes the idea discussed?
5. Is each new paragraph started on a new line?
6. Is the first word of the paragraph indented?
7. Are there any run-on or fragmented sentences?

In many instances, students are able to evaluate their own written paragraphs. Ideally, the teacher and student will be able to establish a mechanism by which the student proofreads his or her own work (using prescribed criteria) prior to submitting it for review. Readers desiring additional information of proficiency skills should see Greene and Petty (1967) for an excellent discussion of this topic.

[3]Dallman, M. *Teaching the language arts in the elementary school.* (3rd ed.) Dubuque, Iowa: William C. Brown, 1976.

Handwriting

As has been mentioned previously, legible handwriting (or penmanship) is crucial to communicating thoughts in writing. Although this aspect of written expression is totally mechanical in nature, if a reader cannot decipher the handwriting, regardless of how well the passage is composed, its meaning will be lost. Teachers attempting to assess handwriting will find that background information regarding illegible handwriting often found in students' written passages will be helpful. This knowledge should indicate those areas that most likely will present significant problems.

According to Newland (1932) and Pressy and Pressy (1927), relatively few letter malformations account for most of the errors in the handwriting of children and adults. These errors are listed in Table 11-11. The consensus of available research on handwriting stresses that the failure to close letters (e.g., a b, etc.), to close top loops, (e.g., l like t), and to loop non-looped strokes (e.g., i like e) account for 49 percent of all errors. In addition, Horton (1970) has determined that various malformations of the letter *r* are responsible for 12 percent of all errors. Hence, the majority of samples of poor penmanship in students' writings are caused by incorrectly writing relatively few letters. The reason students experience difficulty with these particular letters often is that they require more sophisticated motor control

TABLE 11-11   Common Letter Malformations

Errors	Examples of Errors
a like o	*a*
a like ci	*a*
d like cl	*d*
e closed	*e*
g like y	*y*
h like li	*h*
i with no dot	*i*
l like uncrossed t	*l*
m like w	*m*
r like s	*r*
r like n	*r*
t with cross above	*t*
5 like 3	*3*
6 like 0	*6*
7 like 9	*7*

or they are not taught well in the early grades. In any event, it is important that teachers focus upon these letters, at least initially, when they attempt to assess handwriting ability.

According to Quant (1946), letter formation is perhaps the single most important aspect in producing legible handwriting, but other variables require consideration. Greene and Petty (1967) list seven common deficits in penmanship that also should be noted. (See Table 11–12.) Specifying these causes should help teachers when they observe students engaged in handwriting.

Since penmanship depends greatly on adequate fine-motor coordination, it is imperative that teachers be particularly attuned to a student's *readiness* for handwriting instruction. It is not unusual to find some students in third and fourth grade who still have not developed necessary motor control to manipulate a writing utensil effectively. The first step in handwriting assessment is to make a realistic determination concerning the student's

TABLE 11–12   Common Deficiencies in Penmanship

Defect		Causes
1. Too much slant	a.	Writing arm too near body
	b.	Thumb too stiff
	c.	Point of nib too far from fingers
	d.	Paper in wrong direction
	e.	Stroke in wrong direction
2. Writing too straight	a.	Arm too far from body
	b.	Fingers too near nib
	c.	Index finger alone guiding pen
	d.	Incorrect position of paper
3. Writing too heavy	a.	Pressing index finger too heavily
	b.	Using wrong type of pen
	c.	Penholder too small in diameter
4. Writing too light	a.	Pen held too obliquely or too straight
	b.	Eyelet of pen turned to side
	c.	Penholder too large in diameter
5. Writing too angular	a.	Thumb too stiff
	b.	Penholder too lightly held
	c.	Movement too slow
6. Writing too irregular	a.	Movement lacks freedom
	b.	Movement of hand too slow
	c.	Pen gripping
	d.	Incorrect or uncomfortable position
7. Spacing too wide	a.	Pen progresses too fast to right
	b.	Excessive, sweeping lateral movement

FIGURE 11–2   Basic School Skills Inventory: Handwriting

| Materials: primary pencil |
| lined primary writing paper |
| crayons |
| drawing paper |
| card containing a common word |

All the items on this subscale relate to the child's proficiency in using a pencil. For the most part, these abilities have to be taught by teachers or parents; it is unlikely that a child will master the pencil entirely through incidental experience. Children who do well on the subscale are likely to be ready for instruction in either manuscript or cursive writing.

Does the child print from left to right?

To earn a pass on this item, a pupil should evidence some consistent knowledge of left-right progression in writing. His letters or words may be illegible, poorly formed, misspelled, or otherwise inadequate and still be recorded as a pass if, in the execution of his written efforts, he proceeds in a left-to-right sequence. This sequence does not even have to be on a straight line; diagonal writing is permissible, as long as it is basically left to right.

When printing, does the child exhibit an easy three-finger grasp near the tip of his pencil?

For most pupils, writing is accomplished most easily when the pencil is grasped with the thumb and the next two fingers. Using either hand, the child should hold the pencil loosely near the pencil tip. Holding the pencil in the palm of the hand is a nonscorable grip.

Can the child print his first name?

The intention of this item is to determine whether the child can write (manuscript or cursive) his first name on command. The product does not have to be properly formed. The result must, however, be recognizable as being the child's actual name. Writing one's name from a model is not acceptable here.

Does the child maintain a proper sitting and writing position?

Observe whether the child keeps his head reasonably erect, uses the nonwriting hand to hold the paper in a steady position, etc.

Can the child draw a triangle with three sharp angles and no openings?

This is a copying task; therefore, avoid asking the child to "draw a triangle." Some children may execute the task on command, thus demonstrating both understanding of the term "triangle" and motor competence in drawing the figure. However, this task is designed to determine adequacy in pencil use, not language proficiency. Many children, who may not know the meaning of the word "triangle," have the motor ability to draw the form correctly.

Show the child a model and ask him to draw the same shape. To earn a pass, the child's drawing must have three sharp angles and no openings. It may be constructed with one continuous line or with several lines.

FIGURE 11–2   *Continued*

When given a common word on a card, can the child copy the word correctly on his own paper?

Place a card containing a common word on the child's desk. The pupil must copy the example correctly to receive a plus for the item.

Can the child draw a picture of a person with a recognizable head, body, arms, and legs?

To pass this item, the child's drawing must include the four body parts indicated. Stick figures are permissible, provided the parts are definitely connected and recognizable. Eyes, nose, mouth, ears, neck, fingers, and other details are desirable but not necessary.

When a common word is written on the chalkboard, can the child copy it correctly on his own paper?

A child's ability to copy from the chalkboard requires his focusing on the work at the board, retaining the images of the letters, and transferring the images to his own paper. To earn a pass, the pupil must copy the word correctly.

When printing, can the child stay on the line?

This is a relatively difficult task for many children. In scoring the item, you are concerned with the child's skill at organizing and spacing his letters squarely on the line, not with the legibility or quality of the letters themselves.

Can the child print his last name?

To receive credit for this item, a child should make a solid attempt at writing his last name. The name may be misspelled and some of the letters may be reversed or poorly formed. The point here is that the child has enough of an idea about the written form of his name that he will attempt to write it.

Source: "Handwriting" from *Basic school skills inventory* by Libby Goodman and Donald D. Hammill. Copyright © 1975 by Follett Publishing Company. Used by permission of the publisher.

overall readiness to produce legible handwriting. For this purpose, we recommend the use of the handwriting section of the *Basic School Skills Inventory* (Goodman & Hammill, 1975), which was developed on the basis of teachers' observations of 50 kindergarten and first-grade students. (See Figure 11–2.) The teacher should rate the student via the explanation of the items listed on the scale. If a student can perform the majority of items, it should be assumed that he or she has the minimal capabilities to write legibly.

After a student has been judged to possess sufficient prerequisite motor skills but is still not producing acceptable penmanship, the teacher may wish to use a general *scale* to further analyze a pupil's handwriting. Undoubtedly, the most commonly employed instrument is the evaluation

FIGURE 11-3 Zaner-Bloser Scale for Evaluating Handwriting

Farmers are good friends. They grow some of our food.	High for Grade 2	We have many good things to eat.
Farmers are good friends. They grow some of our food.	Good for Grade 2	We have many good things to eat.
Farmers are good friends. They grow some of our food.	Medium for Grade 2	We have many good things to eat.
Farmers are good friends. They grow some of our food.	Fair for Grade 2	We have many good things to eat.
Farmers are good friends. They grow some of our food.	Poor for Grade 2	We have many good things to eat.

Source: Used with permission from "Creative Growth With Handwriting." Zaner-Bloser, Inc., Copyright © 1975. Columbus, Ohio.

FIGURE 11–4   Letter Finder

scales produced by Zaner-Bloser (1975). These scales provide five specimens of handwriting for each grade level. It is suggested that a sample of a student's penmanship be compared with these five specimens to determine if the handwriting is (1) high, (2) good, (3) medium, (4) fair, or (5) poor. A sample of the Zaner-Bloser scale for Grade 2 is given in Figure 11–3. It is obvious that although this scale is useful for making judgments about a student's handwriting, it does not assist in the specification of error patterns.

The informal assessment of specific faults in handwriting must focus upon procedures developed by teachers themselves. In general, there are six areas that teachers need to consider when they attempt to isolate particular deficits in penmanship, including (1) letter formation, (2) spacing, (3) slant, (4) line quality, (5) letter size and alignment, and (6) rate (Zaner-Bloser, 1937; Burns, 1962). Each of these components and suggested assessment techniques are discussed in the next section.

Letter Formation   The most efficient method to test for *letter formation* is to construct a *letter finder*. (See Figure 11–4.) This can be easily accomplished by cutting a hole in a piece of cardboard a little larger than the letter. Place the hole of the letter finder over each letter or numeral in a passage and indicate those that are illegible. Having the student practice those letters that are consistently malformed should increase the overall readability of written passages.

Spacing   *Spacing* refers to the manner in which letters are distributed within words and in which words are spaced in a phrase. The criteria for spacing within words is that uniformity should be observed and there should be no extremes. The space between words in a phrase should be a little more than one lower-case letter. An example of spacing errors and appropriate markings is given below.

Slant   The *slant* of handwriting, either manuscript or cursive, should be uniform in nature. The simplest procedure for assessing slant is to draw straight lines through the letters. It will be apparent quickly which letters are "off slant." An illustration of this procedure is presented below.

Line Quality   The adequacy of *line quality* can be determined quickly by employing the letter finder discussed previously. Place the hole over each letter and indicate those words that are illegible because of the quality of the line. If all letters are legible but it is apparent that inconsistent line quality is detracting from them, mark the letters or words that are too thick or too fine. Simply bringing these inconsistencies to the student's attention may be enough to correct the deficiency.

Size and Alignment   *Size* and *alignment* can be measured by drawing baselines that touch the tops of as many letters as possible. In addition, it should be noted that, in most handwriting, the lower case letters *i, u, e* are ¼ space high; *d, t,* and *p* are ½ space; capitals and *l, h, k, d, b* are ¾ space high. Lower-loop letters ½ space below the line.

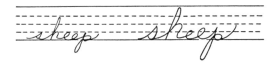

Rate   The *rate* of handwriting becomes more important as students have more demands placed upon them in school. A certain minimum level of speed is essential for a student to accomplish the normal amount of work assigned in class. The usual procedure for determining handwriting speed is to count the number of letters produced per minute. The rate of handwriting (speed) is computed by dividing this figure by the number of minutes allowed for the writing. According to the Zaner-Bloser scales, students should be writing at or close to the following rates.

Grade	1	2	3	4	5	6	7
Rate	25	30	38	45	50	67	74

When teachers attempt to determine the rate of handwriting, the sentences to be assessed should be written on the board, and the students should be allowed to practice them several times. The usual time period for evaluation is 2 minutes.

At the conclusion of these procedures, the teacher will have a detailed analysis of the particular errors made by individual students. It is important that a record be maintained concerning the type and severity of the apparent errors, as well as the amount of progress evidenced in overcoming them. As with other aspects of written expression, students can, in some instances, take responsibility for analyzing (proofreading) their own written work to determine if they are progressing. Teachers should not overlook this potentially valuable assessment technique.

USING WRITTEN EXPRESSION ASSESSMENT TECHNIQUES

When determining a student's proficiency in written expression, teachers should carefully outline the primary objectives of the assessment. They must assess only those aspects that are creating problems for the student. Without the establishment of clearly defined objectives, it is highly likely that the assessment procedures employed will not meet the needs for which they were originally intended (Gronlund, 1976). For example, if it is apparent that a pupil is only exhibiting difficulties in punctuation and capitalization, an in-depth evaluation of word usage and handwriting will not only be a waste of time and energy but also may diagnose problems that do not exist.

In order to circumvent the problem of overdiagnosis, the teacher should begin any assessment effort with a period of structured observation. It also is recommended that, when appropriate, interviews with all school personnel who come into contact with the student be conducted. In many instances, the information provided by such personnel will help clarify the problems and provide direction in choosing those techniques that will best meet the needs of the student. Once the general area of difficulty is specified, the teacher can then employ standardized and informal techniques to probe the observed problem further. Standardized tests will yield a general perspective of aspects of a student's written expression. Informal, teacher-made tests usually are necessary to obtain sufficient data for planning instructional intervention.

When conducting an informal assessment, the teacher needs to obtain representative samples of a student's written work. The use of a chart such as shown in Figure 11-1 will help to categorize the major area(s) in which the student is experiencing difficulties. At this point, a more detailed analysis of discrete problems (e.g., word usage, sentence and paragraph sense, handwriting) can be undertaken. From this analysis, the teacher will be able to isolate the specific problems and to plan appropriate instructional intervention. At the conclusion of the informal assessment process, it should be possible to form both long- and short-range objectives that will constitute the core of remedial activities considered necessary to remedy the disorder. It should be noted that a good assessment procedure proceeds in stages—from the general to the specific.

Suggested Activities

11–1. Obtain or construct picture cards that can be sequenced to depict an event or story. Use these to construct an informal test that will check a child's ability to organize ideas; if desired, use item 2 in Table 11–1 to assist you in the task. Begin by asking a young child to arrange the cards and *tell* a story; ask an older student to *write* the story. Administer this device to three students of the same grade level and summarize your results or findings.

11–2. Select two of the standardized achievement tests listed in Table 11–4 that measure the same aspects of written expression. Make a comparison of these two tests based upon available reliability, validity, standardization, and normative data, and note the format used to test the particular components of written expression.

11–3. Mr. Lee is a sixth-grade teacher in West Middle School. His students come primarily from five elementary schools, two of which use different achievement tests from the other three. Each of the test batteries measure components of written expression; however, the students' scores from the three schools that use one achievement test continually exhibit higher scores than do those from the other two schools. Mr. Lee would like to see if this discrepancy is inherent within the two tests, or among the schools, teachers, or students.

Select any two tests that measure written expression (see Table 11–4), and administer the written expression sections of each to a class of fifth-graders. Score both tests to obtain standard scores, and compare the scores for each student. Discuss any discrepancies, as well as the degree of confidence one might have that the two tests measure the same constructs in an equivalent manner.

11–4. Obtain and administer one or both of the diagnostic tests of written expression discussed in this chapter. Summarize the procedure you have used and the conditions under which you have administered the tests. Summarize the results according to the manual's suggested interpretation and standard scores. In addition, formulate objectives for further instruction in written expression with the particular student assessed.

11–5.   Obtain written compositions from 10 students of any grade level. Analyze the compositions on the basis of productivity, as defined by Myklebust (1965); that is, number of words, number of sentences, and number of words per sentence.

11–6.   For 12 years Mr. Jones has taught language arts to fifth-grade students, but he now finds himself teaching language arts to third-grade students. He fears he will expect either too much or too little from them and, therefore, he has decided to develop a rating scale to assess the class' first assigned composition. Using Table 11–5, construct a rating scale designed to rank each component of written expression, as well as provide an overall ranking for each student in the class.

11–7.   Obtain 10 or more sample compositions from any one grade level. Using Table 11–6, conduct an error analysis for word usage on each composition.

11–8.   Using the procedure by Burns (1974), design a dictation test that will tap those areas of punctuation presented by Dallman (1976), Furness (1960), and Burns (1974). Use the format offered in Table 11–9 to construct a record that will pertain to the test you have constructed. Administer the test to three students and analyze the results.

11–9.   Using the capitalization skills listed by Greene and Petty (1967) earlier in the chapter (and in Table 11–10), construct and administer an informal dictation test to three students.

11–10. Determine several sentences that might be used in eliciting handwriting samples from a specific age group. Be sure that the group of sentences will allow ample opportunity to examine the common errors listed in Tables 11–11 and 11–12. Using this group of sentences, obtain samples from an entire class.

11–11. Using the items listed as causes of poor handwriting (Table 11–12) and any others you feel are necessary, construct an observational checklist that a teacher can use while the student is attempting to perform handwriting tasks. The checklist should be useful in determining appropriate instructional objectives.

11–12. Administer the handwriting subscale of the *Basic School Skills Inventory* (Figure 11–2) to 10 kindergarten or first-grade students. Summarize the group results and suggest remedies where appropriate.

11–13. Ms. Gray would like to use a handwriting scale but she has found that most scales are built around samples employing different letter formations than those she has chosen to teach.

In order to construct a handwriting scale, select four classrooms of the same grade level and obtain handwritten samples from each student. Separate the samples into four or five groups based on general legibility and attractiveness, letter formation, slant, spacing, line quality, and letter size and alignment. Select one sample from each group that represents excellent, good, fair, or poor samples in order to compare them on your newly constructed scale.

References

Anastasiow, N. Review of the picture story language test. In O. K. Burros (Ed.), *Seventh mental measurement yearbook.* Highland Park, N.J.: Gryphon Press, 1972.

Black, M. *The labyrinth of language.* New York: Mentor, 1968.

Burns, P. C. *Improving handwriting instruction in elementary schools.* Minneapolis: Burgess, 1962.

Burns, P. C. *Diagnostic teaching of the language arts.* Itasca, Ill.: F. E. Peacock, 1974.

Cartwright, G. P. Written expression and spelling. In R. M. Smith (Ed.), *Teacher diagnosis of educational difficulties.* Columbus, Ohio: Charles E. Merrill, 1969.

CTB/McGraw-Hill. *Comprehensive tests of basic skills.* New York: CTB/McGraw-Hill, 1968.

Dallman, M. *Teaching the language arts in the elementary school.* (3rd ed.) Dubuque, Iowa: William C. Brown, 1976.

Donoghue, M. R. *The child and the English language arts.* Dubuque, Iowa: William C. Brown, 1971.

Durost, W., Bixler, H., Wrightstone, J., Prescott, G., & Barlow, I. *Metropolitan achievement tests.* New York: Harcourt Brace Jovanovich, 1970.

Ferris, D. R. Teaching children to write. In P. Lamb (Ed.), *Guiding children's language learning.* Dubuque, Iowa: William C. Brown, 1971.

Freeman, F. N. An analytical scale for judging handwriting. *Elementary School Journal*, 1915, *15*, 432–441.

Furness, E. L. Pupils, pedagogues, and punctuation. *Elementary English*, 1960, 187–189.

Goodman, L., & Hammill, D. D. *Basic school skills inventory.* New York: Follett, 1975.

Greene, H. A., & Petty, W. T. *Developing language skills in the elementary schools.* Boston: Allyn and Bacon, 1967.

Gronlund, N. E. *Measurement and evaluation in teaching.* New York: Macmillan, 1976.

Hammill, D. D. Problems in writing. In D. D. Hammill and N.

Bartel (Eds.), *Teaching children with learning and behavior problems.* Boston: Allyn and Bacon, 1975.

Hieronymus, C., & Lindquist, A. P. *Iowa test of basic skills.* Boston: Houghton Mifflin, 1971.

Horton, L. W. Illegibilities in the cursive handwriting of sixth graders. *Elementary School Journal,* 1970, *70,* 446–450.

Johnson, D., & Myklebust, H. R. *Learning disabilities: Educational principles and practices.* New York: Grune & Stratton, 1967.

Lefevre, C. A. *Linguistics, English, and the language arts.* Boston: Allyn and Bacon, 1970.

Madden, R., & Gardner, E. F. *Stanford achievement tests.* New York: Harcourt Brace Jovanovich, 1972.

Myklebust, H. R. *Development and disorders of written language.* New York: Grune & Stratton, 1965.

Newland, T. E. An analytical study of the development of illegibilities in handwriting from the lower grades to adulthood. *Journal of Educational Research,* 1932, *26,* 249–258.

Otto, W., McMenemy, R. A., & Smith, R. J. *Corrective and remedial teaching.* Boston: Houghton Mifflin, 1973.

Pressy, S. L., & Pressy, L. C. Analysis of 300 illegibilities in the handwriting of children and adults. *Educational Research Bulletin,* 1927, *6,* 270–273.

Quant, L. Factors in the legibility of handwriting. *Journal of Experimental Education,* 1946, *14,* 297–316.

Sequential test of basic skills. Palo Alto, Calif.: Educational Testing Service, 1958.

Thorpe, L. P., Lefever, D. W., & Nasland, R. A. *SRA achievement series.* New York: Science Research Associates, 1974.

Tiegs, E. W., & Clark, W. W. *California achievement tests.* New York: CTB/McGraw-Hill, 1970.

Wallace, G., & McLoughlin, J. A. *Learning disabilities: Concepts and characteristics.* Columbus, Ohio: Charles E. Merrill, 1975.

West, W. W. *Developing writing skills.* Englewood Cliffs, N.J.: Prentice-Hall, 1966.

Zaner-Bloser Staff. *Evaluation scale.* Columbus, Ohio: Zaner-Bloser, 1975.

Zaner-Bloser Staff. *Creative growth with handwriting.* Columbus, Ohio: Zaner-Bloser, 1975.

12

Arithmetic Assessment

The types of arithmetic difficulties that children with learning problems experience, along with how to diagnose and remedy these problems, have received very little attention in the professional literature. Teachers working in this area will find that there are fewer assessment devices and remedial materials available in arithmetic than in other academic areas. Hammill and Bartel (1975) speculate that the widespread concern with making children *literate* may be partially responsible for this fact. The considerable emphasis placed upon language arts skills in the primary grades proves this point. Otto, McMenemy, and Smith (1973) also suggest another reason for the lack of arithmetic emphasis in many schools: the feeling that some teachers and parents have that arithmetic is not as vital to future academic success as other areas of the curriculum. An additional reason might be that arithmetic difficulties do not surface as quickly in the classroom as do those in language arts. Children experiencing problems in arithmetic are often able either to compensate for their difficulties or to "hide behind a facade of rote ability in computation" (Hammill & Bartel, 1975, p. 61) with very little understanding of the principles upon which various arithmetic principles are built. Whatever the specific reason is, it is a fact that teachers are forced to be more creative and industrious in their use of arithmetic materials for assessment and remedial purposes because of a lack of published materials in this area.

CAUSES OF ARITHMETIC PROBLEMS

Difficulties in arithmetic achievement may be due to a variety of different reasons—the same intellectual, physical, social, and emotional factors that contribute to difficulties in other academic areas. Reisman (1972), for example, suggests that failure in arithmetic can cause emotional problems among some children. She also suggests that some teachers who are uncomfortable teaching arithmetic will convey these insecurities to the child. Still other children might identify with a parent who has had difficulty in arithmetic.

Lack of Readiness

Recently a number of writers have noted that lack of readiness for learning certain arithmetic skills should be considered in an assessment of all levels of arithmetic achievement (Wallace & McLoughlin, 1975). During the early stages of arithmetic growth, such skills as spatial discrimination, one-to-one correspondence, classification, and serialization are crucial to later success in counting, computating, and measuring. Readiness, however, is not limited to the beginning stages of arithmetic instruction; more advanced skills in arithmetic (e.g., division, multiplication, etc.) also depend upon a knowledge and an understanding of prerequisite abilities. The importance of arithmetic readiness skills only recently has been recognized by educators, and as a result, more attention is now being focused upon this area.

Poor Teaching

Wallace and Kauffman (1978) note that it is axiomatic that learning problems may occur because of inadequate or inappropriate teaching. Many children do not learn because the teacher has failed to teach, or because the teacher has not provided the child with sufficient experiences with manipulative devices for understanding the variety of abstract arithmetic concepts.

Poor teaching or inappropriate teaching techniques often are a result of a lack of sufficient training. Remedial arithmetic teaching methods are simply not included in many teacher training programs. Furthermore, ongoing, inservice programs for teachers in remedial arithmetic techniques are almost nonexistent. Consequently, teachers are unaware in many cases of newer materials or assessment techniques and, in some cases, of the fundamental principles upon which remedial instruction should be based.

Inappropriate Emphasis

In teaching inappropriate emphasis on unimportant concepts often contributes to a student's lack of arithmetic achievement. Arithmetic is an area in which teachers are apt to emphasize skills without stressing an understanding of the basic concepts upon which the skills are based. Memorization of multiplication tables is a case in point: many children are required to learn these tables by rote. Many of these children later experience difficulties because they do not understand the concepts underlying multiplication or the relationship between addition and multiplication. In addition, the memorization of multiplication tables and other arithmetic combinations often contributes to an intense dislike for the subject because the child does not understand the basis upon which a particular process is formulated.

Lack of Motivation

Many children lack interest in arithmetic because the subject is too difficult for them. Other children, however, are not motivated to succeed because of the reasons noted earlier—poor teaching, inappropriate emphasis, or lack of readiness for learning certain skills. Obviously, children who continually experience arithmetic failure will find it difficult to even feign interest in this area. In view of our prior discussion, Otto, McMenemy, and Smith (1973) suggest that it is remarkable that even more children do not develop antagonistic feelings toward arithmetic. It is fortunate, however, that arithmetic is a subject which can be made more appealing for a child through the use of a variety of manipulative devices and positive experiences. A number of suggestions for doing this are provided in the following sections.

ARITHMETIC SKILL SEQUENCES

Clearly stated teaching goals provide a solid basis for formulating effective assessment and remedial procedures in arithmetic. Specific teaching objectives are usually formulated from a broader list of skills found in curriculum guides. Each of the many scope-and-sequence charts and curriculum guides that are available for planning programs will differ in various aspects; some include more detail, whereas others differ in the presentation of skills by grade level or age level. However, the vast majority of curriculum guides and scope-and-sequence charts include similar information, even though they differ slightly in certain details.

We will illustrate arithmetic skill development with two scope-and-sequence charts (Tables 12–1 and 12–2). Table 12–1 is a scope-and-sequence chart for levels K–6 developed by the Fairfax County, Virginia Public Schools. The broad objectives listed for each level in the chart actually are viewed as supportive of continuous progress and not as

TABLE 12–1 Arithmetic Scope-and-Sequence Chart

Level K

Content			
Numeration	Shows that the number of objects in two or more sets have certain relationships	Recognizes numerals for cardinal numbers and makes correct assignment of numerals to sets of objects (0 through 10)	
Operations			Begins addition and subtraction
Equations and inequalities			Begins to express equalities and inequalities
Money			Identifies coins
Time			Recognizes that certain parts of the day can be identified
			Becomes aware that time is measured

Level 1

Content			
Numeration	Expresses whole number numerals and words (0 through 10)	Expresses whole number numerals (0 through 25)	Expresses whole number numerals (0 through 100)
			Expresses whole numbers in a specified pattern
			Recognizes the existence of fractional and negative numbers
Operations	Begins adding (sums through 10)	Acquires basic addition skills (sums through 10)	Begins adding (sums 11 through 18)

433

TABLE 12-1 *Continued*

Level 1 (Continued)

Operations (Continued)	Begins subtracting (minuends through 10)	Acquires basic subtraction skills (minuends through 10)
		Begins multiplying (products through 18)
		Begins dividing (dividends through 18)
		Begins finding fractional parts of numbers (simple fractions)
Equations and inequalities		Makes simple statement of equality (addition and subtraction)
		Solves selected story problems involving addition or subtraction using objects (whole numbers 1 through 10)
Money		Determines money values
Time		Tells time to the hour and half hour
		Names consecutively the days of the week and states that there are seven days in a week
		Names consecutively the months of the year and states that there are 12 months in a year

Content

Level 2

Numeration	Expresses whole number numerals (0 through 1,000)	Arranges whole numbers in a specified pattern
		Expresses simple fractions

Operations	Acquires basic addition skills (sums 11 through 18)	Applies addition skills to problems involving up to three addends	Applies subtraction skills to problems involving up to three-digit minuends	Expresses numbers as Roman numerals (I through XII)
	Reinforces basic subtraction skills (minuends through 10)	Acquires basic subtraction skills (minuends through 18)	Illustrates the need for negative numbers when trying to subtract a larger number from a smaller number	Acquires basic multiplication skills (products through 25 including 0)
				Divides with whole number divisors (dividends through 18, no remainder)
				Begins finding fractional parts of numbers using objects or pictures
Equations and inequalities			Solves simple equations involving addition or subtraction	Makes simple statements of equality (multiplication and division)
			Solves story problems using simple addition and subtraction facts	Solves simple equations involving multiplication and division
Money				Determines money values through 99¢
Time				Tells time to the minute

Level 3

Content				
Numeration	Expresses whole numbers (0 through 1,000,000)	Arranges numbers in multiplication and division patterns	Expresses selected proper fractions	Continues patterns for simple number sequences
			Distinguishes between positive and negative numbers (integers)	

435

TABLE 12-1 Continued

	Level 3 (Continued)		
Operations	Demonstrates the commutative and associative properties of addition Applies addition skills to problems involving at least four, two-digit addends Applies subtraction skills to problems involving up to four-digit minuends	Recognizes the properties of multiplication of whole numbers Acquires basic multiplication skills (products through 81) Applies multiplication skills to problems involving up to two-digit multipliers and up to four-digit multiplicands Acquires basic division skills, whole number dividends and divisors (1 through 9)	Begins adding two fractional numbers (unit fractions)
Equations and inequalities	Solves simple equations involving addition and subtraction (with grouping symbols)	Solves simple equations involving multiplication or division	Solves selected story problems using simple multiplication and division facts
Money			Determines money values through $10.00 Identifies money values greater than $10.00
Time			Classifies periods of time Solves problems involving time

436

Level 4

Content				
Numeration	Expresses whole number numerals having up to ten digits Recognizes other symbols and systems for expressing numbers		Expresses proper and improper fractions and mixed numerals Begins decimals (tenths)	Expresses numbers as products of factors
Operations	Recognizes the 0 property of addition Applies addition skills to problems involving at least four addends Applies subtraction skills to problems involving minuends with at least four digits	Recognizes the properties of 0 and 1 in multiplication Applies multiplication skills to problems involving up to three-digit factors Recognizes the properties of division of whole numbers Applies division skills to problems involving multiples of 10 (through 90) as divisors and up to three-digit dividends	Acquires skills for adding and subtracting with fractions and mixed numerals	
Equations and inequalities	Solves simple equations involving addition and subtraction	Solves simple equations involving multiplication and division	Solves selected word problems requiring a maximum of two different operations	
Money				Solves problems involving money values
Time				Classifies time zones Solves problems involving time

TABLE 12-1 *Continued*

Content	Level 5		
Numeration	Expresses whole number numerals having up to 13 digits Expresses numbers in other systems	Expresses prime and composite numbers Expresses fractions in lowest terms	Expresses decimals through thousandths Expresses fractions as decimals Expresses the comparisons between two numbers	Expresses the relationships between metric prefixes and place value
Operations	Applies addition skills to whole numbers Applies subtraction skills to whole numbers Applies multiplication skills to problems involving numbers with at least four digits Applies division skills to problems in which the divisor has up to two digits	Acquires skills for adding with fractions Acquires skills for subtracting with fractions Begins multiplying fractional numbers	Acquires skills for adding with decimals Acquires skills for subtracting with decimals	
Money			Performs operations using one money value	
Time			Determines time and time periods Solves word problems involving time and requiring a combination of operations	

Content		Level 6
Numeration	Expresses whole number numerals in exponential	Expresses complex fractions	Expresses decimals through millionths
	Describes sets using set notation		Expresses relationships between fractions and decimals
	Expresses integer numerals		Expresses percents
Operations	Applies addition skills to whole numbers	Acquires skills for adding with mixed numerals	Applies addition skills to decimals
	Applies subtraction skills to whole numbers	Acquires skills for subtracting with mixed numerals	Acquires skills for subtracting with decimals
	Begins adding and subtracting integers	Acquires skills for multiplying fractions	Acquires skills for multiplying with decimals
	Applies multiplication skills to whole numbers	Acquires skills for dividing fractions	Acquires skills for dividing with decimals
	Applies division skills to problems in which the divisor has three or more digits	Acquires skills for dividing with mixed numerals	Solves problems which require naming a fraction as a decimal or a decimal as a fraction
			Solves proportions
			Solves word problems involving proportions and involving percents
Equations and inequalities	Solves mathematical sentences with at least three steps	Solves selected word problems	
Money		Performs operations using two money values	
Time		Determines time and time periods	

Source: Fairfax County Public Schools, *Mathematics program of studies.* Fairfax, Va.: Fairfax County Public Schools, Dept. of Instructional Services, Division of Curriculum Services, 1974, pp. 2–8.

representative of the amount of material that should be mastered within a specified time period (Fairfax County Public Schools, 1974). It is important to note that we have not included the sections of the chart dealing with graphs, statistics and probability, geometry, and measurement.

The sequential arithmetic skills listed in Table 12–2 are based on mental age. The specific skills are arranged in columns by levels of mental ability required to master each skill. This sequential arrangement is based upon data described by Brueckner and Bond (1955).

A knowledge of the arithmetic skills presented in these two tables is fundamental to both assessment and instruction. The sequence of skills provides a teacher with a specific frame of reference for planning daily, weekly, and yearly activities for both individuals and groups. The teacher is able to use this sequence of skills to note *where* a particular breakdown might be occurring if a child is experiencing difficulty. More intensive assessment through use of published and teacher-made tests also might reveal the deficiencies causing particular arithmetic problems. Use of the information in these two tables will serve as a basis for selecting any of the various arithmetic assessment devices that are described in the following sections.

TABLE 12–2 Recommended Gradation of Arithmetic Processes

Mental Age	Whole Numbers	Fractions	Decimals
6–7	1. Counting 2. Identifying numbers to 200 3. Writing numbers to 100 4. Serial idea 5. Using numbers in activities of all kinds	1. Contacts in activity units and in simple measurements	1. Tens as basis of number system
7–8	1. Reading and writing numbers to 1,000 2. Concept development 3. Addition and subtraction facts to 6	1. Recognizing fractional parts	1. Place value 2. Zero as a place holder
8–9	1. Addition and subtraction facts and simple processes	1. Extending uses of fractions in measurements	1. Reading money values

TABLE 12–2   *Continued*

Mental Age	Whole Numbers	Fractions	Decimals
	2. Multiplication and division facts through 3 3. Multiplication by one-place numbers 4. Related even division by one-place numbers	2. Finding part of a number	2. Addition and subtraction of dollars and cents 3. Multiplication and division of cents only
9–10	1. Completion of all multiplication and division facts 2. Uneven division facts 3. All steps with one-place multipliers and divisors	1. Extending use and meaning of fractions 2. Easy steps in addition and subtraction of like fractions by concrete and visual means 3. Finding a part of a number	1. Computing with dollars and cents in all processes
10–11	1. Two-place multipliers 2. Two-place divisors—apparent quotient need not be corrected 3. Zeros in quotients	1. Addition and subtraction of like fractions; also the halves, fourths, eighths	1. Addition and subtraction through hundredths
11–12	1. Three- and four-place multipliers 2. Two-place divisors; apparent quotient must be corrected	1. Addition, and subtraction of related fractions, as 1/3 and 1/6; also of easy unrelated types, 1/2 and 1/3 2. Multiplication 3. Division of whole numbers and mixed numbers by fractions	1. Addition and subtraction extended to thousandths 2. Multiplication and division of decimals by whole numbers

Source: Leo J. Brueckner, Guy L. Bond, *The diagnosis and treatment of learning difficulties,* © 1955, pp. 206–207. Reprinted by permission of Prentice-Hall, Inc., Englewood Cliffs, New Jersey.

ASSESSING ARITHMETIC SKILLS

We will describe in this section the techniques used to assess a child's arithmetic performance. The general procedures for diagnosing strengths and weaknesses in other academic areas are also applicable to arithmetic achievement. Basically, the teacher will be interested in gathering as much information as is necessary to fully understand a child's arithmetic difficulties and subsequently to plan a program of instruction. The amount of diagnostic data obviously will differ according to each child's specific problems.

FORMAL ASSESSMENT TECHNIQUES

Standardized Achievement Tests

An achievement test battery is designed to compare the performance of an individual student, class, or a school district in almost all academic areas with the performance of a normative group (Marks, Purdy, & Kinney, 1958). Most achievement tests consist of sections covering specific areas such as reading, arithmetic, etc. Each section is divided into parts (e.g., arithmetic fundamentals, arithmetic reasoning, or arithmetic problem solving). The information obtained from these tests is not as specific as the information obtained from diagnostic tests. However, standardized achievement tests do provide general instructional levels in arithmetic for an entire class. Also, teachers are able to determine class strengths and weaknesses in certain areas and skills. Some achievement tests that include arithmetic sections are listed in Table 12-3.

Diagnostic Arithmetic Tests

Diagnostic tests in arithmetic are administered if it is necessary to determine the exact nature of specific arithmetic skill deficiencies. Since most diagnostic tests are administered individually, they provide a more comprehensive profile of a child's performance. The range of arithmetic skills assessed in diagnostic tests is broader and more specific than in achievement tests, thus providing the teacher with a choice of sections applicable to a particular child.

The formal training required for administering many diagnostic reading tests usually is not required for administering diagnostic arithmetic tests (Smith, 1974). However, Otto, McMenemy, and Smith (1973) suggest

TABLE 12–3   Achievement Tests with Arithmetic Sections

Name of Test	Grade Level	Arithmetic Skills
California Achievement Tests (Tiegs & Clark, 1963)	1–9	Computational skills, reasoning
Metropolitan Achievement Tests (Durost, Bixler, Wrightstone, Prescott, & Balow, 1971)	3–9	Computational skills, problem solving, and concepts
Peabody Individual Achievement Test (Dunn & Markwardt, 1970)	K–12	Total score with items assessing matching skills through trigonometry concepts
SRA Achievement Series in Arithmetic (Thorpe, Lefever, & Naslund 1964)	1–9	Computational skills, reasoning, and concepts
Wide Range Achievement Test (Jastak & Jastak, 1965)	Preschool and up	Total score with items assessing counting, number symbols, oral problems, and computational skills

that a teacher exercise judgment in selecting a diagnostic arithmetic test, and that the teacher consider the administration and scoring procedures, along with the guidelines for interpreting scores. In addition, it is important that the test evaluates arithmetic skills particularly relevant to the child's specific deficiencies and not skills to which the child has had little exposure.

The five published diagnostic arithmetic tests reviewed in this section (see Table 12–4) are basically number-related assessment techniques. Each test, however, is somewhat different in both the form and scope of its diagnosis. All are commonly used to assess a child's arithmetic performance.

Diagnostic Chart for Fundamental Processes in Arithmetic   The *Diagnostic Chart for Fundamental Processes in Arithmetic* (Buswell & John, 1925) cannot be considered a test in the usual sense, since it is not standardized, and there are no final scores, quotients, or grade equivalents. The chart provides the administrator with specific information concerning the methods a child uses in arithmetic. Buswell and John feel that before a teacher can effectively help a child, he or she must know *exactly* what the child is doing to cause the failure.

This chart's method of diagnosis involves observation of a child's work through use of the Diagnostic Chart, the Pupil's Work Sheet, and the examples described in the Manual of Directions.

The authors developed the Diagnostic Chart from their observations of children in metropolitan Chicago schools. The chart consists of children's

TABLE 12–4   Diagnostic Arithmetic Tests

Name of Test	Arithmetic Skills
Diagnostic Chart for Fundamental Processes in Arithmetic (Buswell & John, 1925)	Four basic arithmetic operations with whole numbers
Key Math Diagnostic Arithmetic Test (Connolly, Nachtman, & Pritchett, 1971)	Basic operations, fractions, numeration, word problems, money, measurement, time, geometry, and symbols
Diagnostic Tests and Self-Helps in Arithmetic (Brueckner, 1955)	Basic operations, fractions, decimals, percent, and measurement
Stanford Diagnostic Arithmetic Test (Beatty, Madden, & Gardner, 1966)	Basic operations, decimals, fractions, percent, and counting
Basic Educational Skills Inventory: Math (Adamson, Shrago, & Van Etten, 1972)	Readiness skills, basic operations, decimals, fractions, time, and money

work habits in each of the four fundamental processes, arranged according to their frequency of occurrence in the observed children. Table 12–5 lists these work habits. The most common habit in subtraction that was observed, for example, was making errors in combinations, and the second most common habit was not to allow for having borrowed. The least common habit listed was basing subtraction upon multiplication combinations. The Diagnostic Chart includes habits that were observed in five or more children.

During the administration of this chart, the student is provided with the Pupil Work Sheet, which consists of a graded series of arithmetic examples arranged in order of increasing difficulty in each of the four fundamental processes. The student is directed to work each of the examples *aloud* in a usual manner so that the examiner will know just *how* the student obtains each answer. The examiner encourages the child *to do all thinking aloud.* The examiner should not attempt to correct the child or suggest alternative methods of working out examples, since the success of the diagnosis depends upon the discovery of *normal* work habits.

The same set of examples that appear on the Pupil Work Sheet are included on the Teacher's Diagnostic Chart. However, a blank space is provided to the right of each example on the teacher's chart for noting the child's problem-solving habits. A portion of the addition section with an examiner's notes is illustrated in Figure 12–1. As indicated in the second example at the bottom, left portion of the figure, the child has made an error in adding 8 and 4. This error also has been checked by the teacher in the list of habits (a1).

TABLE 12–5   Frequent Arithmetic Habits Observed in Elementary Students

Addition

Errors in combinations
Counting
Added carried number last
Forgot to add carried number
Repeated work after partly done
Wrote number to be carried
Irregular procedure in column
Carried wrong number
Grouped two or more numbers
Split numbers into parts
Used wrong fundamental operation
Lost place in column
Depended on visualization
Disregarded column position
Omitted one or more digits

Errors in reading numbers
Dropped back one or more tens
Derived unknown combination from
   familiar one
Disregarded one column
Error in writing answer
Skipped one or more decades
Carried when there was nothing to
   carry
Used scratch paper
Added in pairs, giving last sum as
   answer
Added same digit in two columns
Wrote carried number in answer
Added same number twice

Subtraction

Errors in combinations
Did not allow for having borrowed
Counting
Errors due to zero in minuend
Said example backwards
Subtracted minuend from subtrahend
Failed to borrow; gave zero as answer
Added instead of subtracted
Error in reading
Used same digit in two columns
Derived unknown from known
   combination
Omitted a column
Used trial-and-error addition
Split numbers
Deducted from minuend when

borrowing was not necessary
Ignored a digit
Deducted 2 from minuend after
   borrowing
Error due to minuend and subtrahend
   digits being same
Used minuend or subtrahend as
   remainder
Reversed digits in remainder
Confused process: which division or
   multiplication
Skipped one or more decades
Increased minuend digit after
   borrowing
Based subtraction on multiplication
   combination

Multiplication

Errors in combinations
Error in adding the carried number
Wrote rows of zeros
Carried a wrong number
Errors in addition
Forgot to carry
Used multiplicand as multiplier
Error in single zero combinations,
   zero as multiplier
Errors due to zero in multiplier
Used wrong process—added
Error in single zero combinations,
   zero as multiplicand

Confused products when multiplier
   had two or more digits
Repeated part of table
Multiplied by adding
Did not multiply a digit in multiplicand
Based unknown combination on
   another
Errors in reading
Omitted digit in product
Errors in writing product
Errors in carrying into zero
Counted to carry
Omitted digit in multiplier

TABLE 12–5 *Continued*

Multiplication (Continued)

Errors due to zero in multiplicand	Split multiplier
Error in position of partial products	Wrote wrong digit of product
Counted to get multiplication combinations	Multiplied by same digit twice
	Reversed digits in product
Illegible figures	Wrote tables
Forgot to add partial products	

Division

Errors in division combinations	Derived unknown combinations from known one
Errors in subtraction	Had right answer, used wrong one
Errors in multiplication	Grouped too many digits in dividend
Used remainder larger than divisor	Error in reading
Found quotient by trial multiplication	Used dividend or divisor as quotient
Neglected to use remainder within problem	Found quotient by adding
Omitted zero resulting from another digit	Reversed dividend and divisor
	Used digits of divisor separately
Counted to get quotient	Wrote all remainders at end of problem
Repeated part of multiplication table	Misinterpreted table
Used short division form for long division	Used digit in dividend twice
Wrote remainders within problem	Used second digit of divisor to find quotient
Omitted zero resulting from zero in dividend	Began dividing at units digit of dividend
Omitted final remainder	Split dividend
Used long division form for short division	Counted in subtracting
Said example backwards	Used too large a product
Used remainder without new dividend figure	Used endings to find quotient

Source: G. T. Buswell & Leonore John. *Diagnostic Studies in Arithmetic.* Chicago: University of Chicago Press, 1926. Used with permission of the publisher.

After the child has completed the worksheet to his or her best ability (usually 15–20 minutes), the examiner summarizes the errors consistently made throughout the test. Buswell and John note that this summary provides the teacher with a clear understanding of *how* the child solves various arithmetic examples. In addition, the Manual of Directions provides some excellent remedial suggestions for substituting proper work habits for the poor habits that were noted.

Although the Diagnostic Chart was published more than 50 years ago, its usefulness is still valid today. The detailed, individualized diagnosis provided by the Diagnostic Chart certainly is not necessary for all children experiencing arithmetic problems; however, it can be used effectively in

FIGURE 12-1   Sample Administration Sheet of the Diagnostic Chart

Teacher's Diagnosis
for pupil _13_

TEACHER'S DIAGNOSTIC CHART
FOR
INDIVIDUAL DIFFICULTIES
FUNDAMENTAL PROCESSES IN ARITHMETIC
Prepared by G. T. Buswell and Lenore John

Name _John_ _____ School _Lincoln_ _____ Grade _4_ Age _10_ IQ ___

Date of Diagnosis:_____Add._____; Subt._____; Mult._____; Div._____

Teacher's preliminary diagnosis _slow and inaccurate in fundamental operations_

ADDITION: (Place a check before each habit observed in the pupil's work)

X a1 Errors in combinations	——a15 Disregarded column position
X a2 Counting	——a16 Omitted one or more digits
—— a3 Added carried number last	——a17 Errors in reading numbers
X a4 Forgot to add carried number	——a18 Dropped back one or more tens
—— a5 Repeated work after partly done	X a19 Derived unknown combination from familiar one
—— a6 Added carried number irregularly	——a20 Disregarded one column
—— a7 Wrote number to be carried	X a21 Error in writing answer
—— a8 Irregular procedure in column	——a22 Skipped one or more decades
X a9 Carried wrong number	——a23 Carrying when there was nothing to carry
——a10 Grouped two or more numbers	——a24 Used scratch paper
——a11 Splits numbers into parts	——a25 Added in pairs, giving last sum as answer
X a12 Used wrong fundamental operation	——a26 Added same digit in two columns
——a13 Lost place in column	——a27 Wrote carried number in answer
——a14 Depended on visualization	——a28 Added same number twice

Habits not listed above._____

(Write observation notes on pupil's work in space opposite examples)

(1)			(5)		
5 2 — 7	6 3 — 9	_Correct_	$6+2=12$ $3+4=12$		multiplied instead of added. (Habit #12)

(2)			(6)		
2 9 — 11	8 4 — 13	Error in combination (Habit #1)	52 13 — 65	40 39 — 79	_Correct_

(3)			(7)		
12 2 — 14	13 5 — 18	"13 and 15 are—10 and 5 and 15, 11 and 5 are 16, 12 and 5 are 17, 13 and 5 18" (Habit #19)	78 71 — 149	46 92 — 38	"6 and 2 are 8, 9 and 4 are 13" Error in writing answer, omitted the "1" in 13. (Habit # 21)

(4)			(8)		
19 2 — 11	17 9 — 71	"9 + 2 is 11 bring down the 1." (Habit # 4) "7 and 9 is 16, 6 and 1 is 7" carried wrong number (Habit #9)	3 5 2 — 18	8 7 9 7 — 31	Counted on fingers. Said, "18 and 7 are 15 and 9 are—16, 17, 18, 19, 20, 21, 22, 23, 24, and 7 are —25, 26, 27, 28, 29, 30, 31. "Touched one finger for each count. (Habit # 2)

assessing the faulty work habits of many children. Since the Diagnostic Chart has not been standardized on any particular age group, it can be used with any group for whom it would be applicable. Nonetheless, the results will be most helpful to the teacher of children in Grades 2 and above.

Key Math Diagnostic Arithmetic Test The *Key Math Diagnostic Arithmetic Test* (Connolly, Nachtman, & Pritchett, 1971) is an individually administered diagnostic test of arithmetic skills for children in preschool through Grade 6, with no upper limits for remedial usage. The test includes 14 subtests that are organized into three distinct areas: *content, operations,* and *applications.* The organization and content of *Key Math* are outlined in Table 12–6.

Connolly, et al., suggest that the *content* area should focus on basic knowledge of mathematics and those concepts necessary for performing operations and making meaningful applications. The *operations* area, on the other hand, includes four traditional computational processes plus two additional subtests containing items that require more than one computational step for their solution. The final area, *applications,* is unique to *Key Math.* This group of subtests places considerable emphasis on the functional use of mathematics through application in money, time, measurement, etc.

TABLE 12–6   Content and Organization of *Key Math Diagnostic Arithmetic Test*

Area I
Content
Numeration
Fractions
Geometry and symbols
Area II
Operations
Addition
Subtraction
Multiplication
Division
Mental computation
Numerical reasoning
Area III
Applications
Word problems
Missing elements
Money
Measurement
Time

Items within each subtest are sequenced in order of increasing difficulty, and since the child responds orally to open-ended items, only a minimal amount of reading and writing is required. Paper-and-pencil items are found only in the four subtests of computational processes. Consequently, children with specific reading or written-language problems are not necessarily hampered by these additional requirements. This particular feature of *Key Math* is an obvious advantage for children with multiple learning problems.

The actual administration of the test involves establishing a *basal level* (three consecutive correct responses) and a *ceiling level* (three consecutive errors) for each particular subtest. It is estimated that the entire test can be administered in approximately 30 minutes. The authors feel that the most important factor in the effective administration of the test is the examiner's familiarity with the material. Consequently, the test may be used by a wide range of educational personnel.

Key Math provides the administrator with four levels of diagnostic information with each successive level becoming more specific about the student's arithmetic performance. Level 1 provides a grade-equivalent score based on the student's total test performance. Level 2 provides scores based on performance in each of the three general areas of the test (content, operations, and applications). Level 3 provides information on the student's relative performance in each of the 14 subtests through a diagnostic profile; strengths and weaknesses across each of these skill areas are noted in this profile. Level 4 focuses on a description of each item's content expressed in behavioral terms and the student's mastery of each skill.

Normative data for *Key Math* were gathered from 1,200 children in grades K through 7. The manual reports that the subjects were drawn randomly from 42 schools in 22 school districts in 8 states. Total test-score reliabilities are reported for each grade from K through 7. The obtained correlations are in the 0.94 to 0.97 range, with median subtest reliabilities in the 0.64 to 0.84 range. Little information is provided on validity in the test manual. However, the authors point out that the developmental sequence and selection of content to be measured were based on an analysis of 10 major mathematics programs.

The *Key Math* test is a good example of a comprehensive arithmetic battery that provides an overall indication of a child's arithmetic skills, along with more detailed information for teaching specific skills. However, in order for this information to be useful, the test results must be examined closely and analyzed carefully, since the methods used by each child to solve individual problems are not included among the standard findings. All possible explanations for test behaviors must be considered if test results are to be beneficial in planning remedial programs.

Diagnostic Tests and Self-Helps in Arithmetic   Three closely integrated groups of materials actually comprise the *Diagnostic Tests and Self-Helps* in *Arithmetic* (Brueckner, 1955). The first four *Screening Tests* quickly assess a child's abilities with whole numbers, with common fractions, with decimals, and in general arithmetic skills. The screening test for whole numbers, for example, appears in Figure 12–2.

Twenty-three analytical *Diagnostic Tests* comprise the second part of the series. These tests are geared directly to the screening tests, since

FIGURE 12–2   Screening Test for Whole Numbers

Diagnostic Tests and Self-Helps in Arithmetic
DEVISED BY LEO J. BRUECKNER
I. Screening Test in Whole Numbers

Name...Grade or Course..Age.................

School.......................................Teacher..Room.............Date.....................

Addition

					No. Correct

1.   2 5 3
   +1 4 6
	2. 9 6 5
	   +3 7 5
		3. 8 0 9
		   7 0 3
		   +6 0 8
			4. 8 9 7
			   4 6 9
			   8 5 6
			   9 8 8
			   +8 3 5
					If less than 4, see Related Tests 1 & 6

Subtraction

					No. Correct

1.   8 5 7
   −3 4 2
	2. 8 6 2
	   −3 9 5
		3. 8 0 3 2
		   −2 4 3 7
			4. 9 0 0 0
			   −3 6 4 7
					If less than 4, see Related Tests 2 & 7

Multiplication

Part I

				No. Correct

1. 3 0 4
   ×2
	2. 8 3 7
	   ×9
		3. 7 0 8
		   ×5
			4. 7 0 1 9
			   ×4
				Part I_____
				Part II_____

Part II

				If less than 4 in either Part, see Related Tests 3 & 8

1.   2 7
   ×6 0
	2. 4 8
	   ×7 4
		3. 4 2 9
		   ×3 0 8
			4. 5 9 6
			   ×9 2 6	

Division

Part I

				No. Correct
1. 2)8 0 4	2. 5)1 7 5	3. 4)7 9 2	4. 6)3 6 5	Part I_____ Part II_____ If less than 4 in either Part, see Related Tests 4, 5, 9, & 10

Part II

1. 20)1 7 6	2. 53)3 9 2 2	3. 94)3 8 1 6 4	4. 38)2 8 1 0 0

the results of the screening tests determine which, if any, of the *Diagnostic Tests* should be administered. The *Diagnostic Tests* each consist of one arithmetic process. Table 12–7 lists the 23 diagnostic tests.

The *Diagnostic Tests* are closely related to the 23 *Self-Helps* and corrective exercises, the third part of the series, which provide information for remedying deficiencies revealed by the tests. The *Self-Helps* appear on the reverse side of each diagnostic test sheet. These exercises actually provide students with a program for self-testing, study, and practice, if they have not mastered the skills included in the tests. The *Self-Helps* also enable students to see how they should have solved the problems, how they should have performed intermediate steps, and how they could have avoided errors.

To administer these tests, teachers use the screening tests, and then those diagnostic tests that seem necessary as a result of the initial screening. The *Self-Helps* are used primarily to teach the specific arithmetic processes evaluated by each diagnostic test.

The sets of examples in each test are arranged in a carefully graded sequence of steps. As we can see in Figure 12–2, the boxes to the right of each row of examples in the *Screening Tests* are cross-referenced to related *Diagnostic Tests* in the series. In addition, at the bottom of each

TABLE 12–7   List of Subtests for Diagnostic Tests and Self-Helps in Arithmetic

Test	1	Addition Facts
Test	2	Subtraction Facts
Test	3	Multiplication Facts
Test	4	Division Facts
Test	5	Uneven Division Facts
Test	6	Addition of Whole Numbers
Test	7	Subtraction of Whole Numbers
Test	8	Multiplication of Whole Numbers
Test	9	Division by One-Place Numbers
Test	10	Division by Two-Place Numbers
Test	11	Regrouping Fractions
Test	12	Addition of Like Fractions
Test	13	Subtraction of Like Fractions
Test	14	Addition of Unlike Fractions
Test	15	Subtraction of Unlike Fractions
Test	16	Multiplication of Fractions
Test	17	Division of Fractions
Test	18	Addition of Decimals
Test	19	Subtraction of Decimals
Test	20	Multiplication of Decimals
Test	21	Division of Decimals
Test	22	Percent
Test	23	Operations with Measures

Diagnostic Test numbers are given corresponding to those *Diagnostic Tests* that relate to the operation being tested.

Brueckner believes that the interrelationships among the *Diagnostic Tests* are an important consideration, since the primary cause of some difficulties might be closely associated with a skill included in a preceding test(s). A problem in multiplication, for example, might be due to problems in addition. Appropriate Diagnostic Tests must therefore be administered in order to determine whether particular difficulties are related to other basic number operations.

The tests in the series are suitable for both group and individual diagnosis. Although Brueckner lists specific grade levels for each test, it is our belief that the complete series can be used effectively wherever the tests and self-helps seem appropriate for individual needs.

The *Diagnostic Tests and Self-Helps in Arithmetic* are not standardized and, consequently, no normative data are provided. We agree with Brueckner's suggestion that the series must be viewed essentially as teaching material, which enables teachers to locate and identify specific, as well as general, areas of difficulty in arithmetic. The series also provides an effective basis for planning remedial work.

Stanford Diagnostic Arithmetic Test   There are two levels of the *Stanford Diagnostic Arithmetic Test* (Beatty, Madden, & Gardner, 1966). Level I is intended to be used with children in the latter part of Grade 2 to the middle of Grade 4; Level II is intended to be used with children in the latter part of Grade 4 to the middle of Grade 8. However, both levels can be used diagnostically with low-achieving students. The subtests for both levels are listed in Table 12–8.

The entire test is designed to diagnose a student's specific weaknesses in working with numbers. Beatty, Madden, and Gardner believe that difficulties in many aspects of arithmetic, including problem solving and measuring, often are traceable to weaknesses in working with numbers. Consequently, all of the subtests for both levels are concerned primarily with skills related to numbers. The amount of reading required of the child throughout the test is minimal. It is recommended that Level I be administered in six separate sittings and that Level II be administered in seven sittings.

Raw scores from both levels are converted into stanine and grade-level scores for most parts of the tests. The authors also spend considerable time and space in the accompanying manual describing how the test results should be interpreted. Briefly, they outline a three-step procedure involving: (1) *diagnosis,* (2) *evaluation,* and (3) *planning.*

In the *diagnostic* phase, the teacher analyzes each student's performance for relative strengths and weaknesses. During the *evaluation* phase, the teacher relates the scores on the test to other knowledge about the child,

TABLE 12–8   Subtests of *Stanford Diagnostic Arithmetic Test*

Level I	Level II
Concepts of Numbers and Numerals	Concepts of Numbers and Numerals
Part A. Number System, Counting	Part A. Number System and
Part B. Operations	Operations
Part C. Decimal Place	Part B. Decimal Place Value
Computation	Computation with Whole Numbers
Part A. Addition	Part A. Addition and Subtraction
Part B. Subtraction	Part B. Multiplication
Part C. Multiplication	Part C. Division
Part D. Division	Common Fractions
Number Facts	Part A. Understanding
Part A. Addition	Part B. Computation
Part B. Subtraction	Decimal Fractions and Percent
Part C. Multiplication	Number Facts
Part D. Division	Part A. Addition
	Part B. Subtraction
	Part C. Multiplication
	Part D. Division
	Part E. Carrying

including information about the child's daily work and on how the child works. The last phase involves *planning* a teaching program that will help the child overcome specific difficulties and build upon known strengths. Many sample cases and suggestions for remedial instruction are included in the manual to help teachers implement findings and recommendations.

Normative data are based upon a standardization sample of approximately 8,000 children. Split-half reliability coefficients reported in the test manual in the 0.77 to 0.97 range for Level I subtests and in the 0.57 to 0.96 range for Level II subtests. Little validity information is presented in the test manual.

The Stanford tests can be used effectively with children experiencing arithmetic problems. Many teachers have found the detailed sections on interpreting test scores and implementing remedial instruction especially helpful.

Basic Educational Skills Inventory—Math   The *Basic Educational Skills Inventory—Math* (BESI) (Adamson, Shrago, & Van Etten, 1972) is a nonstandardized, criterion-referenced arithmetic inventory available for two levels. Level A primarily involves arithmetic readiness skills and is best used with younger children; Level B consists of number-related skills (addition, subtraction, etc.). Table 12–9 provides a listing of all BESI subtests.

TABLE 12–9   Math Subtests of the *Basic Educational Skills Inventory*

Level A

1. Quantity—Verbal Quantitative Meanings
2. Naming Printed Numbers
3. Matching Numbers
4. Counting Pictured Objects
5. Dot to Dot—Sequences Numbers
6. Counting Orally
7. Writing Numbers
8. Number Sequencing—Before and After
9. Ordinal and Cardinal Concept
10. Number Words

Level B

1. Addition Facts	11. Subtraction of Fractions
2. Subtraction Facts	12. Multiplication of Fractions
3. Multiplication Facts	13. Division of Fractions
4. Addition Problems	14. Addition of Decimals
5. Subtraction Problems	15. Subtraction of Decimals
6. Multiplication Problems	16. Multiplication of Decimals
7. Division Problems	17. Division of Decimals
8. Fractional Parts	18. Decimal-Fraction-Percent
9. Reasoning (Reduction) of	Transformation
Fractions	19. Time
10. Addition of Fractions	20. Money

The BESI may be administered in whole or in part, to an individual or a small group. It provides a knowledge of a child's specific skill deficiencies and strengths. Each of the subtests in both levels of the BESI actually serve as a series of informal tests from which the teacher is able to gather diagnostic information. The informal nature of the BESI allows the teacher an opportunity to observe *how* the child works out specific arithmetic problems and to listen to what children say as they reason out particular responses.

The inventory of basic skills provides the teacher with a score of correct and incorrect answers. No other scores are supplied by the instrument. However, the items included within each subtest can be expanded easily into teaching units, which the teacher can use to remedy the deficiencies noted. The BESI also can serve as a posttest inventory. Scores derived from administering the tests a second time indicate the effectiveness of any teaching that might have occurred.

Classroom volunteers or teacher aides can be taught easily to administer the directions and procedures, thus providing the teacher with an additional advantage. It is important to reiterate that the profile of skills obtained is a valuable feature of this arithmetic inventory: the knowledge of specific strengths and weaknesses often is immediately useful to the teacher.

INFORMAL ASSESSMENT TECHNIQUES

Teacher Observation

Observation is one of the most beneficial informal assessment procedures that can be used in analyzing a student's arithmetic skills. Written seat-work assignments offer many opportunities for observing a child's work habits and types of arithmetic errors. Teachers also can observe the point at which an arithmetic breakdown occurs while the child is solving problems at the chalkboard. Spencer and Smith (1969) note that the chalkboard, as an informal diagnostic tool, has the advantage of allowing a teacher to survey the work of several children simultaneously.

Another part of observation is the teacher's interview with the child. In this approach the child is asked to describe orally how a particular answer to a problem was arrived at. The child actually reworks the problem aloud, while the teacher listens and questions in order to determine if the child has misunderstood or is using incorrect procedures.

The data a teacher collects during these periods of observation must be analyzed and recorded systematically. In fact, Smith (1974) believes that the key to proper informal observation is systematized efforts and an easy record-keeping system. For this reason, anecdotal records, checklists, and rating scales have been among the most widely used procedures for recording and analyzing arithmetic data obtained from observations.

Anecdotal Records Most teachers find it helpful to keep a pad or a notebook at hand in order to record detailed descriptions of a particular behavior or an incident. Usually it is recommended that teachers avoid making specific judgments about behaviors until adequate observations are concluded (Dutton & Adams, 1961). Over a period of time anecdotal recordings can reveal concentrated areas of strength and weakness. They also can serve as a record of progress within a certain skill area.

Checklists The use of a checklist during periods of observations usually results in observations that are more precise, because the teacher must attend to the specific behaviors noted on the checklist. Checklists can be used with an individual or with an entire class to determine specific strengths and weaknesses, to check continual progress, or to note a child's interest (or lack of) in arithmetic. Checklists can be devised for practically any arithmetic skill by listing the types of behaviors that teachers wish to assess. An informal arithmetic checklist is illustrated in Figure 12–3.

Rating Scales The advantages of a checklist also are applicable to rating scales, since both instruments are similar in design. Instead of placing a

FIGURE 12–3   Examples of Arithmetic Checklists

Individual

The child is able to:

_____ 1. Count numbers (1, 2, 3, 4, etc.)
_____ 2. Associate quantity with numerals (1 = △; 2 = △△; 3 = △△△, etc.)
_____ 3. Provide numbers *before* and *after* specific numbers (*5 6 7; 11 12 13;* 27 28 29, etc.)
_____ 4. Count by two's (2, 4, 6, 8, etc.)
_____ 5. Count by five's (5, 10, 15, etc.)
_____ 6. Count by ten's (10, 20, 30, etc.)
_____ 7. Count backward (5, 4, 3; 17, 16, 15; 95, 94, 93, etc.)
_____ 8. Supply missing numbers (3, __, 5; 17, __, 19; 86, __, __, 89, etc.)
_____ 9. Note sequence in counting a series (1, 4, 7, __; 17, 24, 31, __; 11, 21, __, etc.)

Group

	Counting by numbers	Associating quantity to numbers	Before and after numbers	Counting by two's	Counting backward	Supplying missing numbers
1. John P.	Sept. 16	Sept. 16		Sept. 20		
2. Chris W.		Oct. 10				
3. Laurel L.	Sept. 22		Oct. 1	Oct. 3		
4. Charlie S.	Sept. 16					

check before the observed behavior, the teacher uses a sliding scale of quality to appraise the behavior (Dutton & Adams, 1961). For example, many rating scales use the following scale to appraise arithmetic behaviors:

Never   Sometimes   Almost Always

This scale can be used to note a number of arithmetic behaviors, for example, how often a child uses fingers for counting, or how a child solves problems. Further gradations of the scale can be devised according to the specific purpose of the scale.

Teacher-made Tests

Teacher-made tests in arithmetic serve many different purposes. Sometimes these tests are administered as an informal inventory at the beginning of a school year to determine the general arithmetic level of a class, to assess a child's knowledge of a certain skill, or to verify the effectiveness of certain teaching procedures. Whatever the reason for administering a teacher-made test, it is vitally important that the teacher be clearly aware of the purpose for developing the test. For example, a teacher interested in assessing only a child's grasp of the regrouping process certainly would include more problems regarding this skill than the teacher who is interested in evaluating all arithmetic skills.

Once a teacher has decided the purpose of the test, it is important that the child be provided with enough situations so that samples of the behavior(s) under study can actually be secured (Smith, 1974). Some writers have suggested that a major obstacle to obtaining good results from teacher-made tests is the inability of some teachers to prepare appropriate test items that are representative of the skill(s) being assessed.

> Too often the items selected do not proportionately represent the important content of a unit. There is a great temptation . . . to use items which measure rote learnings rather than understandings of mathematical principles (Peterson, 1973, p. 596).

In constructing a teacher-made test for a specific grade level, it is important that the teacher incorporate all of the skills included on the scope-and-sequence chart for that grade level. The arithmetic skills listed on any particular scope-and-sequence chart (see Table 12–1) actually serve as a cross-reference for constructing test items, since these skills reflect the content of lesson plans for certain grade levels. In selecting items for the test, it is also suggested that at least several items for each skill be included on the test to insure reliability. Test items should be sequenced in order of increasing difficulty. Sentence structure and reading should also be minimized so as not to confuse the specific skills being tested.

A teacher-made test will provide an overview of students' arithmetic abilities, as well as an approximate level of achievement in arithmetic skills for individual children. The test results usually are used to divide the class into groups. In addition, a child's need for further assessment will be indicated if the child is performing poorly on the test. The arithmetic survey test illustrated in Figure 12–4, for example, provides an informal assessment of addition, subtraction, multiplication, division, measurement and time, and understanding numbers.

In contrast to survey tests that assess a broad range of arithmetic skills, teacher-made tests measure a specific skill in depth. This type of test usually is useful to the teacher, since exact skills are assessed. Scope-and-sequence charts help in constructing these tests. Over a period of time, many teachers build up a catalog of these tests for various assessment purposes. Table 12–10 provides three examples of teacher-made tests in different areas of arithmetic. The tests are intended to assess the particular skill

FIGURE 12–4   Survey Test of Basic Arithmetic Skills

Addition

5	7	21	30	17
+2	+0	+13	+57	+3

78	8	20	256	867	639
+24	7	30	+23	+55	752
	+3	+50			+417

Subtraction

9	15	34	54	249	876
−8	−9	−21	−39	−135	−399

Multiplication

5	6	23	57	63
×2	×7	×2	×8	×22

58	486	209
×35	×23	×60

Division

2) 8   3) 12   9) 108

11) 121   25) 125

Measurement

This pencil is about _____ inches long.

_____ cups make 1 quart.   18 inches make _____ feet.

_____ o'clock   Show 2:45

Understanding Numbers

Show as numerals:

    seven _____

    twelve _____

    one fourth _____

FIGURE 12–4   *Continued*

Write out:

    6 _____

   21 _____

 103 _____

Place value:

  46 = _____ ten's and _____ one's

     9 hundred's and 3 ten's and 0 one's = _____

completely through a series of examples that become increasingly more difficult. After administering these teacher-made tests, the teacher is able to pinpoint specific areas of difficulty, which probably will need remedial work.

Each of the tests illustrated in Table 12–10 is sequenced in difficulty from relatively simple to more difficult. The test for the addition of whole numbers, for example, proceeds from the addition of single numbers to adding three-place numbers. An analysis of a child's performance probably will pinpoint the specific difficulties the child is encountering with these subskills. It is important that the teacher makes sure an adequate sample is included for each particular subskill in order to assess each arithmetic process accurately.

Teacher-made tests can be administered either individually or in groups. It is important to point out, however, that the opportunity for more intensive observation of pertinent behaviors is always greater during individually administered tests.

Teacher-made tests can be constructed for any group of arithmetic skills. However, certain guidelines must be followed so that the test can be both reliable and valid. The suggestions provided by Reisman (1972, pp. 121–122) are particularly appropriate in this regard.

1. Select content for the diagnostic test by identifying areas of weakness for the class (or individual) through results of arithmetic achievement tests, teacher survey tests, etc.
2. Isolate one arithmetic concept or skill to be diagnosed in depth, and sequentially arrange the subskills involved in that concept.
3. Determine the level of learning for the individual (or the level of performance for the majority of students in a class).
4. Decide on the behavior which you would like the child to display in order for [her or] him to demonstrate that the particular concept has been acquired.
5. Write a table of specifications (see example) which includes the set of behaviors and the concept components to serve as the structure for the diagnostic test from which items will be taught.

Example of Table of Specifications for Equivalent Sets

	B E H A V I O R S				
Equivalent Sets	A. To recognize	B. To name	C. To match	D. To identify	E. To pair
1. Sets of objects					
2. Picture of sets					
3. Sets of numerals or words					

6. Build the test by asking the following questions:
   a. Will it be all paper and pencil or will concrete objects need to be included?
   b. Will the test be a reflection of instruction by parallelling test items after the teaching situation?
   c. Will extrapolation activities be included for demonstrating transfer of knowledge to new situations?
7. Interview the individual (or the class) to determine the validity of the items. Attempt to find out if items were missed because of misinterpretations.

Source: A guide to the diagnostic teaching of arithmetic by Fredricka K. Reisman (Charles E. Merrill Publishing, Columbus, OH, 1972).

TABLE 12–10   Teacher-made Arithmetic Tests

Associating Quantity with Numeral
(Circle the correct numeral.)

		2	3	1
1.				
2.		4	5	6
3.		6	8	7
4.		8	7	9
5.		14	12	13
6.		17	19	15

TABLE 12–10 *Continued*

Multiplication of Whole Numbers

5	7	8	4	9
×4	×3	×6	×5	×7

24	61	43	12	72
×2	×4	×3	×4	×3

47	33	58	437	617
×2	×7	×6	×2	×5

23	41	52	73	44
×22	×34	×42	×33	×12

57	83	95	77	59
×35	×74	×42	×63	×28

55	36	35	75	87
×30	×15	×12	×16	×90

Addition of Whole Numbers without Regrouping

5	7	5	4	6
+1	+2	+3	+4	+3

14	11	15	12	16
+5	+7	+4	+6	+3

11	13	23	45	54
+17	+12	+24	+32	+34

10	20	40	70	30
+18	+19	+27	+15	+26

542	371	213	434	754
+235	+522	+686	+462	+245

USING ARITHMETIC ASSESSMENT TECHNIQUES

Assessment must be viewed as an ongoing part of the teaching process. Unfortunately, the concept of assessment in arithmetic often has been considered as occurring apart from teaching. We believe, however, that the teacher should take both an active and a responsible part in assessing the achievement of children in arithmetic, since the data obtained from the assessment often will influence selection of teaching materials and techniques.

The variety of procedures used for assessing arithmetic achievement can include, as we have outlined, commercial tests, informal observations,

TABLE 12–11   Evaluation of Some Aspects of Arithmetic

| | | | | | | Techniques for |
Main Objectives	Stan-dard-ized Tests	Teacher-made Tests	Check-lists	Oral In-terviews	Attitude Scales	Anec-dotal Records
1. Computes with accuracy and efficiency	√		√			√
2. Shows under-standing of place value in funda-mental processes		√		√		
3. Has favorable attitudes toward arithmetic				√	√	√
4. Achieves basic knowledge ac-cording to maturity and ability	√	√				
5. Applies arith-metic skills and abilities in solv-ing practical problems						

Source: Wilbur H. Dutton, L. J. Adams, *Arithmetic for teachers,* © 1961, p. 356. Reprinted by permission of Prentice-Hall, Inc., Englewood Cliffs, New Jersey.

formal observations, and teacher-made tests. The specific procedure(s) that are used for various situations will depend upon the amount of information required and available time and effort (Marks, Purdy, & Kinney, 1958). In many cases, financial concerns also dictate the use of certain procedures. Nevertheless, all of the arithmetic assessment techniques discussed in this chapter have distinct advantages for certain situations and individuals. In many cases, a variety of data probably will be necessary so that the teacher can make solid recommendations concerning student progress.

Table 12–11 provides a good example of how many arithmetic objec-tives can be met by using a variety of assessment procedures. Determining a child's accuracy and efficiency in computation, for example, can be ob-tained from a number of published tests described in this chapter. How-ever, these skills also can be observed by the teacher during everyday

Collecting Data

Vocabulary Test	Application of Principles	Problems Found in Other Subjects	Class Discussions	Samples of Work	Recording Data
					Cumulative record and pupil record book
			√		Teacher record book and pupil record book
					Cumulative record
√				√	Cumulative record and pupil records
	√	√	√	√	Class records and pupil record book

classroom activities and subsequently recorded in anecdotal records and checklists.

Very often behaviors that are informally observed in classroom situations need to be validated for accuracy through teacher-made or commercial tests. The teacher who notices a child's difficulties with concepts of placement beyond the one's column probably will need to determine the accuracy of this observation by administering a teacher-made test or a subtest of a published inventory dealing with this topic. Smith (1969) believes that continual cross-checking will add credibility to the teacher's observations. Ultimately, however, each teacher must decide which assessment procedure(s) will provide the most accurate information for his or her own particular situation. Nevertheless, assessment should go only as far as is necessary (Otto, McMenemy, & Smith, 1973). All children do *not* require a detailed diagnosis that involves time-consuming and expensive assessment tests. In most cases, teachers can plan appropriate and effective teaching programs in arithmetic based upon informal observations and survey tests of arithmetic skills. Extensive diagnostic testing, involving some of the instruments discussed in this chapter, is necessary only for those children who are experiencing severe problems in arithmetic. In these cases, it is necessary to appraise a student's skills completely in order to develop an appropriate teaching program.

Suggested Activities

12–1.   Mrs. Williams, a fourth-grade teacher, is interested in measuring the range of arithmetic abilities within her class. Using the arithmetic scope-and-sequence chart provided in this chapter as a guide (Table 12–1), construct an informal arithmetic survey test that measures skills at the fourth-grade level.

12–2.   Design an observational checklist that Mr. Roberts can use during his observation of a small group of six to eight average second-graders while they complete subtraction combinations at the chalkboard. Mr. Roberts is particularly interested in noting specific areas of difficulty so that he can provide remedial assistance.

12–3.   As a result of informal observations, Ms. Brown has noticed that two children in her third-grade class experience difficulty in subtraction when they have to regroup more than once in a problem, for example,

$$\begin{array}{r} 571 \\ -387. \\ \hline \end{array}$$

Construct an informal skills test that Ms. Roberts can use to gather more specific data concerning this particular subtraction skill.

12–4.   Administer one of the teacher-made tests illustrated in this chapter to a child who is experiencing difficulties in arithmetic. Evaluate the results in terms of specific strengths and weaknesses, and note any implications for further testing and remedial programming.

12–5.   Vincent's fifth-grade teacher has noticed that Vincent performs better with various arithmetic combinations when he is presented examples as paper-and-pencil tasks. During oral questioning, on the other hand, Vincent usually seems confused and his responses often are incorrect.

   Discuss possible reasons for Vincent's performance and how his teacher might be able to pinpoint his particular difficulty. List a number of remedial teaching techniques designed to overcome Vincent's problem.

12–6.   Mr. Rand is a middle-school teacher who works with children experiencing severe academic disabilities. He is continually dissatisfied with his attempt to use appropriate assessment and teaching techniques with students operating at grade level in arithmetic, yet functioning at lower levels in reading.

Suggest various testing and teaching strategies that Mr. Rand can implement when he presents arithmetic exercises requiring more advanced reading skills.

12–7.   During the process of adding fractions, Karen consistently adds fractions incorrectly, as follows:

$$\frac{1}{2} + \frac{1}{3} = \frac{2}{5} \qquad\qquad \frac{1}{4} + \frac{3}{5} = \frac{4}{9}$$

$$\frac{5}{7} + \frac{1}{7} = \frac{6}{14} \qquad\qquad \frac{2}{3} + \frac{5}{6} = \frac{7}{9}$$

Find Karen's error pattern, and describe a number of teaching activities that would help her to correct this particular problem.

12–8.   During an informal arithmetic skills test in addition, Gertrude completed the following examples:

```
  2 7        1 8        3 5        4 2        3 7
+   8      +   2      +   5      +   3      +   7
-----      -----      -----      -----      -----
  1 7        1 1        1 3          9        1 7
```

Carefully examine Gertrude's answers, and identify the error pattern with which she is experiencing difficulty. Describe a number of activities designed to help Gertrude overcome this problem.

12–9.   Mr. Wayne has noted that 7-year-old Floyd's use of his fingers for counting is particularly detrimental when Floyd tries to complete addition combinations involving two-digit numbers (e.g., $12 + 13 = $ _____). Floyd's reasoning depends entirely on counting with his fingers. Therefore, adding numbers larger than 10 is very confusing to him.

Outline a teaching strategy that will help Floyd overcome his specific problem.

12–10. In analyzing Marshall's performance on an informal arithmetic skills test, his teacher has observed that Marshall experiences difficulty in completing problems that required more than one arithmetic process (e.g., $9 + 3 - 6 = $ _____; $6 - 5 + 8 = $ _____, etc). Further analysis shows that Marshall can correctly add three one-digit numbers (e.g., $5 + 6 + 2 = $ _____, etc.) and can complete various subtraction examples.

List a number of corrective teaching procedures that might help Marshall to overcome this particular difficulty.

12–11. Note the readiness skills mastered by each child below.

	Ann	TJ	Lee	Bob	Elmo
1. Counts to 10	√				
2. Discriminates sizes	√	√		√	√
3. Understands one-to-one correspondence	√				
4. Discriminates quantities	√	√		√	√

The arithmetic readiness information for the five kindergarten children noted was gathered from observations and other informal assessment techniques.

Based upon this data, outline a teaching program in arithmetic for these children. Include any further assessment recommendations and teaching suggestions for developing these arithmetic readiness skills.

12–12. The results of an informal test on time concepts indicates that 12-year-old Jackie is experiencing serious difficulties in this area. Although she is able to recognize hourly intervals, she cannot estimate certain time intervals, such as how long it takes to eat an apple or to walk to the other side of the room. Furthermore, Jackie consistently confuses the meaning of days, weeks, and months. She does not know the difference between seconds and minutes. Based upon this information, outline a teaching program for Jackie, and list both short- and long-term goals, along with any additional assessment data that might be required.

References

Adamson, G., Shrago, M., & Van Etten, G. *Basic educational skills inventory: Math* (Level A and Level B). Olathe, Kans.: Select-Ed., 1972.

Beatty, L. S., Madden, R., & Gardner, E. F. *Stanford diagnostic arithmetic test* (Level I and Level II). New York: Harcourt Brace Jovanovich, 1966.

Brueckner, L. J. *Diagnostic tests and self-helps in arithmetic.* Monterey, Calif.: CTB/McGraw-Hill, 1955.

Brueckner, L. J., & Bond, G. L. *The diagnosis and treatment of learning difficulties.* New York: Appleton-Century-Crofts, 1955.

Buswell, G. T., & John, L. *Diagnostic chart for fundamental processes in arithmetic.* Indianapolis: Bobbs-Merrill, 1925.

Connolly, A. J., Nachtman, W., & Pritchett, E. M. *Key math diagnostic arithmetic test.* Circle Pines, Minn.: American Guidance Service, 1971.

Dunn, L. M., & Markwardt, F. C. *Peabody individual achievement test.* Circle Pines, Minn.: American Guidance Service, 1970.

Durost, W., Bixler, H., Wrightstone, W., Prescott, B., & Balow, I. *Metropolitan achievement tests.* New York: Harcourt Brace Jovanovich, 1971.

Dutton, W. H., & Adams, L. J. *Arithmetic for teachers.* Englewood Cliffs, N.J.: Prentice-Hall, 1961.

Fairfax County Public Schools. *Mathematics program of studies.* Fairfax, Va.: Fairfax County Public Schools, Dept. of Instructional Services, Division of Curriculum Services, 1974.

Hammill, D. D., & Bartel, N. R. *Teaching children with learning and behavior problems.* Boston: Allyn and Bacon, 1975.

Jastak, J. F., & Jastak, S. R. *Wide range achievement test.* Wilmington, Del.: Guidance Associates, 1965.

Marks, J. L., Purdy, C. R., & Kinney, L. B. *Teaching arithmetic for understanding.* New York: McGraw-Hill, 1958.

Otto, W., McMenemy, R. A., & Smith, R. J. *Corrective and remedial teaching.* (2nd ed.) Boston: Houghton Mifflin, 1973.

Peterson, D. L. *Functional mathematics for the mentally retarded.* Columbus, Ohio: Charles E. Merrill, 1973.

Reisman, F. K. *A guide to the diagnostic teaching of arithmetic.* Columbus, Ohio: Charles E. Merrill, 1972.

Smith, R. M. (Ed.). *Teacher diagnosis of educational difficulties.* Columbus, Ohio: Charles E. Merrill, 1969.

Smith, R. M. *Clinical teaching: Methods of instruction for the retarded.* (2nd ed.) New York: McGraw-Hill, 1974.

Spencer, E. F., & Smith, R. M. Arithmetic skills. In R. M. Smith (Ed.), *Teacher diagnosis of educational difficulties.* Columbus, Ohio: Charles E. Merrill, 1969.

Thorpe, L. P., Lefever, D. W., & Naslund, R. A. *SRA achievement series in arithmetic.* Chicago: Science Research Associates, 1964.

Tiegs, E. W., & Clark, W. W. *California achievement tests.* Monterey, Calif.: California Test Bureau, 1963.

Wallace, G., & Kauffman, J. M. *Teaching children with learning problems.* (2nd ed.) Columbus, Ohio: Charles E. Merrill, 1978.

Wallace, G., & McLoughlin, J. A. *Learning disabilities: Concepts and characteristics.* Columbus, Ohio: Charles E. Merrill, 1975.

13

Career Education
Assessment

The concept of career education for students of all ages has received much support by educators today in many of today's schools. In part, this movement is a result of the observation that many, if not most, students currently progressing through elementary and secondary curricula do not have any interest in attending college. However, the predominant theme in education continues to revolve around the assumption that if students do not acquire at least some college credits, they will not be able to find decent jobs or to earn adequate livings. The practice of forcing children into preparing for only one goal—the attainment of a baccalaureate degree—is indeed unfair, as well as irrelevant and unresponsive to the current demands in society.

The problems with the philosophy and rationale underlying career education are, perhaps, most appropriate to students who for many reasons experience moderate to severe difficulties in mastering certain subjects. These students at a relatively early age frequently are disenchanted with the traditional school curriculum and are merely marking time until they are old enough to discontinue their education. Because these children are inadequately prepared to enter the working world, they usually are employed (if at all) as unskilled laborers in jobs that have few opportunities for career satisfaction or advancement (Herr & Cramer, 1972). It is apparent that educators must broaden their own horizons regarding career choices that are appropriate and available to *all* students. This chapter will acquaint teachers with (1) the definition and rationale of career education, (2) proposed structures of career education, and (3) assessment techniques appropriate for estimating a student's best career choice.

DEFINITION AND RATIONALE
OF CAREER EDUCATION

As with any new educational endeavor, there has been difficulty in defining career education in a manner that is acceptable to the majority of educators. A cursory survey of appropriate literature leaves little doubt that there are nearly as many definitions of career education as there are persons trying to define it. One definition that has received considerable attention has been formulated by Hoyt, Pinson, Laramore, and Mangum (1973). This definition, one of the first since career education was launched as a movement in 1971, is as follows:

> Career education represents the total effect of public education and the community to help all individuals become familiar with the values of a work-oriented society, to integrate those values into their personal value structure, and to implement those values in their lives in ways that make work possible, meaningful, and satisfying to each individual [p. 19].

In general, most definitions of career education stress that it (1) relates to preparing students for the world of work, (2) involves more than merely teaching vocational skills, (3) should be part of the curriculum for all students, and (4) is the responsibility of other community agencies as well as the school. If a school is to prepare students with knowledge and skills that are marketable, then the goals of education must be altered. Subject matter should be made more personally relevant whenever possible by restructuring it around a career development theme. Students should be given counseling and guidance that permits development of self-awareness and self-direction, occupational awareness and aspirations, and appropriate attitudes about the personal and social significance of work. In addition, all students should complete high school possessing the knowledge and skills necessary to find a job or to seek further training. In sum, these new educational goals should help students to

1. have reason to want to work;
2. acquire the skills useful to work;
3. enter the world of work as a productive contributor; and
4. continue to grow in a productive and satisfying career (Hoyt, Evans, Mackin, & Mangum, 1974, p. 16).

As we consider the goals of career education, it becomes immediately apparent that many significant modifications will need to be made to educational thought. According to Clark (1974), several key concepts emerge as being fundamental to effectively using career education in schools.

1. Preparation for successful working careers shall be a key objective of *all* education. This implies that it is assumed to be appropriate for all

469

persons pursuing an instructional program at all levels of education, beginning in pre-school and extending through adult education. It is appropriate for youth and adults, boys and girls, those academically talented and those who are handicapped, those who choose college and those who make other choices.

2. Preparation for careers will encompass the mutually important aspects of
   a. work attitudes,
   b. human relations,
   c. orientation to the realities of working environments,
   d. exposure to alternatives in choice of occupations,
   e. acquisition of actual job skills.

3. Every teacher in every subject matter area that has career relevance will emphasize the contribution that academics can make to a successful career.

4. "Hands on" occupationally oriented experiences will be used as a standard method of teaching and motivating the learning of abstract academic concepts.

5. Instruction and guidance for career education will not be limited to the boundaries of a classroom, but will be expanded into the home, community, and employing establishments.

6. Career education will seek to extend its time boundaries, beginning in early childhood and continuing through the regular school years and adult years, allowing the flexibility for an individual to leave school for some work experience and return to school for further education or training when he chooses. In addition, it would include opportunities for adults to upgrade and/or update their skills or, if indeed, change occupational roles. Further, it would give attention to the productive use of leisure time and the years of retirement.

7. Career education in no way conflicts with other legitimate educational objectives, e.g., basic education, educational objectives, culture, and family responsibility. It is, however, a basic and pervasive approach to all education that provides a focus and unifying theme to which young and old, advantaged and disadvantaged, and intellectually and physically able and disabled can relate.[1]

Although the goals of career education have been accepted, there is still confusion among educators regarding the forces that have provided impetus to the movement. For the most part, the call for career education has been generated from a growing dissatisfaction with American education at all levels on the part of students, teachers, parents, and society (Bailey & Stadt, 1973). The most common criticism of the standard school curriculum is that it is suited for only one type of student, is unresponsive to the majority of students who do not aspire to a college diploma, and is irrelevant in preparing children to function as productive members of society.

[1]Clark, G. M. Career education for the mildly handicapped. *Focus on Exceptional Children,* 1974, 5, 1–10. Used with permission of the publisher.

The reasons for this dissatisfaction are readily apparent when we consider recent statistics regarding the status of today's elementary and secondary student. Hoyt, et al., (1973) state that it is now recognized that 80 percent of secondary students are preparing to do what 80 percent in fact will *not* do; that is, complete college. To state this another way, approximately eight out of ten secondary students are enrolled either in college preparatory or a general (i.e., nonremedial) education curriculum that adequately prepares them to work only after some college experience. Interestingly, however, three-quarters of those students who begin high school complete it, one-half of those who do so go on to college, and one-half of those who enter college graduate (Hoyt, et al., 1973). Clearly, alternative approaches for understanding the needs of both students and society are necessary.

The problem of inadequately providing career education to students can be viewed from the perspective of the elementary school. For example, of every 500 children who enter first grade, only 100 will acquire a baccalaureate degree. This is the case even though the majority of all students—because their parents and educators force them—usually are placed in classes that are designed to prepare them to enter college. This is quite alarming when we note that current U.S. Department of Labor Statistics indicate that less than 20 percent of all jobs in the 1970–1980 period require a college degree.

An additional area of criticism regarding American education is that one-fourth of all students never graduate from high school. High school dropouts have been described in various ways: as "dumb," "troublesome," and "unmotivated." Regardless of how they are perceived, it is apparent that the schools have failed them for one reason or another. Hoyt, Pinson, Laramore, and Mangum (1973) have made several comments regarding dropouts.

> Of those who drop out of high school, more than half can be identified before they complete the fifth grade; i.e., they were "turned off" to the public school system long before they became high school students. Whether we labeled such students as "unmotivated," as "reluctant learners," or by some other descriptive term, it is obvious that for whatever set of caused reasons, school does not make sense to them [p. 13].

Career education is one of the newer educational approaches that shows some promise in dealing meaningfully with this problem.

In summary, career education presents a growing force as traditional curricular approaches are adapted and made more relevant to students' lives. The career education that is currently available to students must be broadened to include teaching methods, not only for those who are college bound, but also for those who will not go on to college. Career education is concerned with "merging liberal education and vocational development such that it facilitates the *process of living* and is not limited to facilitating the *process of making a living* (Clark, 1974, p. 10)." Obviously, this shift is essential if the career needs of all students are to be realized and managed effectively.

CURRICULUM MODELS FOR CAREER EDUCATION

Although the concept and philosophy of career education have expanded rapidly, conceptual models designed to facilitate the actual development of career education programs in schools and communities have developed more slowly. Initial efforts were begun during the fiscal years 1971–1972 when the U.S. Office of Education (USOE) began formulating four operational models for career education, discussed in a USOE (1972) "briefing paper." Each of these models relates to current educational practices and is discussed below.

The *School-Based Model* is predicated upon the infusion of career development objectives into comprehensive educational programs in Grades K-14. The purpose of these activities is to acquaint students with the wide diversity of career opportunities available in each subject. Extensive guidance and counseling activities allow students to develop self-awareness, self-confidence, and mature attitudes, and to match their interests and abilities with potential careers. Apparently, obtaining an entry-level job or further education is one of the primary goals of each student in the School-Based Career Education projects. Keller (1972) has provided a summary of the specific goals of the model by educational level.

The *Home/Community-Based Model* represents an attempt to enhance the employability and career options of students who have dropped out of school but who wish to receive further education. Through the use of referral centers, mass media, counseling, and community resources, dropouts are able to identify aspirations as they match their capabilities. It is the basic goal of this model to coordinate, through the Career Education Extension Service, the use of mass media and the existing career education resources in order to help reach and respond to the career education needs of home/community-based populations.

The *Rural/Residential-Based Model* is designed to (1) provide rural families with employment capabilities suitable to the area; (2) provide leverage in the economic development of the area; and (3) improve family living. The goal of this model is residential centers located in each specific region of interest. Each center is responsible for designing programs and providing services for the entire family, some of which include: day care; kindergarten, elementary, and secondary education; career and technical education; young adult and parental education; family living assistance; counseling; and recreational opportunities for single and married students and their families. In addition to these activities, the centers work to improve the economic viability of the region and the regional expansion programs authorized under existing local, state, and federal programs in economic development.

Although these models illustrate governmental efforts to facilitate career education, they are designed for maximum flexibility within existing school and community systems. One curriculum model that offers an integrated, developmental structure for Grades K-12 has been formulated by Bailey and Stadt (1973). This approach is composed of four phases that correspond to the educational levels of elementary, intermediate, junior, and senior high school. In addition, six areas of behavior are identified within each level and are considered as essential "subprocesses" of career education. The domains specified are: (1) self-concept, (2) occupational, educational, and economic concepts and skills, (3) sense of agency, i.e., sense of responsibility and initiative felt by students as they work to articulate occupational choices, (4) information-processing skills, (5) interpersonal relationships, and (6) work attitudes and values. The relationships among the six subprocesses and the four developmental stages are given in Table 13–1.

The *awareness stage* extends through Grades K–3. The function of career education during this stage is to assist students in understanding the basic elements involved in career education as well as developing skills important in analyzing components of common forms of employment. The goals of this stage include

A1. Awareness of self
A2. Awareness of different types of occupational roles
A3. Awareness of individual responsibility for own actions
A4. Development of the rudiments of classification and decision-making skills
A5. Learning cooperative social behaviors
A6. Development of respect for others and their work.

The *accommodation stage,* conducted through Grades 4–6, is based on the idea that children can solve problems and give explanations in terms of concrete data. There appears to be a continuous progression from the use of variable to the use of stable concepts in all curricular areas. Consequently, the goals of this stage are geared to formalizing and complementing those attained in the *awareness stage.* The components of this level are

B1. Development of self-concepts
B2. Development of concepts related to the world of work
B3. Assumption of increased responsibility for planning one's time

TABLE 13–1   A Developmental Curriculum Model for Career Education

Domains of Career Development Behaviors	A. Awareness K-3	B. Accommodation 4-6	C. Orientation 7-8	D. Exploration and Preparation 9-12
1. Concepts of self	A1	B1	C1	D1
2. Occupational, educational and economic concepts and skills	A2	B2	C2	D2
3. Sense of agency	A3	B3	C3	D3
4. Information processing skills	A4	B4	C4	D4
5. Interpersonal relationships	A5	B5	C5	D5
6. Work attitudes and values	A6	B6	C6	D6

Source: Bailey, L. J., & Stadt, R. W. *Career education: New approaches to human development,* p. 350. Bloomington, Ill.: McKnight Publishing Co., 1973. Used with permission of the publisher.

B4.   Application of decision-making and classification skills

B5.   Development of desirable social relationships

B6.   Development of work attitudes and values.

The crucial point in the *orientation stage* occurs at the conclusion of junior high school, when the student must make a curriculum decision prior to entering high school. Bailey and Stadt (1973) state that the potential effects of this decision on later available options are "... in a very real sense, as much a career choice as an educational one (p. 363)." At this age, most adolescents are capable of dealing *intellectually* with tasks. Curricular goals at this stage include

C1.   Clarification of self-concept

C2.   Understanding of the structure and interrelatedness of the American economic, occupational, and technological systems

C3.   Assumption of responsibility for career planning

C4.   Development of individual inquiry and problem-solving skills

C5.   Development of socially responsible behavior and more mature social relationships

C6.   Appreciation of work as a valued and enduring social institution.

In the *exploration-and-preparation stage* the student must finalize an occupational choice and demonstrate commitment to that choice by entering specialized educational or training programs or by finding employment upon leaving school. In essence, at this level adolescents must expand and refine their knowledge and behavior from earlier stages. Obviously, the stakes associated with the end of this period are considerably higher than at the end of previous ones. The curricular goals of the exploratory and preparation stage are

D1. Crystallization and implementation of a self-concept
D2. Execution of plans that will qualify for career objectives
D3. Commitment to implementation of a career plan
D4. Application of problem-solving skills
D5. Understanding of the dynamics of group behavior in a work situation
D6. Acquisition of discipline.

In addition to the basic curricular model and associated goals, Bailey and Stadt (1973) also provide sample objectives that further define each of the four stages. From the information given, it is possible to generate a comprehensive and integrated career-education curriculum for most grade levels. Apparently, the primary elements of concern to teachers who wish to assist students in making viable career choices involve accurately estimating (1) aptitude, (2) values and interests, and (3) career maturity. The evaluation of these components of career choice will be discussed in the following section.

CAREER ASSESSMENT

If students have been prepared adequately for appropriate career opportunities through evaluation of their aptitudes, interests, and attitudes, as well as counseling, then their choices ultimately will influence their sense of well-being. On the other hand, if students have not been prepared for appropriate career choices, then it is likely that they will experience some discomfort and frustration. In order to assist students in planning effective career choices, teachers should be familiar with tests that are designed to probe students' aptitudes, attitudes, values, and maturity. The information received from these tests can help in advising students to choose appropriate careers, given their particular abilities and skills.

Although the tests described in this chapter are beneficial for career planning, several limitations should be kept in mind. The most significant drawback of many of them is that they require reading proficiency at at least a sixth-grade level. For students who do not read at this level, it is necessary to assess basic academic competency (see Chapters 7, 8, 9, 10, 11, and 12). Teachers should feel free to modify suggested testing procedures and to employ the results in a *criterion-test fashion;* that is, not to compare a student's score with normative tables but, rather, to use the data only in order to advise the student. In addition, the majority of tests have been standardized on predominantly white groups and should be interpreted with caution when they are administered to groups from different cultural, ethnic, or experiential backgrounds.

APTITUDE TESTS

When persons possess traits and abilities that enable them, for example, to perform mathematical calculations quickly, to speak a foreign language easily, or to manipulate tools well, they have an *aptitude* for that particular activity. The aptitudes that an individual student possesses sometimes are not readily apparent and will not be evidenced unless the environment is favorable and opportunities are provided. In many cases, training is necessary before an aptitude is revealed.

In form, aptitude tests are not markedly different from intelligence or achievement tests. Interestingly, the contents of these measures are similar because, in reality, they all are tests of aptitude (Gronlund, 1976). Aptitude tests *predict* future chances for success in a given field; as with all tests concerned with prognosis, however, additional input from observations, interviews, and other informal measures also must be obtained to validate impressions yielded from specific test scores. The following measures have been proven useful in assessing the aptitudes of adolescents.

General Aptitude Test Battery

The *General Aptitude Test Battery* was designed by the U.S. Department of Labor (1970) to determine career aptitudes of students of high school age or older. It is composed of 12 tests measuring nine basic aptitudes, as follows:

1. *Intelligence-General Learning Ability*—the ability to understand instructions and underlying principles to reason, and to make judgments
2. *Verbal Aptitude*—the ability to understand meanings of words and ideas associated with them, to comprehend language and relationships among words, to understand meanings of whole sentences and paragraphs, and to present ideas clearly
3. *Numerical Aptitude*—the ability to perform mathematical operations accurately and quickly

4. *Spatial Aptitude*—the ability to comprehend forms in space and relationships between solid and plane objects (frequently described as the ability to *visualize* objects of two or three dimensions)
5. *Form Perception*—the ability to determine pertinent details in objects or in pictorial or graphic material, to make visual comparisons and discriminations, and to see minimal differences in shapes and shadings of figures and widths and lengths of lines
6. *Clerical Perception*—the ability to derive pertinent detail in verbal or tabular material, to observe differences in copy, to proofread words and numbers, and to avoid errors in mathematical calculations
7. *Motor Coordination*—the ability to coordinate eyes and hands/fingers quickly and accurately in making precise movements, to make a movement accurately and swiftly
8. *Finger Dexterity*—the ability to move the fingers and manipulate small objects quickly and accurately
9. *Manual Dexterity*—the ability to move the hands with ease and skill, to work with the hands in placing and turning motions.

Administration of the GATB requires approximately 145 minutes and can be administered in groups. Two forms are provided: one with an expendable booklet and the other with separate answer sheets. An additional feature of this battery is a screening exercise and a pretesting practice exercise for disadvantaged individuals. The GATB, in comparison with other devices, has high reliability and validity data. According to reviews in Buros' *Seventh Mental Measurement Yearbook*, however, the test needs to be updated to take into account the change in composition of the work force as well as the uses of the computer in order to arrive at a more precise prediction model.

Nonreading Aptitude Test Battery

The *Nonreading Aptitude Test Battery* (NATB) (U.S. Department of Labor, 1970) is a nonreading adaptation of the GATB intended to be used with semiliterate and disadvantaged groups. It measures the same aptitudes as the GATB through 10 subtests:

1. Picture-Word Matching
2. Oral Vocabulary
3. Coin Matching
4. Design Completion
5. Tool Matching
6. Three-dimensional Space
7. Form Matching

8. Coin Series
9. Name Comparison
10. Mark Making, Placing, Turning, Assembling, and Disassembling.

The NATB is a pencil-and-paper test presented in eight separate booklets. There are no separate answer sheets, and the students mark their answers in the booklets. Administration time is about 230 minutes, and a maximum of six students can be tested at any one time. Directions for administering and scoring the test are conveniently contained in the accompanying test manual. A machine-scoring service is available for scoring the test booklets, converting raw scores to aptitude scores, and matching aptitude scores with Occupational Aptitude Patterns. Normative data are the same for the GATB and are, perhaps, questionable in view of the fact that the GATB was designed for a reading population and the NATB was not.

Differential Aptitude Test

The *Differential Aptitude Test* (DAT) (Bennett, Seashore, & Wesman, 1969) is used with students in Grades 8–12. The DAT is composed of seven subtests that yield separate scores, and include

1. *Verbal Reasoning*—an analogies test designed to assess the ability to understand verbal relations
2. *Numerical Ability*—a mathematics test covering a wide range of operations
3. *Abstract Reasoning*—assesses the ability to solve problems expressed in diagrams and figures; little language skill required
4. *Space Relations*—evaluates the ability to describe a three-dimensional object from a two-dimensional pattern
5. *Clerical Speed and Accuracy*—measures the speed with which an individual can perform a variety of clerical tasks
6. *Mechanical Reasoning*—assesses the ability to solve problems of simple to moderate difficulty involving mechanical calculations
7. *Language Usage*—two tests (scored separately) test the ability to use mechanical aspects of written expression (e.g., spelling, punctuation, capitalization, etc.).

Percentile norms are supplied for Grades 8–12, for the total score, and for individual subtests. Reliability coefficients are reported for each test, sex, and grade. Validity data have been established effectively with correlations reported between the DAT and school grades, other aptitude tests, and occupational success. At least 180 minutes are required for administration of the test, and it may be given in groups.

Flanagan Aptitude Classification Tests

The primary purpose of *Flanagan Aptitude Classification Tests* (FACT) (Flanagan, 1960) is to generate accurate occupational predictions by testing a diversity of separate aptitudes. The constructs evaluated include (1) inspection, (2) coding, (3) memory, (4) precision, (5) assembly, (6) scales, (7) coordination, (8) judgment and comprehension, (9) arithmetic, (10) patterns, (11) components, (12) tables, (13) mechanics, (14) expression, (15) reasoning, (16) ingenuity, (17) vocabulary, and (18) planning. Administration time is 258 minutes divided into two sessions. Individual subtests range from 3 to 35 minutes. Flanagan cautions that subtests do not meet acceptable reliability criteria, but rather, are intended for use in combination and, when used that way, are high enough for specific predictions. It is recommended that this test is best used with individuals rather than with groups.

INTEREST AND ATTITUDE TESTS

Interest and attitude tests consist of questions regarding a student's interests, values, preferences, and feelings over a wide range of occupational activities. In most instances, the questions asked do not require students to divulge personal data and, consequently, students usually do not object to answering the questions. Time requirements are not as lengthy as with aptitude tests and do not demand the same commitment and expense for scoring. Results of these tests can give teachers an idea of a student's career aspirations. In addition, clues can also be obtained regarding students' personality traits that will be helpful in the counseling process. Selected interest and attitude tests for adolescent students are presented below.

Strong-Campbell Interest Inventory

The purpose of the *Strong-Campbell Interest Inventory* (SCII) (Campbell, 1974) is to provide (1) students with information about themselves that will assist them in making sound career plans, (2) teachers and other professionals who make decisions about others with information, (3) data appropriate for studying groups of persons. In total, 325 items are included, most of which are presented in a "Like-Indifferent-Dislike" form and are listed in seven sections. The specific sections include: Occupations, School Subjects, Activities, Amusements, Types of People, Preference between Two Activities, and Your Characteristics. Three types of scores can be obtained from the SCII: 6 General Occupational Themes, 23 Basic Interest Scales, and 124 Occupational Scales.

Most students require less than 30 minutes to complete the inventory. Scoring is complex, and a scoring service is usually used. It is possible to derive profiles that relate to General Occupational Themes, Basic Interests, and Occupational Scales. In addition, some scoring services also provide interpretations of individual scores printed by a computer. Reliability and validity statistics generally are acceptable for school use. In particular, extensive evidence regarding the predictive validity of the Basic Interest Scales is available (Campbell, 1971).

Kuder Occupational Interest Survey

The *Kuder Occupational Interest Survey* (KOIS) (Kuder, 1966) is designed to evaluate individual preferences, likes, and dislikes for activities and occupations and to compare them with those of other persons in a diversity of careers. The rationale for this process is to limit the range of occupational choices for more in-depth exploration. The 100 items used in this survey are arranged in triads made up of three activities. In each triad the individual chooses the most preferred and least preferred activity. A scoring sheet is employed that must be machine scored. A total of 30 minutes is needed to complete the survey.

The interpretation of this survey is built around 114 occupational scales, 37 of which were derived using female criterion groups and 77, using male criterion groups. Interestingly, 48 college-major scales are also provided. A verification scale is included to determine if carelessness and insincerity were factors in an individual's responses. It is possible to report scores on all scales for either sex. Some norms are given in the survey manual. Although reliability statistics appear to be adequate, no evidence of predictive validity is available. If the KOIS is used effectively, it can help teachers in limiting the number of occupational fields or academic majors appropriate for a student.

Reading-Free Vocational Interest Inventory

The *Reading-Free Vocational Interest Inventory* (R-FVII) (Becker, 1975) is a nonreading vocational preference test for semiliterate and mentally retarded persons. Illustrations or drawings that relate to certain careers are used in a forced-choice format. Presumably, presenting pictured activities of individuals engaged in their job tasks eliminates the reading barrier for those with limited verbal or reading ability. The R-FVII provides scores in 11 male and 8 female interest areas. The male areas are: automotive, building trades, clerical, animal care, food service, patient care, horticulture, janitorial, personal service, laundry service, and materials handling. The female areas include: laundry service, light industrial, clerical, personal service, food service, patient care, horticulture, and housekeeping.

Scores in each of the male and female interest areas are derived from pictorial items presented in 55 male triads and 40 female triads in separate booklets. In each triad the student is instructed to select one activity he or she would most like to do. It is possible to handscore the inventory. An individual profile sheet is provided as an aid to interpreting results. Approximately 45 minutes are required for complete administration of the R-FVII. In general, the female requires less time and fewer triads are offered. Normative tables permit percentiles to be compared among students and with nationwide results. Reliability and validity coefficients are provided in the inventory manual.

Minnesota Vocational Interest Inventory

The *Minnesota Vocational Interest Inventory* (MVII) (Clark & Campbell, 1966) is designed specifically to assess the interests of males 15 years of age and older in nonprofessional areas. There are 158 forced-choice triads in the Occupational Activity Scales. As in other tests employing triads, students are forced to choose most and least preferred items. Twenty-nine Occupational Scales, such as carpenter, printer, farmer, etc., are available. Nine area scales are given: Mechanical, Health Service, Sales Office, Office Work, Electronics, Food Service, Carpenter, Clean Hands, and Outdoors. Hand scoring is possible, although it is recommended that machines be used. From 45–90 minutes are needed for administering the MVII. A verification of the MVII has been devised; however, it has not been incorporated into the inventory (Campbell & Trockman, 1963). The norms, and reliability and validity statistics are stated clearly in the accompanying manual and can be used with confidence. Presently, the MVII is the most useful inventory for assessing nonprofessional interests of male adolescents.

Although these inventories are commonly used in schools, other devices are also used to measure career interests and attitudes. Readers interested in additional scales may wish to consult the Vocational Interest and Sophistication Assessment (Parnicky, Kahn, & Burdett, 1970), the Kuder General Interest Survey (Kuder, 1964), and the California Occupational Preference System (Knapp & Knapp, 1975).

CAREER MATURITY AND VALUES

In addition to the measurement of aptitudes and interests, determining a student's values and career maturity also provides teachers information helpful in career counseling. Instruments designed to test these areas provide an estimate of the student's *need for assistance* in selecting a career that is appropriate to his or her values and competencies. Two devices are used extensively for this purpose: the *Career Maturity Inventory* and *Super's Work Values Inventory.*

Career Maturity Inventory

The *Career Maturity Inventory* (CMI) (Crites, 1973) evaluates the maturity of student's attitudes and competencies, which are necessary for making a sound career decision. This inventory also assesses a student's need for counseling and the effectiveness of career education and counseling programs. Two major parts are incorporated into the CMI: the Attitude Scale, which is composed of 50 true-false questions, and the Competency Test, which uses a multiple-choice format. The Attitude Scale measures five dimensions: Involvement in the Choice Process, Orientation towards Work, Independence in Decision Making, Preference for Career-Choice Factors, and Conceptions of the Choice Process. The Competency Test measures five career-choice competencies: Self-Appraisal, Occupational Information, Goal Selection, Planning, and Problem Solving. The examiner's manual suggests that administration of the inventory should be limited to 20 minutes each for the Attitude Scale and for each subtest in the Competency Test (a total of 2 hours). Answer sheets can be either hand or machine scored. Scores available in the test profile are raw scores, percentiles, and a right-response scale helpful for ascertaining a student's specific problems.

The norms provided for the CMI extend from Grades 6–13 on the Attitude Scale and Grades 6–12 on the Competency Test. Little information is given related to true representativeness of the norms. Crites suggests that teachers develop local norms that can be generated when groups of answer sheets are machine scored. Reliability and validity statistics have been established and are reasonable, particularly as they relate to the Attitude Scale. Careful discussion is given to the effects of sex and socioeconomic status on career maturity when an interpretation of individual test scores is made.

Super's Work Values Inventory

Super's Work Values Inventory (WVI) (Super, 1970) assesses the extrinsic work values of adolescent boys and girls and adult males and females with regard to making career choices and making the possibility of job satisfaction a reality. The WVI consists of 45 statements that test value judgment; the student ranks each statement on a 5-point scale from very important to unimportant. The statements are clear and easily comprehended by most eighth-graders. No limit is given, but the WVI usually requires from 15–20 minutes for completion. Hand-scoring takes 20–25 minutes. In total, 15 values are measured: Altruism, Creativity, Intellectual Stimulation, Achievement, Independence, Prestige, Management, Economic Returns, Security, Surroundings, Supervisory Relations, Associates, Way of Life, and Variety.

The grade and sex norms provided for the WVI are very extensive and carefully designed. Norms are reported in percentile scores, along with means and standard deviations for every scale. Super suggests that the grade norms given in the accompanying manual also can be employed for college pupils and adults. Interpretation of the scores is possible with regard to determining the relative hierarchy of the student's values, as well as the relationship of these values to both sex and grade norms. Test-retest reliabilities are provided for the WVI, as are data regarding construct, content, and concurrent validity. Factor analysis of all items indicates four major value dimensions: Material, Goodness of Life, Self-Expression, and Behavior Control. Although detailed instructions for using results are not provided in the manual, readers will find Super's (1973) discussion of career interests and values very informative for this purpose. Shah (1969) and Singer and Stefflre (1954) also provide data regarding the importance of values to career aspirations, job satisfaction, and curriculum selection.

In addition to the two instruments just described, readers may also wish to consult the *Hall Occupational Inventory* (Hall, 1968) and the *Rating Scales of Vocational Values, Vocational Interests, and Vocational Aptitudes* (Demos & Grant, 1966), which will also yield information about an adolescent's values and career maturity.

USING CAREER EDUCATION ASSESSMENT DATA

The movement to introduce career education into all aspects of the school curriculum has received widespread support from both education and labor. The purpose of these efforts is to produce students who have acquired (1) a reason for wanting to work, (2) the necessary skills and abilities essential for successful work experiences, and (3) knowledge regarding various work opportunities. Prepared with this information, students will be able to enter the world of work as productive contributors and will be able to develop emotionally and intellectually throughout satisfying careers.

In order to institute career education with any students effectively, teachers must become familiar with those tests that determine specific aptitudes, values, and interests necessary for career counseling. In many cases, students who have a history of school failure will be found lacking in basic academic competencies that are prerequisite to adequate job performance. In such cases, tests (both formal and informal) described in previous chapters can be used to determine the degree of deficiency as well as to provide a basis for remedial planning. Quite obviously, until a student masters basic skills in reading, writing, spelling, written expression, and arithmetic, it is highly unlikely that the student will be able to pursue a career in which he or she shows an aptitude and interest. Frequently, teachers find that once a low-achieving student becomes aware that the end of formal schooling is at hand and that a career choice must soon be made, efforts to improve basic skills are greatly increased.

If it has been determined that a student has at least basic academic competency (or is receiving the necessary assistance to acquire this competency), the teacher should focus upon the student's particular aptitudes, interests, and values in order to outline the most optimal career choice(s). This task can be accomplished through the use of formal devices described in this chapter or through simple observation and interviews with the student. Information gathered by teachers from observing students in everyday situations will provide important data. When possible, holding a conference with an individual(s) who is already engaged in that career should be arranged, as well as on-the-job work experiences. It should be kept in mind that, at all times, a student's potential career choices should be kept flexible to allow for changes as new interests are uncovered.

Ultimately, to be successful career education must be an integral part of the curriculum from elementary grades through senior high school. At all levels teachers must incorporate continuous evaluation to ensure that students understand the implications of their curriculum to career choices. The end result of this process will, hopefully, demonstrate to students that the school curriculum is meaningful.

Suggested Activities

13-1. Select two of the aptitude tests discussed in this chapter and compare them according to procedures used, constructs measured, and standardization, reliability, and validity data. Summarize the most appropriate uses and the advantages of each test.

13-2. Select two of the aptitude measures discussed in this chapter, and administer each of the tests to three students. Tabulate the results in the form of standard scores and, if applicable, compare the results of specific subtests. Summarize the degree of confidence one might have concerning the results of the tests and implications for their use.

13–3. Obtain additional information for any three interest inventories discussed in this chapter. Compare each measure according to reliability and validity information, standardization groups, and suggested uses of the results.

13–4. Select two of the interest inventories discussed in this chapter and administer each to five students. Then compare the results from the two instruments. In addition, provide a report on each student concerning potential career choices. Summarize any implications or suggestions you may have for the student's educational program.

References

Bailey, L. J., & Stadt, R. W. *Career education: New approaches to human development.* Bloomington, Ill.: McKnight, 1973.

Becker, R. L. *Reading-free vocational interest inventory.* Washington, D.C.: American Association on Mental Deficiency, 1975.

Bennett, H., Seashore, G., & Wesman, A. G. *Differential aptitude tests.* New York: Psychological Corporation, 1969.

Campbell, D. P. *Handbook for the Strong vocational interest blank.* Stanford, Calif.: University of Stanford Press, 1971.

Campbell, D. P. *Strong-Campbell interest inventory.* Stanford, Calif.: University of Stanford Press, 1974.

Campbell, D. P., & Trockman, R. W. A verification scale for the Minnesota Vocational Interest Inventory. *Journal of Applied Psychology,* 1963, 47, 276–279.

Clark, G. M. Career education for the mildly handicapped. *Focus on Exceptional Children,* 1974, 5, 1–10.

Clark, K. E., & Campbell, D. P. *Minnesota vocational interest inventory.* New York: Psychological Corporation, 1966.

Crites, J. O. *Career maturity inventory.* Monterey, Calif.: CTB/McGraw-Hill, 1973.

Demos, G. D., & Grant, B. *Rating scales of vocational values, vocational interests, and vocational aptitudes.* Chicago: Educational and Industrial Testing, 1966.

Flanagan, J. C. *Flanagan aptitude classification tests.* Chicago: Science Research Associates, 1960.

Gronlund, N. E. *Measurement and evaluation in teaching.* New York: Macmillan, 1976.

Hall, V. *Hall occupational inventory.* New York: Follett, 1968.

Herr, E. L., & Cramer, S. H. *Vocational guidance and career development in the schools: Toward a system approach.* Boston: Houghton Mifflin, 1972.

Hoyt, K. B., Evans, R. N., Mackin, E. F., & Mangum, G. L. *Career education: What is it and how to do it.* Salt Lake City: Olympus, 1974.

Hoyt, K. B., Pinson, N. M., Laramore, D., & Mangum, G. L. *Career education and the elementary school teacher.* Salt Lake City: Olympus, 1973.

Keller, L. J. *Career education in-service training guide.* Morristown, N.J.: General Learning Corporation, 1972.

Knapp, R. R., & Knapp, L. *California occupational preference system.* San Diego: Educational and Industrial Testing Service, 1975.

Kuder, G. F. *Kuder occupational interest survey.* Chicago, Ill.: Science Associates, 1964.

Kuder, G. F. *Kuder occupational interest survey.* Chicago, Ill.: Science Research Associates, 1966.

Parnicky, J. J., Kahn, H., & Burdett, A. D. *Vocational interest and sophistication instrument.* Columbus, Ohio: University of Ohio Press, 1970.

Shah, V. Work values and job satisfaction. Unpublished doctoral dissertation, Teachers College, Columbia University, 1969.

Singer, S. A., & Stefflre, B. The relationship of job values and desires to vocational aspirations of adolescents. *Journal of Applied Psychology,* 1954, *38,* 419–422.

Super, D. E. The work values inventory. In D. E. Zytowski (Ed.), *Con-* 1970.

Super, D. E. The work values inventory. In D. E. Zytowski (Ed.), *Contemporary approaches to interest management.* Minneapolis: University of Minnesota Press, 1973.

U.S. Department of Labor. *Manual for the USES nonreading aptitude test battery.* Washington, D.C.: U.S. Government Printing Office, 1970.

U.S. Department of Labor. *Manual for the USES nonreading aptitude test battery.* Washington, D.C.: U.S. Government Printing Office, 1970.

Index